This book comes with access to more content online.

Watch videos, take practice tests, and study with flashcards!

Register your book or ebook at
www.dummies.com/go/getaccess.

Select your product, and then follow the prompts
to validate your purchase.

You'll receive an email with your PIN and instructions.

2021/2022 ASVAB

with Online Practice

by Angie Papple Johnston

2021/2022 ASVAB For Dummies® with Online Practice

Published by: **John Wiley & Sons, Inc.,** 111 River Street, Hoboken, NJ 07030-5774, www.wiley.com

Copyright © 2021 by John Wiley & Sons, Inc., Hoboken, New Jersey

Published simultaneously in Canada

No part of this publication may be reproduced, stored in a retrieval system or transmitted in any form or by any means, electronic, mechanical, photocopying, recording, scanning or otherwise, except as permitted under Sections 107 or 108 of the 1976 United States Copyright Act, without the prior written permission of the Publisher. Requests to the Publisher for permission should be addressed to the Permissions Department, John Wiley & Sons, Inc., 111 River Street, Hoboken, NJ 07030, (201) 748-6011, fax (201) 748-6008, or online at http://www.wiley.com/go/permissions.

Trademarks: Wiley, For Dummies, the Dummies Man logo, Dummies.com, Making Everything Easier, and related trade dress are trademarks or registered trademarks of John Wiley & Sons, Inc., and may not be used without written permission. All other trademarks are the property of their respective owners. John Wiley & Sons, Inc., is not associated with any product or vendor mentioned in this book.

For general information on our other products and services, please contact our Customer Care Department within the U.S. at 877-762-2974, outside the U.S. at 317-572-3993, or fax 317-572-4002. For technical support, please visit https://hub.wiley.com/community/support/dummies.

Wiley publishes in a variety of print and electronic formats and by print-on-demand. Some material included with standard print versions of this book may not be included in e-books or in print-on-demand. If this book refers to media such as a CD or DVD that is not included in the version you purchased, you may download this material at http://booksupport.wiley.com. For more information about Wiley products, visit www.wiley.com.

Library of Congress Control Number: 2021930612

ISBN 978-1-119-78417-3 (pbk); ISBN 978-1-119-78418-0 (ebk); ISBN 978-1-119-78419-7 (ebk)

Manufactured in the United States of America

SKY10026565_042621

Contents at a Glance

Table of Contents

Introduction

I f you're reading this book, there's a good chance that you want to join the United States military. Perhaps it's been your lifelong dream to drive a tank, fire a machine gun, or blow things up (legally). Maybe you've always wanted to learn how to cook for 2,000 people at a time. Possibly you were attracted to the military because of education and training opportunities, the chance to travel, or huge enlistment bonuses. In any event, by now you've discovered that you can't just walk into a recruiter's office and say, "Hey, I'm here. Sign me up!" These days, you have to pass the ASVAB.

The ASVAB (short for Armed Services Vocational Aptitude Battery) is unlike any test you've ever taken. It covers standard academic areas, such as math and English, but it also measures your knowledge of mechanics, electronics, science, and assembling objects.

The good news is that you need to do well on some of the subtests but not necessarily all of them. In this book, you find out what you need to know to do well on *all* the subtests. You also get the information you need to figure out which subtests require good scores for your dream job. I include charts and tables that tie together military jobs and test scores, information you may see on the test, and even practice questions in each area to help you determine how much you need to study to get the right scores for your personal goals.

About This Book

The computer enlistment version of the ASVAB has ten separate subtests that result in a total of nine scores, and the paper version of the test has nine subtests to provide you with those same nine scores (two of the subtests are combined). This book shows you what to expect on each subtest, offers strategies for studying each subject area, gives you test-taking (and guessing) tips, and provides three full-length practice tests that help you determine your strengths and weaknesses. These practice tests also help you prepare mentally for taking the real test — you can use them to get in the zone. I've thrown in two extra tests that cover the four most important subtests of the ASVAB that make up the AFQT (Armed Forces Qualification Test) score at no extra cost.

Although much of the material covered on the ASVAB is taught in practically every high school in the country, you may have slept through part of the info or performed a major brain-dump as soon as the ink was dry on your diploma. For that reason, you also get a basic review of the relevant subject areas to help refresh your memory, as well as some pointers on where to find more information if you need it.

Foolish Assumptions

While writing and revising this book, I made a few assumptions about you — namely, who you are and why you picked up this book. I assume the following:

» You've come here for test-taking tips and other helpful information. You may be a nervous test-taker.

» You want to take a few ASVAB practice tests to measure your current knowledge in various subject areas to help you develop a study plan.

» You want the military job of your dreams, and passing the ASVAB (or certain sections of it) is really important to you.

» You're in a high school that participates in the ASVAB Career Exploration Program, and you want to know what to expect on the test.

Icons Used in This Book

Throughout this book, you find icons that help you use the material in this book. Here's a run-down of what they mean:

This icon alerts you to helpful hints regarding the ASVAB. Tips can help you save time and avoid frustration.

This icon reminds you of important information you should read carefully.

This icon flags actions and ideas that may prove hazardous to your plans of conquering the ASVAB. Often, this icon accompanies common mistakes or misconceptions people have about the ASVAB or questions on the test.

This icon points out information that is interesting, enlightening, or in-depth but that isn't necessary for you to read.

This icon points out sample test questions that appear in review chapters.

Beyond the Book

In addition to what you're reading right now, this book comes with a free access-anywhere Cheat Sheet that includes tips to help you prepare for the ASVAB. To get this Cheat Sheet, simply go to www.dummies.com and type **ASVAB For Dummies Cheat Sheet** in the Search box.

You also get access to seven full-length online practice tests (six ASVAB and one AFQT) and hundreds of flashcards. To gain access to the online practice, all you have to do is register. Just follow these simple steps:

1. **Register your book or ebook at Dummies.com to get your PIN.** Go to www.dummies.com/go/getaccess.

2. **Select your product from the drop-down list on that page.**

3. **Follow the prompts to validate your product, and then check your email for a confirmation message that includes your PIN and instructions for logging in.**

If you do not receive this email within 2 hours, please check your spam folder before contacting us through our Technical Support website at http://support.wiley.com or by phone at 877-762-2974.

Now you're ready to go! You can come back to the practice material as often as you want — simply log on with the username and password you created during your initial login. No need to enter the access code a second time.

Your registration is good for one year from the day you activate your PIN.

But wait! There's more! This book also comes with some helpful online videos that cover all the topics that you need to study to do well on the ASVAB. Check them out at www.dummies.com/go/asvabvideos.

Where to Go from Here

You don't have to read this book from cover to cover to score well. I suggest that you begin with Chapters 1 and 2. That way, you can get a feel for how the ASVAB is organized (along with the most up-to-date changes on the test) and which subtests may be important for the military service branch and job of your choice. This plan of attack helps you set up logical and effective goals to maximize your study efforts.

You may want to start by taking one of the practice tests in Part 6. By using this method, you can discover which subjects you're strong in and which subjects you could spend a little more time reviewing. If you choose this technique, you can use the other practice tests to measure your progress after reading through and studying the subject chapters.

If you're taking the ASVAB for the purpose of enlisting in the U.S. military, you may want to skip entire chapters, depending on your career goals. For example, if the military careers you're interested in don't require a great score on the Mechanical Comprehension subtest, you may want to spend less time studying that topic and concentrate your study time on chapters focusing on developing knowledge or skills that your dream job does require.

I wish you luck on taking this battery of tests, and if you want to join the military, I hope you have a tremendously successful journey!

1

Getting Started with the ASVAB

Chapter 1

Putting the ASVAB under a Microscope

The Armed Services Vocational Aptitude Battery (ASVAB) consists of ten tests that cover subjects ranging from general science principles to vocabulary. Your ASVAB test results determine whether you qualify for military service and, if so, which jobs you qualify for. The ASVAB isn't an IQ test. The military isn't trying to figure out how smart you are. The ASVAB specifically measures your ability to be trained to do a specific job.

The famous Chinese general Sun Tzu said, "Know your enemy." To develop an effective plan of study (check out Appendix B) and score well on the ASVAB, it's important to understand how the ASVAB is organized and how the military uses the scores from the subtests. This chapter describes the different versions of the ASVAB, the organization of the subtests, how the AFQT score is calculated, and the various service policies for retaking the ASVAB.

Knowing Which Version You're Taking

The ASVAB comes in five versions, depending on where and why you take it. The varieties of the test are essentially the same; they're just administered differently. Table 1-1 boils them down.

The vast majority of military applicants are processed through a MEPS, where they take the computerized format of the ASVAB (called the CAT-ASVAB, short for *computerized-adaptive testing* ASVAB), undergo a physical exam, and run through a security screening, many times all in one trip. The paper-and-pencil (P&P) version is most often given in high school and at Mobile Examination Test (MET) sites located throughout the United States. Most MET sites use paper versions of the test.

TABLE 1-1   Versions of the ASVAB

Version	How You Take It	Format	Purpose
Student	Given to juniors and seniors in high school; it's administered through a cooperative program between the Department of Education and the Department of Defense at high schools across the United States	Paper	Its primary purpose is to provide a tool for guidance counselors to use when recommending civilian career areas to high school students (though it can be used for enlistment if taken within two years of enlistment). For example, if a student scores high in electronics, the counselor can recommend electronics career paths. If a student is interested in military service, the counselor then refers her to the local military recruiting offices.
Enlistment	Given through a military recruiter at a Military Entrance Processing Station (MEPS) or at a satellite testing site	Usually computer, may be paper	This version of the ASVAB is used by all the military branches for the purpose of enlistment qualification and to determine which military jobs a recruit can successfully be trained in.
Enlistment Screening Test (EST)	Given at the discretion of a military recruiter for a quick enlistment qualification screening	Computer	These mini-ASVABs aren't qualification tests; they're strictly recruiting and screening tools. The EST contains about 50 questions similar but not identical to questions on the AFQT portion of the ASVAB. The test is used to help estimate an applicant's probability of obtaining qualifying ASVAB scores.
Pre-screening, internet-delivered Computerized Adaptive Test (PiCAT)	Online, on your own time after receiving an access code from your recruiter	Computer	The PiCAT is an unproctored, full version of the ASVAB. You take it on your own time, but you must take a verification test at a MEPS to validate your score. The verification test typically takes 25 to 30 minutes to complete.
Armed Forces Classification Test (AFCT)	Given at installation educational centers to people already in the military through the Defense Manpower Data Center	Computer	At some point during your military career, you may want to retrain for a different job. If you need higher ASVAB scores to qualify for such retraining, or if you're a commissioned officer who wants to become a warrant officer, you can take the AFCT. The AFCT is essentially the same as the other versions of the ASVAB.

Mapping Out the ASVAB Subtests

The computerized format of the ASVAB contains ten separately timed subtests, with the Auto & Shop Information subtest split in two. The paper format of the test has nine subtests (the Auto & Shop Information subtests are combined). The two formats differ in the number of questions in each subtest and the amount of time you have for each one. Table 1-2 outlines the ASVAB subtests in the order that you take them in the enlistment (computerized or paper) and student (paper only) versions of the test; you can also see which chapters to turn to when you want to review that content.

The CAT-ASVAB now often contains *tryout questions.* These questions haven't been used on an officially scored ASVAB; test-makers use your responses to them to ensure the questions are good enough to use on future versions of the test. Each tester sees 15 tryout questions in two, three, or four of the subtests. These questions don't count toward your score, but you still have to answer them. The tryout questions are only on the computerized version of the test; they're not on the paper version. When you get tryout questions in a subtest, you get extra time to complete it.

TABLE 1-2   The ASVAB Subtests in Order

Subtest	Questions/Time without Tryout Questions (CAT-ASVAB)	Possible Questions/Time with Tryout Questions (CAT-ASVAB)	Questions/Time (Paper Version)	Content	Chapter
General Science (GS)	15 questions, 10 minutes	30 questions, 20 minutes	25 questions, 11 minutes	General principles of biological and physical sciences	Chapters 10, 11, and 12
Arithmetic Reasoning (AR)	15 questions, 55 minutes	30 questions, 113 minutes	30 questions, 36 minutes	Word problems involving high school math concepts that require calculations	Chapter 9
Word Knowledge (WK)	15 questions, 9 minutes	30 questions, 18 minutes	35 questions, 11 minutes	Correct meaning of a word; occasionally antonyms (words with opposite meanings)	Chapter 4
Paragraph Comprehension (PC)	10 questions, 27 minutes	25 questions, 75 minutes	15 questions, 13 minutes	Questions based on passages (usually a couple of hundred words) that you read	Chapter 5
Mathematics Knowledge (MK)	15 questions, 23 minutes	30 questions, 47 minutes	25 questions, 24 minutes	High school math, including algebra and geometry	Chapters 6, 7, and 8
Electronics Information (EI)	15 questions, 10 minutes	30 questions, 21 minutes	20 questions, 9 minutes	Electrical principles, basic electronic circuitry, and electronic terminology	Chapter 16
Auto & Shop Information (AS)	10 Auto Information questions, 7 minutes; 10 Shop Information questions, 6 minutes	25 Auto Information questions, 18 minutes; 25 Shop Information questions, 17 minutes	25 questions, 11 minutes	Knowledge of automobiles, shop terminology, and tool use	Chapters 13 and 14
Mechanical Comprehension (MC)	15 questions, 22 minutes	30 questions, 42 minutes	25 questions, 19 minutes	Basic mechanical and physical principles	Chapter 15
Assembling Objects (AO)*	15 questions, 17 minutes	30 questions, 36 minutes	25 questions, 15 minutes	Spatial orientation	Chapter 17

*The Assembling Objects subtest isn't part of the student version of the test.

Deciphering ASVAB Scores

The Department of Defense is an official U.S. Government agency, so (of course) it provides plenty of detail regarding your scores. When you receive your ASVAB score results, you don't see just one score; you see several. Figure 1-1 shows an example of an ASVAB score card used by high school guidance counselors (for people who take the student version — see "Knowing Which Version You're Taking" for details).

ASVAB Summary Results Sheet					
ASVAB Results	**Percentile Scores**			**11th Grade Standard Score Bands**	**11th Grade Standard Score**
	11th Grade Females	11th Grade Males	11th Grade Students		
Career Exploration Scores					
Verbal Skills	62	64	63		55
Math Skills	44	45	45		46
Science and Technical Skills	66	43	54		51
ASVAB Tests					
General Science	56	43	49		49
Arithmetic Reasoning	36	34	35		44
Word Knowledge	75	74	75		57
Paragraph Comprehension	44	56	50		51
Mathematics Knowledge	49	56	53		48
Electronics Information	77	52	65		53
Auto and Shop Information	68	35	51		48
Mechanical Comprehension	76	48	62		52
Military Entrance Score (AFQT) 39					

FIGURE 1-1: A sample ASVAB score card used by high school guidance counselors.

© *John Wiley & Sons, Inc.*

Figure 1-2 depicts an example of an ASVAB score card used for military enlistment purposes.

So what do all these different scores actually mean? Check out the following sections to find out.

Defining all the scores

When you take a test in high school, you usually receive a score that's pretty easy to understand — A, B, C, D, or F. (If you do really well, the teacher may even draw a smiley face on the top of the page.) If only your ASVAB scores were as easy to understand.

In the following list, you see how your ASVAB test scores result in several different kinds of scores:

WARNING

>> **Raw score:** This score is the total number of points you receive on each subtest of the ASVAB. Although you don't see your raw scores on the ASVAB score cards, they're used to calculate the other scores.

> You can't use the practice tests in this book (or any other ASVAB study guide) to calculate your probable ASVAB score. ASVAB scores are calculated by using raw scores, and raw scores aren't determined by adding the number of right or wrong answers. On the actual ASVAB, harder questions are worth more points than easier questions are.

>> **Standard scores:** The various subtests of the ASVAB are reported on the score cards as standard scores. A *standard score* is calculated by converting your raw score based on a standard distribution of scores with a mean of 50 and a standard deviation of 10.

SAMPLE CAT-ASVAB TEST SCORE REPORT

Testing Site ID: 521342   Service: AF

Testing Session: Date: 2013/05/18   Starting Time: 15:30

Applicant: Jane P. Doe   SSN: 333-33-3333

Test Form: 02E   Test Type: Initial

Standard Scores:	GS	AR	WK	PC	MK	EI	AS	MC	AO	VE
	63	59	60	52	56	81	64	62	52	58

COMPOSITE SCORES:

Army:	GT	CL	CO	EL	FA	GM	MM	OF	SC	ST
	118	121	128	130	127	132	134	129	128	125

Air Force:	M	A	G	E
	91	76	83	96

Navy/CG:	GT	EL	BEE	ENG	MEC	MEC2	NUC	OPS	HM	ADM
	117	259	234	120	185	173	235	225	177	114

Army:	MM	GT	EL
	139	122	134

SAMPLE CAT-ASVAB TEST SCORE REPORT

FIGURE 1-2: A sample ASVAB score card used for military enlistment purposes.

© John Wiley & Sons, Inc.

WARNING

Don't confuse a standard score with the graded-on-a-curve score you may have seen on school tests — where the scores range from 1 to 100 with the majority of students scoring between 70 and 100. With standard scores, the majority score is between 30 and 70. That means that a standard score of 50 is an average score and that a score of 60 is an above-average score.

>> **Percentile scores:** These scores range from 1 to 99. They express how well you did in comparison with another group called the *norm.* On the student version's score card, the norm is fellow students in your same grade (except for the AFQT score).

On the enlistment and student score cards, the AFQT score is presented as a percentile with the score normed using the *1997 Profile of American Youth,* a national probability sample of 18- to 23-year-olds who took the ASVAB in 1997. For example, if you receive a percentile score of 72, you can say you scored as well as or better than 72 out of 100 of the norm group who took the test. (And by the way, this statistic from 1997 isn't a typo. The ASVAB is usually "re-normed" every 15 to 20 years; the last time was in 2004, and the sample group used for the norm was those folks who took the test in 1997.)

>> **Composite scores (line scores):** Composite scores are individually computed by each service branch. Each branch has its own particular system when compiling various standard scores into individual composite scores. These scores are used by the different branches to determine job qualifications. Find out much more about this topic in Chapter 2.

Understanding the big four: Your AFQT scores

The ASVAB doesn't have an overall score. When you hear someone say, "I got an 80 on my ASVAB," that person is talking about his or her percentile on the Armed Forces Qualification Test (AFQT) score, not an overall ASVAB score. The AFQT score determines whether you even qualify to enlist in the military, and only four of the subtests are used to compute it:

» Word Knowledge (WK)

» Paragraph Comprehension (PC)

» Arithmetic Reasoning (AR)

» Mathematics Knowledge (MK)

Each job in the military, from food service positions to specialty jobs in the medical field, requires a certain combination of line scores that can include the scores you get on the AFQT. The subtests that aren't part of the AFQT are used only to determine the jobs you qualify for. (See Chapter 2 for information on how the military uses the individual subtests.)

TIP

Figure out which areas to focus on based on your career goals. If you're not interested in a job that requires a great score on the Mechanical Comprehension subtest, you don't need to invest a lot of time studying for it. As you're preparing for the ASVAB, remember to plan your study time wisely. If you don't need to worry about the Assembling Objects subtest, don't bother with that chapter in this book. Spend the time on Word Knowledge or Arithmetic Reasoning. Keep in mind, though, if you don't have a desired job or aren't sure about your options, it's best to study this book and take the practice tests, focusing on all areas of the ASVAB. Doing well on each subtest will broaden your available job choices and make you a more desirable candidate.

Calculating the AFQT score

The military brass (or at least its computers) determines your AFQT score through a very particular process:

1. **Add the value of your Word Knowledge score to your Paragraph Comprehension score.**

2. **Convert the result of Step 1 to a scaled score, ranging from 20 to 62.**

   This score is known as your *Verbal Expression* or VE score.

3. **To get your raw AFQT score, double your VE score and then add your Arithmetic Reasoning (AR) score and your Mathematics Knowledge (MK) score to it.**

   The basic equation looks like this:

   Raw AFQT Score = 2VE + AR + MK

4. **Convert your raw score to a percentile score, which basically compares your results to the results of thousands of other ASVAB test-takers.**

   For example, a score of 50 means that you scored as well as or better than 50 percent of the individuals the military is comparing you to.

Looking at AFQT score requirements for enlistment

AFQT scores are grouped into six main categories based on the percentile score ranges in Table 1-3. Category III and Category IV are divided into subgroups because the services sometimes use this chart for internal tracking purposes, enlistment limits, and enlistment incentives. Based on your scores, the military decides how trainable you may be to perform jobs in the service.

TABLE 1-3 **AFQT Scores and Trainability**

Category	Percentile Score	Trainability
I	93–99	Outstanding
II	65–92	Excellent
III A	50–64	Above average
III B	31–49	Average
IV A	21–30	Below average
IV B	16–20	Below average
IV C	10–15	Below average
V	1–9	Not trainable

The U.S. Congress has directed that the military can't accept Category V recruits or more than 4 percent of recruits from Category IV. No more than 10 percent of new recruits may have a high school equivalency certificate rather than a diploma. The military also requires at least 60 percent of all new recruits to fall into Categories I, II, or III A. If your score falls into Category III B or anywhere in Category IV, your chances of being able to enlist are smaller (especially if other Category IV recruits beat you to it).

Depending on whether you have a high school diploma or a passing score on your state's approved high school equivalency test (such as the GED), the military has different AFQT score requirements. Check out Table 1-4.

TABLE 1-4 **AFQT Score Requirements**

Branch of Service	Minimum AFQT Score with High School Diploma	Minimum AFQT Score with High School Equivalency Test Certificate	Special Circumstances
Air Force	36	50	In very rare cases, if you possess special skills (such as speaking a foreign language that the Air Force considers critical), the minimum AFQT score can be waived. The Air Force allows less than 1 percent of its enlistees each year to have a high school equivalency test certificate instead of a high school diploma.
Army	31	50	The Army sometimes approves waivers for applicants with high school equivalency test certificates and AFQT scores below 31.
Coast Guard	36	Varies	If you have a high school equivalency certificate, the minimum AFQT score doesn't apply. If your ASVAB line scores qualify you for a specific job and you're willing to enlist in that job, the recruiter may be able to put in a waiver. Very few people (about 5 percent) each year are allowed to enlist with a high school equivalency certificate.
Marine Corps	31	50	You must have at least 15 college credits to enlist with a high school equivalency certificate.
Navy	31	50	If you enlist with a high school equivalency certificate, you must have 15 college credits.

The minimum scores required in each branch can — and do — change frequently because the military has different needs at different times. For example, at the height of Operation Iraqi Freedom, the Army accepted recruits with GEDs who scored 31 on the AFQT.

Checking out the military's AFQT requirements for special programs

Achieving the minimum required AFQT score established by an individual branch gets your foot in the door, but the higher you score, the better. For example, if you need a medical or criminal history waiver in order to enlist, the military personnel who make those decisions are more likely to take a chance on you if they think you're a pretty smart cookie than they would be if you barely made the minimum qualifying score.

Individual branches of the military tie many special enlistment programs to minimum AFQT scores:

>> **Army:** The Army requires a minimum AFQT score of 50 to qualify for most of its incentive programs, such as a monetary enlistment bonus, the college-loan repayment program, and the Army College Fund.

>> **Marine Corps:** Like the Army, the Marine Corps requires a minimum AFQT score of 50 for most of its incentive programs, including the Geographic Area of Choice Program, the Marine Corps College Fund, and enlistment bonuses.

>> **Navy:** Applicants who want to participate in the Navy College Fund or college-loan repayment program need to achieve a minimum score of 50.

MILITARY OPENS COMBAT ROLES TO WOMEN

Jobs that were traditionally open only to male members of the U.S. Armed Forces are now open to women — but it took 378 years for the military to change the way it does business.

The first militias in the New World began organizing in 1636, and men were the only ones who served. Even after June 14, 1775, the official "birthday" of the U.S. Army, the military denied women the opportunity to enlist. However, females sometimes traveled with the troops to act as nurses, laundresses, and cooks if they could prove their usefulness to troop commanders.

History occasionally reveals a woman who disguised herself as a man to join the fight between 1776 and 1948. (During the Civil War, a nominal number of females served as spies while others continued to fight on the front lines disguised as men.)

Congress passed the Women's Armed Services Integration Act on June 12, 1948, which gave women the right to enlist during peacetime and to collect veteran benefits.

Sixty-seven years later, on December 3, 2015, Secretary of Defense Ash Carter ordered the full integration of women in the Armed Forces. Under that order, all military occupational specialties are now open to women — including ground combat roles and special operations, such as Navy SEALS, Army Rangers, and Air Force Special Tactics.

New, gender-neutral job titles replaced traditional titles such as "artilleryman" and "reconnaissance man." Now those jobs are referred to as *artillery technician* and *reconnaissance Marine.*

REMEMBER

Enlistment programs are subject to change without notice based on the current recruiting needs of the service. Your recruiter can give you the most up-to-date information.

TIP

If you don't know which kind of job you want to do in the military, the ASVAB helps you and the military determine your potential ability for different types of jobs. If you're in this situation, review all the chapters in this book, brushing up on the basic principles of everything from science to electronics, but focus on the four subtests that enable you to qualify for enlistment: Word Knowledge, Paragraph Comprehension, Arithmetic Reasoning, and Mathematics Knowledge. Following this plan ensures a relatively accurate appraisal of your aptitude for various military jobs.

Do-Over: Retaking the ASVAB

An AFQT score between 0 and 9 tells the military that you're not trainable, so no branch of the service accepts people who score in that range. Even if you score higher than that, you can fail to achieve a score high enough to enlist in the service branch you want. This means you need to work on one (or more) of the four core areas: Mathematics Knowledge, Arithmetic Reasoning, Paragraph Comprehension, and Word Knowledge. Parts 2 and 3 of this book are specifically designed to help you improve your scores on these four subtests.

When you're sure you're ready, you can apply (through your recruiter) to take the ASVAB. After you take the ASVAB for the first time, you can retake the test after one month (taking the ASVAB in high school does count for retest purposes). After the first retest, you must wait another month to test again. From that point on, you must wait at least six months before taking the ASVAB again.

You can't retake the ASVAB on a whim or whenever you simply feel like it. Each of the services has its own rules concerning whether it allows a retest, and I explain them in the following sections.

REMEMBER

ASVAB test results are valid for two years, as long as you aren't in the military. In most cases, after you join the military, your ASVAB scores remain valid as long as you're in. In other words, except in a few cases, you can use your enlistment ASVAB scores to qualify for retraining years later.

U.S. Army retest policy

The Army allows a retest in one of the following instances:

>> The applicant's previous ASVAB test has expired.

>> The applicant failed to achieve an AFQT score high enough to qualify for enlistment.

>> Unusual circumstances occur, such as if an applicant, through no fault of his or her own, is unable to complete the test.

REMEMBER

Army recruiters aren't authorized to have applicants retested for the sole purpose of increasing aptitude area scores to meet standards prescribed for enlistment options or programs.

U.S. Air Force retest policy

For the U.S. Air Force, the intent of retesting is for an applicant to improve the last ASVAB scores so the enlistment options increase. Before any retest is administered, the recruiting flight chief must interview the applicant in person or by telephone and then give approval for the retest.

Here are a few other policies to remember:

» The Air Force doesn't allow retesting for applicants after they've enlisted in the Delayed Entry Program (DEP).

» Current policy allows retesting of applicants who aren't holding a job/aptitude area reservation and/or who aren't in DEP but already have qualifying test scores.

» Retesting is authorized when the applicant's current line scores (mechanical, administrative, general, and electronic) limit the ability to match an Air Force skill with his or her qualifications.

U.S. Navy retest policy

The Navy allows retesting of applicants

» Whose previous ASVAB tests have expired

» Who fail to achieve a qualifying AFQT score for enlistment in the Navy

TRACING THE TESTING TRAIL

In 1948, Congress made the Department of Defense develop a uniform screening test to be used by all the services. The Defense Department came up with the Armed Forces Qualification Test (AFQT). This test consisted of 100 multiple-choice questions in areas such as math, vocabulary, spatial relations, and mechanical ability. The military used this test until the mid-1970s. Each branch of the service set its own minimum qualification (AFQT) score.

When the military decides to do something, it often acts with the lightning speed of a snail carrying a backpack. So in the 1960s, the Department of Defense decided to develop a standardized military selection and classification test and to administer it in high schools. That's where your old buddy, the ASVAB, came from. The first ASVAB test was given in 1968, but the military didn't use it for recruiting purposes for several years. In 1973, the draft ended and the nation entered the contemporary period in which all military recruits are volunteers. In 1976, the ASVAB became the official entry test used by all services.

The ASVAB remained unchanged until 1980, when it underwent its first revision. The subtest areas remained the same, but several of the questions were updated to keep up with changes in technology.

In 1993, the computerized version was released for limited operational testing, but it didn't begin to see wide-scale use until 1996. The questions on the computerized version of the ASVAB were identical to the questions on the paper version. It wasn't until the end of 2002 that the ASVAB finally underwent a major revision. Two subtests (Coding Speed and Numerical Operations) were eliminated, and a new subtest (Assembling Objects) was added to the computerized version. Also during the 2002 revision, all the questions were updated, and the order of the subtests was changed. The revised ASVAB was first rolled out in the computerized format, and the paper versions of the test were updated during the next year. The most recent update occurred in 2008. The ASVAB was revised to better sync the line scores with the applicants' qualified jobs.

In most cases, individuals in the Delayed Entry Program (DEP) can't retest.

U.S. Marine Corps retest policy

The Marine Corps authorizes a retest if the applicant's previous test has expired. Otherwise, recruiters can request a retest if the initial scores don't appear to reflect the applicant's true capability, considering the applicant's education, training, and experience.

REMEMBER

For the Marine Corps, the retest can't be requested solely because the applicant's initial test scores didn't meet the standards prescribed for enlistment options or programs.

U.S. Coast Guard retest policy

For Coast Guard enlistments, six months must have elapsed since an applicant's last test before he or she may retest solely for the purpose of raising scores to qualify for a particular enlistment option.

The Coast Guard Recruiting Center may authorize retesting after one calendar month has passed from an initial ASVAB test if substantial reason exists to believe the initial test scores or subtest scores don't reflect an applicant's education, training, or experience.

Chapter **2**

Knowing What It Takes to Get Your Dream Job

The Armed Forces Qualification Test (AFQT) portion of the ASVAB is your most important score because it determines whether you can join the service branch of your choice. However, qualifying to join is only part of the picture. Unless you'd be content to spend your military career painting things that don't move, you need to understand how the ASVAB relates to various military job opportunities.

Civilian employers generally use a person's education and experience level when selecting candidates for a job position, but in the military, the vast majority of all enlisted jobs are entry-level positions. The military doesn't require you to have a college degree in computer science before you're hired to become a computer programmer. You don't even have to have any previous computer experience, nor does the military care if you do. The military sends you to advanced individual training (the school you must complete after basic training) to teach you everything it wants you to know.

Sounds like a good deal, right? So what's the catch? Well, believe me — the military spends big bucks turning high school graduates into highly trained and skilled aircraft mechanics, language specialists, and electronic-doodad repair people. In an average year, the services aim to enlist about 150,000 new recruits. Any way you look at it, that's a lot of combat boots! Each and every recruit has to be sent to a military school to train for a job. Uncle Sam needs a way to determine whether these recruits have the mental aptitude to succeed at that job — preferably before he spends people's hard-earned tax dollars.

Enter the ASVAB. The services combine various ASVAB subtest scores into groupings called composite scores or line scores. Through years of trial and error, the individual military services have each determined what minimum composite scores are required to successfully complete its various job-training programs. In this chapter, you discover how those test scores translate into finding the military job of your dreams.

Eyeing How ASVAB Scores Determine Military Training Programs and Jobs

Each service branch has its own system of scores. Recruiters and military job counselors use these scores, along with factors such as job availability, security clearance eligibility, and medical qualifications, to match up potential recruits with military jobs.

REMEMBER

During the initial enlistment process, your service branch determines your military job or enlistment program based on established minimum *line scores:* various combinations of scores from individual subtests (see the next section for details). If you get high enough scores in the right areas, you can get the job you want — as long as that job is available and you meet other qualification factors.

For active duty, the Army is the only service that looks at the scores and offers a guaranteed job for all its new enlistees, aside from those enlisting in the infantry or trying out for Special Forces. In other words, nearly every single Army recruit knows what his or her job is going to be before signing the enlistment contract. The other active duty services use a combination of guaranteed jobs or guaranteed aptitude and career areas:

>> **Air Force:** About 40 percent of active duty Air Force recruits enlist with a guaranteed job. The majority enlists in one of four guaranteed aptitude areas, and during basic training, recruits are assigned to a job that falls into that aptitude area.

>> **Coast Guard:** The Coast Guard rarely, if ever, offers a guaranteed job in its active duty enlistment contracts. Instead, new Coast Guardsmen enlist as undesignated seamen and spend their first year or so of service doing general work ("Paint that ship!") before finally applying for specific job training.

>> **Marine Corps:** A vast majority of Marine Corps active duty enlistees are guaranteed one of several job fields, such as infantry, avionics, logistics, vehicle maintenance, aircraft maintenance, munitions, and so on. Each of these fields is further divided into specific sub-jobs, called Military Occupational Specialties (MOSs). Marine recruits often don't find out their actual MOSs until about halfway through basic training.

>> **Navy:** Most Navy recruits enlist with a guaranteed job, but several hundred people each year also enlist in a guaranteed career area and then *strike* (apply) for the specific job within a year of graduating boot camp.

>> **Space Force:** You can't yet enlist directly into the U.S. Space Force (USSF). As of 2021, you can only transfer in from your current position in the Air Force. The USSF expects to accept transfers from the Army and Navy by fiscal year 2022/2023 and may open enlistment to new applicants after that.

SEMPER SUPRA: THE ASVAB AND THE ALL-NEW SPACE FORCE

The sky isn't the limit anymore. The United States Space Force, the sixth military branch, operates under the U.S. Air Force (like the way the Marines are a department of the Navy). Right now, the branch is only accepting current airmen who transfer from the regular Air Force. Eventually, when the Space Force begins to accept new enlistees, it'll come up with its own AFQT and line score requirements. If you're reading this book with the intention of eventually transferring to the USSF, you should set your sights on Air Force Specialty Code 1C6 (Space Systems Operations) or a job in acquisitions, engineering, intelligence, or cyber operations. Your recruiter can give you the most up-to-date information.

All enlistment contracts for the reserve forces (regardless of branch) contain guarantees for a specific job. Why? Because reserve recruiters recruit for vacancies in specific reserve units, usually located within 100 miles of where a person lives.

Understanding How Each Branch Computes Line Scores

A *line score* combines various standard ASVAB scores to see which jobs or training programs you qualify for. The *standard scores* are your scores on the individual ASVAB subtests (with Word Knowledge and Paragraph Comprehension combined as a Verbal Expression score):

>> General Science (GS)

>> Arithmetic Reasoning (AR)

>> Auto & Shop Information (AS)

>> Mathematics Knowledge (MK)

>> Mechanical Comprehension (MC)

>> Electronics Information (EI)

>> Assembling Objects (AO)

>> Verbal Expression (VE), the sum of Word Knowledge (WK) and Paragraph Comprehension (PC)

Each of the military services computes its line scores differently. Some calculations even include *dummy scores* — average scores received by thousands of test-takers — for Numerical Operations (NO) and Coding Speed (CS), subtests that are no longer part of the ASVAB. The following sections outline how each branch comes up with its line scores.

Line scores and the Army

To compute line scores for job qualification, the Army combines the various scores into ten separate areas by simple addition of the ASVAB standard scores. Table 2-1 shows the line scores and the ASVAB subtests that make them up.

TABLE 2-1 The U.S. Army's Ten Line Scores

Line Score	Standard Scores Used	Formula Used
Clerical (CL)	Verbal Expression (VE), Arithmetic Reasoning (AR), and Mathematics Knowledge (MK)	VE + AR + MK
Combat (CO)	Arithmetic Reasoning (AR), Coding Speed (CS), Auto & Shop Information (AS), and Mechanical Comprehension (MC)	AR + CS + AS + MC
Electronics (EL)	General Science (GS), Arithmetic Reasoning (AR), Mathematics Knowledge (MK), and Electronics Information (EI)	GS + AR + MK + EI
Field Artillery (FA)	Arithmetic Reasoning (AR), Coding Speed (CS), Mathematics Knowledge (MK), and Mechanical Comprehension (MC)	AR + CS + MK + MC
General Maintenance (GM)	General Science (GS), Auto & Shop Information (AS), Mathematics Knowledge (MK), and Electronics Information (EI)	GS + AS + MK + EI

(continued)

TABLE 2-1 *(continued)*

Line Score	Standard Scores Used	Formula Used
General Technical (GT)	Verbal Expression (VE) and Arithmetic Reasoning (AR)	VE + AR
Mechanical Maintenance (MM)	Numerical Operations (NO), Auto & Shop Information (AS), Mechanical Comprehension (MC), and Electronics Information (EI)	NO + AS + MC + EI
Operators and Food (OF)	Verbal Expression (VE), Numerical Operations (NO), Auto & Shop Information (AS), and Mechanical Comprehension (MC)	VE + NO + AS + MC
Surveillance and Communications (SC)	Verbal Expression (VE), Arithmetic Reasoning (AR), Auto & Shop Information (AS), and Mechanical Comprehension (MC)	VE + AR + AS + MC
Skilled Technical (ST)	General Science (GS), Verbal Expression (VE), Mathematics Knowledge (MK), and Mechanical Comprehension (MC)	GS + VE + MK + MC

Line scores and the Navy and Coast Guard

The Navy and Coast Guard use the standard scores directly from the ASVAB: the individual subtest scores and Verbal Expression (VE) score, which is the sum of Word Knowledge (WK) and Paragraph Comprehension (PC).

Although the Navy and Coast Guard don't use their line scores for officially determining jobs, the scores provide recruiters, job counselors, and recruits with a snapshot of which broad career areas recruits may qualify for. For example, the Navy regulation that lists the qualifications to become an Air Traffic Control Specialist states that an ASVAB score of VE + AR + MK + MC = 220 (or higher) is required for that job.

Table 2-2 shows the Navy and Coast Guard line scores that show up on the ASVAB score sheet.

TABLE 2-2 **The U.S. Navy and Coast Guard's Line Scores**

Line Score	Standard Scores Used	Formula Used
Engineman (ENG)	Auto & Shop Information (AS) and Mathematics Knowledge (MK)	AS + MK
Administrative (ADM)	Mathematics Knowledge (MK) and Verbal Expression (VE)	MK + VE
General Technical (GT)	Arithmetic Reasoning (AR) and Verbal Expression (VE)	AR + VE
Mechanical Maintenance (MEC)	Arithmetic Reasoning (AR), Auto & Shop Information (AS), and Mechanical Comprehension (MC)	AR + AS + MC
Health (HM)	General Science (GS), Mathematics Knowledge (MK), and Verbal Expression (VE)	GS + MK + VE
Mechanical Maintenance 2 (MEC2)	Assembling Objects (AO), Arithmetic Reasoning (AR), and Mechanical Comprehension (MC)	AO + AR + MC
Electronics (EL)	Arithmetic Reasoning (AR), Electronics Information (EI), General Science (GS), and Mathematics Knowledge (MK)	AR + EI + GS + MK

Line Score	Standard Scores Used	Formula Used
Nuclear Field (NUC)	Arithmetic Reasoning (AR), Mechanical Comprehension (MC), Mathematics Knowledge (MK), and Verbal Expression (VE)	AR + MC + MK + VE
Engineering and Electronics (BEE)	Arithmetic Reasoning (AR), General Science (GS), and two times Mathematics Knowledge (MK)	AR + GS + 2MK
Operations (OPS)	Arithmetic Reasoning (AR) and Mathematics Knowledge (MK)	AR + MK

Line scores and the Marine Corps

The Marine Corps computes its three line scores for job qualification by adding scores from various ASVAB subtests, as Table 2-3 shows.

TABLE 2-3 The Marine Corps's Line Scores

Line Score	Standard Scores Used	Formula Used
Mechanical Maintenance (MM)	General Science (GS), Auto & Shop Information (AS), Mathematics Knowledge (MK), and Mechanical Comprehension (MC)	GS + AS + MK + MC
General Technical (GT)	Verbal Expression (VE) and Arithmetic Reasoning (AR)	VE + AR
Electronics (EL)	General Science (GS), Arithmetic Reasoning (AR), Mathematics Knowledge (MK), and Electronics Information (EI)	GS + AR + MK + EI

Line scores and the Air Force

The U.S. Air Force uses standard scores from the ASVAB subtests to derive scaled scores in four aptitude areas called MAGE (mechanical, administrative, general, and electronics). The Air Force MAGE scores are calculated as *percentiles*, ranging from 0 to 99, that show your relationship to thousands of others who've taken the test. In other words, a percentile score of 51 indicates you scored better in this aptitude area than 50 percent of the testers who were used to establish the norm.

Table 2-4 lays out the four areas, the subtests used, and the formula used to calculate the score for each particular area. After calculating the score for a particular area, the test-scorer converts that score to a percentile.

TABLE 2-4 The U.S. Air Force's MAGE Scores

Line Score	Standard Scores Used	Formula Used
Mechanical	General Science (GS), Mechanical Comprehension (MC), and two times Auto & Shop Information (AS)	GS + MC + 2AS
Administrative	Numerical Operations (NO), Coding Speed (CS), and Verbal Expression (VE)	NO + CS + VE
General	Arithmetic Reasoning (AR) and Verbal Expression (VE)	AR + VE
Electronics	General Science (GS), Arithmetic Reasoning (AR), Mathematics Knowledge (MK), and Electronics Information (EI)	GS + AR + MK + EI

SCORE! SPEAKING THE LINGO

When you sit down with your recruiter to discuss your ASVAB scores and what you qualify for, you may think he suddenly decided to speak in a foreign language. For job-qualification purposes, remember three key terms and their definitions:

- **AFQT score:** Calculated from the math and English subtests of the ASVAB, the Armed Forces Qualification Test (AFQT) score is used by the military to determine overall enlistment qualification. Chapter 1 explains exactly how this critical score is computed.

- **Line score:** A line score combines various standard scores and is used by the services for job qualification purposes.

- **Standard score:** A standard score refers to individual ASVAB subtest scores (that is, Verbal Expression, Arithmetic Reasoning, Mathematics Knowledge, and so on).

Chapter **3**

Getting Acquainted with Test-Taking and Study Techniques

How many times have you heard someone say (or even said yourself), "I just can't take tests"? A lot of people feel that way, but that mind-set isn't an option on the ASVAB or in the military. In basic training, your drill sergeant will convince you that the words "I can't" don't even *exist* in the military. If you don't believe me, try telling your drill sergeant, "I just can't do push-ups." You'll find that with sufficient practice — and your drill sergeant will ensure you get a lot of practice — you can do push-ups just as well as the next person. (Actually, I don't recommend testing this, for reasons that should be obvious.) The truth is that those who do well on tests are those who've figured out how to study efficiently and how to use a dash of test-taking psychology.

This chapter includes information on how to prepare for the test. I explain how to study, as well as how and why you should take the practice exams. In addition, you get some inside info, such as secrets for guessing when you don't know the answer to a question (although if you study for the test, you won't need to guess, right?). The tips and techniques provided in this chapter can help you get a jump on the ASVAB and your military career.

Taking the Test: Computerized or Paper?

Many versions of the ASVAB exist, but you don't have any say in which one you take. The versions primarily boil down to two basic differences: the computerized version and the paper version. Each version has advantages and disadvantages, which I discuss in the following sections.

If you're taking the ASVAB as part of the student program in high school, you'll take the paper version of the test — the one that doesn't include the Assembling Objects subtest.

If you're taking the ASVAB to enlist in the military, you'll take the enlistment ASVAB. This version comes in two formats: computerized (CAT-ASVAB) and paper-and-pencil (P&P). You may even take the Pre-screening, internet-delivered Computerized Adaptive Test (PiCAT) on your own time. In any event, there's a great chance that you'll take a computerized version, because to save time and money, recruiters often accompany their applicants to the nearest Military Entrance Processing Station (MEPS) for testing, medical examination, and enlistment (one-stop shopping). MEPS only uses the computerized version, and the P&P version is offered only at Military Entrance Test (MET) sites that aren't within an easy traveling distance to MEPS. If your high school schedules a testing event, you'll most likely take the P&P version as well. Your recruiter might be able to schedule an ASVAB-only test session and bring you back in for a follow-on physical (and to sign your contract) if you can't complete everything in one day. There are 65 MEPS locations in the United States and in Puerto Rico, and MET sites are located in each state (often at National Guard armories or local high schools).

Cheating gets you thrown out of the testing location. But even if you were able to get away with looking at your neighbor's paper or computer screen, you'd fail the test. There are several versions of the test, and the people sitting around you have different questions presented in different orders.

Going paperless: The pros and cons of the computerized test

The computerized version of the ASVAB uses *computerized adaptive testing* to make sure each applicant gets questions tailored to his or her ability level. This version, called the CAT-ASVAB, presents test questions in a different format. It adapts the questions it offers you based on your level of proficiency (that's why it's called *adaptive*). Translation: The first test item is of average difficulty. If you answer this question correctly, the next question may be more difficult. If you answer that first question incorrectly, the computer will most likely follow with an easier question. By contrast, on the paper ASVAB, easy and hard questions are presented randomly.

The CAT-ASVAB also has fewer questions than the paper-and-pencil version has— the people who designed it did that on purpose. With this type of testing, the computer can quickly determine how much you know without asking you a full range of very easy to very hard questions.

Maybe it's because people today are more comfortable in front of a computer than with a pencil, but military recruiters have noted that among applicants who've taken both the paper-based and computerized versions of the ASVAB, many applicants tend to score slightly higher on the computerized version of the test.

You don't have to be a computer guru to appreciate the advantages of the computerized version of the ASVAB:

>> **It's impossible to record your answer in the wrong space on the answer sheet.** Questions and possible answers are presented on the screen, and you press the key that corresponds to your answer choice before moving on to the next question. Often, only the A, B, C, and D keys are activated when you take the test.

>> **The difficulty of the test items presented depends on whether you answered the previous question correctly.** On the two math subtests of the ASVAB, harder questions are worth more points than easier questions are, so this method helps maximize your AFQT score.

THE PiCAT: THE ASVAB'S STAY-AT-HOME COUSIN

The Pre-screening, internet-delivered Computer Adaptive Test, or PiCAT, is the military's way of operating more efficiently and speeding up the enlistment process. It allows recruiters to give applicants a special access code to take a full-length, unproctored ASVAB on any computer. After a recruit completes the PiCAT — provided his or her scores are high enough to enlist in the military — the recruiter can take the recruit to MEPS for verification testing. Verification testing takes 25 to 30 minutes, and its purpose is simple: to make sure the recruit wasn't at home looking up answers to ASVAB test questions. When PiCAT scores are verified (meaning the recruit most likely didn't cheat on the test), the recruit is good to go for enlistment. When the scores *aren't* verified (meaning the recruit scored poorly on the verification test compared to how he or she scored on the PiCAT), the recruit must take a full-length ASVAB at MEPS. The resulting ASVAB score will be the score of record. Not all recruiters use the PiCAT, and those who do may not use it for all applicants.

>> **You get your scores right away.** The computer automatically calculates and prints your standard scores for each subtest and your line scores for each service branch. (For more on line scores, see Chapter 2.) This machine is a pretty smart cookie — it also calculates your AFQT percentile score on the spot. You usually know whether you qualify for military enlistment on the same day you take the test and, if so, which jobs you qualify for.

On the downside, you can't skip questions or change your answers after you enter them on the CAT–ASVAB. Instead of being able to go through and immediately answer all the questions you're sure of, you have to answer each question as it comes. This can make it difficult to judge how much time to spend on a tough question before guessing and moving on. Also, if you have a few minutes at the end of the test, you can't go back and make sure you marked the correct answer to each question. Finally, the CAT–ASVAB is the only version of the test that includes tryout questions (see Chapter 1 for more information), which can stretch out your total test-taking time — but on a positive note, the tryout questions don't affect your score.

Writing on hard copy: The advantages and disadvantages of the paper version

The questions on the CAT–ASVAB are the same questions you get on the paper version. Some people feel that the P&P ASVAB provides certain advantages:

>> **You can skip questions that you don't know the answer to and come back to them later.** This option can help when you're racing against the clock and want to get as many answers right as possible. You can change an answer on the subtest you're currently working on, but you can't change an answer on a subtest after the time for that subtest has expired.

>> **You may not make any marks in the exam booklet; however, you may make notes on your scratch paper.** If you skip a question, you can lightly circle the item number on your answer sheet to remind yourself to go back to it. If you don't know the answer to a question, you can mentally cross off the answers that seem unlikely or wrong to you and then guess based on the remaining answers. Be sure to erase any stray marks you make on your answer sheet before time is called for that subtest.

Killing trees isn't the only disadvantage of the paper-based test. Other drawbacks include the following:

>> **Harder questions are randomly intermingled with easier questions.** This means you can find yourself spending too much time trying to figure out the answer to a question that's too hard for you and may miss answering some easier questions at the end of the subtest, thereby lowering your overall score.

>> **The paper answer sheets are scored by using an optical mark scanning machine.** The machine has a conniption when it comes across an incompletely filled-in answer circle or a stray pencil mark and will often stubbornly refuse to give you credit, even if you answered correctly.

>> **Getting your scores may seem like it takes forever.** The timeline varies; however, your recruiter will have access to your score no later than 72 hours (3 days) after you finish the test (not counting days the MEPS doesn't work, such as weekend days or holidays).

Tackling Multiple-Choice Questions

Both the computerized and paper versions of the ASVAB are multiple-choice tests. You choose the correct (or most correct) answer from among the four available choices. Here are some tips to keep in mind as you approach the choices:

>> **Read the directions carefully.** Most ASVAB test proctors agree — the majority of the time when there's an issue with an applicant's scores, misreading directions is a prime offender. Each subtest is preceded by a paragraph or two describing what the subtest covers and instructions on how to answer the questions.

>> **Make sure you understand the question.** If you don't understand the question, you're naturally not going to be able to make the best decision when selecting an answer. Understanding the question requires attention to three particular points:

- **Take special care to read the questions correctly.** Most questions ask something like, "Which of the following equals 2×3?" But sometimes, a question may ask, "Which of the following does not equal 2×3?" You can easily skip right over the word *not* when you're reading, assume that the answer is 6, and get the question wrong.

WARNING

- **On the math subtests, be especially careful to read the symbols.** When you're in a hurry, the $+$ sign and the $\div$ sign can look very similar. Blowing right by a negative sign or another symbol is just as easy.

- **Make sure you understand the terms being used.** When a math problem asks you to find the product of two numbers, be sure you know what finding the product means (you have to multiply the two numbers). If you add the two numbers, you arrive at the wrong answer. If you're having a tough time remembering what equals what in math terminology, check out Chapter 6.

>> **Take time to review all the answer options.** On all the subtests, you select the correct answer from only four possible answer options. On the ASVAB, you're supposed to choose the answer that is most correct. (Now and then you do the opposite and choose the answer that's least correct.) Sometimes several answers are reasonably correct for the question at hand, but only one of them is the best answer. If you don't stop to read and review all the answers, you may not choose the one that's most correct. Or if you review all the answer options, you may realize that you misread the question.

REMEMBER

Often, a person reads a question, decides on the answer, glances at the answer options, chooses the option that agrees with his or her answer, marks it on the answer sheet, and then moves on. Although this approach usually works, it can sometimes lead you astray.

>> **If you're taking a paper test, mark the answer carefully.** A machine scores the paper-based ASVAB answer sheets. You have to mark the answer clearly so the machine knows which answer you've selected. This means carefully filling in the space that represents the correct letter. You've done this a million times in school, but it's worth repeating: Don't use a check mark, don't circle the answer, and don't let your mark wander into the next space. If you must erase, make sure all evidence of your prior choice is gone; otherwise, the grading machine may credit you with the wrong choice or disregard your correct answer and give you no credit at all.

WARNING

Incorrectly marking the answer sheet (answering Question 11 on the line for Question 12, Question 12 on the line for Question 13 — you get the idea) is a very real possibility. Be especially careful if you skip a question that you're going to return to later.

Incorrectly marking the answers can cause a real headache. If you fail to get a qualifying score, the minimum amount of time you must wait before retaking the ASVAB is one month. Even then, your journey to military glory through ASVAB torment may not be over. If within six months of a previous test, your retest AFQT score increases by 20 points or more, you'll be required by MEPCOM regulation to take an additional ASVAB test, called a *confirmation test.* (Confirmation tests can be taken only at MEPS facilities, by the way.) If you're not careful, you'll be taking three ASVABs when all you really needed to take was one. Sound fun? Chapter 1 discusses how and when you can retake the ASVAB.

When You Don't Know an Answer: Guessing Smart

On the ASVAB, guessing is sometimes okay. Guessing can help you on the paper-and-pencil version because of how the test is scored. Here's how the point system breaks down:

>> If you choose the correct answer, you get one point (or more, depending on how the question is weighted).

>> If you don't answer a question, you get nada.

>> If you guess on a question and get the question wrong, you get nada — no worrying about losing points or getting any sort of penalty!

WARNING

Don't make wild guesses if you can make educated guesses. However, if you're nearing the end of a subtest on the CAT-ASVAB and you know you won't have time to finish, try to select answers for every question. If you fail to complete a subtest, you'll be penalized; the system will score the items you didn't complete as though you answered them randomly.

The ASVAB's computer system rarely has to penalize a test-taker. On average, the computerized test takes about two hours to complete, and most people have enough time to finish (or at least come very close to finishing) the test.

TIP

Because ASVAB questions have four possible answers, you have at least a 25 percent chance of guessing correctly, which means you have chances to increase your score. There's nearly always at least one answer that isn't even close to the correct answer, so by using simple deduction, you can often narrow your choices down to three answers or fewer. Here are some things to keep in mind when eliminating answer choices:

>> Don't eliminate an answer based on how frequently that answer comes up. For example, if Choice (B) has been the correct answer for the last five questions, don't assume that it must be the wrong answer for the question you're on just because that would make it six in a row.

>> An answer that has *always, all, everyone, never, none,* or *no one* is usually incorrect.

>> The longer the answer, the more likely that it's the correct answer. The test-makers have to get all those qualifiers in there so you can't find an example to contradict the correct answer. If you see phrases like "in many cases" or "frequently," that's often a clue that the test-makers are trying to make the answer most correct.

>> If two choices are very similar in meaning, neither of them is probably the correct choice. On the other hand, if two answer options contradict each other, one of them is usually correct.

WARNING

If you have to guess, never, ever go back and change the answer, unless you're absolutely, 100 percent, positively convinced that you're changing it to the correct answer and you answered incorrectly only because you had sweat in your eyes and didn't read the choices properly. The United States Air Force Senior NCO Academy conducted an in-depth study of several Air Force multiple-choice test results, taken over several years, and found that when students changed answers on their answer sheets, they changed from a right answer to a wrong answer more than 72 percent of the time!

In each of the chapters in Parts 3, 4, and 5, you find more hints for making educated guesses that are specific to those topics.

TIP

If you guess on more than one question throughout the test, choosing the same answer for every guess is a smart way to go. For example, all your guesses could be Choice (B). This technique slightly increases your chances of getting more answers correct. However, if you can eliminate Choice (B) as a wrong answer, then, by all means, choose a different answer option for that question.

Studying and Practicing for the ASVAB

The practice tests that come with this book are valuable study aids. Before you begin studying, take one of the tests. Try to duplicate the testing environment — take the entire exam at one time, time yourself, and don't allow interruptions.

TIP

The military has a saying, "Train as you fight." The same is true of the ASVAB. If you'll be taking the CAT-ASVAB, spend most of your time practicing with online tests. If you plan to take the paper-and-pencil version of the ASVAB, concentrate most of your efforts on the written practice tests in this book.

Get a sense of how long it takes you to complete each subtest so you know how much time you have to spend on educated guessing. After you complete each practice test, check your answers to see where you need improvement.

TIP

When you study for the ASVAB, fall in line with these study habits to make the most of your time:

>> **Focus on the subtests that matter to you.** If you have a clear interest in pursuing a career in electronics, the Electronics Information subtest should be at the top of your list to ace. Although you'll want to make sure all your line scores are good (in case your desired job isn't available or you want to retrain later in your career), focusing on your expertise in certain areas of interest makes you a more desirable candidate. (See Chapter 2 and Appendix A for lists of the subtests that affect your acceptance into the job areas you're pursuing.)

>> **Concentrate on subject areas that need improvement.** It's human nature to find yourself spending your study time on subject areas that you have an interest in or that you're good at. If you're a whiz at fixing cars, don't waste your time studying for the Auto & Shop Information subtests. You're already going to ace that part of the test, right? On the other hand, if you had a hard time in math during your high school years, you need to spend extra time brushing up on your arithmetic skills.

>> **Be a loner.** You may want to study with a partner now and then so the two of you can brainstorm answers and quiz each other, but most of your studying should be done on your own.

>> **Try to reduce distractions.** Always study in a well-lit, quiet area away from pets, loud music, and the TV.

>> **Study in long blocks of time.** Studying for an hour or two once or twice a day is much more effective than studying 15 minutes six times a day.

>> **Schedule your study times when you are rested.** Don't try to cram studying into your schedule. Quality over quantity!

>> **Keep study breaks short.** A few minutes every hour is sufficient. Don't ignore breaks completely, however. Studies show that taking short breaks while you study improves how well you're able to remember information.

>> **Practice the actual act of test-taking.** Practice marking answers correctly on the answer key and time yourself to see how long it takes you to answer questions.

TIP

If you're unsure of how to begin studying for the ASVAB, check out the 12-week study strategy in Appendix B. If you don't have 12 weeks left before you take the test, you can accelerate the schedule and zero in on what's most important.

After you do some additional studying, take the second practice exam. Again, try to duplicate testing conditions. Check your answers. Compare your scores to the scores from your first test. Have you improved? If so, continue studying as you have been. If not, reconsider how you're studying or whether you're setting aside enough time to study. A school counselor or teacher can give you additional study pointers. Continue practicing with the next few tests.

A couple of weeks before the ASVAB, take the next-to-last practice test. Brush up on any of those nagging areas that still give you fits. Check to see which areas you need help with and spend more time studying those areas.

A week before your test date, take the last test. This test helps you calm your nerves before taking the ASVAB — how the test works will be fresh in your mind.

REMEMBER

Don't waste time memorizing the practice questions in this guide or any other ASVAB study guide. You won't see the same questions on the ASVAB. Use this guide and the sample tests for two purposes:

>> **To determine the subject areas in which you need to improve:** Use the tips and techniques, along with standard study materials (like high school textbooks), to improve your knowledge of each specific subject.

>> **To familiarize yourself with the types of test questions and the way they're presented on the test:** Getting a good idea of what all the subtests look like will improve your test-taking speed. You won't have to spend time trying to figure out how a question looks. You can spend your time answering the question.

Making Last-Minute Preparations: 24 Hours and Counting

TIP

You want some good advice? On the night before the test, get some sleep — at least eight hours. Don't drink alcohol the night before — headaches, dehydration, and the ASVAB don't work well together. And don't pull an all-night cram session. If you don't know the material the night before the test, it's too late. Staying up all night only guarantees that you'll do poorly on the test, because you'll be too tired in the morning. Here are some other suggestions:

>> **On the morning of the test, eat a light meal.** Anything too heavy will make you drowsy, but not eating enough will make it hard for you to concentrate.

Try to avoid eating a breakfast high in carbohydrates and sipping energy drinks. Although the carbs and caffeine will initially make you feel energetic, a couple of hours into the test, you may come crashing down. Select foods high in protein instead.

>> **Get exercise the day before and even the morning of the test.** Doing so gets your blood pumping and helps you remain mentally sharp.

>> **If you're sick, upset, or injured, consider rescheduling the test.** Right before the test starts, the proctor will ask if there's anything, such as sickness or injury, that may affect your test performance. After the test actually starts, it's considered an "official test," and you'll have to wait a certain time period before any possibility of a retest. See Chapter 1 for details.

>> **Don't bring personal supplies to the test.** Your test administrator will provide you with pencils and scratch paper. Don't bring calculators, personal electronic devices (smartphones, tablets), backpacks, or a cooler of munchies to the testing site. You won't be allowed to have them with you. (But if you wear eyeglasses, bring them.)

>> **Bring a watch to help you keep track of time if you're taking the paper version.** The computerized version has a clock on the screen.

>> **Don't drink a lot of liquids just before the test.** You don't want to waste valuable test time in the restroom!

>> **Make sure you arrive at the test site with plenty of time to spare.** In the military, arriving on time means you're 5 minutes late. You should plan to be in your seat at least 15 minutes before the scheduled testing time. Unless your recruiter is driving you (which is often the case), you may want to do a test run a day or two before your testing date to make sure you know where the test is, the availability of parking, and how to find the testing room.

>> **Bring your ID.** You'll have to show proof of your identity when you arrive at MEPS.

2

Words to Live By: Communication Skills

Brush up on vocabulary lessons that will help you ace the Word Knowledge subtest. Review prefixes, suffixes, and roots, and distinguish between synonyms and antonyms.

Get help tackling the Paragraph Comprehension subtest, and check out the different types of questions you'll encounter.

Work some practice questions at the end of each chapter to help you determine where you excel and where you could use some more review.

Chapter **4**

Word Knowledge

To make it to basic combat training, you need a pretty decent vocabulary that helps you score well on the Word Knowledge subtest of the ASVAB. Not only do you have to know how to spell to some degree (so you can differentiate among words), but you also need to know what the words on the test mean. The military wants to know how big your vocabulary is so it can determine whether you'll be a good fit in its ranks. If you're on a military base and you're hungry, don't bother looking for a sign that says Chow Hall. Instead, you need to find the Dining Facility. If you want to work out after your big lunch, forget about the gym. You're looking for the Fitness and Wellness Center.

So, what if you don't know the difference between a carbine and a carbon? Never fear — I'm here to give you a helping hand (bestow upon you inestimable guidance and encouragement — that's Word Knowledge speak). With the help of this chapter and a little work on your part, you can whip your word-knowledge skills right into shape. And then at the end of the chapter, you can check out the practice questions to test those skills.

Grasping the Importance of Word Knowledge

Word Knowledge isn't part of the ASVAB just because the military likes to use big words. It's included because words stand for ideas, and the more words you understand, the more ideas you can understand (and the better you can communicate with others). A decent vocabulary is essential in the military if you want to get ahead. The military operates on paperwork, and whether you're trying to get more supplies (submit necessary logistical requisitions) or get the assignment you want (via application for personnel career-enhancement programs), you need to develop a good vocabulary. The military considers clear communication so important that it's taught and graded at all levels of leadership training.

REMEMBER

The Word Knowledge subtest is one of the four most important subtests on the ASVAB (along with Paragraph Comprehension, Mathematics Knowledge, and Arithmetic Reasoning). This subtest makes up a significant portion of the AFQT score — the score that determines your eligibility for military service. You also need to do well on the Word Knowledge subtest to qualify for many military jobs, such as air traffic controller, military intelligence, and even firefighting.

Table 4-1 shows the military line scores that are calculated by using your Word Knowledge subtest score.

TABLE 4-1 Military Line Scores That Use the Word Knowledge Score

Branch of Service	Line Score
U.S. Army	Clerical, Combat, General Technical, Operators and Food, Skilled Technical, and Surveillance and Communications
U.S. Air Force	Administrative, General, and Mechanical
U.S. Navy/Coast Guard	Administrative, General Technician, Hospital, Nuclear, and Operations
U.S. Marine Corps	Clerical and General Technician

Chapter 2 has more information about military line scores. Check out Appendix A for more information on the scores you need to get the job you want.

Checking Out the Word Knowledge Question Format

The Word Knowledge portion of the ASVAB measures your vocabulary. The questions usually come in one of two types:

>> The first type asks for a straight definition.

>> The second type gives you an underlined word used in the context of a sentence.

When you're asked for a straight definition, your task is quite simple: Choose the answer closest in meaning to the underlined word. Look at the following example:

EXAMPLE

<u>Abate</u> most nearly means

(A) encourage.

(B) relax.

(C) obstruct.

(D) terminate.

Abate means to suppress or terminate. In this case, the correct answer is Choice (D).

When you see an underlined word in a sentence, your goal is to choose the answer closest in meaning to the underlined word. *Remember: Closest in meaning* doesn't mean *the exact same thing.* You're looking for similar or related words. For example:

EXAMPLE

His house was <u>derelict</u>.

(A) solid

(B) run-down

(C) clean

(D) inexpensive

Here, the answer is Choice (B).

When you take the Word Knowledge subtest on the computerized version of the ASVAB, you have 9 minutes to answer only 15 questions, which means you have 36 seconds to answer each question. (If your Word Knowledge subtest includes tryout questions, which I explain in Chapter 1, you have 18 minutes to answer 30 questions.) On the paper version, the schedule's a little tighter. You have 11 minutes to answer 35 questions (or less than 20 seconds for each question). Either way, it's plenty of time, as long as you stay focused and don't waste time daydreaming about your future in the military (sorry, I mean becoming lost in reverie as you consider your impending enlistment).

These days most candidates take the computerized version of the ASVAB, which is designed to ask you questions that gauge your ability. You start with a question of medium difficulty. If you answer correctly, you see a harder question next; if you answer incorrectly, you see an easier question next. Some people find that the ASVAB is easier — or harder — than they expect, but that's only because the test adapts itself to the test-taker's ability.

TIP

Keep in mind that although you may know the word in the question, you may not know one or more of the words in the multiple-choice answers. If this is the case, use the process of elimination to help you narrow down your choices. Eliminate the words that you know are wrong and then choose the one that's most likely correct from what's left.

Building Words from Scratch: Strategies to Help You Decipher Word Meanings

Webster's New World Dictionary lists more than 170,000 primary English words and who knows how many derivatives of those words. Wow! Any way you look at it, that's a lot of memorization. Fortunately, you don't need to study all those words. It's possible to decipher English word meanings even if you've never heard a particular word before.

Developing a large vocabulary takes time — often years. However, just because you have a limited amount of time to study doesn't mean you should give up hope. Instead, focus on the tips throughout this section to help you improve your Word Knowledge score.

From beginning to end: Knowing prefixes and suffixes

Prefixes, roots, and suffixes are the main parts that make up words. Not every word has all three, but most have at least one. A word's *prefix* — the first syllable — affects its meaning. A *suffix* is the last syllable in a word, and it, too, affects the word's meaning. *Roots* are the parts that lie in the middle of a word. Think of roots as the base of the word and prefixes and suffixes as word parts that are attached to the base to modify its meaning. (Check out the following section for more info on — you guessed it — roots.)

These basic word parts generally have the same meaning in whatever word they're used. For instance, the prefix *pro-* means *in favor of, forward,* or *positive,* whether you use it in the word *proton* or the word *proceed.*

Tables 4-2 and 4-3 list some common prefixes and suffixes. Each list has the word part, its meaning, and one word that uses each word part. Write down additional words that use each word part to help you memorize the list. You can find even more prefixes, suffixes, and roots in Appendix C.

TABLE 4-2 **Prefixes**

Prefix	Meaning	Sample Word
a-	no, not	atheist
ab- or abs-	away, from	absent
anti-	against	antibody
bi-	two	bilateral
circum-	around	circumnavigate
com- or con-	with, together	conform
contra- or counter-	against	contradict
de-	away from	detour
deca-	ten	decade
extra-	outside, beyond	extracurricular, extraordinary
fore-	in front of	foretell
geo-	earth	geology
hyper-	above, over	hyperactive
il-	not	illogical
mal- or male-	evil, bad	malediction
multi-	many	multiply
ob-	blocking	obscure
omni-	all	omnibus
out-	external	outside
que-, quer-, or ques-	ask	question, query
re-	back, again	return
semi-	half	semisweet
super-	over, more	superior
tele-	far	telephone
trans-	across	transatlantic
un-	not	uninformed

Suffixes are busy little word segments. They affect the meaning of a word and usually tell you what part of speech a word is (which comes in handy when you're navigating through Word Knowledge questions that you can't answer immediately).

TABLE 4-3   **Suffixes**

Suffix	Part of Speech It Indicates	Meaning	Original Word: Suffixed Word
-able or -ible	Adjective	capable of	agree: agreeable
-age	Noun	act of	break: breakage
-al	Adjective	relating to	function: functional
-ance or -ence	Noun	instance of an action	perform: performance
-ation	Noun	action, process	liberate: liberation
-en	Adjective, verb	made from	silk: silken
-ful	Adjective	full of	help: helpful
-ic	Adjective	relating to, like	anemia: anemic
-ical	Adjective	possessing a quality of	magic: magical
-ion	Noun	result of, act of	legislate: legislation
-ish	Adjective, noun	resembling	child: childish
-ism	Noun	condition or manner	hero: heroism
-ist	Noun	one who or that which does	anarchy: anarchist
-ity	Noun	quality of or state of	dense: density
-less	Adjective, noun	not having	worth: worthless
-let	Noun	small one	book: booklet
-ly	Adjective, adverb	like	fearless: fearlessly
-ment	Noun	act or process of	establish: establishment
-ness	Adjective, noun	possessing a quality	good: goodness
-or, -er	Noun	one who does a thing	orate: orator
-ous	Adjective	state of	danger: dangerous

TIP

If you memorize prefixes, suffixes, and roots, you have a better chance of figuring out the meaning of an unfamiliar word when you see it on the ASVAB. Figuring out the meaning of unfamiliar words is how people with large vocabularies make them even larger. (They look up words in the dictionary, too.)

Determining the root of the problem

Root words are word parts that serve as the base of a word. In English, one root word can be changed slightly to perform all sorts of roles — it can act as a noun, a verb, an adjective, or an adverb with just a little modification. If you recognize a root, you can generally get an idea of what the word means, even if you're not familiar with it. For example, if you know what the root word *attach* means, you can figure out what the word *attachment* means. If you know *adhere*, you can deduce what *adherence* means.

Table 4-4 lists some common roots. Memorize them. When you sit down to take the ASVAB, you'll be glad you did.

TABLE 4-4 **Roots**

Root	Meaning	Sample Word
anthro or anthrop	relating to humans	anthropology
bibl	relating to books	bibliography
brev	short	abbreviate
cede or ceed	go, yield	recede
chrom	color	monochrome
cogn	know	cognizant
corp	body	corporate
dict	speak	diction
domin	rule	dominate
flu or fluc	flow	influx
form	shape	formulate
fract or frag	break	fragment
graph	writing	biography
junct	join	juncture
liber	free	liberate
lum or lumen	light	illuminate
oper	work	cooperate
path or pathy	suffer, feeling	pathology
port	carry	portable
press	squeeze	repress
scrib or script	write	describe
sens or sent	feel	sentient
tract	pull	traction
voc or vok	call	revoke

TIP

When you see an unfamiliar word, try dropping a couple of letters from the beginning and/or the end of the word to see whether you recognize what's left — the root. If so, you can make a good guess about the meaning of the word. You can find more root words to help maximize your vocabulary in Appendix C.

Word families: Finding related words

When you see an unfamiliar word on the Word Knowledge section, don't get upset and pound on the computer (they make you pay for those things if you break them). You may know the word after all — just in a different form. Suppose you run across the word *beneficent* on the Word Knowledge portion:

Beneficent most nearly means

(A) kind.

(B) beautiful.

(C) unhappy.

(D) troubled.

You sit there and begin to sweat. You've never seen the word before, and it's all over for you, right? Well, maybe not. Take a closer look. What other word starting with the letters *benefi* do you know? How about the word *benefit*? A *benefit* is something that helps or aids. It'd be a good bet that the word *beneficent* is related to helping or aiding. So, when you look over the possible choices, you can choose the one that has something to do with helping.

But wait! None of the answers states help or aid. Now what? Just use the process of elimination. If someone is helpful (beneficent), she probably isn't troubled or unhappy. She may be beautiful, but more likely, she's kind. So, the best answer would be Choice (A).

Remember when your high school guidance counselor recommended that you take French or Spanish? You should thank her when you score well on this subtest. Why? Because knowledge of other languages can help you puzzle out the meaning of many English words. For example, if you know that *salud* means "health" in Spanish, you may be able to puzzle out the meaning of the English word *salutary* (favorable to or promoting health). Knowing that *sang* means "blood" in French may help you figure out what the English word *sanguine* means (try to puzzle this one out on your own; then check a dictionary to see how close you are).

Deconstructing words

Pulling apart words is a great strategy when you're not sure what something means. Even knowing what part of a word means can help you make a smarter choice — and on the ASVAB, every question counts.

Try to pull apart the word in this question to see whether you can figure out its meaning.

Detractor most nearly means

(A) critic.

(B) driver.

(C) expert.

(D) adulatory.

Take apart the word *detractor:*

>> *de-* is the prefix

>> *tract* is the root

>> *-or* is the suffix

If you've learned what any part of the word means, whether it's the prefix, root, or suffix, finding the correct answer is easier. (Check Tables 4-2, 4-3, and 4-4 if you're not sure yet.)

The prefix *de-* means "away from," *tract* means "pull," and the suffix *-or* means "one who does a thing." After you've broken down the word *detractor,* you can see that it means a person who pulls away from something.

Remember, too, that the suffix *-or* often makes a word a noun (a word that names a person, place, thing, or idea), so you can immediately rule out Choice (D). That leaves three choices: *critic, driver,* and *expert.*

If you guessed that *detractor* most nearly means *critic,* Choice (A), you're right. It's the only one that makes sense when you know what each part of the word means.

Yin and Yang: Understanding Synonyms and Antonyms

A *synonym* is a word that has the same meaning as or a very similar meaning to another word. *Smile* and *grin* are synonyms. They may not mean exactly the same thing, but their meanings are very similar. An *antonym* is a word that has an opposite or nearly opposite meaning as another word. *Smile* and *frown* are antonyms.

TIP

To help remember the definitions of synonym and antonym, think of a synonym as the same (both also start with an *s*) and an antonym as the enemy.

The ASVAB may ask you to find the word that most nearly means the same thing as a given word, which is a synonym. Or you may be asked to find the word that most nearly means the opposite of a given word, which is an antonym. Most of the questions on the Word Knowledge subtest ask you to find synonyms, although a few may ask you to find antonyms.

TIP

How can you study and find the synonym of a word (or the antonym, for that matter)? Take a look at these suggestions:

>> **Start in the dictionary.** Many dictionary entries include the abbreviation *syn.,* which means synonym. The words that follow this abbreviation are synonyms of the entry word. You may also see the abbreviation *ant.,* which stands for antonym; the word or words that follow it mean the opposite of the entry word.

>> **Make a list of synonyms and antonyms of the words you learn.** As you study vocabulary words for the Word Knowledge subtest, add them to your list.

>> **Use the root-word list from Table 4-4 (earlier in the chapter).** Using a dictionary and/or thesaurus, come up with a list of synonyms and antonyms for each word listed in the Sample Word column. (Of course, not every word has synonyms and antonyms, but many do.)

Many of the ASVAB Word Knowledge questions require you to know a one-word definition for another word. There's no better study aid for this concept than a thesaurus, a book of synonyms.

ASVAB Word Knowledge Strategy: Finding the Answer When You Just Don't Know

Although it's helpful to have a massive vocabulary at your disposal, you can still ace the Word Knowledge subtest if you have a few strategies up your sleeve. Read through this section and then practice these strategies as you answer the Word Knowledge questions at the end of this chapter and on the practice tests in Part 6.

Creating your own context

Some of the Word Knowledge questions you'll see on the ASVAB don't have any context that can offer you clues about their meaning (some are in sentences, which can make them easier to decode). The good news: You may be able to give a word *your own* context, and when you do, you may find that you actually know the answer.

When you see a word you don't know, try to place it in context. Ask yourself, "Have I heard this word before?"

EXAMPLE

<u>Afoul</u> most nearly means

(A) correctly.

(B) wrongly.

(C) easily.

(D) disgusting.

Have you heard the word *afoul* in a sentence before? If you've heard of someone "running afoul of the law," you can surmise that the word doesn't mean correctly, easily, or disgusting — and that leaves you with Choice (B), which happens to be the right answer. It might be a fuzzy definition, but sometimes that's all you need.

Think of phrases you've heard that include these words (or variations of them), and then see whether you can guess their meanings.

> » **Abstain:** "We had abstinence-only education in school."
>
> » **Deduce:** "I'll try to deduce the answer based on what I know."
>
> » **Malignant:** "The tumor is malignant."
>
> » **Credible:** "Can you back that up with a credible source?"

(*Abstain* is a verb that means to restrain oneself from doing something. *Deduce* is a verb that means to arrive at a conclusion by reasoning. *Malignant* is an adjective that means life-threatening, spiteful, or mean. *Credible* is an adjective that means believable.)

How's it feel? Letting the words speak to you

Words can be positive or negative, and you can often tell which they are through context. In Word Knowledge questions that require you to find a word's meaning based on the sentence it's in, you can use the warm-fuzzy or cold-prickly feeling you get to rule out incorrect answers.

EXAMPLE

David hoped that going to the amusement park would help him shake his <u>melancholy</u> mood.

(A) joyful

(B) sorrowful

(C) thoughtful

(D) excited

As long as it's not raining, most people have fun at an amusement park (it's nearly as much fun as basic training, where "If it ain't raining, you ain't training" is often the motto of the day). The sentence also says that David wants to "shake his melancholy mood," which means *melancholy* can't be a very good feeling. It must have a negative connotation (that cold-prickly feeling). You can rule out Choices (A) and (D), then, and think about what's the opposite of fun — and that's most likely Choice (B), because *sorrowful* means "down in the dumps."

Words and phrases such as "dread," "looking forward to," and "shied away from" all give you hints about a sentence's tone, which can help you pick the right answer when you're unsure. Even ruling out one or two incorrect answers can make a big difference in your score.

Compare and contrast: Picking up on signals

Many sentence-based Word Knowledge questions have context clues that can help you decipher the underlined word's meaning. If you can pick up on the signal words that tell you about contrast and similarity, you'll be able to boost your score *and* your vocabulary.

Signal words can be especially helpful in helping you predict a word's meaning. Table 4-5 lists some common signal words and whether they indicate similarity or contrast.

TABLE 4-5 **Signal Words**

Signal Word	Indicates	Example
indeed	Similarity	"The children were happy; *indeed*, they couldn't control their excitement."
like	Similarity	"When I shook the soda bottle, it erupted *like* a volcano."
too	Similarity	"The seniors were upset, and they were angry, *too*."
although	Contrast	"*Although* she was hesitant, Cheryl voted to reopen the school."
but	Contrast	"The class is difficult *but* fun."
despite	Contrast	"The dog ate the ice cream *despite* having eaten 10 minutes before."
however	Contrast	"Sadie applied at several colleges. *However*, only one accepted her."
rather than	Contrast	"The movie is boring *rather than* enjoyable."
while	Contrast	"Many troops are resourceful, *while* others are unimaginative."

EXAMPLE

He <u>recoiled</u> as if he had just seen a ghost.

(A) cringed

(B) laughed

(C) shouted

(D) endured

The signal phrase in the question is "as if," which is very similar to "like." Knowing that, what's the most likely answer? If you saw a ghost, you probably wouldn't laugh, shout, or endure. (I'd run.) The most correct answer is Choice (A), *cringed*, because that's far more likely to be your response than any of the other choices are.

One of these things is not like the other: Ruling out wrong answers

One of the most successful ASVAB strategies involves ruling out answers that aren't likely to be correct before settling on the one you think is right. When two answer choices mean almost the same thing, or when some choices don't match the prefix, suffix, or root word, you can cross them off as possibilities.

EXAMPLE

<u>Inhabit</u> most nearly means

(A) vacate.

(B) reside.

(C) depart.

(D) leave.

Choices (A), (C), and (D) are all very similar in meaning, leaving only Choice (B), *reside,* as the clear front-runner.

On the ASVAB, your choices aren't likely to be this obvious, but you may be able to rule out two choices and give yourself a 50-50 chance of finding the correct answer.

EXAMPLE

<u>Deform</u> most nearly means

(A) cure.

(B) heal.

(C) contort.

(D) tragedy.

Choices (A) and (B) are essentially the same, so you can eliminate those two. Now look at the prefix, *de-,* and compare it to what you find in Table 4-2 or other words that begin with the same prefix. *De-* means "away from." In Table 4-4, you can see that the root word *form* means "shape." That means Choice (C), *contort,* is the right answer for this question. (Combining ASVAB test-taking strategies gives you an extra edge!)

Mind filling in? Replacing the word with the answer choices

When you encounter a Word Knowledge question that asks you to define a word in a sentence, you may find that swapping out the underlined word with each of your choices leads you to the correct answer.

EXAMPLE

The CDC hasn't been able to identify the <u>pathogen</u> that these people ingested before turning into zombies.

(A) person

(B) carrier

(C) event

(D) bacteria

Replace *pathogen* with *person, carrier, event,* and *bacteria.* (The word *ingested* is a big clue. The words *person, carrier,* and *event* just don't make sense in the sentence.)

This strategy can work in conjunction with other strategies, too:

EXAMPLE

Maria was worried that the cockroaches in the apartment would have a <u>deleterious</u> effect on her daughter's health.

(A) helpful

(B) harmful

(C) erasing

(D) backward

Replace *deleterious* with each of the answer choices. Choice (B), *harmful*, is the only one that makes sense — especially because the sentence says, "Maria was worried," which shows you that the correct answer won't be something positive.

Say what? Parts of speech matter

When you see a Word Knowledge question that asks you to define a word in a sentence, you might be able to weed out one or two incorrect choices by knowing the parts of speech. Table 4-6 lists the eight parts of speech, notes what roles they play in sentences, and gives you some examples.

TABLE 4-6 **Parts of Speech**

Part	Role	Examples
Noun	Names a person, place, thing, or idea	Mr. Hall, lawyer, United States, suffix
Verb	Expresses an action or state of being	to write, to read, to eat, to play, to be
Adjective	Describes a noun	green, sleepy, hungry, fast, beautiful
Adverb	Modifies a verb, adjective, or another adverb	tremendously, very, cautiously, dangerously, sneakily
Pronoun	Replaces a noun	he, she, it, this, I, you
Preposition	Relates a noun or pronoun to another word	in, on, around, after, under
Conjunction	Connects clauses to sentences	and, but, if
Interjection	Expresses emotions or feelings	cool, awesome, holy cow, uh-oh, eek

REMEMBER

A suffix can tell you what part of speech a word is, so when you encounter a word you don't know, you'll be able to eliminate possible answer choices that you *do* know by looking at the suffixes.

Suffixes are usually only part of nouns, verbs, and adjectives. If the ASVAB asks you to define *analogous*, but you don't know what it means, you can use your knowledge of the suffix to help you rule out answers that don't make any sense. Because the suffix *-ous* typically modifies nouns and turns words into adjectives, you know that the correct answer probably won't be a noun.

EXAMPLE

<u>Analogous</u> most nearly means

(A) inclusive.

(B) danger.

(C) write.

(D) comparable.

Of those answer choices, *inclusive* and *comparable* are the only adjectives. *Danger* is a noun, and *write* is a verb. You can rule out Choices (B) and (C) to make a more educated choice — and improve your chances of answering the question correctly — if you know that the suffix *-ous* usually refers to adjectives. Choice (D) is correct here; *analogous* means comparable in certain respects, especially when it clarifies the relationship between two things that are being compared ("The relationship between a drill sergeant and a new recruit is analogous to the relationship between a hungry fish and a worm on a hook").

EXAMPLE

Cameron knew that the only <u>viable</u> option was to invest 10 percent of his savings.

(A) succeed

(B) glowing

(C) reasonable

(D) life

The underlined word, *viable,* describes Cameron's option; *option* is a noun in this sentence, so that makes *viable* an adjective. Look through the answer choices and figure out what part of speech each word is. Choice (A), *succeed,* is a verb because it describes an action (the action of succeeding). Choice (B), *glowing,* is an adjective because it modifies a noun (for example, "the glowing candle"), so that's a possible answer. Choice (C), *reasonable,* is also an adjective because it modifies nouns (as in, "That's a reasonable alternative"), so that's another option. Choice (D), *life,* is a noun (and it wouldn't make any sense in this sentence), so it's off the table.

Choices (B) and (C) are the most likely of the four to be correct. If you haven't tried it yet, replace *viable* with each choice. You'll see that Choice (C), *reasonable,* makes the most sense in the sentence.

If all else fails, break your word

If you're stumped on a Word Knowledge question, you can resort to breaking apart the word (read about that in "Deconstructing words" earlier in this chapter). Even taking off a prefix or suffix can point you in the right direction, especially if you've studied Tables 4-2 and 4-3 and the extensive lists in Appendix C.

Predict the meanings of these words to test your skills:

>> Desensitize

>> Decode

>> Deplume

These words all have something in common, and it's the prefix *de-.* Knowing that *de-* usually means "away from," you can guess what each word will mean.

Predict the meanings of these words:

>> Approachable

>> Serviceable

>> Governable

The common theme with these words is the suffix *-able,* which typically signifies "capable of." You can use that to your advantage when you're taking the ASVAB, too.

Guess what! It's okay on the ASVAB

In some cases, it's okay to guess on the ASVAB — but only if you do it strategically.

You won't be penalized for guessing on the paper-and-pencil version of the ASVAB (aside from choosing the wrong answers, that is). You can complete each section at your own pace within the time limits, and you're allowed to review and change your answers in the current section. After time expires and the test proctor tells you to close your booklet, you won't be permitted to go back to that portion of the test.

You *will* be penalized for guessing on the CAT-ASVAB (the computerized version of the test) that new recruits take at MEPS. If you look at the clock and start clicking random answers in a rush because you're almost out of time for that section, your score will go down. You can take the entire CAT-ASVAB at your own pace, but you can't review or change any answers after you've submitted them. You can't go back to the beginning of the subtest after you start. If you're running out of time, *do not guess!* Keep trying to answer each question to the best of your ability, using the test-taking strategies outlined in this chapter.

REMEMBER

You'll have 9 minutes to answer 15 questions if you're taking the CAT-ASVAB and your subtest has no tryout questions, which leaves you about 36 seconds for each one. If you're taking the paper-and-pencil version, you'll have 11 minutes to answer 35 questions. That's about 18 seconds per question (if you want to check the math, refer to Chapter 6).

TIP

If you *must* guess on the ASVAB, eliminate choices that you know are incorrect first. You have a 25 percent chance of getting each question right without reading it, but you can increase those chances if you eliminate even one incorrect choice. That's why these test-taking strategies are so important — the better you perform on the Word Knowledge section, the higher your score will be, which opens doors to more desirable jobs and helps you get your military career off to a good start.

You Are What You Speak: Improving Your Vocabulary, Improving Yourself

Having an extensive vocabulary can help you do well on the Word Knowledge subtest. But even if you don't have a huge vocabulary, the strategies in this section can help you make up for that.

REMEMBER

You can acquire vocabulary words in the short term as well as over a long period of time. Combining both approaches is best, but if you're pressed for time, focus on short-term memorization and test-taking skills.

Reading your way to a larger vocabulary

In a world of constant social media updates and 17 billion streaming platforms, the pastime of reading for enjoyment is quickly fading. To build your vocabulary, you have to read — it's that simple. Studies consistently show that those who read for enjoyment have a much larger vocabulary than those who dislike reading. You have to see the words in print, not just hear someone say them. Besides, people can read and understand many more words than they could ever use in conversation.

That doesn't mean you have to start with *Advanced Astrophysics*. In fact, if you don't read much, you can start with your daily newspaper, a news magazine, or any type of reading material that's just a notch or two above what you ordinarily read. Choose topics that interest you. If you're interested in the subject matter, you'll enjoy reading more. Plus, you may learn something new!

When you encounter a word you don't know, try to understand what it means by looking at the context in which the word is used. For example, if you read, "The scientist extrapolated from the data," and you don't know what *extrapolated* means, you can try substituting words you do know to see whether they'd make sense. For example, the scientist probably didn't hide from the data. She probably used the data to make some sort of decision, judgment, or guess. To confirm your understanding of the word, check your dictionary. Making predictions like this can help you remember a definition for the long term.

You may even consider keeping a running list of terms you come across as you read, along with their definitions (see the following section). On the Word Knowledge subtest of the ASVAB, you often won't be able to guess what a word means from its context (in many cases, there's no context in the test because the words aren't used in sentences). You also won't be able to look the word up in the dictionary. But considering context and consulting a dictionary are two great ways to discover vocabulary words during your test preparation.

Keeping a list and checking it twice

Not long ago, an 11-year-old girl went through the entire dictionary and made a list of all the words she didn't know. (The process took several months.) She then studied the list faithfully for a year and went on to win first place in the National Spelling Bee finals. You don't have to go to this extent, but even putting in a tenth of her effort can dramatically improve your scores on the Word Knowledge subtest.

One way to improve your vocabulary is to keep a word list. Here's how that list works:

1. **When you hear or read a word that you don't understand, jot it down or make note of it in your smartphone.**

2. **When you have a chance, look up the word in the dictionary and then write the meaning on your list.**

3. **Use the word in a sentence that you make up.**

   Write the sentence down, too.

4. **Use your new word in everyday conversation.**

   Finding a way to work the word *zenith* into a description of last night's basketball game requires creativity, but you won't forget what the word means.

Arrange your list by related items so the words are easier to remember. For example, list the words having to do with your work on one page, words related to mechanical knowledge on another page, and so on.

You can also find websites that offer lists of words if you spend a few minutes surfing. Try using search phrases such as "vocabulary words" and "SAT words." Here are a few resources:

>> **Vocabulary.com:** This site (www.vocabulary.com) offers thousands of vocabulary words and their definitions, as well as interactive, adaptive games to help you learn.

>> **Dictionary.com and Thesaurus.com:** Dictionary.com (www.dictionary.com) includes a great online dictionary and word of the day. The related site Thesaurus.com (www.thesaurus.com), which links back to the dictionary, gives you the same word of the day as well as lists of synonyms and antonyms.

>> **Merriam-Webster online:** Merriam-Webster online (www.merriam-webster.com) is another useful site with a free online dictionary, thesaurus, and word of the day.

A ton of books exist to help build your vocabulary. Try *Vocabulary For Dummies* by Laurie E. Rozakis or *SAT Vocabulary For Dummies* by Suzee Vlk, both published by Wiley. These books are great resources designed to help you improve your word-knowledge skills.

Crosswords: Making vocabulary fun

My grandma always kept a book of crossword puzzles in the center of her kitchen table — and she always kept an ink pen inside to complete the puzzles. (You know somebody's good if she's doing crossword puzzles in ink!) So, what was her secret? She'd been doing crosswords since the 1940s, long before you could play word games on a smartphone.

One of the great things about crossword puzzles (other than fun) is that you can find them at all levels of difficulty. Start with one that has a difficulty consistent with your word-knowledge ability and then work your way up to more difficult puzzles. Before you know it, you'll be a lean, mean word machine and have loads of fun in the process. Dozens of free crossword apps are available for phones, so you don't even need to buy a book in the checkout lane at the supermarket.

Sounding off by sounding it out

Sometimes you actually know a word because you've heard it in conversation, but you don't recognize it when you see it written down. For instance, a student who'd heard the word *placebo* (pronounced "plah-*see*-bow") knew that it meant an inactive substance, like a sugar pill. But when she came across it in writing, she didn't recognize it. She thought it was a word pronounced "plah-*chee*-bow," which she'd never heard before.

TIP

When you see a word on the ASVAB that you don't recognize, try pronouncing it (not out loud, please) a couple of different ways. The following pronunciation rules can help you out:

>> Sometimes letters are silent, like the *b* in *subtle* or the *k* in *knight*. A letter at the end of a word may be silent, especially if the word is French; for instance, *coup* is pronounced *coo*.

>> Some sounds have unusual pronunciations in certain contexts. Think of the first *l* in *colonel,* which is pronounced like *kernel.*

>> The letter *c* can sound like *s (lice)* or *k (despicable).*

>> The letter *i* after a *t* can form a sound like *she.* Think of the word *initiate.*

>> The letter *x* at the beginning of a word is generally pronounced like *z (Xerox).*

>> A vowel at the end of a word can change the pronunciation of letters in the word. The word *wag* has a different *g* sound than the word *wage.*

>> When several vowels are right next to each other, they can be pronounced many different ways (consider *boo, boa,* and *bout*). Try a couple of different possibilities. For instance, if you see the word *feint,* you may think that it should be pronounced *feent* or *fiynt,* but it in fact sounds like *faint.* It means fake or pretend.

Word Knowledge Practice Questions

In the stem of each of the following Word Knowledge practice questions, you see an underlined word. Select the choice that best answers the question in relation to the underlined word.

REMEMBER

Pay attention to the wording of each question. Some questions ask you to select the choice closest in meaning to the underlined word. Some questions may ask you to select the word most opposite in meaning. On other questions, you see the underlined word used in a sentence. In that case, your task is to select the choice most similar in meaning to the underlined word as it is used in the context of the sentence.

1. <u>Acclaim</u> most nearly means
   - (A) enthusiastic approval.
   - (B) religion.
   - (C) help.
   - (D) program.

2. The college student met with the <u>bursar</u> to discuss tuition payment options.
   - (A) planner
   - (B) treasurer
   - (C) politician
   - (D) ghost

3. <u>Estrange</u> most nearly means
   - (A) sharp.
   - (B) small.
   - (C) alienate.
   - (D) shiny.

4. <u>Momentous</u> most nearly means
   - (A) significant.
   - (B) small.
   - (C) reality.
   - (D) postpone.

5. The mother <u>chastised</u> her child.
   - (A) comforted
   - (B) carried
   - (C) lectured
   - (D) supervised

6. <u>Obtrude</u> most nearly means
   - (A) condition.
   - (B) absorb.
   - (C) prepare.
   - (D) impose.

7. We often wondered why Daniel lived in such an <u>opulent</u> apartment.
   - (A) run-down
   - (B) lavish
   - (C) far away
   - (D) hideous

8. Now that you've read through it once, it's time to <u>recapitulate</u> the Word Knowledge chapter.
   - (A) discuss
   - (B) summarize
   - (C) test
   - (D) reread

9. <u>Clemency</u> most nearly means
   - (A) mercy.
   - (B) force.
   - (C) imprisonment.
   - (D) compliment.

10. This year the Paris fashion industry has decided to <u>eschew</u> short skirts and high heels.
    - (A) favor
    - (B) manufacture
    - (C) shun
    - (D) sell

11. <u>Pollute</u> most nearly means
    - (A) eliminate.
    - (B) contaminate.
    - (C) clean.
    - (D) confuse.

12. Latent most nearly means
    (A) hidden.
    (B) dull.
    (C) pretentious.
    (D) active.

13. Paul sent all of his friends a salutary message on the Internet.
    (A) beneficial
    (B) profane
    (C) funny
    (D) interesting

14. The word most opposite in meaning to reflect is
    (A) ponder.
    (B) consider.
    (C) ignore.
    (D) speculate.

15. The word most opposite in meaning to blame is
    (A) attribute.
    (B) reprove.
    (C) muster.
    (D) exalt.

16. Amenable most nearly means
    (A) amended.
    (B) prepared.
    (C) guided.
    (D) cooperative.

17. Calamity most nearly means
    (A) desert.
    (B) disaster.
    (C) remorse.
    (D) overeating.

18. The word most opposite in meaning to forthright is
    (A) honest.
    (B) polite.
    (C) blunt.
    (D) outspoken.

19. The word most opposite in meaning to profound is
    (A) thorough.
    (B) mild.
    (C) absolute.
    (D) intense.

20. The attendant charged Karen a nominal fee to park in the crowded lot.
    (A) expensive
    (B) insignificant
    (C) large
    (D) crazy

21. The loving couple celebrated their fidelity over the years on their anniversary.
    (A) complications
    (B) faithfulness
    (C) regrets
    (D) treachery

22. The Army commander decided to avert trouble by heading back to headquarters.
    (A) help
    (B) complicate
    (C) prevent
    (D) attack

23. The word most opposite in meaning to keen is
    (A) fervent.
    (B) reluctant.
    (C) zealous.
    (D) appetent.

24. Quell most nearly means
    (A) launch.
    (B) support.
    (C) enrich.
    (D) suppress.

25. Truncate most nearly means
    (A) shorten.
    (B) fixate.
    (C) pretend.
    (D) turn.

26. The <u>kinetic</u> energy was converted to electricity.

   (A) regulated

   (B) disbursed

   (C) frantic

   (D) moving

27. The witness was happy to <u>corroborate</u> the man's explanation.

   (A) exaggerate

   (B) destroy

   (C) confirm

   (D) question

28. Barry thought he could <u>forge</u> the paperwork without getting caught.

   (A) trash

   (B) destroy

   (C) fabricate

   (D) forget

Answers and Explanations

Use this answer key to score the Word Knowledge practice questions.

1. A. Used as a noun, *acclaim* means a shout of approval, so the answer is Choice (A).

2. B. *Bursar* is similar to the word *reimburse*. The question gives context clues about tuition payment, and that should give you enough clues to select the correct answer, Choice (B).

3. C. *Estrange* means to alienate, Choice (C). Note that *estrange* is a verb, and the only answer choice that's also a verb is Choice (C); the others are adjectives.

4. A. *Momentous* is an adjective and means very significant, Choice (A).

5. C. *Chastised* means disciplined or punished, so Choice (C) is the most correct choice. Choices (A), (B), and (D) are unrelated.

6. D. The correct answer is Choice (D). *Obtrude* means to intrude or to impose oneself on another. The other choices are unrelated.

7. B. *Opulent* is an adjective that means wealthy, rich, or affluent. Choice (B) is the answer closest in meaning. The other choices are unrelated or opposite of the meaning.

8. B. *Recapitulate* is a verb that means to summarize. It's also the longer version of the word *recap*. The correct answer is Choice (B). Choice (A) is somewhat close, but Choice (B) is the closest in meaning.

9. A. *Clemency* means forgiveness or leniency in punishing a person. Choice (A) is the correct answer. The other choices are unrelated.

TIP

Knowing prefixes can be useful when determining the definitions of many words. For example, you may have heard the word *inclement* used to describe stormy, severe weather. If you know that the prefix *in-* can mean *not*, you can conclude that *clement* is likely to be mild and gentle, traits related to mercy.

10. **C.** *Eschew* is a verb that means to avoid or keep away from. Choice (C) is the correct answer, and the other answers are unrelated.

11. **B.** *Pollute* means to contaminate, Choice (B).

12. **A.** *Latent* means present but not visible or noticeable, so Choice (A) is the correct answer. *Latent* can also mean dormant, but none of the answer choices relates to that definition.

13. **A.** *Salutary* is an adjective meaning beneficial, so Choice (A) is correct. If you took Spanish in high school, you may remember that a related word, *salud,* relates to health and well-being, making Choice (A) a good guess.

14. **C.** *Reflect* is a verb that means to think deeply about, demonstrate, or give back. *Ignore* would be most opposite in meaning from the choices given.

15. **D.** *Blame* can be both a noun and a verb; as a verb, it means to condemn, place responsibility, or accuse. So, *exalt* is most opposite in meaning.

16. **D.** *Amenable* is an adjective meaning willing and cooperative.

17. **B.** *Calamity* is a noun meaning disaster.

18. **B.** *Forthright* is an adjective meaning straightforward and honest, so of the choices given, *polite* is the closest to the opposite.

19. **B.** *Profound* is an adjective meaning thoughtful, intellectual, and intense, so *mild* is the most opposite in meaning.

20. **B.** *Nominal* is an adjective meaning insignificant or lower than the actual or expected value.

21. **B.** *Fidelity* is a noun meaning faithfulness and loyalty in a relationship.

22. **C.** *Avert* is a verb meaning to turn something away or prevent it from happening.

23. **B.** *Keen* is an adjective meaning interested and enthusiastic, so *reluctant* is the choice most opposite in meaning.

24. **D.** *Quell* is a verb meaning to defeat or suppress.

25. **A.** *Truncate* is a verb meaning to shorten or abbreviate.

26. **D.** *Kinetic* is an adjective meaning relating to or characterized by motion.

27. **C.** *Corroborate* is a verb meaning to back up or confirm a story.

28. **C.** *Forge* is a verb meaning to counterfeit or fabricate.

Chapter **5**

Paragraph Comprehension

A ny other organization would call this section of the ASVAB the Reading Comprehension subtest, but the Department of Defense is a stickler for precision. You'll be reading paragraphs, darn it, so you're being tested on how well you understand paragraphs! Not words, not sentences, not essays, but paragraphs!

One thing you get from basic training is that comprehending the drill sergeant's orders and the information in your instruction manuals is important. The ability to read and understand the written directions in your basic training manual can save you and your buddies hundreds of push-ups (trust me on this one). The Paragraph Comprehension subtest measures your ability to understand what you read and draw conclusions from that material. It contains a number of written passages and questions about those passages.

After you enlist, you'll discover that the military runs on paperwork. If you can't read and understand a regulation, how are you going to follow it?

Understanding the Importance of Paragraph Comprehension for Military Jobs

The Paragraph Comprehension subtest is an important part of your AFQT score, which is the most important score because it determines whether a particular branch of service lets you join. The score is so important that I plan to keep on repeating it until you're mumbling "The AFQT is the most important score" in your sleep.

The vast majority of military jobs require a decent score on the Paragraph Comprehension subtest. In fact, you'll have a hard time qualifying for any branch if the ASVAB shows the military that you won't understand the written orders you'll receive. For example, if the directions in a military recipe make your head spin, how are you going to use it to cook an edible meal for 2,000 troops? (Assuming you want to become a military cook, that is.) Table 5-1 shows the military job qualification line scores that are calculated by using your Paragraph Comprehension subtest score.

Chapter 2 has more information about military line scores. See Appendix A for more information on the scores you need to get the job you want.

TABLE 5-1 **Military Line Scores That Use the Paragraph Comprehension Score**

Branch of Service	Line Score
U.S. Army	Clerical, General Technical, Operators and Food, Surveillance and Communications, and Skilled Technical
U.S. Air Force	Administrative and General
U.S. Navy and Coast Guard	Administrative, General Technical, Health, and Nuclear
U.S. Marine Corps	General Technical and Clerical

Eyeing the Physique of the Paragraph Comprehension Subtest

When you get to the Paragraph Comprehension subtest, you have several passages to read. Most passages are only one paragraph long, and rarely are they longer than two paragraphs. Each passage contains between 50 and 200 words. (Look at it this way: At least you won't be required to read *War and Peace*!)

The ASVAB test authors may ask you to answer only one question about a given reading passage, or they may ask you to answer as many as five questions about one passage. Unfortunately, this subtest doesn't consist of the most interesting passages you'll ever read. (You won't find paragraphs from your favorite sci-fi novel here.) It's important that you set your attention span dial to the maximum setting. On the paper-and-pencil version, you have 13 minutes to answer 15 questions. If you're taking the computerized version of the ASVAB, you have 27 minutes to read the passages and answer 10 questions. If you get tryout questions in the Paragraph Comprehension subtest of the CAT-ASVAB, you have 75 minutes to complete 25 questions. I cover tryout questions in Chapter 1.

In order to understand what you read — which is what the Paragraph Comprehension subtest is all about — you need to develop several abilities, which I cover later in this chapter:

>> Finding the main idea or argument that the author is making

>> Remembering specific details about the reading

>> Drawing conclusions from what you've read

>> Understanding relationships between ideas

>> Paraphrasing or summarizing what you've read

Trying the Four Flavors of Comprehension Questions

The Paragraph Comprehension questions on the ASVAB usually take one of four forms:

>> Finding specific information

>> Recognizing the main idea

» Determining word meaning in context

» Drawing an implication from a stated idea

Each type of question asks you to perform a different kind of analysis of the reading passage. If a passage has more than one question associated with it, chances are each question falls under a different category. The following sections spell out the differences among these four types of questions.

Treasure hunt: Finding specific information

This type of Paragraph Comprehension question asks you to pick out (you guessed it) specific information from a passage. Sounds easy, right? Take a look at the following passage, which clearly states the answer to the question that directly follows it:

> An industry trade association found that more than 13,000 martial arts schools exist in the United States with nearly 6 million active members. Of the 13,000 schools, nearly 7,000 offered tae kwon do lessons.

EXAMPLE

According to this passage, how many people actively participated in martial arts lessons?

(A) 13,000

(B) 7,000

(C) 6 million

(D) It can't be determined.

The correct answer is Choice (C).

At times, the information that a question asks about isn't directly stated in the question, but you can infer the information from the text. Remember, in the military, the only easy day was yesterday.

WARNING

When questions are phrased in the negative, you may be confused about what the question is asking. (This is especially true when the information being sought isn't directly stated in the passage.) Misreading a negative question is also easy. Research has shown that people often skip over a negative word, such as *not*, when they read. Questions on the Paragraph Comprehension portion of the ASVAB are sometimes stated in the negative. When you see a negative word, an alarm should go off in your head to remind you to read the question more carefully.

Cutting to the chase: Recognizing the main idea

Sometimes the Paragraph Comprehension questions ask you to identify the main point of a passage. The main point can be directly stated, or it can be implied.

TIP

If you're not sure what the main point of a paragraph is, reread the first sentence and the last sentence. Chances are one of these two sentences contains the main point. (Flip to "What's the big idea? Determining the main idea in a paragraph" later in this chapter for more information on identifying main ideas.)

If the shoe fits: Determining word meaning in context

Sometimes the Paragraph Comprehension subtest asks you to determine the meaning of a word when it's used in a passage. The correct definition that the question is looking for can be the most common meaning of the word, or it can be a less well-known meaning. In either case, you have to read the passage, make sure you understand how the word is being used, and select the answer option that's closest in meaning to the word as it's used in the passage. Consider this example:

> In the 18th century, it was common for sailors to be pressed into service in Britain. Young men found near seaports could be kidnapped, drugged, or otherwise hauled aboard a ship and made to work doing menial chores. They weren't paid for their service, and they were given just enough food to keep them alive.

EXAMPLE

In this passage, <u>pressed</u> means

(A) hired.

(B) ironed.

(C) enticed.

(D) forced.

The descriptions of the conditions these sailors found themselves in should help you decide that they weren't hired or enticed; ironed is one meaning of the word *pressed*, but it isn't correct in this context. The correct answer is Choice (D). Here's another example:

> Since the 1980s, computers have become an indispensable part of American business. Computers can be used for thousands of applications, from word processing and running spreadsheets to keeping one's checkbook updated.

EXAMPLE

In this passage, <u>applications</u> means

(A) functions.

(B) sizes.

(C) requests.

(D) types.

Try putting the answer choices in this sentence: "Computers can be used for thousands of applications." You can see that *functions* is closest in meaning to applications, although in a different context, some of the other answer choices may be correct. The correct answer is Choice (A).

Reading between the lines: Understanding implications

Some Paragraph Comprehension questions ask you to draw an inference from a stated idea. This simply means that you may need to draw a conclusion from what you've read. This conclusion should always be based on the reading, not your own particular opinions about a subject.

REMEMBER

The conclusion — which may be called an *inference* or *implication* — must be reasonably based on what the passage says. You have to use good judgment when deciding which conclusions can be logically drawn from what you've read. Give it a shot:

Twenty-five percent of all automobile thefts occur when the doors of a car are left unlocked. People often forget to lock their doors, find it inconvenient, or tell themselves, "I'll only be a minute." But it only takes a minute for an accomplished car thief to steal a car. And thieves are always alert to the opportunities that distracted or rushed people present them with.

EXAMPLE

To prevent auto theft, it's a person's responsibility to

(A) leave the doors unlocked.

(B) never be in a rush.

(C) prevent the opportunity.

(D) be willing to perform a citizen's arrest.

Although the paragraph doesn't state, "It's your own responsibility to prevent car thieves from having an opportunity to break into your car," this idea is certainly implied. The correct answer is Choice (C). There's no implication that people should be willing to (or can) perform a citizen's arrest. Leaving the doors unlocked is the opposite of what one should do, and never being in a rush is probably unlikely.

An example of an unreasonable conclusion drawn from the passage would be something like "if everyone locked his or her doors, there would be no crime" or "all car thieves should be sentenced to 30 years in prison." Nothing in this particular passage supports such a conclusion.

TIP

One way to help determine whether you've drawn a reasonable conclusion is to ask yourself, "Based on what I've just read, would the author agree with the conclusion I've reached?" If the answer is yes, your conclusion is probably reasonable. If the answer is no, it's time to think up a new conclusion.

Check out another example:

Boiler technicians operate main and auxiliary boilers. They maintain and repair all parts, including pressure fittings, valves, pumps, and forced-air blowers. Technicians may have to lift or move heavy equipment. They may have to stoop and kneel and work in awkward positions.

EXAMPLE

According to this job description, a good candidate for this job would be

(A) a person with joint problems.

(B) an individual unaccustomed to heavy lifting.

(C) a person who isn't mechanically minded.

(D) a person who's physically fit.

Although the passage doesn't state, "This job requires a physically fit person," the duties listed imply that this is so. The correct answer is Choice (D). A person with joint problems may not be able to stoop or kneel or work in awkward positions. A person who's unaccustomed to heavy lifting may not be able to lift or move the heavy equipment as needed. A person who isn't mechanically minded may not have the knowledge necessary to maintain and repair boilers and all their parts. This leaves Choice (D) as the answer, and it's true that a person who's physically fit would be a good choice for the job.

Do You Get My Point? Breaking down Paragraphs

All good writing has a point. Some writing has more than one point. *Points* are ideas that the writer is trying to convey to the reader. The primary purpose of the writing is known as the *main point* or *main idea*. Points used to support or clarify the main point are called *subpoints* or *supporting points*. You should know how to identify main points and subpoints when you practice reading.

What's the big idea? Determining the main idea in a paragraph

Questions on the Paragraph Comprehension subtest frequently ask you to identify the main point of a reading passage. How do you get better at identifying main ideas? Practice. The *main idea*, which is the most important point the author is making, is sometimes stated and sometimes implied in a piece of writing.

Finding a topic sentence

Often, the author begins or ends a paragraph or passage with the main idea, which is located in what's called a *topic sentence*. A topic sentence, reasonably enough, describes the topic that the author is writing about.

TIP

If you're looking for the main idea, start off by checking the first and last sentences of the passage. (No, this doesn't mean that you should skip the rest of the passage.) For example, suppose you read the following paragraph:

> The local school district is facing a serious budgetary crisis. The state, suffering a revenue shortfall of more than $600 million, has cut funding to the district by $18.7 million. Already, 65 teachers have been laid off, and more layoffs are expected.

No, the primary theme of this passage isn't "schools in our area suck." The main point of this paragraph can be found in the opening sentence, "The local school district is facing a serious budgetary crisis." What follows are details regarding the budget crisis.

Sometimes a passage builds up to its main idea, and sometimes the main idea is implied instead of stated. Consider the following paragraph:

> The farmers' market reopened on the second weekend of May. Amid the asparagus and flowers, shoppers chatted about the return of temperatures in the 70s. Across the street, children (and their dogs) played Frisbee in the park. Finally, spring has come to town.

In this paragraph, you may think that the farmers' market's reopening is the main point, but the other information about the temperature and the kids playing Frisbee tells you that the main idea is something a bit broader than the market's opening. The main idea is stated in the last sentence: "Finally, spring has come to town."

TIP

In boot camp, your drill instructor may say, "Some of you better check to see that your bunks are properly made." Or he may rip your bunk bed apart and say, "Now make this bunk the right way!" Both comments mean the same thing. In the first statement, the drill instructor implies the meaning (and you'd better go check your bunk); the second statement is a bit more direct.

In other words: Rephrasing passages

TIP

One of the best ways to identify the main point of a paragraph is to put the paragraph into your own words (*paraphrase* it) or to sum up the basic idea of the paragraph (*summarize* it). By quickly doing this when you take the Paragraph Comprehension portion of the ASVAB, you can be confident that you're answering the question correctly. In other words (to paraphrase), you'll know you understand *what* the paragraph is talking about.

You likely won't have time to write down the main point or to jot down your paraphrase or summary. Instead, as you're reading, simply try to mentally keep track of what's being said by putting it into your own words.

Look at the following paragraph:

> The local school district is facing a serious budgetary crisis. The state, suffering a revenue shortfall of more than $600 million, has cut funding to the district by $18.7 million. Already, 65 teachers have been laid off, and more layoffs are expected.

Now put down this book and spend a few moments paraphrasing the preceding paragraph. Come on. Pick up that pencil and get those brain cells firing. When you're done, come back to this page and compare your ideas to the passage. If you wrote something like the following, you're right on track:

> The school district has a budget crunch because the state has a budget crunch. The state cut funding to the school district. Some teachers have been laid off already. More may be laid off soon.

Now, if you wrote something like, "It's finally May, and shoppers and kids-at-play are out and about, enjoying the warmer temperatures of spring," then you're not paying attention.

TIP

As you study for the ASVAB, practice paraphrasing reading passages. You can paraphrase or summarize any short passage you read — a few sentences or a paragraph or two. Read different passages from a book or magazine and then set them aside. Get a pencil and jot down your paraphrases. (Remember, you won't have time to do this on the test itself, but the practice helps you mentally prepare for when you take the test.)

Extra, extra! Identifying subpoints

If a writer stuck to just one point, the Paragraph Comprehension subtest would be a breeze. However, an author usually doesn't make just one point in a piece of writing, so you also need to understand the other points the author makes. These details, or *subpoints*, may include facts or statistics, or they may be descriptions that support the main point of the passage. Subpoints help you see what the author's saying. For instance, look at this passage (from the preceding section):

> The local school district is facing a serious budgetary crisis. The state, suffering a revenue shortfall of more than $600 million, has cut funding to the district by $18.7 million. Already, 65 teachers have been laid off, and more layoffs are expected.

The subpoints help you understand the main point, which is that the school district is facing a severe budgetary crisis. The subpoints help you understand why: "The state, suffering a revenue shortfall of more than $600 million, has cut funding to the district by $18.7 million." You can see that the budgetary crisis is part of a larger problem, which is the state is suffering a severe revenue shortfall. The subpoints also help you understand what this crisis means: "Already, 65 teachers have been laid off, and more layoffs are expected." By using these facts and figures, the author helps you grasp not only the main point but also the implications of that main point.

Analyzing What You've Read: Guessing at What the Writer Really Means

The Paragraph Comprehension subtest of the ASVAB also requires you to analyze what you've read. Analysis is more than simply picking out the point of the text. Analyzing a passage requires you to draw conclusions from what you've read and understand relationships among the ideas presented in the text.

By drawing conclusions about the meaning of a passage, you reach new ideas that the author implies but doesn't come right out and state. You must analyze the information the author presents in order to make inferences from what you've read. For instance, look at the following paragraph:

> The local school district is facing a serious budgetary crisis. The state, suffering a revenue shortfall of more than $600 million, has cut funding to the district by $18.7 million. Already, 65 teachers have been laid off, and more layoffs are expected.

Although the author doesn't say so, you can draw the conclusion that if the state revenue shortfall could somehow be corrected — by increasing state sales tax, for example — the local school district's budgetary crisis could be resolved. The $18.7 million cut from the school budget could be restored. The author never actually makes this point in the paragraph, but by using logic, you can draw this conclusion from the facts presented.

REMEMBER

Making inferences and drawing conclusions requires you to use your judgment. You don't want to read too much into a passage. For example, nothing in the example paragraph suggests that electing a new governor is necessary or that increasing federal income taxes would help the problem.

Look at the next paragraph:

> The farmers' market reopened on the second weekend of May. Amid the asparagus and flowers, shoppers chatted about the return of temperatures in the 70s. Across the street, children (and their dogs) played Frisbee in the park. Finally, spring has come to town.

Suppose you're asked the following question about this paragraph:

EXAMPLE

It can be inferred from the passage that

(A) Frisbee playing in the park doesn't happen in winter.

(B) the warm weather is unusual for this time of year.

(C) the shoppers were disappointed in the farmers' market produce.

(D) rain is imminent.

If the point of the passage is that spring has come to town and the author uses Frisbee playing as evidence of the arrival of spring, then it's likely that Frisbee playing doesn't occur in the winter but does begin again in spring. The answer is Choice (A).

Faster than a Speeding Turtle: Tips for Slow Readers

REMEMBER

Today's military is much more complex than attending basic training, learning how to shoot a gun, and shipping off to war. After boot camp, you attend intensive classroom training to learn your military job. If you can't read well, you're going to have a very hard time. But the good news is that it's never too late to work on improving your reading skills.

For many people, 13 to 27 minutes is enough time to read all the passages, understand the questions, and choose the correct answers. But slow readers may have more difficulty answering all the questions before time is up. Don't despair: Take the suggestions in this section to help build your reading speed. Of course, they require work, but you knew the mission came with its challenges, right?

Read more, watch less

If you're a slow reader, chances are you don't do a lot of reading. If you have plenty of time before you're due to take the ASVAB, start reading more — right now. It's in your best interest.

TIP

You don't have to pick up *A Tale of Two Cities* or *War and Peace*; you can start with the newspaper, a biography of a person you admire, or magazines you find at the library. (Sorry, but the instruction guide to your favorite video game doesn't count.) You don't need to enroll in a speed-reading course. If you devote at least one hour a day simply to reading, you'll see your reading comprehension and speed increase within a month or so.

TECHNICAL STUFF

Several studies have shown that folks who enjoy reading as a pleasurable pastime score better on reading comprehension tests than individuals who dislike reading. Sounds obvious, right? So why study it? The idea is if you grow to enjoy reading, you'll want to read more. You'll become a better reader and thereby score better on reading comprehension tests. How do you discover an enjoyment of reading? Simple — choose reading material in subject areas that interest you.

Become a lean, mean word machine

People sometimes read slowly because they don't have a large vocabulary and don't understand everything they read. If you can identify with this situation, improving your vocabulary is your first step toward increasing your reading comprehension and your reading speed. (Chapter 4 gives you info on building your word knowledge. Check it out.)

TIP

Keep a pocket dictionary or a smartphone dictionary app handy while reading so you can look up words you don't know. If you're reading articles on the Internet, keep a tab open to one of the online dictionaries (such as `www.dictionary.com`, `www.yourdictionary.com`, or `www.m-w.com`) so you can quickly find the definition of words you find confusing. Your reading will become more enjoyable, and you'll be adding to your vocabulary knowledge to boot.

Build your confidence

Another reason people read slowly is that they don't have confidence in themselves. They're not convinced that they understand what they're reading, so they read a passage several times, trying to make sure they haven't missed anything. But just like people who check that the front door is locked 15 times before leaving for vacation and still lie awake at night wondering whether they locked the door, you'll find that reading and rereading a passage doesn't give you confidence that you understand the text. You get confidence from proving that you understand it.

TIP

How do you prove to yourself that you understand what you're reading? Here are a few tips:

>> **Get out a textbook or reference book (preferably one that contains some subject matter that interests you) and read one or two paragraphs straight through without going back and rereading anything.** Then set the book aside (keeping your place marked) and write, in your own words, a brief description of what you've read. Finally, turn back to the passage and compare your description to the information on the page.

>> **Play the 20-questions game.** Read an article from a magazine, reference book, or textbook. Then ask someone to pick out facts from the article and ask you questions.

>> **Create motivation and interest by reading the daily newspaper or news magazines.** Discuss the news events with your classmates, friends, or co-workers. Stronger interest equals greater comprehension.

Is your written version of the article close in meaning to the original? Are you getting most of the 20 questions correct? Do you feel comfortable discussing current events with others? If so, you understand what you're reading, and that should build your confidence. If not, don't toss the book or magazine aside in frustration or go ballistic on your mom for asking you tough questions. Keep working on it, and your comprehension will improve. Do the preceding confidence-building drills a few times a day until you feel like you can read any paragraph or two and understand the content without having to reread the information.

REMEMBER

The Paragraph Comprehension subtest tests your ability to understand what you read, not how quickly you can read it. When you sit down to take this subtest, try to go as quickly as you can without sacrificing accuracy. Being methodical in your reading isn't a bad thing as long as you're getting the answers right. Just try to read a little faster than normal without panicking or missing the point. It's better to read the paragraphs carefully and answer the questions correctly on half of the questions and guess on the other half of the questions than it is to speed through all the reading and get none of the answers right.

Test-Taking Tips for Reading and Gleaning

Although no shortcuts exist for improving your reading comprehension skills (besides practice), you can do a few things on test day to make sure you score as high as possible on this part of the ASVAB.

REMEMBER

If you're running out of time on this subtest or you're not sure whether you can identify the main idea of a passage, take a guess. (But be careful: Guessing and getting too many questions wrong at the end of the subtest may result in a penalty against your score.) If you think that's a good piece of advice, check out these tried-and-true tactics for test day:

>> **Read first, ask questions later.** Read the passage all the way through before glancing at the question and answer options.

>> **Take it one question at a time.** Some passages have more than one question associated with them, but look at only one question at a time.

>> **Understand each question.** What's the question asking you to do? Are you supposed to find the main point? Draw a conclusion? Find a word that's nearest in meaning? Make sure you know what the question is asking before you choose among the answer options. This tip may seem obvious, but when you're in a hurry, you can make mistakes by misunderstanding the questions.

» **Read each answer option carefully.** Don't just select the first answer that seems right. Remember, on the Paragraph Comprehension subtest, one answer is often most right and others are almost right. You want to choose the most right answer, not the almost right answer. And to do that, you have to read all the answers.

» **Check your feelings at the door.** Answer each question based on the passage, not your own opinions or views on the topic.

» **Don't choose vague answer options.** They're incorrect 99.99 times out of 100. (Oh heck, call it 100 times out of 100.) If an answer strikes you as not quite true but not totally false, that answer is incorrect. The ASVAB test authors have put those answers in there to throw you off. Don't give them the satisfaction of falling for their trap!

» **(Almost) never select *never*.** For the most part, answer options that are absolutes are incorrect. *Never, always,* and related words are often a sign that you should select a different answer. Words like *generally* and *usually* are more likely to be correct.

Paragraph Comprehension Practice Questions

The following questions are designed to present you with an opportunity to practice your Paragraph Comprehension skills. Read each short paragraph, followed by one or more questions regarding information contained in that passage. Make sure to read the paragraph carefully before selecting the choice that most correctly answers the question.

Passage one

Mercedes was dismayed to find out that her final exam fell on her birthday — and Russian exams were *hard*. Still, after nearly a year at the Defense Language Institute, she was ready to wrap things up and begin her Air Force career outside the schoolhouse. The whole day would be a mess, though. The test began at 8:00 a.m., and each airman was allowed exactly 90 minutes to complete all the questions. Then, at 10:00 a.m., everyone had to begin writing a 1,000-word essay. Mercedes pressed her fingers to her temples; just thinking about what kind of topics were in the pool (and the fact that she had to finish the essay by noon) conjured a familiar ache. She knew she was ready, and she knew the language inside and out, but test-taker anxiety started to creep in.

1. How does Mercedes feel about taking her final exam?

(A) She is anxious.

(B) She's angry.

(C) She's over-confident.

(D) She wants to celebrate her birthday instead.

2. Why did Mercedes press her fingers to her temples?

(A) It helps her concentrate.

(B) She was beginning to get a headache.

(C) It's an old habit.

(D) All of the above.

Passage two

Some people argue that baking is an art, but Chef Debra Dearborn says that baking is a science. She says that if you follow a recipe carefully, assembling the ingredients accurately, cooking at the specified temperature for the specified period of time, your cookies will always turn out right. Chef Dearborn says the best baking is like the best experiment — anyone can duplicate it.

3. In this passage, the word *assembling* most nearly means

(A) measuring.

(B) putting together.

(C) buying.

(D) storing.

4. According to the passage, a person who's all thumbs in the kitchen

(A) should get out of the kitchen.

(B) is an artist.

(C) isn't following the recipe carefully.

(D) is Chef Dearborn.

Passage three

At dinner-time tonight I was feverish to do three things at once: write out my day's journal, eat my food, and read *The Journal of Marie Bashkirtseff*. Did all three — but unfortunately not at once, so that when I was occupied with one I would surreptitiously cast a glance sideways at the other — and repined.

5. Which of the following was the author NOT planning to do?

(A) go shopping

(B) eat food

(C) write a journal

(D) read a journal

Passage four

To motivate your people, give them tasks that challenge them. Get to know your people and their capabilities, so you can tell just how far to push each one. Give them as much responsibility as they can handle and then let them do the work without looking over their shoulders and nagging them. When they succeed, praise them. When they fall short, give them credit for what they've done and coach or counsel them on how to do better next time.

6. According to the paragraph, if your subordinates fail to adequately perform their tasks, you should

    (A) punish them.

    (B) praise them.

    (C) counsel them.

    (D) both B and C.

7. After assigning responsibility for the tasks at hand to your subordinates, you should

    (A) supervise them closely to ensure the tasks are performed correctly.

    (B) let them do the work on their own.

    (C) check their progress at the end of each day.

    (D) schedule sufficient work-breaks to avoid job burnout.

Passage five

Approximately 15,000 years ago the first Native Americans may have appeared in Colorado. The earliest inhabitants were hunters and nomadic foragers on the plains, as well as the western plateau. Agricultural settlements began appearing along river valleys in the eastern part of Colorado from approximately 5,000 B.C. as people learned farming techniques from the Mississippi River Native Americans.

8. The first Native Americans in Colorado were

    (A) farmers.

    (B) traders.

    (C) hunters and gatherers.

    (D) originally from the Mississippi River region.

Passage six

Organizational leaders influence several hundred to several thousand people. They do this indirectly, generally through more levels of subordinates than do direct leaders. The additional levels of subordinates can make it more difficult for them to see results. Organizational leaders have staffs to help them lead their people and manage their organizations' resources. They establish policies and the organizational climate that support their subordinate leaders.

9. Organizational leaders provide

    (A) direct leadership.

    (B) general policies.

    (C) organizational budgets.

    (D) daily work schedules.

10. In order to become more efficient, organizational leaders make significant use of

    (A) computer technology.

    (B) rules and regulations.

    (C) efficiency and management reports.

    (D) staffs.

Passage seven

His name is Frank Clarke, but his real name isn't really as real as the one the children gave him — The Toyman — because he's always making the kids things, such as kites and tops, sleds and boats, jokes and happiness and laughter. His face is as brown as saddle leather, with a touch of apple red in it from the sun. His face is creased, too, because he laughs and jokes so much. Sometimes when The Toyman appears to be solemn you want to laugh most, for he's only pretending to be solemn. And, best of all, if you hurt yourself or if your pet doggie hurts himself, The Toyman knows how to fix it to make it all well again.

11. Frank Clarke's face could best be described as

    (A) rugged.

    (B) pink and smooth.

    (C) fair.

    (D) feminine.

12. Clarke received his nickname because he was always

    (A) fixing toys.

    (B) making toys for the children.

    (C) telling stories about toys.

    (D) playing with toys.

Passage eight

Let me now take you on to the day of the assault. My cousin and I were separated at the outset. I never saw him when we forded the river; when we planted the English flag in the first breach; when we crossed the ditch beyond, and, fighting every inch of our way, entered the town.

It was only at dusk, when the place was ours, and after General Baird himself had found the dead body of Tippoo under a heap of the slain, that Herncastle and I met.

13. What would be a good title for the passage?

    (A) "Attacking Japan"

    (B) "War without Violence"

    (C) "Moving to the Mountains"

    (D) "My Account of the War"

14. How long was the main character fighting in the area?

    (A) two hours

    (B) from day to dusk

    (C) a few days

    (D) none of the above

15. In this passage, what is the meaning of the word *heap*?

    (A) pile

    (B) rubbish

    (C) marker

    (D) note

16. According to the passage, you can assume the main character is

    (A) at a community function.

    (B) in a war.

    (C) dreaming.

    (D) moving to a new town.

Passage nine

The third leading cause of unintentional injury death the world over is drowning. Sad to say, most of these deaths could have been prevented if the simple rules of water safety had been applied. Most drownings are preventable if the victim does not become panicked; therefore, the first and most important safety rule is to remain calm. The ability to swim may save your life, but even an experienced swimmer can panic with fear and stop making rational decisions and begin to flounder. When this happens, the swimmer has taken the first step to drowning. The key to preventing panic is relaxation. When confronted with an emergency, the swimmer must make himself remain calm and in charge, making conscious efforts to escape the situation.

17. According to this passage, what is the first step in drowning?

    (A) going underwater

    (B) giving in to fear

    (C) not wearing a life preserver

    (D) not knowing how to swim

18. The word *flounder*, as used in this passage, most nearly means

    (A) a fish.

    (B) a building foundation.

    (C) to splash about helplessly.

    (D) to float.

19. According to the passage, what is the best prevention for drowning?

    (A) staying out of the water

    (B) learning how to swim

    (C) having a buddy nearby

    (D) remaining calm

Braille was based on a military code called *night writing*, developed in response to Napoleon's demand for a means for soldiers to communicate silently at night and without light. A soldier invented a tactile system of raised dots. Napoleon rejected it as too complicated, but Louis Braille simplified it for use by the blind. Braille is still used today, consisting of one to six raised dots, representing the alphabet, that a person can feel with his or her fingertips.

20. Why was Napoleon interested in Braille?

(A) He was blind.

(B) He wanted to help the blind.

(C) He couldn't read.

(D) He wanted a code that could be read at night.

21. How many raised dots are used to form each letter of the alphabet in Braille?

(A) three

(B) six

(C) one to six

(D) none of the above

22. What was Louis Braille's contribution to the invention of this reading system?

(A) He taught blind people how to read.

(B) He urged Napoleon to have it developed.

(C) He named it.

(D) He simplified someone else's complicated idea.

23. The word *tactile*, as used in this passage, most nearly means

(A) a sharp object.

(B) words on a printed page.

(C) something that is sticky.

(D) something that can be felt with the fingers.

There seem to be abundant job opportunities for nurses these days. Plus, nurses receive decent salaries and benefits. Nursing jobs are very flexible with work schedules. There is an array of specialties when it comes to nursing positions in a variety of settings. It is true that nursing offers room for advancement and raises. Overall, the biggest advantage to being a nurse must be the satisfaction you get from knowing you are helping others.

24. According to the paragraph, what is the best part about being a nurse?

(A) getting good benefits

(B) helping people

(C) having three days off in a row

(D) having room for advancement

25. According to the passage, which of the following is not a benefit of being a nurse?

(A) room for advancement

(B) array of specialties

(C) convenient uniforms

(D) flexible scheduling

26. What is the main thought of the paragraph?

(A) There are a lot of nurses.

(B) There are a lot of nursing jobs.

(C) Nursing pays well.

(D) Nursing has many benefits.

27. In this paragraph, what is the meaning of the word *abundant*?

(A) excellent

(B) plenty

(C) few

(D) competitive

Answers and Explanations

Use this answer key to score the Paragraph Comprehension practice questions.

1. **A.** The correct answer is Choice (A) — Mercedes is anxious about taking the test, which you can tell with context clues such as "The whole day would be a mess" and "test-taker anxiety started to creep in."

2. **B.** The correct answer is Choice (B). The passage says, "just thinking about what kind of topics were in the pool (and the fact that she had to finish the essay by noon) conjured a familiar ache."

3. **B.** Although measuring is something you do when baking, it doesn't most nearly mean the same thing as *assembling.* Putting together does. Therefore, Choice (B) is the correct answer.

4. **C.** The passage states that if you follow a recipe carefully, "your cookies will always turn out right." The correct answer is Choice (C).

5. **A.** The passage's first sentence tells you everything you need to know — it mentions writing and reading journals and eating food. Shopping isn't mentioned, so the correct answer is Choice (A).

6. **D.** If you didn't read the passage, praising someone who didn't measure up may seem like a bad idea. However, the last sentence states you should give your subordinates credit for the parts of the task they performed correctly and counsel them how to do better the next time. Although that sentence doesn't use the word *praise,* you can infer that giving someone credit means the same thing. The correct answer is Choice (D).

7. **B.** Choices (C) and (D) sound like good ideas, but they aren't suggestions discussed in the paragraph. Remember to avoid the trap of answering based on your personal feelings. Choice (A) is the opposite of what the passage suggests — the writer says to "let [employees] do the work without looking over their shoulders." Choice (B) is the correct answer.

8. **C.** The second sentence states that the original inhabitants "were hunters and nomadic foragers," and because none of the other answer options include hunters, you can deduce that *nomadic foragers* means gatherers. The correct answer is Choice (C).

9. **B.** The passage mentions direct leaders but only to contrast them with organizational leaders, so Choice (A) is wrong. According to the passage, organizational leaders "establish policies and the organizational climate that support their subordinate leaders." The correct answer is Choice (B).

10. **D.** Organizational leaders have staffs to help them efficiently lead their subordinates and manage the organization. Therefore, Choice (D) is the correct answer.

11. **A.** According to the passage, Frank's face is "brown as saddle leather," and he has wrinkles from laughing often. Choice (A) is the correct answer.

12. **B.** The first sentence in the passage explains why the children gave Frank the nickname of The Toyman. Frank knows how to fix things, but that's not how he got his name. The correct answer is Choice (B).

13. **D.** Choice (A) doesn't make much sense because the group put up an English flag in the first breach. Choice (B) doesn't work because the passage talks about fighting and dead bodies. Choice (C) isn't the best answer because it doesn't directly relate to the passage. Choice (D) is correct because the main character is speaking of his experiences of a particular war.

14. **B.** The passage states in the beginning that the assault began in the day. Later in the passage, the author explains that the town was theirs by dusk, so you can conclude the time frame was from daytime into dusk.

15. **A.** *Heap* is a noun meaning a group of things placed, thrown, or lying one on another — in other words, a pile — so Choice (A) is the correct answer.

16. **B.** The main character is describing a scene relative to that of a war, even mentioning an English flag, a general, and dead bodies. The paragraph never states he is doing something for the community, is planning to stay at the town, or is in a dream, so you can conclude that the main character is in some sort of war.

17. **B.** The passage states that fear leads a swimmer to stop making rational decisions, the first step in drowning.

18. **C.** To *flounder* in the water is to splash around helplessly.

19. **D.** The paragraph doesn't discourage the reader from going in the water, nor does it mention having someone nearby. It says knowing how to swim can save your life, but the main focus of the passage is on the importance of remaining calm when trouble strikes.

20. **D.** Napoleon wanted to devise a code that could be read at night, so one of his soldiers invented a system of raised dots that later became Braille.

21. **C.** The passage states that each letter of the alphabet is represented in Braille by raised dots and that each letter uses from one to six dots.

22. **D.** Napoleon rejected the idea for a code that could be read at night because it was too complicated. Louis Braille took that idea and simplified it for use by blind people.

23. **D.** The word *tactile* refers to something that can be felt with one's hands.

24. **B.** According to the last sentence, the biggest satisfaction of being a nurse comes from knowing you make a difference in people's lives, so Choice (B), helping people, is correct.

25. **C.** The passage describes many benefits of being a nurse, but it doesn't talk about the uniforms nurses may wear.

26. **D.** The passage says that nursing has not only good monetary and work benefits but also rewarding self-satisfaction benefits.

27. **B.** *Abundant* is an adjective meaning marked by great plenty. The passage describes abundant job opportunities, meaning there are a lot of jobs from which a nurse can choose.

3

Making the Most of Math: Arithmetic Skills

Chapter **6**

Mathematics Knowledge and Operations

Rumor has it that Albert Einstein once said, "Do not worry about your problems with mathematics. I assure you mine are far greater." The good professor obviously never had to worry about taking the ASVAB! But you don't have to be a mathematical theoretician to score well on the Mathematics Knowledge subtest. This subtest asks questions about basic high school mathematics. No college or graduate degrees needed.

On the computerized version of the ASVAB, the Mathematics Knowledge subtest consists of 15 questions, and you have 23 minutes to complete it. The paper-and-pencil ASVAB serves up 25 questions that you have to answer in 24 minutes. If you're one of the lucky ones who gets tryout questions on this subtest (see Chapter 1), you answer 30 questions in 47 minutes. You don't necessarily have to rush through each calculation, but the pace you need to set doesn't exactly give you time to daydream. If you're taking the P&P version of the test, you can skip questions you're not sure of and come back to them after answering other, easier questions (just be careful to fill in the right blanks on your answer sheet). You have to focus and concentrate to solve each problem quickly and accurately. And no calculators allowed! Test proctors give you all the scratch paper you can handle, though, and they'll make sure you have plenty of sharpened pencils on hand.

REMEMBER

You don't have the luxury of skipping questions when you're taking the CAT-ASVAB because you have to answer the question you're on before moving to the next. Remember, too, that you may find the CAT-ASVAB harder (or easier) than you thought you would. That's because the program is designed to adapt to your ability. It does that by offering you a medium-difficulty question to kick things off and then chooses the difficulty of the next question based on whether you answer the first correctly. If you're knee-deep in the test and you find yourself saying, "This is harder than what the book covered," that most likely means you're getting a lot of the questions right.

Most of the time, the Mathematics Knowledge subtest contains only one or two questions testing each specific mathematical concept. For example, one question may ask you to multiply fractions, the next may ask you to solve a mathematical inequality, and the question after that may ask you to find the value of an exponent. (If you're freaked out by the last sentence, calm down. I cover each of these concepts in this book.)

All this variety forces you to shift your mental gears quickly to deal with different concepts. You can look at this situation from two perspectives. These mental gymnastics can be difficult and frustrating, especially if you know everything about solving for *x* but nothing about finding a square root. But variety can also help save you on the test. If you don't know how to solve a specific type of problem, that oversight may cause you to get only one or two questions wrong.

You can get more practice for the Mathematics Knowledge subtest — and the rest of the AFQT subtests — with *1,001 ASVAB AFQT Practice Questions For Dummies* by yours truly (Wiley).

REMEMBER

To qualify for military enlistment, you have to score well on this subtest (it's part of the AFQT discussed in Chapter 1). You also have to perform well in Mathematics Knowledge to land certain jobs in the military. Turn to Appendix A to find out more about the subtest scores needed for specific military jobs.

In this chapter, I go over the basic arithmetic you need to know. This info also comes in handy when solving word problems on the Arithmetic Reasoning subtest, which I cover in Chapter 9.

Just When You Thought You Were Done with Vocab: Math Terminology

Math has its own vocabulary. In order to understand what each problem on the Mathematical Knowledge subtest asks, you need to understand certain mathematical terms:

>> **Integer:** An *integer* is any positive or negative whole number or zero. The ASVAB often requires you to work with integers, such as –6, 0, or 27.

>> **Numerical factors:** Factors are integers (whole numbers) that can be divided evenly into another integer. To *factor* a number, you simply determine the numbers that you can divide into it. For example, 8 can be divided by the numbers 2 and 4 (in addition to 1 and 8), so 2 and 4 are factors of 8. The *prime factorization* of the number 30 is written $2 \times 3 \times 5$.

Numbers may be either composite or prime, depending on how many factors they have:

- **Composite number:** A *composite* number is a whole number that can be divided evenly by itself and by 1, as well as by one or more other whole numbers; in other words, it has more than two factors. Examples of composite numbers are 6 (whose factors are 1, 2, 3, and 6), 9 (whose factors are 1, 3, and 9), and 12 (whose factors are 1, 2, 3, 4, 6, and 12).

- **Prime number:** A *prime* number is a whole number that can be divided evenly by itself and by 1 but not by any other number, which means that it has exactly two factors. The number 1 is not a prime number. Examples of prime numbers are 2 (whose factors are 1 and 2), 5 (whose factors are 1 and 5), and 11 (whose factors are 1 and 11).

>> **Base:** A *base* is a number that's used as a factor a specific number of times — it's a number raised to an exponent. For instance, the term 4^3 (which can be written $4 \times 4 \times 4$, and in which 4 is a factor three times) has a base of 4.

>> **Exponent:** An exponent is a shorthand method of indicating repeated multiplication. For example, 15×15 can also be expressed as 15^2, which is also known as "15 squared" or "15 to the second power." The small number written slightly above and to the right of a number is the *exponent,* and it indicates the number of times you multiply the base by itself. Note that 15^2 (15×15), which equals 225, isn't the same as 15×2 (which equals 30).

To express $15 \times 15 \times 15$ using this shorthand method, simply write it as 15^3, which is also called "15 cubed" or "15 to the third power." Again, 15^3 (which equals 3,375) isn't the same as 15×3 (which equals 45).

>> **Square root:** The *square root* of a number is the number that, when multiplied by itself (in other words, *squared*), equals the original number. For example, the square root of 36 is 6. If you square 6, or multiply it by itself, you produce 36. (Check out "Getting to the Root of the Problem" later in this chapter.)

>> **Factorial:** A *factorial* is an operation represented by an exclamation point (!). You calculate a factorial by finding the product of (multiplying) a whole number and all the whole numbers less than it down to 1. That means 6 factorial (6!) is $6 \times 5 \times 4 \times 3 \times 2 \times 1 = 720$.

REMEMBER

A factorial helps you determine *permutations* — all the different possible ways an event may turn out. For example, if you want to know how many different ways six runners could finish a race (permutation), you would solve for 6!: $6 \times 5 \times 4 \times 3 \times 2 \times 1$.

>> **Reciprocal:** A *reciprocal* is the number by which another number can be multiplied to produce 1; if you have a fraction, its reciprocal is that fraction turned upside down. For example, the reciprocal of 3 is $\frac{1}{3}$. If you multiply 3 times $\frac{1}{3}$, you get 1. The reciprocal of $\frac{1}{6}$ is $\frac{6}{1}$ (which is the same thing as 6); $\frac{1}{6} \times 6 = 1$. The reciprocal of $\frac{2}{3}$ is $\frac{3}{2}$. The number 0 doesn't have a reciprocal. Get the idea?

>> **Rounding:** *Rounding* is limiting a number to a certain number of significant digits (replacing some digits with zeros). You perform rounding operations all the time — often without even thinking about it. If you have $1.97 in change in your pocket, you may say, "I have about two dollars." The rounding process simplifies mathematical operations.

TIP

Often, numbers are rounded to the nearest tenth. The ASVAB may ask you to do this. If the number you're eliminating is 5 or over, round up; for any number under 5, round down. For example, 1.55 rounded to the nearest tenth can be rounded up to 1.6, and 1.34 can be rounded down to 1.3.

Many math problems require rounding — especially when you're doing all this without a calculator. For example, pi (π) represents a number approximately equal to 3.14159265358979323846264383 (and on and on and on). However, in mathematical operations and on the ASVAB, it's common to round π to 3.14.

Operations: What You Do to Numbers

When you toss numbers together (mathematically speaking), you perform an *operation*. When you add or multiply, you perform a *basic operation*. But because math functions according to yin-yang-like principles, each of these basic operations also has an opposite operation called an *inverse operation*. Thus, the additive inverse (of addition) is subtraction, and the multiplicative inverse (of multiplication) is division. And of course, the inverse of subtraction is — you got it — addition. The inverse of division is multiplication.

NAMING THE ANSWERS

The result of each operation — addition, subtraction, multiplication, or division — goes by a different name:

- When you add two numbers together, you arrive at a *sum.*

- When you subtract, all that remains is a *difference.*

- When you multiply, you come up with a *product.*

- When you divide, you're left with a *quotient.*

WARNING

Don't confuse *opposite* with *inverse.* When you're doing mathematical operations, such as adding and multiplying, the inverse operation is the opposite operation. But when you're talking numbers, *opposite* and *inverse* don't mean the same thing. The opposite of a positive number is a negative number, so the opposite of x is $-x$. But the multiplicative inverse of a number is its reciprocal — that number turned on its head! The reciprocal of x is $\frac{1}{x}$. The inverse of $\frac{1}{5}$ is $\frac{5}{1}$ (or just 5).

First things first: Following the order of operations

Operations must be performed in a certain order. For example, when you have parentheses in a math problem, you must do the calculation in the parentheses before you do any calculations outside of the parentheses. In the equation $2 \times (16 + 5) = ?$, you first add 16 to 5 to arrive at 21, and then you multiply by 2 to come up with a total of 42. You get a different (and wrong) answer if you simply calculate from left to right: $2 \times 16 = 32$, and $32 + 5 = 37$. And you better believe that both results will be choices on the test!

REMEMBER

To figure out which mathematical operation you should perform first, second, third, and so on, follow these rules, otherwise known as the *order of operations:*

1. **Parentheses take precedence.**

   You should do everything contained in parentheses first. In cases where parentheses are contained within parentheses, do the innermost parentheses first. This rule also goes for brackets and braces.

   Note: If you're dealing with a fraction, treat the top as though it were in parentheses and the bottom as though it were in parentheses, even if the parentheses aren't written in the original state. Suppose you have the problem $\frac{3}{1+2} =$. Add the numbers below the fraction bar before dividing. The answer is $\frac{3}{3} = 1$. (For more on fractions, see the later section "Working on Both Sides of the Line: Fractions.") The square root sign $\left(\sqrt{}\right)$ is also a grouping symbol, so you solve for whatever's under the top bar of the square root sign before doing any other operation in the problem.

2. **Exponents come next.**

   Remember that the exponent goes with the number or variable that it's closest to. If it's closest to a parenthesis, then you already should've performed the calculation inside the parentheses in Step 1. For example, $(5 \times 2)^2 = 10^2 = 100$. The square root sign $\left(\sqrt{}\right)$ is also treated as an exponent, so you take the square root during this step.

3. **Multiplication and division are next.**

Do these operations in left-to-right order (just like you read).

4. **Addition and subtraction are last.**

Perform these operations from left to right as well.

Check out the following example for a little practice with order of operations:

$$(15 \div 5) \times 3 + (18 - 7) = ?$$

Do the work in parentheses:

$$3 \times 3 + 11 = ?$$

No exponents are present, so division and multiplication come next (in this problem, only multiplication is needed):

$$9 + 11 = ?$$

Finally, do the addition and subtraction (in this problem, only addition is needed). Your final answer is 20.

TIP

Use the acronym PEMDAS, or "Please Excuse My Dear Aunt Sally," to remember the order of operations. It stands for parentheses, exponents, multiplication, division, addition, and subtraction.

Completing a number sequence

The Arithmetic Reasoning (AR) subtest often includes questions that test your ability to name what comes next in a sequence of numbers. Generally, these problems are the only AR questions that aren't word problems (which I cover in Chapter 9). However, sequence questions do test your ability to do arithmetic and to reason, because you have to determine how the numbers relate to each other. And to do this, you must be able to perform mathematical operations quickly.

Suppose you have a sequence of numbers that looks like this: 1, 4, 7, 10, ?. Each new number is reached by adding 3 to the previous number: $1 + 3 = 4$, $4 + 3 = 7$, and so on. So the next number in the sequence is $10 + 3 = 13$, or 13.

But of course, the questions on the ASVAB aren't quite this simple. More likely, you'll see something like this: 2, 4, 16, 256, ?. In this case, each number is being multiplied by itself, so $2 \times 2 = 4$, $4 \times 4 = 16$, and so on. The next number in the sequence is 256×256, which equals 65,536 — the correct answer.

You may also see sequences like this: 1, 2, 3, 6, 12, ?. In this sequence, the numbers are being added together: $1 + 2 = 3$, and $1 + 2 + 3 = 6$. The next number is $1 + 2 + 3 + 6 = 12$. So the next number would be 24.

Finding the pattern

To answer sequence questions correctly, you need to figure out the pattern as quickly as possible. Some people, blessed with superior sequencing genes, can figure out patterns instinctively. The rest of the population has to rely on a more difficult, manual effort.

Finding a pattern in a sequence of numbers requires you to think about how numbers work. For instance, seeing the number 256 after 2, 4, 16 should alert you that multiplication is the operation, because 256 is so much larger than the other numbers. On the other hand, because the values in 1, 2, 3, 6, 12 don't increase by much, you can guess that the pattern requires addition.

Dealing with more than one operation in a sequence

Don't forget that more than one operation can occur in a sequence. For example, a sequence may be "add 1, subtract 1, add 2, subtract 2." That would look something like this: 2, 3, 2, 4, ?.

Because the numbers in the sequence both increase and decrease as the sequence continues, you should suspect that something tricky is going on.

Make sure to use your scratch paper! Jot down notes while you're trying to find the pattern in a sequence. Writing down your work helps you keep track of which operations you've tried.

Averaging mean, median, and mode in a range

An average number is one that expresses a typical value in a set of data. In plain English, that means what you can expect as an outcome. For example, if you take the ASVAB three times (which I advise against — I just want you to take it once and score really well!) and get an AFQT score of 80, 85, and 90, respectively, your average score is 85. Things get a little sticky when the numbers aren't so nicely rounded, though. If someone's scores are 35, 35, and 50, her average is 40.

This type of average is technically called the *mean*. To figure out a mean, add all the numbers in a data set (in this case, that's 35, 35, and 50). Divide the sum by how many numbers there are. Because there are three numbers in this data set, your math looks like this:

$$35 + 35 + 50 = 120$$
$$120 \div 3 = 40$$

You might also counter other types of averages on the ASVAB, including *median* and *mode*.

>> **Median:** The median is the middle value in a set of ordered numbers. You can find it by putting your numbers in numerical order, from smallest to largest. In the data set 47, 56, 58, 63, 100, the median is 58.

>> **Mode:** Mode is the value or values that occur most often in a list of numbers. If no numbers are repeated, there's no mode. But in the data set with the test scores above — 35, 35, and 50 — the mode is 35 because it appears most often.

Working on Both Sides of the Line: Fractions

I don't know why, but it seems almost all math textbooks explain fractions in terms of pies. (I think most mathematicians must have a sweet tooth.) But I like pizza, so I'm going to use pizza instead. If a *whole number* is a pizza, a *fraction* is a slice of pizza. A fraction also illustrates the slice's relationship to the whole pizza. For example, consider the fraction $\frac{3}{5}$. If you accuse your cousin of eating $\frac{3}{5}$ of the pizza when he comes over for movie night, you're saying that the pizza is divided into five equal-sized slices — fifths — and your cousin ate three of those five slices.

REMEMBER

The number above the fraction bar — the three slices your cousin ate — is called the *numerator*. The number written below the fraction bar — the total number of slices the pizza is divided into — is called the *denominator*.

Common denominators: Preparing to add and subtract fractions

To add and subtract fractions, the fractions must have the same denominator (bottom number), which is called a *common denominator*. If the fractions don't have a common denominator, you have to find one. There are two basic methods to use. Sound fun? Read on.

Method one

Finding a common denominator can be easy, or it can be as hard as picking off anchovies.

Suppose you want to add $\frac{3}{5}$ and $\frac{3}{10}$. Getting a common denominator is easy here, and you use this process whenever you can evenly divide one denominator by another. Follow these steps:

1. **Divide the larger denominator by the smaller denominator.**

   If there's a remainder, then you can't use this method, and you have to use method two (see the next section). In this case, 10 can be divided evenly by 5. The quotient (answer) that results is 2.

2. **Take the fraction with the smaller denominator $\left(\frac{3}{5}\right)$; multiply both the numerator (top number) and the denominator (bottom number) by the answer that resulted in Step 1.**

   Multiply 3 by 2, and the result is 6 — that's your new numerator. Multiply 5 by 2, and the result is 10 — that's your new denominator.

3. **Replace the numerator and denominator with the numbers from Step 2.**

   You can also express $\frac{3}{5}$ as $\frac{6}{10}$. (If you cut the pizza into 10 slices instead of 5 and your cousin eats 6 slices instead of 3, he's eaten exactly the same amount of pizza.)

After you've found a common denominator, you add the two fractions by simply adding the numerators together: $\frac{6}{10} + \frac{3}{10} = \frac{9}{10}$. Think of it this way: If your cousin eats $\frac{6}{10}$ of the pizza (which is just another way of saying $\frac{3}{5}$) and you eat $\frac{3}{10}$ of the pizza, together you've eaten $\frac{9}{10}$ of the pizza.

Method two

Suppose your cousin eats $\frac{3}{5}$ of one pizza and your sister eats $\frac{1}{6}$ of another pizza (one that was cut into 6 slices instead of 5), and you want to know how much pizza has been eaten. In this case, you need to add $\frac{3}{5}$ and $\frac{1}{6}$.

Adding these fractions is a bit more difficult because you can't divide either denominator by the other. You have to find a common denominator that both 5 and 6 divide into evenly. Here's how:

1. **Multiply the denominator of the first fraction by the denominator of the second fraction.**

   In the preceding example, $5 \times 6 = 30$. The common denominator for both fractions is 30.

2. **Express the first fraction in terms of the new common denominator.**

   $\frac{3}{5} = \frac{?}{30}$

3. **Multiply the numerator by the number that you multiplied by to result in the new denominator.**

To convert the denominator (5) to 30, you multiply by 6, so multiply the numerator (3) by 6. The result is 18. Therefore, the fraction $\frac{3}{5}$ can be expressed as $\frac{18}{30}$.

When you're trying to find an equivalent fraction for a fraction, always multiply the numerator and the denominator by the same number. Otherwise, you change the value of the fraction.

REMEMBER

With this example, you multiply the numerator and the denominator by 6, discovering that $\frac{3}{5}$ is the same thing as $\frac{18}{30}$. But if you were to multiply only the denominator by 6, you'd have a new number; $\frac{3}{5}$ and $\frac{3}{30}$ don't have the same value.

4. **Next, express the second fraction in terms of the new common denominator.**

$$\frac{1}{6} = \frac{?}{30}$$

5. **Multiply the numerator of the second fraction by the number you used to result in the denominator.**

To get 30, you have to multiply 6 by 5. Multiply the numerator by the same number: You find that $1 \times 5 = 5$, so the fraction $\frac{1}{6}$ can be expressed as $\frac{5}{30}$.

After all that work, you can finally add the fractions: $\frac{18}{30} + \frac{5}{30} = \frac{23}{30}$. Now pause and take a bite of pizza.

Finding common denominators for three or more fractions

If you have more than two fractions with different denominators, you have to find a common denominator that all the denominators divide into. Suppose you need to add $\frac{1}{2} + \frac{2}{3} + \frac{3}{5}$.

A simple way to find a common denominator is to take the largest denominator (in this case, 5) and multiply it by whole numbers, starting with 1, 2, 3, 4, and so on until you find a denominator that the other denominators also divide into evenly.

If you multiply 5 by 2, you get 10, but 3 doesn't divide evenly into 10. So keep going: $5 \times 3 = 15$, $5 \times 4 = 20$, and so on until you find a number that 2, 3, and 5 can divide into evenly. In this case, 30 is the first number you can find that 2, 3, and 5 can divide into evenly, so 30 is your common denominator.

Multiplying and reducing fractions

REMEMBER

Multiplying fractions is easy. You just multiply the numerators and then multiply the denominators. So look at the following equation: $\frac{1}{2} \times \frac{3}{4} \times \frac{3}{5} = ?$. You multiply $1 \times 3 \times 3 = 9$ (the numerators) and then $2 \times 4 \times 5 = 40$ (the denominators) to result in $\frac{9}{40}$.

Occasionally, when you multiply fractions, you end up with an extremely large fraction that can be simplified or reduced. To express a fraction in its *lowest terms* means to put it in such a way that you can't evenly divide the numerator and the denominator by the same number (other than 1).

A number that you can divide into both the numerator and the denominator is called a *common factor*. If you have the fraction $\frac{6}{10}$, both the numerator (6) and the denominator (10) can be divided by the same number, 2. If you do the division, $6 \div 2 = 3$ and $10 \div 2 = 5$, you find that $\frac{6}{10}$ can be expressed in the simpler terms of $\frac{3}{5}$. You can't reduce (simplify) $\frac{3}{5}$ any further; the only other number that both the numerator and denominator can be divided by is 1, so the result would be the same, $\frac{3}{5}$.

TIP

Remember, you can't use a calculator on the ASVAB, so multiplying large numbers can take extra steps and valuable time. You can make your work easier by *canceling out* common factors before multiplying.

For example, suppose you have the problem $\frac{20}{21} \times \frac{14}{25}$. Multiplying the numerators $(20 \times 14 = 280)$, then multiplying the denominators $(21 \times 25 = 525)$, and finally reducing the fraction $\left(\frac{280}{525} = \frac{8}{15}\right)$ may require you to write out three or more separate multiplication/division problems. But you can save time if a numerator and denominator have common factors. Here, the numerator of the first fraction (20) and the denominator of the second (25) have a common factor of 5, so you can divide both of those numbers by 5: Your problem becomes $\frac{4}{21} \times \frac{14}{5}$. The numerator of the second fraction (14) and the denominator of the first fraction (21) are both divisible by 7, so you can cancel out a 7: Divide 14 and 21 by 7. This changes the equation to $\frac{4}{3} \times \frac{2}{5} = \frac{8}{15}$, a much simpler math problem.

Dividing fractions

Dividing fractions is simple if you remember this rule: Dividing a fraction by a number is the same as multiplying it by the multiplicative inverse (reciprocal) of that number. Of course, there are always exceptions. You can't use this operation on zero. Zero has no multiplicative inverse.

REMEMBER

You obtain the reciprocal of a number by flipping the number. That means that if you want to divide a fraction by 5, you simply multiply the fraction by the inverse of 5, which is $\frac{1}{5}$. You can understand this process more easily if you remember that 5 is the same thing as $\frac{5}{1}$. In other words, 5 divided by 1 equals 5 (that is, $5 \div 1 = 5$). And the reciprocal of $\frac{5}{1}$ is $\frac{1}{5}$. To come up with the reciprocal of a number, simply stand the number on its head.

To divide a fraction, use the inverse of the number that follows the division symbol ($\div$) and substitute a multiplication symbol ($\times$) for the division symbol. Therefore, $\frac{1}{3} \div 2$ is expressed as $\frac{1}{3} \times \frac{1}{2}$, and you already know how to multiply fractions. (If not, check out the "Multiplying and reducing fractions" section earlier in the chapter.) $1 \times 1 = 1$ and $3 \times 2 = 6$, so the product of $\frac{1}{3} \times \frac{1}{2} = \frac{1}{6}$. Therefore, $\frac{1}{3} \div 2 = \frac{1}{6}$.

Converting improper fractions to mixed numbers . . . and back again

If you have a fraction with a numerator larger than or equal to its denominator, you have an *improper fraction*. For example, $\frac{7}{3}$ is an improper fraction. To put an improper fraction into simpler (proper) terms, you can change $\frac{7}{3}$ into a *mixed number* (a number that includes a whole number and a fraction). Simply divide the numerator by the denominator: 7 divided by 3 gives you a quotient of 2 with a remainder of 1. There's something left over because 3 doesn't divide evenly into 7. The remainder becomes a numerator over the original denominator, so $\frac{1}{3}$ is left over. Therefore, $\frac{7}{3}$ is the same as $2\frac{1}{3}$.

REMEMBER

If you want to multiply or divide a mixed number, you need to convert it into a fraction — an improper fraction. To make the change, convert the whole number into a fraction and add it to the fraction you already have. Here's how:

1. **Multiply the whole number by the denominator (bottom number) of the existing fraction to arrive at a new numerator.**

Suppose you have $7\frac{2}{3}$. Multiply 7 by 3: $7 \times 3 = 21$.

2. **Place this new numerator over the existing denominator.**

$\frac{21}{3}$

3. **Add that fraction to the original fraction to get the final answer.**

$\frac{21}{3} + \frac{2}{3} = \frac{23}{3}$

Check out the "Common denominators: Preparing to add and subtract fractions" section earlier in this chapter for the complete scoop on adding fractions.

Or if you want to get technical, you can look at the whole process this way, too:

$7\frac{2}{3} = \frac{7 \times 3 + 2}{3} = \frac{23}{3}$

Expressing a fraction in other forms: Decimals and percents

A fraction can also be expressed as a decimal and as a percent. Here's how to convert between forms:

» **To change a fraction into a decimal:** Divide the numerator (top number) by the denominator (bottom number). Given that handy explanation, $\frac{3}{5}$ (or $3 \div 5$) converted into decimal form is 0.6. (Refer to the section "Dividing decimals" later in this chapter.)

Some fractions convert to *repeating decimals* — a decimal in which one digit is repeated infinitely. For instance, $\frac{2}{3}$ is the same as 0.66666 (with the sixes never stopping).

Repeating decimals are often rounded to the nearest hundredth; therefore, $\frac{2}{3}$ rounds to 0.67. (***Remember:*** The first space to the right of the decimal is the *tenths* place, the second space is the *hundredths* place, and the third is the *thousandths,* and so on.)

» **To make a decimal into a percent:** Move the decimal point two spaces to the right and add a percent sign. For example, 0.6 becomes 60%.

See the following sections for more thorough discussions of decimals and percents.

Adding and subtracting decimals

To add and subtract decimals, put the numbers in a column and line up the decimal points. Then add or subtract as if the decimals were whole numbers, keeping the decimal point in the same position in your answer.

Here are two examples:

$$
\begin{array}{r}
1.4583 \\
+0.5500 \\
\hline
2.0083
\end{array}
\qquad
\begin{array}{r}
1.4583 \\
-0.5500 \\
\hline
0.9083
\end{array}
$$

TIP

You can add zeros to the end of a decimal if performing the calculations this way is easier for you. So 0.1 can be 0.100 without changing its value. In the preceding problems, 0.55 can be 0.5500 to help you line up the decimal points and perform the operation.

Multiplying decimals

Multiplying a decimal is like multiplying a regular, everyday whole number, except that you have to place the decimal point in the correct position after you reach an answer.

1. **Multiply as though you were multiplying whole numbers, without the decimal points.**

Suppose you're multiplying 3.77×2.8. In this example, $377 \times 28 = 10,556$.

2. **Count and add the number of decimal places (to the right of the decimal point) in the numbers being multiplied.**

If one of the numbers you're multiplying is 3.77, you have two decimal places. If the other number you're multiplying is 2.8, you have one more decimal place, so the total number of decimal places in your answer will be three.

REMEMBER

If you're multiplying a number that has only zeros to the right of the decimal point, then those decimals don't count. For instance, 3 can also be expressed as 3.0, but you wouldn't count the 0 as a decimal place. All the zeros to the right of the decimal point don't count unless a number other than zero comes after them. For instance, 3.000007 has six decimal spaces, 3.0070 has three decimal spaces, and 3.000 has none, at least not for the purpose of multiplying (and as long as you're not including those 0s in the multiplication).

3. **In the answer, move the decimal point back to the left by the number of places you counted in Step 2.**

This time, zeros do count. You counted three total decimal places in 3.77 and 2.8, so you move the decimal point in 10566 back to the left three places. The resulting product is 10.556.

REMEMBER

If your answer doesn't include enough numbers for the decimal spaces you need, then add as many zeros as necessary to the left of the answer. Suppose your answer is 50, and you have to move the decimal point to the left three spaces. There aren't three spaces in 50, so you add a zero to the left to make it 050 and put the decimal point in its proper position: 0.050 is your answer.

Here's another example: 0.04×0.25. Multiply the decimals as if they were whole numbers: $4 \times 25 = 100$. Count and add the number of decimal places in the original two numbers; there are four. Then put the decimal point in the correct place in the answer. For 100, count from right to left four places, and put the decimal point there: 0.0100, or 0.01. Here's the method behind the madness:

$$
\frac{4}{100} \times \frac{25}{100} = \frac{100}{10,000} = \frac{1}{100} = 0.01 \ (\text{or } 0.0100)
$$

Dividing decimals

Decimals are divided according to slightly different rules, depending on whether both numbers in the problem are decimals.

DIVIDING DECIMALS BY WHOLE NUMBERS

REMEMBER

Here's how to divide a decimal by a whole number:

1. **Move the decimal point over to the right until the decimal is a whole number, counting the number of decimal places.**

   For example, if you want to find $1.25 \div 4$, change 1.25 to 125 by moving the decimal two decimal places to the right. Remember how many places you moved the decimal — you need that info later.

2. **Perform the division operation on the whole number.**

   $125 \div 4 = 31.25$

3. **In your answer, move the decimal point to the left the number of places you moved it in Step 1.**

   To make up for moving the decimal point two places to the right when you made 1.25 into a whole number, move the decimal point two places to the left in 31.25. Your answer is 0.3125.

DIVIDING DECIMALS BY DECIMALS

Here's how to divide a decimal by another decimal in which there are the same number of places after the decimal point:

1. **Make the *divisor* (the decimal going into the other number) into a whole number: Move the decimal point all the way to the right, counting the number of places you move it.**

   Suppose you want to divide 0.15 by 0.25 (that is, $0.15 \div 0.25$). Move the decimal point in 0.25 two places to the right: It then becomes 25.

2. **Move the decimal in the *dividend* (the number being divided) the same number of decimal places.**

   Move the decimal point in 0.15 two places: 0.15 becomes 15.

3. **Divide.**

   When you divide 15 by 25, the result is 0.60. You don't need to move any more decimals around — 0.60 is your final answer.

Unlike multiplying decimals, where you place the decimal point after the computation, when dividing decimals you place the decimal point first. If your problem is $0.42\overline{)2.394}$, move the decimal point to the right in the divisor until you have a whole number. In this case, you have to move the decimal point two places to the right in both the divisor and the dividend:

$$0.42_\wedge\overline{)2.39_\wedge4}$$

When you move both decimal points to the right two places, the problem now reads $42\overline{)239.4}$. When you divide, put your decimal point in the quotient above its place in the divisor, like this:

$$42\overline{)\begin{matrix}5.7\\239.4\end{matrix}}$$

Playing with percents

A percent is a fraction based on one-hundredths. Five percent (5%) is the same as $\frac{5}{100}$ or 0.05. The ASVAB often asks you to calculate "10% off" or "an increase of 15%" on the Arithmetic

Reasoning subtest. You need to be able to convert percents to fractions or decimals to answer these questions correctly.

TIP

To add, subtract, multiply, or divide using percents, change the percent to a fraction or a decimal. Here are some helpful hints for figuring percents:

>> Remember, a percent is just hundredths, so 3% is $\frac{3}{100}$ or 0.03, 22% is $\frac{22}{100}$ or 0.22, and 110% is $\frac{110}{100}$ or 1.10.

>> To convert a percent to a decimal, just drop the percent sign and move the decimal point two places to the left, adding zeros as needed.

>> The decimal point always starts to the right of a whole number, so 60 is the same thing as 60.0. Moving the decimal point two spaces to the left leaves you with 0.6.

After you do the conversion, follow the rules outlined in the earlier sections for performing specific operations on fractions or decimals.

Showing comparisons with ratios

A *ratio* shows a relationship between two things. For example, if Margaret invested in her tattoo parlor at a 2:1 (or 2 to 1) ratio to her business partner, Julie, then Margaret put in $2 for every $1 that Julie put in. You can express a ratio as a fraction, so 2:1 is the same as $\frac{2}{1}$.

Or suppose you fill up your shiny, brand-new SUV, and you want to compute your gas mileage — miles per gallon. You drive for 240 miles and then refill the tank with 15 gallons of gas, so the ratio of miles to gallons is 240:15. You can compute your gas mileage by dividing the number of miles by the number of gallons: 240 miles ÷ 15 gallons. You're getting 16 miles per gallon. Time for a tuneup!

In this section, I cover some uses for ratios, including scale drawings and rates such as speed.

Navigating scale drawings

Scale, particularly when used on the ASVAB, relates to scale drawings. For example, a map drawn to scale may have a 1-inch drawing of a road that represents 1 mile of physical road in the real world. The Arithmetic Reasoning portion of the ASVAB often asks you to calculate a problem based on scale, which can be represented as a standard ratio $\left(1\text{ inch}:1\text{ mile}\right)$ or a fraction $\left(\frac{1\text{ inch}}{1\text{ mile}}\right)$.

On a map with a scale of 1 inch to 1 mile, the ratio of the scale is represented as 1:1. But questions are never this easy on the ASVAB. You're more likely to see something like, "If a map has a scale of 1 inch to every 4 miles. . . ." That scale is expressed as the ratio $1:4$, or $\frac{1}{4}$.

Try your hand with the following common scale problem:

EXAMPLE

If the scale on a road map is 1 inch = 250 miles, how many inches would represent 1,250 miles?

The problem wants you to determine how many inches on the map represent 1,250 miles if 1 inch is equal to 250 miles. You know that 1 inch = 250 miles, and you also know that some unknown number of inches, which you can call *x*, equals 1,250 miles. The problem can be expressed as two ratios set equal to each other, known as a proportion: $\frac{1}{250} = \frac{x}{1,250}$. Now all you have to do is solve for x by multiplying each side of the equation by 1,250:

$$\frac{1}{250} = \frac{x}{1,250}$$

$$\frac{1}{250} \times 1,250 = \frac{x}{1,250} \times 1,250$$

$$\frac{1,250}{250} = x$$

$$x = 5$$

So if 1 inch is equal to 250 miles, then 5 inches would be equal to 1,250 miles. If this problem causes you to scratch your head, check out Chapter 7 for info on solving for x.

REMEMBER

Almost every military job makes use of scales, which is why scale-related questions are so common on the ASVAB. Whether you're reading maps at Mountain Warfare School or organizing trash pickup (what the military calls "area beautification") around the base, you need to use and interpret scales frequently.

Remembering important rates

A *rate* is a fixed quantity — a 5% interest rate, for example. It can mean the speed at which someone or something works (John reads at the rate of one page per minute), or it can mean an amount of money paid based on another amount (life insurance may be purchased at a rate of $1 per $100 of coverage). A rate is often a speed — something per a unit of time.

REMEMBER

Word problems often ask you to solve problems that involve speed or simple interest rates. Here are two rate formulas you should commit to memory:

>> **Simple interest:** $I = Prt$, where I represents the amount of interest, P is the principal (the initial amount invested), r is the interest rate written as a decimal, and t is the length of time in years the money is invested.

>> **Distance:** $d = rt$, where d represents the distance traveled, r is the rate (speed) of travel, and t is the amount of time traveled.

TIP

In a rate, you can generally think of the word *per* as a division sign. For instance, suppose someone drives 141 miles in 3 hours, and you have to find the average speed. You want the rate of speed in miles per hour, so you take miles (distance) divided by hours (time): 141 miles ÷ 3 hours = 47 miles/hour. Using algebra, you can rearrange the distance formula to say the same thing: $d \div t = r$.

A Powerful Shorthand: Writing in Scientific Notation

Scientific notation is a compact format for writing very large or very small numbers. Although it's most often used in scientific fields, you may find a question or two on the Mathematics Knowledge subtest of the ASVAB asking you to covert a number to or from scientific notation.

Scientific notation separates a number into two parts: a number between 1 and 10 and a power of ten (such as 10^7, 10^{21}, or 10^{-18}; see the earlier section "Just When You Thought You Were Done with Vocab: Math Terminology" for info on powers and exponents). Therefore, 1.25×10^4 means 1.25×10

to the fourth power, or 12,500; 5.79×10^{-8} means $5.79 \div 10$ to the eighth power, or 0.0000000579. The exponent tells you how many places to move the decimal point and whether to move it left (if it's negative) or right (if it's positive).

Getting to the Root of the Problem

A *square root* is the factor of a number that, when multiplied by itself, produces the number. Take the number 36, for example. One of the factors of 36 is 6. If you multiply 6 by itself (6×6), you come up with 36, so 6 is the square root of 36. The number 36 has other factors, such as 18. But if you multiply 18 by itself (18×18), you get 324, not 36. So 18 isn't the square root of 36.

All whole numbers are grouped into one of two camps when it comes to roots:

>> **Perfect squares:** Only a few whole numbers, called *perfect squares,* have exact square roots. For example, the square root of 25 is 5.

>> **Irrational numbers:** Other whole numbers have square roots that are decimals that go on forever and have no pattern that repeats (nonrepeating, nonterminating decimals), so they're called *irrational numbers.* The square root of 30 is 5.4772255 with no end to the decimal places, so the square root of 30 is an irrational number.

REMEMBER

The sign for a square root is called the *radical sign.* It looks like this: $\sqrt{}$. Here's how you use it: $\sqrt{36}$ means "the square root of 36" — in other words, 6.

Perfect squares

Square roots can be difficult to find at times without a calculator, but because you can't use a calculator during the test, you're going to have to use your mind and some guessing methods. To find the square root of a number without a calculator, make an educated guess and then verify your results.

To use the educated-guess method (see the next section), you have to know the square roots of a few perfect squares. One good way to do this is to memorize the squares of the square roots 1 through 12:

>> 1 is the square root of 1 $(1 \times 1 = 1)$

>> 2 is the square root of 4 $(2 \times 2 = 4)$

>> 3 is the square root of 9 $(3 \times 3 = 9)$

>> 4 is the square root of 16 $(4 \times 4 = 16)$

>> 5 is the square root of 25 $(5 \times 5 = 25)$

>> 6 is the square root of 36 $(6 \times 6 = 36)$

>> 7 is the square root of 49 $(7 \times 7 = 49)$

>> 8 is the square root of 64 $(8 \times 8 = 64)$

>> 9 is the square root of 81 $(9 \times 9 = 81)$

>> 10 is the square root of 100 $(10 \times 10 = 100)$

>> 11 is the square root of 121 $(11 \times 11 = 121)$

>> 12 is the square root of 144 $(12 \times 12 = 144)$

Irrational numbers

When the ASVAB asks you to figure square roots of numbers that aren't perfect squares, the task gets a bit more difficult. In this case, the ASVAB usually asks you to find the square root to the nearest tenth.

Suppose you run across this problem:

$\sqrt{54}$

Think about what you know: You know that the square root of 49 is 7, and 54 is slightly greater than 49. You also know that the square root of 64 is 8, and 54 is slightly less than 64. So if the number 54 is somewhere between 49 and 64, the square root of 54 is somewhere between 7 and 8. Because 54 is closer to 49 than to 64, the square root will be closer to 7 than to 8, so you can try 7.3 as the square root of 54.

Multiply 7.3 by itself: $7.3 \times 7.3 = 53.29$, which is very close to 54. Now try multiplying 7.4 by itself to see if it's any closer to 54: $7.4 \times 7.4 = 54.76$, which isn't as close to 54 as 53.29. Therefore, 7.3 is the square root of 54 to the nearest tenth without going over.

Other roots

The wonderful world of math is also home to concepts like cube roots, fourth roots, fifth roots, and so on. A *root* is a factor of a number that when cubed (multiplied by itself three times), taken to the fourth power (multiplied by itself four times), and so on produces the original number. A couple of examples seem to be in order:

>> The cube root of 27 is 3. If you cube 3 (also known as raising it to the third power or multiplying $3 \times 3 \times 3$), the product is 27.

>> The fourth root of 16 is the number that, when multiplied by itself four times, equals 16. Any guesses? Drumroll, please: 2 is the fourth root of 16 because $2 \times 2 \times 2 \times 2 = 16$.

Test-Taking Techniques for Your Mathematical Journey

As with all the other subtests on the ASVAB, guessing on the Mathematics Knowledge subtest may be a good idea — especially if you're taking the paper-and-pencil version. If you're unsure of an answer (and you're not rushing at the end of the subtest), pick an answer, any answer. If you don't, your chances of getting that answer right are zero. But if you take a shot at it, your chances increase to 25%, or 1 in 4. In the following sections, you find some tips that can help you improve those odds, even when you don't know how to solve the problem.

If you're not confident in your math skills, you may want to invest some extra study time. Check out *Algebra I For Dummies* by Mary Jane Sterling, *Geometry For Dummies* by Mark Ryan, and *SAT Math For Dummies* by Mark Zegarelli — all published by Wiley.

Knowing what the question is asking

The Mathematics Knowledge subtest presents the questions as straightforward math problems, not word problems, so knowing what the question is asking you to do is relatively easy. However, reading each question carefully, paying particular attention to plus (+) and minus (−) signs (which can really change the answer), is still important. Finally, make sure you do all the calculations needed to produce the correct answer. Check out this example:

Find the value of $\sqrt{81^2}$.

(A) 9

(B) 18

(C) 81

(D) 6,561

If you're in a hurry, you may put 9 down as an answer because you remember that the square root of 81 is 9. Or, in a rush, you may multiply 9 (the square root of 81) by 2 instead of squaring it, as the exponent indicates you should. Or you may just multiply 81 by 81 to get 6,561 without remembering that you also need to then find the square root, which gives you the correct answer, Choice (C). So make sure you perform all the operations needed (and that you perform the correct operations) to find the right answer. Here, noticing that you're both squaring 81 and taking the square root of 81^2 should make it easy for you to recognize that the answer is actually just 81 without having to work out the multiplication.

Figuring out what you're solving for

Read the question carefully right out of the gate. Some questions can seem out of your league at first glance, but if you look at them again, a light may go on in your brain. Suppose you get this question:

Solve for s: $s = \frac{2}{5} \times \frac{1}{2}$

(A) $2\frac{1}{2}$

(B) 2

(C) $\frac{1}{5}$

(D) $\frac{1}{10}$

At first glance, you may think, "Oh, no! Solve for an unknown, s. I don't remember how to do that!" But if you look at the question again, you may see that you're simply multiplying a fraction. So you take $\frac{2}{5}$ times $\frac{1}{2}$ and arrive at $\frac{2}{10}$, but you should reduce that fraction to get $\frac{1}{5}$. The correct answer is Choice (C).

Solving what you can and guessing the rest

Sometimes a problem requires multiple operations for you to arrive at the correct answer. If you don't know how to do all the operations, don't give up. You can still narrow down your choices by doing what you can.

EXAMPLE

Suppose this question confronts you:

What's the value of $(0.03)^3$?

(A) 0.0027

(B) 0.06

(C) 0.000027

(D) 0.0009

Say you don't remember how to multiply decimals. All isn't lost! If you remember how to use exponents, you know that you have to multiply $0.03 \times 0.03 \times 0.03$. So if you simplify the problem and just multiply $3 \times 3 \times 3$, without worrying about those pesky zeros, your answer will have a 27 in it. With this pearl of wisdom in mind, you can see that Choice (B), which adds 0.03 to 0.03, is wrong. It also means that Choice (D), which multiplies 0.03 and 0.03, is wrong. Now you have two possible answers, and you've improved your chances of guessing the right one to 50 percent! Multiply $3 \times 3 \times 3$ to get 27, and don't forget to put the decimal points back in. You have six places to make up, so move the decimal from 27 six places to the left to get 0.000027. The correct answer is Choice (C).

Using the process of elimination

Another method for when you run into questions and draw a total blank is to plug the possible answers into the equation and see which one works. Say the following problem is staring you right in the eyes:

EXAMPLE

Solve for x: $x - 5 = 32$

(A) $x = 5$

(B) $x = 32$

(C) $x = -32$

(D) $x = 37$

If you're totally stumped and can't think of any possible way of approaching this problem, simply plugging in each of the four answers to see which one is correct is your best bet.

Choice (A): $5 - 5 = 32$, which you know is wrong

Choice (B): $32 - 5 = 32$, which is wrong

Choice (C): $-32 - 5 = 32$, which is wrong

Choice (D): $37 - 5 = 32$, which is correct

TIP

Don't forget that plugging in all the answers is time-consuming, so save this tactic for when you've answered all the problems you can answer on the pencil-and-paper ASVAB. If you're taking the computer version, you can't skip a question, so remember to budget your time wisely. If you don't have much time, just make a guess and move on. You may be able to solve the next question easily.

Math Knowledge and Operations Practice Questions

Run through these practice questions to flex your math muscles. You'll be able to check your answers and figure out how much time you need to devote to studying basic mathematical concepts before you move on to tougher calculations.

1. Solve: $(4 \times 3) \times 3 - 6 \times (9 \div 3)$
   - (A) 54
   - (B) 14
   - (C) 18
   - (D) 28

2. Which of the following fractions is the largest?
   - (A) $\frac{2}{3}$
   - (B) $\frac{5}{8}$
   - (C) $\frac{11}{16}$
   - (D) $\frac{3}{4}$

3. What's the product of $\sqrt{36}$ and $\sqrt{49}$?
   - (A) 1,764
   - (B) 42
   - (C) 13
   - (D) 6

4. Which of the following is expressed as an improper fraction?
   - (A) $1\frac{5}{28}$
   - (B) $\frac{9}{7}$
   - (C) $\frac{1}{2}$
   - (D) $\frac{345}{346}$

5. $2^3 \times 2^4 =$
   - (A) 16
   - (B) 108
   - (C) 128
   - (D) 148

6. Express 403,000,000,000,000 in scientific notation.
   - (A) 4.03×10^{14}
   - (B) 4.03×10^{-14}
   - (C) 4.03×10
   - (D) 0.43×10

7. 27.65×31.3
   - (A) 865.445
   - (B) 835.556
   - (C) 867.5309
   - (D) 842.1

8. What's the prime factorization of 90?
   - (A) $2 \times 3 \times 5$
   - (B) $2 \times 3^2 \times 5$
   - (C) $2^2 \times 3^2$
   - (D) $2 \times 3 \times 5^2$

9. $\frac{1}{4} \times \frac{2}{3}$
   - (A) $\frac{3}{4}$
   - (B) $\frac{1}{4}$
   - (C) $\frac{1}{6}$
   - (D) $\frac{1}{3}$

10. Continue the pattern:

    . . . 5, 10, 9, 15, 20, 19, 25 . . .
    - (A) 30, 35, 41
    - (B) 30, 29, 35
    - (C) 26, 30, 35
    - (D) 26, 30, 31

11. What is the mean average of the following?

    101, 15, 62, 84, and 55

    (A) 55
    (B) 63.4
    (C) 75.5
    (D) 56.25

12. Find the mode:

    46, 29, 47, 22, 100, 47, 157, 138, 47, 22, 184

    (A) 22
    (B) 47
    (C) 76.3
    (D) 184

13. Express the ratio of 48 privates to 2 drill instructors.

    (A) 1:24
    (B) 2:48
    (C) 48:2
    (D) 48:1

14. $\sqrt{121} =$

    (A) 12
    (B) 9
    (C) 21
    (D) 11

15. $\frac{1}{5} \cdot \frac{2}{3} =$

    (A) $\frac{2}{15}$
    (B) $\frac{3}{15}$
    (C) $\frac{2}{5}$
    (D) $\frac{1}{15}$

16. $3 \div \frac{3}{4} =$

    (A) $2\frac{1}{4}$
    (B) 4
    (C) $3\frac{3}{4}$
    (D) 5

17. How far will your platoon go if you march for 3 hours at 6 miles per hour?

    (A) 9 miles
    (B) 6 miles
    (C) 18 miles
    (D) 12 miles

18. Your convoy has to travel a straight line across 4.7 grid squares on a military map. Every grid square equals 1,000 meters. How many meters will your convoy travel?

    (A) 4.7 meters
    (B) 470 miles
    (C) 470 meters
    (D) 4,700 meters

19. Five students take a math test, scoring 97, 92, 81, 90, and 73. What is the median score in the group?

    (A) 90
    (B) 86.6
    (C) 73
    (D) 92

20. David's dogs, Cujo and Achilles, got into a bag containing 250 dog treats. Together, the dogs ate 200 of the treats. What percentage of the treats remain?

    (A) 75
    (B) 25
    (C) 80
    (D) 20

Answers and Explanations

Use this answer key to score the practice questions.

1. **C.** Solve by using the order of operations:

$$\begin{aligned}
&(4 \times 3)3 - 6(9 \div 3) \\
&= (12)3 - 6(3) \\
&= 36 - 18 \\
&= 18
\end{aligned}$$

2. **D.** To arrive at the answer, find a common denominator that all the denominators divide into evenly. In this case, the common denominator is 48. Next, convert all fractions to 48ths. In the case of Choice (A), multiply $\frac{2}{3} \times \frac{16}{16}$ to reach $\frac{32}{48}$. Perform the same type of calculation for all the other fractions, figuring out what number times the denominator gives you 48, and then multiplying each numerator by that number; then compare numerators. The largest numerator is the largest fraction. The other fractions are equal to $\frac{30}{48}$, $\frac{33}{48}$, and $\frac{36}{48}$. Choice (D) is the correct answer.

3. **B.** The square root of 36 is 6, and the square root of 49 is 7. The product of those two numbers (6×7) is 42. The correct answer is Choice (B). *Remember:* Product indicates you multiply.

4. **B.** An *improper fraction* is a fraction in which the numerator is larger than or equal to the denominator.

5. **C.** $2^3 \times 2^4 = 2^7 = 2 \times 2 \times 2 \times 2 \times 2 \times 2 \times 2 = 128$. Choice (C) is the correct answer.

6. **A.** The correct way to write the number in scientific notation is 4.03×10^{14}. When the exponent is positive, the decimal point moves said number of places to the right. When the exponent is negative, the decimal point moves said places to the left. The exponent in Choice (A) is a positive 14, which means you move the decimal point 14 places to the right. Choice (A) is the correct answer.

7. **A.** When you multiply decimals, you move the decimal directly back into its spot after the ones place.

8. **B.** When you figure which prime numbers you need to multiply together to get the original number, you're using *prime factorization*. Here, $90 = 9 \times 10 = 3 \times 3 \times 2 \times 5 = 2 \times 3^2 \times 5$. The correct answer is Choice (B). If you don't know how to solve this problem, you can guess by finding the value of each answer choice. Choice (A) is 30, Choice (B) is 90, Choice (C) is 36, and Choice (D) is 150.

9. **C.** $\frac{1}{4} \times \frac{2}{3} = \frac{2}{12} = \frac{1}{6}$. The correct answer is Choice (C).

10. **B.** The pattern is the next two multiples of 5, minus 1:

    . . .5, 10, 9, 15, 20, 19, 25, 30, 29, 35, 40 . . .

11. **B.** To find the average, add the numbers and divide by 5 (the total number of items in the set):

    $$101 + 15 + 62 + 84 + 55 = 317$$
    $$317 \div 5 = 63.4$$

12. **B.** The mode in a number range is the value that appears most frequently. In this case, it's the number 47, which shows up three times. If you added all the numbers and divided by 11, you were looking for the mean — and you would've chosen Choice (C), which isn't what the question asked for.

13. **C.** There are 48 privates for every 2 drill instructors, so you express that ratio 48:2. Your drill instructor would say, "These privates outnumber us 48 to 2." If you were going to simplify the ratio, you could divide both sides by two to arrive at 24:1, but the question doesn't ask you to do that.

14. **D.** The square root of 121 is 11, because 11^2, or $11 \cdot 11 = 121$.

15. **A.** To multiply fractions, go straight across the numerator and denominator, like this:
$\frac{1}{5} \cdot \frac{2}{3} = \frac{1 \cdot 2}{5 \cdot 3} = \frac{2}{15}$.

16. **B.** Find the reciprocal of the fraction first, then multiply and simplify:
$3 \div \frac{3}{4} = \frac{3}{1} \cdot \frac{4}{3} = \frac{3 \cdot 4}{1 \cdot 3} = \frac{12}{3} = 4$.

17. **C.** Using the distance formula, which is $d = rt$, where d represents distance, r represents rate (speed), and t represents time, you can figure out how far your platoon will get: $d = 3 \cdot 6$ $d = 18$.

18. **D.** The problem tells you that each grid square measures 1,000 meters, and your convoy must travel across 4.7. Multiply 4.7 by 1,000 meters, which equals 4,700 meters.

19. **A.** Median is the middle number in a series when the numbers are in order. Putting the list in order from smallest to largest, you have: 73, 81, 90, 92, 97. In this case, the median number is 90.

20. **D.** The two dogs ate 200 out of the 250 treats that were in the bag, or $\frac{200}{250}$. You can solve it in your head or go through the math, dividing 200 by 250, but the ASVAB only allows you a limited time to solve math problems — and you can't use a calculator. First, simplify the fraction: $\frac{200}{250} = \frac{20}{25}$. You need the denominator to equal 100 when you're figuring out a percent, so multiply by 4: $\frac{20}{25} \cdot 4 = \frac{20 \cdot 4}{25 \cdot 4} = \frac{80}{100}$. That tells you that the dogs ate 80 percent of the treats, but the question asks you what percentage of the treats remain. The dogs left only 20 percent of the treats behind.

Chapter **7**

Algebra

The Mathematics Knowledge subtest on the computerized version of the ASVAB requires you to answer 15 questions in 23 minutes (or 30 questions in 47 minutes if your subtest includes tryout questions, which I cover in Chapter 1). If you're taking the paper-and-pencil version, you'll have to answer 25 questions in 24 minutes. You can't use a calculator on the test, but you can use as much scratch paper as you need.

Some people freak out just hearing the word *algebra*. But algebra is just a way to put problems into mathematical language using the simplest mathematical terms possible. In fact, solving most word problems is almost impossible without some use of algebra. In this chapter, I cover all the basic algebra knowledge you need to nail the Mathematics Knowledge subtest of the ASVAB — and the concepts you review here will also come in handy on the Arithmetic Reasoning subtest, which I cover in Chapter 9.

REMEMBER

The questions on the Mathematics Knowledge subtest aren't all algebra-related. Many involve basic math concepts like fractions, percentages, scientific notation, and square roots (see Chapter 6 for more information). And some are related to geometry, which you can brush up on in Chapter 8.

REMEMBER

The CAT-ASVAB adapts to your ability as you answer questions, so it may not meet your expectations as far as difficulty goes.

Coming to Terms with Basic Algebra Lingo

Algebra has its own language, and knowing how to speak it can take you a long way on the ASVAB. Some of the most common algebraic terms you encounter, both in this book and on the test, include the following:

» **Term:** One or more numbers and/or letters all connected by multiplication or division.

» **Algebraic expression:** An *algebraic expression* is one or more terms in a phrase. It's not a whole "sentence," so an expression doesn't include an equal sign. Here's an example: $4x + 2y + 38c$.

>> **Equation:** An *equation* is a mathematical statement that states that two mathematical expressions are equal. An equation always includes an equal sign, like this example: $7a + 3b = 588$.

>> **Variable:** A *variable* is a number in disguise. In this expression, x and y are the variables: $7x + 10y = 27$. They're called variables because the numbers they represent can vary from problem to problem.

If the same letter appears more than once in a given equation or expression, it stands for the same number in all instances in that equation/expression. In $3x + 2x = 10$, the first x doesn't represent a different number from the second x. In this case, $x = 2$ (both times).

>> **Coefficient:** A *coefficient* is the number part of an algebraic term. In this equation, 8 and 12 are the coefficients: $8a - 12b = -4$.

>> **Constant:** A *constant* is a term in an algebraic expression that contains only a number; it's a term without a variable attached to it. In this equation, 5 is the constant: $14d + 12a + 5$.

>> **Real numbers:** *Real numbers* are actual quantities, like amounts, ages, distances, and temperatures. A real number can be an integer, fraction, or decimal, and it can be rational or irrational. They're numbers that appear on a number line, like this:

>> **Rational numbers:** *Rational numbers* are the set of real numbers, fractions, and terminating decimals. Rational numbers can always be written as the ratio or quotient of two integers. These are examples of rational numbers: $\frac{1}{2}$, 5, 0.25.

>> **Irrational numbers:** *Irrational numbers* can't be expressed as a quotient or ratio of two integers. With irrational numbers, the decimal form is nonrepeating and nonterminating, like pi. You can't write pi as a quotient of two integers, and its decimal form goes on forever. The same goes for square root and other roots.

>> **Exponents:** An *exponent* tells you how many times to use a value (its *base*) in multiplication. In this equation, 2 and x are both exponents: $s^2 + 3^x = 470$.

>> **Polynomial:** A *polynomial* is an expression that contains one or more terms, like constants, variables, and exponents. The exponents on the variables in a polynomial are always whole numbers. Here's an example of a polynomial: $3ab - 2x^2 + 2y^3 - 7$. Other special names for polynomials signal whether they have one, two, or three terms. For example, $2ab^7$ is a monomial because it has one term. $6x - 3$ is a binomial because it has two terms, and $4a + 7b^3 - 5$ is a trinomial because it has three terms.

>> **Like terms:** In algebra, you combine *like terms* — terms that have matching variables in the expression or equation. The variables must have the same power to be *like terms*. These are all like terms: $4xy$, $7xy$, $32xy$. Because xy is the same, you can combine them if you're working with an equation, like this:

$$4xy + 7xy + 32xy = 215$$
$$43xy = 215$$

Solving for x

In algebra, you often hear about "solving for x" or "solving for the unknown," but what's the unknown? The *unknown* is the answer you want find. Check out this example:

EXAMPLE

Rod's mom worked up a powerful thirst solving a ton of math problems and asked Rod to run to the corner store and get her one of those super-duper gigantic nuclear soft drinks. If a regular-sized soft drink costs $0.50 and the super-duper gigantic nuclear size costs three times the price of the regular size, how much will Rod have to spend?

You can express this problem in terms of x, with x being the cost of the super-duper-sized drink: x equals 3 (the price difference) $\times 50$ cents. Written a bit more formally, the equation looks like this: $x = 3(0.50)$ or $3(0.50) = x$.

What if you don't know how much the regular-sized soft drink costs? You can express this missing piece of information in an equation as well: x (how much it will cost to buy a super-duper size) equals 3 (the cost increase) times p (the price of one regular-sized drink). Once again, written a bit more formally, the equation looks like this: $x = 3p$ or $x = 3 \times p$.

TIP

You can remove the multiplication symbol in algebraic expressions when using a combination of letters and numbers. Therefore, the equation $x = 3 \times p$ can also be written $x = 3p$. The multiplication symbol is implied. It's also common to use parentheses or the dot multiplication symbol, $\cdot$, to indicate multiplication. Most people avoid using the $\times$ because it looks so close to the letter x.

When All Things Are Equal: Keeping an Algebra Equation Balanced

Algebra problems can be equations, which means that the quantities on both sides of the equal sign are equal — they're the same. For instance, $2 = 2$, $1 + 1 = 2$, and $3 - 1 = 2$. In all these cases, the quantities are the same on both sides of the equal sign. To solve an algebra equation, you find out what the variable equals by getting it by itself on one side of the equal sign. So if $x = 2$, then x is 2 because the equal sign says so.

REMEMBER

You can perform any calculation on either side of an equation as long as you do the same thing to both sides of the equation. That keeps the equation equal.

You can also combine like terms lying on one side of the equation when operating on algebraic expressions: $3x + 3x = (3 + 3)x = 6x$. However, $3x + 3y$ doesn't equal $6xy$, nor does $x^2 + x^3 = x^5$. (See the earlier section "Coming to Terms with Basic Algebra Lingo" for more on like terms and the later section "Explaining Exponents in Algebra" to find out more about algebra involving exponents.)

Solving one-step equations involving addition and subtraction

If $x + 1 = 2$, then x must be 1, because only 1 added to 1 is 2. So far, so simple, so good. But what if the equation is a little more complicated?

$$x + 47,432 = 50,000$$

To solve the problem, you need to isolate x on one side of the equal sign. To get that job done, move any other numbers on the x side of the equal sign to the other side of the equal sign.

By looking at the x side of the equation, you can see that it's an addition problem. To move the number on the x side to the opposite side, you have to perform the inverse operation. The inverse operation of addition is subtraction. (For a full rundown on inverse operations, check out Chapter 6.)

So to move 47,432 from the *x* side to the non-*x* side of the equation, simply subtract that number from both sides:

$$x + 47{,}432 - 47{,}432 = 50{,}000 - 47{,}432$$

Performing these operations removes the 47,432 from the *x* side of the equation ($47{,}432 - 47{,}432 = 0$, so that side of the equation is $x + 0$ or simply *x*) and gives you 2,568 on the non-*x* side of the equation ($50{,}000 - 47{,}432 = 2{,}568$). You're left with the final answer: $x = 2{,}568$.

To double-check that this answer is correct, you can plug your answer into the original problem:

$$x + 47{,}432 = 50{,}000$$
$$2{,}568 + 47{,}432 = 50{,}000$$

If you plug in the answer and it doesn't work, you've made an error in your calculations. Start again; remember that you're trying to isolate *x* on one side of the equation.

Multiplying and dividing

REMEMBER

In multiplication and division, if the two terms being operated on (on either side of the equal sign) are both positive numbers or both negative numbers, the answer will be a positive number. If one number is negative and the other is positive, the answer will be negative.

To solve the problem $-6x = 36$ (don't forget, 6*x* is the same thing as $6 \times x$), you need to isolate *x*. So perform an inverse operation; the inverse operation of multiplication is division. Division in algebra is usually represented with a fraction bar:

$$\frac{-6x}{-6} = \frac{36}{-6}$$
$$x = -6$$

The answer is a negative number because the two terms, 36 and −6, have different signs.

Solving multistep equations

Not all algebra problems have one-step solutions. (That would be too easy, and you wouldn't sweat nearly as much.) Solving algebra problems on the ASVAB often requires you to perform several steps.

An example of a multistep equation is one in which *x* shows up on both sides of the equal sign. Then you have to get rid of *x* on one side of the equation by moving *x* terms from one side to the other. You do this by performing the inverse operation.

Suppose you want to solve this equation: $3x + 3 = 9 + x$. To remove the *x* from one side of the equation, perform the inverse operation. The right side of the equation adds an *x*, so subtract *x* from both sides of the equation:

$$3x + 3 - x = 9 + x - x$$
$$3x + 3 - 1x = 9 + 0$$
$$2x + 3 = 9$$

To get the *x* term, 2*x*, by itself, subtract 3 from each side of the equation:

$$2x + 3 - 3 = 9 - 3$$
$$2x = 6$$

Divide both sides of the equation by 2 to isolate x:

$$\frac{2x}{2} = \frac{6}{2}$$
$$x = 3$$

REMEMBER

When you have a variable by itself, such as x, it's always equal to 1 times that variable (or one of that variable), like $1x$, even if the 1 isn't written out. In fact, any number is equal to 1 times itself, so you could also say $2 = 2 \times 1$.

Simplifying equations

Before you evaluate or solve an algebraic expression or equation, you need to simplify it. Simplifying makes your calculations a lot easier — and it saves you valuable time on the ASVAB. Here are the basic steps to simplify an expression:

1. Remove whatever parentheses you can by multiplying factors.

If your expression is $3(2 + x) + 4(4x + 3) - (x^2)^2$, the first thing to do is get rid of the parentheses. Using the distributive property, which lets you multiply the factors times the terms inside the parentheses, you can get rid of two sets right off the bat.

The first set works like this: After you multiply the factors times the terms inside the parentheses, $3(2 + x)$ is equal to $6 + 3x$ because $3 \cdot 2 = 6$ and $3 \cdot x = 3x$. Now the original expression is $6 + 3x + 4(4x + 3) - (x^2)^2$.

Remove the second set of parentheses the same way: $4(4x + 3) = 4 \cdot 4x = 16x$ and $4 \cdot 3 = 12$, so $4(4x + 3) = 16x + 12$. Now the original expression is $6 + 3x + 16x + 12 - (x^2)^2$.

2. Use exponent rules to remove any remaining parentheses (if applicable).

When a term with an exponent is raised to a power, you multiply the exponents. That means $(x^2)^2 = x^4$. All the parentheses are gone. The original expression is now $6 + 3x + 16x + 12 - x^4$.

3. Combine like terms.

The like terms in the original equation are $3x$ and $16x$, which together are $19x$. The original expression is now $6 + 19x + 12 - x^4$.

4. Combine constants.

The constants in this expression are 6 and 12, and together, they add up to 18. The original expression is now $19x + 18 - x^4$.

You may see questions on the ASVAB that ask you to simplify expressions, so knowing how to get rid of all the excess can help you sail right through.

Using FOIL

FOIL is a technique for distributing two binomials in algebra. FOIL stands for First, Outer, Inner, and Last, and it refers to problems like this one: $(x + 2)(x + 5)$.

Here's what each part of FOIL means:

>> **First** means multiply the terms that occur first in each binomial.

>> **Outer** means multiply the terms that occur on the outermost ends of the product (the first and last).

>> **Inner** means multiply the innermost terms of the product (the second and third).

>> **Last** means multiply the last terms in each binomial.

FOIL looks like this: $(x+2)(x+5)$, where First is $x \cdot x$, Outer is $x \cdot 5$, Inner is $2 \cdot x$, and Last is $2 \cdot 5$.

That means $(x+2)(x+5) = x \cdot x + x \cdot 5 + 2 \cdot x + 2 \cdot 5$. Combine like terms to further simplify the problem: $x^2 + 7x + 10$.

Tackling Two-Variable Equations

When you have two-variable equations, which you'll see when you're working with graphs and in some other instances, there are usually multiple solutions. When you have two or more of these equations and they all have exponents of 1, the equations are called *linear systems*, and to solve them, you either have to use substitution or combine equations.

Substitution

When a system is simple, like this one, substitution is the way to go.

$$x + 3 = y$$
$$3x + y = 7$$

In this system, you know that $y = x + 3$. Plug $x + 3$ into the second equation, in place of y, to find the value of x, and then simplify and solve:

$$3x + x + 3 = 7$$
$$4x + 3 = 7$$
$$4x + 3 - 3 = 7 - 3$$
$$4x = 4$$
$$\frac{4x}{4} = \frac{4}{4}$$
$$x = 1$$

Because $x = 1$, substitute that value into the original equation, $y = x + 3$, to determine that $y = 4$.

Combining equations

When a system is more complicated, like this one, you need to combine them.

$$12x - 9y = 37$$
$$8x + 9y = 23$$

You have to add these two equations to figure out just one of the variables, like this:

$$12x - 9y = 37$$
$$\underline{+8x + 9y = 23}$$
$$20x \quad\quad = 60$$

When you solve for x, you see that $x = 3$. Plug 3 in for the value of x in either of the original equations to figure out the value of y.

$$8(3) + 9y = 23$$
$$24 + 9y = 23$$
$$9y + 24 - 24 = 23 - 24$$
$$9y = -1$$
$$y = -\frac{1}{9}$$

Combining equations may require you to change one equation entirely to figure out the answer. Here's another system as an example:

$$7x + 10y = 36$$
$$2x - y = -9$$

To solve by combining, multiply the bottom equation by 10. The equation becomes $20x - 10y = -90$. Add it to the first equation to eliminate y. The result is $27x = -54$. Divide to find the value of x:

$$\frac{27x}{27} = \frac{-54}{27}$$
$$x = -2$$

Take the value of x, which is -2, and substitute it into one of the original equations to solve for y (I use the second):

$$2x - y = 9$$
$$2(-2) - y = 9$$
$$-4 - y = 9 - 4$$
$$y = 5$$

Explaining Exponents in Algebra

Exponents are an easy way to show that a number is to be multiplied by itself a certain number of times. For example, 5^2 is the same as 5×5, and y^3 is the same as $y \times y \times y$. The number or variable that's multiplied by itself is called the base, and the number or variable showing how many times it is to be multiplied by itself is called the exponent or power.

REMEMBER

Here are important rules when working with exponents in algebra:

>> Any base raised to the power of one equals itself: $x^1 = x$.

>> Any base raised to the zero power (except 0) equals 1: $x^0 = 1$.

>> To multiply terms with the same base, add the exponents: $x^2(x^3) = x^{2+3} = x^5$.

>> To divide terms with the same base, subtract the exponents: $x^5 \div x^2 = x^{5-2} = x^3$.

>> If a base has a negative exponent, it's equal to its reciprocal (inverse) with a positive exponent: $x^{-3} = \frac{1}{x^3}$.

>> When a product has an exponent, each factor is raised to that power: $(xy)^3 = x^3y^3$.

A Step Back: Factoring Algebra Expressions to Find Original Numbers

Now and then, the ASVAB gives you a product (the answer to a multiplication problem), and you have to find the original numbers that were multiplied together to produce that product. This process is called *factoring*. You use factors when you combine like terms and add fractions.

Pulling out the greatest common factor

Your task may be to pull out the greatest common factor from two or more terms. Take, for example, this product: $4xy + 2x^2$. To factor this product, follow these steps:

1. **Find the greatest common factor — the highest number that evenly divides all the terms in the expression and the lowest power of each variable.**

Look at both the constants (numbers) and variables. In this case, the highest number that divides into 4 and 2 is 2. And the highest variable that divides into both xy and x^2 is x. You can see that the greatest common factor is $2x$.

2. **Divide both terms in the expression by the greatest common factor.**

When you have a fraction, such as $\dfrac{4xy + 2x^2}{2x}$, the resulting terms are $2y + x$.

3. **Multiply the entire expression (from Step 2) by the greatest common factor (from Step 1) to set the expression equal to its original value.**

Doing so produces $2x(2y + x)$.

Factoring a three-term equation $\left(x^2 + bx + c\right)$

Time to try something a little more complicated: factoring a trinomial (an expression with three terms). Suppose you start with $x^2 - 12x + 20$. Follow these steps:

1. **Find the factors of the first term of the trinomial.**

The factors of the first term, x^2, are x and x $\left(x \cdot x = x^2\right)$. Put those factors *(x and x)* on the left side of two sets of parentheses: $(x\quad)(x\quad)$.

2. **Determine whether the parentheses will contain positive or negative signs.**

You can see that the last term in the trinomial (+20) has a plus sign. That means the signs in the parentheses must be either both plus signs or both minus signs.

Two positive numbers multiplied by each other equal a positive number, and two negative numbers multiplied by each other equal a positive number. A negative number times a positive number equals a negative number.

REMEMBER

Because the second term (–12x) is a negative number, both factors must be negative: $(x -\quad)(x -\quad)$.

3. **Find the two numbers that go into the right sides of the parentheses.**

This part can be tricky. The factors of the third term, when added together or subtracted, must equal the second term of the trinomial.

In this example, the third term is 20 and the second term is –12x. You need to find the factors of 20 (the third term) that add to give you –12. The two factors you want are -2 and –10, because $(-2)(-10)=20$ (the third term) and $-2+-10=-12$ (the second term). Plug in these numbers: $(x-2)(x-10)$.

Thus, the factors of $x^2-12x+20$ are $(x-2)$ and $(x-10)$.

Making Alphabet Soup: Solving Quadratic Equations

REMEMBER

A *quadratic equation* is an equation that includes the square of a variable. The exponent in these equations is never higher than 2 (because it would then no longer be the square of an unknown but a cube or something else). Here are some examples of quadratic equations:

» $x^2-4x=-4$

» $2x^2=x+6$

» $x^2=36$

REMEMBER

Simple quadratic equations (those that consist of just one squared term and a number) can be solved by using the square root rule:

If $x^2=k$, then $x=\pm\sqrt{k}$, as long as k isn't a negative number.

Remember to include the $\pm$ sign, which indicates the answer is a positive or negative number. Take the following simple quadratic equation: $7y^2=28$.

First, get rid of the pesky 7 by dividing both sides by 7: $y^2=4$. Using the square root rule, take the square root of both sides of the equation. You know that $\sqrt{y^2}=y$ and $\sqrt{4}=\pm2$, so $y=\pm2$.

When you're solving a complex quadratic equation, you put all the terms on one side of the equal sign, making the equation equal zero. In other words, get the quadratic equation into this form: $ax^2+bx+c=0$, where a, b, and c are numbers and x is unknown. Take a look at the following equation: $x^2-2x=15$. You can convert this equation to standard form by subtracting 15 from both sides of the equation: $x^2-2x-15=0$.

The most efficient way to solve most quadratic equations is by factoring the equation and then setting each separate factor equal to zero. See the section "A Step Back: Factoring Algebra Expressions to Find Original Numbers" earlier in this chapter for info on factoring.

Look at the factored equation:

$$x^2-2x-15=0$$
$$(x-5)(x+3)=0$$

For the left side of the equation to equal zero, one of the quantities in parentheses has to equal zero (because zero times any number equals zero). That means you can split the equation in two, setting each factor equal to zero:

$$\begin{array}{ll} x-5=0 & x+3=0 \\ \quad x=5 & \quad x=-3 \end{array} \text{ or }$$

The solution for $x^2-2x-15$ is $x=5$ or -3.

All Math Isn't Created Equal: Solving Inequalities

Some algebra problems state that two quantities aren't equal to each other; thus, they're *inequalities*. Just like with equations, the solution to an inequality is a value that makes (or values that make) the inequality true. For the most part, you solve inequalities the same as you would solve a normal equation. You need to keep some facts of inequality life in mind, however. Short and sweet, here they are:

>> Negative numbers are less than zero.

>> Zero is less than positive numbers but greater than negative numbers.

>> Positive numbers are greater than zero.

A regular algebraic equation includes the equal sign (=), because the very basis of the equation is that one side of the equation must equal the other. Quite the opposite is true with inequalities, and they have their own special symbols, used to express the differences:

>> $\neq$ means "does not equal" in the way that 3 does not equal 4, or $3 \neq 4$.

>> $>$ means "greater than" in the way that 4 is greater than 3, or $4 > 3$.

>> $<$ means "less than" in the way that 3 is less than 4, or $3 < 4$.

>> $\leq$ means "less than or equal to" in the way that x may be less than or equal to 4, or $x \leq 4$.

>> $\geq$ means "greater than or equal to" in the way that x may be greater than or equal to 3, or $x \geq 3$.

To solve an inequality, you follow the same rules you would for solving an equation. For example, check out this inequality: $3 + x \geq 4$.

To solve it, simply isolate x by subtracting 3 from both sides of the equation:

$$3 + x - 3 \geq 4 - 3$$
$$x \geq 1$$

Therefore, 1 or any number greater than 1 makes this inequality true.

REMEMBER

The only special rule for inequalities takes effect when you multiply or divide both sides of the inequality by a negative number. In that case, the inequality sign is reversed. So if you multiply both sides of the inequality $3 < 4$ by -4, your answer is $-12 > -16$. And if you divide both sides of $-2x < 14$ by -2, your answer is $x > -7$.

TIP

You may encounter ASVAB questions that ask you to identify the correct number line for an inequality. Inequalities are characterized by one of these symbols: $>$, $<$, $\geq$, $\leq$ and $\neq$, although you're not likely to see any number line questions featuring the $\neq$ symbol on the ASVAB (I'm only including that symbol because technically, it means two expressions are inequal). Here's how each looks on a number line:

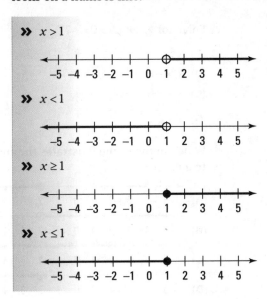

» $x > 1$

» $x < 1$

» $x \geq 1$

» $x \leq 1$

Algebra Practice Questions

The practice questions here are straightforward math; no word problems. Remember, these questions are designed for high school level and below. You won't be solving equations to calculate the orbit of Mars around the sun — you're just doing basic algebra.

1. Solve for x: $2x - 3 = x + 7$

(A) 10

(B) 6

(C) 21

(D) −10

2. Solve for x:

$x + 5 = y$

$3x + y = 12$

(A) 1

(B) $1\frac{5}{8}$

(C) 12

(D) $1\frac{3}{4}$

3. Simplify $8x^2 - 3x + 4xy - 9x^2 - 5x - 20xy$.

(A) $5x^2 + 9xy$

(B) $8x - 9x^2$

(C) $-x^2 - 8x - 16xy$

(D) $8x + 9x^2$

4. Evaluate $3x^2$, if $x = -2$.

(A) 12

(B) −12

(C) 6

(D) −6

5. Combine like terms: $4a + 3ab + 5ab + 6a$

(A) $10a + 8ab$

(B) 18ab

(C) $8a + 10ab$

(D) $2ab - 2a$

6. Solve for s: $30s + s = 62$

(A) $30s^2$

(B) 30

(C) 2

(D) 5

7. Solve for x: $4x + 8 > 2x + 7$

(A) x > 1

(B) x > −1

(C) $x > -\frac{1}{2}$

(D) $x > \frac{2}{3}$

8. Which number line illustrates the answer to $2a > 4$?

9. Solve for y: $3y + 25y = 145 - y$

(A) 5

(B) 9

(C) 130

(D) 27

10. Simplify: $7y^2 \cdot 8y^7 \cdot 8y^5$

(A) 448^{14}

(B) $447y^{15}$

(C) $448y^{14}$

(D) $448y^{70}$

11. There are 25 males in your platoon. There are three more males than two times the number of females. How many females are in your platoon?

(A) 8

(B) 11

(C) 16

(D) 22

12. One number is 10 more than another. The sum of twice the smaller number plus three times the larger number is 55. What is the larger number?

(A) 15

(B) 5

(C) 50

(D) 55

13. The price of a pair of jeans has increased by 15 percent. The original price of the jeans was $20. What is the new price?

(A) $23

(B) $23.50

(C) $24.75

(D) $25

14. It takes 2 minutes for a chef to wrap 3 burritos. What equation expresses this rate if x is the number of minutes and y is the number of burritos?

(A) $x = \frac{2}{3}y$

(B) $y = mx + b$

(C) $x = \frac{3}{2}y$

(D) $\frac{2}{3}xy$

15. Jesse has taken four tests in his English class and scored 89, 83, 78, and 92 percent. His final exam is worth two test grades. What score does he need on the final exam to get 90 percent in the class?

(A) 94

(B) 95

(C) 97

(D) 99

16. Abby is one-third her mom's age. In 12 years, she'll be half her mom's age. How old is Abby now?

(A) 8

(B) 10

(C) 12

(D) 13

17. You have 25 coins in nickels and dimes that total $1.65. How many nickels do you have?

(A) 10

(B) 17

(C) 18

(D) 21

18. The vending machine at the zoo has $17 in it. It only accepts $1 coins and quarters, and it has a total of 26 coins inside. How many $1 coins does the vending machine contain?

(A) 8

(B) 9

(C) 14

(D) 22

19. Private Joe Snuffy spent $35 at the post exchange. That was $7 less than three times what he spent at the commissary. How much did he spend at the commissary?

(A) $14

(B) $32

(C) $48

(D) $51

20. The sum of two numbers is 72, and one of the numbers is five times the other. What are the two numbers?

(A) 12 and 60

(B) 5 and 35

(C) 2 and 36

(D) 14 and 21

Answers and Explanations

Use this answer key to score the practice questions.

1. **A.** Isolate the x's on the left side of the equation by subtracting x from both sides: $2x - 3 - x = x + 7 - x$, or $x - 3 = 7$. Continue to perform operations to isolate x: Add 3 to both sides of the equation to get rid of the -3 on the left: $x - 3 + 3 = 7 + 3$, or $x = 10$. The correct answer is Choice (A).

2. **D.** In this system, use substitution to find the value of x. Start by replacing y in the second equation with $x + 5$. Then combine like terms, simplify, and solve:

$$x + 5 = y$$
$$3x + (x + 5) = 12$$
$$4x + 5 - 5 = 12 - 5$$
$$\frac{4x}{4} = \frac{7}{4}$$
$$x = 1\frac{3}{4}$$

   If you needed to solve for y, you'd plug in the x value to either one of the equations and solve. Some questions on the ASVAB will require you to do that, so be ready!

3. **C.**

$$8x^2 - 3x + 4xy - 9x^2 - 5x - 20xy$$
$$= (8x^2 - 9x^2) + (-3x - 5x) + (4xy - 20xy)$$
$$= -x^2 - 8x - 16xy$$

   The correct answer is Choice (C).

4. **A.** Just substitute -2 for x:

$$3x^2 = 3(-2)^2$$
$$= 3(4)$$
$$= 12$$

5. **A.** Group the two term categories (a and ab):

$$3ab + 5ab = 8ab$$
$$4a + 6a = 10a$$

6. **C.** First, combine like terms: $30s + s = 62$ is really $31s = 62$. Then solve for s:

$$31s = 62$$
$$\frac{31s}{31} = \frac{62}{31}$$
$$s = 2$$

7. C. Solve an inequality just like you'd solve an equation, by isolating the variable:

$$4x + 8 > 2x + 7$$
$$4x + 8 - 2x > 2x + 7 - 2x$$
$$2x + 8 > 7$$
$$2x + 8 - 8 > 7 - 8$$
$$2x > -1$$
$$\frac{2x}{2} > -\frac{1}{2}$$
$$x > -\frac{1}{2}$$

8. D. Solve the inequality and choose the number line that corresponds with it:

$$2a > 4$$
$$\frac{2a}{2} > \frac{4}{2}$$
$$a > 2$$

The number line that corresponds with $a > 2$ is Choice (D).

9. A. Combine like terms, then solve for y:

$$3y + 25y = 145 - y$$
$$28y + y = 145 - y + y$$
$$29y = 145$$
$$\frac{29y}{29} = \frac{145}{29}$$
$$y = 5$$

10. C. Simplify this expression with exponents by adding the exponents together, then multiplying like terms. Because the variable attached to each number is y, you can multiply them in order.

11. B. Let f represent the number of females in your platoon. The problem tells you that 25 is three more than two times f, so your equation looks like this: $25 = 2f + 3$. Solve for f:

$$25 = 2f + 3$$
$$25 - 3 = 2f - 3$$
$$22 = 2f$$
$$\frac{22}{2} = \frac{2}{2}$$
$$11 = f$$

You can check your math by working through the problem with 11 females. Multiply 11 by 2 to get 22, then add 3 to get 25. That means you found the correct answer choice.

12. **A.** Let x represent the smaller number. The larger number is 10 more, or $x + 10$. Create an equation to figure out what numbers you're dealing with based on what the problem tells you:

$$2x + 3(x + 10) = 55$$
$$2x + 3x + 30 = 55$$
$$5x = 55 - 30$$
$$5x = 25$$
$$x = 5$$

This tells you that the smaller number is 5, so the larger number — which is 10 more than the smaller number — is 15.

13. **A.** You can solve this problem in two ways. First, you can find 15 percent of the original price by converting 15 percent into a decimal and performing these calculations:

$$x = \$20 + (0.15 \cdot 20)$$
$$x = \$20 + \$3$$
$$x = \$23$$

You could also multiply the original amount ($20) by 1.15, because the new price is 100 percent of the original price plus 15 percent. Either way, the correct answer is $23.

14. **A.** Write an equation that relates the number of burritos the chef can wrap in 3 minutes: $\dfrac{2 \text{ minutes}}{3 \text{ burritos}} = \dfrac{\text{how many minutes}}{1 \text{ burrito}}$. Let x represent the number of minutes and y represent the number of burritos, then simplify your equation:

$$\frac{2}{3} = \frac{x}{1y}$$
$$3x = 2y$$
$$x = \frac{2}{3}y$$

15. **D.** This weighted average problem requires you to find the value of an unknown, so let x represent the score for one test grade. Because Jesse's final exam counts as two test grades, use $2x$ to represent the score he needs. Set up your math like this: $\dfrac{89 + 83 + 78 + 92 + 2x}{6} = 90$. (The denominator 6 represents the fact that the final score, 90, needs to be the average of six test scores.) Solve for x:

$$\frac{89 + 83 + 78 + 92 + 2x}{6} = 90$$
$$\frac{89 + 83 + 78 + 92 + 2x}{\cancel{6}} \cdot \frac{\cancel{6}}{1} = 90 \cdot 6$$
$$342 + 2x = 540$$
$$2x + 342 - 342 = 540 - 342$$
$$2x = 198$$
$$\frac{2x}{2} = \frac{198}{2}$$
$$x = 99$$

Jesse needs to score 99 percent on his test to get a 90 in the class.

16. C. Let a represent Abby's age. Because her mom is three times as old as Abby is, let $3a$ represent her age. The problem asks you to calculate Abby's age 12 years in the future, when she'll be half her mom's age, so set up your equation like this and solve for a:

$$a + 12 = \frac{1}{2}(3a + 12)$$
$$2 \cdot (a + 12) = 3a + 12$$
$$2a + 24 = 3a + 12$$
$$3a - 2a = 24 - 12$$
$$a = 12$$

Abby is 12 years old now, and her mom is 36. In 12 years, Abby will be 24 and her mom will be 48 — and that's exactly what the problem said would happen (she'll be half her mom's age).

17. B. Let n represent the number of nickels you have and let d represent the number of dimes you have. Together, $n + d = 25$ because you have 25 coins. Describe each coin using its value, like this: $(0.05)(n) + (0.10)(d) = 1.65$. Then find the value for one of the variables so you can work through the equation. Because $n + d = 25$, $d = 25 - n$. You can multiply both sides of the equation by 100 to get $5n + 10(25 - n) = 165$ so you don't have to work with decimals. Then, combine one n with the other:

$$5n + 250 - 10n = 165$$
$$-5n + 250 = 165$$
$$-5n = 165 - 250$$
$$-5n = -85$$
$$\frac{-5n}{-5} = \frac{-85}{-5}$$
$$n = 17$$

If the problem had asked you to figure out how many dimes you had, $25 - 17 = 8$ would tell you that you have 8 dimes. (I'd just take the coins out of my pocket and count them, but that's the easy way out.)

18. C. Let q represent quarters and d represent dollars so that $26 - q = d$ (there are 26 coins in total). $25q$ represents the value in cents of all the quarters together. Because the dollar coins have a value of 100 cents each, you have to determine how many cents he has from the dollar coins. That's $100(26 - q)$. Create a table to help you keep all these coins straight, like this:

	Number of Coins	Cents per Coin	Total Cents
Quarters	q	25	$25q$
Dollars	$(26 - q)$	100	$100(26 - q)$
Total	26		1,700

Add the total value of the quarters to the dollar coins' value:

$$25q + 100(26 - q) = 1,700$$
$$25q + 2,600 - 100q = 1,700$$
$$-75q + 2,600 = 1,700$$
$$-75q = -900$$
$$q = 12$$

The machine contains 12 quarters but a total of 26 coins. That means the 14 remaining coins are $1 coins.

19. **A.** Private Snuffy spent x dollars at the commissary. To figure out just how much lighter his bank account is, create an equation that shows he spent three times as much at the post exchange, less \$7: $3x - 7 = \$35$. Then solve for x:

$$3x - 7 = 35$$
$$3x - 7 + 7 = 35 + 7$$
$$3x = 42$$
$$\frac{3x}{3} = \frac{42}{3}$$
$$x = \$14$$

20. **A.** The problem tells you that one number is five times the other and that the sum of both numbers is 72, so there's only one variable. Set up an equation like this: $x + 5x = 72$. Remember that $5x$ is standing in for the second number. Then solve for x:

$$x + 5x = 72$$
$$6x = 72$$
$$\frac{6x}{6} = \frac{72}{6}$$
$$x = 12$$

That tells you that the first number is 12. Multiply that by 5 (that's where the $5x$ comes in) to find the second number, which is 60. The two numbers are 12 and 60.

» Shaping up for calculations involving common forms

» Zeroing in on coordinates and graphs

Chapter **8**

Geometry

Geometry is the branch of mathematics that deals with the properties of shapes, lines, points, angles, and other such objects and the relationships among them.

The computerized ASVAB's Mathematics Knowledge subtest consists of 15 questions, and you have 23 minutes to complete them all; if your test includes tryout questions, which I explain in Chapter 1, you have 47 minutes to complete 30 questions. The paper-and-pencil ASVAB has 25 questions, and you have 24 minutes to answer them all. Not all those questions deal with geometry, but you're very likely to encounter at least a few that do. You may finish a question about algebra and head right into a question that asks you to find the volume of a cylinder, the circumference of a circle, or the slant of an angle. Or you may have to deal with something entirely different, like adding fractions, messing with percentages, or working with scientific notation (but don't worry — I cover all those things in Chapter 7).

You're not allowed to use a calculator, but you can use as much scratch paper as you need — the test proctors hand it out like candy.

REMEMBER

The CAT-ASVAB is designed to test how much you know and do it quickly. The test usually kicks off with a question of medium difficulty. If you answer correctly, you get a harder question, but if you answer incorrectly, you get an easier question. The whole test works like that, which means you may not see very many "easy" questions at all — or you may not see any "hard" questions at all and think that the practice exams in Part 6 are much harder than they need to be.

REMEMBER

Before you read any further, you should note a few things:

>> Arcs of a circle and sizes of angles are measured in *degrees* and (not very often) in *minutes* or even *seconds;* 1 degree equals 60 minutes, and 1 minute equals 60 seconds.

>> A *circle* has 360 degrees (360°). Any arc that isn't a complete circle measures less than 360°.

>> A *quadrilateral* (a shape with four sides, such as a square or rectangle) has angles that add up to 360°.

Outlining Angles

Angles are formed when two lines intersect (cross) at a point. You typically measure angles in degrees. The greater the number of degrees, the wider the angle is:

> » A *straight line* is 180°.
>
> » A *right angle* is exactly 90°.
>
> » An *acute angle* is more than 0° but less than 90°.
>
> » An *obtuse angle* is more than 90° but less than 180°.
>
> » A *reflex angle* measures more than 180°.
>
> » *Complementary angles* are two angles that equal 90° when added together.
>
> » *Supplementary angles* are two angles that equal 180° when added together.

An angle's *vertex* is the point where two rays intersect to form an angle.

Take a look at the different types of angles in Figure 8-1.

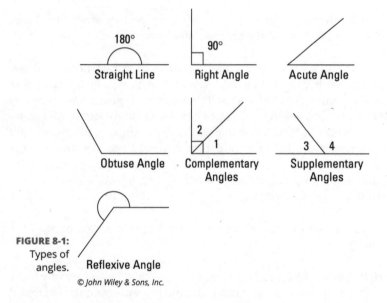

FIGURE 8-1:
Types of
angles.

© John Wiley & Sons, Inc.

Vertical angles oppose each other when two lines cross. They're always equal, like they are in Figure 8-2. Angles *a* and *b* are equal, and angles *x* and *y* are equal. In this case, the term *vertical* refers to where the lines cross each other; it has nothing to do with direction.

FIGURE 8-2:
Vertical
angles.

© John Wiley & Sons, Inc.

Parallel lines

Parallel lines never intersect. Lines are considered *parallel* if they're always the same distance apart (the technical term for this attribute is *equidistant*) and they'll never meet. They also point in the same direction. When another line, called a *transversal*, crosses parallel lines, the angles formed makes pairs that have the same measure, just as they are in Figure 8-3. Each type of angle in this situation has its own name.

>> **Corresponding angles** have the same measure. They're on the same side of the transversal and both either above or below the parallel lines. The pairs in Figure 8-3 are *a* and *w*, *d* and *z*, *b* and *x*, and *c* and *y*. These angles have to be equal if the lines are parallel.

>> **Alternate interior angles** are on opposite sides of the transversal and between the parallel lines, like *d* and *x* are in Figure 8-3. Equality between these angles means you have parallel lines on your hands.

>> **Alternate exterior angles** are on opposite sides of the transversal, like *a* and *y* are in Figure 8-3. When these angles are equal, you guessed it — parallel lines.

>> **Consecutive interior angles** are on the same side of the transversal, between the parallel lines, like *d* and *w* are in Figure 8-3. If these two angles add up to 180°, you're dealing with parallel lines.

FIGURE 8-3: Pairs of angles on parallel lines.

© John Wiley & Sons, Inc.

Naming angles

Angles have descriptors like acute, obtuse, and complementary, but you can also name angles by using the vertex point and a point on each of the angle's rays. You may see problems where angles are named ∠*ABC*, ∠*CMZ*, or ∠*DRJ*. The middle letter in this type of label is the vertex. Also, angles can be named using only the vertex, as long as it's clear which angle you're talking about (not two angles sharing the same vertex).

Here's what an angle labeled ∠*DRJ* may look like:

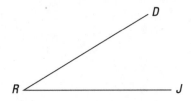

Pointing Out Triangle Types

A *triangle* consists of three straight sides that intersect at the three vertices. All three angles always add up to 180°. Triangles can be classified according to the relationship among their angles or the relationship among their sides:

>> **Isosceles triangle:** An *isosceles triangle* has two equal sides; the angles opposite the equal sides are also equal.

>> **Equilateral triangle:** An *equilateral triangle* has three equal sides; each of the angles measures 60°.

>> **Right triangle:** A *right triangle* has one right angle (90°); therefore, the remaining two angles are complementary (add up to 90°). The side opposite the right angle is called the *hypotenuse,* which is the longest side of a right triangle. The other two sides are called *legs.*

>> **Obtuse triangle:** An *obtuse triangle* has an angle greater than 90°.

>> **Scalene triangle:** A *scalene triangle* has three unequal sides.

Check out Figure 8-4 to see what these triangles look like.

FIGURE 8-4:
The three basic types of triangles.

Isosceles Triangle

If sides *a* and *c* are equal, then angles 1 and 2 are equal.

Equilateral Triangle

Sides *a*, *b*, *c* are equal. Angles 1, 2, 3 are equal.

Right Triangle

$a^2 + b^2 = c^2$

© John Wiley & Sons, Inc.

REMEMBER

You can find the *perimeter* — the distance around a shape — of a triangle by adding together the lengths of the three sides. The *area* — the space within a shape — of a triangle is one-half the product of the base (*b*, the bottom or the length) and the height (*h*, the distance drawn perpendicular from the base to the opposite vertex), or $A = \frac{1}{2}bh$.

The *Pythagorean theorem* (also known as Pythagoras's theorem) says that when a triangle has a right angle and you make squares on all three sides, the biggest square has the exact same area as the other two squares put together. It doesn't sound like something you'll ever use, but it really comes in handy when you know the lengths of two sides of a triangle and need to figure out the third.

REMEMBER

The Pythagorean theorem only works with right-angled triangles.

The formula for this theorem is $a^2 + b^2 = c^2$, where *a* and *b* are the triangle's legs and *c* is its longest side. On paper, it looks like Figure 8-5.

FIGURE 8-5:
The Pythagorean theorem in action.

© John Wiley & Sons, Inc.

EXAMPLE

Find the length of *c*.

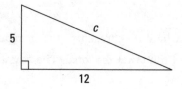

(A) 13

(B) 17

(C) 26

(D) 169

Remember that *c* is always the hypotenuse, which is what you need to find. Take the measurements from the figure and apply them to the Pythagorean theorem:

$$a^2 + b^2 = c^2$$
$$5^2 + 12^2 = c^2$$
$$25 + 144 = c^2$$
$$169 = c^2$$

The square root of 169 is 13, so the triangle's hypotenuse is 13. The correct answer is Choice (A).

Back to Square One: Quadrilaterals

Quadrilaterals — shapes with four sides — all contain angles totaling 360°. Many types of quadrilaterals exist (see Figure 8-6):

> ❯❯ *Squares* have four sides of equal length, and all the angles are right angles.

> ❯❯ *Rectangles* have all (four) right angles, and the opposite sides have equal lengths.

> ❯❯ *Parallelograms* have opposite sides that are parallel, and their opposite sides and angles are equal. The angles don't have to be right angles.

> ❯❯ *Rhombuses* have four sides of equal length, but the angles don't have to be right angles.

> ❯❯ *Trapezoids* have exactly two sides that are parallel.

FIGURE 8-6:
Types of quadrilaterals.

Square   Rectangle   Parallelogram   Rhombus   Trapezoid

© John Wiley & Sons, Inc.

You can find the area of a square and a rectangle with the formula $A = lw$, where *A* represents area, *l* represents length of one side, and *w* represents width.

To find the area of a parallelogram, you need the formula $A = bh$, where A represents area, b represents base, and h represents height. The height is measured from the base perpendicular to the parallel side.

The area of a rhombus is a bit trickier. It's $A = \frac{pq}{2}$, where A represents area, p represents the length of one diagonal, and q represents the length of the other diagonal. The variables in this formula look like this:

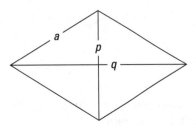

The formula to find the area of a trapezoid is $A = \frac{a+b}{2}h$, where A represents area, a represents the length of one base (one of its parallel lines), and b represents the length of the other base (the other parallel line). In this formula, h represents height as measured between the two parallel lines, like this:

REMEMBER

Knowing these formulas may come in handy if you're answering "hard" Mathematics Knowledge or Arithmetic Reasoning questions on the ASVAB. But the test doesn't have that many questions (15 if you're taking the CAT-ASVAB without tryout questions and 25 if you're taking the pencil-and-paper version). Most people only see a handful of geometry-related questions.

Going around in Circles

A *circle* is formed when its points are all located an equal distance from its center. A circle always has 360°. Here are some key circle terms (see Figure 8-7, which shows the parts of a circle):

>> **Circumference (C):** The points forming the circle — that is, the distance around the circle — is called its *circumference*.

>> **Radius (r):** The *radius* of a circle is the straight-line measurement from the center of the circle to any point on the circumference of the circle.

>> **Diameter (d):** The *diameter* of the circle is measured as a line passing through the center of the circle, from a point on one side of the circle all the way to a point on the other side of the circle. Any line that passes through a circle and connects two points on the circle is called a *chord*. The diameter is the longest chord.

FIGURE 8-7:
The parts of
a circle.

REMEMBER

The diameter of a circle is always twice as long as the radius of a circle: $d = 2r$.

Navigating the circumference

To measure the circumference of a circle, use the number pi (π). Although π is a lengthy number, it's generally rounded to 3.14 or approximated as $\frac{22}{7}$. If you round π so you can solve a problem, you don't use the equal sign because the answer isn't equal to the actual length. You use the approximation symbol ($\approx$) instead.

REMEMBER

The formula for circumference is circumference = $\pi \times$ diameter, or $C = \pi d$. Because the radius of a circle is half its diameter, you can also use the radius to determine the circumference of a circle. Here's the formula: $C = 2\pi r$.

Suppose you know that the pie you just baked has a diameter of 9 inches. You can determine its circumference by using the circumference formula:

$C = \pi d$

$C \approx 3.14 \times 9$

$C \approx 28.26$ inches

Mapping out the area of a circle

REMEMBER

Determining the area of a circle also requires the use of π. Area = $\pi \times$ the square of the circle's radius, or $A = \pi r^2$.

To determine the area of a 9-inch-diameter pie, multiply π by the square of 4.5. Why 4.5 and not 9? Remember, the radius is always half the diameter, and the diameter is 9 inches.

$A = \pi r^2$

$A \approx 3.14 \times 4.5^2$

$A \approx 3.14 \times (4.5 \times 4.5)$

$A \approx 3.14 \times 20.25$

$A \approx 63.585$ square inches

Fillin' It Up: Calculating Volume

Volume is the space a solid (three-dimensional) shape takes up. You can think of volume as how much a shape would hold if you poured water into it. Volume is measured in cubic units. The formula for finding volume depends on the object, which, when the sides are all polygons (flat figures), is a *prism:*

>> **Rectangular prisms:** For rectangular prisms, you multiply length × width (depth) × height. You can do so because the length, width, and height of a rectangle are consistent throughout the whole shape. The formula looks like this: $V = lwh$.

   Remember that a cube is also a box; its sides are all the same length, and you use the same formula as you would with a rectangular box.

>> **Cylinders:** A cylinder has two circles for its bases. The volume equals π × the radius squared × height, or $V = \pi r^2 h$.

   Basically, you're multiplying the area of the cylinder's circular base $\left(A = \pi r^2 \right)$ times the height *(h)* of the cylinder.

>> **Spheres:** Finding the volume of a sphere (a ball-shaped object) requires this formula: $V = \frac{4}{3}\pi r^3$, where *V* represents volume and *r* represents the sphere's radius. (Like circles, spheres have diameter and radius.)

EXAMPLE

Find the volume of this rectangular prism:

2 in.

4 in.

10 in.

(A) 40 in.³

(B) 80 in.²

(C) 80 in.³

(D) 160 in.³

Use the formula for the volume of a rectangular object, $V = lwh$, where *V* represents volume, *l* represents length, *w* represents width, and *h* represents height. Plug in the values to solve:

$$V = lwh$$
$$V = 10 \cdot 2 \cdot 4$$
$$V = 80$$

Volume is measured in cubic inches (represented by in.³), so don't let Choice (B) mess you up. The answer is Choice (C).

EXAMPLE

Find the volume of this cylinder:

8 in.

4 in.

(A) 401.92 in.³

(B) 396.56 in.³

(C) 403.12 in.³

(D) 112.8 in.³

Replace the variables in the formula for the volume of a cylinder with what you see in the diagram:

$$V \approx \pi r^2 h$$
$$V \approx (3.14) \cdot 4^2 \cdot 8$$
$$V \approx 3.14 \cdot 16 \cdot 8$$
$$V \approx 401.92$$

The variables fit right into the formula, and using 3.14 to represent pi, you can perform the calculations on your scratch paper. The correct answer on this question is Choice (A).

Scratching the surface area of solids

Surface area is all the area on the exterior of a solid, and some questions on the Mathematics Knowledge or Arithmetic Reasoning subtests of ASVAB may ask you to calculate it. The surface area of an object is the sum of all the areas of all the shapes that cover the surface of it.

The formula for surface area is different for different objects:

» **Surface area of a cube:** $SA = 6s^2$, where s represents the length of the side of each edge

» **Surface area of a rectangular prism:** $SA = 2ab + 2bc + 2ac$, where a, b, and c represent the lengths of the three sides

» **Surface area of any prism:** $SA = 2B + ph$, where B represents the area of the base, p represents the perimeter of the base, and h represents height

» **Surface area of a cylinder:** $SA = 2\pi r^2 + 2\pi rh$, where r represents radius and h represents height

EXAMPLE

Find the surface area of this cube:

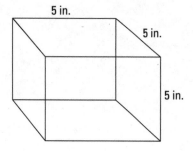

5 in.

5 in.

5 in.

(A) 100 in.²

(B) 150 in.²

(C) 300 in.²

(D) 900 in.²

Each side of the cube is 5 inches long, and the formula for the surface area of a cube is $SA = 6s^2$. Replace s in the formula with 6 and work through the equation:

$$SA = 6s^2$$
$$SA = 6(5 \cdot 5)$$
$$SA = 6(25)$$
$$SA = 150$$

The correct answer is Choice (B). Remember that surface area is measured in square inches, which is abbreviated in.².

EXAMPLE

Find the surface area of this rectangular prism:

10 in.

4 in.

4 in.

(A) 150 in.²

(B) 172 in.²

(C) 192 in.²

(D) 215 in.²

The formula for the surface area of a rectangular prism is $SA = 2ab + 2bc + 2ac$, so choose what you want to fill in for a, b, and c (any side will do) from the figure. Put it into the formula:

$$SA = 2ab + 2bc + 2ac$$
$$SA = (2 \cdot 4 \cdot 4) + (2 \cdot 4 \cdot 10) + (2 \cdot 4 \cdot 10)$$
$$SA = 32 + 80 + 80$$
$$SA = 192$$

The answer, Choice (C), is a measurement of every square inch of the outside of the rectangular prism in the figure.

Breaking down combined figures

On the ASVAB, you may come across nonstandard shapes — they're like a mashup of two (or more) shapes. When you have to find the area, volume, or surface area of one of these figures, you have to break apart the figure and perform multiple sets of calculations (one for each shape you're left with). Figure 8-8 shows some examples of combined figures.

FIGURE 8-8: Combined figures.

© John Wiley & Sons, Inc.

EXAMPLE

Find the area of this figure:

(A) 54 ft.²

(B) 16 ft.²

(C) 70 ft.²

(D) 74 ft.²

You can solve this problem two ways: You can find the area of the figure as if it were one whole figure, subtracting the part that's missing (the 4-foot-by-4-foot segment in the upper right corner), or you can find the sum of the areas of two rectangles stuck together (one that measures 4 feet by 5 feet and one that measures 6 feet by 9 feet). On the ASVAB, you have a limited amount of time to answer each question, so do what's easiest for you.

In this case, it may be easier to figure out what the area would be if this figure were a whole rectangle, and then subtract the area of the missing part. If this shape were a whole rectangle, its measurements would be 10 feet by 9 feet, so use the formula for the area of a rectangle: $A = lw$. Because $10 \cdot 9 = 90$, the whole rectangle's area would be 90 ft.². Subtract the area of the missing piece, which is 16 ft.² (because $4 \cdot 4 = 16$). $90 - 16 = 74$, so the answer is Choice (D).

Find the area of this figure:

10 in.

5 in.

(A) 65.32 in.²

(B) 59.81 in.²

(C) 45.23 in.²

(D) 31.41 in.²

The figure depicts two shapes: a half-circle and a rectangle. You have to perform calculations to find the area of a circle, divide your answer in half (because it's a half-circle), and also find the area of the rectangle. You can perform the calculations in whatever order is easiest for you.

The rectangle's area is 50 in.² because the formula for the area of a rectangle is $A = lw$, and the diagram says one side is 5 inches long and the other is 10 inches long.

The formula for the area of a circle is $A \approx \pi r^2$. Radius is half a circle's diameter, and the figure shows that the circle's diameter is 5 inches. That means this circle's radius is 2.5 inches, so replace r in the formula to find the first part of the answer:

$$A \approx \pi (2.5)^2$$
$$A \approx 3.14(6.25)$$
$$A \approx 19.625$$

That gives you the area of the whole circle, but you have to cut it in half. $19.625 \div 2 = 9.8125$, and because the answer choices only have two numbers to the right of the decimal, you can round that down to 9.81.

The last step in this problem is adding the areas of the two shapes together: $50 + 9.81 = 59.81$. The correct answer is Choice (B).

A good guessing strategy on the ASVAB is to rule out answer choices you know can't be correct. In this case, Choices (C) and (D) are impossible — they're both smaller than what you know the area of the rectangle is. If you were going to guess on this question, you'd have a 50-50 chance of getting it right by eliminating those two choices.

TIP

Mapping Out Coordinates

Geometry coordinates are a little different from what you'll experience on a military Land Navigation Course, but chances are pretty good you'll use this skill to get from Point A to Point B on a military map — and you may need to use it on the ASVAB, too.

In geometry, a *coordinate grid* is a grid that includes a horizontal *x*-axis and a vertical *y*-axis. The two axes meet at the *origin*, and its coordinates are (0, 0). Every point on the grid has a pair of coordinates. In this figure, Point A's coordinates are (−8, 8), Point B's coordinates are (3, 4), and Point C's coordinates are (−5, −2). Coincidentally, you read these grids just like you read military maps.

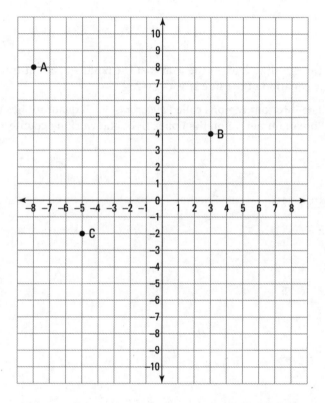

You can represent a line on a coordinate grid by using a formula called the *slope-intercept form* of a linear equation. That formula is $y = mx + b$, where m represents the line's slope, b represents the point where the line crosses the *y*-axis, and x and y represent coordinates of points that lie on the line.

EXAMPLE

Find the *y*-intercept of the straight line that has a slope of 4 and passes through the point (−1, −6).

(A) −2

(B) −3

(C) 2

(D) 3

Using slope-intercept form, which is $y = mx + b$, plug in what you know. Remember to read coordinates the right way, which is (*x*, *y*).

$$y = mx + b$$
$$-6 = (4 \cdot -1) + b$$
$$-6 = -4 + b$$
$$-6 + 4 = b$$
$$-2 = b$$

The correct answer is Choice (A). The line crosses the *y*-axis at the point −2, and it travels through points −1 and −6. The equation of the line is $y = 4x - 2$.

The *x* and *y* axes divide the plane into four regions called *quadrants*. Each quadrant has its own number, beginning with the Roman numeral I on the upper right and working counterclockwise with II, III, and IV.

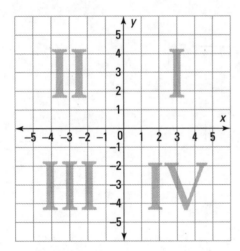

Geometry Practice Questions

On the ASVAB's mathematics knowledge subtest, you're very likely to encounter problems that include figures and formulas. If you're taking the computerized version of the test, you'll probably kick off with a question of medium difficulty; if you get it right, the questions will get harder until you get one wrong, and if you get that first question wrong, the questions will get easier until you get one right. You may see a lot of difficult questions, a lot of easy questions, or a mix — it all depends on how you're doing on the test.

1. Find the perimeter:

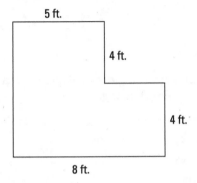

(A) 32 ft.

(B) 33 ft.

(C) 34 ft.

(D) 35 ft.

2. The radius of a circle is 2 inches. What is its approximate circumference?

(A) 12 inches

(B) 12.56 inches

(C) 23.23 inches

(D) 26.2 inches

3. What is the value of YZ? (*Note:* This figure is not drawn to scale.)

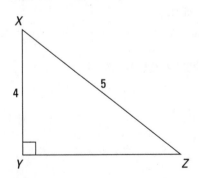

(A) 3

(B) 2

(C) 6

(D) 5

4. Find the area of the rectangle:

(A) 48 in.²

(B) 65 in.²

(C) 90 in.²

(D) 135 in.²

5. Identify the angle:

(A) acute

(B) obtuse

(C) complementary

(D) right

6. What is the area of the trapezoid?

(A) 32 cm²

(B) 157 cm²

(C) 110 cm²

(D) 220 cm²

7. What is the measure of *x*?

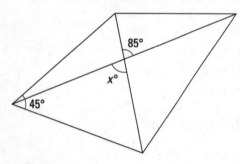

(A) 85°

(B) 135°

(C) 95°

(D) 20°

8. A circle has a radius of 15 feet. What's most nearly its circumference?

(A) 30 feet

(B) 225 feet

(C) 94 feet

(D) 150 feet

9. At 3:00 p.m., the angle between the hands of the clock is

(A) 90 degrees

(B) 180 degrees

(C) 120 degrees

(D) 360 degrees

10. Find the area of a circle with a radius of 5 cm.

(A) 87.5 cm²

(B) 78.5 cm²

(C) 17.5 cm²

(D) 8.5 cm²

11. In any triangle, the sum of the interior angles adds up to how many degrees?

(A) 90

(B) 180

(C) 270

(D) 360

12. One complementary angle is 62 degrees. What is measure of the other angle?

(A) 158 degrees

(B) 28 degrees

(C) 62 degrees

(D) 26 degrees

13. In which quadrant does the point (7, −8) lie?

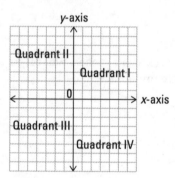

(A) Quadrant I

(B) Quadrant II

(C) Quadrant III

(D) Quadrant IV

14. Find the slope of the line $y = 2x + \frac{2}{7}$.

(A) 2

(B) $\frac{7}{2}$

(C) $\frac{2}{7}$

(D) $2\frac{2}{7}$

15. Find the surface area:

(A) 58 in.²

(B) 96 in.²

(C) 112 in.²

(D) 200 in.²

16. Find the area:

(A) 12 in.²

(B) 15 in.²

(C) 24 in.²

(D) 48 in.²

17. Find the circumference:

(A) 92.5 in.

(B) 94.2 in.

(C) 143.2 in.

(D) 150 in.

18. What letter represents the vertex?

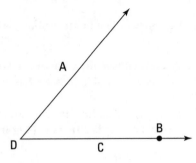

(A) A

(B) B

(C) C

(D) D

19. What is the measurement of Angle D?

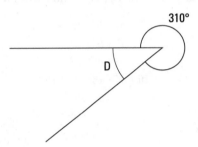

(A) 50°

(B) 60°

(C) 45°

(D) 310°

20. What is the area of the larger circle less the area of the smaller circle?

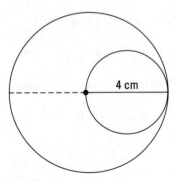

(A) 50.24 cm²

(B) 40 cm²

(C) 37.68 cm²

(D) 12.56 cm²

Answers and Explanations

Use this answer key to score your performance on geometry practice questions.

1. **A.** Perimeter is the total of the length of each side. Although not all the segments are labeled, every side totals 8 feet in length. That makes Choice (A) the correct answer.

2. **B.** The formula for the circumference of a circle is $C = 2\pi r$, and the problem tells you the circle's radius is 2 inches. Plug in the numbers you know and solve:

$$C \approx 2\pi r$$
$$C \approx 2 \cdot 3.14 \cdot 2$$
$$C \approx 12.56$$

   Use 3.14 as an approximation of pi, and you should come up with the correct answer, which is Choice (B).

3. **A.** Use the Pythagorean theorem:

$$a^2 + b^2 = c^2$$
$$4^2 + b^2 = 5^2$$
$$16 + b^2 = 25$$
$$16 + b^2 - 16 = 25 - 16$$
$$b^2 = 9$$
$$b = \sqrt{9}$$
$$b = 3$$

4. **D.** The formula for the area of a rectangle is $A = lw$, and this rectangle is 15 inches long by 9 inches wide. $15 \cdot 9 = 135$, so the answer is Choice (D).

5. **D.** The angle depicted in the figure is a right angle, which has a measurement of 90° (you can tell because of the small square in the corner). An acute angle has a measurement that's more than 0° but less than 90°, an obtuse angle measures more than 90° but less than 180°, and complementary angles add up to 90°.

6. **C.** The area of a trapezoid is

$$A = \frac{a+b}{2}h$$

   Plug in the values and solve:

$$A = \left(\frac{7+15}{2}\right)10$$
$$A = \left(\frac{22}{2}\right)10$$
$$A = (11)10$$
$$A = 110 \text{ cm}^2$$

7. **A.** Angle x and the angle marked 85° are vertical angles — they're opposite each other where two lines cross. Vertical angles are always equal. It doesn't matter what other angles are labeled in the figure. You don't need to do any math to find out that the answer is Choice (A).

8. C. The circumference of a circle is π times the diameter; the diameter equals two times the radius. Therefore, $3.14 \times 30 \approx 94.2$ feet. The correct answer is Choice (C).

9. A. At 3:00 p.m., one hand is on the 12, and the other is on the 3. This creates a right angle — a 90° angle. The correct answer is Choice (A).

10. B. The formula for the area of a circle is $A = \pi r^2$. Plug in the values and solve:

$$A \approx (3.14)(5)^2$$
$$A \approx (3.14)(25)$$
$$A \approx 78.5 \text{ cm}^2$$

11. B. All angles of a triangle always add up to 180°.

12. B. Complementary angles are angles that add up to 90°: $90° - 62° = 28°$.

13. D. The coordinates $(7, -8)$ are read "7 right, 8 down," so the point lies in Quadrant IV.

14. A. The formula to find the slope of a line is $y = mx + b$, where m represents the slope. The formula in the problem has 2 in place of the m variable, so you don't need to do any math — the answer is right in the question.

15. C. The formula to find the surface area of a prism is $SA = 2ab + 2bc + 2ac$. Choose a variable for each measurement in the diagram, such as $a = 10$ in., $b = 2$ in., and $c = 3$ in. Then fill in what you know from the diagram:

$$SA = 2ab + 2bc + 2ac$$
$$SA = (2 \cdot 10 \cdot 2) + (2 \cdot 2 \cdot 3) + (2 \cdot 10 \cdot 3)$$
$$SA = 40 + 12 + 60$$
$$SA = 112$$

The surface area of the rectangular prism depicted in the question is 112 in.²

16. A. The formula to find the area of a triangle is $A = \frac{1}{2}bh$, and the diagram says the base is 4 inches and the height is 6 inches. Work out the math like this:

$$A = \frac{1}{2}bh$$
$$A = \frac{1}{2}(4 \cdot 6)$$
$$A = \frac{1}{2}(24)$$
$$A = 12$$

The answer is Choice (A).

17. B. Find the circumference of a circle with the formula $C \approx 2\pi r$. The radius of the circle in the diagram is 15 inches, so fill in the formula and use 3.14 for pi:

$$C \approx 2\pi r$$
$$C \approx 2\pi(15)$$
$$C \approx 2 \cdot 3.14 \cdot 15$$
$$C \approx 94.2$$

18. **D.** The vertex of an angle is where the two rays converge. In this case, it's Choice (D).

19. **A.** A circle has 360 degrees, and this angle cuts into a circle. The reflex angle is 310 degrees, as shown in the diagram, which means the only possible measurement of Angle D is 50 degrees.

20. **C.** Determine the area of both circles using $A \approx \pi r^2$. The radius of the circle is 4 centimeters, as shown in the diagram. Use 3.14 for pi and figure out the large circle's area:

$$A \approx \pi r^2$$
$$A \approx 3.14 \cdot 4^2$$
$$A \approx 50.24$$

The large circle's area is 50.24 cm². Now figure out the smaller circle's area the same way:

$$A \approx \pi r^2$$
$$A \approx 3.14 \cdot 2^2$$
$$A \approx 12.56$$

Subtract the smaller circle's area from the larger circle's area: $50.24 - 12.56 = 37.68$. The correct answer is Choice (C).

Chapter 9

Arithmetic Reasoning: Math Word Problems

How many miles per gallon does your brand-new SUV get? How long does it take to go over the river and through the woods to Grandmother's house? How much wood would a woodchuck chuck? These are examples of everyday questions that can be answered by arithmetic reasoning. (Okay, maybe not the woodchuck situation.)

The rest of the world calls this type of question math *word problems*. The ASVAB calls them *Arithmetic Reasoning*. No matter what they're called, these problems help you apply mathematical principles to the real world (at least the real world according to the people who think up word problems). Your job is to read a word problem, determine what the question asks, and select the correct answer.

Arithmetic Reasoning is an important part of the Armed Forces Qualification Test (AFQT) score, which is used to determine your general qualification for enlistment in all the service branches (see Chapter 1 for more information). Also, certain military jobs require that you score well on this subtest (see Appendix A).

The test administrator will supply you with scratch paper and a trusty No. 2 pencil, but one thing he or she won't give you (or even let you bring) is a calculator. You can use your paper and lead to clarify the data, write formulas, and mathematically solve the problems. You can even use them to draw pretty pictures to help you understand the problem. Don't get too artistic, though — you have 55 minutes to answer 15 questions if you're taking the CAT-ASVAB (or 113 minutes to answer 30 questions if your subtest includes tryout questions, which I explain in Chapter 1). You have 36 minutes to answer 30 questions if you're taking the paper version. As long as you're focused on problem-solving, you should have plenty of time.

To do well on the Arithmetic Reasoning subtest, you have to remember that there are two parts: arithmetic and reasoning. You usually have to use both skills for each problem. The arithmetic part comes in when you have to perform mathematical operations such as addition, subtraction, multiplication, and division. The reasoning comes in when you figure out which formulas and numbers to use in your calculations. In other words, Arithmetic Reasoning tests how you apply your ability to perform calculations to real-life problems. If you slept through high school math, don't worry. This chapter helps you decipher these math problems, focusing on the reasoning part. For additional info on the arithmetic, flip to Chapter 6.

REMEMBER

The CAT-ASVAB, which most people take, gives you questions of varying difficulty. If you answer a question correctly, you get a harder one next. If you answer incorrectly, you get an easier question.

Tackling the Real World of Word Problems

Test-takers often waste a lot of time reading and rereading word problems as if the answer might reveal itself to them by some miracle; however, correctly solving math word problems requires you to perform a series of organized steps:

1. **Read the problem completely.**

2. **Figure out what the question is asking.**

3. **Dig out the relevant facts.**

4. **Set up one or more equations to arrive at a solution and then solve the problem.**

5. **Review your answer.**

I cover these steps in detail throughout this section.

Reading the entire problem

The first step in solving a word problem is reading the entire problem to discover what it's all about. Try forming a picture about the problem in your mind or — better yet — draw a sketch of the problem on your scratch paper. Ask yourself whether you've ever seen a problem like this before. If so, what's similar about it, and what did you do to solve it in the past?

As plain as the nose on a fly: Figuring out what the question is asking

The second and most important step in solving a word problem is to determine exactly what the question is asking. Sometimes the question is asked directly. At other times, identifying the actual question may be a little more difficult. Suppose you're asked the following question:

EXAMPLE

What's the volume of a cardboard box measuring 12 inches long by 14 inches wide by 10 inches tall?

(A) 52 cubic inches

(B) 88 cubic inches

(C) 120 cubic inches

(D) 1,680 cubic inches

The problem directly asks you to determine the volume of a cardboard box. Recall from your high school algebra and geometry classes that the volume of a rectangular container is length × width × height, or $V = lwh$. So $12 \times 14 \times 10 = 1,680$. The correct answer is Choice (D).

Now take a look at the next example:

EXAMPLE

How many cubic inches of sand can a cardboard box measuring 12 inches long by 14 inches wide by 10 inches tall contain?

(A) 52 cubic inches

(B) 88 cubic inches

(C) 120 cubic inches

(D) 1,680 cubic inches

This is the same problem, but the question you need to answer isn't as directly stated. Therefore, you have to use clues embedded in the problem to figure out what the actual question is. Would figuring out the perimeter of the box help you with this question? Nope. Would figuring out the area of one side of the box help you? Nope — you're not painting the box; you're filling it. The question wants you to determine the volume of the container.

TIP

Clue words can be a big help when trying to figure out which question is being asked. Look for the following clue words:

» **Addition:** Sum, total, in all, perimeter, increased by, combined, added

» **Division:** Share, distribute, ratio, quotient, average, per, out of, percent

» **Equals:** Is, was, are, were, amounts to

» **Multiplication:** Product, total, area, cubic, times, multiplied by, of

» **Subtraction:** Difference, how much more, exceed, less than, fewer than, decreased

Digging for the facts

After you figure out which question you're answering, the next step is to figure out which data is necessary to solve the problem and which data is extra. Start by identifying all the information and variables in the problem and listing them on your scratch paper. Make sure you attach units of measurement contained in the problem (miles, feet, inches, gallons, quarts, and so on). After you've made a list of the facts, try to eliminate those facts that aren't relevant to the question. Look at the following example:

EXAMPLE

To raise money for the school yearbook project, Tom sold 15 candy bars, Becky sold 12 candy bars, Debbie sold 17 candy bars, and Jane sold the most at 50. How many candy bars were sold by the girls?

The list of facts may look something like this:

Tom = 15 bars

Becky = 12 bars

Debbie = 17 bars

Jane = 50 bars

? = total the girls sold

Because the question is the total number of candy bars sold by the girls, the number of bars sold by Tom isn't relevant to the problem and can be scratched off the list. Just add the remaining bars from your list. The answer is 79.

Setting up the problem and working your way to the answer

EXAMPLE

You need to decide how the problem can be solved and then use your math skills to arrive at a solution. For instance, a question may ask the following:

Joan just turned 37. For 12 years, she's dreamed of traveling to Key West to become a beach bum. To finance this dream, she needs to save a total of $15,000. How much does Joan need to save each year if she wants to become a beach bum by her 40th birthday?

Write down, in mathematical terms, what the question is asking you to determine. Because the question is asking how much money Joan needs to save per year to reach $15,000, you can say y (years Joan has to save) × m (money she needs to save each year) = $15,000. (Assume she saves the same amount each year.) Or to put it more mathematically,

$$ym = \$15,000$$

You don't know the value of m (yet) — that's the unknown you're asked to find. But you can find out the value of y — the number of years Joan has to save. If she's 37 and wants to be a beach bum by the time she's 40, she has 3 years to save. So now the formula looks like this:

$$3m = 15,000$$

To isolate the unknown on one side of the equation, you simply divide each side by 3, so $3m \div 3 = 15,000 \div 3$. (If you don't remember how to isolate unknowns, flip to Chapter 6.) Therefore, your answer is

$$m = 5,000$$

Joan needs to save $5,000 each year for 3 years to reach her goal of $15,000 by the time she's 40. You may be tempted to include the 12 years Joan has been dreaming of this trip in your formula. This number was put into the problem as a distraction. It has no bearing on solving the problem.

Drawing a diagram

TIP

Sometimes it's easier to work through a problem when you can visualize it. You can use as much scratch paper as you need on the ASVAB, so you may want to draw diagrams to help work out some of the questions.

For example, if you encounter a question that asks you how much tile you need to floor a six-walled room that measures 15 feet on one side, 14 feet on another, 8 feet on another, and 6 feet on a fourth, it can be really helpful to draw a diagram like this:

As you work through the practice questions in this book and complete the practice tests, use scratch paper to help you visualize what you're working through — that way, you'll know when drawing a quick sketch or creating a diagram will help you when you take the ASVAB.

Reviewing your answer

TIP

Before marking your answer sheet or punching in that choice on the computer, review your answer to make sure it makes sense. Review by asking yourself the following questions:

» **Does your solution seem probable?** Use your common sense. If you determine that a 12-by-16-foot roof is covered in only 12 shingles, you've probably made a mistake in your calculations.

» **Does it answer the question asked?** Reread the problem. For example, if a question asks you to calculate the number of trees *remaining* after 10% of the total was cut down, the correct answer wouldn't be 10% of the trees but rather the 90% still standing. Both answers will most likely be choices.

» **Are you sure?** Double-check your answer. Those tricky test-makers often supply false answers that are very, very close to the correct answer.

» **Is your answer expressed using the same units of measurement as used in the problem?** A question may ask how many cubic feet of concrete are required to cover a driveway. Your answer in cubic yards would have to be converted to cubic feet so you can select the correct answer choice.

WARNING

Although you may have been taught in school to round up for 5 or more and down for less than 5, rounding real-world problems requires a different mindset. For example, if someone needs 2.2 cans of paint for a particular job, she really needs 3 cans of paint to make sure she has enough, even though you'd generally round down. And if someone gets a 15-minute break for every 4 hours of work but works only 7 hours, he'd get only one break, even though 7 divided by 4 equals 1.75, which is generally rounded up to 2.

You may find that the solution you arrived at doesn't fit the facts presented in the problem. If this is the case, back up and go through the steps again until you arrive at an answer that seems probable.

The Guessing Game: Putting Reason in Your Guessing Strategy

Guessing wrong on any of the ASVAB subtests doesn't count against you, unless you guess incorrectly on a bunch of questions in a row at the end of the subtest when taking the CAT-ASVAB. If you don't guess, your chances of getting that answer right are zero, but if you take a shot at it, your chances increase to 25%, or 1 in 4. Eliminate two wrong answers, and you have a 50-50 shot.

If you're taking the paper version of the ASVAB, you can always skip the tough questions and come back to them after you've finished the easier ones. If you're taking the computerized version of the ASVAB, the software won't let you skip questions, so you need to make your guess right then and there.

WARNING

If you're taking the paper version of the test and elect to skip questions until later, make sure you mark the next answer in the correct space on the answer sheet. Otherwise, you may wind up wearing out the eraser on your pencil when you discover your error at the end of the test. Or even worse, you may not notice the error and wind up getting several answers wrong because you mismarked your answer sheet.

Using the process of elimination

TIP

Guessing doesn't always mean "pick an answer, any answer." You can increase your chances of picking the right answer by eliminating answers that can't be right. To eliminate some obvious wrong answers, you can do the following:

» **Make sure the answer is realistic in relation to the question asked.** For example, if a question asks you how much water would be required to fill a child's wading pool, 17,000 gallons isn't a realistic answer. You can save time by eliminating this potential answer choice immediately.

» **Pay attention to units of measurement.** If a question asks how many feet of rope you'll need, answer choices listed in inches or cubic feet are probably incorrect.

» **Consider easier answer choices first.** Remember, you're not allowed to use a calculator on the ASVAB, so math answers that you'd arrive at by using complicated formulas are probably not correct.

Solving what you can and guessing the rest

TIP

Sometimes you may know how to solve part of a problem but not all of it. If you don't know how to do all the calculations — or don't have time for them — don't give up. You can still narrow down your choices by doing what you can. Here's how partially solving problems can help:

» When adding mixed numbers (a whole number and a fraction), add the whole-number parts first; then immediately eliminate answer choices that are too low. Or when adding lengths, add full feet first and cross off choices that are too small, even before considering the inches.

» Multiply just the last digits and cross off all answers that don't end in the right numbers (assuming the answers aren't rounded).

Making use of the answer choices

TIP

If you're stuck on a particular problem, sometimes plugging possible answers into an equation can help you find the right answer. Here's how using the answer choices can improve your guessing:

» **Plug in each remaining answer choice until you get the right answer.** Plugging in all the answer choices is time-consuming, so make sure you eliminate obviously wrong choices first.

» **Estimate and plug in numbers that involve easy mental calculations.** For instance, if Choice (A) is 9 and Choice (B) is 12, plug in 10 and solve the equation in your head. Think about whether the right answer has to be higher or lower than 10, and choose from there.

>> **Using a little logic, do calculations with an obviously wrong answer choice.** Sometimes a wrong answer choice — especially one that differs drastically from the other answers — represents an intermediate step in the calculations, so you can use it to solve the problem. For instance, take this example:

EXAMPLE

A security guard walks the equivalent of six city blocks when he makes a circuit around the building. If he walks at a pace of eight city blocks every 30 minutes, how long will it take him to complete a circuit around the building, assuming he doesn't run into any thieves?

(A) 20.00 minutes

(B) 3.75 minutes

(C) 22.50 minutes

(D) 24.00 minutes

Choice (B) is obviously way too low to be the right answer, but it would be a logical guess for the security guard's rate for a single block. Multiply 3.75 minutes/block by 6 blocks, and you probably have a good candidate for the right answer — 22.50 minutes, Choice (C).

Arithmetic Reasoning (Math Word Problems) Practice Questions

Arithmetic Reasoning questions are math problems expressed in a story format. Your goal is to determine what the question is asking by picking out the relevant factors needed to solve the problem, set up mathematical equations as needed, and arrive at the correct solution. Sounds easy, right? Try your hand at the following questions.

1. If apples are on sale at 15 for $3, what's the cost of each apple?

   (A) 50 cents

   (B) 25 cents

   (C) 20 cents

   (D) 30 cents

2. A noncommissioned officer challenged her platoon of 11 enlisted women to beat her record of performing a 26-mile training run in 4 hours. If all the enlisted women match her record, how many total miles will they have run?

   (A) 71.5 miles

   (B) 6.5 miles

   (C) 286 miles

   (D) 312 miles

3. Diane takes her client to an expensive restaurant in town to discuss new legal strategies. The restaurant adds a 15% gratuity for the server. If her meal and drinks cost $85 and her client's meal and drinks cost $110, how much did the restaurant add as a gratuity?

   (A) $22.50

   (B) $29.25

   (C) $20.00

   (D) $224.25

4. A bag of sand holds 1 cubic foot of sand. How many bags of sand are needed to fill a square sandbox measuring 5 feet long and 1 foot high?

   (A) 25 bags

   (B) 5 bags

   (C) 10 bags

   (D) 15 bags

5. An Army battalion in Hawaii has four companies. Two of the companies, Alpha and Charlie, each have 70 soldiers. Bravo Company has 44 soldiers, while Delta Company has 84. What is the average number of soldiers in a company in this battalion?

   (A) 67 soldiers

   (B) 45 soldiers

   (C) 70 soldiers

   (D) 62 soldiers

6. Farmer Beth has received an offer to sell her 320-acre farm for $3,000 per acre. She agrees to give the buyer $96,000 worth of land. What fraction of Farmer Beth's land is the buyer getting?

   (A) $\frac{1}{4}$

   (B) $\frac{1}{10}$

   (C) $\frac{1}{5}$

   (D) $\frac{2}{3}$

7. A large wall map is drawn so that 1 inch equals 3 miles. On the map, the distance from Kansas City to Denver is $192\frac{1}{2}$ inches. How far is the round trip from Kansas City to Denver in miles?

   (A) $192\frac{1}{2}$ miles

   (B) $577\frac{1}{5}$ miles

   (C) 385 miles

   (D) 1,155 miles

8. Margaret and Julie can sell their tattoo parlor for $150,000. They plan to divide the proceeds according to the ratio of the money they each invested in the business. Margaret put in the most money at a 3:2 ratio to Julie's contribution. How much money should Julie get from the sale?

   (A) $50,000
   (B) $30,000
   (C) $60,000
   (D) $90,000

9. Mr. Cameron purchased a shirt for $20. He sold it for $26. By what percentage did he increase the price?

   (A) 5
   (B) 20
   (C) 30
   (D) 25

10. In the military, $\frac{1}{4}$ of an enlisted person's time is spent sleeping and eating, $\frac{1}{12}$ is spent standing at attention, $\frac{1}{6}$ is spent staying fit, and $\frac{2}{5}$ is spent working. The rest of the time is spent at the enlisted person's own discretion. How many hours per day does this discretionary time amount to?

    (A) 6.0 hours
    (B) 1.6 hours
    (C) 2.4 hours
    (D) 3.2 hours

11. A designer sells a square yard of carpet for $15.00. The same carpet can be purchased at the carpet outlet store for $12.50. As a percentage, how much more expensive is the designer's carpet?

    (A) The designer's carpet costs 17% more than the outlet-store carpet.
    (B) The designer's carpet costs 20% more than the outlet-store carpet.
    (C) The designer's carpet costs 25% more than the outlet-store carpet.
    (D) The designer's carpet costs 12% more than the outlet-store carpet.

12. Terry got paints for $32.50, canvas for $112.20, and paintbrushes for $17.25. How much total money did she spend at the art supply store?

    (A) $167.45
    (B) $144.70
    (C) $161.95
    (D) $156.95

13. If mailing the first ounce of a letter costs $0.49, and it costs $0.21 to mail each additional ounce, how much does it cost to mail a 5-ounce letter?

    (A) $1.85
    (B) $1.05
    (C) $1.54
    (D) $1.33

14. Larry travels 60 miles per hour going to a friend's house and 50 miles per hour coming back, using the same road. He drives a total of 5 hours. What is the distance from Larry's house to his friend's house, rounded to the nearest mile?

    (A) 110
    (B) 126
    (C) 136
    (D) 154

15. Joe ran around a pentagon-shaped track with sides each measuring 1,760 feet. If he made three complete trips around the track, how far did he run?

    (A) 37,500 feet
    (B) 15,300 feet
    (C) 20,150 feet
    (D) 26,400 feet

16. It takes Steve 56 hours to paint his fence. If his 3 children each work 7 hours per day with him, how many days will it take Steve and the children to paint the fence, assuming they all work at the same rate?

    (A) 2
    (B) 4
    (C) 2.5
    (D) 1

17. To buy a new car priced at $32,000, Martha takes out a five-year loan with a simple interest rate of 6.5%. By the time she owns the car, how much will she have paid including principal and interest?

(A) $45,000

(B) $41,500

(C) $40,000

(D) $42,400

18. What is the width of a rectangular vegetable garden whose perimeter is 150 feet and length is 50 feet?

(A) 100 feet

(B) 25 feet

(C) 200 feet

(D) 50 feet

19. Mike took Jen bowling for the first time. He bowled two games with scores of 157 and 175. Jen had never bowled before and scored 78 and 98. What was Mike's average score?

(A) 88

(B) 127

(C) 156

(D) 166

20. The cost of 4 shirts, 4 pairs of dress pants, and 2 ties is $560. A shirt costs twice as much as a tie, and a pair of pants costs $70 more than a tie. What is the total cost of 1 shirt, 1 pair of dress pants, and 1 tie?

(A) $150

(B) $230

(C) $175

(D) $195

21. A can of pork and beans has a radius of 3 inches and a height of 7 inches. What is the volume of the can?

(A) 198 cubic inches

(B) 156 cubic inches

(C) 21 cubic inches

(D) 42 cubic inches

22. Edward's electric bill for the month of July was $90.12. The electric company charges a flat monthly fee of $20.00 for service plus $0.14 per kilowatt-hour of electricity used. Approximately how many kilowatt-hours of electricity did Edward use in July?

(A) 361.11

(B) 424.12

(C) 500.86

(D) 567.17

23. Billy left the house without his wallet. When he went to purchase his lunch, he had to dig into his change stash to buy it. How much did he have left if he had 15 quarters, 15 dimes, 22 nickels, and 12 pennies and the lunch cost $5.52?

(A) $0.45

(B) $1.15

(C) $0.95

(D) $1.03

24. What will it cost to carpet a room 10 feet wide and 12 feet long if carpet costs $12.51 per square yard?

(A) $166.80

(B) $213.50

(C) $186.23

(D) $165.12

25. Jack eats three hot dogs per minute, while Jeff eats two hot dogs per minute. How many total hot dogs do they eat in 12 minutes?

(A) 35

(B) 40

(C) 60

(D) 65

26. The simple interest on Jerry's fixed sum of money depends on the length of time the money is invested. If it draws $60 in 4 months, how much will it draw in 1.5 years?

(A) $320

(B) $240

(C) $270

(D) $200

27. A rancher is driving along the edge of a circular sinkhole on his property. The sinkhole's diameter is 14 kilometers. If he walked around the sinkhole, how far would he walk?

(A) 34 kilometers

(B) 54 kilometers

(C) 44 kilometers

(D) 35 kilometers

28. What is the price of a $200 item after successive discounts of 10% and 15%?

(A) $75

(B) $175

(C) $153

(D) $150

Answers and Explanations

Use this answer key to score the Arithmetic Reasoning practice questions.

1. **C.** Divide $3 by 15. The answer is $0.20, so the correct answer is Choice (C). Remember to simplify; 15 for $3 is the same as 5 for $1.

2. **C.** Multiply 26×11. The other information in the question is irrelevant — it's there to throw you off. The correct answer is Choice (C). You can immediately eliminate Choice (B) because it isn't a reasonable answer. Identifying unreasonable answers (through the process of elimination) can help you choose the correct answer choice faster.

3. **B.** Add 85 and 110 to get the cost of the services $\left(\$85 + \$110 = \$195 \right)$; then multiply the answer by 0.15 (15%) to find the gratuity. The question asks for the amount of the tip, so the correct answer is Choice (B), $29.25. You can immediately eliminate Choice (D), because the amount is far too high to make sense.

4. **A.** To find the volume of the sandbox, you take length times width times height $\left(V = lwh \right)$. Don't forget that the measurements are for a square sandbox, so you can assume that if the box is 5 feet long, then it's also 5 feet wide. So $5 \times 5 \times 1$ is 25 cubic feet. Each bag holds 1 cubic foot of sand, and $25 \div 1 = 25$. Choice (A) is the correct answer. If you were thinking answer Choice (B) sounded good, remember that the answer should make sense. Five cubic feet of sand would not fill a very large sandbox, would it?

5. **A.** Add all the soldiers in the battalion: 70 + 70 + 84 + 44 = 268. Divide 268 by 4 to find the average, which is 67. The average company in the battalion has 67 soldiers.

6. **B.** The buyer's price, $96,000, divided by $3,000 (price per acre) equals 32 acres. Thirty-two acres divided by 320 acres (total of the farm) equals 10%, or $\frac{1}{10}$, of the land. The correct answer is Choice (B).

7. **D.** Multiply 192.5×3 to get the distance in miles, and then double the answer to account for both legs of the trip. Choice (D) is the correct answer. *Note:* A quick approach here involves rounding. The distance is about 200 inches, or 400 inches round trip. Multiply that by 3, and you get 1,200 miles. The only choice that comes close is Choice (D).

8. **C.** According to the ratio, Margaret should get $\frac{3}{5}$ of the money and Julie should get $\frac{2}{5}$ of the money. You calculate the fractions by adding both sides of the ratio together $(3+2=5)$ to determine the denominator — Margaret gets 3 parts of the total, and Julie gets 2 parts, so there are 5 total parts. Each side of the ratio then becomes a numerator. Multiply the total amount of money by the fraction representing Julie's share: Multiply $150,000 by 2, and then divide the answer by 5 to determine Julie's share of the money. The correct answer is Choice (C). (You can also divide $150,000 by 5 and then multiply that total by 2 to get the same answer.)

9. **C.** Let x = the percentage of profit. Set up the following proportion and solve for x by cross-multiplying:

$$\frac{x}{100} = \frac{6}{20}$$
$$20x = 600$$
$$x = 30$$

Mr. Cameron increased the price by 30% on the shirt he sold.

10. **C.** Calculate this answer by first assigning a common denominator of 60 to all the fractions and adjusting the numerators accordingly: $\frac{15}{60}, \frac{5}{60}, \frac{10}{60},$ and $\frac{24}{60}$. Add the fractions to find out how much time is allotted to all of these tasks. The total time is $\frac{54}{60}$, which leaves $\frac{6}{60}$ or $\frac{1}{10}$ of the day to the enlisted person's discretion. One-tenth of 24 hours is 2.4 hours. Therefore, Choice (C) is the correct answer.

11. **B.** You want the cost of the designer's carpet in terms of the outlet-store carpet, so divide the difference in costs by the lower price: $15.00 − $12.50 = $2.50, and $2.50 ÷ $12.50 = 0.20 = 20\%$. The correct answer is Choice (B) — the designer's carpet is 20% more expensive.

12. **C.** Simply add the amounts together: $32.50 + $112.20 + $17.25 = $161.95. Choice (C) is the correct answer.

13. **D.** The first ounce costs $0.49. The next 4 ounces cost $0.21 each. Multiply $0.21 × 4$ and then add $0.49 to determine how much mailing a 5-ounce letter costs: $0.21 × 4 = $0.84, and $0.84 + $0.49 = $1.33, the cost of mailing a 5-ounce letter. Choice (D) is the correct answer.

14. **C.** Let x be the distance traveled to Larry's friend's house. The time it takes to drive to the house looks like this:

$$\frac{\text{distance}}{\text{speed}} = \frac{x}{60}$$

The time it takes to return looks like this:

$$\frac{\text{distance}}{\text{speed}} = \frac{x}{50}$$

The total time to travel and return is 5 hours. Therefore,

$$\frac{x}{50} + \frac{x}{60} = 5$$

Next, find the common denominator in order to add the fractions and solve for x:

$$\frac{6x}{300} + \frac{5x}{300} = 5$$
$$\frac{11x}{300} = 5$$
$$11x = 1,500$$
$$x \approx 136.36$$

The answer is 136 miles (rounded to the nearest mile), Choice (C).

15. **D.** A pentagon has 5 sides. If each side measures 1,760 feet, the formula for finding the total feet Joe ran looks like this:

$$1,760(5)(3) = 8,800(3) = 26,400 \text{ feet}$$

16. **A.** Four people are working on the fence for 7 hours a day; therefore, the family is spending $(4)(7) = 28$ person-hours on the job each day. Divide the total number of hours needed to complete the job by the total number of person-hours to find the total number of days: $56 \div 28 = 2$. It will take 2 days for the team to finish painting the fence.

17. **D.** The formula for interest is Interest = Principal × Rate × Time. Simply substitute what you know to solve this problem:

$$\text{Interest} = 32,000(0.065)(5)$$
$$\text{Interest} = 10,400$$

Now add the interest to the principal: $32,000 + 10,400 = 42,400$

Martha is paying $42,400 for her new car.

18. **B.** Use the formula for perimeter to find the answer; $w =$ width and $l =$ length:

$$\text{Perimeter} = 2w + 2l$$
$$150 = 2w + 2(50)$$
$$150 = 2w + 100$$
$$50 = 2w$$
$$25 \text{ feet} = w$$

19. **D.** Don't let Jen's scores throw you off. They're completely irrelevant. To solve this problem, first add up Mike's scores and then divide by 2:

$$157 + 175 = 332$$
$$332 \div 2 = 166$$

20. **A.** Let $s =$ the price of one shirt.

Let $p =$ the price of one pair of dress pants.

Let $t =$ the price of one tie.

Here's what you know: A shirt costs twice as much as a tie, so the value of one shirt is $2t$, which means $s = 2t$. A pair of pants costs \$70 more than a tie, so the value of one pair of pants is $t + 70$, which means $p = t + 70$. To find out how much 1 shirt, 1 pair of dress pants, and 1 tie costs, multiply these values by 2, 4, and 4, respectively, to get a sum of 560, which corresponds with the number of clothing items in the original problem:

$$(2t) + (2t \times 4) + ((t+70)4) = 560$$
$$2t + 8t + 4t + 280 = 560$$
$$14t + 280 = 560$$
$$14t = 280$$
$$\frac{14t}{14} = \frac{280}{14}$$
$$t = 20$$

Now you know that a tie costs \$20, so a shirt (\$20 × 2) costs \$40, and a pair of dress pants (\$20 + 70) is \$90. The cost of 1 shirt, 1 pair of dress pants, and 1 tie is \$20 + \$40 + \$90, which adds up to \$150.

21. **A.** To solve this problem, you have to know the formula for volume of a cylinder:

$$V = \pi r^2 h$$

where h is the height and r is the radius. Simply plug in the numbers from the question to solve:

$$V \approx 3^2 (3.14)(7)$$
$$V \approx 9(3.14)(7)$$
$$V \approx 63(3.14)$$
$$V \approx 197.82$$

Round to the nearest whole number to get Choice (A).

22. **C.** First, subtract the monthly fee from the bill to find the total amount actually spent on electricity:

$$\$90.12 - \$20.00 = \$70.12$$

Now divide your answer by the charge per kilowatt-hour:

$$\frac{70.12}{0.14} \approx 500.857$$

Choice (C) is the winner here.

23. **C.** Add the change to see how much Billy has before he buys lunch:

$$15(\$0.25) + 15(\$0.10) + 22(\$0.05) + \$0.12$$
$$= \$3.75 + \$1.50 + \$1.10 + \$0.12$$
$$= \$6.47$$

Subtract the cost of the lunch:

$$\$6.47 - \$5.52 = \$0.95$$

24. **A.** The room measures $10 \times 2 = 120$ square feet. Because there are 3 feet in a yard, 1 square yard = 9 square feet. Use this conversion factor to find out how many square yards you need to carpet:

$$\frac{120}{9} = 13\frac{1}{3} \text{ square yards}$$

Now just multiply to find the total price of the carpet: $13.333 \times \$12.51 = \$166.80$.

25. **C.** If Jack eats 3 hot dogs in 1 minute, you know he eats $3(12) = 36$ in 12 minutes. If Jeff eats 2 per minute, he eats $2(12) = 24$ in 12 minutes. Add $36 + 24 = 60$ and you have your answer. That's a lot of hot dogs.

26. **C.** Let i = the interest earned in 1.5 years and convert 1.5 years to months ($12 \times 1.5 = 18$ months). Then set up a proportion that represents the ratios of interest earned to time invested:

$$\frac{60}{i} = \frac{4}{18}$$
$$\frac{60}{i} = \frac{2}{9}$$

Cross-multiply to solve:

$$2i = 540$$
$$i = \$270$$

Jerry will make $270, Choice (C).

27. **C.** Use the formula Circumference $= \pi d$, where d is the diameter, to solve this problem:

$$C = \pi(14)$$
$$C \approx 3.14(14)$$
$$C \approx 43.96$$

Rounded to the nearest whole number, the sinkhole's circumference is 44 kilometers, Choice (C).

28. **C.** The item originally sold for $200. The first reduction was 10%, taking the item down to $180:

$$200 - 0.1(200)$$
$$= 200 - 20$$
$$= 180$$

The second reduction was 15%, taking the item down to $153:

$$180 - 0.15(180)$$
$$= 180 - 27$$
$$= 153$$

Choice (C) is the right answer.

4

Examining General Science under a Microscope

Explore biological processes and figure out what makes plants and animals tick under the umbrella of life sciences.

Pour yourself into a chemistry mindset to come up with solutions to common questions. Work through physics principles and leverage a better ASVAB score.

Dig into earth science topics that you may encounter on the General Science subtest. Zero in on space science topics that can help you ace the test.

Answer some practice questions at the end of each chapter to help you determine where you excel and where you could use some more review.

IN THIS CHAPTER

» **Figuring out the scientific method**

» **Grasping measurements**

» **Examining human and plant biology**

» **Considering cell structures and processes**

» **Getting into genetics**

» **Using scientific strategies to improve your score**

Chapter **10**

General Science and Life Science

As you study for the General Science subtest, you may feel overwhelmed by facts and figures. General Science requires a lot of straight-up memorization. You're presented with questions about facts you probably learned in high school in various science classes, such as health, Earth science, biology, and chemistry. If you don't know that Earth is the third planet from the sun, then all the other science knowledge you have won't help you one bit when the question asks, "What is the third planet from the sun?"

TIP

Instead of trying to remember nine million individual facts, spend some time reviewing the general principles behind the facts. Think about how the facts relate to each other. Looking at the big picture is an effective learning technique.

You have 10 minutes to answer 15 General Science questions on the CAT-ASVAB (20 minutes to answer 30 questions if your subtest includes tryout questions, which I cover in Chapter 1). If you take the paper version, you get 11 minutes to answer 25 questions. That comes out to a maximum of 40 seconds per question, so there's no time to daydream. For the most part, you either know the answer or you don't. If you don't know the answer, you can always guess (check out Chapter 3 for tips on guessing on the ASVAB).

You can relax this time around . . . well, just a little. The General Science subtest has no bearing on your Armed Forces Qualification Test (AFQT) score. On the other hand, your score on this subtest is used to calculate some of the military composite scores that are used for job qualification purposes (see Appendix A for more information).

If the job you want requires a good score on this subtest, dedicate yourself to the information in this chapter, Chapter 11, and Chapter 12 to boost your General Science score. You may also want to check out *Biology For Dummies* (Wiley) by René Fester Kratz, PhD, for more information.

REMEMBER

The computerized version of the ASVAB is designed to ferret out your scientific knowledge quickly and efficiently. That means it chooses question difficulty based on whether you've answered the preceding question correctly. This approach helps the military figure out the probable extent of your knowledge without keeping you at a testing site for weeks on end.

There's a Scientific Method to the Madness

Scientists are pretty skeptical. They don't necessarily believe anything said by anyone else unless it's been shown to be true (time after time after time) using a process called the *scientific method*. Scientists know that personal and cultural biases may influence perceptions and interpretations of data, so they've derived a standard set of procedures and criteria to minimize those influences when developing a theory. Because the scientific method is prevalent in all fields of science, you can expect to see a few questions about the process on the General Science subtest.

Here are the usual steps to solving a problem using the scientific method:

1. **Observe some aspect of the universe.**

2. **Ask a question about why this thing is happening.**

3. **Develop a testable explanation *(hypothesis)* based on the theory.**

4. **Make a prediction based on the hypothesis.**

5. **Experiment and observe to test the prediction.**

6. **Use the results of the experiment to create new hypotheses or predictions.**

If a theory holds up to repeated testing, scientists gain confidence in it, and a hypothesis that's supported consistently over time eventually comes to be considered a law, fact, or principle.

The terms *law* and *theory* mean different things to scientists than they do to the average person. Scientifically speaking, a *law* is a statement about something that happens: When you jump off a diving board, you're going to travel in a downward direction. A scientific law doesn't say *why* you fall toward the pool — only that you *do* fall toward the pool. Laws usually rely on a mathematical equation, and they're always true. (In case you were wondering, the formula for gravity is $F = \dfrac{G(m_1 m_2)}{r^2}$, where F represents the force due to gravity between two masses, which are represented by m_1 and m_2, and G represents the gravitational constant.)

SCIENTIFIC LAWS AND THEORIES YOU ALREADY KNOW

Every moment you're awake, you observe scientific laws in action. You're holding this book in your hands, which means you're an active participant in Newton's third law: The book is exerting force on your hands, while your hands are exerting equal and opposite force on the book. You're not floating on the ceiling right now, which means the law of gravity is working on you. The fact that you aren't identical to your parents, who aren't identical to their parents (and on and on) is part of the theory of evolution, which states that living things on Earth have origins in other, preexisting types and that the ways you're different from your ancestors are due to modifications in your DNA over generations.

A *theory* is a detailed explanation of the phenomenon. It consists of one or more hypotheses that have been supported through repeated testing. Theories are widely accepted as true in the scientific community, but in order to hold that status, they must never have been proven wrong. If a theory doesn't hold up, it's been disproved. Theories can also evolve based on new evidence, which doesn't mean the original theory was wrong; it simply means it was incomplete.

Understanding Forms of Measurement

Because science is based on developing objective facts — evidence and results that are measurable and experiments that can be reproduced — measurements are an important part of science. And because this subtest is all about science, you can expect to run into a few questions about measuring scientifically on the ASVAB.

The metric system, or SI (abbreviated for the French *le Système International d'Unités,* which translates to the International System of Units), is based on a decimal system of multiples and fractions of ten. Scientists almost always use the metric system for precise measurement so a standard exists among scientists around the world. In fact, the majority of countries around the globe use the metric system — the United States is one of the few countries that still teach and use the Imperial (non-metric) system.

REMEMBER

Here are some units of measurement you need to know for the General Science subtest of the ASVAB:

>> The meter (m) is a unit of length.

>> The liter (L) is a unit of volume.

>> The gram (g) is a unit of mass (similar to weight).

You can attach prefixes to these base units to indicate units that are larger or smaller. Check out Table 10-1 for metric prefixes and Table 10-2 for some abbreviations of common metric measurements. Table 10-3 has the most common conversion formulas.

TABLE 10-1 **Metric Prefixes**

Prefix	Symbol	What It Means
milli-	m	One-thousandth (0.001)
centi-	c	One-hundredth (0.01)
deci-	d	One-tenth (0.1)
deca-	da	10
hecto-	h	100
kilo-	k	1,000
mega-	M	1,000,000

TABLE 10-2 **Common Metric Units and Their Abbreviations**

Length	Liquid Volume	Mass
millimeter (mm)	milliliter (mL)	milligram (mg)
centimeter (cm)	centiliter (cL)	centigram (cg)
meter (m)	liter (L)	gram (g)
kilometer (km)	kiloliter (kL)	kilogram (kg)

TABLE 10-3 **Imperial to Metric Conversions**

Imperial	Conversion Formula	Metric
Inches	$inches \times 2.54 = centimeters$	1 inch = 2.54 centimeters
Feet	$feet \times 0.3 = meters$	1 foot = 0.3 meters
Yards	$yards \times 0.9 = meters$	1 yard = 0.9 meters
Miles	$miles \times 1.6 = kilometers$	1 mile = 1.6 kilometers
Square inches	$square\ inches \times 6.45 = square\ centimeters$	1 square inch = 6.45 square centimeters
Square feet	$square\ feet \times 0.09 = square\ meters$	1 square foot = 0.09 square meters
Quarts	$quarts \times 0.94 = liters$	1 quart = 0.94 liters
Gallons	$gallons \times 3.78 = liters$	1 gallon = 3.78 liters
Ounces	$ounces \times 28.3 = grams$	1 ounce = 28.3 grams
Pounds	$pounds \times 0.45 = kilograms$	1 pound = 0.45 kilograms

Uncovering Biology, from Big to Small

It would be impossible to cover all the areas of biology in this book, and I'm not going to try. Luckily, the General Science subtest of the ASVAB measures your knowledge of scientific disciplines at the average high school level. You remember studying the Animal kingdom, the human body, plant physiology, and cell structures in high school, right? If not, the following sections can serve as a short refresher course.

Relating to your world through ecology

Ecology is the study of the environment — more specifically, the relationship between organisms and the world around them. All plants and animals are part of an *ecosystem* (a biological community of interacting organisms and their environment). An ecosystem includes producers that make their own food and consumers that eat other things. An ecosystem also has decomposers, such as bacteria, that break down dead plants, animals, and the waste of all organisms.

REMEMBER

Animals can't produce their own food, so they're consumers, which are classified in three categories:

» **Carnivores** eat only meat. Some examples include lions, tigers, polar bears, snakes, crocodiles, hawks, and eagles.

» **Herbivores** eat only plants. Cows, moose, giraffes, and elk are herbivores.

» **Omnivores** eat both plants and other animals. People are omnivores, and so are pigs, mice, raccoons, chickens, crows, and foxes.

Conditions in the world either encourage or prevent the establishment of individual ecosystems. For plants (producers) to grow, adequate sunlight, good soil, moderate temperatures, and water must be part of the environment. If plants aren't around, plant-eating consumers can't be sustained, which means predators (who eat other animals) can't be sustained, either. For consumers, mates are as essential as a food supply. Diseases and enemies can prevent an animal from establishing itself in an ecosystem. Human actions, such as wasting natural resources and polluting the air, water, or soil, can disrupt or destroy an entire ecosystem.

Variety is the spice of life: Biodiversity

Biodiversity is the term scientists use to talk about the variety of life in the world-at-large or in specific habitats and ecosystems. Scientists have already named and classified just under 2 million species of plants and animals, but experts suspect between 8 and 10 million haven't been discovered yet. Every species has an important role to play in natural sustainability, from the smallest bacterium to the biggest animal.

The continuation of life on this planet depends on biodiversity; if one species that was food for another species dies out, it creates a domino effect that disrupts the entire food chain (all the way up to humans). It's not only about food, though. It's also about depending on other organisms to perform functions that keep the world turning (such as bees pollinating plants or big trees taking carbon dioxide out of the air and replacing it with oxygen).

When any species has good genetic diversity, it has a larger gene pool to pull from during the process of evolution — and that makes organisms more adaptable to changing conditions over time so species can survive. About 40 percent of the medicines we use today come from natural compounds in plants, fungi, and animals, too. Biodiversity is nature's checks-and-balances system, and without it, conditions for every species on Earth would quickly go downhill.

Categorizing Mother Nature

A long time ago, scientists looked at the world, noticed the hundreds of thousands of plants and animals around them, and decided that all these organisms (living things) needed to be labeled and grouped. To effectively study and discuss plants, animals, and other living creatures, all scientists needed to use the same names. Thus, a system of scientific classification was developed.

The most common classification system was created by Swedish botanist Carl Linnaeus, who published ten editions of his works from 1753 to 1758. Scientists often refer to this system as *taxonomy*. Not only does taxonomy provide official names for every plant and animal, but it also helps scientists understand how living creatures are related to one another. Modern-day taxonomy has its roots in the Linnaean taxonomic system.

No one is privy to the actual questions asked on the ASVAB (test materials are considered "controlled items" and are locked up in safes when not in use). In this category, questions can range anywhere from "How many kingdoms are there?" to "What's the genus for *Canis familiaris?*"

Counting down the classification system

The scientific classification system notes the relationships and similarities among organisms. It consists of eight main levels:

» **Domain:** A *domain* is a group of organisms that are similar based on characteristics such as chemistry and cell structure. The three domains are the broadest classifications and include the most kinds of organisms.

» **Kingdom:** *Kingdoms* group organisms by developmental characteristics and whether they make their own food. The relationships between organisms in a kingdom can be extremely loose, so members may share only a few characteristics. According to scientists, five or six kingdoms exist.

» **Phylum:** *Phylum* (plural *phyla*) is the next major taxonomic group. Within the kingdoms, organisms are divided into 36 phyla by general characteristics. For example, in the Animal kingdom, animals with backbones (vertebrates) are placed in a separate phylum from animals without backbones.

» **Class:** Organisms in a phylum are divided into *classes*. In the Animal kingdom, for example, birds, mammals, and fish all go in their own classes. Among plants, all flowering plants comprise the *Angiosperm* class, and all trees that bear cones, such as pines and spruces, comprise the *Conifer* class.

» **Order:** Scientific groupings create *orders,* which separate organisms based on the characteristics of the major groups in their class. For example, humans, chimps, gorillas, and gibbons are all part of the order *Primate* because they all share large brains and opposable thumbs, use tools, and have social groups. The order *Rodentia* includes gnawing mammals with continuously growing teeth, like squirrels, hamsters, and rats.

» **Family:** Families further divide organisms of the same order by similar characteristics. For example, humans are part of the *Hominidae* family, where gibbons split off into their own family: *Hylobatidae.*

» **Genus:** Two or more species that share unique body structures or other characteristics are closely related enough to be placed in a single *genus.* A genus may include only a single species if no other organism has characteristics similar enough for it to be considered the same genus. Here's where humans split from gorillas; we're part of the genus *Homo,* while they're in the genus *Gorilla.*

» **Species:** A *species* is the most specific level, so it contains the fewest types of organisms. Organisms of the same species have very similar characteristics. The human species is *sapiens,* while a gorilla's species is *gorilla* (and yes, that means they're classified as *Gorilla gorilla,* because species are conventionally written with the genus and the species together).

If the classification system gets you mixed up, try the mnemonic "Dear King Phillip, come over for good spaghetti." The first letter of each word represents part of the classification system, in order from broadest (domain) to most narrow (species). Figure 10-1 shows you the taxonomic system in action.

To get a better idea of how the scientific classification system works, Table 10-4 shows you how a few species are classified.

FIGURE 10-1: The Linnaean taxonomic classification system.

Homo sapien   *Fragaria ananassa*

© John Wiley & Sons, Inc.

TABLE 10-4 **Taxonomy of Different Organisms**

Taxonomic Group	Human	Strawberry	House cat	Staphylococcus aureus
Domain	Eukarya	Eukarya	Eukarya	Bacteria
Kingdom	Animalia	Plantae	Animalia	Eubacteria
Phylum	Chordata	Spermatophyta	Chordata	Firmicutes
Class	Mammalia	Dicotyledonae	Mammalia	Bacilli
Order	Primate	Rosales	Carnivora	Bacillales
Family	Hominidae	Rosaceae	Felidae	Staphylococcaceae
Genus	*Homo*	*Fragaria*	*Felis*	*Staphylococcus*
Species	sapiens	ananassa	silvestris	aureus

Visiting the kingdoms

Most scientists agree that there are five or six kingdoms. Check out the kinds of organisms that fall under each:

» **Animals:** This is one of the two largest kingdoms, and it includes many-celled organisms that, unlike plants, don't have cell walls, chlorophyll, or the capacity to use light to make energy (photosynthesis). Members of this kingdom can move. The Animal kingdom includes more than one million species. (Check out Figure 10-3 later in the chapter for a better look at cells.)

» **Plants:** Plants are also one of the two largest kingdoms. This kingdom includes organisms that can't move, don't have obvious nervous or sensory systems (the Venus flytrap is one exception), and possess cell walls made of cellulose. More than 250,000 species belong to the Plant kingdom.

» **Fungi:** Examples of common fungi are mushrooms and yeast. Fungi don't *photosynthesize* (use light to create energy) like plants do, but they do have cell walls made of a carbohydrate called *chitin.* More than 100,000 species belong to the Fungi kingdom.

» **Protists:** Protists include one-celled organisms that do have a nucleus, such as the protozoan, which you may remember from biology class. This kingdom consists of more than 250,000 species.

» **Eubacteria:** This kingdom, which used to be considered Monerans, is made up of single-celled organisms that don't have distinct nuclei or *organelles* (small, specialized structures within cells that act like organs). Bacteria are found everywhere, including your body and the depths of the ocean.

» **Archaebacteria:** Archaea is a kingdom comprising single-celled organisms that have no distinct nuclei or organelles; they have different genetic structures and metabolic processes than bacteria do.

Just name it: Showing off your genius about the species

Each organism is given a scientific name that consists of two words (usually derived from Latin) — the genus and the species of the organism. The genus is the first word, and the species is the second. Thus, *Homo sapiens* refers to humans. *Canis familiaris* is the family dog, and *Canis lupus* is the family wolf. Because wolves and dogs share many similarities, they share the same genus (no, no, not the same genes, the same genus).

TECHNICAL STUFF

When writing a scientific name, the genus name is capitalized, and the species name is all lowercase. Both names are italicized.

Perusing the Human Body Systems

Your body consists of several major systems that work together to keep you alive. (And staying alive is a good thing, so be sure to thank your circulatory system and all the rest!) These systems include the ones listed in Table 10-5 and described in the following sections.

TABLE 10-5 **Human Body Systems**

System	Components	What the System Does
Nervous system	Cerebrum, cerebellum, medulla, spinal cord, and nerves	Receives, processes, and responds to all physical stimuli; for example, if you burn your hand on the stove, this system prompts you to remove your hand from the stove
Cardiovascular and circulatory systems	Heart, arteries, veins, capillaries, and blood	Delivers oxygenated blood and nutrients from the heart to the rest of the body, whisks away waste products, and returns the blood to the heart to oxygenate it again
Renal system and urinary system	Kidneys, bladder, and urethra	Filters toxins from the blood and sends them out with urine
Respiratory system	Nose, nasal cavity, trachea, and lungs	Inhales air, uses the oxygen in the air to release energy, and exhales the carbon dioxide that results from this process
Digestive system and excretory system	Mouth, esophagus, stomach, and intestines	Breaks down food into smaller substances that the body can absorb and process into energy; eliminates waste from the body
Muscular system	Smooth, cardiac, and skeletal muscles	Allows organs to contract and allows bodily movement
Skeletal system	Bones, joints, tendons, and cartilage	Supports the body's muscles and organs; allows bones and joints to move
Endocrine system	Thyroid, pituitary, adrenal, pineal, and reproductive glands; pancreas; and hormones	Communicates through hormones
Lymphatic system and immune system	Lymph nodes, spleen, tonsils, and lymph	Helps rid the body of toxins, waste, and other materials the body doesn't need; fights infection
Integumentary system and exocrine system	Skin, hair, nails, and exocrine glands such as sweat glands	Protects the body from damage, such as overheating, injuries, abrasion, and loss of water from the outside
Reproductive system	Sex organs and reproductive organs	Enables and controls the production of offspring

Your nervous system is at the wheel, controlling everything that happens in your body. Your cardiovascular system pumps blood to spread oxygen to all your organs and tissues — but it couldn't do that if your respiratory system wasn't bringing in the oxygen in the first place. Your musculoskeletal system enables you to keep bringing in food by eating, and your digestive system turns the food into fuel for your nervous system (and all your other systems).

Some of these functions are involuntary, like breathing and pumping blood through your body. Others, such as eating, running, and scratching the itch on your foot, are voluntary — they require you to actively choose to do something (even if it happens within a split second) and then act on your impulse. When your nervous system takes in stimuli (either through one of your external senses or through an internal stimulus, like hunger), it kicks into high gear. It sends chemical and electrical signals out to the organs that need to participate in what's happening next, and they take action.

Picking your brain: The nervous system

The human brain is part of the *nervous system,* which also includes the spinal cord and billions of nerve cells called neurons. The *central nervous system* contains the cerebrum, which is responsible for thinking, hearing, seeing, and other functions. The cerebellum is also part of the central nervous system; it's the group of nerves responsible for your balance and muscle coordination. The medulla connects your brain to your spinal cord, and it handles all your involuntary actions (including your heartbeat). The spinal cord — the last major component of the central nervous system — is the highway that carries nerve impulses so your brain and organs can communicate. The *peripheral nervous system* is everything else, and it includes every other neuron in your body.

Flowing through the heart, blood, and circulatory system

The *circulatory system* keeps blood with oxygen and nutrients flowing to all your organs so they continue to work. At its core is the *heart,* a four-chambered organ that contracts and relaxes several times each minute. Two chambers collect blood coming in (each is called an atrium, but together, they're atria), and two, called ventricles, pump it back out. Heart valves close after blood leaves, preventing it from coming back in the Exit door.

When blood leaves the heart, it rushes through *arteries* — the largest and thickest tunnels in the circulatory system. These blood-carrying tubes have to be thick and strong, because the heart pumps out oxygenated blood fast, which creates a lot of pressure. Arteries branch out several times (each branch is called an *arteriole*) to send blood into the tissues through tiny tunnels called *capillaries.* Capillaries let out oxygen and nutrients while they take in carbon dioxide and waste in a process called *diffusion* (arteries and veins don't).

Veins carry blood back to the heart, and they don't have thick walls because they don't need them; when blood makes its return trip, it's not under a lot of pressure to get there quickly. The blood going back to the heart is dark red because it's deoxygenated (it drops off all its oxygen to organs and systems when it travels from the heart).

Blood is made up of cells suspended in plasma. Red blood cells carry oxygen, white blood cells fight infection, and platelets are pieces of cells that cause blood to clot. The cells for blood are made in *bone marrow* (the spongy stuff inside the cavities of bones). Types A, B, AB, and O are all the types of blood, which can be positive or negative.

When you donate blood, or when someone donates it to you, your blood types need to match. The exceptions to this rule are Type O negative and Type AB positive. Type O negative blood is considered the *universal donor;* it can be donated to anyone. Type AB positive is the *universal recipient,* which means a person with this blood type can receive any other kind of blood.

Renal 9-1-1: Emergency toxin filtering

The *renal system*, home to the kidneys, ureters, bladder, and urethra, is the main toxin-filtering component of your body. The kidneys filter blood to remove waste, and they produce urine. Together, the ureters, bladder, and urethra form the *urinary tract* — the pathway that carries urine from the body.

The kidneys control excretion of several minerals, so if the body has too many, the kidneys get rid of them. These wonder-organs also monitor and control blood pressure, and they help maintain *homeostasis* (the body's ability to regulate its inner environment so it remains stable, even when outside conditions aren't).

Breathing in and out: The respiratory system

The process of bringing in oxygen and getting rid of carbon dioxide is respiration, and all the magic happens in your nose, mouth, throat, and lungs (with support from your muscles and heart). When you breathe in — a result of your chest cavity expanding, which causes your lungs to suck in air — your nasal cavity filters, warms, and moistens the air. Another filter in the *pharynx* (what usually hurts when you have a sore throat) catches pathogens before they go through your *epiglottis* (the bit that makes a mistake when you choke on food). The final filter is in your *trachea*, which is the area right below the hard lump you can feel in your throat (that's the *larynx*, or voice box).

After all that, the air you breathe goes into your lungs through the left and right bronchi. The bronchi separate into smaller tunnels, called *bronchioles*, and each one ends in a tiny sac, or alveolus (plural alveoli), that puts oxygen into your bloodstream.

You are what you eat: The digestive system

When you pick up an apple, a bag of chips, or a glass of milk, your *digestive system* is gearing up to do its job. This essential system lets you break down food into fuel your body can use. It all starts when you think about food: Your mouth starts to water, and your stomach may start to growl. Those are the signs your digestive system is up and running.

When you eat, your teeth and tongue break the food into smaller parts while your saliva starts to break down starch. Your chewed-up food moves into your esophagus when you swallow, and the esophagus contracts to push the food into your stomach. Gastric acids and a chemical called *pepsin* break the food down further, but the most intense part of the process doesn't start until the food reaches your small intestine.

The small intestine in a normal adult is about 23 feet long, and it produces enzymes that work with other enzymes made in the pancreas and liver to turn fat, carbs, and proteins into useful substances for your body. The large intestine is about 5 feet long; it reabsorbs water and minerals into your body. The kidneys filter liquid waste and secrete it through urine. The solid waste matter left over stays in your rectum until you evacuate it.

Muscling your way through life

Your body has three types of muscles: cardiac, smooth, and skeletal. Some of them you choose to move, while others don't give you any say in the matter. (Remembering to tell your heart to beat would be a pain, anyway.)

» **Cardiac muscle** is only present in your heart. The fibers of these cylindrical, involuntary muscles interlock with each other so that your heart can pump blood. Your heart muscles contract involuntarily — they act on their own, outside your control.

» **Smooth muscle** is the muscle of choice for hollow organs (such as your stomach, lungs, and intestines). These muscles are arranged in parallel lines to form sheets of tissue. Like cardiac muscles, smooth muscles contract involuntarily.

» **Skeletal muscle** is what makes you run, jump, and use the remote control to stream your favorite TV shows. They're *striated* (they appear striped under a microscope) and cylindrical. These muscles are voluntary because you can consciously decide to use them.

Taking the skeletons out of the closet

Your *skeletal system* is the frame that holds your body together, keeps you upright, and in some ways protects you from injury. Humans have an *endoskeleton* — one that's inside the body and covered by soft tissue. Other animals (such as armadillos, grasshoppers, and lobsters) have *exoskeletons* that protect their soft tissues. Some animals, such as jellyfish, don't have skeletons at all.

The skeletal system includes bones, cartilage, ligaments, and tendons. Bones start their lives as cartilage, but over time, the cartilage is replaced by calcium and phosphorus in a process called *ossification.* (That's the technical term for bone formation.) Cartilage is much more flexible than bone is, but because bone is still living tissue, it can repair itself when it's damaged or broken.

The human body has several types of joints, but they all share one thing in common: They enable two or more bones to move relative to each other. Here are the seven major types of joints:

» **Hinge joints,** such as those at your elbows and knees, work like a door hinge or the binding of a book.

» **Ball and socket joints,** like those in your shoulders and hips, consist of a ball-like end that fits into a bowl-shaped receptacle. They work like a joystick, allowing you a wide range of motion.

» **Pivot joints** allow you to rotate one bone around another because one bone fits into a ring formed by another bone. You find them in your neck's first and second vertebrae (that's what allows you to move your head back and forth).

» **Fixed joints** are places where two separate bones meet, but there's no room or ability for movement. Your skull has fixed joints.

» **Saddle joints** are joints that let you move one bone in an oval motion. Rotate your thumb to see a saddle joint in action.

» **Condyloid joints** allow back-and-forth and side-to-side movement. You find condyloid joints in your knuckles (the ones connected to your hand bones, not the ones halfway up your fingers). They give you the range of motion you need to signal that you want five cheeseburgers and to make a fist.

» **Gliding joints** occur between the surfaces of two bones held together by ligaments. They're in your wrists and ankles and between the tiny bones in your feet.

Ligaments and tendons help your bones move so you can move. *Ligaments* join the bones (think of them like rubber bands), while *tendons* connect muscle tissue to bones and other structures in your body (like your eyeballs).

Ending up in the endocrine system

The glands that produce hormones to regulate reproduction and sexual function, growth and development, tissue function, sleep, mood, and a whole host of other actions are part of the *endocrine system*. This system uses hormones to communicate with organs and other glands.

The lymphatic system: When things go haywire

The body's *lymphatic* and *immune systems* include *lymph* (a fluid that contains white blood cells that fight infection). These systems can fight off many bacteria and viruses, which are everywhere. *Bacteria* are single-celled organisms that cause illnesses such as pneumonia and staph infections, and *viruses* cause illnesses like colds and HIV. The bacteria and viruses that cause diseases evolve — sometimes very quickly, such as when antibiotic resistance pops up — and the lymphatic system responds quickly to new challenges from newly evolved organisms.

Antibiotics can be used to treat bacterial infections, but they don't work on viruses. Scientists have had a tough time defeating most viruses, except through prevention by way of vaccines. Vaccinations prevent disease and pick up where the immune system leaves off.

TECHNICAL STUFF

Human bodies are always in a balancing act between staying healthy and falling apart. Some illnesses and diseases are caused by diet and lifestyle, so they're preventable. Others are genetic and ingrained in DNA. Still others come through pathogens, such as bacteria and viruses; sometimes these illnesses and diseases are preventable, too. Disease-carrying organisms are called *vectors*, and they include mosquitoes, rats, and ticks.

Damage control through the integumentary system

The *integumentary system* protects you from getting scuffed up, losing all the water in your body, and smashing your bones when you miss the nail and hit your thumb with a hammer. The largest organ in your body — your skin — is part of this essential system. It also includes your fingernails, hair, and sweat glands, as well as *sebaceous glands* (the ones responsible for oily skin) and *ceruminous* glands (the purveyors of earwax). The whole system protects you from more severe injuries, but it's also there to produce vitamin D that your body needs.

THE FIRST TROOP INOCULATION: SMALLPOX

General George Washington, the commander-in-chief of the Continental Army, was also the first person ever to command his troops to be inoculated against disease. In 1777, Washington ordered that his soldiers be exposed to mild forms of the smallpox virus to prevent them from getting a more serious version of the disease. His decision was based on the fact that about 5,000 Continental soldiers came down with smallpox after a skirmish near Quebec — but most of the British, Canadians, and Native Americans who were also involved didn't even get sick. Some historians believe that if Continental troops had been inoculated earlier, the Revolutionary War would've ended sooner (and the spoils may have included some or all of Canada). The actual smallpox vaccine wasn't invented until 1796, 13 years after the revolution ended.

Today, troops are tested for immunity to a variety of diseases as soon as they arrive at basic training. Any who aren't immune receive vaccinations to protect them against diseases they can pick up here or overseas, from the flu and chickenpox to smallpox and anthrax.

Continuing the species through the reproductive system

Like any species, humans have to reproduce to ensure long-term survival. Sex organs, including external organs and internal ones like testes, ovaries, fallopian tubes, the uterus, sperm and eggs (ova) work together to pass the genes down to the next generation. I discuss how genetics and DNA combine to make new humans (the tiny kind) in the later section "Swimming in the Gene Pool: Genetics."

Human reproduction can't occur unless a male's sperm fertilizes a female's ovum. Women release an egg from an ovary approximately once every 28 days. The egg travels down the fallopian tube and into the uterus, where it waits for fertilization. If it's not fertilized, the endometrial lining comes off in a process called menstruation — but if sperm does fertilize it, the egg turns into a zygote. If conditions are right, the zygote can implant itself in the uterus and eventually develop into a fetus.

Keeping the body in peak operating condition

In order to work properly (so all those functions can keep on keepin' on), your body needs plenty of fuel — and that comes in the form of food, vitamins, minerals, and water. You need the following:

>> **Carbohydrates for energy:** Carbohydrates come from starches and sugars, such as bread, pasta, fruit, and candy bars.

>> **Fats for energy:** Too much fat is bad, but you do need some in your diet. Fats fall into three categories: saturated, monounsaturated, and polyunsaturated. Polyunsaturated fats are required for normal body functions, but your body can't make them, so you have to eat foods that contain them (such as many vegetable oils, walnuts, and some fish). Saturated fats come from meat, shellfish, eggs, and dairy. Monounsaturated fats come from olives, avocados, and some nuts.

>> **Fiber for getting rid of waste products:** Leafy green vegetables, beans, potatoes, and fruits have plenty of fiber.

>> **Minerals for various bodily functions:** A few necessary minerals include iron to develop red blood cells, calcium to keep your bones strong, and potassium to keep your heart's electrical activity in check. A well-balanced diet ensures you're getting the minerals you need, but some people need supplements.

>> **Protein for growth, maintenance, and repair:** Humans consume protein through meat, fish, beans, nuts, and a handful of other sources.

>> **Vitamins for various bodily functions:** You can usually get all the 13 essential vitamins from fruits, veggies, and the sun. Your body uses them for things such as blood clotting, processing food, and regulating your hormones.

>> **Water to keep your cells from shriveling up and withering away:** Most foods contain water, but you still need to drink water as well. Humans lose about four pints of water each day, and you have to replace it or face serious health consequences, such as headaches, cramps, and even death.

TECHNICAL STUFF

While you're in basic training, your diet is extremely balanced. You may not have time to actually *taste* your food (which can be a good thing in some military dining facilities), but rest assured that the military is making sure you get what you need to become a lean, mean, fighting machine.

Digging through Plant Physiology

Plants, like animals, are made from cells and tissues. Plants have organs, too, but they're quite a bit different from humans' organs. Most plants have two organ systems. One consists of its underground roots, and the other consists of above-ground shoots (stems, leaves, flowers, and seeds).

The roots bring in nutrients and anchor the plant to the ground. The stem is like the plant's spine, supporting it above ground and serving as a highway for nutrients and water between roots and leaves. The leaves collect energy from the sun and host the processes that make food for the plant through photosynthesis.

Types of plants

Scientists usually put plants in one of four major groups based on the types of tissues they have and how they reproduce. Plants fall under the Linnaean taxonomic system, too (which you can read about in the "Categorizing Mother Nature" section earlier in this chapter).

>> **Angiosperms** are flowering plants. These plants have vascular tissue (tissue that transports fluid and nutrients internally, which is similar to human veins) and produce flowers and seeds. Angiosperms include roses and all the flowers in your garden; palm trees; and apple trees.

>> **Bryophytes** are plants that don't have a vascular system and don't produce flowers or seeds. They reproduce by releasing spores. Lichen, liverwort, and many types of mosses are bryophytes.

>> **Ferns** are plants with vascular tissue, but they don't produce seeds.

>> **Gymnosperms** are plants that produce cones and seeds rather than flowers, and they have vascular tissue, too. Your Christmas tree is a gymnosperm, as are California's giant sequoias and most non-flowering shrubs.

Where plant processes take place

Plants sustain themselves by pulling nutrients and water from the soil, capturing energy from the sun, and taking carbon dioxide from the air. Table 10-6 shows how plants use their organs to stay alive and well, and Figure 10-2 shows the basic anatomy of a plant.

TABLE 10-6 Plant Systems and Functions

System	Components	What the System Does
Root	Vascular tissue, primary roots, and secondary roots (branches)	Absorbs water and nutrients from the soil, holds the plant in place, and stores nutrients
Shoot	Vascular tissue, stem or stalk, leaves, flowers, cones	Allows the plant to grow taller, absorbs light energy from the sun, converts energy, absorbs carbon dioxide, and releases oxygen

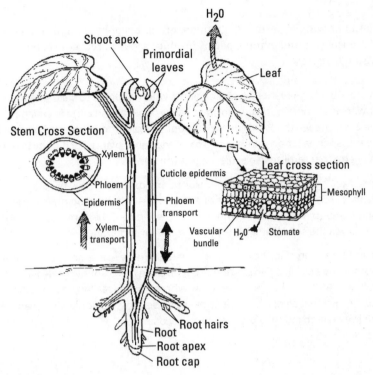

FIGURE 10-2:
The
anatomy
of a plant.

© John Wiley & Sons, Inc.

A plant's stem is technically part of its shoot system, but it has several big jobs. It moves water and nutrients between roots and leaves, holds the plant upright so it can grow taller (and access more sun so it can grow even taller), and redirects the plant's growth.

Plants make their own food through *photosynthesis,* which takes place in the leaves. All they need are carbon dioxide, water, and sunlight. Photosynthesis occurs in two stages: light-dependent reactions and the Calvin cycle.

Light-dependent reactions happen when chlorophyll (the chemical substance that makes plants green) and other pigments absorb energy from sunlight. The energy splits water molecules into hydrogen and oxygen (I explain molecular structures in Chapter 11), and the oxygen evaporates into the atmosphere when temperatures heat up. The hydrogen that's left behind combines with carbon dioxide the plant absorbs to form glucose — that's what plants "eat."

The Calvin cycle is a series of chemical reactions that take place during photosynthesis. These reactions can only happen after the plant has captured energy from sunlight.

TECHNICAL STUFF

Every living organism on earth is carbon-based. Carbon atoms form the backbone of nearly every molecule that makes up creatures and plants that can live in Earth's environment. Carbon, as an element, is really, *really* good at bonding to other elements. It's so good that it can bond with itself to create long carbon chains and rings — and without it, DNA wouldn't be possible.

Plant reproduction

Plants, like all other organisms, need to reproduce. They can do so sexually (when two cells carrying half the DNA necessary for a new, whole cell join) or asexually (when one cell splits into two identical cells).

More advanced plants are angiosperms or gymnosperms; bryophytes and ferns are considered primitive plants. Angiosperms and gymnosperms produce seeds to reproduce, but bryophytes and ferns reproduce through spores.

>> **Angiosperms** are the most advanced types of plants when it comes to sexual reproduction. They create flowers that contain *stigma,* which produces pollen, and *carpels,* which catch pollen. A bug, a bird, or even the wind can pick up pollen from one flower and deposit it on the stigma of the same species (or on another stigma of the same plant). Each particle of pollen grain contains sperm that fertilizes an *ovule* (egg) in the flower.

>> **Gymnosperms** sexually reproduce in ways similar to angiosperms. They produce naked seeds — seeds that aren't wrapped in a fruit or seed pod — that develop on the upper surfaces of cone scales (pine trees are gymnosperms, and pine cones are where seeds develop). Wind carries the seeds where they need to be for fertilization.

>> **Bryophytes and ferns** reproduce sexually and asexually. They use spores, which contain male and female reproductive organs. Fertilization occurs before the plant ever releases a spore. After a plant releases a spore, the spore can grow where it lands (as long as conditions are right). Scientists believe that all plants were once spore-bearing, and only after plants evolved and adapted to live on land did they begin to form seeds.

Thinking Small: A Look at Cells

Living things are made up of cells that share certain characteristics. Cells come in different sizes and shapes, depending on what they do. In the human body, a muscle cell looks very different from a brain cell. Cells combine to create tissues, which form structures like bones and skin.

Inspecting cell structure

Nearly all cells have four things in common. Each has a nucleus, cytoplasm, a membrane, and ribosomes.

>> **Nucleus:** The *nucleus* (plural *nuclei*) controls cellular activity. It's like the brains behind the cell, and it holds the cell's genetic material — DNA.

Bacteria are *prokaryotes,* which means their cells don't have nuclei. Their genetic material floats in the cytoplasm instead of being held inside a membrane *(nuclear envelope).*

>> **Cytoplasm:** The *cytoplasm* is a gel-like substance, composed mostly of water, that's inside the cell membrane and outside the nucleus. Cytoplasm contains many chemicals that carry out the life processes in the cell.

>> **Cell membrane (plasma membrane):** This thin membrane holds the cell together, protecting the nucleus and cytoplasm.

>> **Ribosomes:** *Ribosomes* manufacture proteins that the cell uses to perform work. They're necessary for biochemical reactions inside cells that allow them to survive.

See Figure 10-3 for a description of other cell structures.

Plant Cell

1. Chloroplast: Contains chlorophyll, which produces food
2. Cell wall: Protects the cell
3. Nucleus: The "brain" of the cell
4. Chromatin: Thin fibers containing genes
5. Nucleoplasm: Protoplasm (living material) in the nucleus
6. Ribosome: Combines amino acids into proteins
7. Cytoplasm: The cell's factory
8. Mitochondria: Produce the energy for cellular activity
9. Cell membrane: Contains the cellular material within it
10. Vacuole: Storage area

Animal Cell

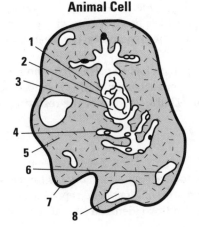

1. Nucleus
2. Chromatin
3. Nucleoplasm
4. Ribosome
5. Cytoplasm
6. Mitochondria
7. Cell membrane
8. Vacuole

FIGURE 10-3: Basic structures of plant and animal cells.

© John Wiley & Sons, Inc.

REMEMBER

Plant cells differ from animal cells in several ways:

>> Plant cells have a firm cell wall that supports and protects the cell. Animal cells don't have such a structure.

>> Plant cells have larger *vacuoles* (storage areas) than those found in animal cells.

>> Unlike animal cells, many plant cells contain *chloroplasts,* which contain *chlorophyll,* a chemical that helps plants create food with the help of sunlight.

>> Animal cells contain *centrioles* (cylindrical structures involved in cell division). Most plant and fungus cells don't.

>> Animal cells have *lysosomes* (sacs of enzymes), which aren't found in plant cells.

Profiting from cell processes

Cells perform various processes to function at an optimum level. Here are a few of these processes:

>> **Metabolism:** Chemical processes within a cell that are necessary to maintain life

>> **Osmosis:** Movement of liquid through the cell membrane (and the main way that water goes in and out of cells)

>> **Phagocytosis:** Acquisition of particles of material from outside the cell; it's accomplished by surrounding the particles and passing them through the cell membrane

>> **Photosynthesis:** Conversion of light energy from the sun to chemical energy that the cell can use

>> **Cellular respiration:** Process in which biochemical energy from nutrients turns into products the cell can use; one of the ways a cell releases chemical energy to fuel its activity

Swimming in the Gene Pool: Genetics

You might have your grandma's eyes, your great-grandpa's nose, or your great-great-grandfather's height. Whether you like it or not, it happens because parents pass their traits on to their offspring. Understanding genetics — how traits are physically passed from parents to offspring and what happens when the process goes wrong — helps scientists pinpoint the causes of diseases and disorders and can help them develop treatments and cures.

REMEMBER

In human genetics, a healthy person has 23 pairs of *chromosomes* (the structure that contains the genes). The mother and the father each supply one chromosome per pair. Genes contained in the chromosomes determine many characteristics of the resulting child.

Copying genes

When body cells multiply to produce tissues and organs (and eventually a complete living thing), they reproduce their genetic material. Most cells reproduce by *mitosis,* in which the nucleus of a cell divides, forming two cells and two identical sets of chromosomes.

However, sex cells (eggs and sperm) reproduce differently. Through *meiosis,* each cell divides into four cells, each containing only half the number of chromosomes as a nonsex cell. This process takes place so the sex cells of one person (with 23 chromosomes) can hook up with the sex cells of another person (with 23 chromosomes) to produce 46 chromosomes, or 23 pairs. Otherwise, way too many chromosomes would be floating around.

Sometimes cells don't copy themselves and divide perfectly. This frequently results in a fetus who doesn't live or in a fetus with a genetic disease or disorder. For example, Down syndrome is the result of a fetus's having 47 rather than 46 chromosomes.

Determining your sex with two little letters

The genes on one pair of chromosomes, called the *sex chromosomes,* determine whether a child will be a biological male or female. In females, the two sex chromosomes are alike, and they're labeled XX. In males, the chromosomes are different and are labeled XY.

TECHNICAL STUFF

The child always receives an X chromosome from the mother (who only has XX chromosomes). The father (who has XY chromosomes) can contribute either an X or a Y chromosome, so Papa actually determines the sex of the child.

Knowing which genes get passed down the family line

Many characteristics that you possess (from the way your nose turns up at the end to the color of your eyes) are determined by a pair of genes (or multiple pairs of genes). These two genes may be alike, or they may not.

Some genes are dominant, and some genes are recessive. If you have two unlike genes, the characteristic that they produce comes from the *dominant gene;* the gene that doesn't overshadow the other is called the *recessive gene.* If each parent has two unlike genes, both parents will have the dominant trait, but they can have a child with the recessive trait — because each parent contributes a gene to the offspring, each parent may contribute a recessive gene to the child. Whew!

Using Common Sense to Hypothesize about Answers

If you don't know the answer to a question right off the bat, don't panic. You can often eliminate a few incorrect choices simply by using common sense. Even if you can't determine the answer, keep in mind that this subtest doesn't penalize you for guessing (unless you guess incorrectly on several questions in a row at the end of the subtest when taking the CAT-ASVAB). Guessing makes sense; you have a 25% chance of guessing the right answer even if you can't eliminate any obviously wrong answers. If you can eliminate just one wrong answer, you improve your chances to 33%.

REMEMBER

Most people don't have to rush to finish the General Science subtest, but then again, you don't have much leisure time to stop and think about all the questions at length, either. If you don't know the answer to a question right away, do your best to eliminate wrong answers quickly, make your best guess, and move along. (For help on making these eliminating decisions, check out Chapter 3.)

Try the process of elimination on the following question:

EXAMPLE

The knee joint is known as a

(A) pivot joint.

(B) fixed joint.

(C) ball-and-socket joint.

(D) hinge joint.

Looking at the choices, you can eliminate Choice (A), pivot joint, because if you picture something that pivots, you think of it moving in a circular or at least a semi-circular manner. Your knee doesn't do that, so that choice is out the window. Choice (B), fixed joint, can't be right either; your knee isn't stuck in one position (or if it is, it shouldn't be). A ball-and-socket joint is one that permits limited movement in any direction (your shoulder joint is a ball-and-socket joint). Your knee doesn't do that, so you can strike off Choice (C) and choose Choice (D), hinge joint, as the most likely answer. Your knee moves like a door on a hinge.

General and Life Science Practice Questions

General science and life science are both broad topics. To score well on this subtest, you pretty much have to wade through the textbooks and memorize the facts. See how well you do on the following 10 practice questions.

1. A cell nucleus is often referred to as the

    (A) control center.

    (B) cytoskeleton.

    (C) cell membrane.

    (D) chromosome.

2. The human circulatory system

    (A) uses air to release energy.

    (B) processes food and eliminates waste.

    (C) moves oxygenated blood throughout the body.

    (D) controls movement of joints.

3. Proteins come from all the following sources except

    (A) beans.

    (B) water.

    (C) meat.

    (D) eggs.

4. Animals that eat only plants are called

    (A) vegivores.

    (B) carnivores.

    (C) omnivores.

    (D) herbivores.

5. The nasal cavity is part of which system?

    (A) respiratory

    (B) cardiac

    (C) muscular

    (D) lymphatic

6. The gram is a unit of

    (A) liquid measurement.

    (B) mass.

    (C) distance.

    (D) temperature.

7. The first step in the scientific method is to

    (A) ask questions.

    (B) test hypotheses.

    (C) make observations.

    (D) create a theory.

8. In the term *Homo sapiens*, the word *sapiens* describes the organism's

    (A) genus.

    (B) domain.

    (C) species.

    (D) phylum.

9. Most cells reproduce by

    (A) meiosis.

    (B) mitosis.

    (C) photosynthesis.

    (D) osmosis.

10. Where would you find a hinge joint in the human body?

    (A) the neck

    (B) the elbow

    (C) the hip

    (D) the toes

Answers and Explanations

Use this answer key to score the General Science practice questions.

1. **A.** The nucleus contains most of the cell's genetic material and is often referred to as the control center of the cell, so the correct answer is Choice (A).

2. **C.** The respiratory system uses air to release energy, the digestive system processes food and eliminates waste, and the musculoskeletal system controls the movement of joints. The correct answer is Choice (C).

3. **B.** Beans, meat, and eggs all contain protein necessary for body functions, but water doesn't. That makes Choice (B) the right answer.

4. **D.** An herbivore is an animal that eats only plants, so Choice (D) is correct. Carnivores eat meat, and omnivores eat both meat and plants. (And for the record, vegivores aren't a thing.)

5. **A.** The nasal cavity, where air enters your body, is part of the respiratory system. Other parts of this system include the nose, lungs, and trachea.

6. **B.** The gram is a unit of mass in the metric system, making Choice (B) the only right answer.

7. **C.** The scientific method starts with observation. Scientists then ask questions, develop a hypothesis, make predictions about what will happen, and test the hypothesis.

8. **C.** Species is the most specific classification in the Linnaean taxonomic system, and *sapiens* is a species. Domain is the broadest, and phylum and genus are between the two. (*Homo* in this question is the genus.)

9. **B.** Most cells reproduce by mitosis, the process of dividing into two separate cells with identical DNA, so Choice (B) is correct. By contrast, meiosis is the process of cells separating into four separate cells. Photosynthesis refers to plants making energy from light, and osmosis is the transfer of liquid between cell walls.

10. **B.** Hinge joints are found at the elbows and knees, and they allow bones to move back and forth (like a door that opens and closes).

IN THIS CHAPTER

» **Unearthing elements**

» **Compounding chemistry facts**

» **Seeing what's up with SI units**

» **Studying matter, mass, and motion**

» **Finding out about physics topics like frequencies and magnets**

Chapter **11**
Physical Sciences

B rushing up on your chemistry and physics knowledge for the General Science subtest on the ASVAB is essential if you want to snag a good score for a particular job. And don't worry — this subtest doesn't factor into your Armed Forces Qualification Test (AFQT) score, so you can still join the military if you don't know an atom from Adam. (See Appendix A to figure out which military jobs require a solid General Science score.)

As you study, remember that understanding the principles behind the facts is what's important. You don't see these exact questions (or questions from any other test-prep book) on the ASVAB, but you do encounter the principles I cover in this chapter.

You have 10 minutes to answer 15 questions on the General Science subtest if you're taking the CAT-ASVAB (and 20 minutes for 30 questions if your test includes the tryout questions I describe in Chapter 1). If you're going the old-fashioned paper-and-pencil route, you get 11 minutes to answer 25 questions. As long as you focus on finding the right answers (and you've checked out the tips for guessing in Chapter 3), you should have plenty of time. The questions in this subtest are pretty cut-and-dried, which means you know the answers or you don't.

WARNING

When you answer an easy question correctly on the CAT-ASVAB, you're most likely going to get a question of medium difficulty next. Get that one right, and you'll be facing down a hard question. If you get hard questions right, you see more of them, but if you get them wrong, the computer dials back to medium and easy questions. Making sure you have the basics nailed down before you start studying (or even brushing up on) more advanced subjects is usually a good idea.

If the job you want requires a good score on the General Science subtest, this chapter is one you need to bookmark. You can also check out *Chemistry For Dummies* by John T. Moore, along with *Physics I For Dummies* and *Physics II For Dummies* by Steven Holzner, PhD (all from Wiley).

Chemistry: Not Blowing Up the Lab

Chemists study matter, and everything that has mass and takes up space — including your old Chevy that's up on blocks and the mosquito buzzing around the room — is matter. All matter is made up of basic substances (building blocks) called *elements*.

REMEMBER

In order to study matter, chemists use exactly what scientists in other fields use: the scientific method, which I discuss in Chapter 10. The careful steps scientists follow help ensure they cover all their bases. Figure 11-1 shows the way the scientific method works in a loop so scientists can continue learning (even when they think they already know the answers).

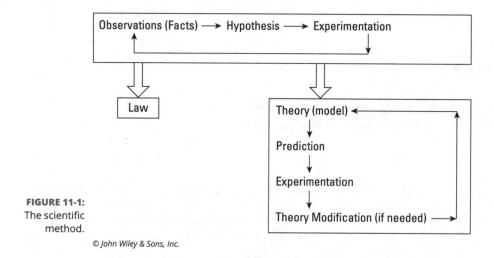

FIGURE 11-1:
The scientific method.

© John Wiley & Sons, Inc.

How chemists look at things

Chemists see the world two ways: on a macroscopic level and on a microscopic level. *Macroscopic* refers to the world-at-large — all the stuff you can see right now. *Microscopic* refers to a much smaller level, where gas particles bump into each other and atoms bind together.

They use the information they gather to analyze substances, create compounds (a process called *synthesis*), create models and test theories, and measure substances' physical properties.

EVERYDAY CHEMISTRY

Everything on Earth is made from chemical elements — your desk, this book, your dog, and even your body. In fact, your body contains a significant amount of a chemical called dihydrogen oxide, and the same substance covers about 71 percent of the Earth.

Dihydrogen oxide is just water, but in scientific terms, it's still a chemical. Many of the things around you are made from chemicals that have been engineered to make your life better (the result of the scientific method). Look under your kitchen sink at the cleaning supplies — all engineered to kill germs and cut through grime. What about your clothes? Chemists worked in a lab to develop nylon, rayon, and polyester. Even your food is made up of chemical elements (some natural, some concocted in a lab).

Chemists typically use the SI system for measurements (flip to Chapter 10 for details) so they can communicate in the same scientific language as other chemists around the world. The base unit for length in the SI system is the *meter*, the unit for mass is the *kilogram*, and the main units of volume are the *cubic meter* and *liter*. Temperature is measured in *kelvins*, and pressure is measured in *pascals* and *newtons*. Finally, energy is measured in *joules* and *calories*.

Understanding the elements, my dear Watson

The *atom* is the smallest part of an element that still retains the characteristics of that element. Every atom has particles — pieces of matter that are very, very small. *Electrons* are negatively charged particles that float around the atom's *nucleus*, or core, which is made up of *neutrons* (particles with no charge) and *protons* (positively charged particles).

REMEMBER

Each element has its own atomic number that's equal to the number of protons it has. If an atom has one proton in its nucleus, it has the atomic number 1. Hydrogen is the only element with just one proton in its nucleus. Magnesium, which has 12 protons in its nucleus, is given the atomic number 12.

Atoms can combine with each other to form *molecules.* If those atoms are of two or more different elements, the molecule is called a *compound.* A compound can have very different properties from the elements that make it up. For example, table salt, which is mostly harmless, consists of two lethal elements — sodium and chlorine. But when combined, these elements make a compound that people ingest every day: salt.

Sitting down at the periodic table

The *periodic table* (also known as the table of elements) classifies all elements, because scientists love to classify things. Elements are listed according to their atomic numbers (number of protons) and are arranged into *families* of similar elements.

The periodic table lists the atomic number, the abbreviation for each element, and its *atomic weight,* which is the average mass of one atom of the element. Looking at Figure 11-2, you can see that copper (Cu, atomic number 29) has an atomic weight of 63.546, which means that copper is much, much heavier than helium (He, atomic number 2), which has an atomic weight of 4.0026.

You don't have to memorize these charts to do well on the ASVAB, but knowing the atomic numbers for common elements such as hydrogen (1), helium (2), carbon (6), nitrogen (7), and oxygen (8) can't hurt.

Changing states: Physical and chemical moves for molecules

Particles of matter are always in motion. How much kinetic energy (motion energy) a particle has determines whether the matter is a solid, liquid, or gas in its normal state. (The later section "Measuring work, force, energy, and power" has more on kinetic energy.) Gas particles move around very quickly, liquid particles move more slowly, and solid particles move much more slowly than either of the other two.

When heat or cold is applied to matter, the kinetic energy of the matter changes; therefore, the nature of the substance can change. Heat applied to water changes the water from a liquid to a gas (steam), and cold applied to water changes it from a liquid to a solid (ice). When physical changes occur, the molecule itself remains the same. For example, water is still made of hydrogen and oxygen, no matter which state it's in.

FIGURE 11-2:
The periodic
table.

© John Wiley & Sons, Inc.

Scientists can distinguish these states (shown in Figure 11-3) at the macroscopic level *and* the microscopic level.

» **Solids** have particles or molecules that are close together and don't move much, and they have a definite shape. In many cases, that's because the molecules are bound together in a very rigid structure of repeating patterns. The structure is called *crystal lattice.* The molecules are still moving, but not much.

» **Liquids** have particles that are a bit more spread out than they are in solids. The big difference? They move around a lot more. Liquids don't have definite shapes, but they do have a definite volume. (Picture one cup of orange juice in a plastic box and one cup of orange juice in a coffee mug. They both have the same volume — one cup — but they definitely have different shapes.)

» **Gases** have particles that are much more spread out than they are in solids or liquids, and they move faster, too. Gases have no definite shape and no definite volume. The molecules move independently of one another, so gases expand to fill the area that contains them. You can compress gases (such as in a SCUBA tank) or release them (like when you turn the knob and release the gas from the same SCUBA tank).

FIGURE 11-3:
States of
matter.

(a) solid   (b) liquid   (c) gas

© John Wiley & Sons, Inc.

Matter can — and does — change states. It usually takes extreme conditions to change the state of matter, like boiling or freezing. For example, an ice cube is a solid, but it quickly becomes a liquid when you leave it on the sidewalk in the sun. Soon after that, it evaporates into a gas. As molecules heat up, they move more quickly and become more spread out.

Boiling and freezing

When you're making spaghetti for dinner, the first thing you do is boil a pot of water so you have an environment that's hot enough to change the spaghetti from a very solid piece of pasta to a softer (and much tastier) piece of pasta without catching it on fire. You eat the pasta while it's transitioning between states; it's still a solid, but it's a much *softer* solid. If you leave the pasta in boiling water for too long, it'll turn into mush and eventually become a liquid.

Heating water changes its state. The molecules begin to move faster as they absorb heat, and the temperature rises until water reaches its boiling point. (Water's boiling point varies based on atmospheric pressure, but if you're at sea level, it's 100 degrees Celsius or 212 degrees Fahrenheit.) The temperature stays constant until all the liquid *evaporates* into a gas (water turns into steam). Steam contains the same molecules water does (H_2O), but in each state, the molecules are at different distances and moving at different speeds.

Cooling water changes its state, too. *Condensation* — the process of a substance changing from a gas to a liquid — is the first phase change liquids go through as they cool; it's the opposite of evaporation. When your glasses fog up when you open the dishwasher, when you see dew on the grass in the morning, or when your cup of cold liquid "sweats" on a hot day, you're watching liquids condense. These events happen because your glasses, the ground, and your cup are colder than the environment they're in; they cause water molecules in the air to gather together and form a liquid.

Freezing is another way to change a molecule's state. The molecule's freezing point is the same as its melting point; it's just that the thermostat is moving in the opposite direction. Cooling a substance slows down the motion of its molecules until it becomes a solid.

TECHNICAL STUFF

Most substances go through the same progression of events to change states, but some elements go through the process of sublimation instead. *Sublimation* occurs when a substance goes directly from a solid state to a gaseous state with no liquid state in-between. One example is dry ice. Dry ice is solid carbon dioxide, and it's often used to create a smoke or fog effect in magic shows (and nightclubs). Dry ice turns into a colorless gas, but it creates a white cloud as it evaporates (the white cloud it forms is actually condensation of water vapor in the air because the dry ice is so cold). The reverse of sublimation is called *deposition*, where a gaseous substance becomes a solid without a liquid state in-between.

Compounds, mixtures, and reactions: When elements get together

Elements that combine can join together in specific ratios, mix and mingle in different ratios, or react to each other to create different substances.

Compounds: Adding elements together

Compounds are elements that have joined by chemical bonds in a specific ratio. The water that comes out of your tap is a compound made of two elements: hydrogen (represented by H in the periodic table) and oxygen (represented by O in the periodic table). These elements together make water if they're combined only in a very specific way: two hydrogen atoms for every one oxygen atom (that's why you see the compound written as H_2O). The little number 2 between the two elements tells you the compound has two hydrogen atoms; because there's no number after the O, you can assume that the compound has just one of them.

REMEMBER

As you read a chemical formula, you have to deal with molecules and compounds in shorthand. The number of molecules is listed in front of the molecule, so you write "five molecules of helium" as "5He." You write the number of atoms in a molecule in subscript after the elemental symbol, so hydrogen with two atoms is H_2. Sometimes formulas have brackets, just like algebraic formulas do, to separate them when they're complex. Table 11-1 gives you examples of how to read chemical formulas. Use Figure 11-2 (the periodic table) earlier in the chapter to figure out which elements are in each compound.

TABLE 11-1 ## Examples of Chemical Formulas

Formula	Shorthand	Number of Molecules	Number of Atoms	Name
$NaHCO_3$	Na = sodium	1 sodium	1 sodium	Baking soda
	H = hydrogen	1 hydrogen	1 hydrogen	
	C = carbon	1 carbon	1 carbon	
	O = oxygen	1 oxygen	3 oxygen	
NaCl	Na = sodium	1 sodium	1 sodium	Table salt
	Cl = chlorine	1 chlorine	1 chlorine	
$C_3H_5(NO_3)_3$	C = carbon	1 carbon	3 carbon	Nitroglycerin
	H = hydrogen	1 hydrogen	5 hydrogen	
	N = nitrogen	1 nitrogen	3 nitrogen	
	O = oxygen	1 oxygen	9 oxygen	
$AgNO_3$	Ag = silver	1 silver	1 silver	Silver nitrate
	N = nitrogen	1 nitrogen	1 nitrogen	
	O = oxygen	1 oxygen	3 oxygen	
$C_{10}H_{14}N_2$	C = carbon	1 carbon	10 carbon	Nicotine
	H = hydrogen	1 hydrogen	14 hydrogen	
	N = nitrogen	1 nitrogen	2 nitrogen	

The ASVAB may dish up a question or two that asks you to identify one (or more) of the components of a chemical formula. Though you don't have to memorize the symbols for each element, knowing how formulas work (and how to break them apart) can help boost your score. If you think of atoms like LEGO blocks that you can arrange into different structures (and make parts for an even bigger structure), you can visualize the letters and numbers inside brackets as parts that can be added to other molecules. Those parts are called *functional groups*. Like atoms, you indicate how many of these groups there are with the subscript number. $(NO_3)_3$ means that there are three NO_3 functional groups.

Here's an example: I always add two (sometimes more) teaspoons of good, old-fashioned $C_{12}H_{22}O_{11}$ (that's sugar) to my coffee in the morning. Look at Figure 11-2 earlier in the chapter. Based on sugar's molecular formula, you can tell that it has 12 carbon atoms, 22 hydrogen atoms, and 11 oxygen atoms in each molecule. These three elements together, in this ratio only, make up sugar.

If one is off, even by one atom, my coffee would taste a lot different (and may even be toxic). Acetone, which removes paint, serves as an ingredient in rubber cement, and does a bunch of other non-food-related tasks, is also made up of carbon, hydrogen, and oxygen. (In case you were wondering, acetone's chemical makeup is $(CH_3)_2 O$, and it's nasty in coffee.)

Mixtures: Physical combinations of pure substances

In chemistry, a *mixture* is a physical combination of pure substances that don't have a constant composition. The composition of the mixture depends on who makes it. Bread tastes different when it comes from two different bakers because each uses a slightly different mixture even though they use all the same ingredients. In a mixture, though, each substance keeps its own chemical characteristics (the flour, oil, and water keep the same molecular structures from start to finish).

Chemical reactions

Boiling and freezing are changes in a substance's state (as I discuss earlier in the chapter), but a *chemical reaction* is a process that rearranges a substance's molecular structure. No matter what its physical state, water is still made up of H_2O. But if you compound it with another element, its atoms are redistributed to create a new substance. For example, when iron rusts, a chemical change occurs. The rust isn't the same molecule as the iron is.

In a normal chemical reaction, matter is neither created nor destroyed. That means the total mass of *reactants* (the elements that are changing) is the same as the total mass of *products* (the elements that have changed).

There are several types of chemical reactions, but the most common are these:

>> **Combination:** *Combination reactions* occur when two or more reactants merge to form one product. One example is the way sodium and chlorine combine to create sodium chloride (that's table salt).

>> **Decomposition:** *Decomposition reactions* are the opposite of combination reactions because a single compound breaks down into two or more simpler substances. This process happens when water decomposes into hydrogen and oxygen gases, for example.

>> **Combustion:** *Combustion reactions* typically involve carbon and oxygen in the process known as burning. This type of reaction occurs in your car, in open fires, and when some people try to cook.

Covering all the bases (and the acids, too)

Aqueous chemical compounds, substances, and mixtures (those that contain water) can be bases, acids, or neutral (neither an acid nor a base).

A *base* is a substance that gives up negatively charged hydroxyl ions when dissolved in water; they're often called *alkaline* substances. Liquid soap, ammonia, and baking soda are all bases. An *acid* gives up positively charged hydrogen ions when dissolved in water. Some examples of acids include vinegar, orange juice, and sulfuric acid.

Whether a solution is basic or acidic, it can be measured on a pH scale. The pH scale ranges from 0 to 14, with 0 being the most acidic (that's where you find battery acid) and 14 being the most basic (that's where liquid drain cleaner hangs out). Pure water falls right in the middle, at a very neutral 7. Figure 11-4 shows the pH scale with common household substances on it.

FIGURE 11-4:
The pH
scale.

Battery Acid		Soda		Bananas		Pure Water		Baking Soda		Ammonia	Soapy Water		Drain Cleaner

0   3   5   7   9   11   12   14

© John Wiley & Sons, Inc.

Each whole pH value below 7 — the most neutral number on the scale — is ten times more acidic than the value after it. That means something with a pH of 3 is 10 times more acidic than something with a pH of 4 and 100 times more acidic than something with a pH of 5.

TECHNICAL STUFF

pH stands for the Latin *potentia hydrogenii* — in English, potential hydrogen. The scale is based on the logarithm $pH = -\log(H+)$, where log is the base 10 logarithm and H+ is the hydrogen ion concentration measured in moles per liter.

Physics: It Matters (and It's Matter)

Physics is the branch of science that delves into matter and energy. It includes mechanics, heat, light, and other radiation. Physicists also study sound, magnetism, electricity, and the makeup and structure of atoms. You need a basic understanding of physics for both the General Science subtest and the Mechanical Comprehension subtest of the ASVAB. (You can brush up on what you need to know for Mechanical Comprehension in Chapter 15.)

New theories in physics don't always bring about new answers. In fact, more often than not, they bring up even more questions. In an attempt to answer them, physicists try to find relationships between what they already know and what's most likely to be true — and they often do so by using mathematical formulas.

Keeping track with SI units of measurement

Scientists around the world need a common language to share and explain their discoveries, so they use SI units of measurement I introduce in Chapter 10. Table 11-2 shows the base quantities, names, and abbreviations that physicists and other scientists use to communicate. (For easy conversion formulas, flip to Chapter 10.)

TABLE 11-2 **Measurement, SI Base Quantities, and Abbreviations**

Measurement	SI Base Quantity	Abbreviation
length	meter	m
mass	kilogram	kg
time	second	s
electric current	ampere	A
thermodynamic temperature	kelvin	K
amount of substance	mole	mol
luminous intensity	candela	cd

SI *derived units* are measurements you can get by using a system of equations. Table 11-3 shows the most common measurements, SI derived units, and the abbreviations and symbols that represent them.

TABLE 11-3   Measurements, SI Derived Units, and Symbols/Abbreviations

Measurement	SI Derived Unit	Symbol
area	square meter	m^2
volume	cubic meter	m^3
speed and velocity	meter per second	m/s
magnetic field strength	ampere per meter	A/m
luminance	candela per square meter	cd/m^2
force	newton	N
energy, work, and quantity of heat	joule	J
power	watt	W
electric resistance	ohm	f
electric charge and quantity of electricity	coulomb	C
electric potential difference and electromotive force	volt	V
frequency	hertz	Hz
pressure or stress	pascal	Pa

Weight and mass

Weight and mass are two different things. Look at it this way: If you were on the moon, you'd weigh a lot less than you do here on Earth. Your body composition hasn't changed, so your mass would remain the same.

» **Weight** is a measure of the force gravity exerts on an object or the force needed to support it. You're being pulled to the Earth at an accelerating rate of 9.81 meters per second squared, or m/s^2, but if you were on the moon, you'd be pulled to it at a rate of 1.62 m/s^2. You weigh less on the moon than you do on Earth.

» **Mass** is a measure of an object's inertial property — the amount of matter it contains. The mass of an object doesn't change, whether it's on the moon, in a compression device, or anywhere else.

Newton's laws: The science of motion

Sir Isaac Newton, a brilliant English physicist and mathematician who lived in the late 17th and early 18th centuries, developed the principles of modern physics. He illustrated the laws of motion and made discoveries in mathematics and optics as well. He's even credited with developing essential theories of calculus. (It's safe to say he would've gotten a pretty high score on the ASVAB.)

Newton came up with three laws that describe motion and gravity, which I cover in the following sections.

As I explain in Chapter 10, the words *law* and *theory* don't mean the same things to scientists that they mean to the average person. Theories can evolve over time as new information becomes available, but they're pretty much accepted as true across the scientific community. Laws, on the other hand, are always true (that's why there are few laws and many theories), and they're often expressed in a simple statement.

Newton's first law of motion

Newton's first law of motion says that an object at rest tends to stay at rest, and an object in motion tends to stay in motion with the same speed and in the same direction, unless acted upon by an unbalanced force.

What that means is that without *friction* to slow down a moving object (and nothing to knock the object off its path), the object would keep going the same speed, on the same path. Newton's first law, which is sometimes called the *law of inertia*, basically means that objects tend to keep doing what they're doing unless something interrupts them. *Inertia* means a tendency to do nothing or to remain unchanged, and all matter resists changes in motion.

The key phrase in Newton's first law is *unbalanced force.* The first law of motion only works if forces are balanced — that is, if there's nothing to change the object's course. In that case, the object is in a state of *equilibrium* (the condition in which all forces balance) and won't accelerate, decelerate, or change course.

You've probably experienced the law of inertia yourself. When you're in the car with a hot cup of coffee and the driver hits the brakes, your coffee keeps moving in the same direction it's been moving the entire time you've been in the car, at the same speed (so you'd better have the lid on tight). The same is true for you; if you're in a crash and the car stops abruptly, you keep going in the same direction at the same speed (and right through the windshield, if you're not wearing a seat belt that acts as an unbalanced force to stop you).

Sometimes other forces, such as gravity, also act on objects. That's why when you throw a baseball from left field to first base, it follows an upward path but begins to drop by the time it (hopefully) reaches the first baseman, and why when you fire your M4 carbine at a 300-meter target, the bullet hits a little lower than it would've if you'd been firing at a 50-meter target.

Newton's second law of motion

Newton's second law of motion says that when dealing with an object for which all existing forces are not balanced, the acceleration of that object (as produced by the net force) is in the same direction as the net force and directly proportional to the magnitude of the net force, and is inversely proportional to the object's mass.

That's expressed by the mathematical formula acceleration = net force ÷ mass. If you're using this formula, you need to rely on these units of measurement: m/s², N, and kg. You can express Newton's second law of motion as $\vec{a} = \dfrac{\vec{F}}{m}$, where $\vec{a}$ represents acceleration, $\vec{F}$ represents net force, and m represents mass. The formula's equivalent form (to figure out force) is $\vec{F} = m\vec{a}$.

The greater an object's mass, the greater the force you need to overcome its inertia, which is described in Newton's first law of motion (see the preceding section).

Starting or stopping a moving 50-car train carrying lead is a lot harder than starting or stopping a toy car in motion. That's because the force necessary to overcome an object's inertia is inversely proportional to its mass. If you use the same force to push the toy car as you use to push the train, the toy car is going to accelerate a lot faster because it has less mass than the train does.

Newton's third law of motion

Newton's third law of motion says that for every action, there is an equal and opposite reaction. That means that when an object exerts a force on another object, the second object exerts an equal force in an opposite direction on the first object.

In every interaction between objects, a pair of forces is acting on the objects that are interacting. The forces on the first object equal the forces on the second object, but the direction of the forces are opposite. Forces always come in pairs, called *action-reaction force pairs*.

Birds can fly because of action-reaction force pairs. A bird's wings push air down, but because every action has an equal and opposite reaction, the air is pushing the bird's wings upward. (They're attached to the bird, so the whole bird stays airborne.) When your car rolls down the road, your wheels push the road backward. The road exerts the same force on your wheels (but in the opposite direction), which makes your car move forward.

Newton's law of universal gravitation

Newton also developed the law of universal gravitation, which says that all objects in the universe attract each other with an equal force that varies directly as a product of their masses, and inversely as a square of their distance from each other. This force is known as *gravity.*

The mathematical equation that Newton's law of universal gravitation relies on is expressed this way: $\vec{F}_g = \dfrac{G(m_1 m_2)}{r^2}$, where $\vec{F}$ represents the force of gravity between two objects, G represents the gravitational constant, m_1 and m_2 represent the mass of the first and second objects, and r represents the distance.

The sun and the Earth have a gravitational relationship. Because scientists know the law of universal gravitation, we know that if the Earth's mass was doubled, the force on Earth would double. If the sun's mass was doubled, the force on Earth would double. The force the sun exerts on the Earth is equal and opposite the force the Earth exerts on the sun, which brings in Newton's third law (see the preceding section).

Measuring work, force, energy, and power

Physicists define *work* as far more than "showing up at the right place at the right time in the right uniform" (you hear that phrase often in the military). To a physicist, a force performs *work* on an object when it causes the object to move. You can calculate the work performed on an object by multiplying the force by how much the object moves. The equation for work is $W = Fd$, where W represents work, F represents force, and d represents displacement. Units of work are measured in newton-meters (Nm) or joules (J) under the SI system, but under the U.S. system, they're measured in pounds.

Force is something that causes a change in an object's motion, such as a push or pull resulting from the object's interaction with another object. It can refer to gravity, pushing against something with your muscles, or smashing into something with a car; it's anything that takes away an object's inertia. Forces only exist as a result of an interaction between two objects, and it's typically measured in pounds (lbs.).

TECHNICAL STUFF

The SI system is used in most of the world, but in the U.S., many common applications (and most engineering functions) use U.S. Standard Units. You may see either system on the ASVAB, which is designed to test the depth of your existing knowledge, but what you won't see is a mixture of the two systems in the same problem. Table 11-4 highlights some of the key differences between them.

TABLE 11-4 **SI versus U.S. Standard Units**

System	Mass	Acceleration	Force
SI	kilogram (kg)	meters/second/second (m/s²)	newtons (N)
U.S.	slug	feet/second/second (ft/sec²)	pounds

EXAMPLE

Tech Sergeant Yost pushes a box of dental equipment across the dental clinic. He uses 60 newtons of force to move the box 2 meters away. How much work does Tech Sergeant Yost perform against the box?

(A) 120 joules

(B) 30 joules

(C) 15 joules

(D) 90 joules

Use the formula for work:

$$W = Fd$$
$$W = 60 \text{ newtons} \cdot 2 \text{ meters}$$
$$W = 120 \text{ joules}$$

Tech Sergeant Yost performed 120 joules of work on the box, Choice (A).

Energy, which is also measured in joules, is the capacity for doing work. It can exist in several forms, such as electrical, chemical, and thermal, but it's always either kinetic or potential. *Kinetic energy* is the energy an object possesses because of its motion, and *potential energy* is the energy an object stores due to its position or configuration. Potential energy turns into kinetic energy when an object begins moving.

When you shoot a rubber band at your brother and it's flying through the air, the rubber band has kinetic energy. Go back to the moment before you shot it, though — when you stretched the rubber band as far as it would go. When you began stretching it, it started to develop potential energy because of its position. As soon as you fired it, the potential energy turned into kinetic energy. If it has enough kinetic energy and your brother's arm is the force that stops it, it's going to sting!

Power is the rate of doing work or the rate of converting energy per unit of time. You can calculate it with the formula $P = \frac{w}{t}$, where P represents power, W represents work, and t represents time. Power is measured in watts, and one watt is defined as one joule per second. (If you don't know how much work was exerted when you're tackling an ASVAB problem, figure it out using the formula for work.)

Did you hear that? Understanding sound waves

Your favorite song, the bell ringing before class starts, and your mom reminding you to pick up your room all travel to your ears through *sound waves*. Sound waves are actually fast-moving waves of pressure that result in the vibrations of particles in the medium carrying them (most of the time, that's air). If you bang on a drum, you're causing the drum's tight surface to vibrate. In turn, that makes the air around the drum vibrate, sending energy out of the drum in all directions. When the vibrating air hits your eardrums, you perceive it as a sound; you're hearing energy making a journey. If that vibrating air hits a wall or another surface, it bounces back in the form of an echo, which is technically called *sound reflection*.

TECHNICAL STUFF

Sound waves travel very quickly. At sea level, they speed through the air at about 760 miles per hour. When you hear about ultra-fast jets breaking the sound barrier, that means the jet is accelerating so quickly that it goes faster than the sound waves it's creating. The result is a *sonic boom* — a tremendous, explosion-like sound caused by the shock waves the jet makes.

Sound waves travel in ripples, like water (that's why you can hear around corners), and they spread out as they go. Sound is measured in *amplitude* and *wavelength*, as Figure 11-5 shows. The higher a sound's amplitude is, the more intense — and loud — it is. The higher a sound's wavelength (the number of sound waves it creates per second) is, the higher its pitch sounds. A violin makes more sound waves per second than a bass guitar does, so its pitch sounds higher. Wavelength and frequency are also related; the shorter the wavelength, the higher the frequency. Frequency is typically measured in hertz (Hz).

FIGURE 11-5:
A sound wave.

© John Wiley & Sons, Inc.

The rainbow of frequencies on the electromagnetic spectrum

Visible light is only one part of the electromagnetic spectrum (shown in Figure 11-6), which covers all the wavelengths and frequencies of radiation. Radiation that produces long wavelengths and low frequencies falls on one side of the electromagnetic spectrum, while radiation that produces short wavelengths and high frequencies falls on the other.

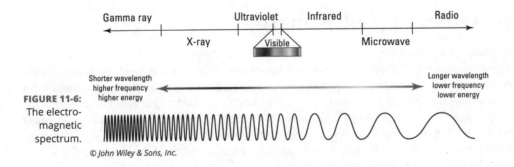

FIGURE 11-6:
The electromagnetic spectrum.

© John Wiley & Sons, Inc.

On the electromagnetic spectrum, wavelengths are measured by the distance from the peak of one wave to the peak of the next wave. They're measured in kilometers (km), meters (m), centimeters (cm), millimeters (mm), and nanometers (nm). Frequencies are measured by how many waves occur per second, in hertz (Hz), kilohertz (kHz), megahertz (MHz), and gigahertz (GHz), with one Hz being one wave per second.

TECHNICAL STUFF

Your favorite FM radio station broadcasts radiation at about 100 MHz. A microwave oven generates a few GHz (one GHz equals 1 billion cycles per second), and X-ray machines create between 10^{18} and 10^{20} Hz.

The light you see falls near the middle of the electromagnetic spectrum. The frequency of a light wave determines the color it produces. The colors visible to the eye are the results of wavelengths between about 400 and 800 nanometers. Sunlight appears white because it emits over all visible frequencies.

Light is a little bit like sound because it travels out from a specific source (see the preceding section); however, unlike sound, light can travel without a medium. Light waves can travel through empty space (a vacuum), and they move much faster than sound waves do.

The speed light travels is directly impacted by *refraction* and *reflection*. It travels faster through empty space (about 186,000 miles per second) and slower when it's passing through water, glass, or other mediums.

>> **Refraction** is the bending of light as it passes from one medium to another. Rainbows, the lenses of your glasses, and magnifying glasses are all possible because of refraction. Light refracts when it travels at an angle from one medium into another, such as from air to water. When the light slows down, it begins traveling at a different angle or in a different direction. The amount that light bends depends on its change in speed and the angle at which it hits the new medium. Rays of light that enter a *convex* lens, which curves outward, gather together at a focal point on the other side of the lens (like your eyeglasses or a magnifying glass). *Concave* lenses bend light away from a focal point and result in a smaller image for the person viewing it — like peepholes, binoculars, telescopes, and your car's mirrors.

>> **Reflection** occurs when light bounces off an object. If it bounces off a smooth, shiny surface (such as glass, water, shiny metal, or a mirror), the light reflects at the same angle it hits; that's called *specular reflection* and is what you see in the mirror or a smooth, mountain lake. When it reflects off a rough surface, you see *diffuse reflection*. Most of the things you see are due to diffuse reflection, which occurs when light hits your dog, your energy drink can, or this book. Light has reflected off each of those things and traveled in nearly all directions; the light that makes it to your eyes shines on your retina (in the back of your eyes), which passes a signal to your brain.

Heating things up with energy

Heat is the flow of energy from a warm object to a cooler object, and all matter contains heat energy (from volcanoes to ice cubes). Often called *thermal energy*, it's the result of atoms, molecules, and ions moving in solids, liquids, and gases. (Flip to Figure 11-3 earlier in the chapter for a quick look at the way particles are arranged when they're in different states.) At higher temperatures, particles have more energy and move faster than slower particles operating at lower temperatures do. When a higher-energy, higher-temperature particle hits a lower-energy, lower-temperature particle, the higher-energy particle transfers some of its energy to the lower-energy particle; that's the transfer of heat.

An ice cube and a glass of vodka both have heat energy. If you put the ice cube in the vodka, the vodka will transfer some of its heat energy into the ice cube. The ice will eventually melt, and the vodka and the water from the ice will be the same temperature. When this happens, the contents of the glass have reached a state of *thermal equilibrium*, a condition in which no heat is flowing between them anymore (see the following section for more information).

Faster-moving particles tend to "excite" particles near them. If a solid has enough heat, the movement causes the particles to break free from the bonds holding them together. The resulting change is what you know as *melting* — when matter changes from a solid to a liquid. If the heat keeps up, the particles can break their bonds even further and turn into a gas during the process of *evaporation*.

Heat energy can transfer in three ways: convection, conduction, and radiation.

>> **Conduction** transfers thermal energy in solids. The moving particles in a warm solid can increase the thermal energy in particles of a cooler solid by directly transferring it, particle by particle. In solids, the particles are closer together (see Figure 11-3), and that makes them better conductors of heat than liquids or gases are. Some materials are really good at conducting heat, like metal (think about how hot a pan gets on the stove), so they're called *conductors*. Other materials, such as plastic, foam, and wood, aren't so good at conducting heat, so they're known as *insulators*.

>> **Convection** transfers thermal energy through gases and liquids. The air heats up and gives particles thermal energy, and the particles move faster and farther apart while carrying the heat energy with them. If you're sitting in a warm room right now, thank convection.

>> **Radiation** doesn't require particles to carry thermal energy. Instead, it uses infrared waves (see Figure 11-6 earlier in the chapter), which radiate out in all directions and travel at the speed of light until they hit something else. When the waves hit an object, the object can absorb or reflect the thermal energy they carry.

Fire uses all three methods of heat transfer. First, the substance that's burning uses conduction; the moving particles make other particles in nearby solids hot enough to catch (and stay) on fire. Convection heats the air above and around the fire, and you warm your hands near the flames because of radiant heat transfer.

The four laws of thermodynamics

The *zeroth law of thermodynamics* says that if two systems are in thermal equilibrium with a third system, then they are in thermal equilibrium with each other. Thermal equilibrium means that no heat transfers from one object to another because they're the same temperature.

TECHNICAL STUFF

The zeroth law of thermodynamics serves as the definition of temperature, but it wasn't created until after the first, second, and third laws of thermodynamics were. The first three laws were already well-known by the time this one came about, but it supersedes all of them. As a result, scientist Ralph H. Fowler — who was also a British soldier during World War I — proposed calling it the "zeroth" law.

All matter adheres to the zeroth law. It's the reason scientists can measure temperature (which they do in kelvins), and it makes the following three laws of thermodynamics possible:

>> **The first law of thermodynamics:** The *first law of thermodynamics* is another version of the law of conservation of energy, which says that energy can be neither created nor destroyed. It can be transferred to other locations, though, and it can be converted to (and from) other forms of energy. However, the total quantity of energy in the universe always stays the same.

>> **The second law of thermodynamics:** The *second law of thermodynamics* describes how energy affects matter, as well as the relationships between thermal energy (heat) and other types of energy. It says that the more energy is transferred or transformed, the more it's wasted. It also says that an isolated system has a tendency to degenerate into a more disordered state.

>> **The third law of thermodynamics:** The *third law of thermodynamics* says that achieving a temperature of absolute zero is impossible. *Absolute zero* is the temperature matter would reach if it contained absolutely no heat energy.

Side effects: Feeling hot and cold

When substances get hot because their molecules are colliding fast, they expand. When things cool down, they shrink. Sometimes the change in size is so small that you don't notice it — but sometimes it's huge. One example of this change happens in burning houses. The air inside the house is hot, and its molecules are moving really quickly. The air expands so much that it creates tremendous pressure, and eventually, the windows explode outward.

Heat expansion is why mercury thermometers worked (back when people still used them, that is). Cold contraction is why a weather balloon looks emptier as it floats higher into the atmosphere.

The reason objects feel so hot or cold to the touch is because of the state their molecules are in. When you stick a metal spoon into a pot of boiling water, it excites the spoon's molecules — and remember, even in solids, the molecules are always moving. If you stick that same spoon in the freezer, you'll slow down its molecules so much that it will feel cold when you touch it. For example, you can test out how cold a metal light pole is by sticking your tongue on it during winter. (Wait! Bad idea. Please don't lick anything metal during winter. I just wanted to make sure you were still paying attention!)

Essentially, when you cool down an object, you're "freezing" the movement of its molecules.

TECHNICAL STUFF

You've heard that ice expands, and that's true. Although ice is frozen and its molecules aren't moving as much as they are in liquid form, its hydrogen bonds create a crystal lattice pattern (see Figure 11-3 earlier in this chapter for a peek at what a solid's molecules look like). In that pattern, each water molecule is held away from the molecules next to it at a distance equal to the length of its hydrogen bonds. Technically, cooling water shrinks until it starts to develop that crystal lattice pattern — then, because of the way the molecules arrange themselves, it expands.

Opposites attract: Magnetism and polarization

Hold two magnets up to each other. Sometimes they snap together, and other times they push against each other. This phenomenon occurs because magnets have two poles: north and south, just like the Earth. When you try to put two norths together, they repel each other; the same applies to two souths. But when you put a north and a south together, the old saying "opposites attract" is in full effect — the two magnets stick together.

Earth is magnetized and has a North Pole and a South Pole. Magnetic compasses work because their needles are magnetized, too. The point of the needle is the magnet's south pole, so it's automatically attracted to Earth's North Pole.

Physical Science Practice Questions

Physical science questions are sprinkled throughout the ASVAB's General Science subtest. Work your way through these 15 practice questions to see what areas need most of your attention if you're trying to ace this part of the test.

1. Energy is measured in
   (A) joules.
   (B) newtons.
   (C) calories.
   (D) both Choice (A) and Choice (C).

2. The formula you need to determine force is
   (A) $m = F\vec{a}$.
   (B) $\vec{F} = m\vec{a}$.
   (C) $\vec{F} = mg$.
   (D) $\vec{a} = \dfrac{\vec{F}}{m}$.

3. Compasses work by
   (A) measuring heat in the air.
   (B) reacting to magnetic fields.
   (C) repulsing wave currents.
   (D) reacting to iron in the Earth's core.

4. Mass is a measure of
   (A) how much matter an object contains.
   (B) the force of gravity on an object.
   (C) weight.
   (D) the amount of force necessary to move an object.

5. The element with the lowest atomic number is
   (A) hydrogen.
   (B) helium.
   (C) lithium.
   (D) uranium.

6. An element's atomic number indicates its number of
   (A) neutrons.
   (B) kelvins.
   (C) protons.
   (D) negatively charged ions.

7. The electromagnetic spectrum measures
   (A) sound waves.
   (B) only visible light.
   (C) radiation.
   (D) rainbows.

8. Which of the following is not a state of matter?
   (A) ether
   (B) liquid
   (C) gas
   (D) solid

9. Compounds are elements that have
   (A) mixed in various ratios.
   (B) combined as liquids and solids.
   (C) created toxic chemicals.
   (D) joined together in specific ratios.

10. What is the term for an element or molecule that results from a chemical reaction?
    (A) reactant
    (B) product
    (C) molecule
    (D) chemical

11. A chemical reaction

   (A) can only be set off by adding negative ions.

   (B) rearranges an element's molecular structure.

   (C) requires fire or water.

   (D) is always dangerous.

12. An object at rest

   (A) releases heat energy.

   (B) tends to stay at rest.

   (C) contains no potential energy.

   (D) cannot move with very slight force.

13. A substance with a pH of 3 is

   (A) more acidic than a substance with a pH of 10.

   (B) less acidic than a substance with a pH of 1.

   (C) a base.

   (D) none of the above.

14. How many atoms of hydrogen are in the chemical compound $H_2 Pr_5 I_{10}$?

   (A) 2

   (B) 7

   (C) 10

   (D) 17

15. Which of the following is not true of gases?

   (A) They have no definite volume.

   (B) They have no definite shape.

   (C) Gases cannot evenly fill a container.

   (D) They are also called vapors.

Answers and Explanations

Use this answer key to score the General Science practice questions.

1. **D.** Energy is measured in joules (J). In case you were wondering, pressure is measured in pascals (Pa), which makes Choice (D) the one you should've picked.

2. **B.** To determine how much force is exerted on an object, use the formula $\vec{F} = m\vec{a}$, where F represents force, m represents the object's mass, and a represents acceleration. Choice (B) is the right answer.

3. **B.** A compass is a magnetized device that's attracted to the North Pole. Choice (B) is the correct answer.

4. **A.** Mass is a measurement of how much matter an object contains.

5. **A.** Hydrogen has an atomic number of 1. The atomic numbers for the other elements listed are 2 (helium), 3 (lithium), and 92 (uranium). The correct answer is Choice (A).

6. **C.** An element's atomic number indicates how many protons the element has and determines its place in the periodic table.

7. **C.** The electromagnetic spectrum measures radiation, from radio waves to gamma rays. It doesn't measure sound waves or only visible light, which makes Choices (A) and (B) wrong. Though rainbows do fall on the electromagnetic spectrum, they're only a tiny fraction of it (they're classified as visible light). Choice (C) is the correct answer. Be careful when you see an answer choice on the ASVAB that includes the word *only*, *always*, or *never* because those answers are usually wrong.

8. **A.** Matter can be a liquid, solid, or gas, which makes Choice (A) the only correct answer. The question asks which of the answer choices is *not* a state of matter.

9. **D.** Compounds are elements that have joined together by forming chemical bonds in specific ratios. Elements that are joined together in various ratios are considered mixtures, not compounds, so Choice (D) is the only correct answer.

10. **B.** A *product* is a new element or molecule that results from a chemical reaction.

11. **B.** Chemical reactions rearrange a substance's molecular structure. They don't require negative ions, or fire or water, so Choices (A) and (C) are wrong. They're not always dangerous, either, which rules out Choice (D).

12. **B.** Newton's first law of motion says that an object at rest tends to stay at rest, and an object in motion tends to stay in motion with the same speed and in the same direction, unless acted upon by an unbalanced force.

13. B. The pH scale measures acids and bases. The lower a substance's pH is, the more acidic the substance is. The most acidic substances have a pH of 0; on the other end, the most basic substances have a pH of 14. Water has a pH of about 7.

14. A. The compound $H_2 Pr_5 I_{10}$ contains two hydrogen atoms. The small number in subscript immediately to the right of the H is what tells you how many atoms an element contains in a compound.

15. A. Gases can, and do, evenly fill containers. The molecules in gases spread out once they're contained and don't pool at one end or another, like those in a liquid do.

Chapter **12**
Earth and Space Sciences

Earth and space science — the two branches of science that deal with everything from the Earth's core to the farthest galaxies (and beyond) — are important if you want to ace the General Science subtest of the ASVAB. Whether you're going to shoot for the stars as a future astronaut in the Space Force or you want to be an Army meteorologist, this chapter is for you. The General Science subtest isn't used to calculate your Armed Forces Qualification Test (AFQT) score, which determines whether you're eligible to enlist in the military, but it does factor into several ASVAB line scores, such as your Electronics (EL), General Maintenance (GM), and Skilled Technical (ST). Head to Chapter 2 to see which subtest scores feed into line scores so you know where to focus your study-time energy, and see Appendix A to figure out what line scores you need to get the job you want.

When you take the computerized version of the ASVAB, which most people do, you get 10 minutes to answer 15 General Science questions unless you're taking a General Science subtest with tryout questions, which I discuss in Chapter 1; then you get 20 minutes to answer 30 questions. If you take the paper-and-pencil version, you have 11 minutes to answer 25 questions. Most new recruits find that they have time to spare after the General Science subtest, but if you're racing against the clock, use the tips for guessing I outline in Chapter 3.

If a high score on this subtest is on the horizon for you, but you still need more practice, check out *Geology For Dummies* by Alecia M. Spooner, *Weather For Dummies* by John D. Cox, *Archaeology For Dummies* by Nancy Marie White, and *Astronomy For Dummies* by Stephen P. Maran, PhD (all published by Wiley).

Staying Down to Earth with Geology and Meteorology

The study of the physical makeup of Earth is often called Earth science. *Geology* describes Earth's physical appearance, and *meteorology* deals with the atmosphere and weather.

Peeling back the layers of the planet

Earth is like an onion in that it consists of several layers, which you can see in Figure 12-1. Scientists categorize Earth's layers by the elements and minerals found in each. The *crust* is Earth's surface, and there are two types: *continental*, which forms each of the continents and is about 12 miles thick, and *oceanic*, which lies beneath the oceans and is about 5 miles thick. The solid rock below the crust is the *mantle*, which accounts for about two-thirds of Earth's mass. The *core* is Earth's superheated metal center, and it has two parts: the inner core and the outer core. The *outer core* is about 1,800 miles (2,900 kilometers) below your feet, and the *inner core* is about 3,200 miles (5,200 kilometers) down.

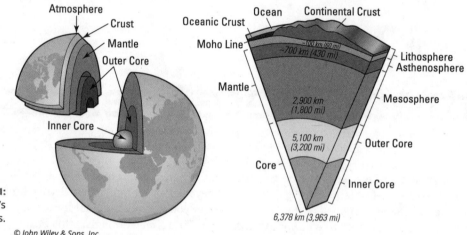

FIGURE 12-1:
Earth's
layers.

© John Wiley & Sons, Inc.

TECHNICAL STUFF

Scientists haven't been able to sample the Earth's core, but based on experiments and interpretations, they believe the core is made from heavy metals such as nickel and iron. Nobody can measure the temperature of the inner or outer core, but it's hot. Geophysicists — scientists who study Earth using gravity and magnetic, electrical, and seismic methods — estimate that the temperatures in Earth's core range between 5,000 degrees Fahrenheit and 15,000 degrees Fahrenheit. (For comparison, the sun's surface temperature is 9,941 degrees Fahrenheit.)

Within the mantle, which is just outside the outer core, are rocks made of light elements and heavy elements. Scientists have classified the mantle into layers based on the composition of the elements in each and the way each responds to earthquakes. The layers of mantle are

>> **Mesosphere:** The *mesosphere* is located in the lower mantle, surrounding Earth's outer core. In the mesosphere, temperatures are high enough to melt rock, but a tremendous amount of pressure keeps all the materials solid.

>> **Asthenosphere:** The *asthenosphere* is in the middle part of the mantle. The rocks there are solid, but they move like glaciers do. (It's called *plastic flow*.) The temperatures in the asthenosphere are still very high, which can lead to some melting.

>> **Lithosphere:** The *lithosphere* is the uppermost part of Earth's mantle, and it's attached to the crust. The rocks in the lithosphere are solid, thick, and brittle, like the crust, but they're not officially part of the crust because they're made from different minerals than the crust is.

Sedimentary, metamorphic, and igneous rocks

Geologists classify rocks into three major categories: sedimentary, metamorphic, and igneous.

>> **Sedimentary:** Formed by sediment (such as particles of sand, seashells, and other materials), *sedimentary* rocks "grow" in layers. Over a long period of time, sediment hardens — but it's still considered soft, as far as rocks go. This type of rock most often contains the fossils I discuss later in this chapter.

>> **Metamorphic:** *Metamorphic* rocks form because of the heat and pressure below Earth's surface. These rocks sometimes have shiny crystals inside them and may form layers that look like ribbons, such as marble and gneiss.

>> **Igneous:** *Magma,* the super-heated molten rock simmering below Earth's crust and above its mantle, collects in pockets called *magma chambers* beneath volcanoes that eventually erupt. (It's ultra-hot — between 1,000 degrees Fahrenheit and 3,000 degrees Fahrenheit.) When magma comes out through a volcano, it's lava. Cooled lava forms *igneous* rocks. Magma that cools quickly is shiny and glasslike; when it cools slowly, crystals can form. Obsidian and granite are types of igneous rock.

What's shakin'? A word on earthquakes

Earthquakes are usually, but not always, caused by rock underground breaking along a *fault* — the space between Earth's *tectonic plates.* Tectonic plates have rough edges that push against each other, but they don't move until the pressure causes one to break or slide past the other. Pressure can build for hundreds of years, producing a huge earthquake when the plates finally move. This sudden release of energy causes seismic waves that make the ground shake. Figure 12-2 shows the three major types of faults in Earth's crust.

FIGURE 12-2: Types of faults.

Reverse fault   Normal fault   Strike-slip fault

© John Wiley & Sons, Inc.

The *Richter magnitude scale* is a mathematical formula that scientists use to compare the size of earthquakes. Because it's based on a logarithm, each whole-number increase on the scale represents a quake ten times larger and releasing 31 times more energy than the next lowest whole number. Earthquakes can strike anywhere, at any time, but geologists have identified three zones where they usually occur: the Pacific Rim, the Alpide seismic belt (it extends from Java to Sumatra, running through the Himalayas and the Mediterranean), and the mid-Atlantic ridge, which is underwater. Scientists have never put an upper limit on the scale, but the largest earthquake ever recorded occurred about 100 miles off the coast of Chile on May 22, 1960. It registered as a magnitude 9.5 and caused an 80-foot tsunami, destroying cities all along the coast.

Seeing the sea through a different lens

Oceanographers study the physical and biological properties of the seas. They look at temperatures, rising and falling levels, sea creatures, and the geologic frameworks that make the oceans, well, the oceans. Earth has only one global ocean, which covers nearly 72 percent of the planet and holds 97 percent of the planet's water, but scientists have divided it into five named oceans: the Atlantic, Pacific, Indian, Arctic, and Southern.

HAPPY BIRTHDAY, PLANET EARTH

Earth itself is about 4.54 billion years old, which scientists determined by studying the oldest mineral grains on Earth (tiny zirconium silicate crystals that are at least 4.3 billion years old), the moon, and Earth's other celestial neighbors, where there are no magma recycling rocks. Samples from the moon show it's between 4.4 and 4.5 billion years old, and samples of meteorites that fell to Earth from space are 4.5 billion years old. (The Earth is less than half the age of the Milky Way galaxy, whose last birthday brought it up to about 13.2 billion years old, and the rest of the universe, which is 13.8 billion years old.)

Because of its massive size, scientists have explored only about 5 percent of the global ocean, but it's the main driving force of Earth. The ocean drives weather, regulates temperature, and supports all living organisms. It distributes heat around the planet after absorbing it near the equator, and it feeds into the rains that crops need. It's also home to a tremendous amount of biodiversity (see Chapter 10 to learn more about why that's so important) and ensures that life on the third rock from the sun can continue.

Outta this world: Checking the atmosphere

The atmosphere contains many layers of gases surrounding Earth's surface, and it's about 300 miles thick — although most of it is located within 10 miles of the surface. Starting with the layer closest to Earth and extending outward, Table 12-1 names those layers.

TABLE 12-1 Layers of Earth's Atmosphere

Layer Name	Location	Details
Troposphere	Extends between 6 and 12 miles above Earth and is higher at the equator than it is at the poles	This layer is where the jet stream (fast-flowing, narrow air currents) is located and where almost all weather changes occur.
Stratosphere	Extends about 30 miles	A major reported cause of ozone depletion is the presence of chlorofluorocarbons (CFCs) in Earth's stratosphere. CFCs undergo a series of chain reactions, which ultimately lead to the destruction of the ozone layer.
Mesosphere	Extends about 50 miles	Millions of meteors burn up daily in the mesosphere as a result of collisions with the gas particles contained there.
Ionosphere	Extends about 70 miles	This layer reflects most radio waves, making it important to communications. **Note:** Scientists disagree among themselves as to whether the ionosphere is a separate atmospheric layer or whether it's part of the thermosphere.
Thermosphere	Extends about 350 miles	The International Space Station has a stable orbit within the upper part of the thermosphere, between 208 and 285 miles up.
Exosphere	Extends about 6,200 miles	It's only from the exosphere that atmospheric gases, atoms, and molecules can escape into outer space. No boundary exists between the exosphere and space; therefore, *exosphere* is sometimes used synonymously with *outer space*.

Gases in the atmosphere

The entire atmosphere is made from a variety of gases — trace amounts of neon, helium, krypton (you can find that element on the periodic table in Chapter 11), methane, and hydrogen, as well as the following compositions:

» **Nitrogen:** 78 percent

» **Oxygen:** 21 percent

» **Argon:** 0.93 percent

» **Carbon dioxide:** 0.04 percent

Each of these gases has its own place in the atmosphere, and they need to stay in balance to keep things running smoothly down here on the surface. Methane, which is only supposed to be around in small amounts, is a major contributor to climate change. Scientists call it a "feedback loop" and say that methane hydrate being released from glacier deposits warms the atmosphere. The warming causes additional glacial melt, which releases even more methane, and the loop continues. All this methane is speeding up the warming of the planet. Carbon dioxide is on the rise, too, because there aren't enough plants and trees to keep up with human CO_2 output. (Chapter 10 has information on how plants pull CO_2 from the air.)

The magnetosphere: A polarizing force

Earth's *magnetosphere* is a globe of space around the planet that's controlled by our *magnetic field.* It's not part of the atmosphere, but it's important because it deflects solar wind, which I discuss later in this chapter in "Where Few Have Gone Before: Astronomy." Earth's magnetic field is invisible, but because Earth's core is made from iron and other hot, liquid metals that create electrical currents, it's there — and its protective forces come out of the Southern Hemisphere (where the South Pole is) and travel back into the planet in the Northern Hemisphere (where the North Pole is). Figure 12-3 shows how the magnetosphere works.

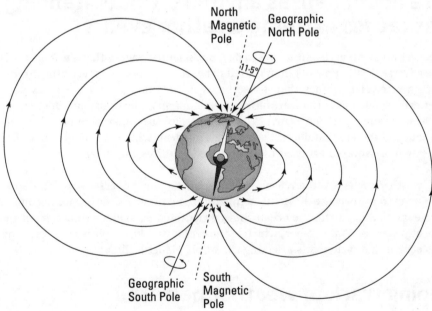

FIGURE 12-3:
The magnetosphere.

© *John Wiley & Sons, Inc.*

Warming up to cold fronts

Most weather events take place in the troposphere, where you're sitting right now. This layer of atmosphere begins on Earth's surface and extends between 6 and 12 miles up. Air is warmest near ground-level in the bottom of the troposphere, and it becomes colder at higher levels; that's why you can sometimes see snow on the peaks of big mountains in the summer and why jets leave white trails, called *contrails,* in the sky. The hot, humid exhaust from jets' engines mixes with the atmosphere, and the water vapor in the exhaust condenses or freezes.

When the sun shines, land and water absorb its warmth. Land warms up more quickly than water does, so air over land is warmer than air over water during most of the day. At night, the air over land cools more quickly than air over water does. The angle of the sun also affects air density (the sun shines directly over the equator but not the poles).

Temperature affects *air density* (how closely packed the air molecules are). Cold air is denser than warm air. Because it's denser, cold air has high pressure, compared to warm air's low pressure. (A *barometer* measures atmospheric pressure.) Air moves from areas of high pressure to areas of low pressure, creating wind.

Air masses have certain characteristics depending on where they form:

>> If an air mass forms over land, it's dry, and if it forms over water, it's wet.

>> Air masses formed in Earth's northern and southern regions are cold, and those formed at the equator are warm.

When two different air masses meet, they don't mix. They form a boundary called a *front.* When cold air meets warm air, a *cold front* develops. The warm air may be pushed up to form clouds, causing heavy rain. When a warm air mass meets a cold air mass, a *warm front* develops. The warm air passes over the cold air, forming a different kind of cloud, which causes light rain.

We're not in Kansas anymore: Understanding what causes extreme weather events

The weather on Earth varies from day to day, but scientists agree that the world is falling victim to more adverse weather events than it used to because the planet is warming. Areas closer to the equator have fewer extremes than those between the equator and the poles do, but extreme weather events, such as tornadoes, hurricanes, tsunamis, blizzards, and dust storms, can occur at any time in any place. Since 1970, the average global temperature has risen by 0.9 degrees Fahrenheit, and though that doesn't seem like a big deal (what's one degree in either direction?), it's causing more severe heat waves, drought, and wildfires each year.

Natural weather cycles are the reason we experience many adverse weather events, but they're made more extreme because of Earth's temperature increase. As the oceans become warmer, they evaporate more. Since 1970, the oceans have evaporated an average of 4 percent more moisture into the atmosphere. Water vapor, which is a greenhouse gas, amplifies the warming effect — so Earth is caught in a cycle that's affecting the whole planet's climate.

Keeping track of weather patterns

Meteorologists predict the weather with a number of tools, including weather balloons, radar systems, ocean buoys, sensors, satellites, and computer models that rely on past data. Often, the best meteorologists can do is make predictions about what is most likely to happen; too many unpredictable variables can come into play and sweep away a thunderstorm or usher in a tornado.

Climate scientists use the data that meteorologists collect to track weather over specific periods of time. These weather patterns are what make up Earth's *climate*. The National Oceanic and Atmospheric Administration (NOAA) and several international agencies look at the patterns of the past to watch for changes in atmospheric conditions and the relationships between the ocean, land, and sun. They look at air chemistry, temperatures, precipitation and cloud cover, and wind today and compare it with data from the past to create an accurate picture of what's happening on Earth. Climate scientists also study *paleoclimate* — prehistoric climate clues they obtain from natural records such as fossils, coral skeletons, sediment, and glaciers — to create longer-term models of the planet's climate patterns.

REMEMBER

Weather is different from climate. The term *weather* refers to daily atmospheric conditions, while *climate* refers to patterns in weather over time (usually 30 years or more). Weather fluctuates — sometimes it's 30 degrees Fahrenheit and sometimes it's 110 degrees Fahrenheit — and the term only refers to the weather you can see, feel, and remember in the recent past. Climate is an average pattern of weather across the whole Earth or in a specific region. For example, Alaska has a colder climate than Florida does.

Classifying clouds

Clouds are made from small droplets of water or bits of ice that are spread out from each other. Rain (or snow) falls when the drops get too big and heavy to stay in the cloud. Clouds have three main types, and the ASVAB may ask you a question or two about their characteristics, which I detail in Table 12-2.

TABLE 12-2 Types of Clouds

Cloud Type	Description	What It Forecasts
Cirrus	Thin, wispy, high clouds that usually form between altitudes of 20,000 feet and 40,000 feet	Cirrus clouds generally indicate rain or snow in the near future, when they thicken and lower, becoming other types of clouds.
Cumulus	White, puffy pillows, often flat-bottomed with rounded tops that usually form at altitudes between 1,000 and 5,000 feet	Cumulus clouds are common during fair weather, but when they gather, they cause heavy rains.
Stratus	Broad, flat, and low-hanging (gray blanket) clouds that usually form below 2,000 feet but sometimes form as high as 4,000 feet	If close to the ground, stratus clouds may produce drizzle.

Additionally, the cloud name frequently includes a prefix or suffix to indicate which level of the atmosphere the cloud is in or whether it's producing *precipitation* (rain, sleet, snow, and the like):

>> *Cirro-* is the prefix given to high clouds (base above 20,000 feet).

>> *Alto-* is the prefix given to midlevel clouds (base between 6,000 and 20,000 feet).

>> *Nimbo-* added to the beginning of a cloud name or *-nimbus* added to the end means the cloud is producing precipitation.

Therefore, a *cirrocumulus* cloud is a white, puffy, flat-bottomed, rounded-topped cloud at high altitude. *Altostratus* clouds are gray, broad, flat clouds at mid-altitude.

Figuring out temperature conversions

When you think of temperature, you may think of the Fahrenheit and Celsius scales, which measure temperatures in degrees. Scientists actually use three different scales to report temperature:

>> **Fahrenheit (°F):** This scale is more common in the United States. On the Fahrenheit scale, water freezes at 32 degrees Fahrenheit and boils at 212 degrees Fahrenheit.

>> **Celsius or Centigrade (°C):** This scale is the metric standard worldwide. On the Celsius scale, the freezing point for water is 0 degrees Celsius, and the boiling point for water is 100 degrees Celsius.

>> **Kelvin (K):** Scientists have theorized that the coldest anything can get is –273.15 degrees Celsius. They believe that at this temperature, molecular motion would stop. That's pretty darn cold! This temperature, often called *absolute zero,* is assigned the number 0 on the Kelvin scale (with the units the same size as degrees on the Celsius scale). On this scale, the freezing point of water is 273.15 K, and the boiling point is 373.15 K.

The word *degrees* isn't used when stating temperature in kelvins. Scientists who work with thermodynamics, such as physicists and astronomers, measure temperature using kelvins. For instance, the surface temperature of planets is always stated in kelvins.

REMEMBER

An ASVAB question may ask you to convert temperatures from one scale to another, so here are some formulas to commit to memory (C stands for the temperature in degrees Celsius, and F is the temperature in degrees Fahrenheit):

>> To convert from Celsius to Fahrenheit, use this formula:

$$F = \frac{9}{5}C + 32$$

>> To convert from Fahrenheit to Celsius, use the following formula:

$$C = \frac{5}{9}(F - 32)$$

>> To get temperatures in the Kelvin scale, add 273.15 degrees to the Celsius temperature:

$$K = C + 273.15$$

To go from kelvins to degrees Celsius, do the opposite: Subtract 273.15 from the Kelvin temperature. Then you can convert the Celsius temperature to Fahrenheit if you want to.

TIP

Here's a quick temperature conversion system that may be easier to remember. (*Note:* This process only works with Celsius and Fahrenheit.)

1. **Add 40 to the temperature you want to convert.**

2. **Multiply this sum by $\frac{5}{9}$ if converting from Fahrenheit to Celsius or $\frac{9}{5}$ if converting from Celsius to Fahrenheit.**

3. **Subtract the 40 you added at the beginning to yield the result.**

TIP

An easy way to remember whether to use $\frac{9}{5}$ or $\frac{5}{9}$ in the conversion is to associate the *f* in *Fahrenheit* with *Fraction* ($\frac{5}{9}$ is a proper fraction); similarly, $\frac{9}{5}$ can be *Converted* to a mixed number $\left(1\frac{4}{5}\right)$ — *c* is for *convert* and *Celsius.*

Paleontology: Can You Dig It?

Paleontologists — scientists who, in general, study fossil animals and plants — spend plenty of time working in a variety of subdisciplines, including these:

>> **Invertebrate paleontology:** These paleontologists study invertebrate animal fossils, such as mollusks, brachiopods, and arthropods (like crabs, shrimp, and barnacles).

>> **Vertebrate paleontology:** Is that a wooly mammoth or a tyrannosaurus rex? Vertebrate paleontologists can tell you. These scientists study vertebrate fossils, including fish and mammals.

>> **Human paleontology:** Comparing anatomy between the apelike creatures that preceded humans and dating paleohuman (prehistoric) remains is a job for human paleontologists. This field is a little similar to the field of anthropology called paleoanthropology, which studies human culture, society, and biology.

>> **Paleobotany:** These not-quite-garden-variety paleontologists deal with fossil plants to study their evolutionary history.

>> **Micropaleontology:** Armed with microscopes and other tools, micropaleontologists study microscopic fossils from the ocean floor and all over land. Micropaleontology is the largest discipline within paleontology because the microorganisms these scientists study are so abundant.

>> **Palynology:** Sifting through archaeological and geological deposits to study pollen grains and other spores is just another day at the office for a paleontologist who focuses on palynology.

>> **Taphonomy:** Scientists who study taphonomy are looking at the process of how organisms decay and become fossils.

>> **Ichnology:** Ichnology is a branch in several scientific disciplines (including biology and geology), but paleontologists who focus on it study fossil tracks, footprints, and trails.

>> **Paleoecology:** Paleontologists who study paleoecology investigate the relationships between ancient organisms and their responses to changing environments.

Plants, germs, dinosaurs, and humans

No matter which area a paleontologist focuses on, she's looking at fossils, the fossil record, and data about how Earth and its inhabitants operated and evolved in the past. Sure, the scientists who dig up dinosaur bones get the most attention, but paleontologists all over the world are uncovering history's mysteries each day. Many paleontologists are also evolutionary biologists who study the origin, development, and evolution in species over time. The oldest fossils on Earth are more than 3.5 billion years old, so these scientists have plenty of time periods to choose from when they're evaluating these rock-like formations.

Studying the past with today's tools

Paleontologists use fossil remains and data from other sources to understand different aspects of extinct and living organisms. Using just one well-preserved fossil, a scientist might learn when an organism lived (and in what type of environment), what it consumed for food, and even how it died. Other fossils that contain whole fossilized specimens, such as amber, can hold the keys to a more complete picture of an organism's life cycle. Paleontologists look at the big picture, too, by evaluating sites where there are thousands of skeletons and fossils, to determine whether prehistoric animals traveled and lived in herds.

Table 12-3 shows Earth's many eras and why they cover specific time periods. Like the Linnaean taxonomic system I describe in Chapter 10, Earth's geologic eras are broken into large groups called *eons*, subgroups called *eras*, and very specific windows of history called *periods*.

TABLE 12-3 **Earth's Geologic Eras**

Eon	Era	Period	What Occurred
Phanerozoic (540 million years ago–today)	Cenozoic	Quaternary (1.8 million years ago–today)	First humans, mammoths, mastodons, and saber-toothed cats lived
		Neogene (24 million years ago–1.8 million years ago)	Australopithecus appears; first sheep, cattle, modern whales, bears, mice, rats, apes, monkeys, dogs, and modern birds appear
		Paleogene (65 million years ago–24 million years ago)	First deer, cats, pigs, rhinos, elephants, horses, owls, hedgehogs, and rabbits evolve
	Mesozoic	Cretaceous (146 million years ago–65 million years ago)	First flowering plants, snakes, and crocodilians appear; mass extinction kills off dinosaurs
		Jurassic (208 million years ago–146 million years ago)	Dinosaurs roamed Earth; first birds appear
		Triassic (245 million years ago–208 million years ago)	First dinosaurs, mammals, frogs, turtles, and crocodyliforms appear
	Paleozoic	Permian (280 million years ago–245 million years ago)	Sail-back reptiles appear; amphibians are abundant; Pangea forms; ends with mass extinction
		Carboniferous (360 million years ago–280 million years ago)	First reptiles and winged insects appear
		Devonian (408 million years ago–360 million years ago)	First amphibians, sharks, bony fish, and spiders appear
		Silurian (438 million years ago–408 million years ago)	First insects and vascular plants appear on land
		Ordovician (505 million years ago–438 million years ago)	First land plants, corals, and nautiloids appear; ends with mass extinction
		Cambrian (540 million years ago–505 million years ago)	First shellfish, primitive fish, and mollusks appear
Proterozoic (2.5 billion years ago–540 million years ago)		Vendian (600 million years ago–540 million years ago)	First sponges and multicelled animals appear; Supercontinent Rodinia is formed
		Early Proterozoic (2.5 billion years ago–600 million years ago)	Oxygen builds up on Earth and the first life appears

Modern innovations allow paleontologists to learn more than ever about fossilized remains. Using neutron tomography, photogrammetry, microscopes, X-rays, lasers, MRIs, and CT scans, paleontologists can put data into computer models to create two- and three-dimensional visions of organisms to better understand them. These scientists also use techniques such as radiometric dating, stratigraphic dating, and index fossils to determine how old fossils are.

What fossils tell us

Fossils are like windows into the past. Some fossils are found in groups, which let paleontologists know that there were clusters of plants or animals living or traveling together. Others, like amber, trap and preserve ancient specimens (even air) that scientists can use to learn about prehistoric conditions. Fossils can also provide evidence of some organisms' evolution — that happens when paleontologists find fossils of extinct animals that are closely related to modern animals. Climatologists, anthropologists, and other scientists also use fossils to learn about changes in Earth's climate over time and cultures that existed in the past.

Dating a caveman

If you visualize Earth's history as a 24-hour clock, modern humans didn't arrive until a little after 11:58 p.m. (that's 23:58 in military time, which you become very familiar with after you pass the ASVAB). Scientists can determine when the first apelike creatures appeared (which eventually evolved into humans over a 6-million-year period) based on where the fossils are found, the tools and other evidence found near or with the fossils, and what the fossils themselves contain. The earliest hominid (humanlike species) has been dated at 4.4 million years old, although other, older species have been identified and may eventually be classified as hominids.

Scientists use dozens of methods to determine the ages of fossils, but some of the most important are:

>> **Radiometric dating:** This technique involves observing the natural decay of radioactive elements.

>> **Relative dating:** This technique involves evaluating the layers of sediments and rock in which the fossil was found; some layers and types of rock are older than others are, so scientists compare what they already know to what they find.

>> **Paleomagnetism:** This method compares magnetic particles in sediment layers, which can be used for relative dating, to known worldwide shifts in the Earth's magnetic field.

>> **Biochronology:** Animal fossils can often be dated by comparing them to other, well-dated species.

Where Few Have Gone Before: Astronomy

Earth's solar system is only a tiny part of its galaxy, the Milky Way. The Milky Way alone has a few hundred billion stars and planets. It's part of what astronomers call the *Local Group of Galaxies,* which are our neighbors in space. Beyond that, the Virgo Cluster is the closest group of galaxies (but it's about 54 million light-years away). There are tremendous *superclusters* (groups of many individual groups of galaxies) past that, and astronomers have even discovered *Great Walls* — light-years upon light-years of superclusters. Quite a bit of the universe is considered a cosmic void, though, with few detectable galaxies.

TECHNICAL STUFF

Because the space between most of the objects in the galaxy (and beyond) is so large, astronomers measure in light-years and astronomical units (AU). A *light-year* is a unit of astronomical distance equivalent to the distance that light travels in one year, which is nearly 6 trillion miles. One AU measures a distance of about 93 million miles, the average distance from Earth to the sun, which translates into about 8 *light-minutes.*

Taking a bite out of the Milky Way

The Milky Way galaxy (shown in Figure 12-4) doesn't have a rich, creamy center, but it does have a supermassive black hole called Sagittarius A, and all the stars, planets, asteroids, and other matter in the galaxy are spiraling around it.

© John Wiley & Sons, Inc.

FIGURE 12-4: The Milky Way galaxy.

Earth's solar system, which takes up only a fraction of the Milky Way galaxy, consists of the sun and a number of smaller bodies (such as planets, the planets' moons, and asteroids) that the sun's mass holds in orbit. The sun's mass creates gravity, and this gravity controls the movements of the smaller bodies.

Taking a quick glimpse at the sun

The sun is the largest and most important object in our solar system. It's a yellow dwarf star that contains 99.8 percent of the solar system's mass (quantity of matter). The sun provides most of the heat, light, and other energy that makes life possible. It's huge; the distance from the sun's center to its surface (the sun's radius) is about 109 times the radius of Earth. (To visualize this, hold a dime up to a jumbo beach ball.)

The sun's heat comes from its gravity and mass. All the matter is being pulled to the sun's core, where there's tremendous pressure — so much pressure that nuclear fusion takes place there, changing hydrogen to helium. Nuclear fusion produces tons of energy, released as light and heat over long periods of time.

The sun's outer layers are hot and stormy. Some of the streams of gas rising from the solar surface are even larger than Earth's diameter. The hot gases and electrically charged particles in those layers continually stream into space and often burst out in solar eruptions. This flow of gases and particles forms the *solar wind*, which bathes everything in the solar system.

TECHNICAL STUFF

At about 4.6 billion years old, the sun is nearly halfway through its life. When it runs out of nuclear fuel — its hydrogen — and the nuclear fusion turns off, it will begin to contract. The sun will become a red giant, shedding its outer layers in a massive push that will engulf Mercury, Venus, and Earth as it swells to about 150 times its present size. Gravity will reignite the sun's nuclear fusion process, but only for a short time; the sun will briefly become about

2,100 times brighter than it is now until it collapses again. Finally, it'll turn into a white dwarf and fizzle out.

Perusing the planets

A *planet* is a celestial body larger than an asteroid or comet, illuminated by light from a star that the planet revolves around (the planet doesn't emit its own light). The solar system consists of eight planets and five known dwarf planets. In order from closest to the sun to farthest from the sun, they are Mercury, Venus, Earth, Mars, Jupiter, Saturn, Uranus, and Neptune. (The five identified dwarf planets are Pluto, Ceres, Eris, Haumea, and Makemake, but NASA says the solar system may contain dozens that haven't been classified yet.)

Earth's orbit

Earth revolves around the sun in an oval-shaped pattern called an ellipse. Every $365\frac{1}{4}$ days, Earth completes its orbit around the sun and starts again. Earth rotates (spins) on its axis, completing a rotation every 24 hours. Because of Earth's tilt at a 23.5-degree angle, hours of daylight and darkness aren't equal, except for on two days a year. There are four important days during each revolution:

>> **Vernal equinox:** The first day of spring — the *vernal equinox* — is the day the sun crosses from south of the equator to north of it.

>> **Summer solstice:** *Summer solstice* is the day the sun reaches the farthest point north on the ecliptic (the path the sun takes each year).

>> **Autumnal equinox:** The sun crosses the equator toward the south and kicks off fall on the *autumnal equinox*.

>> **Winter solstice:** *Winter solstice* is the day the sun is as far south as possible on the ecliptic.

Planetary composition

The inner (first) four planets consist chiefly of iron and rock. They're known as the *terrestrial* (earthlike) planets because they're somewhat similar in size and composition. The outer planets, known as *Jovian* (Jupiter-like) planets, are giant worlds with thick, gaseous outer layers. Almost all their mass consists of hydrogen and helium, giving them compositions more like that of the sun than of Earth. Beneath their outer layers, the giant planets have no known solid surfaces. The pressure of their thick atmospheres turns their insides liquid, though they may have rocky cores.

Rings of dust, rock, and ice chunks encircle all the giant planets. Saturn's rings are the most familiar, but thin rings also surround Jupiter, Uranus, and Neptune.

To the Kuiper Belt and beyond

The Kuiper Belt, a region beyond Neptune and about 50 astronomical units from the sun, contains about 100,000 icy bodies, and it's where Pluto hangs out. Astronomers believe that the Kuiper Belt contains some remains from the earliest development of the solar system, and that it's the source of short-period comets. Beyond the Kuiper Belt, on the edges of the solar system, the Oort Cloud is an extended shell of icy objects that most likely produces long-period comets. (You can read more about short- and long-period comets in the later section "Watching for meteors, comets, and asteroids.")

Shooting for the moons

Moons (sometimes called *satellites*) orbit all the planets except Mercury and Venus because of each planet's gravitational pull. The moon you refer to as *the moon* revolves around Earth in the phases shown in Figure 12-5. It makes a complete revolution every $27\frac{1}{3}$ days and is slowly moving away from Earth at a rate of about 1.5 inches per year. When the moon moves into Earth's shadow, a *lunar eclipse* results; Earth is positioned between the sun and the moon. When Earth moves into the moon's shadow, a *solar eclipse* results; the moon is positioned between Earth and the sun.

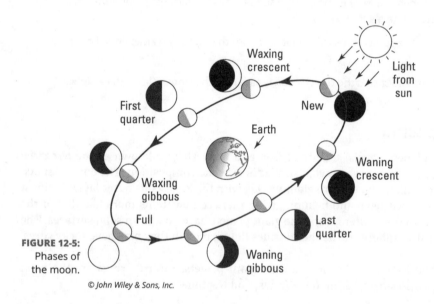

FIGURE 12-5:
Phases of
the moon.

© John Wiley & Sons, Inc.

The inner planets have few moons. The giant planets probably have more small moons not yet discovered. See Table 12-4 for a lineup of the planets and their moon counts.

TECHNICAL STUFF

Jupiter's four largest moons are known as the *Galilean satellites* because the Italian astronomer Galileo Galilei discovered them in 1610 with one of the first telescopes. The largest Galilean satellite — and the largest satellite in the solar system — is Ganymede, which is even bigger than Mercury and Pluto. The largest of Saturn's moons, Titan, has an atmosphere thicker than Earth's and a diameter larger than that of Mercury or Pluto. Pluto's largest moon, Charon, is more than half the size of Pluto.

TABLE 12-4 **The Number of Moons per Planet in Earth's Solar System**

Planet	Number of Moons
Mercury	0
Venus	0
Earth	1
Mars	2
Jupiter	63
Saturn	61
Uranus	27
Neptune	13

Watching for meteors, comets, and asteroids

A *meteor* occurs when a rock from space (a *meteoroid*) hits Earth's atmosphere and glows as it heats up, resulting in a brief streak of light. It's often called a *shooting star.* When a meteoroid enters Earth's atmosphere, it usually burns up (and that's a good thing). If a meteoroid actually strikes Earth, it's called a *meteorite.*

Comets are snowballs composed mainly of ice and rock. When a comet approaches the sun, some of the ice in its nucleus (center) turns into gas. The gas shoots out of the sunlit side of the comet. The solar wind then carries the gas outward, forming it into a long tail. Astronomers divide comets into two main types:

>> *Long-period comets,* which take 200 years or more to orbit the sun and originate in the Oort Cloud

>> *Short-period comets,* which complete their orbits in fewer than 200 years and most likely originate in the Kuiper Belt

TECHNICAL STUFF

The most famous of all comets, Halley's Comet (also referred to as Comet Halley after Edmond Halley), is a comet that can be seen every 75 to 76 years, making it a short-period comet. Halley is the only short-period comet that is visible to the naked eye and will return within a human lifetime. Its many appearances over the centuries have had a notable effect on human history. Halley's Comet last appeared in the inner solar system in 1986 and will next appear in mid-2061.

Asteroids are sometimes called *minor planets* because they're small bodies that orbit the sun. Some have elliptical orbits that pass inside the orbit of Earth or even that of Mercury. Others travel on a circular path among the outer planets. Most asteroids circle the sun in a region called the *asteroid belt,* between the orbits of Mars and Jupiter. The belt contains more than 200 asteroids larger than 60 miles (100 kilometers) in diameter. Scientists estimate that more than 750,000 asteroids with diameters larger than $\frac{3}{5}$ mile (1 kilometer) exist in the belt. There are millions of smaller asteroids, and astronomers have even found several large asteroids with smaller asteroids orbiting them.

Getting Back to Your Latin Roots to Improve Your Test Score

TIP

Just when you thought vocabulary study was over, leave it to me to bring it up again. Many scientific words come from Latin or Greek. If you know the meaning of the Latin or Greek word, you can often figure out the meaning of the scientific word. Often, a Latin or Greek root word is used to create a longer, more specific word. (For common word roots, see Chapter 4.)

For example, the Latin root *homo* means human being, and the Greek root *homo* means same. *Homo sapiens* refers to members of the human species, but *homogeneous* means "of the same kind." If you were to run across the word *homologous* on the General Science subtest, you'd know that it has something to do with humans or with things that are the same.

Take a look at the following example question:

EXAMPLE

Which of the following instruments might an oceanographer be expected to use?

(A) aspirator

(B) hydrophone

(C) calorimeter

(D) centrifuge

Even if you don't have a clue about what any of these instruments do, if you know that hydro relates to water, you've significantly increased your chances of getting the right answer, Choice (B).

Earth and Space Science Practice Questions

Earth and space sciences are broad fields, so to do well on these questions on the ASVAB's General Science subtest, you need to have a firm grasp on the basics. See how well you do on the following 15 practice questions.

1. If the temperature in Fahrenheit is 212 degrees, the temperature in Celsius is

   (A) 0 degrees.

   (B) 32 degrees.

   (C) 100 degrees.

   (D) 106 degrees.

2. Earthquakes occur along

   (A) faults.

   (B) magma chambers.

   (C) the troposphere.

   (D) valleys.

3. Dinosaurs existed during the

   (A) Paleozoic era.

   (B) Mesozoic era.

   (C) Cenozoic era.

   (D) Vendian period.

4. What element makes up most of Earth's atmosphere?

   (A) water

   (B) helium

   (C) oxygen

   (D) nitrogen

5. The process that takes place inside the sun's core is

   (A) gravity.

   (B) rotational pull.

   (C) nuclear fusion.

   (D) solar flares.

6. Most weather events take place in Earth's

   (A) ionosphere.

   (B) stratosphere.

   (C) mesosphere.

   (D) troposphere.

7. Absolute zero is equivalent to

   (A) 0 degrees Kelvin.

   (B) 0 kelvins.

   (C) −273.15 degrees Kelvin.

   (D) −273.15 kelvins.

8. A comet's tail is visible when

   (A) the metal alloys react to the atmospheric change.

   (B) the ice and rock collide.

   (C) the comet is close enough to the sun.

   (D) the comet passes the Kuiper Belt.

9. Which of the following is not a terrestrial planet?

   (A) Earth

   (B) Venus

   (C) Saturn

   (D) Mercury

10. Cooled lava forms

    (A) igneous rock.

    (B) sedimentary rock.

    (C) metamorphic rock.

    (D) shale.

11. Climate is

    (A) the weather conditions outside now.

    (B) patterns of weather over long periods of time.

    (C) not an area of scientific study.

    (D) a series of chemical reactions involving heat and cold.

12. Radiometric dating involves

   (A) evaluating layers of sediment that contain fossils.

   (B) comparing magnetic particles in sediment layers.

   (C) observing the natural decay of radioactive elements in a fossil.

   (D) comparing a newer fossil to an older fossil.

13. What phenomenon occurs when Earth travels between the sun and the moon?

   (A) lunar eclipse

   (B) vernal equinox

   (C) solar eclipse

   (D) summer solstice

14. What are fast-flowing, narrow air currents located in Earth's atmosphere called?

   (A) density

   (B) air mass

   (C) jet streams

   (D) air chambers

15. Why are regions of Earth unequal in daylight and darkness?

   (A) because Earth rotates on a tilted axis

   (B) because the sun changes direction halfway through the year

   (C) because Earth's orbit is slower during different seasons

   (D) because Earth's axis moves around during rotation

Answers and Explanations

Use this answer key to score the Earth and space science practice questions.

1. **C.** Measured in Celsius, the boiling point of water is 100 degrees. If you don't have this memorized, you can calculate it. To convert from Fahrenheit to Celsius, use the formula $C = \frac{5}{9}(F - 32)$. The correct answer is Choice (C).

2. **A.** Earthquakes occur along faults — the spaces between tectonic plates — as a result of pressure causing the plates to give way and move past each other.

3. **B.** Dinosaurs made their first and last appearances during the Mesozoic era, between 230 and 66 million years ago.

4. **D.** Earth's atmosphere is made primarily of nitrogen, which clocks in at about 78 percent.

5. **C.** Nuclear fusion, the result of the sun's mass and its gravity, takes place inside the sun's core.

6. **D.** Nearly all weather events occur in Earth's troposphere, which is the atmospheric layer that extends between 6 and 12 miles above the surface.

7. **B.** Absolute zero is −273.15 degrees Celsius, which is equivalent to 0 kelvins. Temperatures stated in the Kelvin scale are measured by using units of kelvins, not degrees. The correct answer is Choice (B).

8. **C.** Comets are balls composed mainly of ice and rock. The comet's tail is formed when the ice turns into gas from the heat of the sun; therefore, the comet must be closer to the sun for the tail to be visible. The correct answer is Choice (C).

9. **C.** Saturn is a Jovian planet, but the other three — Earth, Venus, and Mars, plus Mercury — are terrestrial planets. The other Jovian planets are Jupiter, Uranus, and Neptune.

10. **A.** When lava cools, it forms igneous rock. Sedimentary rock is formed by layers of sediment, and metamorphic rock forms due to the pressure and heat below Earth's surface.

11. **B.** Climate is a pattern of weather over long periods of time — typically 30 years or more. It's different from weather, which refers only to immediate conditions like rain, heat, and cold.

12. **C.** Radiometric dating is the process of observing the natural decay of radioactive elements. Scientists know how long it takes radioactive elements to decay and disappear entirely, so they can sometimes use radiometric dating to compare timelines with the radioactive elements inside a fossil.

13. **A.** When Earth travels between the sun and the moon, it blocks the sun's rays from reaching the moon's surface, resulting in a lunar eclipse.

14. **C.** Jet streams are narrow air currents that flow in between the troposphere and the stratosphere.

15. **A.** Except for two days per year (known as the vernal and autumnal equinoxes), the hours of daylight and darkness are unequal because Earth spins on its axis on a tilt (think about your friends in Alaska).

5

The Whole Ball of Facts: Technical Skills

Check out the basic automotive systems and various shop tools and fasteners that you may be asked about on the Auto & Shop Information subtest.

Practice identifying parts of simple machines and making calculations involving mechanical principles to prepare for the Mechanical Comprehension subtest.

As you get ready for the Electronics Information subtest, shock yourself with how much you know about the principles of electricity and how these principles work in the real world.

Discover what's required to ace the Assembling Objects subtest by looking at puzzle pieces and determining how they fit together.

Answer some practice questions at the end of each chapter to help you determine where you excel and where you could use some more review.

Chapter **13**

Auto Information

Ever wonder why automobile mechanics can charge so much money for labor to work on your car, even when the parts are cheap? Because if their jobs were easy, everyone would do them.

Fortunately, to do well on the Auto & Shop Information subtest(s) of the ASVAB, you don't have to get your hands greasy or chance hitting your thumb with a hammer. The questions on these subjects are pretty basic. Automotive questions usually ask about basic automotive systems and malfunctions.

REMEMBER

The CAT-ASVAB presents Auto Information and Shop Information (which I cover in Chapter 14) as separate subtests but combines your results on them into one score (AS). The pencil-and-paper (P&P) version of the exam tests these topics in one subtest.

On the CAT-ASVAB, you have 7 minutes to answer 10 questions on Auto Information (18 minutes for 25 questions if you're taking a version of the test with tryout questions; see Chapter 1). If you happen to take the paper-and-pencil version, the Auto & Shop Information subtest consists of 25 questions you have to answer in 11 minutes (that's about 26.4 seconds for each question). About half of these 25 questions measure your basic knowledge of automotive principles, and half query you about shop tools and basic shop principles.

REMEMBER

The military uses the AS score to determine your qualifications for certain jobs only. It's not used in the calculation of your AFQT score. Turn to Appendix A to find the jobs that require a good AS score. If you don't need to do well on these subjects to qualify for the kind of job you want, you may be better off studying for a different part of the ASVAB, but it's better to try to get the best possible score on every subtest. Doing so makes you a more desirable candidate and may open the door for more job opportunities if your first choice doesn't work out.

Checking under the Hood

The engines of planes, trains, and automobiles (and motorcycles, boats, and recreational vehicles) are complex machines that have undergone almost 150 years of evolution. Before Henry Ford made headlines for mass-producing automobiles, Karl Benz received the first patent for a gas-fueled car on January 29, 1886 in Germany. Ford and Benz would probably be shocked to see what cars have become — and how fast they can go — compared to the horseless carriages of the 1800s.

The modern car is divided into several primary and secondary systems. I cover these systems in the next few sections.

Chassis and frame: Holding it all together

A vehicle's *chassis* keeps all its systems and components together. It accommodates the frame, gearbox, engine, axles, and every other system. Think of the chassis as a vehicle's skeleton, because without it, the vehicle is just a heap of parts sitting on the ground.

The frame is the main structure of the chassis, like the backbone. The frame supports the vehicle's body and all its mechanical components as well as the weight of passengers and cargo inside. It has a lot of other jobs, too: It deals with the torsional and vertical twisting caused by driving over uneven surfaces, torque from the engine and transmission, and tensile forces from starting, acceleration, and stopping.

TECHNICAL STUFF

Most modern cars and trucks feature *unibody* construction, which means the chassis (including the frame) and body are integrated into one piece. Older cars and most modern trucks feature *body-on-frame* construction, using two separate components for the body and frame.

The engine: Different strokes

How does an engine work? You turn the key or push the ignition button, and it starts, right? That's true, but there's more to it than that. Cars and other vehicles use an internal combustion engine, which burns a mixture of fuel and air. Gasoline and diesel are the most common fuels, but some vehicles use propane, natural gas, or alcohol. In the military, you'll most likely use a fuel called JP-8, which is kerosene-based.

Burning the fuel mixture makes it expand quickly — so quickly that it's an explosion. The energy from this explosion is transferred through several mechanical systems to make the vehicle move. Technically, what's happening is that the internal combustion engine is converting the air-fuel mixture's chemical energy into heat energy and then converting the heat energy into mechanical energy. (I explain energy in Chapter 11.)

Inside an internal combustion engine, this energy conversion happens over and over in a cycle. That's what makes the engine run. Most internal combustion engines use a *four-stroke cycle*, which means a piston in the engine must move four times to complete one cycle. The piston has two distinct positions: top dead center, or TDC, and bottom dead center, or BDC. Here are the four strokes that make up a cycle (Figure 13-1 illustrates a four-stroke engine):

1. **Intake stroke:** The intake valve opens as the connecting rod pulls the piston down from its TDC position, creating a vacuum that sucks the air-fuel mix into the cylinder. The piston goes to the BDC position. The intake valve closes, sealing the air-fuel mixture inside the combustion chamber portion of the cylinder.

2. **Compression stroke:** The connecting rod pushes the piston up, compressing the air-fuel mixture inside the combustion chamber. This compression builds up energy because it excites the molecules and generates heat. The flywheel helps compress the *charge* (the volume of compressed air-fuel mixture trapped inside the combustion chamber). The mixture ignites through a chemical reaction — combustion — when the piston is almost back at TDC and a spark plug releases a spark. The spark heats the gases in the combustion chamber even more, which causes an explosion of energy.

3. **Combustion stroke:** The explosion forces the piston down. Because the intake and exhaust valves are still closed, the explosion pushes down on the connecting rod, turning the crankshaft; the crankshaft turns the flywheel, which keeps the engine going.

4. **Exhaust stroke:** The exhaust valve opens as the connecting rod moves the piston back up, pushing out the leftover gases from the explosion. At this point, their energy is spent. The valves are timed, of course, using push rods attached to the camshaft. Complete expulsion of the exhaust prepares the engine to repeat the intake stroke.

FIGURE 13-1:
A four-stroke engine.

REMEMBER

Sometimes people refer to their engines as *four-cycle* engines. This isn't really true. It's a *four-stroke*, *one-cycle* engine. The intake stroke, compression stroke, combustion stroke, and exhaust stroke are one engine cycle. The crankshaft must rotate twice to complete an entire cycle. When the *tachometer* (an instrument measuring revolutions per minute [rpm]) on your dashboard shows 4,800 rpm, for example, that means the crankshaft is performing 4,800 rotations every minute (and that equals a total of 2,400 cycles).

In order for the cycle to happen at all, fuel must be properly mixed with air and transported within the cylinder at the right time. Various components perform this function. Depending on how old a car is, it may use a carburetor or fuel injectors:

>> **Carburetors:** Carburetors are used on most older cars (those made before the early 1990s) to mix the fuel and air mechanically. As air moves quickly through the carburetor, it creates a vacuum, which draws more and more fuel into the mixture. While no major car manufacturers currently use carburetors, some manufacturers build motorcycles with them.

>> **Fuel injectors:** Fuel injectors have replaced carburetors on newer cars to perform the air-fuel mixture function. (Fuel injectors have been around since the late 1950s, but they weren't widely introduced until the late 1980s and early 1990s.) The fuel injector acts as the fuel-dispensing nozzle. It injects liquid fuel directly into the engine's air stream. In almost all cases, this requires an external pump.

All mass-produced cars today use an electronic fuel injection system, or EFI, which receives commands from the powertrain control module (PCM) computer. The PCM receives information from the sensors in the fuel, air, and exhaust system, and from that information it determines how much fuel the engine needs to operate at optimum levels.

A *throttle* is mechanically connected to the carburetor or electronically connected to the EFI computer. Advancing (opening) the throttle causes more fuel to be transferred to the carburetor or the fuel injectors. The accelerator (the gas pedal) is connected to the throttle by electrical connections and — in older vehicles — mechanical linkages. The harder you push on the gas pedal, the farther the throttle is advanced (opened). Thus, more fuel is transported to the carburetor or fuel injectors.

Whatever floats your boat: Considering common components of internal combustion engines

Most internal combustion engines have the same components within the engine block (the framework that holds it all together) to make a vehicle run:

>> **Pistons:** A *piston* is a cylindrical object with a solid crown at the top. One piston moves up and down in each cylinder.

>> **Piston rings:** *Piston rings* seal the piston to the cylinder. They prevent gases from leaking out. Similarly, oil rings stop engine oil from getting into the combustion chamber.

>> **Cylinders:** A *cylinder* houses a piston and other components. It's where the piston and the air-fuel mixture work together to transfer energy.

>> **Cylinder head:** A *cylinder head* is the part of the cylinder located above the piston. It's where you find the combustion chamber as well as the intake and exhaust valves and ports.

>> **Combustion chamber:** A *combustion chamber* is inside the cylinder head, right above the piston. The air-fuel mixture combusts inside the chamber.

>> **Intake valves:** An *intake valve* lets the air-fuel mix enter the combustion chamber. It seals after the mixture is inside.

>> **Exhaust valves:** The *exhaust valve* lets waste gases exit the combustion chamber after combustion.

>> **Crankshaft:** The crankshaft turns a piston's up-and-down motion into a rotary motion (like a crank).

>> **Camshaft:** A *camshaft* is what opens and closes the intake and exhaust valves. It turns at half the speed of the crankshaft.

>> **Wrist pins:** A *wrist pin* connects the piston to the connecting rod.

>> **Connecting rods:** A connecting rod connects each piston and wrist pin assembly to the crankshaft.

Running on all your cylinders

Most car engines have four, six, or eight cylinders, while motorcycles have between one and six. Engines with more cylinders can combust more fuel, which creates more movement to turn the crankshaft — and more power to move the vehicle. Engines with fewer cylinders tend to be more efficient, but they're usually less powerful than engines with more cylinders are. Generally, you have to trade power for efficiency when you buy a vehicle with an internal combustion engine.

Usually, cylinders are arranged in-line, V-type, or horizontally opposed, which you can see in Figure 13-2.

FIGURE 13-2: Common cylinder arrangements.

In-Line   V-Type   Horizontally Opposed

© John Wiley & Sons, Inc.

Diesel: Discovering the more powerful alternative

Diesel engines, also called *compression ignition engines*, are internal combustion engines, but they're a little simpler than standard gasoline engines are. Many of the vehicles you'll use in the military are diesel-powered. Diesel engines don't rely on a spark to ignite the fuel. Instead, the engine injects fuel right into the combustion chamber of a cylinder, where the air is so compressed (and hot) that it ignites the fuel without a spark. Glow plugs assist in heating the air, but they don't produce an electrical spark.

MAKING THE GRADE: OCTANE RATINGS

Octane ratings measure gasoline's ability to resist *engine knock,* a rattling or pinging sound that results from premature ignition of the compressed air-fuel mixture in one or more cylinders. Most gas stations offer three octane grades: regular (usually 87 octane), midgrade (usually 89 octane), and premium (usually 91, 92 or 93). By federal law, the ratings must be posted on bright yellow stickers on each gasoline pump.

The octane rating correlates to how much the gasoline can be compressed before it ignites spontaneously. When gasoline ignites this way, instead of by the spark of a spark plug, the engine begins knocking. That's not a good thing because early ignition can cause engine damage over time.

But don't be fooled — that doesn't mean using higher octane gas is better. In most cases, using a higher octane gasoline than your owner's manual recommends offers absolutely no benefit. It won't make your car perform better, go faster, get better mileage, or run cleaner. The only time you may need to switch to a higher octane level is if your car engine knocks when you use the recommended fuel. This happens to a small percentage of cars. Buying higher octane gasoline can be a waste of money, too. Premium gas can cost at least 30 to 40 cents per gallon more than regular gas does. That can add up to hundreds of dollars a year in unnecessary spending.

How can you tell if you're using the right octane level? Read your owner's manual and listen to your car's engine. If it doesn't knock when you use the recommended octane, you're probably using the right grade of gasoline.

These engines are more powerful and more efficient with their fuel than gasoline-powered engines are (because they don't rely on throttling or a spark). This power is also available at lower RPMs, which can make diesel engines more efficient at heavy-duty work like towing. Most modern diesels produce less carbon dioxide than gas-powered engines do, thanks to emissions control devices, but they still produce significant amounts of nitrogen oxide and nitrogen dioxide, as well as fine particulate matter that's harmful to human health.

Charging into the future with electric vehicles

Electric vehicles (EVs) are a lot like their gasoline- and diesel-powered counterparts, but they have one or more electric motors that take power from a large (and very heavy) battery. Some electric vehicles have a smaller electric motor at each wheel, which eliminates the need for a transmission, drive shaft, and axles, ultimately making them simpler than other types of engines. On-board computers control the amount of electricity sent to each motor for precise performance. Because they use electric motors, EVs have instant torque at their wheels and can reach high speeds very quickly.

Mixing things up with hybrid vehicles

Hybrid vehicles use widely available gasoline or diesel fuel to help power electric motors. A small gasoline or diesel engine powers the vehicle *and* a generator; the generator provides electricity to the vehicle's electric motors. Sometimes the vehicle stores energy in a small battery bank, which allows it to run purely as an electric vehicle for a short time. Hybrids were originally designed for efficiency, and they're becoming increasingly popular — you'll even find them in some military applications.

Electrical and ignition systems: Starting up

Your car requires more than just gasoline to operate. It also needs a supply of electricity. In the old days, automotive electrical systems operated on 6 volts. Shortly after World War II, as electrical accessories became more prevalent in automobiles, 12 volts became the standard.

The battery powers an electrical motor that starts the engine when you turn the key or push the ignition button. This motor is called a *starter* (for obvious reasons). An *alternator* sends an electric current back to the battery, keeping it charged, and powers the electronics on your car when the engine is running.

The *ignition system* supplies a high-voltage current to the spark plugs to ignite the fuel mixture in the cylinders. (See the section "The engine: Different strokes" earlier in this chapter.) The system takes the 12-volt current from the battery, steps it up to about 20,000 volts, and then sends the current to the spark plugs.

In older cars and diesel engines, this increase of voltage is accomplished by means of a device called a *coil*, which uses electromagnetic induction to step up the voltage. The current then passes through an electrical/mechanical switching device called a *distributor*. A rotating shaft and a switch within the distributor, called *breaker points*, route the current through wires to the spark plugs. A *condenser* absorbs excess current and protects the breaker points from damage by the high-voltage surge. The distributor and other devices control the timing of the spark-plug discharges.

In the 1970s, the electronic ignition systems were introduced. In modern ignition systems, the distributor, coil, points, and condenser have been replaced by solid-state electronics controlled by a computer. A computer controls the ignition system and adjusts it to provide maximum efficiency in a variety of driving conditions.

Cooling systems: Preventing a meltdown

Engines need a built-in cooling system because of the high temperature at which fuel ignites, and because most vehicle engines only convert 20 to 30 percent of the chemical energy they create into work (with the remaining 70 to 80 percent being released as heat energy). Without a cooling system, the engine would melt, and you'd have to use your LPCs to get around (that's your *leather personnel carriers,* or combat boots).

Most modern internal combustion engines are liquid-cooled. A *water pump* pushes liquid coolant through *water jackets,* which surround the parts of the engine that reach the highest temperatures. The coolant picks up heat and carries it through the engine's *radiator,* where the heat disperses when the coolant is exposed to outside air.

The water in the system is usually mixed with coolant (antifreeze), which raises the boiling point of the water (which keeps the water from boiling away) and lowers its freezing point (which keeps the system from freezing up during cold weather).

Lubrication systems: Keeping the engine moving smoothly

When metal grinds against metal, it breaks down. The solution: engine oil. An *oil pump* circulates oil through the engine; oil flows through the crankshaft and connecting rods, lubricating as it goes. Oil does more than lubricate moving parts, though. When oil touches hot engine parts, like the pistons, it picks up the heat and transfers it elsewhere. It also acts as a sealer between things like the piston rings and cylinder walls. Motor oil is often mixed with additives that also snatch up contaminants and drop them off in the engine's oil filter. Even better, oil makes engines run more quietly (so your radio doesn't have to work as hard).

A standard lubrication system includes the following:

>> **Oil pump:** The *oil pump* pushes the motor oil through the engine. Usually, the camshaft controls the oil pump.

>> **Oil galleries:** *Oil galleries* are pathways that oil takes through the engine.

>> **Oil pan:** The *oil pan* is the reservoir where all the oil pools. It's at the bottom of the engine.

>> **Pickup tube and screen:** The *pickup tube* sends oil into the oil pump, and the *screen* filters out solid materials that could clog up the system.

>> **Oil filter:** The *oil filter* cleans out contaminants before the oil gets circulated back through the engine.

Exhaust systems: Where byproducts go to die

The byproducts of combustion and other engine functions have to go somewhere, and they have to be able to escape the engine freely. The exhaust system manages all of an engine's byproducts using these components:

>> **Exhaust manifold:** The *manifold* connects to the exhaust ports on the cylinder head, where combustion takes place.

>> **Catalytic converter:** The *catalytic converter* contains a honeycomb-like set of passageways or small ceramic beads coated with catalysts that create chemical reactions. These chemical

reactions transform the most toxic compounds in exhaust to less-harmful compounds, like carbon dioxide and water.

>> **Muffler:** The *muffler* provides a place for gases to expand (quietly) because it's made from sound-absorbing material.

>> **Tailpipe:** The *tailpipe* is the exit door for exhaust.

When toxic fumes leave the exhaust ports, they gather in the exhaust manifold before making an unceremonious exit through steel exhaust pipes. The pipes take these gases to the catalytic converter (or two or three separate catalytic converters), where chemical reactions take place to neutralize them. When they're as neutral as they're going to get, the gases go to the muffler and out the tailpipe.

Emissions-control systems: Filtering out pollutants

Exhaust systems (see the preceding section) aren't the only systems that deal with emissions. Think of the engine as a giant cigarette and the emissions–control system as a filter. The exhaust from automobiles contains pollutants, including carbon monoxide. These pollutants are a result of the combustion process (or they're partially combusted or unburned fuel). To prevent these pollutants from poisoning the atmosphere, manufacturers place emissions–control systems on cars. These systems include the following:

>> **Positive-crankcase ventilation:** An old method (still in use) that forces unspent or partially spent fuel back into the cylinder so the fuel can burn

>> **Air-injection system:** System that forces air into the engine's exhaust system to reuse unburned or partially burned fuel before the fuel comes out the exhaust pipe

>> **Catalytic converter:** Oxidizes hydrocarbons and carbon monoxide into water vapor and carbon dioxide (the same thing people exhale); doesn't control other types of pollutants such as nitrogen oxides

>> **Exhaust-gas-recirculation system:** Helps control nitrogen-oxide emissions by forcing some of the gases back into the cylinders

Drive systems: Taking it for a spin

Having a working engine is all fine and dandy, but the power of the engine still has to be transferred to the wheels to make them move. This is the job of the *drive system.* Cars have *drivetrain* systems that run on axles. The *axle* is the shaft on which the wheels revolve. The *universal joint* allows the axle to move up and down without breaking the *drive shaft.* The drive shaft is the connecting component that carries torque and transmits rotation. Gears on the axle allow the vehicle to make turns. Axle shafts turn the wheels. The wheels on vehicles turn in three different ways:

>> **Rear-wheel drive:** The rear wheels push the car. The drive shaft extends from the transmission to the rear axle.

>> **Front-wheel drive:** The front wheels pull the car. The drive shaft extends from the transmission to the front axle.

>> **All-wheel drive (four-wheel drive):** All wheels push and pull the car at the same time. The drive shaft extends from the transmission to both axles.

TECHNICAL STUFF

Four-wheel drive vehicles typically have locking differentials (the handy mechanical components that allow powered wheels to turn at different speeds). The driver can choose to engage two wheels or all four. In all-wheel drive vehicles, which are common in SUVs, a computer controls braking and other functions to provide traction in slippery conditions.

The drive system also includes a *transmission*. The transmission changes the speed of the engine in relation to the speed of the rear wheels (in rear-wheel drive), the front wheels (in front-wheel drive), or all the wheels (in four-wheel or all-wheel drive). Vehicles have two types of transmissions: automatic or manual (stick shift).

The transmission consists of several gears that allow the driver to control the amount of torque used. When the terrain is difficult (for example, steep) the wheels need more *torque* (the force that produces rotation) in order to move. You need less torque when you're driving on slippery surfaces to help prevent your wheels from spinning. The transmission increases torque as needed. In an automatic transmission, the torque change is automatic thanks to a *torque converter.* In a manual transmission, the driver shifts the gears by compressing the *clutch,* which disconnects the engine from the drive shaft, and moving the *gear shift* inside the car by hand. Changing to a different gear (torque) requires temporarily disconnecting the engine. The clutch also allows the engine to run when the car isn't moving.

REMEMBER

People often refer to torque by assigning it a gear. Lower gears equal more engine power. For example, first gear produces the largest amount of torque; it's enough to get a heavy car moving when the car is at a dead stop. Automatic transmissions shift into higher gears (and drivers switch gears manually) when a vehicle is already rolling and doesn't need as much power to keep up its momentum.

Suspension and steering systems: Keeping it on the road

No matter how powerful an engine is, it's no use if you can't control the vehicle. The suspension system, steering system, and tires, with some help from on-board computers, tackle that big job.

The *suspension system* maximizes friction between the tires and the road surface by keeping the two in contact as much as possible, which gives a driver the ability to handle the car well. Without a suspension system, every little bump would transfer energy into the car's chassis — and riding in a car would be a lot more like riding in a jerking, jolting old horse carriage. (I discuss the chassis earlier in this chapter.) The springs and shock absorbers create a smoother ride as the vehicle rolls over bumps, potholes, and debris in the road.

Here's a rundown of the most important parts of a suspension system, which you can see in Figure 13-3:

>> **Struts:** *Struts* support the weight of the vehicle and keep it from collapsing to the ground. Typically, a strut has an attached spring that helps the vehicle adapt to irregularities in the road.

>> **Shock absorbers:** Also simply called *shocks,* these handy gadgets are part of the struts in modern cars. They consist of a piston inside a hydraulic fluid-filled, sealed tube. When the tire hits a bump (or anything else), it pushes up the piston inside the tube instead of jolting the vehicle's chassis.

>> **Tires:** The tires are a vehicle's first — and hopefully only — contact with the road. The air inside the tires helps with stability and handling. The rubber creates traction caused by friction.

>> **Springs:** Springs hold the chassis up and work with the shocks to let the wheels move up and down smoothly.

>> **Steering knuckle:** The *steering knuckle* is the connection point between a tie rod and a wheel, and it's the point that controls where the wheel turns.

>> **Control arms:** Also called *A-arms*, these long, metal pieces connect to the steering knuckle with ball joints and keep it vertical when the wheels move up and down. You find an upper and a lower arm on each steering knuckle.

>> **Tie rods:** *Tie rods* transfer force from the steering linkage or steering rack to the steering knuckle, which causes a wheel to turn.

FIGURE 13-3:
A basic suspension system.

© John Wiley & Sons, Inc.

A vehicle's steering system lets the driver control where the wheels go. A driver can use light force to steer a heavy car because most cars use one of two systems: rack-and-pinion or Pitman arm steering. Both of these types of steering are often power-assisted, which makes turning the steering wheel and getting a response from the vehicle's wheels easier.

Brake system: Pulling out all the stops

When a vehicle is in motion, you apply brakes to stop the car from moving. Each wheel has a brake that applies friction to the wheel to stop its rotation. The friction takes motion energy and turns it into heat energy (which is why you shouldn't ride your brakes — they'll overheat and degrade).

All types of brake systems share several components. First, the *brake pedal* provides the connection between the driver and the braking mechanism. The *master cylinder* is just on the other side of the brake pedal, and its job is to push *brake fluid* through *brake lines* that operate the brake assemblies at the wheels. (That fluid comes from — and goes back to — the *fluid reservoir*, which sits on top of the master cylinder.) What happens next depends on the type of brakes:

>> **Drum brakes:** In a drum brake, the lines are connected to a *hydraulic cylinder* on each wheel. This cylinder contains pistons that move outward and force two *brake shoes* against the metal drum that rotates with the wheel.

>> **Disc brakes:** In a *disc-brake system*, the master cylinder forces a caliper containing a piston or pistons, with brake pads on each side, to squeeze against a rotor disc in each wheel, thus stopping your car by using fluid and pressure on both sides of the rotor.

THE MAGIC OF ABS

In the modern world of cars, most vehicles are equipped with an *antilock brake system* (ABS). The ABS is a four-wheel system (usually) that prevents the wheels from locking up. The system does this by automatically adjusting the brake pressure during an emergency stop. This enables the driver to maintain steering control and to stop in the shortest possible distance under most conditions.

The theory behind ABS is simple. If your car isn't equipped with ABS and you have to stop quickly, your wheels simply stop turning when you hit the brakes. If your tires don't have much traction on the road, your car may continue forward in a skid, even though the wheels are locked. You don't stop as quickly as you would with ABS, and you won't be able to steer. However, with ABS, your wheels are slowed to a stop as quickly as possible, without locking up, which gives you much better control during an emergency stop situation.

TECHNICAL STUFF

Most modern cars use both drum brakes and disc brakes. Drum brakes are usually installed on the rear wheels, and disc brakes are generally installed on the front wheels. A drum brake system usually consists of a rotating drum with shoes that expand to rub the inside of a drum. This differs from the disc brake, which uses pads that pinch both sides of a rotating disc, effectively doubling the stopping power.

Cruising toward a Better Score

If you haven't picked up much automotive knowledge by this point in your life and want to do well on this part of the ASVAB, one thing you can do is get a car manual and take your car apart (hoping that you can get it back together again).

Or you can check out your local community college, which may be a more practical solution. Many community colleges offer basic automotive repair classes. You may also want to take a gander at the following books published by Wiley:

>> *Auto Repair For Dummies* by Deanna Sclar

>> *Car Hacks & Mods For Dummies* by David Vespremi

On this part of the exam, you usually either know the answer or you say, "Huh?" However, you can answer some questions you run into by using the common-sense approach. For example, say you run into a question on the ASVAB that reads something like the following:

EXAMPLE

The system responsible for cleaning toxic emissions from spent automobile fuel is the

(A) drivetrain.

(B) heating and cooling system.

(C) exhaust system.

(D) both Choice (B) and Choice (C).

Even if you haven't read up on the vehicle exhaust system, you probably know a car's exhaust is toxic. That means the common-sense answer would be Choice (C), which in this case is the correct answer.

Try another one:

EXAMPLE

Antifreeze mixed with water in an engine's coolant system will

(A) lower the boiling point of the water.

(B) lower the freezing point of the water.

(C) keep the boiling point of the water the same.

(D) raise the freezing point of the water.

In this case, the best answer would be Choice (B). It's an anti-freezing compound (hence the name), which means the temperature must be colder than normal (the normal freezing point of water is 32 degrees Fahrenheit and 0 degrees Celsius) for the coolant to freeze solid.

REMEMBER

When all else fails, guessing is okay. If you guess, you have a 25 percent chance of guessing the right answer. If you leave the answer blank, you have a 0 percent chance. If you're taking the computerized version of the ASVAB, you don't have a choice, of course, because you must provide an answer before you're presented with the next question. For general guessing hints, check out Chapter 3.

Auto Information Practice Questions

If you like to tinker with cars and your idea of a fun weekend is to rebuild the engine, you should do well on this subtest without too much additional study. If your idea of fixing your car involves calling that guy down the street, a little extra study may be in order.

1. The component of a water-cooled engine that dissipates heat is the

    (A) radiator.

    (B) oil gallery.

    (C) water jacket.

    (D) manifold.

2. A carburetor has the same function as a/an

    (A) distributor.

    (B) fuel-injection system.

    (C) alternator.

    (D) exhaust system.

3. An engine's rotational energy is stored by using which mechanical device?

    (A) connecting rod

    (B) rear axle

    (C) flywheel

    (D) cylinder

4. A catalytic converter

    (A) charges the battery while the engine is running.

    (B) creates chemical reactions.

    (C) converts heat energy into power.

    (D) controls the drivetrain.

5. Which of the following is NOT normally part of a routine automotive tuneup?

    (A) Replace the air filter.

    (B) Replace the spark plugs.

    (C) Replace the CV axles.

    (D) Check the fluids.

6. Antifreeze is used to

    (A) prevent the engine from overheating.

    (B) prevent water in the cooling system from freezing.

    (C) prevent damage to the engine block.

    (D) all of the above.

7. What assembly is pictured?

© John Wiley & Sons, Inc.

    (A) exhaust

    (B) compressor

    (C) carburetor

    (D) radiator

8. Why might you be hesitant to offer a jump start to another vehicle?

    (A) The battery terminals are not corroded.

    (B) One of the vehicles has a digital ignition system.

    (C) One of the vehicles makes a clicking sound when attempting to start.

    (D) The vehicle is really dirty.

9. What is most likely to occur if a spark plug's gap is too wide?

   (A) It could damage the motor.

   (B) It could misfire.

   (C) The car could swerve.

   (D) A fire could start in the engine.

10. What is the primary purpose of an intake manifold?

    (A) to burn fuel

    (B) to distribute the air/fuel mixture

    (C) to ignite the spark plugs

    (D) to circulate coolant

11. Identify the vehicle part shown here.

© John Wiley & Sons, Inc.

    (A) water pump

    (B) fuel filter

    (C) oil pump

    (D) air compressor

12. What engine component keeps running power to a vehicle's electronics when the engine is running?

    (A) spark plugs

    (B) battery

    (C) alternator

    (D) rectifier

13. The system that controls how much power goes to a vehicle's wheels is its

    (A) transmission.

    (B) fuel injector.

    (C) spark plug TDC.

    (D) spark plug BDC.

14. A catalytic converter

    (A) injects fuel into the combustion chamber.

    (B) converts chemical energy into mechanical energy.

    (C) runs the exhaust manifold.

    (D) reduces toxic emissions.

15. What part of the vehicle supports its weight?

    (A) shocks

    (B) struts

    (C) A–arms

    (D) frame

Answers and Explanations

Use this answer key to score the Auto Information practice questions.

1. **A.** Coolant (typically antifreeze mixed with water) runs through the radiator, which exposes it to outside air so heat energy can escape.

2. **B.** The alternator, exhaust system, and distributor all have very different purposes from the carburetor, which combines the fuel and air mixture and sends it to the engine, just as the fuel-injection system does.

3. **C.** The flywheel accelerates a rotor to a high speed and uses rotational energy to maintain and store the energy to keep the engine speed constant as the flywheel and rotor work together. As for the other devices, the drive shaft turns the rear axle. The cylinder contains the piston that moves the connecting rod that's connected to the crankshaft, which turns the flywheel.

4. **B.** The catalytic converter creates chemical reactions that makes toxic gases less harmful.

5. **C.** A general automotive tuneup consists of checking or replacing the following: air and fuel filter, belts, spark plugs, battery, fluids, ignition timing, and tire pressure. You can also change the positive crankcase ventilation valve and change the points and condenser if you have an older vehicle. Replacing the CV (constant velocity) axles is something that happens when they become worn, which occurs after many routine replacements of plugs, filters, oil, and so on.

6. **D.** Antifreeze raises the boiling point of water and lowers the freezing point. This process keeps the water in the cooling system from overheating or freezing. Either condition can cause damage to the engine.

7. **C.** A *carburetor* is an assembly used in an engine (mostly used in older cars and machines) that mixes fuel and air to an appropriate amount in order for the engine to run properly.

8. **B.** Capacitive discharge ignitions, like digital ignition systems, store charged energy for the spark in a capacitor within the vehicle, releasing it to the spark plug on demand. Because all the energy is stored in the capacitor for the vehicle to release the energy, using the battery doesn't help give or receive power and could result in an overload.

9. **B.** A spark plug that has too wide a gap may not fire at all, or it may misfire at high speeds.

10. **B.** The primary purpose of an *intake manifold* is to evenly distribute the air/fuel mixture to the cylinders in an internal combustion engine.

11. **C.** An *oil pump* is a small pump located in the crankcase that circulates the oil from the oil pan to the moving parts of the engine.

12. **C.** The alternator converts mechanical to electrical energy and uses it to operate the electronic accessories. It continues to circulate power through the vehicle and charge the battery while the vehicle is running.

13. A. The transmission's job is to make sure the right amount of power gets to the vehicle's wheels so it can move at a certain speed. The transmission works because it contains a series of gears, and the lower the gear, the more power (but slower speed) it generates. First gear is the largest.

14. D. A catalytic converter creates chemical reactions that help neutralize toxins in a vehicle's exhaust.

15. B. Struts support a vehicle's weight. They contain a coil spring and shock absorbers, and they shift the weight of the car to its tires.

Chapter **14**

Shop Information

f you're afraid you'll end up hitting your thumb with a hammer studying to get a good score on the Auto & Shop Information subtest(s) of the ASVAB, don't worry. The shop questions generally just ask you to identify a tool or fastener or the purpose of such.

REMEMBER

The computerized exam (CAT-ASVAB) tests Shop Information and Auto Information (which I cover in Chapter 13) in separate subtests but combines your results on them into one score (AS). If you take the pencil-and-paper (P&P) test, you see these topics together in one subtest.

On the CAT-ASVAB, you have 6 minutes to answer 10 questions on Shop Information. If you're taking a computerized test that includes tryout questions, which I explain in Chapter 1, you'll have 17 minutes to answer 25 questions. The Auto & Shop Information subtest consists of 25 questions on the paper-and-pencil version. You get 11 minutes to answer those questions on the paper version of the test, and about half of the questions ask you about shop tools and basic shop principles.

REMEMBER

The AS score is a way for the military to gauge how qualified you are for certain jobs. It's not part of your AFQT score, which determines whether you're even eligible to join the military. Check out Appendix A to see whether the military job you want requires you to get a good score on this part of the ASVAB. If it doesn't, your efforts may be better spent studying for another subtest. Remember, though, that performing well on the entire battery of tests helps keep your options open.

Picking Up the Tools of the Trade

You've probably heard the phrase "Use the right tool for the job." The ASVAB folks also believe in using the right tool for the job, and many of the questions on the Shop Information portion of the exam ask you to identify the best tool for certain tasks.

Tools are easiest to understand when you classify them by their functions, so the following sections are divided by function.

Measuring tools

As any shop enthusiast will tell you, the golden rule of shop is to "measure twice and cut once." It's frustrating to cut a piece of material only to find it's just a little bit too short to fit in the place you intended or to have to make another cut to trim something down. You can check out some of the most common measuring tools in Figure 14-1.

FIGURE 14-1: Common measuring tools.

Sliding Calipers
Scale
Locking Device
Micrometer
Depth Gauge
Outside Calipers
Inside Calipers
Digital Thickness Gauge

© John Wiley & Sons, Inc.

Tape rules (tape measures), rigid steel rules, steel (or fiberglass) tape rules, and folding rules are all used to measure materials in the shop. *Micrometers* can measure down to thousandths of an inch, so you use them when you need to precisely measure the thickness of a flat object or the outside diameter of a cylinder. You use calipers in a similar way; *outside calipers* measure the external size of an object, and *inside calipers* measure the internal size. *Slide calipers* have a built-in rule.

Depth gauges measure the depth of holes. *Thickness gauges* measure the thickness of small gaps. *Thread gauges* measure the number of threads per inch in threaded fasteners. *Wire gauges* measure the thickness of wire.

Leveling and squaring tools

Levels show whether a horizontal surface is true. A torpedo level has one or more small tubes filled with a liquid (like alcohol) and an air bubble. If the level is placed on a surface and the bubble remains exactly in the center of the tube, the surface is level. When you need to measure trueness across a plane, like a tabletop, you use a bullseye level.

You use a *square* to check the trueness of an angle. Because most squares have a rule, you can also use them for measuring. Squares have two arms: a long one (the *blade*) and a short one (the *tongue*). The two arms meet at a right angle. You can set a square against any angle that's supposed to measure 90 degrees. If a gap exists between the square and the material, the material isn't true — that is, it's not at 90 degrees. A sliding T-bevel has an adjustable blade so you can check different angles.

A *plumb bob* is a heavy weight that's suspended from a line. It indicates vertical trueness. Check out Figure 14-2 to see different types of levels and squares.

FIGURE 14-2: Leveling and squaring tools.

Torpedo Level

Bullseye Level

Plumb Bob

Tongue Blade

Steel Square

Sliding T-Bevel

© John Wiley & Sons, Inc.

Striking tools

Striking tools apply driving force to an object. (Watch your fingers!) These tools include hammers, sledges, and mallets. Here's a brief explanation of all three:

>> **Hammer:** A hammer is generally made of metal and consists of a handle, a head, a face (the part of the hammer that touches the nail or other fastener), a claw (to pull nails), and a wedge that attaches the head to the handle. The face of a hammer may be made of steel, brass, or lead.

>> **Mallet:** A mallet is generally made of metal or plastic but may be made of wood or rubber. It's used to strike another tool or to strike a surface without damaging it. A mallet doesn't have a claw like its cousin, the hammer.

>> **Sledge:** A sledge is generally made of metal. People use it to drive bolts and chisels and to break rock. Although a small sledge may be used with one hand, many are designed for two-hand use. A sledge doesn't have a claw, either.

Fastening tools

Fastening tools apply fasteners, such as screws, to objects. (For more info on fasteners, check out "Sticking Materials Together with Fasteners" later in this chapter.) Numerous tools make up the fastening category, which you can see in Figure 14-3:

>> **Stapler:** A stapler is a fastening tool. Heavy-duty staplers can staple roofing felt to a roof, for instance.

>> **Wrenches:** Wrenches turn nuts and bolts. The bolt or nut fits between the jaws of the wrench, and the wrench turns the bolt. Some wrenches have adjustable jaws. Not only can wrenches be used to turn nuts and bolts, but they may also be used to keep nuts and bolts stationary.

● **Open-end wrenches:** These wrenches have open jaws.

● **Box wrenches:** Box wrenches are closed. Some wrenches have open-end jaws on one end and a box wrench on the other.

Open-End Wrench   Box-End Wrench   Socket Wrench

Torque Wrench   Adjustable Pipe Wrench   Screwdriver

FIGURE 14-3:
Fastening
tools.

Allen Wrench   Needle-nosed Pliers   Vise Grip Pliers

© John Wiley & Sons, Inc.

- **Socket wrenches:** Socket wrenches have box-type sockets of varying sizes that can be attached to a handle, which in turn can be attached to an extension.

  Note: Socket, box, and open-ended wrenches come in standard sizes — either in inches or in millimeters. They're not interchangeable. (Selecting the wrong socket wrench is how mechanics learn to use cuss words.)

- **Torque wrenches:** These wrenches apply measured leverage to a fastener. A torque wrench looks much like a socket wrench but has additional internal mechanisms designed to measure and limit the amount of torque (twisting force) being applied.

- **Pipe wrenches:** Pipe wrenches have serrated jaws and grip round objects.

>> **Screwdrivers:** A screwdriver, in the shop world, turns screws. (In the civilian world, it's a pretty decent drink!) Some special screwdrivers have different tips to fit different types of screws:

- **Flathead screwdriver:** A flathead screwdriver has a flat tip at one end of the shank (the other end of the shank goes into a handle).

- **Phillips screwdriver:** Phillips screwdrivers have a tip that is shaped like a cross; this tip fits into a cross-shaped Phillips screw head.

- **Allen wrench:** An Allen wrench fits hexagonal screw heads. Nobody knows why this tool is called an Allen wrench instead of an Allen screwdriver; after all, it's used on hexagonal screws. It's sometimes also called a hex key.

  The Allen wrench, which was designed in 1910, gets its name from the Allen Manufacturing Company of Hartford, Connecticut.

TECHNICAL STUFF

- **Offset screwdriver:** Offset screwdrivers have the shank set at an angle to the blade to allow the tool to be used in cramped spaces. Offset screwdrivers can have a standard blade, Phillips blade, or any number of other blades.

>> **Pliers:** Pliers can be used to fasten and unfasten fasteners, hold objects, and cut material. When you squeeze the handles, the jaws of the pliers come together.

- **Long-nosed or needle-nosed:** Long-nosed pliers, also called needle-nosed pliers, have tapered jaws that can hold small objects or fit into small spaces.

- **Curved-nose:** These pliers have curved jaws.

- **Slip-joint:** These pliers can be adjusted so the jaws open wider.

- **Wrench and vise-grip:** Wrench pliers and vise-grip pliers have serrated jaws that clamp onto and hold objects of all shapes. Vise-grip pliers are adjustable and can lock into a closed position.

- **Cutting:** These pliers are used to cut wire.

Soldering and welding tools

Soldering and welding are two methods of fastening materials together, but they're unlike the fastening methods I cover in the "Sticking Materials Together with Fasteners" section later in this chapter.

Soldering is a process that joins metals together by bonding a metal alloy (usually a combination of lead and tin) between two surfaces. Most soldering irons and soldering guns — the tools necessary for melting metal alloy — are electrically powered. Usually, you can solder two objects together with fairly low temperatures (less than 800 degrees Fahrenheit) because you are only melting the bonding alloy. The amount of lead in your solder determines how hot your iron or gun needs to be (more lead means a lower melting temperature).

Welding creates incredibly strong joints. Rather than melting a metal alloy to use like glue, welding involves melting the base metal of two surfaces you want to join — and it requires very high temperatures that depend on the types of metal you're joining. The two major types of welding are oxyacetylene welding and electric-arc welding. *Oxyacetylene welding* requires a torch fueled by oxygen and acetylene, which burns hot enough to melt steel and other iron-based metals. *Electric-arc* welding uses electricity to generate heat. Common forms of electric-arc welding are MIG, TIG, and stick welding.

Cutting tools

Cutting tools use sharp blades to cut through metal, wood, or other materials. Cutting tools have teeth. The number of teeth per inch (or points per inch) gives an indication of the type of work the saw can do. Because of the way points and teeth are counted, a saw always has one more point per inch than tooth per inch. A saw with fewer teeth is used for rough work, like cutting wood to size. A saw with more teeth cuts more finely and is used for more delicate work, like sawing joints and lightweight pieces of wood for molding in a house. Check out Table 14-1 for a breakdown of the different cutting tools that may be covered on the ASVAB.

TABLE 14-1 **Cutting Tools**

Cutting Tool	Description/Function
Bolt cutters	Heavy-duty shears that produce enough force when the handles are closed to slice through metal bolts, chains, or rods
Circle snips	Used to cut curves
Coping saw	A type of handsaw that's used to cut curved lines or shapes
Crosscut saw	A type of handsaw that cuts against the grain of the wood; the shape of the teeth and the angle in which they're set are the main differences in this type of saw

(continued)

TABLE 14-1 *(continued)*

Cutting Tool	Description/Function
Hacksaw	A type of handsaw that's used to cut metal; a hacksaw has an adjustable frame that holds thin blades of varying length in place; a handle is set in one end
Pipe cutters and tube cutters	Used to score and cut metal pipes and tubes
Ripsaw	A type of handsaw that cuts with the grain of the wood; the shape of the teeth and the angle in which they're set are the main differences in this type of saw
Snips and shears	Snips and shears have two cutting blades that scissor together when the handles close; the blades can be curved or straight

Drilling, punching, and gouging tools

No, this section isn't about hand-to-hand combat training from basic training. Masters in the art of shop often make holes in the material they're working with in order to build that perfect birdhouse (or whatever they're working on). These holes can be made with a variety of tools, which I cover in the following sections. You can see some examples in Figure 14-4.

FIGURE 14-4: Drilling, punching, and gouging tools.

Power Drill · Augur Bit · Butt Chisel · Mortising Chisel · Cold Chisel · Socket Chisel

© *John Wiley & Sons, Inc.*

Drills and bits

Twist drills use *drill bits*, which are round pieces of steel shaped in a spiral, to create holes. Drill bits are attached to a drill (usually a power drill but sometimes a hand drill operated by manually turning a crank). The point of the drill bit is sharpened, and the shank is smooth and fits into the drill's adjustable chuck.

TECHNICAL STUFF

A *countersink* is a drill bit that enlarges just the surface of a hole so a screw head can be accommodated. A countersink allows the top of the fastener to be set flush with or below the material to which it's attached. Without a countersink, the fastener slightly protrudes from the material to which it's been attached.

Auger bits bore larger holes. They're shaped differently from drill bits. They have a long, deep spiral flute for easy chip removal. They're also much larger. Auger bits are most commonly used with a brace for drilling holes in wood. Their average length varies from 7 to 10 inches, but larger auger bits can be several feet long.

Punches

Punches have a sharp end that's placed against the material to be punctured; the other end is struck with a hammer. A center punch is used to mark where a drilled hole is to be placed; this keeps the drill bit in position and prevents the drill bit from wandering to another part of the material during the first few rotations.

WARNING

Using a Phillips screwdriver as a punch is bad form in the shop world because hitting the handle of a screwdriver with a hammer can damage it (and then you'll get talked about in serious shop circles).

Chisels

Chisels are made of steel and have a sharp cutting edge. They're used to chip or cut metal or wood:

>> **Metal-cutting chisels:** Chisels that cut metal are usually struck with a hammer to make the cut. These chisels have different shapes depending on how they'll be used; *cold chisels* are flat, and they're used for cutting metals without using heating torches or forges, whereas *round chisels* make circular cuts.

>> **Wood-cutting chisels:** Some wood chisels, called *socket chisels,* are struck with a mallet. Other wood chisels require only the pressure of your hands.

Wood chisels also come in different shapes, depending on what they're used for. A *butt chisel* has a short blade and is used for in-close work. A *mortising chisel* has a narrow blade made for chiseling out the narrow mortises in joints. A *framing chisel* has a heavy, strong blade meant for rough work.

WARNING

Because you use chisels with other tools and the pressure of your hands, there's a little bit of a risk involved with this tool. One slip, and these instruments can easily cut large chunks out of your skin, so be careful.

Finishing tools

Filing and finishing shop tools are used to sharpen the blades of other tools and to smooth the edges of cut objects. Files come in a range of coarseness, and the blades can cut in different patterns. Files also come in different shapes to finish different kinds of objects. Here are the different kinds of files:

>> **Single-cut:** Single-cut files are used for finishing work and sharpening blades.

>> **Double-cut:** Double-cut files are used for rough work.

>> **Flat files and half-round:** These files are for general purposes.

>> **Square and round:** These files fit square and round openings.

Planes are a type of finishing tool used to prepare wood for final finishing and to fit doors and trim. A plane body or frame has two handles: a handle to push with and a knob to guide with. A plane has four other parts: a blade or iron, a chip breaker, a lever cap, and a frog, which is used to hold the blade. *Bench planes* are used to smooth surfaces. Longer planes give a more uniform surface by shaving off a portion of the wood.

Clamping tools

A clamping tool is a device used to hold or fasten objects securely so they won't move while you're working on them. Several types of clamping tools are available for many different purposes:

>> **Pliers:** Pliers (discussed in the "Fastening tools" section earlier in the chapter) can be used to hold objects while you're working on them.

>> **Vises:** Vises hold material while it's being sawed, drilled, or glued. Here are some different types of vises:

- **Bench vise:** A bench vise has large, rough jaws that keep the material from slipping.

- **Pipe vise:** Pipe vises hold round material or pipes.

- **Hand screw vise:** A hand screw vise has two hard, wooden jaws connected by two long screws. The screws are tightened to bring the jaws of the hand screw vise together.

>> **Clamps:** Clamps are used when a vise won't work. Vises generally attach to a workbench, while clamps generally connect only to the items being worked with. C-clamps consist of a cast-iron "C" frame and a screw that moves back and forth to open and shut the clamp. Bar clamps hold material together that can measure several feet wide.

Figure 14-5 shows you an example of a vise and a C-clamp.

FIGURE 14-5:
Clamping
tools.

Vise

C-Clamp

© John Wiley & Sons, Inc.

Sticking Materials Together with Fasteners

Although wood and metal (and other materials) can be held together with glue, straps, duct tape, and other brilliant fastening methods, people usually fasten these types of materials with nails, screws, bolts, and rivets. These fasteners offer more strength and stability than the white glue that you used to fasten painted macaroni noodles onto construction paper in the first grade.

Nails

Nails are used to hold pieces of wood together. The nail head is flat, and the shank is usually round. Nail length is designated by the *penny system*, which is abbreviated with a *d*. A ten-penny nail is a 10d nail. Length and thickness generally correspond. The higher the penny size, the longer the nail. Nails that are larger than 20-penny are called *spikes* and are measured in inches.

TECHNICAL STUFF

The penny system is used in the United States. It originates from the price of 100 nails in the 15th century in England.

Other types of nails include the following:

>> **Brads and finishing nails:** They have heads that are made to fit flush with or slightly below the surface of the wood.

>> **Common nails:** These nails are the most commonly used nails. (How about that for a truly difficult vocab word?)

>> **Double-headed nails:** These have two heads, one lower than the other, and a point on the other end. The nail is driven to the lower head but can be pulled out of the material because of the remaining higher head. These nails are used for temporary construction that will be taken apart.

Screws and bolts

Unlike nails, you can easily take screws and bolts out of the wood without causing additional damage to the wood (unless, of course, the threads are stripped). Figure 14-6 shows a few options. These fasteners also hold more tightly than nails. Screws have flat heads, round heads, or oval heads; in addition to this classification, they also have standard heads (for flathead screwdrivers) or Phillips heads (with cross-shape slots). Screw sizes are based on length and the diameter of the unthreaded part of the screw.

Here's the lowdown on these types of fasteners:

>> **Wood screws:** Wood screws are used to fasten wood. (Hmm, ingenious!)

>> **Lag screws:** Lag screws have square- or hexagon-shaped heads and are used for large projects.

>> **Bolts:** Bolts don't thread into wood. They have flat ends (as opposed to the pointed ends of screws). They're held in place by a nut (which is what actually screws into the threads) and washer. The body of the bolt may have few threads or many.

>> **Machine screws:** Machine screws are used to fasten metal parts. Machine screws are sometimes used with nuts. They come in various lengths and widths and have a wide variety of heads.

FIGURE 14-6:
Screws
and bolts.

Flathead Screw   Phillips Head Screw   Bolt

© John Wiley & Sons, Inc.

Nuts and washers

Nuts can be square, but more often they're hexagonal. *Cap nuts* are rounded and smooth; *stop nuts* prevent the screw or bolt from coming loose. *Wing nuts* have flanges on each side so they can be tightened by hand.

Washers prevent damage to the surface of a material by preventing the bolt head from digging into the material. They also help keep the bolt (or screw) in place. *Flat washers*, a simple ring of flat metal, are the most common type of washer. *Shake-proof washers* have teeth to prevent them from slipping, while *split lock washers* apply a small spring force that prevent the nut from vibrating off.

You can see many of these fasteners in Figure 14-7.

Square Nut   Hexagonal Nut

Flat
Washer

Split Lock
Washer

External Tooth
Washer

FIGURE 14-7:
Nuts and
washers.

Wing Nut   Cap Nut

© *John Wiley & Sons, Inc.*

Rivets

Rivets are commonly used to fasten parts together, especially when welding would prevent the parts from being disassembled. You drive standard rivets by using a *bucking bar.* Rivets come in a wide variety of lengths, diameters, and head shapes. The rivet material should match the material being fastened. *Pop rivets* can be used when only one side of a joint is accessible.

Building a Better Score

If you want to do well on this subtest but you don't have a lot of experience in the woodshop yet, you can get a woodworking book and build some furniture for your mom. (Even if you mess it up, Mom always likes gifts from the heart.) Remember, too, that many community colleges offer basic shop classes. You may also want to flip through the following books, both published by Wiley:

>> *Woodworking For Dummies* by Jeff Strong

>> *Home Improvement For Dummies* by Gene Hamilton and Katie Hamilton

On the Shop Information questions, you either know the answers or you don't — in most cases. Sometimes you can use your intuition to figure out the right answer. For example, you may find a question on the ASVAB that looks like this one:

EXAMPLE

When attaching two pieces of wood together, the most secure bond would be formed by using

(A) wood screws.

(B) nails.

(C) wood glue.

(D) both Choice (A) and Choice (C).

If you think about it, screws have threads, which are likely to "grab" wood more securely than a nail would. Glue would likely strengthen that bond even more. It's obvious that the common-sense answer would be Choice (D).

Try a variation of the same question:

The best fastening method to use when attaching pieces of wood together when time is of the essence would be

(A) screws.

(B) cutting mortise and tenon joints.

(C) wood glue.

(D) both Choice (A) and Choice (C).

In this case, the best answer would be Choice (A), because using a drill (or even a screwdriver) to put screws in wood is generally faster than making cuts in the wood or waiting for glue to dry.

If you need to, you can guess on the ASVAB. The military doesn't expect every applicant to know every answer to every question, but it does expect every applicant to try to perform well on the test. (That's why too many incorrect answers at the end of a subtest on the CAT–ASVAB can incur a penalty; the military doesn't want you just clicking through willy-nilly.) Try to rule out obviously incorrect answers before you choose; that way, you'll maximize your chances of getting one right. For general guessing hints, check out Chapter 3.

Shop Information Practice Questions

Do you build birdhouses for leisure and speed through "name that tool" rounds on game shows? If so, you probably don't need a lot of practice for this part of the ASVAB. If you use those rounds as an opportunity to get a snack, on the other hand, you may want to check out the following sample questions to help you nail down some shop concepts.

1. A two-penny nail is

(A) thicker than a 10d nail.

(B) shorter than a 10d nail.

(C) the same thing as a 10d nail.

(D) harder than a 10d nail.

2. A hacksaw is used to cut

(A) with the grain of wood.

(B) against the grain of wood.

(C) round stock.

(D) metal.

3. To drive a cold chisel, the best object to use would be

(A) a hammer.

(B) a sledge.

(C) a mallet.

(D) a plane.

4. The best tool for cutting curves or shapes in wood is a

(A) ripsaw.

(B) crosscut saw.

(C) coping saw.

(D) pliant saw.

5. What is the next step after filling in a hole with plastic filler and letting it dry?

(A) Clean the area with a glass-cleaning solution.

(B) Sand the area with medium-grain sandpaper.

(C) Coat the area with a layer of primer.

(D) none of the above.

6. What type of joint is pictured?

© John Wiley & Sons, Inc.

(A) overlap joint

(B) butt joint

(C) dovetail joint

(D) mortise and tenon joint

7. Why is a cross-shaft lug wrench better than a single-shaft wrench?

(A) It gives more leverage.

(B) It holds lug nuts better.

(C) It fits better in storage because it's smaller.

(D) It doesn't scratch the lug nuts.

8. Which term refers to the measure of thickness of a liquid?

(A) hydrometer

(B) viscosity

(C) fluidity

(D) frequency

9. What is the name of the tool shown here?

(A) bench vise

(B) pipe vise

(C) pipe cutter

(D) ripsaw

10. Without a key, what tool would you use to remove a padlock from a gate?

(A) bolt cutters

(B) a coping saw

(C) slip-joint pliers

(D) a cold chisel

Answers and Explanations

Use this answer key to score the Shop Information practice questions.

1. **B.** *Penny,* abbreviated *d* (for the ancient Roman *denarius* coin), indicates length; a 2d nail is shorter than a 10d nail.

2. **D.** The hacksaw has a blade specifically designed to cut metal, not wood.

3. **A.** A hammer has a smaller, harder striking surface than a mallet does. Mallets don't usually have metal striking surfaces, and a plane is a tool carpenters and woodworkers use to finish a wood surface.

4. **C.** *Coping saws* have thin blades with many teeth and are specifically designed to cut curves and shapes in wood.

5. **B.** After the filler dries completely, the next step is to sand the area to create a smooth surface for painting.

6. **D.** You use a *mortise and tenon joint* when you need it to withstand weight and movement, such as in a piece of furniture (for example, chairs).

7. **A.** A cross-shaft wrench (shaped like a cross) is better than the single-shaft wrench (one long handle) because you can push down and pull up at the same time, resulting in more leverage.

8. **B.** The *viscosity* of a fluid is a measure of its thickness.

9. **B.** *Pipe vises* hold round material or pipes.

10. **A.** *Bolt cutters* are heavy-duty shears that produce enough force to cut through the arms of a padlock.

Chapter **15**
Mechanical Comprehension

When you need to clean your M-4 5.56 mm carbine, knowing how to take it apart and put it back together is going to come in handy. Of course, your drill sergeants in basic training will teach you (and ensure you get *plenty* of practice), but how easily you grasp such tasks depends greatly on your aptitude for understanding simple mechanical operations and *applied physics,* which relates to motion, force, and energy. That's the purpose of the Mechanical Comprehension (MC) subtest of the ASVAB.

The questions on this subtest measure your understanding of simple machines and mechanisms. Many of the questions on this subtest display a diagram, such as a series of connected gears, followed by a question, such as which direction a gear turns or how fast it revolves. The Mechanical Comprehension subtest is almost all about applied physics, so you may want to review some basic physics in Chapter 11 of this book. For even more study, check out *Physics I For Dummies,* by Steven Holzner, PhD (Wiley).

REMEMBER

Only some military jobs require a good score on this subtest. Turn to Appendix A for information about the subtest scores you need to qualify for specific military jobs. If you have no interest in taking apart a fighter aircraft or rebuilding a tank, you're better off reviewing for the Word Knowledge or Arithmetic Reasoning subtests, which make up part of the core exam (the AFQT; see Chapter 1) that you must do well on to even qualify for enlistment. Remember, though, it doesn't hurt to understand mechanical operations. You never know when you'll be offered an interesting job opportunity that requires a good score in this area.

To do well on this subtest, you also have to bone up on your mathematical skills. The Mechanical Comprehension subtest often asks you to make calculations based on formulas to explain mechanical principles. Don't panic; the formulas are easy to understand, but you do have to use math to come up with a final answer. See Part 3 for more information on math. In this chapter, you get the mathematical formulas for commonly asked questions on the ASVAB, so pay especially close attention to these little beauties. (If the information probably isn't on the ASVAB, I don't burden you with it here.)

The CAT-ASVAB (computerized test) has 15 Mechanical Comprehension questions that you're supposed to answer in 22 minutes. If you're taking a CAT-ASVAB with tryout questions, which I cover in Chapter 1, you get 42 minutes to answer 30 questions. For the paper version of the ASVAB, this subtest has 25 questions, and you have 19 minutes to answer them. That's enough time for a mechanically oriented individual to tackle this subtest and put a broken clock back together. Well, maybe not the whole clock.

A-mass-ing Knowledge on Matter, Weight, Density, and Relativity

A lot of people think that weight and mass are the same, and although they're not identical, they're similar. All matter has mass. An object's mass is a measure of how much matter it contains. Weight is a measure of the force that gravity exerts on the object (or the force necessary to support it). Essentially, weight is mass × gravity; weight is a force expressed by the relationship of multiplying an object's mass and gravity.

The simplest way to look at weight versus mass is to think about taking a trip to the moon. Your mass stays the same here on Earth and on the moon because mass is simply the amount of matter inside your body. But you weigh less on the moon than you do here because the moon's gravity is about a sixth as powerful as Earth's is. If you weigh 150 pounds here on Earth, you'd weigh about 25 pounds on the moon (or 380 pounds on Jupiter because it's a larger planet with more gravity). You can even figure out how much you'd weigh on other planets based on their gravity. Of course, that only makes a difference if you end up joining the Space Force.

Matter can vary in *density*, a measure of how much matter is inside an object (its mass) and how much space that matter takes up (its volume). Remember the old joke "Which weighs more: a ton of feathers or a ton of bricks?" They both weigh the same, but the two have different densities; a ton of feathers would probably take up a lot more space than a ton of bricks would.

An object made from a dense material, like iron, has less volume than the same object made from a less-dense material, like water. A one-gallon bag of iron not only *feels* heavier than a one-gallon bag of water but is also heavier because the iron is denser.

TIP

Imagine an elevator in a high-rise building. The elevator starts with just one person in it, but as it moves between floors, it picks up more and more passengers. The space available inside the elevator never changes (that's its volume), but the density of the matter inside it (the people) does change. The people can be packed in like sardines, just like the atoms in a high-density object are.

"Energy equals mass times the speed of light squared" is the long way of saying the world's most famous equation: $E = mc^2$. Albert Einstein's theory of special relativity really says that mass and energy are the same physical entity, and that they can be changed into each other. According to the equation, m represents the mass of an object, c^2 represents the speed of light squared, and E represents that object's total energy (which I discuss later in the chapter). In a nutshell, the amount of mass in an object determines how much energy it has.

Understanding the Forces of the Universe

By applying *force* (a push or pull), you can open the door or close it, speed it up (slam it) or slow it down (catch it before it slams), or make it change direction (push it shut when the wind blows it open). In fact, all mechanical devices need force to move mass.

REMEMBER

In physics, applying force allows changes in the *velocity* (the speed and direction) of an object. A change (such as an increase) in velocity is known as *acceleration.* Here's the mathematical formula to determine force: Force = Mass × Acceleration.

TECHNICAL STUFF

Martial artists use this concept all the time. Although a larger fighter may have more size (mass), a smaller fighter can usually speed up more quickly (have more acceleration), possibly resulting in both fighters applying the same amount of force. This concept is why 110-pound martial artists can break boards and bricks just as well as 200-pound martial artists.

This section gives you the basics of force that you need to know for the ASVAB.

He hit me first! The basics of action and reaction

Sir Isaac Newton sure was one of the sharpest crayons in the box. His third law of motion states that for every action (force) in nature, there's an equal and opposite reaction. In other words, if object A exerts a force on object B, then object B also exerts an equal and opposite force on object A. Notice that the forces are exerted on the opposite object.

Take a look at Figure 15-1. As you sit in your chair, your body exerts a downward force on the chair, and the chair exerts an upward force on your body. There are two forces resulting from this interaction: a force on the chair and a force on your body. These two forces are called *action* and *reaction forces.*

FIGURE 15-1: An example of action and reaction forces.

© *John Wiley & Sons, Inc.*

This force can also be used to describe how a motorboat moves through the water. As the propellers turn, they push the water behind the boat (action). The water reacts by pushing the boat forward (reaction).

Equilibrium: Finding a balance

Forces are *vector* quantities. That means they have both a magnitude (size) and a direction associated with them. Forces applied in the same direction as other forces increase the total force, and forces that move in opposite directions reduce the total force. In general, an object can be acted on by several different forces at any one time.

REMEMBER

A very basic concept when dealing with forces is the idea of *equilibrium* or balance. When two or more forces interact so that their combination cancels the other(s) out, a state of equilibrium occurs. In this state, the velocity of an object doesn't change. The forces are considered to be balanced if the rightward forces are balanced by the leftward forces and the upward forces are balanced by the downward forces.

If an object is at rest and is in a state of equilibrium, then it's at *static equilibrium*. *Static* means being stationary or at rest. For example, a glass of water sitting on a table is at static equilibrium. The table exerts an upward force on the glass to counteract the force of gravity.

Under pressure: Spreading out the force

REMEMBER

Pressure is a measurement of force over an area. Pressure is usually measured in pounds per square inch (psi). The formula for deriving pressure is

$$\text{Pressure} = \frac{\text{Force (in pounds)}}{\text{Area (in square inches)}}$$

If 50 pounds of force is exerted on 10 square inches of surface, the amount of pressure is 5 pounds per square inch $\left(5 = 50 \div 10\right)$.

Consider this: If you're sleeping in bed, the amount of pressure being exerted per square inch is much less than when you're standing on your feet. The surface area of the bottoms of your feet (supporting all that weight) is much less than the surface area of all your body parts that touch the mattress.

TECHNICAL
STUFF

Ever wonder how a person can lie on a bed of nails? The answer involves elementary physics. His or her body rests evenly on hundreds of nails; therefore, no individual nail exerts a great amount of pressure against the skin. Have you ever seen someone stand on a bed of nails? That would be a lot more painful — and because there are fewer nails exerting pressure on a smaller surface area, they'd most likely puncture the feet.

A *barometer* is a gauge that measures atmospheric pressure. Normal atmospheric pressure is 14.7 psi. A change in air pressure means the weather is about to change. For more information on science and barometric pressure, see Chapters 10, 11, and 12.

Looking at kinds of forces

Here are some of the forces that act on objects:

>> **Gravity** is the physical property that draws objects toward the center of Earth (and other objects that have mass), which is generally known as weight. Gravity generates a weight force when multiplied by an object's mass.

>> **Applied force** is force a person or another object applies to an object through contact.

>> **Tension** is transmitted through string, rope, cable, or wire when forces are acting on opposite ends.

>> **Friction** is resistance to the motion of two objects or surfaces that touch.

>> **Recoil** occurs when something regains its original form when an object exerting force on it is removed; it's also referred to as a *spring force*.

>> **Magnetism** is the property of attracting iron or steel.

>> **Static electricity** is the production of stationary electrical charges, often the result of friction.

In this section, I explain a few of these forces in detail.

Gravity: What goes up must come down

Isaac Newton didn't invent gravity, but the famous mathematician *was* the first to study it seriously. Robert Hooke, an English scientist and architect, proposed the idea in 1665. Hooke's idea provided a springboard for Newton's 1687 universal gravitation theory, which is now a scientific law. (Newton deliberately declined to credit Hooke, leading to a scientific spat that lasted until Hooke's death.)

REMEMBER

Newton's *law of universal gravitation* states that every object in the universe attracts every other object in the universe. Earth produces gravity, and so do the sun, other planets, your car, your house, and your body. The amount (force) of the attraction depends on the following:

>> **Mass:** The force of gravity depends on the mass of the object. If you're sitting in front of your television, you may be surprised to know that the television set is attracting you. However, because the mass of the TV is so small compared to the mass of Earth, you don't notice the physical "pull" toward the television set.

   Note that the force of gravity acting on an object is equal to the weight of the object. Of course, other planets have lesser or greater masses than Earth, so the weight of objects on those planets is different. (I discuss mass, and its relation to weight, in "A-mass-ing Knowledge on Matter, Weight, Density, and Relativity" earlier in this chapter.)

>> **Distance:** Newton's law also says that the greater the distance is between two objects, the less the objects attract each other. In other words, the farther away an object is from Earth (or any large body), the less it weighs. If you stand at the top of a high mountain, you'll weigh less than you will at sea level. Don't get too excited about this weight-loss technique, though. The difference is incredibly small. Gravitational pull isn't the next big diet craze. Sorry!

   For an object to really lose weight, it must be far away from Earth (or any other large body). When an object is far enough away from these bodies that it experiences practically no gravitational pull from them, it's said to experience weightlessness — just like the astronauts you see on TV.

Gravity pulls objects downward toward the center of Earth, so the old saying "what goes up must come down" is appropriate when discussing gravity. If you fire a bullet straight up into the air, it'll travel (overcoming the force of gravity) until it reaches its farthest or highest point, and then it'll fall.

When push comes to shove: Applied force

An *applied force* is any type of force that a person or another object exerts on something. If your drill sergeant tells you to mop the parking lot when it's raining, you'll run out there and apply force to the mop. You'll also apply force to the wringer in the mop bucket to get it to squeeze out the water. When one Humvee tows another, the towing vehicle applies force; likewise, when you throw a live grenade in basic training, your hand applies a force on the grenade, so you're looking at applied force in action.

CENTRIFUGAL FORCE: FALSE GRAVITY

An object traveling in a circle appears to experience a gravitational force. This isn't really gravity; instead, it's a concept known as *centrifugal force*. The amount of force depends on the mass of the object, the speed of rotation, and the distance from the center:

- The more massive the object, the greater the force.

- The greater the speed of the object, the greater the force. Faster rotating speed results in higher overall speed.

- The greater the distance from the center, the greater the force.

The centrifugal force, or effect, on an object is actually a fictitious outward force on an object moving along a curved path, which can be equal to the centripetal force on an object. *Centripetal force* points toward the center of an object's circular path, perpendicular to the direction of motion of an object.

If you're riding on a merry-go-round on the playground (whee!), you have to exert a constant force to keep from flying off. This feeling of being pushed outward isn't due to something actually pushing you in that direction but to your body's inertia trying to keep you moving in a straight line. (You can read more about inertia in the "Exerting force to make things happen" section in this chapter.) Because Newton's first law states that moving objects tend to want to travel in one direction, as the merry-go-round turns, your body wants to keep traveling in one direction (*tangent* to the circle, if you like math), so you feel you're being pushed outward.

Stretching out tension

Tension force is the force transmitted through a rope, string, or wire when force is applied to both ends. The force is the amount of tension directed along the rope, string, or wire and pulls equally on the objects at both ends. Tension force is usually measured in either pounds–force (lbf) or newtons (N); 4.45 newtons equal 1 pound–force. See Figure 15-2.

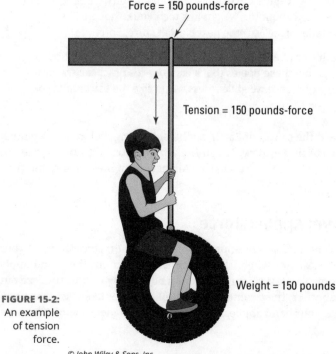

Force = 150 pounds-force

Tension = 150 pounds-force

Weight = 150 pounds

FIGURE 15-2: An example of tension force.

Friction: Resisting the urge to move

When one surface (such as a floor) resists the movement of another surface (the bottom of a box), the result is *frictional* resistance. (This friction isn't like resisting orders to cut the grass. That type of resistance may cause friction between you and your dad, but I'm talking about a different kind of resistance here.)

In order to perform work — that is, to get an object to move in the direction you're pushing or pulling — sometimes you have to overcome friction by applying more force. For example, when you're moving a box across a smooth, vinyl floor, little friction is produced, so the amount of force required to push the box comes from the box's weight and the very minor friction produced by the smooth floor. But when you're moving a box across a carpeted floor, more friction is produced, so you have to push harder to move the same box the same distance. (See the later section "You Call That Work?!" for more information on what's considered work in physics terms.)

Rolling friction (like the friction that occurs when you roll a wheel along the pavement) is always less than sliding friction (which occurs when you shove a box along the floor). If you put wheels on a box (or put the box on a wheeled tool, such as a dolly), it's much easier to push!

You can decrease friction by using a lubricant. Oil, grease, and similar materials reduce friction between two surfaces. So theoretically, if you oil the bottom of a box, it's easier to move! (Oiling the bottom of a box isn't recommended — for reasons involving the appearance of your floor and the contents of the box — but some oil on the bearings of a dolly would be a huge help.)

Elastic recoil: The trampoline of physics

Liquids and gases don't have a specific shape, but solid matter does. Solids are perfectly happy with the way they look and resist changes in shape. If you exert a force on a solid shape, it responds by exerting a force in the opposite direction. This force is called *elastic recoil*. It's also called a *spring force*. All material has a constant property (called a *spring constant*) that's directly proportional to the force it generates based on the distance it's deformed. The mathematical relationship is expressed as Spring Force = Spring Constant × Distance Displaced.

Take a look at Figure 15-3. The cat is standing on a board suspended on two blocks. While the board bends, the cat can feel the force of the board trying to regain its original shape. If the cat steps off the board, the board will recoil to its normal state.

FIGURE 15-3: The concept of elastic recoil.

© John Wiley & Sons, Inc.

The law of attraction: Magnetism

Magnetism comes from the force (attract or repel) that magnets cause. The type of magnetism you're probably most familiar with is *ferromagnetism*, which involves iron; it's the strongest type.

All magnets have north and south poles, and opposite poles are attracted to each other. If you rub a piece of iron across a magnet, all the north-seeking poles in the iron line up in the same direction, and the force they generate creates a magnetic field. That magnetic field pulls or repels other objects, creating a type of force.

TECHNICAL STUFF

Every substance is made from atoms, and every atom has electrons that carry electric charges. These electrons spin and circle the atom's nucleus, which generates an electric current; as a result, each electron acts like a tiny magnet. Most substances have equal numbers of spinning electrons, and half spin in one direction while the other half spin in the other direction. That cancels out their magnetism, and it's why you can't use a refrigerator magnet to pick up a piece of paper or a shard of glass. But the refrigerator magnet is another story; it contains atoms where most of the electrons are spinning in the same direction.

Tapping into electrical forces

When you rub a balloon on your little brother's head and then touch the balloon to the wall, chances are that it'll stick. That's due to electrical force. This kind of force, called *static electricity*, is the buildup of electrical charges on the surface of a substance. Opposite electrical charges attract, so the charge on the balloon and the charge on the wall are literally pulling for each other.

Opening the window to drag forces

Drag forces slow down objects; the amount of drag depends on an object's shape and the substance it's moving through, such as air or water. If you've ever held your hand out of the car window horizontally, then rotated it vertically, you've experienced the increase in drag force that pushed your arm backward. Designers make cars and boats as streamlined as possible to reduce drag, making these vehicles as efficient as possible. (If your drill sergeant at Basic Combat Training calls you a "high-speed, low-drag" troop, it's a compliment — but don't thank her. Trust me on this one.)

You Call That Work?!

REMEMBER

Mechanically speaking, *work* happens when a force (usually measured in pounds) moving over a measurable distance (usually measured in feet) overcomes a resistance. In the United States, the unit of measure for work is often called a *foot-pound*. (**Note:** The rest of the world uses the newton-meter, or joule.) One foot-pound of work occurs when a 1-pound weight is lifted to a height of 1 foot. You can represent this concept in equation form:

$$\text{Work} = \text{Force} \times \text{Distance}$$

Work is different from effort; work is the result of effort. You can think of *effort* as being force and of *work* as being what you produce with that force.

Contrasting the difference between potential and kinetic energy

Energy is the capacity to do work. Every object in the universe has energy, and it's either potential or kinetic. *Potential energy* is stored energy — energy that's not doing anything at the moment but that's in the object by virtue of its position in a field. If this book is resting in your hands right now, the book itself is holding potential energy. If you raise the book over your head, you're increasing its potential energy (thanks to the Earth's gravitational pull). When you accidentally drop it, all its potential energy becomes *kinetic energy,* or energy of motion. When the book hits the ground, its energy becomes potential again. (*Tip:* Don't drop the book if you're reading it as an e-book; replacing your tablet is going to be expensive.)

Potential energy can't be transferred between objects. The more massive an object is, the more potential and kinetic energy it has (so a bowling ball contains more energy than a basketball does). Both these forms of energy are measured in joules.

Exerting force to make things happen

"An object at rest stays at rest and an object in motion stays in motion with the same speed and in the same direction unless acted upon by an unbalanced force." That's Newton's first law of motion, and in plain English, it means that objects just keep on keepin' on until some outside force makes a change.

As I note in Chapter 11, an object's tendency to resist change in its state of motion is called *inertia.* All objects follow this law, even if it doesn't always look like it. Without gravity and physical obstacles, an object in motion would keep going in the same direction at the same speed forever.

Some objects resist changes more than others do, and it all comes down to mass. Mass is solely dependent on the inertia of an object, which means the more inertia an object has, the more mass it has. A more massive object, like a tactical military vehicle, has a greater tendency to resist changes in its state of motion than a smaller object, like a bowling ball, does. The earlier section "A-mass-ing Knowledge on Matter, Weight, Density, and Relativity" has more on mass.

Overcoming resistance

The resistance that the work overcomes isn't the same thing as the weight of the object. (If you've ever tried to put your freaked-out cat in a cat carrier to go to the vet, you know what I mean.) In other words, if you try to move a 1,200-pound piano, you'll probably notice a measurable difference between the amount of work it takes to shove it along the floor and the amount of work it takes to carry it up the stairs. But don't take my word for it — you can demonstrate this concept at home. First, find a 1,200-pound piano and push it across the floor. Next, put it on your back and carry it up the stairs. See the difference? (Really, don't put the piano on your back. I'm just trying to make a point here.)

When you move the piano across the floor, you're really working (pushing) against the frictional resistance (the force that's produced when two surfaces rub together) of the piano rather than its full weight. Under these circumstances, the frictional resistance of the piano offers less resistance than its full weight. There are times when an object's full weight is less than its frictional resistance. Consider trying to push a textbook across a deep-pile carpet. Picking the book up and carrying it is easier. (For more about friction, see the earlier section "Friction: Resisting the urge to move.")

Powering through work

Work, at least in terms of physics, is what happens when a force acts on an object over a length of displacement. The two main ingredients in work are force and displacement. You do work on your duffel bag when you drag it from the bus to the reception area on your first day in basic training. You do work on your groceries when you carry them in from the car. You do work on the barbell when you lift it over your head. In each of those scenarios, you apply force that causes displacement. In each of those scenarios, you apply force over some distance.

Power is the rate at which work is done. Mathematically speaking,

$$\text{Power} = \frac{\text{Work}}{\text{Time}}$$

In this formula, work is usually measured in joules, time is measured in seconds, and power is measured in watts.

In many machines, power is measured in *horsepower*, which you may be more familiar with than watts and joules. Using the same formula to calculate horsepower requires you to measure work in foot-pounds, time in minutes, and power in foot-pounds-per-minute. Horsepower is derived from the estimate that an average horse can do 33,000 foot-pounds of work in 1 minute (according to James Watt). Therefore, 1 horsepower = 33,000 foot-pounds per minute. One horsepower is also the same as 550 foot-pounds per second, which is equivalent to 745.7 watts.

Relying on Machines to Help You Work

Humans have used machines that help make work easier since early hominids (*Homo habilis,* to be specific) created crude wedges about 2 million years ago. The first wheel wasn't used on a chariot until about 3,200 BCE, but machines have steadily evolved to make humans more efficient.

In addition to increasing efficiency, machines are also used to help with work that couldn't be done otherwise. Think of the mechanisms and machines you use every day — from the simple (like the hinge that allows a door to move easily when you push it open) to the more complex (like the hydraulic lift that allows you to lift a car up to check its undercarriage). You could move most doors out of the way without hinges, but you couldn't lift a car over your head without some help.

REMEMBER

Machines give you the ability to magnify and change the direction and magnitude of forces. When a machine multiplies the force you use, it gives you a *mechanical advantage.* This concept can be stated as

$$\text{Mechanical Advantage} = \frac{\text{Resistance}}{\text{Effort}} = \frac{\text{Output Force}}{\text{Input Force}}$$

Some simple machines may give you a mechanical advantage of only 1 or 2. This means that they enable you to do one or two times the amount of work by expending the same effort. But those simple machines are still worth using! Often, even if a machine doesn't multiply your effort (or doesn't multiply your effort by much), it can at least spread your effort out and make it more effective.

Machines make work easier by providing some trade-off between the force applied and the distance over which it's applied. Keep reading to find out more on some basic types of machines.

Using levers to your advantage

You may not think of the seesaw at the neighborhood park as a machine, but it is. It's a lever. Levers are among the simplest machines used to help increase force.

All levers work by using a *fulcrum* (point of support) to reduce resistance and multiply the effect of effort. Resistance (such as a weight force from an object with mass) is exerted at one end of the lever (the *resistance arm*) and effort is exerted at the other (the *effort arm*). The effort arm moves the resistance arm. See Figure 15-4.

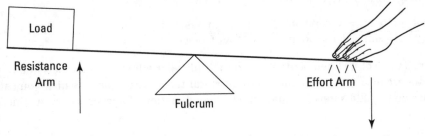

FIGURE 15-4: A simple lever.

REMEMBER

To determine how much a lever reduces the amount of effort needed to do work, use the following formula:

$$\frac{\text{Length of Effort Arm}}{\text{Length of Resistance Arm}} = \frac{\text{Resistance Force}}{\text{Effort Force}}$$

As you can see, the amount of effort needed to move the lever varies depending on how long the effort arm is and how long the resistance arm is. Keep in mind that a short resistance arm, although easier to move, can't move an object as far through space as a longer resistance arm can. Theoretically, you could lift a car off the ground with one hand if you had a half-mile-long lever — but why would you want to?

REMEMBER

The mechanical advantage of using a lever can be stated as

$$\text{Mechanical Advantage} = \frac{\text{Effort Arm}}{\text{Resistance Arm}}$$

If the effort arm is 6 inches and the resistance arm is 3 inches, the mechanical advantage is 2. If the effort arm is 6 feet and the resistance arm is 3 feet, the mechanical advantage is still 2.

Levers fall into classes: 1, 2, and 3. A *Class 1* lever's fulcrum is between the effort and load. Scissors, pliers, old-school seesaws, and the oars on a boat are examples of Class 1 levers, as is Figure 15-4. With a *Class 2* lever, the load is between the effort and the fulcrum; think wheelbarrows, crowbars, and nutcrackers. The fulcrum on a *Class 3* lever is beside the effort and opposite the load. Tweezers, staplers, and brooms are all Class 3 levers. Check out Figure 15-5 for examples of each class of lever.

FIGURE 15-5: Classes of levers.

Ramping up the inclined plane

The *inclined plane*, also called a *ramp*, is another very simple machine that makes moving an object from one point to another easier. The ramp spreads your work out over a longer distance, so less force is needed to do the work.

For instance, suppose you have to lift a 50-pound barrel to a truck bed that's 3 feet off the ground. You'd have to use 50 pounds of force for 3 feet to move the barrel. But if you put a 6-foot ramp in place and pushed the barrel up the ramp, you'd only use half as much force to get the barrel in the truck (assuming there was no friction) because the mechanical advantage of such a ramp is 2.

REMEMBER

The advantage of using a ramp can be expressed as

$$\frac{\text{Length of Ramp}}{\text{Height of Ramp}} = \frac{\text{Weight of Object Being Moved}}{\text{Force Required to Move Object}}$$

REMEMBER

Wedges are a form of inclined plane and can multiply your effort in much the same way as a ramp can. Screws are also inclined planes, only in spiral form. Screw jacks, which you can use to lift your house up to build a new foundation, are a combination of a lever and an inclined plane.

Easing your effort: Pulleys and gears

Pulleys and gears are simple machines that can be used to change the magnitude (size) and direction of force. When you ride in an elevator, step onto an escalator, drive your car, or wind your watch, you're using pulleys and gears.

Block and tackle systems

When used in a *block and tackle* arrangement (see Figure 15-6), pulleys make lifting heavy objects easier. In block and tackle systems, pulleys can also be used to change the direction of your pull. If you tie a 200-pound crate to one end of a rope, run the rope through a pulley, and grab the other end of the rope, you can pull down on the rope to lift the crate up. Without a pulley, you could pull down on the crate all day, and it wouldn't go up. In this case, using a simple pulley, the force of your pull must equal the weight of the object being lifted. The regular pulley doesn't multiply your force, but it makes the process of lifting easier by allowing you to redirect the force.

FIGURE 15-6: A pulley used in a block and tackle system.

© John Wiley & Sons, Inc.

Using a block and tackle system allows you to distribute your force more effectively. Instead of hoisting that entire 200-pound crate in one try, you can pull on a rope to lift it a few inches, pull on the rope some more to lift it a few more inches, and so on, provided you add a ratchet mechanism or trapped roller bearing. The block and tackle requires less force to lift the heavy crate, and the ratchet allows you to perform effort over short distances, creating smaller periods of work. This makes the work easier to perform.

A block and tackle system can also be used to reduce effort by magnifying force. To help understand how this works, look at Figure 15-7:

» Example 1 shows a 100-pound box secured to the ceiling by a single line. The weight supported by the line is equal to the weight of the box.

» In Example 2, the box is secured to the ceiling by using two lines. Each line is supporting one-half the weight of the box.

» In Example 3, a single line is threaded through a pulley. Although the line (as a whole) is supporting the entire weight of the box, each section of the line is supporting only one-half of the box's weight, just as in Example 2.

» In Example 4, a man is using this principle to lift the 100-pound box by applying only 50 pounds of force. In short, this block and tackle system provides the man with a mechanical advantage of 2. In receiving a mechanical advantage of force, the man must pull the rope farther than if he weren't using a pulley. In this example, the man would have to pull 2 feet of rope to raise the box 1 foot.

FIGURE 15-7: Reducing effort by using a block and tackle.

© John Wiley & Sons, Inc.

Additional pulleys can be added to a block and tackle arrangement to further increase the mechanical advantage. Figure 15-8 shows a couple of examples:

» Example 1 is a 2:1 pulley system in which two sections of rope produce a mechanical advantage of 2. Lifting a weight with this pulley arrangement requires only $\frac{1}{2}$ of the effort required to lift the weight directly. However, in order to lift the crate 1 foot, you have to pull 2 feet of rope. The fixed pulley in the upper-right side of the figure only redirects the tension force you need to pull up the weight.

» Example 2 illustrates a block and tackle system with six sections of rope. Using this arrangement provides you with a mechanical advantage of 6, but you have to pull the rope 6 feet for every foot you want to raise the box.

You notice in both examples that the mechanical advantage is determined by the number of rope sections only attached to the top of the box (and the pulley[s] fixed to the top of the box).

Example 1

Example 2

Understanding how gears work

Machines often use gears to transmit motion from one place to another. An additional advantage of using gears is that they can be used to change direction, increase or decrease speed, or increase or decrease force.

REMEMBER

Gears arranged in a series turn in the opposite direction of each other. If you have an even number of gears connected in a series, the first and last gear turn in opposite directions. If you have an odd number of gears aligned in a series, the first and last gear spin in the same direction. Look at Figure 15-9. Gear 1 is rotating counterclockwise, which causes Gear 2 to turn clockwise, resulting in Gear 3 spinning counterclockwise, with Gear 4 turning clockwise.

The speed at which a gear rotates (in relation to the driving gear connected to it) depends on the number of teeth. In Figure 15-10, Gear 1 has six teeth, and Gear 2 has eight teeth. This relation of teeth can be expressed as a ratio of 6:8, which can be reduced to 3:4. That means Gear 1 has to rotate four times in order for Gear 2 to make three revolutions. Or expressed another way, for each rotation made by Gear 1, Gear 2 will make three-quarters of a revolution.

FIGURE 15-10: The ratio of teeth between two gears affects rotational speed.

$$\text{Ratio} = \frac{3}{4}$$

© John Wiley & Sons, Inc.

When gear shafts aren't parallel to one another, *bevel gears* can be used to connect shafts at different angles. The principles of gear rotation remain the same. Figure 15-11 shows an example of bevel gears designed to connect shafts having a 90-degree angle to the other. A car's differential, which takes a drive shaft rotating along the length of the car and sends power 90 degrees out to the rear tires, is an example of a bevel gear.

FIGURE 15-11: Two bevel gears meet at a right angle.

90 Degrees

© John Wiley & Sons, Inc.

Pulley and belt arrangements

In addition to magnifying force as part of a block and tackle system, pulleys have another use. When connected by a system of belts, pulleys can drive other pulleys.

Like gears, pulleys are used to transmit motion from one location to another. However, the physical properties of pulleys are different from those of gears:

>> **Turning direction:** Unless the driving belt is reversed (twisted), pulleys connected in series rotate in the same direction. Figure 15-12 illustrates this concept with two sets of pulleys. In the first set of pulleys, all the pulleys turn in the same direction (counterclockwise) as the

driving pulley. However, in the second set of pulleys, the driving pulley and the lower pulley are rotating counterclockwise, but the right-hand pulley is rotating in a clockwise direction because the belt is twisted.

>> **Speed of rotation:** Although the speed of gear rotation is determined by the number of teeth, how fast a pulley rotates depends on the diameter of the pulley in relation to the diameter of the pulley that's driving it. Have a look at Figure 15-13. Pulley A has a diameter of 1 inch, Pulley B has a diameter of 2 inches, and Pulley C measures 4 inches in diameter. The ratio among the three pulleys is 1:2:4. For every complete revolution made by Pulley A, Pulley B makes half of a revolution. Each time Pulley B makes a full revolution, Pulley C makes half of a revolution. Thus, for every full revolution of Pulley A, Pulley C makes a quarter of a revolution.

FIGURE 15-12:
Pulleys rotate in the same direction unless the belt is reversed.

© John Wiley & Sons, Inc.

FIGURE 15-13:
Pulley rotation speed is based on the pulley's diameter.

Pulley A Diameter = 1 inch
Pulley B Diameter = 2 inches
Pulley C Diameter = 4 inches

© John Wiley & Sons, Inc.

Multiplying your effort: Wheels and axles

The *wheel-and-axle* machine multiplies the effort you use, producing a greater force. When you steer a car by using a steering wheel (which is a wheel-and-axle device), a little effort exerted on the steering wheel turns the wheels of the car in the direction you desire. Turning your car wheels would be a lot more complicated if you didn't have the steering wheel.

In true wheel-and-axle machines, the wheel and the axle are fixed together and turn at the same time. This arrangement multiplies the amount of force you can exert by a considerable amount.

The relationship between the radius of the wheel and the radius of the area to which force is being applied determines the mechanical advantage you receive by using this piece of equipment. (Remember, the *radius* of a circle equals half the diameter; a straight line extending from the center of the circle to the edge is the radius of a circle.) A hand drill may apply 200 pounds of force for your 10 pounds of effort. (A hand drill uses a gear to convert the direction of the force.) See Figure 15-14.

FIGURE 15-14: A hand drill increases mechanical advantage.

Mechanical advantage of wheel and axle =

$$\frac{R}{\frac{1}{2}W} = \frac{S}{E}$$

Force required to turn handle **(E)**

Radius of wheel's circle **(R)**

Resistance offered by material **(S)**

Width of drill tip **(W)**

© John Wiley & Sons, Inc.

Opening up the door to torque

Torque is a twisting or turning force that tends to cause rotation around an axis. Cars and other vehicles use torque to make their engines run (find out more about that in Chapter 13), but it's not just for drag racing. Torques are everywhere else in your life, too.

The simplest way to visualize torque is to open a door. Turning a doorknob and pushing a door open (and turning a key, for that matter) are examples of torque in action. Think of the door as the movement arm and its hinges as the axis. When you push on a door to open it, you push toward the edge that's not hinged to the wall because it's easier to open. (Try to open your front door by pushing on it about 6 inches from the hinges — it's a lot harder than you think.) When you're thinking proportionally, the wider the door is, the more easily you can open it from the side away from the hinges; it becomes harder as you move closer to the hinges. Torque is measured in newton-meters or pound-feet (see Chapter 11 for more SI units of measurement).

HORSEPOWER: A MEASURABLE MARKETING TACTIC

Vehicle and other engines measure power output in *horsepower*, a term that comes from the 18th century. Steam power had been recently invented, and it was poised to send a lot of horses back to the stable. James Watt invented a new version of the steam engine and wanted to market it to buyers, but he had a big problem: He couldn't show people how valuable it was because he had no way to compare it to the amount of work output people were used to seeing from their hoofed helpers. Watt decided to watch mill horses who trod in circles all day, every day, to operate the gears that made mills run. He soon discovered that they usually walked a 24-foot-diameter circle about 144 times per hour, and each horse pulled with a force that he estimated to be 180 pounds. He calculated that one horsepower is equivalent to one horse doing 33,000 foot-pounds of work in one minute. Watt then used his unit of power to show off how much more work a steam engine could do than a horse, and the measurement stuck. It's now used for all kinds of engines, ranging from muscle cars and gas-powered leaf blowers to electric motors in washing machines.

Torque can be static or dynamic. *Static torque* doesn't produce an angular acceleration — it's what happens if you push on a door marked "Pull," or pedal your bike at a constant speed without accelerating. *Dynamic torque* produces an angular acceleration, and it's what you see when a race-car takes off down the track.

Getting a grip on things with vises

Although many mechanisms are designed to transmit motion, some machines have the purpose of keeping things motionless. Vises are very useful because they can close around items and hold them with great force (much greater force than you could do by holding the item in your hands). Figure 15-15 shows an illustration of a standard shop vise.

FIGURE 15-15:
A standard shop vise.

Rotating the handle on the vise causes a screw to turn, which either tightens or loosens the vise. A *screw* is a cylinder wrapped in a continuous spiral. The distance between the ridges of the spiral is called the *pitch* of the thread. The greater the pitch of the thread, the farther the jaws of the vice move for each revolution of the handle. However, there's a trade-off. Larger pitches require more force to rotate the handle than screws with smaller pitches do.

Magnifying your force with liquid: Hydraulic pressure

A *hydraulic jack* uses a nearly incompressible liquid, such as oil, to exert force in order to move an object (see Figure 15-16). As the handle moves, it applies pressure to the oil. Because the oil doesn't compress, the oil transmits whatever force is applied to it to the work cylinder with little or no loss in efficiency. The mechanical advantage is the ratio between the diameters of the two cylinders.

In the figure, the small cylinder has a diameter of 1 inch and the large cylinder has a diameter of 4 inches. This difference in diameter results in a mechanical advantage of 4. If the rocks weigh a total of 100 pounds, only 25 pounds of force has to be applied to the piston in the small cylinder in order to lift the load. However, although the force required is reduced by a factor of 4, the smaller piston has to move 4 feet for every foot the piston in the larger cylinder moves.

FIGURE 15-16:
A hydraulic
jack.

Force

Force

© John Wiley & Sons, Inc.

Working Your Way to a Better Test Score

When you take the Mechanical Comprehension subtest, you may not know the correct answer to a question, or you may not know the mechanical principle involved. You may know the mechanical principle but not remember the formula you need to come up with the right answer. Never fear — you can still stumble through this test without totally crashing and burning.

Using your observations and common sense

Questions on this subtest often include illustrations. The ASVAB test-makers expect you to look at the illustrated device and guess how it operates. When you run across these types of questions, make sure you understand the illustration. Often, parts of the device are labeled. Make certain you read and understand these labels before you try to answer a question about the illustration.

Also, try to use a common-sense approach. You may see something like the following question:

EXAMPLE

Which of the following controls an automatic sump pump?

(A) mechanical switch

(B) manual switch

(C) pneumatic valve

(D) float

You may not know the answer to this question, but you can rule out Choice (B), manual switch, because the question asks you about an automatic sump pump, and anything manual isn't automatic. Eliminating one choice narrows your chances from one in four to one in three. Not a bad start, huh?

A *sump pump* is used to drain water from an area, and if you know that, you have an even better shot at getting this question right. Think about what type of device detects the presence of water, and you may guess correctly that Choice (D), float, is the right answer.

You can answer a lot of the questions correctly if you just think about what you've observed in the world around you. Remember, the Mechanical Comprehension subtest also tests your knowledge of physical principles of the world around you — questions you may expect to find on the General Science subtest. For example, a question may ask something like this:

EXAMPLE

If all the following objects are the same temperature, which one will feel coldest on a cool day?

(A) a wooden spoon

(B) a plastic spoon

(C) a metal spoon

(D) a fiberglass spoon

You don't need to know mechanical or scientific principles to know that a metal spoon will feel colder than the other spoons. So it makes sense to select Choice (C) as your answer, even if you can't explain the science behind this correct answer.

TECHNICAL STUFF

The nerve endings in your skin detect the difference between your inside body temperature and your outside skin temperature. Metal is an excellent conductor of heat, so heat readily flows from your hand into the metal. The heat is conducted rapidly away into the bulk of the metal, leaving your skin surface relatively cool. That's why metal feels cooler than other, less efficient conductors of heat, such as wood, plastic, or fiberglass.

Using the mathematics of mechanics

Mechanical principles are based on mathematical principles. Therefore, a screw making a complete revolution turns 360 degrees, because a mathematical principle states that 360 degrees are in a circle, a complete revolution. If you have to know the surface area of a floor to determine the pounds per square inch that a ton of tile would put on the floor, that's a mathematical principle, too (Area = Length × Width).

Suppose you run across this question:

EXAMPLE

A 3-inch-diameter flanged pipe with six holes is being fitted to a base with six holes. What's the maximum number of degrees the pipe must be rotated in order to line up the holes?

(A) 120 degrees

(B) 180 degrees

(C) 60 degrees

(D) 360 degrees

This isn't really a Mechanical Comprehension question at all — it's a math question. The only part that requires mechanical knowledge is knowing that the holes are spaced equally distant from one another on a flanged pipe. The answer is 360 degrees ÷ 6 = 60 degrees, Choice (C).

Guessing with a mechanical mind

TIP

Like most of the other subtests on the ASVAB, you can and should guess on the Mechanical Comprehension subtest when you don't know the answer (unless you're nearing the end of the CAT-ASVAB; too many incorrect answers at the end of a subtest give the impression you're just guessing and can bring on a penalty). Check out these tips to help you narrow the field:

>> The amount of force needed to move an object (not including friction resistance) is never greater than the weight of the object. Any answer that includes a force that's greater than the weight of the object being moved is probably wrong.

>> The correct answer is a mechanical answer. For example, if the question asks, "What's the purpose of lubricating oil in an engine?" the correct answer won't be "to make the parts look shiny." The answer may be "to reduce friction between moving parts."

>> Any change in a mechanical operation almost always has pluses and minuses associated with it. So when a question proposes a change, the correct answer is probably the one that specifies the good, the bad, and the ugly. For instance, suppose the question says, "Enlarging the wheel on a hand drill will . . .?" The correct answer is the one that says something like "increase the mechanical advantage and decrease the amount of effort needed to operate the drill."

For more general tips on guessing on the ASVAB, flip to Chapter 3.

Mechanical Comprehension Practice Questions

Mechanical Comprehension is all about figuring out how machines and mechanical mechanisms operate. A solid background in mechanical physics is a big advantage in scoring well in this area. Basic math skills are also a plus in this area. Test yourself with the next several questions.

1. The moisture that forms on the inside of a window on a cold day is called

   (A) condensation.

   (B) distillation.

   (C) evaporation.

   (D) tarnation.

2. If a 200-pound barrel must be lifted 4 feet to the bed of a box truck, an inclined plane will reduce the amount of effort required to move the barrel by half if the inclined plane is

   (A) 2 feet long.

   (B) 6 feet long.

   (C) 8 feet long.

   (D) 9 feet long.

3. While throwing a football, Dan exerts a forward force of 50 newtons on the ball and pushes it forward a distance of 1.2 meters. How much work does he do on the football?

   (A) 45 joules

   (B) 60 joules

   (C) 50 joules

   (D) 50.5 joules

4. A block and tackle is used to lift a truck engine with a weight of nearly 7,406 newtons. The input force required to lift this weight using the block and tackle is 308.6 newtons. What is the mechanical advantage of the block and tackle?

   (A) 23.99

   (B) 15

   (C) 25

   (D) 24.75

5. Which of the tanks will overfill?

© John Wiley & Sons, Inc.

   (A) Tank A

   (B) Tanks A and B

   (C) Tank C

   (D) Tanks B and C

6. Two people are carrying a 100-pound crate on a 2-x-8-x-12-foot board. To distribute the load evenly between the two people, the crate should be placed

   (A) 2 feet from the end of the board.

   (B) in the middle of the board.

   (C) 3 feet from the end of the board.

   (D) The load can't be evenly distributed.

7. Wheel A has a diameter of 9 feet. Wheel B has a diameter of 12 feet. If both wheels revolve at the same rate, Wheel B will cover a linear distance of 24 feet

   (A) at the same speed as Wheel A.

   (B) more slowly than Wheel A.

   (C) in half the time of Wheel A.

   (D) more quickly than Wheel A.

8. The shock absorber on a car is a very large spring. If Jonas's car hits a pothole with 600 pounds of force and the shock absorber compresses 3 inches, what is its spring constant in pounds per inch?

(A) 200

(B) 600

(C) 20

(D) 1,800

9. In the following figure, a 600-pound weight is placed on a 10-pound board that has been evenly balanced between two scales. How much does the left scale measure if the weight is $\frac{2}{3}$ closer to the left than to the right?

© John Wiley & Sons, Inc.

(A) 400

(B) 300

(C) 405

(D) 410

10. Daisy's single-speed bicycle has a front gear with 48 teeth and a rear gear with 12 teeth. If Daisy pedaled at 80 revolutions per minute (rpm), how fast would her rear wheel rotate?

(A) 280 rpm

(B) 320 rpm

(C) 70 rpm

(D) 128 rpm

11. Not including friction, a stationary single pulley gives a mechanical advantage of

(A) 2.

(B) 4.

(C) 3.

(D) 1.

12. Four gears are connected in a series. If Gear #1 is turning clockwise, Gear #4 will turn

(A) clockwise.

(B) counterclockwise.

(C) more quickly than Gear #1.

(D) more slowly than Gear #1.

13. James applies force at one end of a hydraulic jack. The area at the other end of the jack is five times the area where James is applying the force. How much larger is the exerted force than what James is applying?

(A) twice as large

(B) half as large

(C) one-fifth as large

(D) five times as large

14. Mr. Roth's children — Jake, Paul, and Jill — weigh 80, 60, and 50 pounds, respectively. They all sit on the same side of a seesaw together. Jake sits 3 feet from the fulcrum, Paul sits 5 feet from the fulcrum, and Jill sits 6 feet from the fulcrum. How far from the fulcrum must Mr. Roth sit on the other side to balance the seesaw if he weighs 200 pounds?

(A) 4.2 feet

(B) 5.5 feet

(C) 5 feet

(D) 4 feet

15. A rope is pulling a 320-pound box up an incline that's 16 feet long. If 80 pounds of force is used to move the box up the incline, how tall is the incline?

© John Wiley & Sons, Inc.

(A) 6 feet

(B) 10 feet

(C) 4 feet

(D) 8 feet

16. The sideways force one feels when a car turns sharply is often called

(A) thrust force.

(B) angle force.

(C) centrifugal force.

(D) positive force.

17. When two or more forces act to balance each other out, the condition is called

(A) equilibrium.

(B) static recoil.

(C) gravitational balance.

(D) concurrent forces.

18. Two balls of the same density, one large and one small, roll toward each other at the same speed. When they collide, what will happen to the larger ball?

(A) It will be propelled backward.

(B) It will jump over the smaller ball.

(C) It will continue forward.

(D) It will stop.

Answers and Explanations

Use this answer key to score the Mechanical Comprehension practice questions.

1. **A.** *Distillation* is the process of extracting or refining a substance using both boiling and condensation. *Evaporation* is the process of removing moisture from the surface of a liquid — the water molecules escape the surface and assume gas form. *Tarnation* is an interjection used to express anger. The correct answer is Choice (A), condensation.

2. **C.** The formula used for determining how an inclined plane reduces effort is Length of Ramp / Height of Ramp = Weight of the Object / Force, or $x \div 4 = 200 \div 100$. The amount of force needed to lift the object is equivalent to the object's weight, but the question wants to reduce that amount of force to half, so half of the object's weight is 100. Now do the math: $x \div 4 \times 4 = 2 \times 4$; $x = 8$. The correct answer is Choice (C).

3. **B.** Work is the amount of energy transferred by a force. To calculate how much work is done, use this formula (note that a newton-meter equals a joule):

$$\begin{aligned} \text{Work} &= \text{Force} \times \text{Distance} \\ &= (50 \, \text{newtons})(1.2 \, \text{meters}) \\ &= 60 \, \text{joules} \end{aligned}$$

4. **A.** To find the mechanical advantage of the block and tackle, use the following formula:

$$\begin{aligned} \text{MA} &= \frac{\text{Output Force}}{\text{Input Force}} \\ &= \frac{7,406}{308.6} = 23.99 \end{aligned}$$

5. **C.** Tank C has an inflow greater than its outflow, so it will eventually overfill.

6. **B.** If the weight is placed closer to one person or the other, that person would carry more of the load, so the weight should be placed in the middle. Choice (B) is the correct answer.

7. **D.** Because Wheel A has a smaller circumference, it covers a shorter linear distance than Wheel B when turning at the same rate. Thus, Wheel B covers the distance of 24 feet faster than Wheel A. Choice (C) is inaccurate because the diameter of Wheel A isn't exactly half the diameter of Wheel B. If both wheels revolve at the same rate, then Wheel A turns 25 percent more slowly than Wheel B, because Wheel A's diameter is three-quarters of Wheel B's. Choice (D) is the correct answer.

8. **A.** The formula for force on a spring is $F = -kx$, with F representing force, k representing the spring constant, and x representing the displacement of the spring. The spring is compressed so the displacement, 3 inches, is negative. Just plug in the values from the question and solve:

$$\begin{aligned} 600 &= -k(-3) \\ 600 &= 3k \\ \frac{600}{3} &= \frac{3k}{3} \\ 200 &= k \end{aligned}$$

9. **C.** Two-thirds of the weight of the block (400 pounds) is supported by the left scale because the block is $\frac{2}{3}$ closer to the left than to the right. The board is evenly placed, so each scale supports $\frac{1}{2}$ of its weight (5 pounds). The total weight being supported by the left scale is 400 pounds + 5 pounds = 405 pounds.

10. **B.** Each full turn of the pedals turns the rear wheel $48 \div 12 = 4$ revolutions. If the pedals were to turn at 80 rpm, the rear wheel would rotate at $4 \times 80 \text{ rpm} = 320 \text{ rpm}$.

11. **D.** A stationary single pulley allows you to change the direction of force but doesn't result in an increased mechanical advantage. The correct answer is Choice (D).

12. **B.** Gears connected in series turn in opposite directions of each other. Gears 1 and 3 rotate clockwise, and Gears 2 and 4 rotate counterclockwise. The size of gears is unknown, so there isn't enough information to determine whether Choice (C) or Choice (D) is correct. The correct answer is Choice (B).

13. **D.** A hydraulic jack uses an incompressible fluid, so the pressure has to be the same everywhere $(P_1 = P_2)$. *Pressure* is force divided by area $(P = F/A)$, so set up a proportion that represents the equal pressures:

$$P_1 = P_2$$
$$\frac{F_1}{A_1} = \frac{F_2}{A_2}$$

If the area at the output end of the jack is five times the area where James is applying the force, then the exerted force is five times the applied force:

$$\frac{F_1}{A_1} = \frac{5F_1}{5A_1}$$

Force is greater where the area is greater.

14. **A.** Let x = Mr. Roth's distance from the fulcrum.

© John Wiley & Sons, Inc.

$$200 \cdot x = (80 \cdot 3) + (60 \cdot 5) + (50 \cdot 6)$$
$$200x = 240 + 300 + 300$$
$$200x = 840$$
$$x = 4.2 \text{ feet}$$

15. **C.** First, determine the mechanical advantage of the ramp by using this formula:

$$\text{MA} = \frac{\text{Output Force}}{\text{Input Force}} = \frac{320}{80} = 4$$

The mechanical advantage of the ramp is also equal to the length of the ramp (16 feet) divided by the height of the ramp (x feet). Thus, the height of the ramp is 4 feet.

16. **C.** Although commonly referred to as centrifugal force, this property isn't actually a force at all but rather a property of inertia, one of Newton's laws of motion. As the car turns, your body is trying to continue traveling in a straight line. The correct answer is Choice (C).

17. **A.** When two or more forces interact so their combination cancels the other(s) out, there's a state of equilibrium. In this state, the velocity (speed and direction) of an object doesn't change. Choice (A) is the correct answer.

18. **C.** Because both balls are moving at the same speed, the ball with more mass (the larger one in this case, because both balls have the same density) will have more momentum. Upon impact, the heavier ball will slow down but continue in the same direction and knock the smaller, lighter ball backward.

Chapter **16**
Electronics Information

When a guy I know was around 12 years old, he impressed his parents by taking an old television set apart and putting it back together. He impressed them right up to the point where he plugged it in and blew up the garage. But the world of electronics is a bit more complex than simply plugging something in and seeing whether it works. This kid (and his garage) learned this lesson the hard way.

Six years later, when he took the ASVAB, he scored very well on the Electronics Information subtest. (Go figure!) This subtest is designed to measure your knowledge of the principles of electricity and how these principles are applied in the real world. You may see questions about transistors, magnets, engines and motors, and radio and television.

You don't have to be an electronics whiz to score well on this subtest. If you're not familiar with this information and you want to pursue a military career that requires you to do well on this subtest, this chapter is calling your name. You also need to have some familiarity with basic mathematical and algebraic principles (see Chapters 6 and 7 for more information).

REMEMBER

Not every military career requires a good score on this subtest. (Turn to Appendix A to find out which military jobs require a score on this — and other — subtests.) If the military feels that the Electronics Information subtest is important to your desired career, study intensively for this test. You can even take a course or two at the local community college if you don't have a strong enough background in this area.

You have 10 minutes to answer 15 questions on the computerized ASVAB or 21 minutes for 30 questions if you get tryout questions (more about those in Chapter 1). If you're taking the paper-and-pencil version of the test, you get 9 minutes to answer 20 questions. Although 9 or 10 minutes is sufficient time to answer the questions, it doesn't provide much time for anything else — if you don't know an answer, guess and go.

Uncovering the Secrets of Electricity

One day in 1752, Benjamin Franklin electrified the scientific community by tying a key to a kite and picking up an ambient electrical charge from a stormy sky. (You've probably heard the story, but what you haven't heard is that if lightning *had* struck the key, it would've killed

Franklin — and in fact, it *did* kill a German physicist who tried to replicate the experiment the following year.) What that led to was an incredibly important discovery, though: that scientists could harness and store electrical energy from lightning.

Although electricity was just a hobby for Ben Franklin, he created many of the terms used today when people talk about electricity: battery, conductor, condenser, charge, discharge, uncharged, negative, minus, plus, electric shock, and electrician.

Electricity is a general term for the variety of phenomena resulting from the presence and flow of electric current. You can't see electricity running through a wire (but you can certainly feel it). You only know electricity is there when you flip on the light switch and the light turns on. Even though electricity appears to be pretty mysterious at first glance, scientists understand a great deal about its properties and how it works.

REMEMBER

Electricity is measured in three ways:

>> **Volts:** Volts measure the difference of potential between two points.

>> **Amperes (amps):** Amps measure the number of electrons that move past a specific point in 1 second.

>> **Ohms:** Ohms measure resistance, including anything that could limit the flow of electrons.

REMEMBER

Here are some other electricity terms that are important for you to know for the ASVAB:

>> **Current:** Electricity is like water — it flows. Electrical current occurs when electrons move from one place to another. The use of *conductors,* such as copper and water, allows the electrons to move freely. *Insulators,* such as rubber and wood, discourage the electric current.

>> **Watt:** A watt measures *power,* the rate at which electrical energy is consumed or transformed into another type of energy, such as light or heat.

>> **Watt-hour:** A *watt-hour* is the amount of energy used in 1 hour at a rate of 1 watt. Most electricity is measured in *kilowatt-hours,* which is how much energy you'd use if you ran a 1,000-watt (1-kilowatt) device for an hour. For example, 10 kilowatt-hours is enough energy to run a 10,000-watt speaker system for an hour-long outdoor concert, or it could run a 5,000-watt air conditioner for 2 hours or a 1,000-watt waffle iron for 10 hours. You find watt-hours by multiplying wattage by time (expressed in hours).

>> **Kilowatt and kilowatt-hours:** One *kilowatt* (kW) equals 1,000 watts, and one *kilowatt-hour* (kWh) is one hour using electricity at a rate of 1,000 watts. Kilowatt-hours are what you see on your electricity bill; they're useful for measuring large amounts of electricity. For more on kWh, head to the later section "Measuring power."

>> **Megawatt:** *Megawatts* (MW) are tremendous. One megawatt is equal to 1,000 kilowatts (and 1,000,000 watts). This unit measures things like power plants or how much electricity an entire city uses.

>> **Gigawatt:** *Gigawatts* (GW) measure the capacity of large power plants (or multiple smaller power plants). One gigawatt is equal to 1,000 megawatts and 1 billion watts. (Rumor has it that 1.21 gigawatts can power a time machine.)

The following sections explain electricity in more detail.

Going subatomic

To understand electricity, you have to start with the basics: atoms. All matter is composed of atoms, the smallest particles that can be broken up without losing their original properties. (You know why you can't trust an atom? Because they make up everything.)

Atoms have a nucleus, just like a cell does. The nucleus is the central hub of the atom, and it's where you find two types of subatomic particles: protons and neutrons. Because *protons* have a positive charge and *neutrons* are neutrally charged, an atom's nucleus is positively charged. Protons and neutrons are packed together in a tiny, dense space, so the nucleus accounts for most of an atom's mass. Each proton and neutron has about 2,000 times more mass than a single electron does. (Check out Chapter 15 for a closer look at density and mass.) Outside the nucleus, in the electron shell, *electrons* (which have a negative charge) are constantly in motion. Atoms have different properties based on the number of basic particles they have and the way in which those basic particles are arranged.

A hydrogen atom (H) contains only one proton, one electron, and no neutrons. Look at the periodic table in Chapter 11. The first element you see is hydrogen, and it has an atomic number of 1. It's the simplest element in the periodic table. Helium, which contains two protons, has an atomic number of 2. Figure 16-1 shows a helium atom, with its pair of protons and electrons, plus two neutrons for good measure. An atom with two protons is helium, no matter what else is happening inside that atom. The same goes for any element and its respective number of protons.

FIGURE 16-1:
A helium atom.

© John Wiley & Sons, Inc

The number of neutrons in an atom doesn't count for much, at least in terms of the atomic number. Scientists count only the number of protons in an atom to determine its atomic number, but they add together both protons and neutrons when determining its average *atomic mass* (written on the bottom of each box in the periodic table within parentheses). Helium's atomic mass is 1.00797.

TECHNICAL STUFF

All the atoms on Earth (and in the rest of the universe) were created 13.7 billion years ago. Quarks came together to form protons and neutrons, and those protons and neutrons teamed up to form nuclei, but they weren't quite atoms yet. The universe took about 380,000 years to cool down enough for the nuclei to capture any electrons, which are necessary parts of atoms. When conditions were right, the first hydrogen and helium atoms (the simplest elements on the periodic table in Chapter 11) began to form. Even today, new atoms are created within hot, dense stars, and they launch into the universe when those stars eventually explode.

Earning the good conduct(or) medal

The number of electrons in the outer electron shell of an atom — called a *valence shell* — determines whether an element is a *conductor, semiconductor,* or *insulator.* Each runs this way:

>> **Conductors** allow electrons to flow freely between different atoms. These valence shells have more empty spots than they have electrons.

>> **Semiconductors** have half-full valence shells (or half-empty, depending on your attitude) and are neither good conductors nor good insulators.

>> **Insulators** have pretty full valence shells (at least more than half), so electrons can't move much (or at all) between atoms. They're very poor conductors.

Electrons are negatively charged, and they attempt to shift from one atom to the next trying to get to a positive charge, such as the positive side of a battery. They're able to shift if the material is a conductor. But if the material is an insulator, the electrons are much, much less able to shift because of the insulating material's molecular structure. This flow is called *electrical current.*

Examining the current of the electrical river

Electrical current is the flow — or, more precisely, the rate of flow — of electrons in a conductor. Electrons carry an electrical charge that's expressed in *coulombs* (C). It's called a coulomb because a guy named Charles de Coulomb discovered it in the late 19th century, and the rules say that if you discover something, someone will stick your name on it.

If 1 coulomb (about 6,241,500,000,000,000,000 electrons) flows past a specified point in 1 second, that's a flow rate of 1 ampere (amp, abbreviated A). An *ampere* represents the movement (flow) of electrons, so electrical currents are measured in amps. Typically current is tiny, so small that it's measured in milliamperes; 1 *milliampere* is one-thousandth of an ampere. Current meters, called *ammeters,* measure the flow of current through a circuit. You can compare the flow of electrons to water coming from a garden hose; amps are equivalent to gallons-per-minute if you're washing your car in the driveway.

The amount of voltage (the difference in potential) and the resistance in a circuit determine the number of amperes along a wire — or whatever you're using to conduct the electricity from one place to another. More voltage (for instance, a higher-voltage battery) means that more amps flow in a wire (or conductor). You can read more about this relationship in the next section, which discusses Ohm's law.

Resistance: Putting the brakes on electrical flow

Current doesn't just flow in any properly working circuit unimpeded. Resistance pops up along the way. If the flow of electricity needs to be regulated, resistance is deliberately set up in a circuit so that electronics work properly. If the flow weren't regulated, the motors powering devices like can openers and microwave ovens would quickly overheat and melt. (But before that happened, hopefully a fuse would blow or a circuit breaker would trip, halting current flow and saving the equipment.) In a sense, even a wire, such as a filament in a light bulb, is a type of resistance and is a way to deliberately create circuit resistance.

Adding or removing resistance

Sometimes a circuit must be opened in order to add or remove resistance. In other words, the flow of the electricity must be interrupted in order to physically change the resistance. Using a *circuit breaker,* which is a device that automatically interrupts the electrical current, is an example of opening a circuit to control the current. When the circuit breaker *trips,* the electrical device can no longer operate.

Some devices use a *rheostat,* which can vary the resistance without opening the circuit — the device can continue to work even as the resistance is altered. If an application doesn't use all the electricity, the rheostat absorbs it. A dimmer switch on a light is an example of a rheostat. You increase the amount of resistance to dim the light and decrease the resistance to brighten the light.

Ohm's law: Relating resistance to current and voltage

The amount of resistance that interferes with the flow is measured in *ohms* (pronounced just like those yoga chants). The symbol for ohm is the Greek letter omega, which looks like an upside-down horseshoe: Ω. Resistance can be measured by dividing the voltage measured at any given point (the voltmeter reading) by the amount of current at the same point in a circuit (the ammeter reading). Or you can measure the resistance directly by an ohmmeter.

If you have a current flowing through a wire, three influences are present:

>> The amount of voltage, measured in volts *(V)* or electromotive force *(EMF)*

>> The resistance to the current, measured in ohms (Ω)

>> The amount of current, measured in amperes and expressed as *I* or *i*

These three units are always present in a specific relationship to each other. If you know the value of any two of the influences, you can find the value of the third. (Yes, this requires more math. Sorry.)

REMEMBER

Ohm's law, which was first stated by Georg Simon Ohm, reads, "The current in a circuit is directly proportional to the applied voltage and inversely proportional to the circuit resistance," but it's actually easier to understand in mathematical terms. When stating the relationship mathematically, abbreviations are used, where *I* is current, *V* is voltage, and *R* is resistance:

$$\text{Current (amperes)} = \frac{\text{Voltage (volts)}}{\text{Resistance (ohms)}}, \text{ or } I = \frac{V}{R}$$

This essentially means that current in a basic circuit is always dependent on the voltage and resistance in the circuit. If you use a higher-voltage battery (increase *V*), the resistance doesn't change, but current in the circuit increases. By the same token, if you leave the same battery in the circuit but increase the resistance (increase *R*), current decreases.

Here are two other ways to write the same formula, solved for voltage and resistance:

>> $\text{Voltage} = \text{Current} \times \text{Resistance, or } V = IR$

>> $\text{Resistance} = \dfrac{\text{Voltage}}{\text{Current}}, \text{ or } R = \dfrac{V}{I}$

Ohm's law works exactly the same, no matter which format you use.

Measuring voltage: Do you have the potential?

Voltage is the difference of the pressure between two points in a circuit. (A *circuit* is just the path of an electrical current; you can read more about circuits in the later section "Getting around to circuits.") It's sometimes called the *voltage drop* or *difference of potential.* So, for instance, a 9-volt battery supplies 9 volts of electricity. To see what the voltage is anywhere in a circuit, you have to compare the voltage at that point to ground. *Ground* is any part of a circuit (or other object that has electricity running through it) that measures 0 volts, such as the case of your radio, the base of a lamp, or the chassis of your car. The negative terminal of a 9-volt battery is at ground potential, so the voltage from the negative terminal to ground measures 0 volts. The voltage from the positive terminal to either ground or the negative terminal of the battery measures 9 volts.

To measure voltage in a circuit, you use a *voltmeter* or a *multimeter,* which has several meters in one instrument. A voltmeter has two leads. To measure voltage, you place one lead somewhere in the circuit and one lead at another location in the circuit. The voltmeter tells you what the voltage is between those two points.

REMEMBER

A *cell* (a storage compartment for electricity in a battery) has a specific voltage. For example, in a particular battery, cells may be 1.5 volts. Therefore, you can figure out the number of cells that battery has by dividing the voltage of the battery by 1.5. Pretty handy stuff, huh?

Getting around to circuits

Although an earlier section suggests that electricity flows like water, it actually flows more like NASCAR. If you want to use its power, electricity must be sent along the path of a closed circle (a circuit), just like all those NASCAR speedsters roaring around the track. The drivers never actually get anywhere; they just keep driving in circles. Electrical charges are a lot like that.

However, electricity does flow like a river in one respect. Electricity follows every path available to it. Most electrons take the path of lowest resistance, but some still take a path of higher resistance. The conventional way in thinking about the electrical flow of current is based on the vacancies left by electrical particles "moving" from the positive (+) terminal to the negative (−) terminal of a battery. This concept is called *conventional current.* However, the military teaches current flow based on the actual flow of the electrons, and electrons, no matter how you look at them, flow from the negative terminal to the positive terminal (see Figure 16-2). This is referred to as *electron flow.*

FIGURE 16-2:
A simple
electric
current.

© John Wiley & Sons, Inc.

Electrical current can't flow without a circuit, and a working circuit must include three components:

>> A voltage source, such as a battery

>> A load, which is a source of resistance that converts electrical energy into another form of energy (like a light bulb)

>> Conductors, which are necessary to carry the current from Point A to Point B

Figure 16-2 shows the way current flows, but Figure 16-3 shows how electricity comes from a voltage source, powers something (like a light bulb), and returns to its original source. It also shows what happens if a circuit is opened, interrupting the flow of electricity. When you flip a light switch to its "Off" position, you open the light's circuit. The electricity can't flow to the light bulb anymore because there's an open gap in the wire. Electricity can't usually flow through air because air is an insulator (see "Earning the good conduct(or) medal" in this chapter), so the light turns off. When you flip the switch to the "On" position, the circuit closes and the electricity can flow uninterrupted, reaching the light bulb and turning it on.

FIGURE 16-3: An open and closed circuit.

© John Wiley & Sons, Inc.

Circuit breakers and fuses

Circuit breakers are designed to break a circuit when too much energy is flowing through an electrical system. The circuit breaker panel in your house is a great example. If your washing machine is sucking too much power from the electrical outlet, putting too much of a load on your electrical system, the circuit breaker literally breaks the circuit to interrupt the flow before it can damage all the wiring in your house.

Fuses work the same way. *Fuses* are thin wires enclosed in a safe insulating material, and they're just part of a circuit. However, they're designed to burn up if the current heats up above a certain level. When the fuse disintegrates, the circuit is interrupted and can't carry any more electricity. Fuses work once only; you have to replace them if one is blown.

TECHNICAL STUFF

In some cases, current does flow through an insulator — if there's enough difference of potential (voltage). When lightning bridges an expanse of air from a cloud to ground (or a tree or a golfer), it's because a huge amount of voltage, on the order of 300 million volts, exists between the source of the lightning and ground.

When current flows, every electron carries its voltage all the way along the conductor. The electrons keep moving forward, pushing the ones in front of them while being pushed by the ones behind them. When even one electron stops, they all stop, and the current instantly becomes zero.

Types of circuits

Circuits come in three main types: series, parallel, and series-parallel.

Series circuits have only one path electrical current can take. A break anywhere in the circuit stops the whole operation. Figure 16-3 earlier in the chapter is a series circuit, but on official electrical diagrams, it's drawn like what you see in Figure 16-4. (What? I just really liked the light bulb's visual effect.) The current flow in a series circuit is the same in every part of the circuit because it has nowhere else to go. If multiple loads are located along a series circuit, their resistances together create an overall sum. That means if R represents resistance, you can represent the loads this way: $R_{(total)} = R_1 + R_2 + R_3 + R_4$ (and so on). Voltage remains the same throughout the circuit based on Ohm's law. (You can read more about voltage in "Measuring voltage: Do you have the potential?" in this chapter.)

FIGURE 16-4: Circuits on electrical diagrams.

© John Wiley & Sons, Inc.

Parallel circuits are very common. In this type of circuit, every load is wired along its own path. If a break occurs in one path to one load, the current continues to flow to the other loads. The voltage in a parallel circuit remains the same throughout each parallel branch of the circuit, but the current flow can vary across each branch. The total current remains the same.

Adding a load in parallel decreases the total resistance of a current; that's because it provides an additional pathway for electrons to take. That's true even if the additional pathway provides more resistance than the first pathway. When you're working with a parallel circuit, you figure out the total resistance this way, where R represents each instance of resistance (each load): $\frac{1}{R_{(total)}} = \frac{1}{R_1} + \frac{1}{R_2} + \frac{1}{R_3} + \frac{1}{R_4}$ and so on.

Series–parallel circuits are the most common arrangement. Most houses are wired this way. These circuits are more complicated because they include more components, such as on/off switches and fuses. Despite their popularity, you aren't likely to have to calculate resistance for series–parallel circuits on the ASVAB; doing so requires you to use the right formula on each group of resistors until you can zero in on a single value.

HOLIDAY (LIGHT) BURNOUT

Holiday lights are an interesting way to look at series and parallel circuits. In some types of holiday lights, when one blue bulb burns out, all of the other blue bulbs go dark. That's because all the blue bulbs run along the same series circuit, and one burned-out or broken bulb interrupts the flow of electricity. However, the red, green, and white lights run on different series circuit paths. Although they're all connected to the same power source, the other colors stay illuminated because the power source isn't the problem; the series circuit containing blue lights is the problem. Sometimes holiday lights are several parallel circuits wired together. In cases like those, none of the other lights are affected when one bulb goes out, because current flows directly to each bulb from the source. If you buy strings of lights you can connect to each other, you create your own series-parallel circuit made from series and parallel circuits (and the technical specs of those are more complicated than anything you're likely to see on the ASVAB).

Note: Most modern holiday lights are wired with shunts, so if one of your blue bulbs goes out this year, it's not going to affect the rest of them. A *shunt* is a device that allows current to continue flowing through a circuit by creating a path of lower resistance. In holiday lights, shunts are small wires wrapped with an insulating substance; when a bulb gets too hot and burns out, it melts the insulating substance so the circuit can continue and your lights keep working.

When any wire accidentally crosses over another wire, causing the electricity to bypass the rest of the circuit and not follow its intended path, you get a *short circuit*. This issue is a circuit problem rather than a circuit type, but it's worth mentioning.

In fact, most people are unlikely to see complex electrical problems that involve mathematical calculations on the ASVAB (if you do, it means you're blowing all the easy and medium questions out of the water with correct answers). The ASVAB tests your basic knowledge to see how trainable you are in each academic area; it's not judging you for not being an electronics expert. Just in case, check out this example about a simple parallel circuit.

EXAMPLE

Determine the total resistance in this series circuit.

(A) 2Ω

(B) 4Ω

(C) 7Ω

(D) 5Ω

The formula for determining resistance in a series circuit is $R_{(total)} = R_1 + R_2 + R_3$, so the total resistance is 7Ω.

EXAMPLE

Determine the total resistance in this parallel circuit.

(A) 0.233Ω

(B) 0.35Ω

(C) 2.33Ω

(D) 4.29Ω

Remember that the formula for determining resistance in a parallel circuit is $\frac{1}{R_{(total)}} = \frac{1}{R_1} + \frac{1}{R_2} + \frac{1}{R_3}$. That means you have to formulate the problem this way: $\frac{1}{R_{(total)}} = \frac{1}{17} + \frac{1}{12} + \frac{1}{11}$. When you apply the mathematical principles in Chapter 6, you get a common denominator of 2,244. (Remember, you can't use a calculator on the ASVAB.) Your problem looks like this: $\frac{132}{2244} + \frac{187}{2244} + \frac{204}{2244} = \frac{523}{2244}$, or 0.233.

That decimal isn't your total resistance, though. The total resistance is in the denominator of the problem (the bottom part of the fraction). That means you need to find the inverse of the fraction. Because $\frac{1}{R_{total}} = \frac{0.233}{1}$, you need to find the inverse to calculate the total resistance: $R_{total} = \frac{1}{0.233}$, or approximately 4.29Ω.

The correct answer is Choice (D).

EXAMPLE

Determine the total resistance in this series–parallel circuit.

80Ω

100Ω   50Ω

(A) 20Ω

(B) 70Ω

(C) 113.3Ω

(D) 230Ω

First find the resistance of the parallel combination using $\frac{1}{R_{(total)}} = \frac{1}{R_1} + \frac{1}{R_2}$, which is $\frac{1}{R_{(total)}} = \frac{1}{100} + \frac{1}{50}$, or 33.3Ω. You can redraw the circuit this way:

80Ω

33.3Ω

Because it's now a series circuit, add the two series resistances (80 and 33.3Ω) to determine that the total resistance is 113.3Ω, which is Choice (C).

Measuring power

Power is measured in *watts*. One watt is a very small amount of power. It would require nearly 750 watts to equal 1 horsepower. One kilowatt represents 1,000 watts.

A *kilowatt-hour* (kWh) — the amount of electricity a power plant generates or a customer uses — is equal to the energy of 1,000 watts working for one hour. Kilowatt-hours are determined by multiplying the number of kilowatts (kW) required by the number of hours of use. For example, if you use a 40-watt light bulb 5 hours a day, you've used 200 watt-hours, or 0.2 kilowatt-hours of electrical energy. The other way to find power (in watts) is by using this formula:

$$\text{Power (watts)} = \text{Voltage (volts)} \times \text{Current (amperes)}$$

TECHNICAL STUFF

The term *watt* was named to honor James Watt, the inventor of the steam engine.

MAGNETIC, ELECTRIC: NO, NOT YOUR PERSONALITY

Certain magnetic effects always accompany an electric current, and these effects follow definite laws. In a wire, the *magnetic lines of force* (imaginary lines used to explain magnetic effects) are perpendicular to the conductor and parallel to each other.

But when you wrap a wire around a core and pass current through it, the wire forms a coil. As the lines of force around the core take on a different shape, the field around each turn of wire links with the fields from the other turns of wire around it. The combined influence of all the turns of wire produces a two-pole magnetic field, very much like the magnetic field of a simple bar magnet — one end of the coil is a north pole; the other end is a south pole.

The strength of the magnetic field depends on several factors. Here are the main ones:

- **Number of turns:** If you increase the number of turns, you increase the field strength.

- **Closeness of the turns:** The closer the turns, the stronger the field.

- **Amount of current:** If you increase current, you increase field strength.

- **Material in the core:** Most coils are classified as either air or soft iron, based on their cores. *Air coils* are usually wrapped around a piece of cardboard; *soft-iron coils* are wrapped around a piece of iron. Soft iron offers a better path for magnetic lines of force because its high permeability offers less reluctance to magnetic flux, resulting in more lines of force. (Think of *magnetic flux* as a measurement of magnetic strength located on a two-dimensional surface. A good example of magnetic flux would be the magnetic strength of one side of a magnet.) The more lines of force, the stronger the magnetic field.

Passing a suspended loop of conductive material (wire) through a magnetic field creates *electromagnetic induction,* which is the basic principle behind the electric generator. When the conductor is standing still, current doesn't flow through it. But when the loop starts to rotate clockwise through the lines of force of the magnets, the lines of force induce free electrons to move through the wire.

Producing electrical effects

Electric currents can produce different effects. These effects are packaged and sold commercially. The following is a description of effects produced by current and some of their commercial applications:

>> **Chemical effect:** Current produces this effect when it passes through a chemical compound and breaks up that compound. Also called *electrolytic decomposition,* this phenomenon is used in *electroplating,* a process used to cover objects with a very thin coating of metal. This effect is used to make less expensive jewelry.

>> **Heat effect:** Conducting electricity causes wires to become heated. Heat develops because the current must overcome the resistance of the wire. This heat energy can be quite obvious or hardly noticeable to touch, depending on the size of the wire and the amount of current. You've used this effect to cook dinner if you have an electric stove.

>> **Magnetic effect:** When a wire is introduced into a magnetic field, electricity flows through the wire and creates a magnetic field that repels a magnet. This effect is used to create energy through *electromagnetic induction,* the basic principle behind the electric generator. If the wire is wrapped around an iron core and a current is sent through the wire, the iron becomes magnetized. (See the nearby sidebar for more on the magnetic effect.) Huge electromagnets help sort out metal at recycling plants.

>> **Physiological effect:** Current produces this effect when it passes through your bicep (or any of your muscles, for that matter) and causes the muscle to contract. This effect is used in medicine.

Switching Things Up with Alternating and Direct Current

A current doesn't always flow in one direction. A *direct current* (DC) does — it only and always flows in one direction. An *alternating current* (AC), however, constantly changes direction in a regular pattern. Higher voltages are easier to obtain with alternating current, and transferring high voltage down a power line is ultimately cheaper than transferring low voltage, so most electricity comes in the form of AC.

>> **Direct current** often comes from a battery. It's what your phone, kids' toys, and flashlights use when you're not charging them in a wall.

>> **Alternating current** comes directly into your home from the power company. It can change direction and voltage from higher to lower current when it encounters a transformer (not Bumblebee or Optimus Prime — the electrical kind).

>> **AC/DC** is a combination of the two. Your laptop uses it, a wall-plug phone charger uses it, and some vehicles use it. AC comes in through the outlet, and the box (the rectifier) between the outlet and the part that plugs into your device transforms it to DC.

The following sections cover some important points about alternating and direct current.

Figuring out frequency

The number of times an alternating current changes direction per second is known as its *frequency*. *Hertz* (Hz) is the unit of measurement for frequency. One hertz (Hz) equals one complete cycle per second. In other words, the current makes two complete alternations of direction.

The AC in your house probably completes 60 alternating cycles per second. Therefore, the AC in your house has a frequency of 60 Hz. Most electronic devices operate at higher frequencies; therefore, frequencies may be measured in kilohertz (kHz, 1,000 hertz), megahertz (MHz, 1 million hertz), or even gigahertz (GHz, 1 billion hertz).

GROUNDING YOURSELF WITH BASIC ELECTRICAL SAFETY

Grounding is an important aspect of working with electricity. In practice, it gives excess electricity a place to go without harming anyone in the process: the ground. Any wiring system can fail, so some systems — most notably, homes — include a series of grounding wires that run parallel to "hot" and "neutral" wires. That way, if a rat gnaws through a live wire that's carrying current, the grounding wires can capture the stray current and send it where it belongs (usually a grounding rod driven deep into the ground outside) so it doesn't shock someone or start a fire.

AM radio stations often broadcast in the 530–1,700 kHz range. Television stations may broadcast at as low as 7 to as high as 1,002 MHz. Traditional radar operates in the 1–40 GHz range.

Impedance: Join the resistance!

Resistance interferes with the flow of current in a circuit. But the flow of current is also impeded by two properties of alternating currents:

- » **Capacitive reactance (capacitance):** *Capacitive reactance* is a measure of a capacitor's opposition to alternating current, and it's measured in ohms. Capacitance is the storage of energy that occurs in a nonconductor, and it's measured in farads *(F).* This property resists any change in voltage in a circuit.

- » **Inductive reactance (inductance):** *Inductive reactance,* also measured in ohms, is the resistance to a change in the flow of current. Inductance is the property that causes current to increase or decrease even more based on changes in current induced in a circuit. This inductance creates an electromotive force and is measured in henrys (H).

These two types of reactance combine to impede the flow of current. Impedance can become incredibly complex, but in its simplest form, it can be expressed as the ratio of electromotive force to the current:

$$\text{Impedance} = \frac{\text{Electromotive force}}{\text{Current}}$$

Electronic devices often require a specific capacitive or inductive reactance to work. *Capacitors* and *inductors* are devices used in circuits to provide the type of reactance needed. Capacitors are rated in microfarads (μF), and inductors are rated in millihenries (mH). For an in-depth look at imped-ance and other information that professional electricians use, check out *Electronics For Dummies,* by Cathleen Shamieh and Gordon McComb (Wiley).

You can relate impedance to Ohm's law in reference to AC circuits. Simply substitute resistance in Ohm's law with impedance and voltage with electromotive force.

SORTING OUT CAPACITORS AND INDUCTORS

Capacitors store or hold a charge of electrons. In an AC circuit, because AC voltage goes positive and neg-ative in each cycle, the capacitor is constantly charging and discharging. The rate of the charging and dis-charging acts as opposition to the changing AC voltage — as a resistive effect called *capacitive reactance.*

Inductors are coils of wire that make use of the properties of a magnetic field. The property specifically desired is the flow of current through the wire. With full current, the magnetic field is at its maximum. However, if you take away the current, the field doesn't disappear immediately. It decays gradually, and the decay continues to push electrons in the path they were going. But in an AC circuit, the current con-stantly reverses. The rate of changing current flow and the resulting collapse and regeneration of the magnetic field in the coil act as opposition to changing AC current — a resistive effect called *inductive reactance.*

Rectifying the situation: Going direct

Certain electronic circuits are engineered to change alternating current to direct current. The process of making the change is called *rectification*, and the circuits that perform the rectification are called *rectifiers*.

Rectifiers contain *semiconductor diodes*, a component made of a material with conductivity somewhere between that of a conductor and an insulator. *Diodes* conduct electricity in only one direction. Rectification also often requires inductors and capacitors (see the preceding section).

Rectification helps appliances run at cooler temperatures and allows them to run at variable speeds. Devices typically need direct current to run properly. The process of rectification changes the incoming AC to DC. Manufacturers often use diodes, which used to be housed in big, glass vacuum tubes, to rectify current in many appliances and electronic devices.

Turning up the transistor radio

A transistor is a *semiconductor* (an object that conducts electricity poorly at low temperatures) that controls the flow of electricity in a circuit. It's usually made of germanium or silicon. This electrical device can amplify a signal, which is why it's used in transistor radios. Transistors have many properties:

>> Unlike rectifier diodes (see the preceding section), a transistor doesn't require a vacuum to operate.

>> Transistors are small, require little power, and last a long time.

>> A transistor contains at least three terminals:

- The *emitter* is the voltage output.

- The *base* acts like a gate, and the voltage at the base controls the flow of current through the transistor (and therefore the voltage).

- The *collector* is the voltage input.

Picture It: Decoding Electrical Circuit Codes

Electronic circuits can be combined to create *complex systems*, such as those required to operate a stereo system. *Block diagrams* are used to show the various combined circuits that form a complex system.

Many of the questions on the Electronics Information subtest require you to identify an electronic component symbol and know what that component does in an electronic circuit. Figure 16-5 shows the most common component symbols. The figure's items are grouped based on similarity of functions. For example, cells, batteries, DC power supplies, and AC power supplies all have similar functions (they supply power to the circuit).

FIGURE 16-5: Symbols in electronic circuit diagrams.

© John Wiley & Sons, Inc.

So what do all these electronic doodads do when connected in a circuit? I cover each item in the following list:

>> **Wires:** Wires are used to pass current from one part of the component to another. Wires that are connected to each other are indicated by a dark circle and are called *joined wires.* Sometimes in complex circuit diagrams, it's necessary to draw wires crossing even though they aren't connected. In this case, the dark circle is omitted, or a hump symbol is drawn to make it clear the wires aren't connected — these are called *unjoined wires.*

>> **Cell:** A cell supplies electrical current. Some call this a battery, but technically a battery is more than one cell. The large terminal (on the left side of the cell image in Figure 16-5) is positive.

>> **Battery:** A battery is two or more cells. The large terminal is positive.

>> **DC power supply:** A DC power supply provides direct current. Direct current always flows in one direction.

>> **AC power supply:** An AC power supply provides alternating current. Alternating current constantly changes direction at a specific frequency.

>> **Fuse:** A fuse is a safety device that *blows* (melts) if the current flowing through it exceeds a specified value. Read more about fuses in the earlier section "Circuit breakers and fuses."

» **Transformer:** A transformer consists of two coils of wire linked by an iron core. Transformers are used to step up (increase) and step down (decrease) AC voltages. No electrical connection exists between the coils. Energy is transferred between the coils by the magnetic field in the core.

» **Ground:** A ground is a connection to the Earth.

» **Transducer:** A transducer is a device that converts energy from one form to another. Here are various types of transducers:

  • **Lighting lamp:** Converts electrical energy to light, such as in a light bulb or automobile headlight

  • **Indicator lamp:** Converts electrical energy to light for such uses as a warning light on a car's dashboard

  • **Motor:** Converts electrical energy to kinetic energy (motion)

  • **Heater:** Converts electrical energy to heat

  • **Bells and buzzers:** Convert electrical energy to sound

  • **Microphone:** Converts sound to electrical energy

  • **Earphones and speakers:** Convert electrical energy to sound

» **Inductor:** An *inductor* is a coil of wire that creates a magnetic field when current passes through it.

» **Switch:** Here are several types of switches:

  • **Push switch:** A push switch allows current to flow only when the button is pressed, such as in a doorbell.

  • **Push-to-break switch:** With this switch, the circuit is normally closed (the device is on); the circuit is open (device is off) only when the button is pressed.

  • **On/off switch:** An on/off switch allows current to flow only when it's in the closed (on) position.

  • **Two-way switch:** A two-way switch directs the flow of current to one of two routes, according to its position.

  • **Dual on/off switch:** This type is often used to switch main electricity because it can isolate both the live and neutral connections.

  • **Relay (relay switch):** A relay is an electrically operated switch that may operate multiple switches at one time. Typically a small current flowing through a coil sets up a magnetic field, which causes the lever(s) to move, effectively changing the (relay) switch's position(s). As an example, a 5-volt signal from your dashboard turns on your 12-volt headlights through a relay.

» **Resistor (nonvariable):** There are two different versions of the basic resistor symbol. Resistors restrict the flow of electric current. Resistors are rated in ohms and have a color code on them to indicate their value, tolerance, and sometimes quality. The band code is as follows:

  • Black is 0.

  • Brown is 1.

  • Red is 2.

  • Orange is 3.

  • Yellow is 4.

  • Green is 5.

- Blue is 6.

- Violet is 7.

- Gray is 8.

- White is 9.

The first and second bands on the resistor are the first two digits in the resistor's value. The next band indicates the multiplier (number of zeros after the first two numbers). So if the first band is red, the second is yellow, and the third band is orange, the resistor's value is 24,000 ohms. A gold or silver band after the first bands indicates tolerance, and a quality band may follow the tolerance band.

>> **Variable resistor:** Variable resistors also restrict the flow of electric current. There are several symbols in use in circuit diagrams for standard variable and preset variable resistors. Types of variable resistors include the following:

- **Rheostat:** A type of variable resistor with two contacts, usually used to control current; examples of controlling current would be adjusting lamp brightness or adjusting motor speed

- **Potentiometer:** A type of variable resistor with three contacts that's used to control voltage

- **Preset variable resistor:** A device that operates with a small screwdriver or similar tool; it's designed to be set when the circuit is made and then left without further adjustment

>> **Capacitor:** Capacitors store electric charge. They're used with resistors in timing circuits because it takes time for a capacitor to fill with charge. They're also used in filter circuits because capacitors easily pass AC (changing voltage) signals but they block DC (constant voltage) signals. Two types of capacitors include the following:

- Polarized capacitors must be connected the correct way in circuit.

- Variable capacitors are used most often in radio tuning circuits.

>> **Diode:** Diodes allow electricity to flow in only one direction. The arrow of the circuit symbol shows the direction in which the current can flow. Diodes are the electrical version of a valve, and early diodes were actually called *valves.* Light-emitting diodes (LEDs) emit light when an electric current passes through them. Specialized diodes, called *Zener diodes,* do allow current in the opposite direction after a threshold is met.

>> **Transistor:** Transistors amplify current. For example, they can be used to amplify the small output current from a logic chip so it can operate a lamp, relay, or other high-current device.

>> **Amplifier:** An amplifier isn't actually an electronic component but instead is a complex circuit. The block diagram symbol shows where an amplifier circuit would be connected. Amplifier circuits are used to magnify power, current, or voltage.

>> **Antenna:** An antenna is a device designed to receive and/or transmit radio signals.

Circuit diagrams show how electronic components are connected together. These diagrams show the connections as clearly as possible with all wires drawn neatly as straight lines. The actual layout of the components is usually quite different from the circuit diagram, however. Circuit diagrams are useful when testing a circuit and for understanding how it works. Figure 16-6 shows a diagram of an adjustable timer circuit. See how many components you can identify.

Adjustable Timer Circuit

FIGURE 16-6:
An adjustable timer circuit.

© John Wiley & Sons, Inc.

Coming in Hot: Wire Color Codes Used in the U.S.

In the United States, electrical wires follow color standards. The process started after the 1940s, so older wiring systems don't necessarily follow the same standards, and different types of wires have different color codes. In electrical terms, *phase* refers to the distribution of a load. A single-phase wire has three wires within the insulation (two hot, or live, wires and one neutral wire). A Phase 2 wire has two live wires, each providing the same voltage but with different peaks and dips in voltage, and one or two neutral wires. A Phase 3 wire contains three hot wires (and sometimes a neutral wire), with each phase AC signal being 120 electrical degrees apart.

WARNING

All electrical wires can carry a current, so no matter how they're labeled, treat them as if they could shock you.

AC wires that travel between the last protective device (such as a circuit breaker) and the load on branch circuits carrying 120, 208, or 240 volts are

>> **Black** for Phase 1

>> **Red** for Phase 2

>> **Blue** for Phase 3

>> **White** if they're neutral

>> **Green, green with a yellow stripe, or bare wire** if they're ground wires

>> **Orange** if the wiring system has one phase at a higher voltage than the others

AC wires in 277- or 480-volt systems are

>> **Brown** for Phase 1

>> **Orange** for Phase 2

>> **Yellow** for Phase 3

>> **Gray** if they are neutral

>> **Green, green with a yellow stripe, or bare wire** if they're ground wires

DC wires are different (such as those you use as jumper cables on your car battery). Those are red for positive, black for negative, and white or gray for ground.

Consider black and brown wires to be live (that is, carrying a current) at all times. They transfer power to switches and outlets. Red wires are secondary live wires, and you can use them in *switch legs* (connections that link a switch to an electrical load). Blue and yellow wires carry a current through a conduit. Netural wires in white or gray connect a conductive piece of metal that attracts electric current so it can be distributed everywhere it needs to go. (And for the record, they may carry a current even though they're called "neutral.") Finally, green wires are the failsafe; they give electricity a place to escape into the ground if it has nowhere else to go. These wires can be live if the system has a fault somewhere.

Eyeing Some Electronics Information Test Tips

When it comes to the electronics test, don't feel like you have to know as much as Ben Franklin to get a passing score. Just use your common sense. If a question asks, "What's the safest way to run an extension cord to a reading light?" the answer "across the middle of the floor" is probably going to be wrong.

You can also figure out quite a few answers if you remember these units of measure:

>> **Current:** Amperes (or amps)

>> **Voltage:** Volts

>> **Resistance:** Ohms

>> **Power:** Watts

>> **Energy:** Watt-hours

Memorizing simple principles

REMEMBER

If you commit the following principles to memory, you'll have an easier time succeeding on the Electronics Information subtest:

>> Ohm's law: $\text{Current} = \dfrac{\text{Voltage}}{\text{Resistance}}$.

>> $\text{Power}\,(\text{watts}) = \text{Voltage}\,(\text{volts}) \times \text{Current}\,(\text{amperes})$, or $P = VI$.

>> Current flows from a negative pole to a positive pole.

>> A closed circuit must exist for electricity to flow. (Think NASCAR.)

>> Alternating current (AC) changes direction constantly at a constant rate. The number of times a current completes two alternations of direction per second is known as its *frequency;* the unit of measurement for frequency is the hertz (Hz).

>> Electronic devices operate at very high frequencies.

>> Electronic devices often require a specific capacitive or inductive reactance to work. Capacitors and inductors are devices used in circuits to provide the type of reactance needed.

>> Devices that change alternating current to direct current are called *rectifiers.*

>> A *transistor* can amplify a signal.

Playing the guessing game

The Electronics Information subtest is the type of test where you either know the answer or you don't. But if you don't know the answer, you should still guess (just be cautious about guessing on the CAT-ASVAB; if you click random answers quickly at the end of the subtest, you may be penalized). Remember, you don't have a lot of time to ponder the answer choices. Guess and move on. To increase your chances of guessing correctly, you can often eliminate an incorrect answer.

Sometimes one answer is obviously wrong, or one answer is more obviously right than another. The electronics answer is usually the right answer. Therefore, an answer that has to do with how much something costs or how pretty it looks is probably wrong.

Not all questions are specifically electronics questions. You may be asked something like, "A milliradian measures what quantity?" Think about how you've seen that prefix used before, such as in the word millimeter. A millimeter, you may remember, is one-thousandth of a meter. And like other SI units of measurement, a *milliradian* is one-thousandth of a radian. For additional guessing help, flip to Chapter 3.

Electronics Information Practice Questions

The questions in this section measure your knowledge of basic electronics principles.

If you need a good score on this subtest to get your military dream job or you want to rebuild that old television set without sacrificing your garage, you may want to check out *Electronics For Dummies* by Gordon McComb and Cathleen Shamieh (Wiley) for additional help.

1. What does the abbreviation DC stand for?

   (A) duplicate charge

   (B) direct charge

   (C) direct current

   (D) diode current

2. Which of the following is the ohm symbol?

   (A) Σ

   (B) Δ

   (C) Φ

   (D) Ω

3. Which of the following has the least resistance?

   (A) iron

   (B) rubber

   (C) copper

   (D) wood

4. What conclusion can you draw based on the following diagram of a flashbulb circuit?

   © John Wiley & Sons, Inc.

   (A) There is no power to the circuit.

   (B) The flashbulb is turned off.

   (C) Only one battery is working.

   (D) The flashbulb is in parallel.

5. What increases or decreases the voltage in a system without the need for an electrical connection?

   (A) terminal

   (B) trigger

   (C) transmitter

   (D) transformer

6. A device used to amplify a signal is called a

   (A) diode.

   (B) transformer.

   (C) rectifier.

   (D) transistor.

7. What process changes incoming alternating current (AC) to direct current (DC)?

   (A) magnetic effect

   (B) rectification

   (C) transformation

   (D) impedance

8. The amount of electrical power is measured in units called

   (A) volts.

   (B) amperes.

   (C) watts.

   (D) ohms.

9. What does the arrow over the resistor symbol represent?

   © John Wiley & Sons, Inc.

   (A) indicator

   (B) direct current

   (C) variable

   (D) live

10. Components designed to store electrical charge are called

    (A) capacitors.

    (B) transformers.

    (C) resistors.

    (D) transistors.

11. In what direction does current go in electron flow notation?

    (A) from negative to positive

    (B) from positive to negative

    (C) any direction

    (D) horizontally

12. In an electronic circuit diagram, the symbol used to show wires connecting is a/an

    (A) X symbol.

    (B) dot.

    (C) dark square.

    (D) T symbol.

13. What occurs when a wire is wrapped around an iron core and a current is sent through the wire?

    (A) chemical effect

    (B) heat effect

    (C) magnetic effect

    (D) physiological effect

14. What is the term for magnetic effects that are perpendicular to the conductor and parallel to each other?

    (A) north pole

    (B) semiconductor

    (C) lines of force

    (D) electroplating

15. What symbol is not shown in the following circuit diagram?

© John Wiley & Sons, Inc.

    (A) transformer

    (B) fuse

    (C) resistor

    (D) transistor

16. What is commonly used in a circuit in which the flow of electricity needs to be regulated for the device to run properly?

    (A) resistance

    (B) transformer

    (C) diodes

    (D) batteries

17. What color wire from the following choices is not considered a "hot" wire?

    (A) red

    (B) black

    (C) gray

    (D) blue

18. What does the following symbol represent?

© John Wiley & Sons, Inc.

    (A) fuse

    (B) ground

    (C) outlet

    (D) resistor

Answers and Explanations

Use this answer key to score the Electronics Information practice questions.

1. **C.** DC stands for *direct current.* I made up the other choices. The correct answer is Choice (C).

2. **D.** Remember, the upside-down horseshoe (the Greek letter omega) is the symbol for ohm, the measure of electrical resistance. The correct answer is Choice (D).

3. **C.** Copper is the best conductor of electricity of those listed here. Therefore, it offers the least resistance to an electric current. The correct answer is Choice (C).

4. **B.** When the switch is in contact with point A (as shown), the charges are being stored. When the switch moves to point B, the flashbulb turns on.

5. **D.** A transformer is an inductor with two or more windings, a *terminal* is a device that connects electrical circuits together, a *trigger* initiates a circuit action, and a *transmitter* is a device used to achieve transmission. *Windings* are magnetic wires that are coated with enamel and wrapped around the core of a transformer. The primary winding is driven by transistors, and the secondary winding is driven by the core's magnetic field, produced by the primary winding. Choice (D) is the correct answer.

6. **D.** A *diode* is a semiconductor that conducts electricity in one direction only; a *transformer* is a device that changes voltage (either "transforming" low voltage to high voltage or high voltage to low voltage); a *rectifier* is a circuit that changes alternating current to direct current. Choice (D) is the correct answer.

7. **B.** Rectification occurs in certain electronic circuits that need to change incoming AC to DC in order to run properly.

8. **C.** A *watt* measures the amount of power, the rate at which energy is produced or used. The correct answer is Choice (C).

9. **C.** A *variable resistor* is a potentiometer with two connecting wires instead of three; it allows for finer control over the current by changing the amount of resistance.

10. **A.** *Capacitors* store electric charge. They're used with resistors in timing circuits because it takes time for a capacitor to store voltage (to become charged). The correct answer is Choice (A).

11. **A.** In conventional flow notation, the motion of charge is shown according to the (technically incorrect) labels of + and −, with the electric charge moving from positive to negative. But in electron flow notation, the actual motion of electrons in the circuit is followed. Negative electrons are always searching for positive charges, so current flows from a negative pole to a positive pole.

12. **B.** Wires connected to each other are indicated by a darkened circle. The correct answer is Choice (B).

13. **C.** When a wire is wrapped around an iron core and a current is sent through the wire, the iron becomes magnetized.

14. C. In a wire, magnetic lines of force are perpendicular to the conductor and parallel to each other.

15. B.

© *John Wiley & Sons, Inc.*

This symbol represents a fuse; the circuit doesn't contain a fuse.

16. A. Resistance is set up in a circuit to regulate the electricity so the device isn't destroyed by electrical heat.

17. C. Red, black, and blue wires are always "hot" and should never be tampered with unless the power is off. The gray wire is a neutral, Earth-connected wire.

18. B. The symbol represents ground. Grounding an electrical circuit provides a safe place to discharge electricity.

Chapter **17**

Assembling Objects

Although much of the ASVAB measures academic knowledge at the high school level, Assembling Objects is a subtest that probably doesn't resemble any of your high school classes (unless your high school offered a course in Jigsaw Puzzles 101).

The Assembling Objects subtest is designed to measure your ability to look at pieces of an object and determine how those pieces should fit together (technically called *visualizing spatial relationships*). Spatial skills, which help people figure out maps and interpret technical drawings, are important to everyday living as well as for performing well in school and on the job. Demand for workers with good spatial skills, including interpretation of graphs, maps, architectural drawings, and X-rays, is growing.

The Assembling Objects subtest of the CAT–ASVAB consists of 15 graphical problems that you have to solve in 22 minutes, unless you're taking a version of the test with tryout questions (which I describe in Chapter 1). In that case, you have 42 minutes to answer 30 questions. The paper version of the ASVAB has 25 questions for you to solve in 15 minutes. That gives you a little less than a minute for each question, which is plenty of time to finish if you're good at jigsaw puzzles.

Getting the Picture about Assembling Objects

The Assembling Objects subtest is relatively new to the ASVAB. It was added when the ASVAB was revised in 2005, when the Numerical Operations and Coding Speed subtests were deleted. First it was added only to the computerized version of the ASVAB, and then it was added to the paper enlistment version about a year later. If you're taking the high school version of the ASVAB, you won't see this subtest.

REMEMBER

At the time of this writing, only the Navy uses the score from the Assembling Objects subtest for job qualification purposes. Additionally, only a few ratings (what the Navy calls *jobs*) require a score in this area. The other branches don't use the results of this subtest at all, but they may in the future. For details about which Navy enlisted jobs require a score in this area, see Appendix A.

The upshot is that unless you're planning to join the Navy, in one of only a handful of Navy enlisted jobs, you can safely ignore this entire chapter. Don't say I never gave you anything.

Two Types of Questions for the Price of One

The Assembling Objects subtest has two types of questions, both of which consist of five separate drawings. In the first drawing, you see a picture with various disassembled parts, followed by four drawings that show the parts assembled or connected. Your task is to choose the drawing that shows what the parts may actually look like after they're assembled or connected properly.

REMEMBER

Both types of Assembling Objects problems require you to perform mental rotation — a process through which you predict what an array of objects would look like if they were rotated or turned by some number of degrees.

Putting tab A into slot B: Connectors

The first type of problem presents you with simple geometric figures such as stars, cloud shapes, letter shapes, circles, and triangles. In the first drawing, you can see shapes and lines labeled with dots and the letters A and B. These letters and dots indicate points of attachment.

The next four drawings show possible solutions of what the shapes would look like if connected at designated points by the line. The shapes may be reoriented or rotated from what you observe in the first drawing. The correct solution shows the line connected correctly to reflect the points shown in the first drawing.

Look at Figure 17-1 and see whether you can solve it. In the first drawing, you see a star and a sort of lopsided T. There's a small dot on the short appendage of the T, labeled *A*, and a dot on one of the points of the star, labeled *B*.

FIGURE 17-1:
Identifying points and shapes.

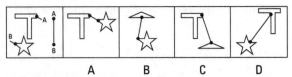

© John Wiley & Sons, Inc.

In Figure 17-1, Choice (A) is the correct solution. Choices (B) and (C) include shapes that aren't included in the first drawing, so they're obviously incorrect. Although Choice (D) has the correct shapes, they aren't connected at the same points depicted in the first drawing.

Okay, that sounds simple, doesn't it? Don't worry; it gets more complicated (sorry to burst your bubble). Figure 17-2 shows the same problem but with a different twist.

FIGURE 17-2:
Rotated shapes make the problem harder.

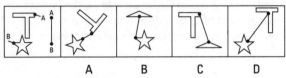

© John Wiley & Sons, Inc.

Choice (A) is the correct solution for the problem in Figure 17-2. In this case, the two shapes have been repositioned and rotated.

On the flip side: Avoiding mirrors

WARNING

Mirroring (or flipping or reflecting) isn't the same as rotation, as Figure 17-3 illustrates. The shape in Box B isn't the same as the shape in Box A. It's a mirror image. No matter how you rotate the shape in Box A, it will never look like the shape in Box B. Think of it this way: You can turn a jigsaw puzzle piece upside down (so the picture side is facing the table), and it may fit, but that's not the proper method of putting the puzzle together. (It wouldn't look very pretty, either.) The Assembling Objects subtest is the same way. The possible solutions may include shapes that are reflections of a shape shown in the first drawing, but they'll never be the correct solution.

FIGURE 17-3:
Figuring out mirrored shapes (A and B) and rotated shapes.

© John Wiley & Sons, Inc.

Crossing over the right places

REMEMBER

If a shape in the first drawing shows a line that goes through any part of the shape, the correct solution must also reflect the same line-shape relationship. Check out Figure 17-4. In the first drawing, Point B is in the center of the star. But note the line intersects the star at one of its indentations and not one of its points. That means the correct solution must show the same intersection.

FIGURE 17-4:
Line-shape relationships.

© John Wiley & Sons, Inc.

In this example, Choice (B) is the correct solution. At first glance, Choice (C) looks like it could be correct. Can you spot the reason it's not the correct solution? Right! The lopsided T shape in the image is a reflection of the shape shown in the first drawing.

Putting it all together

You're starting to see the shape of things! (I'm sorry, but these little zingers just keep popping out.) Try a couple more, just to get into shape. Look at Figure 17-5.

FIGURE 17-5:
Another example of spatial relationships.

© John Wiley & Sons, Inc.

In Figure 17-5, did you select Choice (C) as the correct answer? If so, good job! Choice (A) is incorrect because the line intersects the triangle at the wrong point and the connection point A is misplaced. Choice (B) is incorrect because the weird shape is actually a mirror image of the shape shown in the first drawing. Choice (D) is incorrect because the points don't correlate to the points depicted in the first drawing.

Now try Figure 17-6. The first drawing includes a shape that kind of looks like a Y and a shape that looks like the letter C.

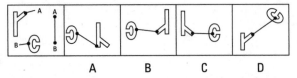

FIGURE 17-6:
More shapes to test your spatial skills.

© John Wiley & Sons, Inc.

The correct answer for the problem shown in Figure 17-6 is Choice (B). Choice (A) is incorrect because the Y shape is a mirror image of the shape shown in the first drawing, and the connection points don't correspond to the first drawing's points. Choice (C) is incorrect because the Y shape is a mirror image of the shape shown in the first drawing. Choice (D) is incorrect because the Y shape is a different shape (the stem is much shorter) than the shape shown in the first drawing and because the connection dot on the C shape is in the wrong location.

Solving the jigsaw puzzle: Shapes

Many people may find the second type of Assembling Objects problem easier than the connection problems. This type of problem is very much like a jigsaw puzzle, except it doesn't result in a picture of the Statue of Liberty or a map of the United States. Also, there's a heck of a lot fewer pieces than that 1,000-piece puzzle your grandma kept wanting you to help her with. The difficulty lies in the fact that you can't use your hands to twist the pieces around on the table in order to see how they fit. You have to rotate and move the pieces mentally.

In Figure 17-7, the solution is pretty straightforward.

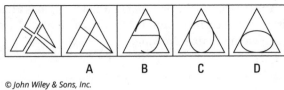

FIGURE 17-7:
A simple jigsaw example.

© John Wiley & Sons, Inc.

By mentally sliding the shapes in the first drawing together, it's easy to see that they fit together to form the picture shown in Choice (A). Now look at Figure 17-8.

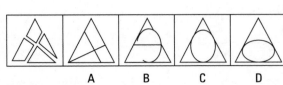

FIGURE 17-8:
Putting pieces together with rotation.

© John Wiley & Sons, Inc.

Choice (A) is the correct answer. The figure shown in Choice (A) is the same as the figure depicted in Choice (A) of Figure 17-7, except it's been rotated.

The previous two figures were warm-up exercises — the questions on the ASVAB are harder. Check out Figure 17-9 for a better representation of the types of questions on the ASVAB.

FIGURE 17-9: A harder example of spatial rotation.

© John Wiley & Sons, Inc.

Pay attention to the curve of the leaf shape inside the square. It's not bowed out as in Choice (B) — the edges have more of a wave shape. Choice (C) has that shape but too thin. If you selected Choice (D) as the correct solution, give yourself a pat on the back. Examining spatial relationships can help locate the correct answer with ease. Try a couple more examples to see if you've gotten the hang of it. Check out Figure 17-10.

FIGURE 17-10: Practice mentally rotating and relocating pieces of puzzles.

© John Wiley & Sons, Inc.

In Figure 17-10, Choice (B) is the correct answer. Mentally rotate and relocate the pieces in the first picture until you can see how they fit together to form the shape in Choice (B). In the puzzle, three pieces have both a curved edge and a single straight edge. Practice eliminating choices that lack these characteristics. Choice (A) lacks these shapes, so you can discount it right away. Notice the curved pieces are all different sizes. Visualize fitting these pieces of the puzzle in your mind and compare the sizes and differences. Now try Figure 17-11.

FIGURE 17-11: Putting the pieces of the puzzle together with your mental spatial skills.

© John Wiley & Sons, Inc.

In Figure 17-11, Choice (A) is the correct answer. If you didn't get this one quite right, don't worry. You can hone your skills with the practice questions at the end of this chapter.

Tips for the Assembling Objects Subtest

In the following sections, I offer some tips for improving your score on the Assembling Objects subtest. I suggest strategies for eliminating wrong answers during the test, and I name some ways you can improve your spatial skills in general (which may come in handy the next time you have to read a map, too).

Comparing one piece or point at a time

TIP

On the Assembling Objects subtest, you can sometimes improve your odds of getting the answer right if you select just one shape from the first drawing and then quickly look at each of the choices to see whether that shape is represented there but in a different orientation. This process can help you quickly eliminate answer choices that are obviously wrong.

On connection-type problems, note the position of the dot on one of the shapes in the first drawing and then quickly scan the possible answers, eliminating any choice that depicts the dot in a different location or that shows the line passing through the shape at a different point than that shown in the first drawing.

REMEMBER

Remember to be aware of mirror images — shapes that are reflected (instead of rotated) from the image shown in the first drawing. The sneaky test-makers often make use of such mirror representations to see whether they can trick your eyes.

Visualizing success: Practicing spatial skills ahead of time

TIP

Researchers at the University of Chicago have determined that your basic foundation for spatial skills is established at a very early age, perhaps as young as age 4 or 5. But don't worry. That doesn't mean all is lost if your parents never got you that model rocket kit you wanted. The same research has concluded that you can still improve spatial skills by engaging in activities that are spatially oriented. Some of those activities include the following:

>> **Practicing reading maps:** Map reading can help you develop the ability to gauge scales of size and direction between related objects (roads, rivers, towns, cities, and so on).

>> **Putting together jigsaw puzzles:** This way is an obvious form of practice for improving your spatial perceptions.

>> **Playing puzzle games online:** Many online puzzle games exercise the skill of identifying spatial relationships and visual similarities.

>> **Playing graphical computer games:** Computer games may help you to improve your spatial skills. A study conducted in the United Kingdom showed that children who played computer games consistently scored higher on spatial aptitude tests than children who didn't play the games.

>> **Sketching:** Look at an object or a picture and attempt to sketch it as viewed from a different view. This exercise can help you to improve your ability to mentally visualize angles.

Assembling Objects Practice Questions

Assembling Objects questions measure your spatial skills. There are two types of questions: connecting questions and putting-pieces-together questions. In connection questions, your task is to choose the answer that shows the shapes properly connected together at the designated points. In the jigsaw puzzle–type questions, you must choose the answer that best shows what the shapes in the first drawing would look like if assembled together.

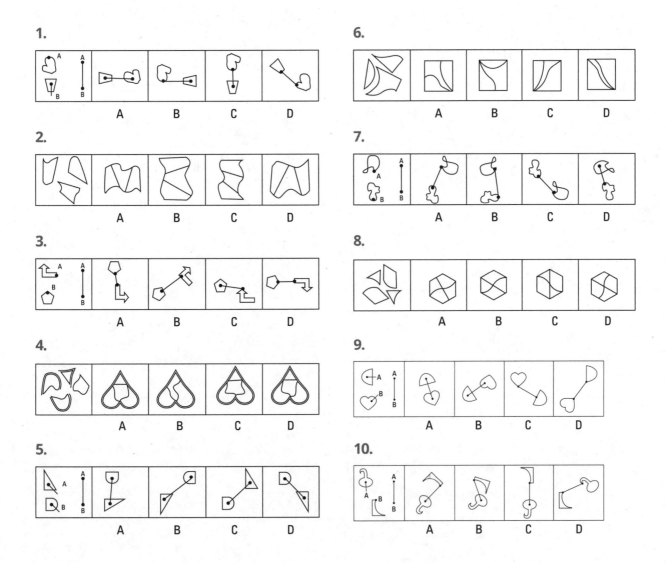

1.
A B C D

2.
A B C D

3.
A B C D

4.
A B C D

5.
A B C D

6.
A B C D

7.
A B C D

8.
A B C D

9.
A B C D

10.
A B C D

11.

A B C D

12.

A B C D

13.

A B C D

14.

A B C D

15.

A B C D

16.

A B C D

Answers and Explanations

Use this answer key to score the Assembling Objects practice questions.

1. **B.** Note that the bottom figure in the first drawing has a line that intersects the short side of the trapezoid shape, so Choices (C) and (D) are wrong. Connection point A is at the tip of the mitten shape, so Choice (A) is wrong as well. The correct answer is Choice (B).

2. **C.** Mentally rotate and reposition the shapes in the first drawing until you can see how they fit together to form the shape shown in Choice (C) — the correct answer. In the first drawing, notice that the shape at the upper right resembles a shark fin — it has two sharp points, and the third point is curved. Choice (C) is the only image that contains this shape (it's at the bottom).

3. **D.** If you selected Choice (A), you were fooled. The arrow shape shown in Choice (A) is a mirror of the shape depicted in the first drawing. The correct answer is Choice (D).

4. **A.** Mentally rotate and reposition the shapes in the first drawing until you can see how they fit together to form the shape shown in Choice (A) — the correct answer. If you had trouble with this one, notice that the piece in the center of the upside-down heart should have a corner that dips a bit on the left. Choice (C) has the dip in the center, and Choice (D) has it on the right, so these answers are wrong. Choice (B) has only three pieces.

5. **D.** Note that both shapes in the first drawing have lines that intersect the shapes at designated points. If you selected Choice (B), your eyes were fooled by mirror images. The correct answer is Choice (D).

6. **B.** Mentally rotate and reposition the shapes in the first drawing until you can see how they fit together to form the shape shown in Choice (B) — the correct answer. Here, you can take a mental snapshot of the largest shape and look for it in the answers — Choice (B) is the only choice that has it. Verify that this is the right answer by recognizing that Choice (B) is also the only answer that contains a segment of a circle, at the top.

7. **A.** Don't be fooled by the mirror shape in Choice (B), because the correct answer is Choice (A).

8. **C.** Mentally rotate and reposition the shapes in the first drawing until you can see how they fit together to form the shape shown in Choice (C), which is the correct answer. Here, you may note that the first drawing contains two shapes that resemble triangles with one side curved inward. Choice (C) is the only image that contains those shapes.

9. **B.** Take note of the point of intersection in the heart in the question; then match it up with the correct answer, Choice (B).

10. **A.** Awkward shapes plus mirrored images make this one a little tricky, but when you look at the points and the positions of the images, you can see that Choice (A) is right.

11. **D.** Choice (D) is the only answer that shows the right intersection between the circle and *L*-shaped object.

12. **A.** Keeping your eye on the points of assembly and staying clear of any mirrored images, you can see that Choice (A) is connected appropriately.

13. **D.** The rectangle in the middle of Choices (C) and (D) is a negative space. You can tell Choice (D) is correct by sizing up the proportions of the three curvy shapes and the triangle.

14. **B.** Counting out the shapes and identifying the right proportions help you see Choice (B) as your shining star.

15. **A.** Awkward shapes can make it difficult to mentally piece together multiple objects with the correct proportions. Don't be distracted by the shapes. Notice the proportions and lines in relation to one another. Make sure each element in the question appears in your answer.

16. **B.** Unusual shapes can be awkward to dissect, but Choice (B) reflects the correct assembly. It has the right number of shapes in the right proportions.

6

Practice ASVAB Exams

Discover your areas of strength and weakness by taking a full-length ASVAB practice test or two (or three).

Sharpen your strategies for math, vocabulary, and reading passage questions by taking two practice AFQTs.

Determine where you went wrong (or right) by reading through answer explanations for practice test questions.

Chapter **18**
Practice Exam 1

This sample test features nine subtests, just like the paper-and-pencil ASVAB. As you may have guessed, the sample tests in this book are paper-based tests. When you take the actual ASVAB, it may be a computer-based or paper-based exam. The computer version has the mostly the same subtests as the paper version, but it separates Auto Information and Shop Information, follows a different time format, and has a different number of questions.

Another difference with the computer-based test is that you can't skip a question and go back to it, and you can't change an answer after you enter it into the computer. You can find out about the computer-based test in greater detail in Chapter 3.

TIP

To get the most out of this sample test, take it under the same conditions as the real ASVAB:

>> Allow yourself about 3 hours to take the entire exam, and take the whole thing at one time.

>> Find a quiet place where you won't be interrupted.

>> Bring a timer that you can set for various lengths of time, some scratch paper (you get two pieces during the exam, but you can get more; just ask for it as needed), and a pencil.

>> At the start of each subtest, set your timer for the specified period of time. Don't go on to the next section until the timer has gone off, and don't go back to a previous section. If you finish early, check your work for that section only.

>> Use the answer sheet that's provided.

>> Don't take a break during any subtest. You can take a short 1- or 2-minute break between subtests if you need it.

After you complete the entire sample test, check your answers against the answers and explanations in Chapter 19.

Your primary goal with this sample test is to determine your strengths and weaknesses. If you miss only one question on the Word Knowledge subtest but you miss 15 on Arithmetic Reasoning, you know where to spend your study time. If you're not going to pursue a career that requires a score on a particular subtest or the type of knowledge a subtest covers, don't worry about your score there. (See Appendix A for information on the subtests that various careers require good scores on.)

Answer Sheet for Practice Exam 1

Subtest 1: General Science

1. Ⓐ Ⓑ Ⓒ Ⓓ 6. Ⓐ Ⓑ Ⓒ Ⓓ 11. Ⓐ Ⓑ Ⓒ Ⓓ 16. Ⓐ Ⓑ Ⓒ Ⓓ 21. Ⓐ Ⓑ Ⓒ Ⓓ
2. Ⓐ Ⓑ Ⓒ Ⓓ 7. Ⓐ Ⓑ Ⓒ Ⓓ 12. Ⓐ Ⓑ Ⓒ Ⓓ 17. Ⓐ Ⓑ Ⓒ Ⓓ 22. Ⓐ Ⓑ Ⓒ Ⓓ
3. Ⓐ Ⓑ Ⓒ Ⓓ 8. Ⓐ Ⓑ Ⓒ Ⓓ 13. Ⓐ Ⓑ Ⓒ Ⓓ 18. Ⓐ Ⓑ Ⓒ Ⓓ 23. Ⓐ Ⓑ Ⓒ Ⓓ
4. Ⓐ Ⓑ Ⓒ Ⓓ 9. Ⓐ Ⓑ Ⓒ Ⓓ 14. Ⓐ Ⓑ Ⓒ Ⓓ 19. Ⓐ Ⓑ Ⓒ Ⓓ 24. Ⓐ Ⓑ Ⓒ Ⓓ
5. Ⓐ Ⓑ Ⓒ Ⓓ 10. Ⓐ Ⓑ Ⓒ Ⓓ 15. Ⓐ Ⓑ Ⓒ Ⓓ 20. Ⓐ Ⓑ Ⓒ Ⓓ 25. Ⓐ Ⓑ Ⓒ Ⓓ

Subtest 2: Arithmetic Reasoning

1. Ⓐ Ⓑ Ⓒ Ⓓ 7. Ⓐ Ⓑ Ⓒ Ⓓ 13. Ⓐ Ⓑ Ⓒ Ⓓ 19. Ⓐ Ⓑ Ⓒ Ⓓ 25. Ⓐ Ⓑ Ⓒ Ⓓ
2. Ⓐ Ⓑ Ⓒ Ⓓ 8. Ⓐ Ⓑ Ⓒ Ⓓ 14. Ⓐ Ⓑ Ⓒ Ⓓ 20. Ⓐ Ⓑ Ⓒ Ⓓ 26. Ⓐ Ⓑ Ⓒ Ⓓ
3. Ⓐ Ⓑ Ⓒ Ⓓ 9. Ⓐ Ⓑ Ⓒ Ⓓ 15. Ⓐ Ⓑ Ⓒ Ⓓ 21. Ⓐ Ⓑ Ⓒ Ⓓ 27. Ⓐ Ⓑ Ⓒ Ⓓ
4. Ⓐ Ⓑ Ⓒ Ⓓ 10. Ⓐ Ⓑ Ⓒ Ⓓ 16. Ⓐ Ⓑ Ⓒ Ⓓ 22. Ⓐ Ⓑ Ⓒ Ⓓ 28. Ⓐ Ⓑ Ⓒ Ⓓ
5. Ⓐ Ⓑ Ⓒ Ⓓ 11. Ⓐ Ⓑ Ⓒ Ⓓ 17. Ⓐ Ⓑ Ⓒ Ⓓ 23. Ⓐ Ⓑ Ⓒ Ⓓ 29. Ⓐ Ⓑ Ⓒ Ⓓ
6. Ⓐ Ⓑ Ⓒ Ⓓ 12. Ⓐ Ⓑ Ⓒ Ⓓ 18. Ⓐ Ⓑ Ⓒ Ⓓ 24. Ⓐ Ⓑ Ⓒ Ⓓ 30. Ⓐ Ⓑ Ⓒ Ⓓ

Subtest 3: Word Knowledge

1. Ⓐ Ⓑ Ⓒ Ⓓ 8. Ⓐ Ⓑ Ⓒ Ⓓ 15. Ⓐ Ⓑ Ⓒ Ⓓ 22. Ⓐ Ⓑ Ⓒ Ⓓ 29. Ⓐ Ⓑ Ⓒ Ⓓ
2. Ⓐ Ⓑ Ⓒ Ⓓ 9. Ⓐ Ⓑ Ⓒ Ⓓ 16. Ⓐ Ⓑ Ⓒ Ⓓ 23. Ⓐ Ⓑ Ⓒ Ⓓ 30. Ⓐ Ⓑ Ⓒ Ⓓ
3. Ⓐ Ⓑ Ⓒ Ⓓ 10. Ⓐ Ⓑ Ⓒ Ⓓ 17. Ⓐ Ⓑ Ⓒ Ⓓ 24. Ⓐ Ⓑ Ⓒ Ⓓ 31. Ⓐ Ⓑ Ⓒ Ⓓ
4. Ⓐ Ⓑ Ⓒ Ⓓ 11. Ⓐ Ⓑ Ⓒ Ⓓ 18. Ⓐ Ⓑ Ⓒ Ⓓ 25. Ⓐ Ⓑ Ⓒ Ⓓ 32. Ⓐ Ⓑ Ⓒ Ⓓ
5. Ⓐ Ⓑ Ⓒ Ⓓ 12. Ⓐ Ⓑ Ⓒ Ⓓ 19. Ⓐ Ⓑ Ⓒ Ⓓ 26. Ⓐ Ⓑ Ⓒ Ⓓ 33. Ⓐ Ⓑ Ⓒ Ⓓ
6. Ⓐ Ⓑ Ⓒ Ⓓ 13. Ⓐ Ⓑ Ⓒ Ⓓ 20. Ⓐ Ⓑ Ⓒ Ⓓ 27. Ⓐ Ⓑ Ⓒ Ⓓ 34. Ⓐ Ⓑ Ⓒ Ⓓ
7. Ⓐ Ⓑ Ⓒ Ⓓ 14. Ⓐ Ⓑ Ⓒ Ⓓ 21. Ⓐ Ⓑ Ⓒ Ⓓ 28. Ⓐ Ⓑ Ⓒ Ⓓ 35. Ⓐ Ⓑ Ⓒ Ⓓ

Subtest 4: Paragraph Comprehension

1. Ⓐ Ⓑ Ⓒ Ⓓ 4. Ⓐ Ⓑ Ⓒ Ⓓ 7. Ⓐ Ⓑ Ⓒ Ⓓ 10. Ⓐ Ⓑ Ⓒ Ⓓ 13. Ⓐ Ⓑ Ⓒ Ⓓ
2. Ⓐ Ⓑ Ⓒ Ⓓ 5. Ⓐ Ⓑ Ⓒ Ⓓ 8. Ⓐ Ⓑ Ⓒ Ⓓ 11. Ⓐ Ⓑ Ⓒ Ⓓ 14. Ⓐ Ⓑ Ⓒ Ⓓ
3. Ⓐ Ⓑ Ⓒ Ⓓ 6. Ⓐ Ⓑ Ⓒ Ⓓ 9. Ⓐ Ⓑ Ⓒ Ⓓ 12. Ⓐ Ⓑ Ⓒ Ⓓ 15. Ⓐ Ⓑ Ⓒ Ⓓ

Subtest 5: Mathematics Knowledge

1. Ⓐ Ⓑ Ⓒ Ⓓ 6. Ⓐ Ⓑ Ⓒ Ⓓ 11. Ⓐ Ⓑ Ⓒ Ⓓ 16. Ⓐ Ⓑ Ⓒ Ⓓ 21. Ⓐ Ⓑ Ⓒ Ⓓ
2. Ⓐ Ⓑ Ⓒ Ⓓ 7. Ⓐ Ⓑ Ⓒ Ⓓ 12. Ⓐ Ⓑ Ⓒ Ⓓ 17. Ⓐ Ⓑ Ⓒ Ⓓ 22. Ⓐ Ⓑ Ⓒ Ⓓ
3. Ⓐ Ⓑ Ⓒ Ⓓ 8. Ⓐ Ⓑ Ⓒ Ⓓ 13. Ⓐ Ⓑ Ⓒ Ⓓ 18. Ⓐ Ⓑ Ⓒ Ⓓ 23. Ⓐ Ⓑ Ⓒ Ⓓ
4. Ⓐ Ⓑ Ⓒ Ⓓ 9. Ⓐ Ⓑ Ⓒ Ⓓ 14. Ⓐ Ⓑ Ⓒ Ⓓ 19. Ⓐ Ⓑ Ⓒ Ⓓ 24. Ⓐ Ⓑ Ⓒ Ⓓ
5. Ⓐ Ⓑ Ⓒ Ⓓ 10. Ⓐ Ⓑ Ⓒ Ⓓ 15. Ⓐ Ⓑ Ⓒ Ⓓ 20. Ⓐ Ⓑ Ⓒ Ⓓ 25. Ⓐ Ⓑ Ⓒ Ⓓ

Subtest 6: Electronics Information

1. Ⓐ Ⓑ Ⓒ Ⓓ 5. Ⓐ Ⓑ Ⓒ Ⓓ 9. Ⓐ Ⓑ Ⓒ Ⓓ 13. Ⓐ Ⓑ Ⓒ Ⓓ 17. Ⓐ Ⓑ Ⓒ Ⓓ
2. Ⓐ Ⓑ Ⓒ Ⓓ 6. Ⓐ Ⓑ Ⓒ Ⓓ 10. Ⓐ Ⓑ Ⓒ Ⓓ 14. Ⓐ Ⓑ Ⓒ Ⓓ 18. Ⓐ Ⓑ Ⓒ Ⓓ
3. Ⓐ Ⓑ Ⓒ Ⓓ 7. Ⓐ Ⓑ Ⓒ Ⓓ 11. Ⓐ Ⓑ Ⓒ Ⓓ 15. Ⓐ Ⓑ Ⓒ Ⓓ 19. Ⓐ Ⓑ Ⓒ Ⓓ
4. Ⓐ Ⓑ Ⓒ Ⓓ 8. Ⓐ Ⓑ Ⓒ Ⓓ 12. Ⓐ Ⓑ Ⓒ Ⓓ 16. Ⓐ Ⓑ Ⓒ Ⓓ 20. Ⓐ Ⓑ Ⓒ Ⓓ

Subtest 7: Auto & Shop Information

1. Ⓐ Ⓑ Ⓒ Ⓓ   6. Ⓐ Ⓑ Ⓒ Ⓓ   11. Ⓐ Ⓑ Ⓒ Ⓓ   16. Ⓐ Ⓑ Ⓒ Ⓓ   21. Ⓐ Ⓑ Ⓒ Ⓓ
2. Ⓐ Ⓑ Ⓒ Ⓓ   7. Ⓐ Ⓑ Ⓒ Ⓓ   12. Ⓐ Ⓑ Ⓒ Ⓓ   17. Ⓐ Ⓑ Ⓒ Ⓓ   22. Ⓐ Ⓑ Ⓒ Ⓓ
3. Ⓐ Ⓑ Ⓒ Ⓓ   8. Ⓐ Ⓑ Ⓒ Ⓓ   13. Ⓐ Ⓑ Ⓒ Ⓓ   18. Ⓐ Ⓑ Ⓒ Ⓓ   23. Ⓐ Ⓑ Ⓒ Ⓓ
4. Ⓐ Ⓑ Ⓒ Ⓓ   9. Ⓐ Ⓑ Ⓒ Ⓓ   14. Ⓐ Ⓑ Ⓒ Ⓓ   19. Ⓐ Ⓑ Ⓒ Ⓓ   24. Ⓐ Ⓑ Ⓒ Ⓓ
5. Ⓐ Ⓑ Ⓒ Ⓓ   10. Ⓐ Ⓑ Ⓒ Ⓓ   15. Ⓐ Ⓑ Ⓒ Ⓓ   20. Ⓐ Ⓑ Ⓒ Ⓓ   25. Ⓐ Ⓑ Ⓒ Ⓓ

Subtest 8: Mechanical Comprehension

1. Ⓐ Ⓑ Ⓒ Ⓓ   6. Ⓐ Ⓑ Ⓒ Ⓓ   11. Ⓐ Ⓑ Ⓒ Ⓓ   16. Ⓐ Ⓑ Ⓒ Ⓓ   21. Ⓐ Ⓑ Ⓒ Ⓓ
2. Ⓐ Ⓑ Ⓒ Ⓓ   7. Ⓐ Ⓑ Ⓒ Ⓓ   12. Ⓐ Ⓑ Ⓒ Ⓓ   17. Ⓐ Ⓑ Ⓒ Ⓓ   22. Ⓐ Ⓑ Ⓒ Ⓓ
3. Ⓐ Ⓑ Ⓒ Ⓓ   8. Ⓐ Ⓑ Ⓒ Ⓓ   13. Ⓐ Ⓑ Ⓒ Ⓓ   18. Ⓐ Ⓑ Ⓒ Ⓓ   23. Ⓐ Ⓑ Ⓒ Ⓓ
4. Ⓐ Ⓑ Ⓒ Ⓓ   9. Ⓐ Ⓑ Ⓒ Ⓓ   14. Ⓐ Ⓑ Ⓒ Ⓓ   19. Ⓐ Ⓑ Ⓒ Ⓓ   24. Ⓐ Ⓑ Ⓒ Ⓓ
5. Ⓐ Ⓑ Ⓒ Ⓓ   10. Ⓐ Ⓑ Ⓒ Ⓓ   15. Ⓐ Ⓑ Ⓒ Ⓓ   20. Ⓐ Ⓑ Ⓒ Ⓓ   25. Ⓐ Ⓑ Ⓒ Ⓓ

Subtest 9: Assembling Objects

1. Ⓐ Ⓑ Ⓒ Ⓓ   6. Ⓐ Ⓑ Ⓒ Ⓓ   11. Ⓐ Ⓑ Ⓒ Ⓓ   16. Ⓐ Ⓑ Ⓒ Ⓓ   21. Ⓐ Ⓑ Ⓒ Ⓓ
2. Ⓐ Ⓑ Ⓒ Ⓓ   7. Ⓐ Ⓑ Ⓒ Ⓓ   12. Ⓐ Ⓑ Ⓒ Ⓓ   17. Ⓐ Ⓑ Ⓒ Ⓓ   22. Ⓐ Ⓑ Ⓒ Ⓓ
3. Ⓐ Ⓑ Ⓒ Ⓓ   8. Ⓐ Ⓑ Ⓒ Ⓓ   13. Ⓐ Ⓑ Ⓒ Ⓓ   18. Ⓐ Ⓑ Ⓒ Ⓓ   23. Ⓐ Ⓑ Ⓒ Ⓓ
4. Ⓐ Ⓑ Ⓒ Ⓓ   9. Ⓐ Ⓑ Ⓒ Ⓓ   14. Ⓐ Ⓑ Ⓒ Ⓓ   19. Ⓐ Ⓑ Ⓒ Ⓓ   24. Ⓐ Ⓑ Ⓒ Ⓓ
5. Ⓐ Ⓑ Ⓒ Ⓓ   10. Ⓐ Ⓑ Ⓒ Ⓓ   15. Ⓐ Ⓑ Ⓒ Ⓓ   20. Ⓐ Ⓑ Ⓒ Ⓓ   25. Ⓐ Ⓑ Ⓒ Ⓓ

Subtest 1: General Science

TIME: 11 minutes for 25 questions

DIRECTIONS: This subtest tests your knowledge of general science principles usually covered in high school classes. Pick the best answer for each question and then mark the space on your answer sheet that corresponds to the letter indicating your choice.

1. Which planet is named after the Greek god who personified the sky?

   (A) Earth

   (B) Mars

   (C) Pluto

   (D) Uranus

2. An animal that eats only meat is called a(n)

   (A) omnivore.

   (B) herbivore.

   (C) carnivore.

   (D) voracious.

3. The chemical process in which electrons are removed from a molecule is called

   (A) respiration.

   (B) recreation.

   (C) oxidation.

   (D) metabolism.

4. What is a single unit of quanta called?

   (A) quantum

   (B) quantumonium

   (C) quantus

   (D) quanfactorial

5. In a vacuum, light waves travel at a rate of about

   (A) 186,000 miles per hour.

   (B) 186,000 miles per minute.

   (C) 18,600 miles per hour.

   (D) 186,000 miles per second.

6. The largest planet in the solar system is

   (A) Earth.

   (B) Mars.

   (C) Saturn.

   (D) Jupiter.

7. The intestines are part of the

   (A) circulatory system.

   (B) nervous system.

   (C) respiratory system.

   (D) digestive system.

8. Joints that hold bones firmly together are called

   (A) hinge joints.

   (B) ball and socket joints.

   (C) fixed joints.

   (D) pivot joints.

9. Of the levels listed, the top or broadest level of the classification system for living organisms is called the

   (A) class.

   (B) phylum.

   (C) kingdom.

   (D) genus.

10. Which planet is the brightest object in the sky, aside from the sun and moon?

    (A) Saturn

    (B) Pluto

    (C) Venus

    (D) Mercury

11. The human heart includes

    (A) 2 chambers.

    (B) 3 chambers.

    (C) 4 chambers.

    (D) 5 chambers.

12. White blood cells

    (A) produce antibodies.

    (B) fight infections.

    (C) carry oxygen and carbon dioxide.

    (D) Both A and B.

GO ON TO NEXT PAGE ➤

13. A measureable amount of protein can be found in all of the following foods EXCEPT

(A) eggs.

(B) meat.

(C) peas.

(D) apples.

14. What is the most abundant element, by mass, in Earth's crust?

(A) carbon

(B) oxygen

(C) gold

(D) salt

15. Osmosis is

(A) diffusion of a solvent.

(B) transfer of oxygen.

(C) low blood sugar.

(D) protein.

16. A meter consists of

(A) 10 centimeters.

(B) 100 millimeters.

(C) 100 centimeters.

(D) 10 millimeters.

17. One light-year is

(A) the distance traveled by light in one year.

(B) the brightness of light at 30,000 miles.

(C) 17 standard Earth years.

(D) the distance Earth must travel around the sun.

18. Electrons are particles that are

(A) positively charged.

(B) neutral.

(C) able to move freely.

(D) negatively charged.

19. The asteroid belt is located

(A) around Mercury.

(B) between Mars and Jupiter.

(C) inside the orbit of Venus.

(D) There is no such thing as an asteroid belt.

20. The atomic number of an atom is determined by

(A) the size of its nucleus.

(B) the number of protons.

(C) the number of electrons.

(D) its location in the periodic table.

21. The "control center" of a cell is called the

(A) nucleus.

(B) compound.

(C) mitochondria.

(D) atom.

22. How many planets in the solar system have rings?

(A) one

(B) two

(C) three

(D) four

23. The temperature at which a substance's solid and liquid states exist in equilibrium is its

(A) melting point.

(B) boiling point.

(C) anti-freezing point.

(D) concentration point.

24. The atmosphere of Mars is composed mostly of

(A) oxygen.

(B) carbon dioxide.

(C) helium.

(D) Mars has no atmosphere.

25. Not counting the sun, the closest star to Earth is

(A) Rigel.

(B) Proxima Centauri.

(C) Antares.

(D) Betelgeuse.

Subtest 2: Arithmetic Reasoning

TIME: 36 minutes for 30 questions

DIRECTIONS: This test contains questions about arithmetic. Each question is followed by four possible answers. Decide which answer is correct and then mark the space on your answer sheet that has the same number and letter as your choice. Use scratch paper for any figuring you want to do. A calculator is not allowed.

1. If a car is towed 12 miles to the repair shop and the tow charge is $3.50 per mile, how much does the tow cost?

   (A) $12.00

   (B) $3.50

   (C) $42.00

   (D) $100.00

2. The sum of two numbers is 70. One number is 8 more than the other. What's the smaller number?

   (A) 31

   (B) 33

   (C) 35

   (D) 36

3. A sales manager buys antacid in bottles by the gross. If he goes through 3 bottles of antacid every day, how long will the gross last?

   (A) 144 days

   (B) 3 days

   (C) 20 days

   (D) 48 days

4. Jenny's test grades are 93, 89, 96, and 98. If she wishes to raise her average to 95, what does she need to score on her next test?

   (A) 100

   (B) 99

   (C) 97

   (D) 95

5. A server earns an average tip of 12% of the cost of the food she serves. If she serves $375 worth of food in one evening, how much money in tips will she earn on average?

   (A) $37

   (B) $45

   (C) $42

   (D) $420

6. How many square feet of carpeting are needed to carpet a 12-foot-x-12-foot room?

   (A) 24

   (B) 120

   (C) 48

   (D) 144

7. Carpet stain protector costs $0.65 per square yard to apply. How much will it cost to apply the protector to a 16-foot-x-18-foot carpet?

   (A) $187.20

   (B) $62.40

   (C) $20.80

   (D) $96.00

8. A printing plant that produces baseball cards has a monthly overhead of $6,000. It costs 18 cents to print each card, and the cards sell for 30 cents each. How many cards must the printing plant sell each month in order to make a profit?

   (A) 30,000

   (B) 40,000

   (C) 50,000

   (D) 60,000

GO ON TO NEXT PAGE ➤

9. Joe received an hourly wage of $8.15. His boss gave him a 7% raise. How much does Joe make per hour now?

(A) $0.57

(B) $8.90

(C) $8.72

(D) $13.85

10. Alice leaves her house, driving east at 45 miles per hour (mph). Thirty minutes later, her husband Dave notices she forgot her cellphone and sets off after her. How fast must Dave travel in order to catch up with Alice 3 hours after he leaves?

(A) 49 mph

(B) 50.5 mph

(C) 52.5 mph

(D) 54 mph

11. A baker made 20 pies. A Boy Scout troop buys one-fourth of his pies, a preschool teacher buys one-third of his pies, and a caterer buys one-sixth of his pies. How many pies does the baker have left?

(A) $\frac{3}{4}$

(B) 15

(C) 12

(D) 5

12. Miriam bought five cases of motor oil on sale. A case of motor oil normally costs $24.00, but she was able to purchase the oil for $22.50 a case. How much money did Miriam save on her entire purchase?

(A) $7.50

(B) $1.50

(C) $8.00

(D) $22.50

13. A security guard walks the equivalent of six city blocks when he makes a circuit around the building. If he walks at a pace of eight city blocks every 30 minutes, how long will it take him to complete a circuit around the building, assuming he doesn't run into any thieves?

(A) 20.00 minutes

(B) 3.75 minutes

(C) 22.50 minutes

(D) 7.5 minutes

14. The population of Grand Island, Nebraska, grew by 600,000 people between 1995 and 2005, one-fifth more than the town council predicted. The town council originally predicted the city's population would grow by

(A) 400,000

(B) 500,000

(C) 300,000

(D) 100,000

15. Joan is taking an admissions examination. If she has to get at least 40 of the 60 questions right to pass, what percent of the questions does she need to answer correctly?

(A) 30%

(B) 40%

(C) $66\frac{1}{3}\%$

(D) $66\frac{2}{3}\%$

16. A teacher deposits $3,000 in a retirement fund. If she doesn't add any more money to the fund, which earns an annual interest rate of 6%, how much money will she have in 1 year?

(A) $180

(B) $3,006

(C) $3,180

(D) $6,000

17. The high school track measures one-quarter of a mile around. How many laps would you have to run in order to run three and a half miles?

(A) 12

(B) 14

(C) 16

(D) 18

18. Karl is driving in Austria, where the speed limit is posted in kilometers per hour. The car's speedometer shows that he's traveling at a rate of 75 kilometers per hour. Karl knows that a kilometer is about $\frac{5}{8}$ of a mile. Approximately how many miles per hour is Karl traveling?

(A) 47

(B) 120

(C) 50

(D) 53

19. A carpenter earns $12.30 an hour for a 40-hour week. His overtime pay is $1\frac{1}{2}$ times his base pay. If he puts in a 46-hour week, how much is his weekly pay?

(A) $602.70

(B) $492.00

(C) $565.80

(D) $110.70

20. An office building has 30 employees and provides 42 square feet of work space per employee. If five more employees are hired, how much less work space will each employee have?

(A) 6 square feet

(B) 7 square feet

(C) 7.5 square feet

(D) 36 square feet

21. Stan bought a monster truck for $2,000 down and payments of $450 a month for five years. What's the total cost of the monster truck?

(A) $4,250

(B) $29,000

(C) $27,000

(D) $34,400

22. Darla spent $120.37 on groceries in January, $108.45 in February, and $114.86 in March. What was the average monthly cost of Darla's groceries?

(A) $343.68

(B) $110.45

(C) $114.86

(D) $114.56

23. Keith is driving from Reno to Kansas City to meet his girlfriend. The distance between the two cities is 1,650 miles. If Keith can average 50 miles per hour, how many hours will it take him to complete his trip?

(A) 8 hours

(B) 30 hours

(C) 33 hours

(D) 82 hours

24. Michael needs 55 gallons of paint to paint an apartment building. He would like to purchase the paint for the least amount of money possible. Which of the following should he buy?

(A) two 25-gallon buckets at $550 each

(B) eleven 5-gallon buckets at $108 each

(C) six 10-gallon buckets at $215 each

(D) fifty-five 1-gallon buckets at $23 each

25. As a member of FEMA, you're required to set up a contingency plan to supply meals to residents of a town devastated by a tornado. A breakfast ration weighs 12 ounces, and the lunch and dinner rations weigh 18 ounces each. Assuming a food truck can carry 3 tons and that each resident will receive 3 meals per day, how many residents can you feed from one truck during a 10-day period?

(A) 150 residents

(B) 200 residents

(C) 250 residents

(D) 300 residents

GO ON TO NEXT PAGE

26. A train headed south for Wichita left the station at the same time a train headed north for Des Moines left the same station. The train headed for Wichita traveled at 55 miles per hour. The train headed for Des Moines traveled at 70 miles per hour. How many miles apart are the trains at the end of 3 hours?

   (A) 210 miles

   (B) 165 miles

   (C) 125 miles

   (D) 375 miles

27. A carpenter needs to cut four sections, each 3 feet, 8 inches long, from a piece of molding. If the board is only sold by the foot, what's the shortest length of board she can buy?

   (A) 15 feet

   (B) 14 feet

   (C) 16 feet

   (D) 12 feet

28. Kiya had only one coupon for 10% off one frozen turkey breast. The turkey breasts cost $8.50 each, and Kiya wanted to buy two. How much did she pay?

   (A) $16.15

   (B) $17.00

   (C) $15.30

   (D) $7.65

29. A recruiter travels 1,100 miles during a 40-hour workweek. If she spends $\frac{2}{5}$ of her time traveling, how many hours does she spend traveling?

   (A) 22

   (B) $5\frac{1}{2}$

   (C) 16

   (D) 8

30. Your car uses gasoline at the rate of 21 miles per gallon. If gasoline costs $2.82 per gallon and you drive for 7 hours at a speed of 48 miles per hour, how much will you pay for gasoline for the trip?

   (A) $38.18

   (B) $45.12

   (C) $47.73

   (D) $59.27

DO NOT TURN THE PAGE UNTIL TOLD TO DO SO   STOP   DO NOT RETURN TO A PREVIOUS TEST

Subtest 3: Word Knowledge

TIME: 11 minutes for 35 questions

DIRECTIONS: This test is about the meanings of words. Each question has a word underlined. You may be asked to decide which one of the four words in the choices most nearly means the same thing as the underlined word or which one of the four words means the opposite. If the underlined word is used in a sentence, decide which of the four choices most nearly means the same thing as the underlined word, as used in the context of the sentence. Mark the corresponding space on your answer sheet.

1. Tim promised to meet us at the <u>apex</u>.

   (A) top

   (B) bottom

   (C) canyon

   (D) river

2. <u>Assimilate</u> most nearly means

   (A) absorb.

   (B) react.

   (C) pretend.

   (D) lie.

3. <u>Brittle</u> most nearly means

   (A) soft.

   (B) fragile.

   (C) study.

   (D) hard.

4. <u>Datum</u> most nearly means

   (A) fiscal year date.

   (B) congruence.

   (C) fact.

   (D) positive result.

5. The exchange student was <u>proficient</u> in French, German, and English.

   (A) poor

   (B) knowledgeable

   (C) adept

   (D) exacting

6. The judge <u>imposed</u> a severe penalty due to Tom's actions.

   (A) scheduled

   (B) made an example of

   (C) levied

   (D) questioned

7. Mary went to the store and bought peanuts <u>galore</u>.

   (A) abundant

   (B) salty

   (C) on sale

   (D) roasted

8. He ran <u>headlong</u> into the fight.

   (A) headfirst

   (B) reluctantly

   (C) happily

   (D) recklessly

9. <u>Frugal</u> most nearly means

   (A) quiet.

   (B) amazing.

   (C) delayed.

   (D) economical.

10. The word most opposite in meaning to <u>stimulate</u> is

    (A) support.

    (B) arrest.

    (C) travel.

    (D) dislike.

GO ON TO NEXT PAGE

11. Illicit most nearly means
   (A) historical.
   (B) unlawful.
   (C) storied.
   (D) willfully.

12. Vacate most nearly means
   (A) crawl.
   (B) impel.
   (C) exhume.
   (D) leave.

13. The sergeant gave his reasoned opinion.
   (A) irate
   (B) logical
   (C) impressive
   (D) uninformed

14. Tacit most nearly means
   (A) loud.
   (B) understood.
   (C) commendable.
   (D) transparent.

15. The brass was not burnished.
   (A) yellow
   (B) dull
   (C) expensive
   (D) polished

16. The commodity was sold.
   (A) product
   (B) stock
   (C) idea
   (D) table

17. Her motives were contrived.
   (A) premeditated
   (B) emotional
   (C) obscure
   (D) amusing

18. Supplicate most nearly means
   (A) to make superior.
   (B) to be unnecessary.
   (C) to beg.
   (D) to be expansive.

19. The word most opposite in meaning to hypocrisy is
   (A) honesty.
   (B) happy.
   (C) angry.
   (D) threatening.

20. Bob found the peaches to be extremely succulent.
   (A) large
   (B) tasteless
   (C) old
   (D) juicy

21. The Army soldiers were ordered to immediate garrison duty.
   (A) field
   (B) combat
   (C) latrine
   (D) fort

22. Furtherance most nearly means
   (A) advancement.
   (B) finance.
   (C) practicality.
   (D) destruction.

23. Domicile most nearly means
   (A) office.
   (B) shopping.
   (C) home.
   (D) vacation.

24. Abrogate most nearly means
    (A) recover.
    (B) aid.
    (C) foreclose.
    (D) abolish.

25. Compensation most nearly means
    (A) religion.
    (B) commission.
    (C) boathouse.
    (D) shower.

26. He gave a brusque account of the events.
    (A) passionate
    (B) lengthy
    (C) uncensored
    (D) abrupt

27. The vote resulted in the demise of the proposed new law.
    (A) passage
    (B) death
    (C) postponement
    (D) abatement

28. We commemorated our veterans during the ceremony.
    (A) denied
    (B) remembered
    (C) thanked
    (D) took pictures of

29. Bore most nearly means
    (A) deepen.
    (B) hide.
    (C) dig.
    (D) jump.

30. That custom still prevails.
    (A) angers
    (B) persists
    (C) surprises
    (D) excites

31. Defray most nearly means
    (A) invade.
    (B) obstruct.
    (C) pay.
    (D) reverse.

32. Chasm most nearly means
    (A) abyss.
    (B) sky.
    (C) mountain.
    (D) valley.

33. Fundamental most nearly means
    (A) radical.
    (B) religious.
    (C) basic.
    (D) excessive.

34. Susceptible most nearly means
    (A) travel.
    (B) resistant.
    (C) limited.
    (D) vulnerable.

35. Emblem most nearly means
    (A) symbol.
    (B) picture.
    (C) statue.
    (D) religion.

DO NOT TURN THE PAGE UNTIL TOLD TO DO SO   STOP   DO NOT RETURN TO A PREVIOUS TEST

Subtest 4: Paragraph Comprehension

TIME: 13 minutes for 15 questions

DIRECTIONS: This test contains items that measure your ability to understand what you read. This section includes one or more paragraphs of reading material followed by incomplete statements or questions. Read the paragraph and select the choice that best completes the statement or answers the question. Mark your choice on your answer sheet, using the correct letter with each question number.

An important stage of personal time management is to take control of appointments. Determined by external obligation, appointments constitute interaction with other people and an agreed-on interface between your activities and those of others. Start with a simple appointment diary. List all appointments, including regular and recurring ones. Now, be ruthless and eliminate the unnecessary. There may be committees where you can't productively contribute or where a subordinate may be able to participate. Eliminate the waste of your time.

1. Effectively managing your appointments allows you to
   - **(A)** spend more time with your subordinates.
   - **(B)** delegate responsibility to subordinates.
   - **(C)** make more efficient use of your time.
   - **(D)** attend only the most important meetings.

The U.S. Congress consists of 100 senators and 435 representatives. Two senators are elected from each state. The number of representatives from each state is based on population, although each state has at least one representative. Senators serve six-year terms, and representatives serve two-year terms.

2. According to this passage,
   - **(A)** there are equal numbers of senators and representatives.
   - **(B)** the number of representatives from each state is decided by a lottery.
   - **(C)** it's possible for a state to have no representatives.
   - **(D)** senators and representatives have different term lengths.

Indo-European languages consist of those languages spoken by most of Europe and in those parts of the world that Europeans have colonized since the 16th century (such as the United States). Indo-European languages are also spoken in India, Iran, parts of western Afghanistan, and in some areas of Asia.

3. The author of this passage would agree that
   - **(A)** Indo-European languages are spoken in areas all over the world.
   - **(B)** Indo-European languages include all the languages spoken in the world.
   - **(C)** only Europeans speak Indo-European languages.
   - **(D)** Indo-European language speakers can easily understand one another.

In privatization, the government relies on the private sector to provide a service. However, the government divests itself of the entire process, including all assets. With privatized functions, the government may specify quality, quantity, and timeliness requirements, but it has no control over the operations of the activity. Also, the government may not be the only customer. Whomever the government chooses to provide the services would likely provide the same services to others.

4. This paragraph best supports the statement that
   - **(A)** the government must closely supervise privatized functions.
   - **(B)** privatized functions consist of a mixture of government employees, military personnel, and private contractors.
   - **(C)** privatized functions are those institutions that provide services only to a government agency.
   - **(D)** privatized functions provide essential services to the government.

The success or failure of a conference lies largely with its leader. A leader's zest and enthusiasm must be real, apparent, and contagious. The leader is responsible for getting the ball rolling and making the attendees feel as if the meeting is theirs and its success depends on their participation. A good, thorough introduction helps establish the right climate.

5. A good title to this paragraph would be

   (A) "Lead by Example."

   (B) "The Importance of Proper Introductions."

   (C) "Leading a Successful Conference."

   (D) "Conference Participation Basics."

Cloud seeding is accomplished by dropping particles of dry ice (solid carbon dioxide) from a plane onto super-cooled clouds. This process encourages condensation of water droplets in the clouds, which usually, but not always, results in rain or snow.

6. From this passage, it's reasonable to assume that

   (A) cloud seeding could be used to end a drought.

   (B) cloud seeding is prohibitively expensive.

   (C) cloud seeding is rarely used.

   (D) cloud seeding can be accomplished by using regular ice.

To write or not to write — that is the question. If assigned a writing task, there's no option. However, if someone is looking for a specific answer, find out if they need a short answer or a detailed one. Can the requirement be met with a telephone call, email, or short note, or is something more necessary? A former CEO of a major corporation once commented that he had looked at 13,000 pieces of paper in a 5-day period. Think how much easier and more economical it would be if people would use the telephone, send an email, or write a short note.

7. The main point of this passage is that

   (A) written records are important because they provide detailed documentation.

   (B) more businesspeople should invest time and energy improving their writing skills.

   (C) writing may not be the best way to communicate information.

   (D) it's pointless for businesspeople to spend time improving their writing skills.

The transistor, a small, solid-state device that can amplify sound, was invented in 1947. At first, it was too expensive and too difficult to produce to be used in cheap, mass-market products. By 1954, though, these cost and production problems had been overcome, and the first transistor radio was put on the market.

8. According to this passage,

   (A) there was no market for transistors before 1954.

   (B) when transistors could be produced cheaply and easily, the transistor radio was put on the market.

   (C) transistors were invented in 1947 by order of the Department of Defense.

   (D) transistors are still expensive to produce.

I returned from the City about three o'clock on that May afternoon pretty well disgusted with life. I had been three months in the Old Country and was fed up with it. If people had told me a year ago that I would've been feeling like that I should've laughed at them; but there was the fact. The weather made me liverish, the talk of the ordinary Englishman made me sick, I couldn't get enough exercise, and the amusements of London seemed as flat as soda water that had been standing in the sun.

9. The author is speaking of his travels in

   (A) Spain.

   (B) Great Britain.

   (C) Germany.

   (D) Scotland.

Surveys show that the average child under the age of 18 watches four hours of television per day. Although some of the programming may be educational, most isn't. Spending this much time watching television interferes with a child's ability to pursue other interests, such as reading, participating in sports, and playing with friends.

10. The author of this passage would agree that

(A) television viewing should be restricted.

(B) parents who let their children watch this much television are neglectful.

(C) reading, participating in sports, playing with friends, and watching television should all be given equal time.

(D) adults over 18 can watch as much television as they want.

Questions 11 and 12 are based on the following passage.

High school and college graduates attempting to find jobs should participate in mock job interviews. These mock interviews help students prepare for the types of questions they'll be asked, make them more comfortable with common interview formats, and help them critique their performance before facing a real interviewer. Because they're such a valuable aid, schools should organize mock job interviews for all their graduating students.

11. The above passage states that mock job interviews

(A) frighten students.

(B) should be offered to the best students.

(C) help prepare students for real job interviews.

(D) should be organized by students.

12. From the above passage, it is reasonable to assume that

(A) mock interviews can increase a student's confidence when he or she goes into a real job interview.

(B) mock interviews are expensive to organize.

(C) few students are interested in mock interviews.

(D) students don't need job interview preparation.

Questions 13 through 15 are based on the following passage.

Due process, the guarantee of fairness in the administration of justice, is part of the 5th Amendment to the U.S. Constitution. The 14th Amendment further requires states to abide by due process. After this amendment was enacted, the U.S. Supreme Court struck down many state laws that infringed on the civil rights guaranteed to citizens in the Bill of Rights.

13. According to the above passage, due process

(A) is an outdated concept.

(B) guarantees fairness in the justice system.

(C) never became part of the U.S. Constitution.

(D) is the process by which winning lottery tickets are selected.

14. According to the above passage, it's reasonable to assume that the 5th Amendment

(A) is about taxes.

(B) guarantees due process in all criminal and civil cases.

(C) guarantees due process in federal law.

(D) should never have become part of the Bill of Rights.

15. The author of the above passage would agree that

(A) without the passage of the 14th Amendment, many laws restricting civil rights would still exist in various states.

(B) the Supreme Court overstepped its jurisdiction when it struck down laws infringing on citizens' civil rights.

(C) the Supreme Court had every right to strike down state laws before the passage of the 14th Amendment.

(D) the 14th Amendment was opposed by all states.

Subtest 5: Mathematics Knowledge

TIME: 24 minutes for 25 questions

DIRECTIONS: This section tests your ability to solve general mathematical problems. Select the correct answer from the choices given, and then mark the corresponding space on your answer sheet. Use scratch paper to do any figuring.

1. If $x = 8$, what's the value of y in the equation $y = (x^2 \div 4) - 2$?

   (A) 14

   (B) 16

   (C) 18

   (D) 20

2. The cube of 5 is

   (A) 125

   (B) 25

   (C) 15

   (D) 50

3. $2.5 \times 3^3 =$

   (A) 22.5

   (B) 75.0

   (C) 67.5

   (D) 675.0

4. The fourth root of 16 is

   (A) 4

   (B) 1

   (C) 3

   (D) 2

5. What's the equation of a line that passes through points (0, −1) and (2, 3)?

   (A) $y = 2x - 1$

   (B) $y = 2x + 1$

   (C) $x = 2y - 1$

   (D) $x = 2y + 1$

6. $(12 \text{ yards} + 14 \text{ feet}) \div 5 =$

   (A) 12 feet

   (B) $5\frac{1}{5}$ feet

   (C) 10 feet

   (D) $2\frac{1}{2}$ feet

7. $x^3 \cdot x^4 =$

   (A) x^{12}

   (B) $2x^7$

   (C) $2x^{12}$

   (D) x^7

8. $(x + 4)(x + 2) =$

   (A) $x^2 + 6x + 6$

   (B) $x^2 + 8x + 8$

   (C) $x^2 + 8x + 6$

   (D) $x^2 + 6x + 8$

9. $1.5 \times 10^3 =$

   (A) 45

   (B) 150

   (C) 1,500

   (D) 15

10. Which of the following is a prime number?

   (A) 27

   (B) 11

   (C) 8

   (D) 4

GO ON TO NEXT PAGE

11. What's the mode of the following series of numbers? 4 4 8 8 8 10 10 12 12

(A) 9

(B) 8

(C) 11

(D) 10

12. If $a = 4$, then $a^3 \div a =$

(A) 4

(B) 12

(C) 64

(D) 16

13. Solve: 5!

(A) 25

(B) 125

(C) 120

(D) 15

14. $(900 \times 2) \div 6 =$

(A) 30

(B) 300

(C) 150

(D) 3,000

15. If $x = 2$, then $xx(x) =$

(A) 8

(B) 2xx

(C) 4

(D) 6

16. If $(5+1)(6 \div 3)(8-5) = (3+3)x$, then $x =$

(A) 12

(B) 3

(C) 4

(D) 6

17. $\sqrt{49} \times \sqrt{64} =$

(A) 56

(B) 15

(C) 42

(D) 3,136

18. Which of the following fractions is the largest?

(A) $\frac{2}{5}$

(B) $\frac{3}{8}$

(C) $\frac{7}{10}$

(D) $\frac{13}{16}$

19. If $2 + x \geq 4$, then $x \geq$

(A) 6

(B) 2

(C) 4

(D) $\frac{1}{2}$

20. If a circle has a radius of 12 feet, what's its circumference most nearly?

(A) 24 feet

(B) 72 feet

(C) 75 feet

(D) 36 feet

21. An aquarium measures 16 inches long x 8 inches deep x 18 inches high. What's its volume?

(A) 2,304 cubic inches

(B) 128 cubic inches

(C) 42 cubic inches

(D) 288 cubic inches

22. Triangle ABC is a(n)

© John Wiley & Sons, Inc.

(A) right triangle.

(B) obtuse triangle.

(C) equilateral triangle.

(D) isosceles triangle.

23. The sum of the measures of the angles of a trapezoid is

    (A) 360 degrees.

    (B) 540 degrees.

    (C) 180 degrees.

    (D) 720 degrees.

24. Angles 1 and 2 are

© *John Wiley & Sons, Inc.*

    (A) supplementary.

    (B) complementary.

    (C) both obtuse.

    (D) both right angles.

25. Convert 24% to a fraction.

    (A) $\dfrac{6}{25}$

    (B) $\dfrac{1}{25}$

    (C) $\dfrac{6}{24}$

    (D) $\dfrac{1}{24}$

DO NOT TURN THE PAGE UNTIL TOLD TO DO SO   **STOP**   **DO NOT RETURN TO A PREVIOUS TEST**

Subtest 6: Electronics Information

TIME: 9 minutes for 20 questions

DIRECTIONS: This test contains questions to challenge your knowledge of electrical, radio, and electronics information. Select the correct response from the choices given and then mark the corresponding space on your answer sheet.

1. Ohm's law states
   - (A) Voltage = Current × Resistance
   - (B) Amperes = Current × Resistance
   - (C) Voltage = Resistance ÷ Amperes
   - (D) Ohms = Current ÷ Voltage

2. A resistor's first three color bands are brown, black, and red. What is its value?
   - (A) 1,000 ohms
   - (B) 500 ohms
   - (C) 500 volts
   - (D) 50 volts

3. In the U.S., all metal equipment, electrical or not, connected to a swimming pool must be
   - (A) freestanding.
   - (B) bonded together.
   - (C) certified.
   - (D) none of the above.

4. Voltage can also be expressed as
   - (A) watts.
   - (B) amps.
   - (C) current.
   - (D) electrical potential difference.

5. Newer cellphones contain a removable memory card, which is often called a
   - (A) SIM card.
   - (B) DIM chip.
   - (C) PIN card.
   - (D) PIN chip.

6. Made from a variety of materials, such as carbon, this inhibits the flow of current.
   - (A) resistor
   - (B) diode
   - (C) transformer
   - (D) generator

7. This is a type of semiconductor that only allows current to flow in one direction. It is usually used to rectify AC signals (conversion to DC).
   - (A) capacitor
   - (B) inductor
   - (C) diode
   - (D) transformer

8. Radar can operate at frequencies as high as
   - (A) 100,000 Hz.
   - (B) 100,000 kHz.
   - (C) 100,000 MHz.
   - (D) 500,000 MHz.

9. What do AC and DC stand for in the electrical field?
   - (A) amplified capacity and differential capacity
   - (B) alternating current and direct current
   - (C) accelerated climate and deduced climate
   - (D) none of the above

10. Changing AC to DC is called what?
    - (A) capacitance
    - (B) impedance
    - (C) rectification
    - (D) induction

11. A 5,000 BTU air conditioner can efficiently cool up to 150 square feet, or a 10-foot-x-15-foot room. What does BTU stand for?

(A) basic thermal unit

(B) basic temperature unit

(C) British thermal unit

(D) none of the above

12. Which is the most correct definition of current?

(A) the measure of electrical pressure

(B) the amount of electricity used in a heater

(C) the electricity used in heating a kilo of water

(D) the presence of electron flow

13. A device that transforms energy from one form to another is called

(A) a capacitor.

(B) a transducer.

(C) a transformer.

(D) magic.

14. Which one of the following is an active element?

(A) 15 kΩ resistor

(B) 10 mH inductor

(C) 25 pF capacitor

(D) 10 V power supply

15. A light bulb is 60 watts. Operated at 120 volts, how much current does it draw?

(A) 0.5 amperes

(B) 5.0 amperes

(C) 50.0 amperes

(D) 7,200 amperes

16. A number-12 wire, compared to a number-6 wire,

(A) is longer.

(B) is shorter.

(C) is smaller in diameter.

(D) is larger in diameter.

17. A fuse with a higher-than-required rating used in an electrical circuit

(A) improves safety.

(B) increases maintenance.

(C) may not work properly.

(D) is less expensive.

18. Neutral wire is always

(A) whitish or natural.

(B) black.

(C) green with stripes.

(D) blue.

19. To measure electrical power, you would use a(n)

(A) ammeter.

(B) ohmmeter.

(C) voltmeter.

(D) wattmeter.

20. What will happen if you operate an incandescent light bulb at less than its rated voltage?

(A) The bulb will burn brighter and last longer.

(B) The bulb will burn dimmer and last longer.

(C) The bulb will burn brighter but won't last as long.

(D) The bulb will burn dimmer but won't last as long.

Subtest 7: Auto & Shop Information

TIME: 11 minutes for 25 questions

DIRECTIONS: This test is about automobiles, shop practices, and the use of tools. Pick the best answer for each question and then mark the corresponding space on your answer sheet.

1. Overheating the engine can cause all of the following problems EXCEPT
   - (A) burned engine bearings.
   - (B) enlarged pistons.
   - (C) melted engine parts.
   - (D) improved fuel efficiency.

2. The device that converts an automobile's mechanical energy to electrical energy is called the
   - (A) converter.
   - (B) alternator.
   - (C) battery.
   - (D) brakes.

3. A primary advantage of the electronic ignition system over conventional ignition systems is that
   - (A) the electronic ignition system is less expensive to repair.
   - (B) the electronic ignition system requires a lower voltage to provide a higher voltage for spark.
   - (C) the electronic ignition system allows for use of a lower octane fuel.
   - (D) all of the above.

4. The primary purpose of piston rings is to
   - (A) seal the combustion chamber and allow the pistons to move freely.
   - (B) connect the piston to the crankshaft.
   - (C) allow fuel to enter the piston cylinder.
   - (D) provide lubrication to the piston cylinder.

5. The crankshaft typically connects to a
   - (A) flywheel.
   - (B) fuel pump.
   - (C) muffler.
   - (D) battery.

6. What component allows the left and right wheels to turn at different speeds when cornering?
   - (A) differential
   - (B) camshaft
   - (C) valve rotator
   - (D) battery

7. If a car's ignition system, lights, and radio don't work, the part that's probably malfunctioned is the
   - (A) cylinder block.
   - (B) water pump.
   - (C) carburetor.
   - (D) battery.

8. A good tool to cut intricate shapes in wood would be a
   - (A) ripsaw.
   - (B) hacksaw.
   - (C) coping saw.
   - (D) pocket knife.

9. A two-stroke engine will normally be found on
   - (A) small cars.
   - (B) large diesel trucks.
   - (C) trucks, vans, and some cars.
   - (D) snowmobiles, chainsaws, and some motorcycles.

10. A belt sander would best be used to
    (A) cut wood.
    (B) finish wood.
    (C) shape wood.
    (D) keep your pants up.

11. A car equipped with limited-slip differential
    (A) can be readily put into all-wheel (four-wheel) drive.
    (B) won't lock up when the brakes are applied steadily.
    (C) transfers the most driving force to the wheel with the greatest amount of traction.
    (D) is rated for off-road driving.

12. Big block engines generally have
    (A) more than 5.9 L of displacement.
    (B) better gas mileage than small block engines.
    (C) less than 6 L of displacement.
    (D) air conditioning.

13. A good tool for spreading and/or shaping mortar would be a
    (A) cement shaper.
    (B) hammer.
    (C) trowel.
    (D) broom.

14. Plumb bobs are used to
    (A) clean pipes.
    (B) check vertical reference.
    (C) fix the toilet.
    (D) carve stones.

15. Rebar is used to
    (A) measure the depth of concrete.
    (B) reinforce concrete.
    (C) stir concrete.
    (D) smooth concrete.

16. Annular ring, clout, and spring head are types of
    (A) hammers.
    (B) saws.
    (C) nails.
    (D) screwdrivers.

17. A ripsaw cuts
    (A) against the grain of the wood.
    (B) with the grain of the wood.
    (C) most materials, including metal.
    (D) only plastic.

18. A cam belt is also known as a
    (A) piston.
    (B) timing belt.
    (C) transmission belt.
    (D) lug nut.

19. To check for horizontal trueness, the best tool to use is a
    (A) steel tape rule.
    (B) plumb bob.
    (C) level.
    (D) sliding T-bevel.

20. A bucking bar is used to
    (A) pull nails.
    (B) pry wood apart.
    (C) form rivet bucktails.
    (D) drive screws.

21. Washers that have teeth all around the circumference to prevent them from slipping are called
    (A) shake-proof washers.
    (B) jaw washers.
    (C) flat washers.
    (D) split lock washers.

GO ON TO NEXT PAGE

22. The tool below measures

© John Wiley & Sons, Inc.

(A) an inside curve.

(B) an outside curve.

(C) the depth of a hole.

(D) the thickness of wire.

23. The object below is a type of

© John Wiley & Sons, Inc.

(A) nut.

(B) washer.

(C) screw.

(D) bolt.

24. The tool below is used to

© John Wiley & Sons, Inc.

(A) finish concrete.

(B) spread joint compound.

(C) smooth wallpaper.

(D) dress wood.

25. The chisel used to cut metal is

No. 1

No. 2

No. 3

No. 4

© John Wiley & Sons, Inc.

(A) No. 1

(B) No. 2

(C) No. 3

(D) No. 4

Subtest 8: Mechanical Comprehension

TIME: 19 minutes for 25 questions

DIRECTIONS: This test is about mechanical principles. Many of the questions use drawings to illustrate specific principles. Choose the correct answer and mark the corresponding space on the answer sheet.

1. An induction clutch works by

(A) magnetism.

(B) pneumatics.

(C) hydraulics.

(D) friction.

2. If a first-class lever with a resistance arm measuring 2 feet and an effort arm measuring 8 feet are being used, what's the mechanical advantage?

(A) 2

(B) 4

(C) 6

(D) 1

3. The bottoms of four boxes are shown below. The boxes all have the same volume. If postal regulations state that the sides of a box must meet a minimum height, which box is most likely to be too short to go through the mail?

© John Wiley & Sons, Inc.

(A) No. 1

(B) No. 2

(C) No. 3

(D) No. 4

4. Looking at the figure below, when Anvil B lands on the seesaw, Anvil A will

© John Wiley & Sons, Inc.

(A) remain stationary.

(B) hit the ground hard.

(C) rise in the air quickly.

(D) enter the stratosphere.

5. Air pressure at sea level is about 15 psi. What's the amount of force exerted on the top of your head, given a surface area of 24 square inches?

(A) 360 pounds

(B) 625 pounds

(C) $\frac{5}{8}$ pound

(D) 180 pounds

6. The force produced when a boxer's hand hits a heavy bag and "bounces" off it is called

(A) response time.

(B) bounce.

(C) recoil.

(D) gravity.

GO ON TO NEXT PAGE

7. In the figure below, if Gear 1 has 25 teeth and Gear 2 has 15 teeth, how many revolutions does Gear 2 make for every 10 revolutions Gear 1 makes?

1

© John Wiley & Sons, Inc.

(A) about $16\frac{2}{3}$

(B) 12

(C) about $\frac{1}{3}$ more

(D) about 20

8. A cubic foot of water weighs about 62.5 pounds. If an aquarium is 18 feet long, 10 feet deep, and 12 feet wide, what's the approximate pressure in pounds per square inch (psi) on the bottom of the tank?

(A) 2 psi

(B) 4 psi

(C) 5 psi

(D) 7 psi

9. Springs used in machines are usually made of

(A) plastic.

(B) bronze.

(C) nylon fiber.

(D) steel.

10. A clutch is a type of

(A) universal joint.

(B) coupling.

(C) gear differential.

(D) cam follower.

11. When Cam A completes one revolution, the lever will touch the contact point

© John Wiley & Sons, Inc.

(A) once.

(B) never.

(C) four times.

(D) twice.

12. A single moveable block-and-fall is called a

(A) fixed pulley.

(B) gun tackle.

(C) runner.

(D) sheave.

13. In the figure below, if the fulcrum supporting the lever is moved closer to the anvil, the anvil will be

© John Wiley & Sons, Inc.

(A) easier to lift and will move higher.

(B) harder to lift but will move higher.

(C) easier to lift but will not move as high.

(D) harder to lift and will not move as high.

14. The mechanical advantage of the block-and-tackle arrangement shown below is

Upper Block

Lower Block

LOAD

© John Wiley & Sons, Inc.

(A) 2

(B) 3

(C) 6

(D) 1

15. In the figure below, if the cogs move up the track at the same rate of speed, Cog A will

© John Wiley & Sons, Inc.

(A) reach the top at the same time as Cog B.

(B) reach the top after Cog B.

(C) reach the top before Cog B.

(D) have greater difficulty staying on track.

16. If a house key, a wooden spoon, a plastic hanger, and a wool jacket are all the same temperature on a cool day, which one feels the coldest?

(A) key

(B) spoon

(C) hanger

(D) jacket

17. In the figure below, assume the valves are all closed. To fill the tank but prevent it from filling entirely, which valves should be open?

© John Wiley & Sons, Inc.

(A) 1 and 2 only

(B) 1, 2, and 3 only

(C) 1, 2, and 4 only

(D) 1, 2, 3, and 5 only

18. If Gear A is turned to the left,

© John Wiley & Sons, Inc.

(A) Gear B turns to the right and Gear C turns to the left.

(B) Gear B turns to the left and Gear C turns to the left.

(C) Gear B turns to the right and Gear C turns to the right.

(D) Gear B turns to the left and Gear C turns to the right.

GO ON TO NEXT PAGE

19. If Gear 1 moves in a clockwise direction, which other gears also turn clockwise?

© John Wiley & Sons, Inc.

(A) 3 and 5

(B) 3, 4, and 5

(C) 2 and 5

(D) 3 and 4

20. The pressure gauge in the figure below shows a reading of

© John Wiley & Sons, Inc.

(A) 15.0

(B) 19.5

(C) 21.0

(D) 23.0

21. A way to determine the amount of power being used is to

(A) multiply the amount of work done by the time it takes.

(B) multiply the distance covered by the time it takes to move a load.

(C) divide the amount of work done by 550 pounds per second.

(D) divide the amount of work done by the amount of time it takes.

22. A wood tool, a silver tool, and a steel tool are placed in boiling water for cleaning. Which tool will get hot most quickly?

(A) steel

(B) wood

(C) silver

(D) All three are equally hot.

23. A whip is being used in the figure shown. How much effort is the boy who's lifting the 50-pound anvil using? Disregard friction, wind resistance, and the weight of the pulley and the rope.

© John Wiley & Sons, Inc.

(A) 50-pound effort

(B) 100-pound effort

(C) 25-pound effort

(D) 10-pound effort

24. In the figure below, at what point was the ball traveling most slowly?

© John Wiley & Sons, Inc.

(A) A

(B) B

(C) C

(D) D

25. In the figure below, which angle is braced most solidly?

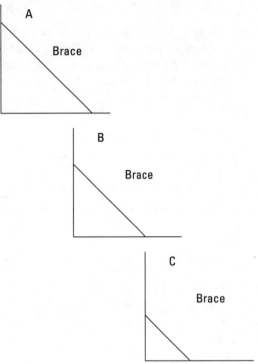

© John Wiley & Sons, Inc.

(A) A

(B) B

(C) C

(D) All are braced equally solidly.

DO NOT TURN THE PAGE UNTIL TOLD TO DO SO **STOP** DO NOT RETURN TO A PREVIOUS TEST

Subtest 9: Assembling Objects

TIME: 15 minutes for 25 questions

DIRECTIONS: The Assembling Objects subtest consists of questions that measure your ability to mentally picture items in two dimensions. Each question is comprised of five separate drawings. The problem is presented in the first drawing, and the remaining four drawings are possible solutions. Determine which of the choices best solves the problem shown in the first picture and then mark the corresponding choice on your answer sheet.

1.

A   B   C   D

2.

A   B   C   D

3.

A   B   C   D

4.

A   B   C   D

5.

A   B   C   D

6.

A   B   C   D

7.

A   B   C   D

8.

A   B   C   D

9.

A   B   C   D

10.

A   B   C   D

11.

A   B   C   D

12.

A   B   C   D

13.

14.

15.

16.

17.

18.

19.

20.

21.

22.

23.

24.

25.

Chapter **19**

Practice Exam 1: Answers and Explanations

With the first practice test out of the way, you're probably anxious to see how well you did. Use the answer keys in this chapter to score yourself on each of the nine subtests. Remember, your scores on this practice exam don't equate to scores on the actual ASVAB. That's because on the enlistment ASVAB, you get more points for answering harder questions correctly than you do for easier questions. The test is scored by comparing your raw score to other people's scores, which produces a scaled score, so missing 20 out of 225 questions doesn't mean that your score is 205. The practice exam, however, is a valuable tool for determining which subject areas you need to brush up on. (Turn to Chapter 1 to find out how the ASVAB is scored.)

Subtest 1: General Science Answers

The General Science subtest tests your knowledge of science facts. If you missed a few questions, reread the questions and try to figure out where you went wrong. If you missed more than a few questions, review Chapters 10, 11, and 12.

TIP

General Science is a broad field, but some of the following books may help you: *Chemistry For Dummies* by John T. Moore, *Biology For Dummies* by Donna Rae Siegfried, *Astronomy For Dummies* by Stephen P. Maran, *Weather For Dummies* by John D. Cox, and *Physics I For Dummies* by Steven Holzner, all published by Wiley. You can find additional practice questions in Chapters 10, 11, and 12.

1. **D.** The planet Uranus was named for the Greek god Uranus, who personified the sky.

2. **C.** From the Latin, *carne* means flesh and *vorare* means to devour — hence the word *carnivore*, a meat-eater. Choice (C) is correct.

3. **C.** In the chemical process of *oxidation*, an atom loses electrons in its *valence shell* (the outermost shell of electrons). Oxidation is usually paired with *reduction*, in which another atom or molecule gains those electrons. Together, reduction and oxidation form a *redox* reaction.

4. A. The plural of *quantum* is *quanta.*

5. D. Light waves travel at 299,792 kilometers (or approximately 186,000 miles) per second. That's why light from the sun takes about 8.3 minutes to reach Earth.

6. D. Jupiter is the largest planet in our solar system.

7. D. Both the large and small intestines are part of the digestive system.

8. C. Joints that hold bones firmly together are called *fixed joints.*

9. C. The levels of classification of living creatures from broadest to narrowest are kingdom, phylum, class, order, family, genus, and species.

10. C. Venus is the brightest planet and is sometimes called the *morning* or *evening star.*

11. C. The left and right ventricles, with the left and right atria, make up the four heart chambers in a human.

12. D. White blood cells produce antibodies and fight infection, making Choice (D) correct.

13. D. Eggs, meat, and peas all contain protein. A negligible amount of protein occurs in apples.

14. B. Oxygen makes up about 46.6 percent of the Earth's crust. Silicon is the next-most abundant, coming in at 27.7 percent.

15. A. *Osmosis* is a passive process in which water or another solvent moves through a partially permeable membrane. If the solution on one side of the membrane has a high concentration of solute and the other has a lower concentration of solute, the water moves through the membrane toward the highly concentrated side until the concentrations are equal.

16. C. A centimeter is one-hundredth of a meter; therefore, you find 100 centimeters in a meter.

17. A. The distance light travels in one year is one *light-year.*

18. D. *Electrons* are the negatively charged parts of an atom.

19. B. The asteroid belt is located between the planets Mars and Jupiter.

20. B. The number of protons in an atom's nucleus determines the atomic number of an atom.

21. A. A cell's nucleus contains its nuclear genome. It's sometimes called the control center.

22. D. Jupiter, Saturn, Neptune, and Uranus are the four planets with rings.

23. A. The melting point of a substance is a state of equilibrium between its solid and liquid states. The melting point is equal to the freezing point.

24. B. Mars's atmosphere is comprised mainly of carbon dioxide.

25. B. Proxima Centauri C (or Alpha Centauri C) is the closest star to the Earth (after our sun).

Subtest 2: Arithmetic Reasoning Answers

Arithmetic Reasoning is one of the four ASVAB subtests that make up your Armed Forces Qualification Test (AFQT) score, which determines whether you qualify to join the service branch of your choice (check Appendix A to see whether the jobs you're interested in require a score in this subtest). If you missed more than five or six questions, dig out that old high school math textbook and wrap your brain around some math problems. The chapters in Part 3 may also help you out.

TIP

Some books that may help you score better on the Arithmetic Reasoning subtest include *Basic Math & Pre-Algebra For Dummies* by Mark Zegarelli, *Algebra I For Dummies* and *Algebra II For Dummies* by Mary Jane Sterling, and *Geometry For Dummies* by Mark Ryan, as well as the related workbooks. You can also check out Mark Zegarelli's *SAT Math For Dummies* and *ACT Math For Dummies* for some math test practice. (All these books are published by Wiley.)

1. **C.** Multiply 12 miles by \$3.50 per mile: $12 \times \$3.50 = \$42.00$.

2. **A.** Let x equal the smaller number and $x + 8$ equal the larger number. Because the sum of the two numbers is 70, you can express this mathematically as $x + x + 8 = 70$. Now all you have to do is solve for x. Combine the like terms: $2x + 8 = 70$. Then subtract 8 from both sides of the equation: $2x + 8 - 8 = 70 - 8$, or $2x = 62$. Divide both sides of the equation by 2, and you find that x is equal to 31.

3. **D.** 144 bottles are in a gross, and $144 \div 3$ (bottles per day) $= 48$ days.

4. **B.** To determine Jenny's average, add the test scores and divide the sum by the number of tests she took. You want to know what she needs on the next test to achieve an average of 95, so let x equal the unknown score. Set up the equation as $(93 + 89 + 96 + 98 + x) \div 5 = 95$. Combine the like terms: $(376 + x) \div 5 = 95$. Multiplying both sides by 5 results in $376 + x = 475$, so $x = 99$.

   Choice (A) is very close to the correct answer, but it isn't the best answer. If Jenny's next test score is 100, her average would be raised to 95.2.

5. **B.** Multiply the total amount spent on food, \$375, by 12% (or 0.12) to determine the amount of tips: $\$375 \times 0.12 = \$45$.

6. **D.** You determine square footage by multiplying length by width: $12 \times 12 = 144$.

7. **C.** First determine the number of square feet of carpet you want to protect: $16 \text{ ft.} \times 18 \text{ ft.} = 288 \text{ ft.}^2$ The carpet stain protector is priced by the square yard, so divide 288 by 9 to convert square feet to square yards (because $1 \text{ yd.}^2 = 3 \text{ ft.} \times 3 \text{ ft.} = 9 \text{ ft.}^2$): $288 \text{ ft.}^2 \div 9 \text{ ft.}^2/\text{yd.} = 32 \text{ yd.}^2$

   Multiply the number of square yards by the cost of protection per square yard, \$0.65, to get the correct answer: $32 \text{ yd.}^2 \times \$0.65/\text{yd.}^2 = \$20.80$.

8. **C.** Let x equal the number of cards printed and sold each month. Each card costs \$0.18 to print and sells for \$0.30. Therefore, the cost is equal to $6,000 + 0.18x$, and revenue is equal to $0.30x$. You're looking for the point where revenue is greater than the cost (revenue > cost). The inequality is $0.30x > 6,000 + 0.18x$.

Now solve for x. Subtract $0.18x$ from both sides of the inequality and then divide both sides by 0.12:

$$0.12x > 6,000$$
$$x > 50,000$$

The printing plant would have to print and sell at least 50,000 cards per month to make a profit.

9. **C.** Joe gets a 7% raise. To calculate the new wage, start off by multiplying $\$8.15 \times 0.07 = \$0.57$. Then add that number (the amount of Joe's raise) to his original hourly wage. Joe's new hourly wage is $\$8.15 + \$0.57 = \$8.72$.

10. **C.** To find distance, you multiply speed by time. First find how far Alice travels before Dave catches up with her. By the time Dave leaves, Alice has already been traveling for half an hour. Three hours later, she would've been traveling for $3\frac{1}{2}$ hours at 45 mph, or 157.5 miles: $3.5 \text{ hr.} \times 45 \text{ mph} = 157.5 \text{ mi.}$ Dave has three hours to cover this distance. Now find his speed. To travel 157.5 miles in 3 hours, Dave would have to travel at 52.5 mph: $157.5 \text{ mi.} \div 3 \text{ hr.} = 52.5 \text{ mph.}$

11. **D.** To find the amount of pie purchased (which, by the way, does not give you the final answer), you have to add the fractions. But first the fractions need to have a common denominator. The denominators (4, 3, and 6) all divide evenly into 12, so use 12 as the common denominator.

To convert the fractions to the least common denominator of 12, do the following:

$$\frac{1}{4} \times \frac{3}{3} = \frac{3}{12}$$
$$\frac{1}{3} \times \frac{4}{4} = \frac{4}{12}$$
$$\frac{1}{6} \times \frac{2}{2} = \frac{2}{12}$$

Now you can add the fractions together:

$$\frac{3}{12} + \frac{4}{12} + \frac{2}{12} = \frac{3+4+2}{12} = \frac{9}{12}$$

Nine-twelfths of 20 pies is the same thing as $\frac{3}{4}$, or 75%, of the 20 pies. That equals 15 pies.

But that's not what the question asks. One more step: Subtract the pies sold (15) from the original 20, leaving 5 pies, which makes Choice (D) correct.

12. **A.** Subtract the sale price from the regular price to find how much she saved on each case: $\$24.00 - \$22.50 = \$1.50$. Multiply the answer by the total number of cases to get your final answer: $\$1.50 \times 5 = \$7.50$.

13. **C.** Divide 30 by 8 to determine how long the security guard takes to walk one city block: $30 \div 8 = 3.75$ minutes. Then multiply 3.75 by 6, the number of blocks it takes to complete the circuit. The answer is 22.50 minutes.

14. **B.** Let x equal the original number of how much Grand Island would grow. An additional $\frac{1}{5}$ would make the population growth $\frac{6}{5}$, or 120%, of x. You can express the equation as $1.2x = 600,000$. To solve for x, divide both sides of the equation by 1.2, which gives you $x = 500,000$.

15. **D.** Divide the number of questions she has to get right (40) by the total number of questions (60) to reach $66\frac{2}{3}\%$.

16. **C.** The interest formula says that interest equals principal times rate times time, or $I = Prt$. To determine the amount of interest earned, multiply the principal ($3,000) by the interest rate (6%) and the number of years interest accrues (1 year): $3,000 \times 0.06 \times 1 = \$180$. Add the interest earned to the principal to show how much total money the teacher would have: $180 + \$3,000 = \$3,180$.

17. **B.** Recognize that if the track is a quarter mile long, then 1 mile equals four laps. Therefore, multiply 4 times 3.5 miles; the answer is 14 laps.

18. **A.** One kilometer is approximately $\frac{5}{8}$ of 1 mile, so you can multiply $75 \times \frac{5}{8} : 75 \times 5 = 375$, and $375 \div 8 =$ about 46.8. Therefore, Karl was traveling at 47 miles per hour.

19. **A.** You need to add the carpenter's base pay and overtime pay to find his total pay for the week. First find his base pay per week: $12.30 / \text{hr.} \times 40 \text{ hr.} = \$492$. Then find his overtime rate per hour, which is $1\frac{1}{2}$ times his base pay: $12.30 / \text{hr.} \times 1.5 = \$18.45$. Multiply this rate by the number of hours of overtime to find his overtime pay: $18.45 / \text{hr.} \times 6 \text{ hr.} = \$110.70$. Finally, add his base pay and overtime pay to find his total pay for the week: $492.00 + \$110.70 = \$602.70$.

20. **A.** The office has 1,260 square feet of space (multiply 42 square feet by 30 employees). With 35 employees, each employee will have 36 square feet of work space $(1,260 \div 35)$, which is 6 square feet less than the amount was originally.

21. **B.** The total cost is the down payment plus 5 years' worth of monthly payments. Five years contain 60 months, so multiply 450 (monthly payment) $\times 60 = \$27,000$ (total payments). Then add $27,0000$ (total payments) $+ \$2,000$ (down payment) $= \$29,000$ (total cost).

22. **D.** Add the three monthly amounts to determine the total amount Darla spent on groceries: $120.37 + \$108.45 + \$114.86 = \$343.68$. Divide the total by 3 to determine the average monthly cost: 114.56.

23. **C.** Distance equals speed times time, so divide the total distance by Keith's average speed to find how long the trip took: $1,650 \text{ mi.} \div 50 \text{ mph} = 33 \text{ hr.}$

24. **B.** Choice (A) doesn't provide enough paint $(2 \times 25 \text{ gal.} = 50 \text{ gal.})$, so it's wrong. Now determine the cost of each of the other options:

Choice (B): $11 \times \$108 = \$1,188$
Choice (C): $6 \times \$215 = \$1,290$
Choice (D): $55 \times \$23 = \$1,265$

The lowest price is $1,188, Choice (B).

25. **B.** First find how many ounces of rations each truck can hold. One ton is 2,000 pounds, so one truck can carry three times that, or 6,000 pounds. There are 16 ounces in a pound, so one truck can carry 96,000 ounces: $6,000 \text{ lb.} \times 16 \text{ oz.} = 96,000 \text{ oz.}$

Then figure out how many daily rations are in a truckload. The total daily ration for each resident is 12 ounces + 18 ounces + 18 ounces, or 48 ounces. You can express the number of daily rations supplied as 96,000 oz. $\div$ 48 oz./daily ration = 2,000 daily rations. These rations need to last 10 days. Dividing 2,000 by 10 days results in 200 residents who can be fed by one truck during this 10-day period.

26. D. The train headed for Wichita traveled 55 miles/hour × 3 hours = 165 total miles. The train headed for Des Moines traveled 70 miles/hour × 3 hours = 210 total miles. Adding the distances together gives you the number of miles apart the two trains are after three hours: 210 + 165 = 375. Another option: You can add the two rates of speed (55 + 70) and multiply the sum by 3 hours (125 × 3 hours = 375).

27. A. Convert the mixed number to inches: 3 feet, 8 inches equals 44 inches (12 in./ft. × 3 ft. = 36 in., and 36 in. + 8 in. = 44 in.). Each section needs to be 44 inches long, and you need four sections. So 44 in. × 4 = 176 in. The total amount of molding needed is 176 inches. To find the amount of molding needed in feet, convert 176 inches into feet by dividing 176 inches by 12 inches.

You get $14\frac{2}{3}$ feet, so the shortest board length necessary is 15 feet.

28. A. One turkey breast costs $8.50 minus 10% of $8.50 (which is $0.85), or $8.50 − $0.85 = $7.65. The other turkey breast is full price, so add the two costs: $7.65 + $8.50 = $16.15.

29. C. Don't let the number of miles traveled confuse you. You don't use them to solve the problem. Finding $\frac{2}{5}$ of a 40-hour workweek is the same thing as multiplying 40 times 2, which is 80, and then dividing 80 by 5, which equals 16 hours the recruiter travels weekly.

30. B. Your first step is to determine the number of miles traveled. Multiply the rate of travel by the time: 48 × 7 = 336 mi. The amount of gas used is the total miles driven divided by the number of miles per gallon: 336 ÷ 21 = 16 gal. used. At the price of $2.82 per gallon, you spent $45.12 for gas: $2.82 × 16 = $45.12.

Subtest 3: **Word Knowledge Answers**

The Word Knowledge subtest is nothing more than a vocabulary test. However, it's very important because it's another one of the four subtests used to make up your AFQT score. If you find you need to improve your vocabulary, see Chapter 4.

A couple of other great study references are *Vocabulary For Dummies* by Laurie E. Rozakis (Wiley) and *SAT Vocabulary For Dummies* by Suzee Vlk (Wiley). Additionally, see Chapter 4 for more practice questions.

1. A. *Apex* is a noun that means the top or highest part of something, especially when it forms a point.

2. A. *Assimilate* is a verb that means to take in and understand or to cause something to resemble another thing.

3. B. *Brittle* is an adjective that means hard but liable to break easily.

4. C. *Datum* is a noun that refers to a piece of information.

5. C. *Proficient* is an adjective that means competent or skilled in doing (or using) something.

6. C. *Impose* is a verb that means to force acceptance of something unwelcome or unfamiliar.

7. A. *Galore* is an adjective that means in abundance.

8. **D.** *Headlong* is an adverb and an adjective, and it means with the head foremost or in a reckless rush.

9. **D.** *Frugal* is an adjective that means sparing or economical, particularly as it relates to money or food.

10. **B.** *Stimulate* is a verb that means to raise levels of physiological or nervous activity within the body or another biological system. It also means to encourage interest or activity in someone or something or to encourage development of increased activity in a state or process. Therefore, the opposite is to arrest, or stop.

11. **B.** *Illicit* is an adjective that means forbidden by law, rules, or customs.

12. **D.** *Vacate* is a verb that means to leave a place that was previously occupied.

13. **B.** *Reasoned* is an adjective that means underpinned by logic or sense.

14. **B.** *Tacit* is an adjective that means understood or implied.

15. **D.** *Burnish* is a verb that means to polish something by rubbing.

16. **A.** *Commodity* is a noun that means a raw material or agricultural product that can be bought or sold; it can also refer to a useful or valuable thing.

17. **A.** *Contrived* is an adjective that means deliberately created instead of arising naturally or spontaneously.

18. **C.** *Supplicate* is a verb that means to ask or beg for something humbly or earnestly.

19. **A.** *Hypocrisy* is a noun that means the practice of claiming standards or beliefs without actually conforming to them. The word most opposite in meaning is *honesty*.

20. **D.** *Succulent* is an adjective that refers to food being juicy, tender, and delicious.

21. **D.** *Garrison* is a noun that refers to troops stationed in a fortress or town to defend it.

22. **A.** *Furtherance* is a noun that refers to the advancement of an interest or scheme.

23. **C.** *Domicile* is a noun that means a permanent home or a place in which someone lives and has a substantial connection with; it often refers to countries (particularly as it relates to U.S. laws), but not always.

24. **D.** *Abrogate* is a verb that means to repeal or do away with.

25. **B.** *Compensation* is a noun that refers to something awarded to someone as reimbursement for loss, injury, or suffering. It can also refer to the money an employer gives to an employee as a salary or wages.

26. **D.** *Brusque* is an adjective that means abrupt or offhand in speech or manner.

27. **B.** *Demise* is a noun that means someone's or something's death.

28. **B.** *Commemorate* is a verb that means to recall and show respect for someone or something; it also means to celebrate or serve as a memorial to something.

29. **C.** *Bore* is a verb that means to make a hole in something or to make one's way through something.

30. **B.** *Prevail* is a verb that means to be victorious, to be widespread, or to be current.

31. **C.** *Defray* is a verb that means to provide money to pay a cost or expense.

32. **A.** *Chasm* is a noun that refers to a deep fissure in the earth, rock, or another surface; it can also refer to a vast difference between two things.

33. **C.** *Fundamental* is an adjective that means forming a needed base or core; it also refers to a central or main rule or principle on which something is based.

34. **D.** *Susceptible* is an adjective that means likely to be influenced or harmed by something.

35. **A.** *Emblem* is a noun that means a device or symbolic object that's used as a badge or something that serves as a symbolic representation of a characteristic or concept.

Subtest 4: Paragraph Comprehension Answers

Like Word Knowledge, your Paragraph Comprehension score goes toward your AFQT score, so pay special attention if you've missed more than a couple of these answers — you need some study time (see Chapter 5). Remember that rereading the paragraph several times to make sure you have the right answer is perfectly fine. You can find additional practice questions in Chapter 5.

1. **C.** Effective appointment management eliminates the waste of your time, as the last sentence of the passage explains.

2. **D.** The passage gives the numbers of senators and representatives, so Choice (A) is incorrect. The passage states that each state's population determines the number of representatives a state has, so Choice (B) is incorrect. As the passage states, each state has at least one representative, so Choice (C) is incorrect.

3. **A.** Many languages are excluded from the Indo-European language group, so Choice (B) is incorrect. Indians, Iranians, Asians, and Afghans aren't Europeans, so Choice (C) is incorrect. The passage gives no evidence to support Choice (D), which isn't true.

4. **D.** Privatized functions operate independently of the government, making Choices (A) and (B) incorrect. The passage states that privatized functions may sell goods and services to other customers as well as the government, so Choice (C) is also incorrect. Choice (D) is the correct answer, because privatized functions do perform essential services to government agencies.

5. **C.** Choice (A) — "Lead by Example" — is a good philosophy but isn't pertinent to the main point of the passage. Choices (B) and (D) are subpoints, which support the main point of the passage: how to lead a successful conference, Choice (C).

6. **A.** You can assume that causing rain or snow would end a drought, Choice (A). Nothing in the passage has to do with expense, so Choice (B) is incorrect. The passage says nothing about how frequently the process is used, so Choice (C) is incorrect. The passage specifies

that dry ice (solid carbon dioxide) is used; regular ice (solid water) is a different substance, so Choice (D) is wrong.

7. **C.** Choices (A) and (B) may be true in certain situations, but they're not the point of this particular paragraph. The passage doesn't say anything about working to improve writing skills being a waste of time, so Choice (D) is incorrect. The main point of the paragraph is that writing may not be the most efficient way of communicating, depending on the situation.

8. **B.** Products with transistors weren't widely sold before 1954 because of the expense and difficulty of production, not because markets didn't exist, so Choice (A) is incorrect. Choice (C) has the right date, but the passage doesn't say who invented the transistor, so it's wrong as well. Choice (D) is wrong because the passage states that the problem of transistors being expensive to produce was solved in 1954. The last sentence notes that the first transistor radio went on the market after cost and production problems were overcome, so Choice (B) is the right answer.

9. **B.** The words *London* and *Englishman* make it clear that the author is speaking of his travels in England, which is part of Great Britain.

10. **A.** The author makes no reference to parents in the passage, so Choice (B) is incorrect. The author doesn't imply anything about all these interests requiring equal time, so Choice (C) is incorrect. The passage is about children under 18; you can't draw a conclusion about what the author thinks people over 18 should do, so Choice (D) is incorrect.

11. **C.** The passage doesn't say anything about mock job interviews being frightening, so Choice (A) is wrong. The passage says that mock job interviews should be available to all students, so Choice (B) is wrong. The passage says that schools, not students, should organize mock interviews, so Choice (D) is incorrect.

12. **A.** Choices (B), (C), and (D) are the opposite of what the paragraph states and implies.

13. **B.** Nothing in the paragraph supports Choice (A), which is incorrect. When an amendment is passed, it becomes part of the Constitution, so Choice (C) is incorrect. The passage doesn't support Choice (D), because the passage doesn't mention anything related to lottery tickets. The passage defines *due process* as "the guarantee of fairness in the administration of justice," so Choice (B) is correct.

14. **C.** Because the 14th Amendment guarantees due process in states' laws, the 5th Amendment must guarantee due process only in federal law, which makes Choice (C) right. Nothing in the passage implies that the 5th Amendment is about taxes, so Choice (A) is wrong. Because the passage states that the 14th Amendment had to be enacted to require states to abide by due process, Choice (B) is incorrect. Choice (D) is neither stated nor implied in the passage.

15. **A.** Because the Supreme Court struck down many state laws after the 14th Amendment was enacted, it's probably true that these laws would still exist if there'd been no 14th Amendment. The passage doesn't support Choices (B), (C), or (D).

Subtest 5: Mathematics Knowledge Answers

This subtest is also used to calculate your AFQT score, so it's important. If you miss more than four or five, consider brushing up on your basic math skills. Chapters 6, 7, and 8 can help with this.

TIP

The following books may also be of some help: *Algebra I For Dummies* and *Algebra II For Dummies* by Mary Jane Sterling, *Geometry For Dummies* and *Calculus For Dummies* by Mark Ryan, and *SAT Math For Dummies* by Mark Zegarelli (all books published by Wiley).

1. A. Substitute 8 for x in the equation and then solve for y:

$$
\begin{aligned}
y &= \left(x^2 \div 4\right) - 2 \\
&= \left(8^2 \div 4\right) - 2 \\
&= \left(64 \div 4\right) - 2 \\
&= 16 - 2 \\
&= 14
\end{aligned}
$$

2. A. The cube of 5 is 5^3, which is $5 \times 5 \times 5 = 125$.

3. C. Because of the order of operations, you need to find 3^3 first and then multiply by 2.5:

$$
\begin{aligned}
2.5 \times 3^3 &= 2.5\left(3 \times 3 \times 3\right) \\
&= 2.5 \times 27 \\
&= 67.5
\end{aligned}
$$

4. D. Because $2^4 = 16$, the fourth root of 16 is 2.

5. A. To get the equation of the line, you need to know the line's slope and y-intercept. The slope of the line is equal to the change in y values divided by the change in x values. The change in y values is $3 - (-1) = 4$. The change in x values is $2 - 0 = 2$. Thus, the slope is $\frac{4}{2} = 2$. The line passes through the point (0, 1), so to find the intercept, substitute 0 for x and -1 for y in the equation $y = 2x + b$:

$$
\begin{aligned}
-1 &= 2(0) + b \\
b &= -1
\end{aligned}
$$

Therefore, $b = -1$, so the full equation is $y = 2x - 1$.

6. C. Do what's in parentheses first. You need consistent units of measurement, so convert 12 yards to feet; then add 14 feet:

$$
\begin{aligned}
&\left(12 \text{ yards} \times 3 \text{ feet/yard}\right) + 14 \text{ feet} \\
&= 36 \text{ feet} + 14 \text{ feet} \\
&= 50 \text{ feet}
\end{aligned}
$$

The original problem asks for $\left(12 \text{ yards} + 14 \text{ feet}\right) \div 5$, so divide by 5 as instructed: $50 \text{ feet} \div 5 = 10 \text{ feet}$.

7. D. If two powers have the same base, you multiply them by keeping the base the same and adding the powers together: $x^3 \cdot x^4 = x^{3+4} = x^7$.

8. D. To find $(x + 4)(x + 2)$, you need to multiply every term in the first set of parentheses by every term in the second set and then add the results. The acronym FOIL (First, Outer, Inner, Last) can help you keep track of which terms you're multiplying:

- **First:** Multiply the first variable in the first set of parentheses by the first variable in the second set of parentheses: $x(x) = x^2$.

- **Outer:** Next, multiply the first variable in the first set of parentheses by the second number in the second set of parentheses: $x(2) = 2x$. So far, the results are $x^2 + 2x$.

- **Inner:** Now multiply the second number in the first set of parentheses by the first variable in the second set of parentheses: $4(x) = 4x$.

- **Last:** Next, multiply the second number in the first set of parentheses by the second number in the second set of parentheses: $4(2) = 8$.

The solution is $x^2 + 2x + 4x + 8$. Combining the like terms results in $x^2 + 6x + 8$.

9. **C.** You need to do powers (exponents) first, so find 10^3 and then multiply by 1.5:

$$1.5 \times 10^3 = 1.5 \times (10 \times 10 \times 10)$$
$$= 1.5 \times 1,000$$
$$= 1,500$$

10. **B.** A *prime number* is a number that can be divided evenly by itself or by 1 but not by any other number. Choices (A), (C), and (D) can all be divided evenly by other numbers.

11. **B.** The *mode* of a series of numbers is the number that appears in the series the most frequently. In this case, it's 8.

12. **D.** Substitute 4 for all *a*'s in the problem and then solve, doing the powers first:

$$4^3 \div 4 = (4 \times 4 \times 4) \div 4$$
$$= 64 \div 4$$
$$= 16$$

13. **C.** The factorial (!) of a number is the number multiplied by the next-smallest whole number, then by the next smallest whole number, and so on down to 1:

$$5! = 5 \times 4 \times 3 \times 2 \times 1 = 120$$

14. **B.** Use the order of operations and do what's in parentheses first:

$$(900 \times 2) \div 6 = 1,800 \div 6 = 300$$

15. **A.** Substitute 2 for all *x*'s in the problem and then simplify, starting with the powers:

$$2 \times 2(2) = 4(2) = 8$$

16. **D.** The problem asks you to solve $(5+1)(6 \div 3)(8-5) = (3+3)x$ for *x*. First find the values in parentheses:

$$(6)(2)(3) = 36$$

Therefore, the whole equation becomes $36 = (3+3)x$, which simplifies to $36 = 6x$. Solve for *x*:

$$36 \div 6 = 6x \div 6$$
$$6 = x$$

To check your answer, substitute 6 for *x*.

17. **A.** The square root of 49 is 7; the square root of 64 is 8. And $7 \times 8 = 56$.

18. **D.** Find a common denominator for the fractions. In this case, 80 works for all the fractions. Convert all the fractions using the following method:

$$\frac{2}{5} \times \frac{16}{16} = \frac{32}{80}$$

$$\frac{3}{8} \times \frac{10}{10} = \frac{30}{80}$$

$$\frac{7}{10} \times \frac{8}{8} = \frac{56}{80}$$

$$\frac{13}{16} \times \frac{5}{5} = \frac{65}{80}$$

Comparing the fractions, you can see that $\frac{65}{80}$ $\left(\text{or } \frac{13}{16}\right)$ is the largest fraction.

19. **B.** Solve as you would solve for any unknown:

$$2 + x \geq 4$$
$$2 + x - 2 \geq 4 - 2$$

Therefore, $x \geq 2$. To check your answer, substitute 2 for x: $2 + 2 \geq 4$. That's true, so the answer is correct.

20. **C.** Circumference equals $\pi \times$ diameter, and diameter is equal to two times the radius (or mathematically, $C = \pi d$ and $d = 2r$). For this problem, $C = \pi \times 24$. If you round π to 3.14, the answer is about 75.36, or about 75 feet.

21. **A.** Volume equals length $\times$ width $\times$ height $(V = lwh)$, so plug in the numbers and solve: $16 \times 8 \times 18 = 2{,}304$ in.^{3}

22. **C.** In an equilateral triangle, all sides are equal and all angles are equal.

23. **A.** All quadrilaterals (four-sided figures) have angles that total 360 degrees.

24. **B.** If the sum of two angles equals 90 degrees, they're called *complementary angles*.

25. **A.** $24\% = \frac{24}{100}$. You further reduce this fraction to $\frac{6}{25}$ by dividing the numerator and denominator by 4.

Subtest 6: Electronics Information Answers

The Electronics Information subtest is particularly important if you want to obtain a job that requires a solid score in this area. You can check Appendix A to see whether any job you're interested in requires a high score in Electronics Information. If so, you shouldn't miss more than five questions in this practice exam. If you do, you may want to review Chapter 16.

TIP

If you need even more study, check out *Electronics For Dummies,* by Cathleen Shamieh and Gordon McComb (Wiley) or consider enrolling in a quick course at a community college.

1. **A.** Ohm's law states that Voltage $(V \text{ or } E)$ = Current $(I) \times$ Resistance (R). All other answers are incorrect expressions of this law.

2. **A.** You read a resistor's color bands from left to right. The first band denotes the first digit, the second band denotes the second digit, and the third band denotes the subsequent number of zeros. In this example, brown is one, black is zero, and red means there are two additional zeros.

3. **B.** Heaters, pumps, stairs, diving boards, railings, and rebar, among other things, must be bonded together by a minimum #8 wire for safety purposes.

4. **D.** *Voltage* is commonly used as a short name for electrical potential difference, and it is measured in volts.

5. **A.** SIM stands for *Subscriber Identity Module.* The card contains information such as your phone number, your billing information, and your address book. The card makes it easier to switch from one cellphone to another.

6. **A.** A resistor is so named because it resists (or inhibits) the flow of current.

7. **C.** A diode has two terminals, the anode and the cathode, which is why it's called a *di*ode. It restricts current flow to only one direction.

8. **C.** Radar can operate as high as 100,000 MHz (megahertz).

9. **B.** *Current* is the flow of charged particles. The difference between alternating current (AC) and direct current (DC) is that the electrons in an AC circuit regularly reverse their direction. In a DC circuit, electrons always flow in the same direction.

10. **C.** Changing AC to DC is a process called *rectification.*

11. **C.** A British thermal unit (BTU) is a measure of heat energy.

12. **D.** *Current* is the presence of electron flow.

13. **B.** *Transducers,* which transform or convert energy, can be switches, strain gauges, temperature sensors, or inductive switches. A transformer is an inductor that increases or decreases voltage.

14. **D.** *Active elements* are electronic devices that can create energy (such as voltage supplies and current supplies). *Passive elements* are electronic devices that cannot create energy.

15. **A.** Power = Current × Voltage or, written another way, Current = Power ÷ Voltage. Plug in the numbers and do the math: 60 watts ÷ 120 volts = 0.5 amperes.

16. **C.** The larger the number, the smaller the diameter of the wire.

17. **C.** Because fuses are designed to prevent current overload at a specific level, a fuse with a high rating may allow a higher current to flow through a circuit not designed to work at that higher current, possibly causing damage to the circuit.

18. **A.** Neutral wire is always whitish or natural colored.

19. **D.** Electrical power is measured in watts, so you use a wattmeter. An ammeter measures amps (current). An ohmmeter measures ohms (resistance). A voltmeter measures volts (voltage).

20. **B.** The bulb will burn dimmer because its full potential isn't used; it'll last longer for the same reason.

Subtest 7: Auto & Shop Information Answers

The Auto & Shop Information subtest is fairly straightforward. You either know the information or you don't. Not knowing the info may not matter to you as long as the career you want doesn't require a subtest score in this area (check Appendix A to see whether the jobs you're interested in require a score in this subtest). But if you do need to do well on this subtest and you've missed more than five answers, review the material in Chapters 13 and 14.

TIP

Reviewing *Auto Repair For Dummies* by Deanna Sclar (Wiley) may also help you score better on this subtest. *Home Improvement All-in-One For Dummies* by Roy Barnhart, James Carey, Morris Carey, Gene Hamilton, Katie Hamilton, Donald R. Prestly, and Jeff Strong (Wiley) can help you get a better handle on basic tools and their uses. You may even want to take a class at a nearby community college or at least hang out at the garage and help some mechanics for a couple of weeks.

1. **D.** Overheating can melt engine parts, enlarge pistons, and burn engine bearings.

2. **B.** Alternators convert mechanical energy (rotary motion) into electrical energy (output current).

3. **B.** Electronic ignition systems use lower input voltages to get higher output voltages (for spark).

4. **A.** Piston rings are seals that keep the exploding gases in the combustion chamber.

5. **A.** The crankshaft is connected to the flywheel, which causes it to rotate, operating the pistons.

6. **A.** A differential lets wheels turn at different rates. When one tire is spinning, the other can have traction.

7. **D.** The ignition system starts a car. If there doesn't seem to be any electricity, check the battery.

8. **C.** You use a coping saw to make intricate cuts in wood.

9. **D.** Snowmobiles, chainsaws, lawn mowers, and some motorcycles need only two-stroke engines.

10. **B.** You often use a belt sander is often used to finish wood because doing so is faster than hand sanding for large areas.

11. **C.** A limited-slip-differential transfers the most driving force to the wheel with greatest traction.

12. **A.** Big block engines generally have greater than 5.9-liter displacement.

13. **C.** A trowel would be a good tool for spreading and/or shaping mortar.

14. **B.** You use a plumb bob to check vertical reference using a pointed weight on a line.

15. **B.** Rebar is an iron bar that is embedded in cement to reinforce it.

16. **C.** Annular ring, clout, and spring head are all types of nails.

17. **B.** A ripsaw cuts wood with the grain, called *ripping,* because it's easier than cutting against the grain.

18. **B.** A cam belt, also known as a *timing belt,* connects the crankshaft to the camshaft.

19. **C.** You use a level to check for horizontal trueness.

20. **C.** A bucking bar is used to form rivet bucktails.

21. **A.** Washers that have teeth all around the circumference are called shake-proof washers.

22. **D.** The tool shown is an outside caliper, and it measures the thickness of wire and other objects.

23. **A.** The object pictured is a nut.

24. **D.** The tool is a plane, and you use it to dress (prepare, smooth, and shave) wood.

25. **A.** Commonly called a cold chisel, this tool cuts through metal screws, bolts, nails, and other metals.

Subtest 8: Mechanical Comprehension Answers

The Mechanical Comprehension subtest is important only if you want to pursue a military career that requires a good score on this subtest (check Appendix A to see whether the jobs you're interested in require a score in this subtest). Otherwise, spend your time studying more important areas of the ASVAB. If you're considering a military job that requires a high mechanical aptitude and you missed more than four or five questions on this subtest, give Chapter 15 another once over.

1. **A.** An induction clutch is a magnetic clutch. When a conductor (wire) is wrapped around a core and electricity is passed through the wire, it sets up a magnetic field. The same wire also acts as an inductor, which produces inductance, during AC current flow. It's similar to resistance in a resistor in that it "resists" current flow, but the value of inductance is based on the value of the inductor (written as L) and the frequency of the AC current. Therefore, an induction clutch uses magnetism to operate.

2. **B.** You can calculate mechanical advantage as Length of Effort Arm ÷ Length of Resistance Arm. Simply plug in the numbers: $MA = 8 \div 2 = 4$.

3. **C.** The box with the largest area on the bottom will have the shortest sides. If Length × Width × Height = Volume and all the boxes have equal volume, then the sides must be shortest on the box with the largest area on the bottom. Calculate the area of each box bottom:

   No. 1 = 20 square inches

   No. 2 = 35 square inches

   No. 3 = 48 square inches

   No. 4 = 27 square inches

   No. 3, which has the largest area, will have the shortest sides.

4. C. Anvil B's landing on the seesaw will propel Anvil A into the air.

5. A. Pressure equals force divided by area in square inches $(P = F \div A)$. You can also state this formula as $F = A \times P$. Substitute the known quantities: $F = 15 \times 24 = 360$ pounds.

6. C. *Recoil* occurs when an object producing a force is kicked back.

7. A. To determine the answer, multiply the number of teeth Gear 1 has (*D*) and the number of revolutions it makes (*R*). Divide that number by the number of teeth Gear 2 has (*d*) to determine the number of revolutions Gear 2 makes (*r*). Because the gears are proportional, this formula shows you the ratio of teeth to revolutions.

$$r = \frac{DR}{d}$$
$$= \frac{25 \times 10}{15}$$
$$= \frac{250}{15} = \frac{50}{3} = 16\frac{2}{3}$$

8. B. You can determine the pressure of all that water by multiplying the volume of the aquarium by the weight of the water. Volume = *lwh*. The bottom of the tank is 18 feet long by 12 feet wide by 10 feet high for a total volume of 2,160 cubic feet: $18 \times 12 \times 10 = 2,160$ ft.^{3} A cubic foot of water weighs approximately 62.5 pounds, so multiply the volume of water by 62.5: $2,160 \times 62.5 = 135,000$.

That gives an approximate pressure on the bottom of the tank of about 135,000 pounds over the entire surface area. The surface area of the bottom of the tank is length $\times$ width. Convert feet to inches and then find the area: $A = (18 \text{ ft.} \times 12 \text{ in./ft.}) \times (12 \text{ ft.} \times 12 \text{ in./ft.}) = 216 \text{ in.} \times 144 \text{ in.} = 31,104 \text{ in.}^2$

Dividing the pressure of 135,000 by the number of square inches of surface area gives an approximate psi of 4.

9. D. Machine springs are usually made of steel, although sometimes they're made of brass or other metal alloys.

10. B. Clutches connect and disconnect parts, so they're a type of coupling.

11. D. When the high point of the cam connects with the lever arm, the lever arm will touch the contact point. Two high points on the cam mean the lever arm will touch the contact point twice with each revolution of the cam.

12. C. A single moveable block-and-fall is called a runner. A runner provides a way to get mechanical advantage by threading a rope through a pulley attached to the load, anchoring one end to a stationary point, and you pulling on the other end of the rope, hoisting the load.

13. C. If the fulcrum is moved closer to the anvil, the length of the effort arm of the lever will be increased, making the anvil easier to raise, but the height to which the anvil can be raised will be reduced.

14. B. In this block-and-tackle arrangement, there are three segments coming off the load, which gives this arrangement a mechanical advantage of 3.

15. C. The larger cog (Cog A) covers a greater linear distance in a given period of time, so Cog A reaches the top first.

16. A. The key will feel coldest because metal is a better conductor than the other materials.

17. **D.** All but Valve 4 should be open. Opening Valves 1 and 2 allows water to enter the tank. Opening Valves 3 and 5 prevents water from filling the tank entirely. Opening Valve 4 allows water to leave the tank.

18. **A.** Gears with their teeth together in mesh turn in opposite directions. Gear A turns Gear B in the opposite direction (right), and Gear B turns Gear C in the opposite direction (left).

19. **A.** Gears with their teeth together in mesh turn in opposite directions. Gear 1 turns clockwise. Gear 2, in mesh with Gear 1, turns counterclockwise. Gear 3, in mesh with Gear 2, turns clockwise. Gear 4, in mesh with Gear 3, turns counterclockwise. Gear 5, in mesh with Gear 2, turns clockwise.

20. **C.** The gauge shows a reading of 21.

21. **D.** The formula for determining power is Power = Work ÷ Time.

22. **C.** Silver is the best conductor, so it will become hotter faster than the other objects because heat transfers faster into materials with greater conductivity than with those with lower conductivity.

23. **A.** Stationary pulleys (often called whips) give no mechanical advantage, so effort equals the weight of the crate, or 50 pounds.

24. **C.** At the height of the arc, the ball has no upward momentum, so it goes the slowest at that point (it has zero upward movement at its highest point).

25. **A.** The brace on Angle A covers more area of the angle, so it's more solidly braced.

Subtest 9: Assembling Objects Answers

If you plan on enlisting in the Navy, check Appendix A to see whether the jobs you're interested in require a score in this subtest. For more information about the Assembling Objects subtest and additional practice questions, see Chapter 17.

TIP

Try to envision the shapes matching each figure before you select an answer. If the right answer doesn't just pop out at you, use strategy to help you rule out incorrect choices.

1. **C.** Connect Point A on the star and Point A on the line. Rotate the star-shaped figure about 45 degrees and connect Point B on the line to Point B on the shape, rotating the shape 90 degrees.

2. **A.** Count the number of shapes in the original image (there are seven). Only one answer choice includes the seven shapes in the original figure. In this case, Choices (B), (C), and (D) just don't have enough shapes — and that makes it easy to get this question correct.

3. **D.** Point B in the original image is on the end of the crescent, which means you can automatically rule out Choice (C), in which the point is in the center of the figure. Choices (A) and (B) are also incorrect, because in the original figure, the line goes directly through the point of the triangle. The only answer that reflects that intersection is Choice (D).

4. **D.** There are three shapes in the original puzzlelike diagram, so you can automatically rule out Choices (A) and (B) — they each have four. If you rotate the shapes depicted in the question, you'll see that there are two sections that are larger than the remaining one. The only reasonable answer is Choice (D), because it shows an oval inside a triangle with more space in two corners than there is in the remaining corner.

5. **A.** Rotate the pentagon to the left so Point A is on the top. Flip the other shape almost 180 degrees so Point B is on the bottom. Connect the two shapes with the line's corresponding points, and you'll have Choice (A) on your hands.

   If you're unsure, you can always rule out answers that you know aren't correct. In this case, you can tell Choice (B) is wrong because Point B is in the wrong place; it doesn't match the original diagram. Choice (C) is incorrect because neither of the points are in the correct places, and Choice (D) is wrong for the same reasons.

6. **A.** Reconfigure the shapes in the original figure so that the two largest are side-by-side and symmetrical, with the uppermost points touching. The remaining two shapes fit right inside, like a puzzle. (On this question, you can immediately rule out *all* the other choices because the shapes don't match the original figure; Choices (C) and (D) even depict too many shapes to be contenders.)

7. **C.** On Assembling Objects questions, pay attention to the original figures. In this question, the line in Shape B starts in the center of the triangle and travels through one of the triangle's points. The only answer choice that depicts Figure B in the correct way is Choice (C), so you can ignore all the other choices.

8. **D.** Start by counting the number of shapes in the original diagram — there are six. Remember that counting shapes doesn't always work to rule out incorrect answers, but you can tell (in this problem, at least) that Choice (B) is incorrect because it depicts only four shapes. If you can't picture the correct answer in your mind, go through the rest of the choices to eliminate those that are clearly wrong. Choice (A) can't be correct, because it depicts two triangle-like shapes that aren't in the original diagram. Choice (C) can't be correct, because the shapes it depicts aren't even similar to those depicted in the question, which leaves Choice (D) as the only possible correct answer.

9. **B.** Choice (B) is correct because Point A on the circle and Point B on the triangle match the original diagram, as does the length of the line. Choice (A) can't be right, because Figure A is flipped and the line connecting the two figures is too short, and Choice (C) shows Point B on the wrong place on the triangle. Choice (D) is wrong, too, because Point A is on the wrong circle.

10. **B.** The shapes in the original diagram are all very similar (and this is one case where counting the number of shapes won't work). The shapes in Choices (A), (C), and (D) don't match those in the original diagram, leaving Choice (B). If you rearrange the three trapezoids in your mind by connecting the points on the longest side of each, you'll see Choice (B) take shape.

11. **A.** Point A is on the long, flat side of the first shape (the one with four points), whereas Point B is just about in the center of the second shape (the one with five points). When you look at the answer choices, you'll see that Choices (B) and (D) both depict the points in the wrong places, so those choices are automatically wrong. Choice (C) looks like it has the points in the correct places, but not so fast — they're attached to the wrong shapes.

12. **D.** Compare the shapes in the question with the shapes in the answer choices. You can see that Choice (A) is incorrect because the shapes don't match; so is Choice (C). The shapes in the question include three figures that are very similar, but two are large and one is small. Choice (B) can't be correct, then, because two of the shapes are small and one is large, creating an oval tucked into the bottom of a triangle. Choice (D) is the right answer, because it takes two larger shapes and one smaller shape to create an upright oval inside a triangle.

13. **D.** Both of the figures in the original diagram are the same; they're just mirror images of each other. Choice (D) is correct because it's the only figure that shows them as mirror images of each other with the points in the correct places.

14. **C.** You can put Choice (A) in the recycle bin right away — it depicts four triangles put together. The same is true for Choice (D), except it depicts a square and three rectangles. Choice (B) shows five triangles, which can't be correct, either (the original diagram shows four shapes, and only three of them are triangles). Choice (C) is the only one that can possibly be correct.

15. **B.** The first thing you should do on a problem like this one is check out where the points are located on the shapes in the original diagram. On this question, you can rule out Choices (A), (C), and (D) because the points are in the wrong places.

16. **A.** One of the figures in the original diagram is a triangle with a line running parallel to one side. Choices (B) and (C) don't show any such shape, so those are out the window. Choice (D) has too many triangles (there are six, but the original figure depicts only four), leaving Choice (A) as the correct answer.

17. **B.** Choices (C) and (D) are incorrect because they each feature shapes that aren't depicted in the original diagram. Choice (A) is also incorrect; although it's a mirror image of the correct answer, Choice (B), it requires you to flip the shapes rather than rotate them.

18. **B.** Look closely at where the points are in the original diagram — particularly Point B, which is on the corner of the square. You know that Choice (D) isn't the answer, because it shows Point B inside the square. Choices (A) and (C) are wrong, too, because they require you to flip the *F* shape, whereas Choice (B) doesn't even require you to rotate it.

19. **C.** Choice (C) is the only choice in which each of the shapes corresponds with a shape in the original diagram.

20. **A.** The only answer choice that doesn't require you to invert a shape and doesn't feature a point in the wrong place on one of the shapes is Choice (A). Choice (B) requires you to flip the shape with Point A on it, and so does Choice (D). Choice (C) has the point on the wrong place inside the hexagon.

21. **B.** Choice (A) depicts four shapes (the smallest of which isn't in the original diagram), so you can rule that one out immediately. Choices (C) and (D) don't use any five-sided shapes, but there's one in the original diagram. Choice (B) is the only figure that uses replicas of the three shapes in the original illustration.

22. **D.** Point B is clearly marked in the original illustration, but in Choices (A), (B), and (C), it's in all the wrong places; that leaves you with Choice (D) as the correct answer.

23. A. Look closely at Choice (C) — it has a part missing, so you know it can't be correct. Choice (A) is the only one that makes use of all the shapes depicted in the original diagram; Choices (B) and (D) use shapes that aren't in the question.

24. C. Point A is located on the lower-right corner of the original figure in the question, so you can ignore Choices (A), (B), and (D) because they don't match.

25. C. Check each shape to see which answer choices it appears in before you try to put together this puzzle. The only answer choice that features the right shapes in the right proportions (those that match the original illustration) is Choice (C). All the other answers have odd shapes that don't match.

Chapter **20**
Practice Exam 2

've designed the second practice test so you can see how much you've improved. This exam is exactly like the first one from Chapter 18, except (of course) the questions are different. I hope you used the results from the first practice exam to pinpoint your weak areas and then spent some time hitting the books and recharging your thinking cap.

TIP

To get the most out of this practice exam, take it like you'd take the real ASVAB under the same conditions:

» Allow yourself about 3 hours to take the entire exam, and take the whole thing at one time.

» Find a quiet place where nothing will interrupt you.

» Bring a timer that you can set for various lengths of time, some scratch paper, and a pencil.

» At the start of each subtest, set your timer for the specified period of time. Don't go on to the next section until the timer has gone off, and don't go back to a previous section. If you finish early, check your work for that section only.

» Use the answer sheet that's provided.

» Keep testing until you've gone through all the subtests. You don't get any breaks in between subtests during the real thing.

After you complete the entire sample test, check your answers against the answer explanations and key in Chapter 21.

Answer Sheet for Practice Exam 2

Subtest 1: General Science

1. Ⓐ Ⓑ Ⓒ Ⓓ   6. Ⓐ Ⓑ Ⓒ Ⓓ   11. Ⓐ Ⓑ Ⓒ Ⓓ   16. Ⓐ Ⓑ Ⓒ Ⓓ   21. Ⓐ Ⓑ Ⓒ Ⓓ
2. Ⓐ Ⓑ Ⓒ Ⓓ   7. Ⓐ Ⓑ Ⓒ Ⓓ   12. Ⓐ Ⓑ Ⓒ Ⓓ   17. Ⓐ Ⓑ Ⓒ Ⓓ   22. Ⓐ Ⓑ Ⓒ Ⓓ
3. Ⓐ Ⓑ Ⓒ Ⓓ   8. Ⓐ Ⓑ Ⓒ Ⓓ   13. Ⓐ Ⓑ Ⓒ Ⓓ   18. Ⓐ Ⓑ Ⓒ Ⓓ   23. Ⓐ Ⓑ Ⓒ Ⓓ
4. Ⓐ Ⓑ Ⓒ Ⓓ   9. Ⓐ Ⓑ Ⓒ Ⓓ   14. Ⓐ Ⓑ Ⓒ Ⓓ   19. Ⓐ Ⓑ Ⓒ Ⓓ   24. Ⓐ Ⓑ Ⓒ Ⓓ
5. Ⓐ Ⓑ Ⓒ Ⓓ   10. Ⓐ Ⓑ Ⓒ Ⓓ   15. Ⓐ Ⓑ Ⓒ Ⓓ   20. Ⓐ Ⓑ Ⓒ Ⓓ   25. Ⓐ Ⓑ Ⓒ Ⓓ

Subtest 2: Arithmetic Reasoning

1. Ⓐ Ⓑ Ⓒ Ⓓ   7. Ⓐ Ⓑ Ⓒ Ⓓ   13. Ⓐ Ⓑ Ⓒ Ⓓ   19. Ⓐ Ⓑ Ⓒ Ⓓ   25. Ⓐ Ⓑ Ⓒ Ⓓ
2. Ⓐ Ⓑ Ⓒ Ⓓ   8. Ⓐ Ⓑ Ⓒ Ⓓ   14. Ⓐ Ⓑ Ⓒ Ⓓ   20. Ⓐ Ⓑ Ⓒ Ⓓ   26. Ⓐ Ⓑ Ⓒ Ⓓ
3. Ⓐ Ⓑ Ⓒ Ⓓ   9. Ⓐ Ⓑ Ⓒ Ⓓ   15. Ⓐ Ⓑ Ⓒ Ⓓ   21. Ⓐ Ⓑ Ⓒ Ⓓ   27. Ⓐ Ⓑ Ⓒ Ⓓ
4. Ⓐ Ⓑ Ⓒ Ⓓ   10. Ⓐ Ⓑ Ⓒ Ⓓ   16. Ⓐ Ⓑ Ⓒ Ⓓ   22. Ⓐ Ⓑ Ⓒ Ⓓ   28. Ⓐ Ⓑ Ⓒ Ⓓ
5. Ⓐ Ⓑ Ⓒ Ⓓ   11. Ⓐ Ⓑ Ⓒ Ⓓ   17. Ⓐ Ⓑ Ⓒ Ⓓ   23. Ⓐ Ⓑ Ⓒ Ⓓ   29. Ⓐ Ⓑ Ⓒ Ⓓ
6. Ⓐ Ⓑ Ⓒ Ⓓ   12. Ⓐ Ⓑ Ⓒ Ⓓ   18. Ⓐ Ⓑ Ⓒ Ⓓ   24. Ⓐ Ⓑ Ⓒ Ⓓ   30. Ⓐ Ⓑ Ⓒ Ⓓ

Subtest 3: Word Knowledge

1. Ⓐ Ⓑ Ⓒ Ⓓ   8. Ⓐ Ⓑ Ⓒ Ⓓ   15. Ⓐ Ⓑ Ⓒ Ⓓ   22. Ⓐ Ⓑ Ⓒ Ⓓ   29. Ⓐ Ⓑ Ⓒ Ⓓ
2. Ⓐ Ⓑ Ⓒ Ⓓ   9. Ⓐ Ⓑ Ⓒ Ⓓ   16. Ⓐ Ⓑ Ⓒ Ⓓ   23. Ⓐ Ⓑ Ⓒ Ⓓ   30. Ⓐ Ⓑ Ⓒ Ⓓ
3. Ⓐ Ⓑ Ⓒ Ⓓ   10. Ⓐ Ⓑ Ⓒ Ⓓ   17. Ⓐ Ⓑ Ⓒ Ⓓ   24. Ⓐ Ⓑ Ⓒ Ⓓ   31. Ⓐ Ⓑ Ⓒ Ⓓ
4. Ⓐ Ⓑ Ⓒ Ⓓ   11. Ⓐ Ⓑ Ⓒ Ⓓ   18. Ⓐ Ⓑ Ⓒ Ⓓ   25. Ⓐ Ⓑ Ⓒ Ⓓ   32. Ⓐ Ⓑ Ⓒ Ⓓ
5. Ⓐ Ⓑ Ⓒ Ⓓ   12. Ⓐ Ⓑ Ⓒ Ⓓ   19. Ⓐ Ⓑ Ⓒ Ⓓ   26. Ⓐ Ⓑ Ⓒ Ⓓ   33. Ⓐ Ⓑ Ⓒ Ⓓ
6. Ⓐ Ⓑ Ⓒ Ⓓ   13. Ⓐ Ⓑ Ⓒ Ⓓ   20. Ⓐ Ⓑ Ⓒ Ⓓ   27. Ⓐ Ⓑ Ⓒ Ⓓ   34. Ⓐ Ⓑ Ⓒ Ⓓ
7. Ⓐ Ⓑ Ⓒ Ⓓ   14. Ⓐ Ⓑ Ⓒ Ⓓ   21. Ⓐ Ⓑ Ⓒ Ⓓ   28. Ⓐ Ⓑ Ⓒ Ⓓ   35. Ⓐ Ⓑ Ⓒ Ⓓ

Subtest 4: Paragraph Comprehension

1. Ⓐ Ⓑ Ⓒ Ⓓ   4. Ⓐ Ⓑ Ⓒ Ⓓ   7. Ⓐ Ⓑ Ⓒ Ⓓ   10. Ⓐ Ⓑ Ⓒ Ⓓ   13. Ⓐ Ⓑ Ⓒ Ⓓ
2. Ⓐ Ⓑ Ⓒ Ⓓ   5. Ⓐ Ⓑ Ⓒ Ⓓ   8. Ⓐ Ⓑ Ⓒ Ⓓ   11. Ⓐ Ⓑ Ⓒ Ⓓ   14. Ⓐ Ⓑ Ⓒ Ⓓ
3. Ⓐ Ⓑ Ⓒ Ⓓ   6. Ⓐ Ⓑ Ⓒ Ⓓ   9. Ⓐ Ⓑ Ⓒ Ⓓ   12. Ⓐ Ⓑ Ⓒ Ⓓ   15. Ⓐ Ⓑ Ⓒ Ⓓ

Subtest 5: Mathematics Knowledge

1. Ⓐ Ⓑ Ⓒ Ⓓ   6. Ⓐ Ⓑ Ⓒ Ⓓ   11. Ⓐ Ⓑ Ⓒ Ⓓ   16. Ⓐ Ⓑ Ⓒ Ⓓ   21. Ⓐ Ⓑ Ⓒ Ⓓ
2. Ⓐ Ⓑ Ⓒ Ⓓ   7. Ⓐ Ⓑ Ⓒ Ⓓ   12. Ⓐ Ⓑ Ⓒ Ⓓ   17. Ⓐ Ⓑ Ⓒ Ⓓ   22. Ⓐ Ⓑ Ⓒ Ⓓ
3. Ⓐ Ⓑ Ⓒ Ⓓ   8. Ⓐ Ⓑ Ⓒ Ⓓ   13. Ⓐ Ⓑ Ⓒ Ⓓ   18. Ⓐ Ⓑ Ⓒ Ⓓ   23. Ⓐ Ⓑ Ⓒ Ⓓ
4. Ⓐ Ⓑ Ⓒ Ⓓ   9. Ⓐ Ⓑ Ⓒ Ⓓ   14. Ⓐ Ⓑ Ⓒ Ⓓ   19. Ⓐ Ⓑ Ⓒ Ⓓ   24. Ⓐ Ⓑ Ⓒ Ⓓ
5. Ⓐ Ⓑ Ⓒ Ⓓ   10. Ⓐ Ⓑ Ⓒ Ⓓ   15. Ⓐ Ⓑ Ⓒ Ⓓ   20. Ⓐ Ⓑ Ⓒ Ⓓ   25. Ⓐ Ⓑ Ⓒ Ⓓ

Subtest 6: Electronics Information

1. Ⓐ Ⓑ Ⓒ Ⓓ   5. Ⓐ Ⓑ Ⓒ Ⓓ   9. Ⓐ Ⓑ Ⓒ Ⓓ   13. Ⓐ Ⓑ Ⓒ Ⓓ   17. Ⓐ Ⓑ Ⓒ Ⓓ
2. Ⓐ Ⓑ Ⓒ Ⓓ   6. Ⓐ Ⓑ Ⓒ Ⓓ   10. Ⓐ Ⓑ Ⓒ Ⓓ   14. Ⓐ Ⓑ Ⓒ Ⓓ   18. Ⓐ Ⓑ Ⓒ Ⓓ
3. Ⓐ Ⓑ Ⓒ Ⓓ   7. Ⓐ Ⓑ Ⓒ Ⓓ   11. Ⓐ Ⓑ Ⓒ Ⓓ   15. Ⓐ Ⓑ Ⓒ Ⓓ   19. Ⓐ Ⓑ Ⓒ Ⓓ
4. Ⓐ Ⓑ Ⓒ Ⓓ   8. Ⓐ Ⓑ Ⓒ Ⓓ   12. Ⓐ Ⓑ Ⓒ Ⓓ   16. Ⓐ Ⓑ Ⓒ Ⓓ   20. Ⓐ Ⓑ Ⓒ Ⓓ

Subtest 7: Auto & Shop Information

1. Ⓐ Ⓑ Ⓒ Ⓓ	6. Ⓐ Ⓑ Ⓒ Ⓓ	11. Ⓐ Ⓑ Ⓒ Ⓓ	16. Ⓐ Ⓑ Ⓒ Ⓓ	21. Ⓐ Ⓑ Ⓒ Ⓓ
2. Ⓐ Ⓑ Ⓒ Ⓓ	7. Ⓐ Ⓑ Ⓒ Ⓓ	12. Ⓐ Ⓑ Ⓒ Ⓓ	17. Ⓐ Ⓑ Ⓒ Ⓓ	22. Ⓐ Ⓑ Ⓒ Ⓓ
3. Ⓐ Ⓑ Ⓒ Ⓓ	8. Ⓐ Ⓑ Ⓒ Ⓓ	13. Ⓐ Ⓑ Ⓒ Ⓓ	18. Ⓐ Ⓑ Ⓒ Ⓓ	23. Ⓐ Ⓑ Ⓒ Ⓓ
4. Ⓐ Ⓑ Ⓒ Ⓓ	9. Ⓐ Ⓑ Ⓒ Ⓓ	14. Ⓐ Ⓑ Ⓒ Ⓓ	19. Ⓐ Ⓑ Ⓒ Ⓓ	24. Ⓐ Ⓑ Ⓒ Ⓓ
5. Ⓐ Ⓑ Ⓒ Ⓓ	10. Ⓐ Ⓑ Ⓒ Ⓓ	15. Ⓐ Ⓑ Ⓒ Ⓓ	20. Ⓐ Ⓑ Ⓒ Ⓓ	25. Ⓐ Ⓑ Ⓒ Ⓓ

Subtest 8: Mechanical Comprehension

1. Ⓐ Ⓑ Ⓒ Ⓓ	6. Ⓐ Ⓑ Ⓒ Ⓓ	11. Ⓐ Ⓑ Ⓒ Ⓓ	16. Ⓐ Ⓑ Ⓒ Ⓓ	21. Ⓐ Ⓑ Ⓒ Ⓓ
2. Ⓐ Ⓑ Ⓒ Ⓓ	7. Ⓐ Ⓑ Ⓒ Ⓓ	12. Ⓐ Ⓑ Ⓒ Ⓓ	17. Ⓐ Ⓑ Ⓒ Ⓓ	22. Ⓐ Ⓑ Ⓒ Ⓓ
3. Ⓐ Ⓑ Ⓒ Ⓓ	8. Ⓐ Ⓑ Ⓒ Ⓓ	13. Ⓐ Ⓑ Ⓒ Ⓓ	18. Ⓐ Ⓑ Ⓒ Ⓓ	23. Ⓐ Ⓑ Ⓒ Ⓓ
4. Ⓐ Ⓑ Ⓒ Ⓓ	9. Ⓐ Ⓑ Ⓒ Ⓓ	14. Ⓐ Ⓑ Ⓒ Ⓓ	19. Ⓐ Ⓑ Ⓒ Ⓓ	24. Ⓐ Ⓑ Ⓒ Ⓓ
5. Ⓐ Ⓑ Ⓒ Ⓓ	10. Ⓐ Ⓑ Ⓒ Ⓓ	15. Ⓐ Ⓑ Ⓒ Ⓓ	20. Ⓐ Ⓑ Ⓒ Ⓓ	25. Ⓐ Ⓑ Ⓒ Ⓓ

Subtest 9: Assembling Objects

1. Ⓐ Ⓑ Ⓒ Ⓓ	6. Ⓐ Ⓑ Ⓒ Ⓓ	11. Ⓐ Ⓑ Ⓒ Ⓓ	16. Ⓐ Ⓑ Ⓒ Ⓓ	21. Ⓐ Ⓑ Ⓒ Ⓓ
2. Ⓐ Ⓑ Ⓒ Ⓓ	7. Ⓐ Ⓑ Ⓒ Ⓓ	12. Ⓐ Ⓑ Ⓒ Ⓓ	17. Ⓐ Ⓑ Ⓒ Ⓓ	22. Ⓐ Ⓑ Ⓒ Ⓓ
3. Ⓐ Ⓑ Ⓒ Ⓓ	8. Ⓐ Ⓑ Ⓒ Ⓓ	13. Ⓐ Ⓑ Ⓒ Ⓓ	18. Ⓐ Ⓑ Ⓒ Ⓓ	23. Ⓐ Ⓑ Ⓒ Ⓓ
4. Ⓐ Ⓑ Ⓒ Ⓓ	9. Ⓐ Ⓑ Ⓒ Ⓓ	14. Ⓐ Ⓑ Ⓒ Ⓓ	19. Ⓐ Ⓑ Ⓒ Ⓓ	24. Ⓐ Ⓑ Ⓒ Ⓓ
5. Ⓐ Ⓑ Ⓒ Ⓓ	10. Ⓐ Ⓑ Ⓒ Ⓓ	15. Ⓐ Ⓑ Ⓒ Ⓓ	20. Ⓐ Ⓑ Ⓒ Ⓓ	25. Ⓐ Ⓑ Ⓒ Ⓓ

Subtest 1: General Science

TIME: 11 minutes for 25 questions

DIRECTIONS: This exam tests your knowledge of general science principles usually covered in high school classes. Pick the best answer for each question and then mark the space on your answer sheet that corresponds to the question number and the letter indicating your choice.

1. What is the change in body form that some insects undergo from birth to maturity?

    (A) transformation

    (B) metamorphosis

    (C) trinity

    (D) transmutation

2. An earthquake that measures 4 on the Richter scale would be how many times stronger than an earthquake that measured 2?

    (A) 2 times stronger

    (B) 4 times stronger

    (C) 10 times stronger

    (D) 100 times stronger

3. Muscles attach to bone with

    (A) nonconnective tissue.

    (B) ligaments.

    (C) tendons.

    (D) rubber bands.

4. The male part of a flower is called

    (A) the stamen.

    (B) the pistil.

    (C) the throttle.

    (D) stubborn.

5. Blood leaving the lungs is

    (A) hydrogenated.

    (B) coagulated.

    (C) watery.

    (D) oxygenated.

6. Of these, which river is the longest?

    (A) Mississippi

    (B) Nile

    (C) Colorado

    (D) Congo

7. The branch of science that studies matter and energy is called

    (A) chemistry.

    (B) physics.

    (C) oceanography.

    (D) trigonometry.

8. Which type of cloud's name comes from the Latin word meaning "rain"?

    (A) nimbus

    (B) cirrus

    (C) strato

    (D) alto

9. Deoxyribonucleic acid is better known as

    (A) antacid.

    (B) carbohydrates.

    (C) triglyceride.

    (D) DNA.

10. The instrument used to measure wind speed is

    (A) barometer.

    (B) anemometer.

    (C) altimeter.

    (D) fanometer.

11. Electric charges can be

    (A) positive or negative.

    (B) positive or neutral.

    (C) negative or neutral.

    (D) neutral only.

12. Which planet in the solar system has the most moons?

    (A) Neptune

    (B) Saturn

    (C) Jupiter

    (D) Uranus

GO ON TO NEXT PAGE

13. The law of universal gravitation was discovered by
    (A) Albert Einstein.
    (B) Isaac Newton.
    (C) Alexander Graham Bell.
    (D) Rod Powers.

14. Which U.S. space program is responsible for putting 12 men on the moon?
    (A) Gemini
    (B) Titan
    (C) Voyager
    (D) Apollo

15. Animals that eat both plants and animals are called
    (A) herbivores.
    (B) carnivores.
    (C) omnivores.
    (D) ambidextrous.

16. Unlike most other fish, sharks have no
    (A) gills.
    (B) bones.
    (C) liver.
    (D) heart.

17. What human organ is responsible for detoxification of blood?
    (A) liver
    (B) kidneys
    (C) intestines
    (D) stomach

18. Kinetic energy is the energy that
    (A) is produced by sound waves.
    (B) an object potentially has.
    (C) is possessed by a moving object.
    (D) results from the attraction of two magnets.

19. The terrestrial planets consist of
    (A) Jupiter, Saturn, Uranus, and Neptune.
    (B) Pluto and Neptune.
    (C) Mercury, Venus, Earth, and Mars.
    (D) any planet.

20. An example of a mineral is
    (A) calcium.
    (B) vitamin C.
    (C) granite.
    (D) almonds.

21. Which animal has the heaviest brain?
    (A) human
    (B) elephant
    (C) rhinoceros
    (D) sperm whale

22. The sun is what type of star?
    (A) O type
    (B) G type
    (C) F type
    (D) M type

23. Molecules are created when
    (A) matter is created.
    (B) matter is destroyed.
    (C) atoms combine together.
    (D) atoms are separated.

24. An example of an embryonic plant would be a
    (A) tree.
    (B) rose.
    (C) seed.
    (D) cabbage.

25. The vernal equinox is
    (A) the first day of winter.
    (B) near the equator.
    (C) the first day of spring.
    (D) a lunar eclipse.

DO NOT TURN THE PAGE UNTIL TOLD TO DO SO   STOP   DO NOT RETURN TO A PREVIOUS TEST

Subtest 2: Arithmetic Reasoning

TIME: 36 minutes for 30 questions

DIRECTIONS: The questions in the arithmetic test are each followed by four possible answers. Decide which answer is correct and then mark the space on your answer sheet that has the same number and letter as your choice. Use scratch paper for any figuring you need to do. Calculators are not allowed.

1. If you roll two six-sided dice, what's the probability of not rolling a five on either die?

   (A) $\frac{1}{36}$

   (B) $\frac{1}{6}$

   (C) $\frac{4}{36}$

   (D) $\frac{25}{36}$

2. Jack loaned Bob $1,500 at an annual interest rate of 7%. If Bob makes no payments, how much will he owe Jack after one year?

   (A) $105

   (B) $1,500

   (C) $1,605

   (D) $1,507

3. A 2-ton truck is taxed at a rate of $0.12 per pound. How much is the total tax bill?

   (A) $480

   (B) $240

   (C) $120

   (D) $600

4. If $ab = 10$ and $a^2 + b^2 = 30$, solve for y in the equation $y = (a + b)^2$.

   (A) 40

   (B) 45

   (C) 50

   (D) 55

5. A half-pint of cream is what part of a gallon?

   (A) $\frac{1}{8}$

   (B) $\frac{1}{4}$

   (C) $\frac{1}{16}$

   (D) $\frac{1}{6}$

6. The cost of a protein bar increased from $2.50 to $2.80. The percent increase to the $2.80 rate was how much?

   (A) 16%

   (B) 10%

   (C) 15%

   (D) 12%

7. An aircraft flies over Boondock Air Force Base at 10:20 a.m. At 10:32 a.m., the aircraft passes over Sea Side Naval Air Station, 120 miles away. How fast is the aircraft traveling?

   (A) 400 mph

   (B) 500 mph

   (C) 600 mph

   (D) 700 mph

8. Last year, Margot grew 50 bushels of corn in her backyard. This year, the yield has increased 8%. How many bushels of corn did Margot grow this year?

   (A) 56

   (B) 52

   (C) 60

   (D) 54

9. Junior has saved money in his piggy bank over the winter. He wants to buy a $30 computer game. If he has 14 one-dollar bills, 16 half dollars, 12 quarters, 8 dimes, 25 nickels, and 10 pennies, how much more does he need to borrow from Dad to buy the game?

   (A) $27.15

   (B) $2.85

   (C) $2.95

   (D) $1.85

GO ON TO NEXT PAGE

10. Debbie receives a weekly salary of $80, plus a 5% commission on any sales. During the week, she has $800 in total sales. What's the ratio of her commission to her salary?

(A) 2:1

(B) 1:2

(C) 3:1

(D) 1:3

11. How many 1-quart cans can be filled from 25 gallons of paint?

(A) 50

(B) 75

(C) 100

(D) 80

12. If a crew of four people can paint the barn in three days, how long will it take a crew of two people?

(A) 4 days

(B) $1\frac{1}{2}$ days

(C) 8 days

(D) 6 days

13. Brian works for five hours and is paid $24. Christina works for three hours and is paid $10.95. How much more per hour does Brian make than Christina?

(A) $1.15

(B) $1.25

(C) $1.35

(D) $1.37

14. Margaret is getting married and must be ready by 11:15 a.m. If it's now 8:30 a.m., how much time does she have to get ready?

(A) $1\frac{1}{2}$ hours

(B) $2\frac{1}{2}$ hours

(C) $2\frac{3}{4}$ hours

(D) $2\frac{1}{3}$ hours

15. An accounting-firm employee is asked to shred 900 documents. If he can shred documents at a rate of 7 per minute, the number of documents remaining after $1\frac{1}{2}$ hours of shredding is

(A) 630

(B) 90

(C) 270

(D) 810

16. A home stereo depreciates by 20% each year. What's the value of a stereo, purchased new for $1,200, after two years?

(A) $768

(B) $693

(C) $827

(D) $654

17. Janet's old pickup truck can only reach a speed of 45 miles per hour. If she drives at top speed, how long will it take her to reach a city 135 miles away?

(A) 3 hours

(B) 2 hours

(C) 4 hours

(D) $2\frac{1}{2}$ hours

18. A blouse normally costs $18.50. How much money is saved if the blouse is purchased at a 20% discount?

(A) $1.85

(B) $14.80

(C) $4.50

(D) $3.70

19. A clerk's weekly salary of $320 is increased to $360. The percent increase is

(A) $10\frac{1}{2}$%

(B) 11%

(C) $12\frac{1}{2}$%

(D) 12%

20. Go-Cart One and Go-Cart Two are on a 360-foot circular track. There is a camera at the center of the track for each go-cart. Camera One is following Go-Cart One, and Camera Two is following Go-Cart Two. If the angle between the two cameras is 40 degrees, how far apart are the two go-carts?

(A) 30 feet

(B) 40 feet

(C) 50 feet

(D) 60 feet

21. Dinner at a nice restaurant costs $35.98. If Joan gave the cashier $40.00, how much change should she get back?

(A) $5.02

(B) $4.02

(C) $3.92

(D) $1.02

22. A balloonist circumnavigated the globe in 13 days, 12 hours, 16 minutes, and 13 seconds. A plane circumnavigated the globe in 4 days, 10 hours, 15 minutes, and 7 seconds. How much longer did it take for the balloon to go around the world?

(A) 12 days, 7 hours, 11 minutes, and 35 seconds

(B) 9 days, 2 hours, 1 minute, and 6 seconds

(C) 8 days, 14 hours, 16 minutes, and 6 seconds

(D) 9 days, 7 hours, 3 minutes, and 20 seconds

23. Darlene bought 12 boxes of cookies for $48.00. What was the cost of each box of cookies?

(A) $4.00

(B) $0.48

(C) $0.40

(D) $4.80

24. A tuneup increases a car's fuel efficiency by 5%. If a car averaged 20 miles per gallon before the tuneup, how many miles per gallon will it average after the tuneup?

(A) 25

(B) 22

(C) $20\frac{1}{2}$

(D) 21

25. A lumberjack wishes to drive a spike through the center of a tree with a circumference of 43.96 feet. What's the minimum length of the spike needed to go completely through the tree, passing through the center?

(A) 14 feet

(B) 15 feet

(C) 16 feet

(D) 17 feet

26. A bin of hard candy holds $10\frac{1}{2}$ pounds. How many $\frac{3}{4}$-pound boxes of candy can be filled from the bin?

(A) 30 boxes

(B) $15\frac{1}{4}$ boxes

(C) $7\frac{7}{8}$ boxes

(D) 14 boxes

27. A patio measures 12 feet by 14 feet. How many 8-inch-square paving stones are needed to pave the patio?

(A) 21

(B) 252

(C) 378

(D) 168

28. A computer programmer is making $25,000 per year, and 28% of her salary is withheld for federal and state deductions. How much is the computer programmer's net pay?

(A) $20,000

(B) $7,000

(C) $18,750

(D) $18,000

GO ON TO NEXT PAGE

29. Pam cuts a pie in half in a straight line. She then cuts a line from the center to the edge, creating a 55-degree angle. What's the supplement of that angle?

(A) 55 degrees

(B) 125 degrees

(C) 70 degrees

(D) 35 degrees

30. A stack of lumber is 6 feet high. If each piece of lumber is 4 inches thick, how many pieces of lumber are in the stack?

(A) 72

(B) 12

(C) 18

(D) 10

DO NOT TURN THE PAGE UNTIL TOLD TO DO SO   STOP   DO NOT RETURN TO A PREVIOUS TEST

Subtest 3: Word Knowledge

TIME: 11 minutes for 35 questions

DIRECTIONS: This test's questions cover the meanings of words. Each question has an underlined word. You may be asked to decide which one of the four words in the choices most nearly means the same thing as the underlined word or which one of the four words means the opposite. If the underlined word is used in a sentence, decide which of the four choices most nearly means the same thing as the underlined word as used in the context of the sentence. Mark the corresponding space on your answer sheet.

1. <u>Abeyance</u> most nearly means
   - **(A)** trustworthiness.
   - **(B)** passion.
   - **(C)** suspension.
   - **(D)** business.

2. It was a <u>sturdy</u> table.
   - **(A)** well-built
   - **(B)** ugly
   - **(C)** thick
   - **(D)** small

3. <u>Bullock</u> most nearly means
   - **(A)** ox.
   - **(B)** inattentive.
   - **(C)** lazy.
   - **(D)** panther.

4. <u>Brevity</u> is the soul of wit.
   - **(A)** beauty
   - **(B)** intelligence
   - **(C)** clarity
   - **(D)** humor

5. <u>Paradigm</u> most nearly means
   - **(A)** twenty cents.
   - **(B)** model.
   - **(C)** heaven.
   - **(D)** basis.

6. He <u>facilitated</u> her promotion.
   - **(A)** hindered
   - **(B)** helped
   - **(C)** disliked
   - **(D)** ignored

7. <u>Quiescence</u> most nearly means
   - **(A)** kill.
   - **(B)** preserve.
   - **(C)** small.
   - **(D)** quiet.

8. The <u>spectator</u> enjoyed the game.
   - **(A)** competitor
   - **(B)** observer
   - **(C)** referee
   - **(D)** organizer

9. Joy <u>reclined</u> against the far wall.
   - **(A)** sat
   - **(B)** leaned
   - **(C)** jumped
   - **(D)** paraded

10. The teacher <u>cited</u> some examples.
    - **(A)** memorized
    - **(B)** finished
    - **(C)** quoted
    - **(D)** examined

11. <u>Surround</u> most nearly means
    - **(A)** line.
    - **(B)** benefit.
    - **(C)** encircle.
    - **(D)** speaker.

12. <u>Illustrious</u> most nearly means
    - **(A)** illustrated.
    - **(B)** famous.
    - **(C)** foolish.
    - **(D)** intelligent.

GO ON TO NEXT PAGE

13. Inhabitant most nearly means

    (A) invalid.

    (B) nun.

    (C) seeker.

    (D) dweller.

14. Tim had a penchant for engaging in subterfuge.

    (A) religion

    (B) intrigue

    (C) gambling

    (D) danger

15. Megan found the adults' costumes to be ghastly.

    (A) hideous

    (B) cute

    (C) large

    (D) comfortable

16. Rigid most nearly means

    (A) strong.

    (B) weak.

    (C) pliable.

    (D) inflexible.

17. Billy yearned to join the fraternal organization.

    (A) brotherly

    (B) large

    (C) fun

    (D) special

18. Deplore most nearly means

    (A) accept.

    (B) insult.

    (C) disapprove.

    (D) salute.

19. Meager most nearly means

    (A) space.

    (B) sparse.

    (C) brief.

    (D) thirsty.

20. Weal most nearly means

    (A) happiness.

    (B) blow.

    (C) scream.

    (D) tire.

21. To be guileless, I think your hair looks ugly.

    (A) helpful

    (B) kind

    (C) frank

    (D) serious

22. The customs agent confiscated the goods.

    (A) bought

    (B) noticed

    (C) seized

    (D) stole

23. Dubious most nearly means

    (A) long.

    (B) beautiful.

    (C) articulate.

    (D) doubtful.

24. Illusion most nearly means

    (A) mirage.

    (B) distant.

    (C) sight.

    (D) perspective.

25. Becky developed a sudden craving for ice cream.

    (A) disgust

    (B) passion

    (C) hatred

    (D) desire

26. Enmity most nearly means

    (A) enemy.

    (B) hostility.

    (C) anger.

    (D) childish.

27. <u>Arbor</u> most nearly means
  - (A) native.
  - (B) tree.
  - (C) travel.
  - (D) delirious.

28. They <u>terminated</u> his contract.
  - (A) bought
  - (B) extended
  - (C) sold
  - (D) ended

29. Tim always considered Chuck to be a big <u>buffoon</u>.
  - (A) clown
  - (B) help
  - (C) liar
  - (D) pain

30. <u>Null</u> most nearly means
  - (A) zero.
  - (B) dull.
  - (C) unskilled.
  - (D) rapid.

31. Tom had to provide proof to the judge that he was not <u>indigent</u>.
  - (A) guilty
  - (B) rich
  - (C) poor
  - (D) ugly

32. <u>Impertinent</u> most nearly means
  - (A) fun.
  - (B) boring.
  - (C) rude.
  - (D) impatient.

33. <u>Lustrous</u> most nearly means
  - (A) expensive.
  - (B) lazy.
  - (C) cold.
  - (D) polished.

34. <u>Pardon</u> most nearly means
  - (A) courtesy.
  - (B) excuse.
  - (C) believe.
  - (D) respect.

35. <u>Veracious</u> most nearly means
  - (A) fast.
  - (B) slow.
  - (C) equal.
  - (D) truthful.

DO NOT TURN THE PAGE UNTIL TOLD TO DO SO **STOP** DO NOT RETURN TO A PREVIOUS TEST

Subtest 4: Paragraph Comprehension

TIME: 13 minutes for 15 questions

DIRECTIONS: This test measures your ability to understand what you read. This section includes one or more paragraphs of reading material followed by incomplete statements or questions. Read the paragraph and select the choice that best completes the statement or answers the question.

Questions 1 and 2 are based on the following passage.

There is not a single town of any size within a distance of forty miles, yet already the rural population of this county is quite large. The whole country, within a wide circuit north, south, east, and west, partakes of the same general character; mountain ridges, half tilled, half wood, screening cultivated valleys, sprinkled with farms and hamlets, among which some pretty stream generally winds its way. The waters in our immediate neighborhood all flow to the southward, though only a few miles to the north of our village, the brooks are found running in an opposite course, this valley lying just within the borders of the dividing ridge. The river itself, though farther south it becomes one of the great streams of the country, cannot boast of much breadth so near its source, and running quietly among the meadows, half screened by the groves and thickets, scarcely shows in the general view.

1. According to this passage,

(A) the author lives in a large city.

(B) the author lives in the country.

(C) the author lives on the seashore.

(D) the author lives on Mars.

2. According to this passage, the brooks are running in which direction within the author's neighborhood?

(A) north

(B) south

(C) east

(D) west

The Panama Canal is a ship canal that cuts through the Isthmus of Panama, connecting the Atlantic and Pacific oceans. Although several foreign companies tried to build the canal throughout the 19th century, none were successful. After the U.S. helped Panama revolt against Colombia, the U.S. was given rights to the land the canal occupied. The U.S. government finished the canal in 1914.

3. According to this passage,

(A) Panama and Colombia fought a war over the Panama Canal.

(B) the U.S. was given rights to the canal land.

(C) foreign companies built the canal before the U.S. stepped in.

(D) Panama built the canal in 1914.

Extreme care must be exercised to ensure proper handling and cleaning of soiled U.S. flags. A torn flag may be professionally mended, but a badly torn or tattered flag should be destroyed. When the flag is in such a condition that it's no longer a fitting emblem for display, destroy it in a dignified manner, preferably by burning.

4. According to this passage, torn flags should be

(A) mended.

(B) burned.

(C) destroyed.

(D) all of the above.

Medieval guilds were similar to modern-day labor unions. These groups of merchants or craftspeople set rules regarding economic activity in order to protect themselves. Some guilds held considerable economic power, but even small guilds protected members. Guilds also served a social purpose.

5. According to this passage, guilds
   (A) had only one purpose.
   (B) had little in common with modern labor unions.
   (C) exploited workers.
   (D) held considerable economic power.

After a series of well-publicized failures by various inventors, Orville and Wilbur Wright succeeded in flying and controlling a heavier-than-air craft on December 17, 1903. The War Department, stung by its investment in a failed effort by Samuel Langley and compounded by the Wrights' own secretiveness, initially rejected the brothers' overtures toward the government to buy the aircraft. Prevailing sentiments held that the immediate future still belonged to the balloon. In August 1908, the two brothers delivered the first Army aircraft to the U.S. Government. That the U.S. government managed to purchase an airplane was a minor miracle. For more than four years after the Wright brothers' successful flight at Kitty Hawk, North Carolina, the government refused to accept the fact that man had flown in a heavier-than-air machine.

6. Which of the following statements is not supported by the above passage?
   (A) The U.S. Government felt that balloons were more practical than airplanes.
   (B) The Wright brothers' own secretiveness contributed to their problems in getting the government interested in their aircraft.
   (C) The historic flight took place on the East Coast.
   (D) It took more than six years for the Wright brothers to interest the U.S. Government in their airplane.

If anyone should be inclined to overrate the state of our present knowledge of mental life, all that would be needed to force him to assume a modest attitude would be to remind him of the function of memory. No psychologic theory has yet been able to account for the connection between the fundamental phenomena of remembering and forgetting; indeed, even the complete analysis of that which one can actually observe has as yet scarcely been grasped. Today forgetting has perhaps grown more puzzling than remembering, especially since we have learned from the study of dreams and pathologic states that even what for a long time we believed forgotten may suddenly return to consciousness.

7. The primary subject of this paragraph is
   (A) bowling.
   (B) puzzles.
   (C) memory.
   (D) government service.

Troy weight is based on a pound of 12 ounces and an ounce of 480 grains. Common, or avoirdupois, weight is based on a pound having 16 ounces and an ounce having 437.5 grains. A common pound has 7,000 grains while a troy pound has 5,760.

8. According to this passage,
   (A) in common weight, an ounce is less than 438 grains.
   (B) a troy pound and a common pound are the same weight.
   (C) common weight and avoirdupois weight are different measures.
   (D) a troy ounce equals 437.5 grains.

Good leaders get involved in their subordinates' careers. People merely obey arbitrary commands and orders, but they respond quickly and usually give extra effort for leaders who genuinely care for them. An often neglected leadership principle in today's environment of technology and specialization is knowing the workers and showing sincere interest in their problems, career development, and welfare. Leadership is reflected in the degree of efficiency, productivity, morale, and motivation demonstrated by subordinates. Leadership involvement is the key ingredient to maximizing worker performance.

9. A key leadership principle that's often ignored is
   (A) leading by example.
   (B) showing sincere interest in the problems of the workers.
   (C) ensuring workers have access to the most modern technology.
   (D) maximizing worker performance.

Leukemia is a blood disease in which white blood cells in the blood or bone marrow reproduce rapidly, interfering with the body's ability to produce red blood cells. Red blood cells are needed to perform vital bodily functions.

GO ON TO NEXT PAGE ➡

10. According to this passage,

    (A) white blood cells perform no vital function in the body.

    (B) no treatment for leukemia exists.

    (C) leukemia makes it hard for the body to produce red blood cells.

    (D) white blood cells are found only in the blood.

Questions 11 and 12 are based on the following passage.

Any discussion of distinctive military capabilities would be incomplete without looking at their relationship to the Joint Service vision of the future. JV 2020 guides all the Services into the next century with its vision of future war fighting. JV 2020 sets forth four overarching operational concepts: dominant maneuver, precision engagement, focused logistics, and full-dimensional protection. Each of these operational concepts reinforces the others. The aggregate of these four concepts, along with their interaction with information superiority and innovation, allows joint forces to dominate the full range of military operations from humanitarian assistance through peace operations to the highest intensity conflict.

11. According to the passage above, which of the following is not an operational concept?

    (A) dominant maneuver

    (B) focused logistics

    (C) high intensity conflict

    (D) precision engagement

12. The document discussed in the above passage is primarily about

    (A) military operations of the past.

    (B) present military operations.

    (C) military operations in the future.

    (D) training for future military operations.

Questions 13 through 15 are based on the following passage.

Genetics is a branch of science dealing with heredity. The field is concerned with how genes operate and the way genes are transmitted to offspring. Subdivisions in the field include cytogenetics, which is the study of the cellular basis of inheritance; microbial genetics, the study of inheritance in microbes; molecular genetics, the study of the biochemical foundation of inheritance; and human genetics, the study of how people inherit traits that are medically and socially important. Genetic counselors are primarily concerned with human genetics. They advise couples and families on the chances of their offspring having specific genetic defects.

13. In the passage above, cytogenetics is defined as

    (A) the study of the psychological impact of genetics.

    (B) the study of the cellular foundation of inheritance.

    (C) the study of molecular genetics.

    (D) the study of human genetics.

14. According to the passage, genetics

    (A) concerns how genes operate and how they're passed along.

    (B) is a field of study populated by quacks, fakes, and frauds.

    (C) is a field of study only concerned with human genetics.

    (D) is a new field of study.

15. According to the passage, it's reasonable to assume that genetic counseling

    (A) is restricted to the very rich.

    (B) is used to diagnose diseases.

    (C) can be used by parents to learn if their offspring are likely to inherit a disease one of the parents has.

    (D) can be used by parents to prevent their offspring from inheriting a specific genetic defect.

DO NOT TURN THE PAGE UNTIL TOLD TO DO SO **STOP** **DO NOT RETURN TO A PREVIOUS TEST**

Subtest 5: Mathematics Knowledge

TIME: 24 minutes for 25 questions

DIRECTIONS: This test is a test of your ability to solve general mathematical problems. Select the correct answer from the choices given and then mark the corresponding space on your answer sheet. Use scratch paper to do any figuring.

1. $x^2(x^4) =$

(A) x^6

(B) x^8

(C) $2x^6$

(D) $2x^8$

2. If a rectangle has a perimeter of 36 feet and is 4 feet wide, what's its area?

(A) 56 square feet

(B) 128 square feet

(C) 112 square feet

(D) 16 square feet

3. The cube root of 64 is

(A) 3

(B) 9

(C) 2

(D) 4

4. Convert 314,000 to scientific notation.

(A) 3.14×10^5

(B) 3.14×10^{-5}

(C) 314×10

(D) 31.4×100

5. The reciprocal of $\frac{1}{6}$ is

(A) 1

(B) 3

(C) 6

(D) $\frac{1}{3}$

6. If $0.05 \div x = 1$, then $x =$

(A) 0.05

(B) 0.5

(C) 50.0

(D) 5.0

7. Factor $x^2 - 6x + 9$.

(A) $(x+6)(x+6)$

(B) $(x-6)(x+6)$

(C) $(x-3)^2$

(D) $(x+3)^2$

8. $(3 \times 2)(7-2)(6+2) = (6 \times 4)x$. What's the value of x?

(A) -5

(B) 5

(C) 10

(D) 1

9. Solve for x: $2x - 6 = x + 5$.

(A) 3

(B) 11

(C) 7

(D) 5

10. If $I = Prt$, and $P = \$1,000, r = 7\%$, and $t = 1$, what does I equal?

(A) $35

(B) $1,000

(C) $700

(D) $70

11. Solve for x in the equation $(x-7)^2 - 4 = (x+1)^2$.

(A) $2\frac{1}{2}$

(B) $2\frac{3}{4}$

(C) $4\frac{1}{2}$

(D) $4\frac{3}{4}$

GO ON TO NEXT PAGE

12. A circle has a radius of 5 inches. What's its approximate area?

(A) 78.5 inches

(B) 70.0 inches

(C) 314.0 inches

(D) 25.0 inches

13. Solve the following inequality: $\frac{2}{3}(6x-9)+4>5x+1.$

(A) $x>6$

(B) $x<6$

(C) $x>-3$

(D) $x<-3$

14. A tube has a radius of 3 inches and a height of 5 inches. What's its approximate volume?

(A) 34 cubic inches

(B) 141 cubic inches

(C) 565 cubic inches

(D) 45 cubic inches

15. Triangle *ABC* (shown below) is a(n)

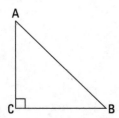

© John Wiley & Sons, Inc.

(A) right triangle.

(B) equilateral triangle.

(C) scalene triangle.

(D) isosceles triangle.

16. The following figure is what type of quadrilateral?

© John Wiley & Sons, Inc.

(A) square

(B) rhombus

(C) trapezoid

(D) parallelogram

17. The angle shown below is a(n)

© John Wiley & Sons, Inc.

(A) complementary angle.

(B) supplementary angle.

(C) acute angle.

(D) obtuse angle.

18. Solve for *x*: $-x^2-x+30=0.$

(A) 4, −8

(B) −6, 5

(C) −4, 5

(D) 6, −3

19. A square box has a volume of 64 cubic inches. What's the perimeter of one of its faces?

(A) 8 inches

(B) 16 inches

(C) 64 inches

(D) 32 inches

20. A cube has a volume of 27 cubic inches. What's its surface area?

(A) 9 square inches

(B) 6 square inches

(C) 54 square inches

(D) 4.5 square inches

21. $\left(x^3\right)^3 =$

(A) $3x^3$

(B) x^6

(C) x^9

(D) $2x^6$

22. $4! =$

(A) 16

(B) 40

(C) 0

(D) 24

23. If $a^3 + b^3 = a^3 + x^3$, then $b =$

(A) $b^3 - a^3$

(B) x

(C) $a^3 - b^3$

(D) a

24. What's the sum of the integers from 1 to 300?

(A) 38,243

(B) 45,150

(C) 49,923

(D) 52,024

25. $\left(y^2\right)^3 + y^2 =$

(A) y^7

(B) $y^6 + y^2$

(C) $y^8 + y^2$

(D) $3y^2$

Subtest 6: Electronics Information

TIME: 9 minutes for 20 questions

DIRECTIONS: This part tests your knowledge of electrical, radio, and electronics information. Select the correct response from the choices given and then mark the corresponding space on your answer sheet.

1. What is used to measure current that is going through a circuit?

   (A) multimeter

   (B) amp gauge

   (C) currentometer

   (D) tri-gauge

2. Which of the following isn't a component of a DC motor?

   (A) rotor bars

   (B) armature

   (C) field poles

   (D) yoke

3. The television broadcast standard in the United States is

   (A) NTSC.

   (B) RGB.

   (C) SECAM.

   (D) RTSC.

4. In a closed electrical circuit,

   (A) one terminal is always positive, and one terminal is always negative.

   (B) both terminals can be positive.

   (C) both terminals can be negative.

   (D) terminals are neither positive nor negative.

5. Electrical current is counted in what measurement?

   (A) hertz

   (B) voltage

   (C) amps

   (D) ohms

6. The following symbol is a/an

© John Wiley & Sons, Inc.

   (A) resistor.

   (B) fuse.

   (C) capacitor.

   (D) inductor.

7. In the United States, what is the specification for an electrical outlet in a bathroom near a sink?

   (A) If within 6 feet of a sink, an outlet must have a childproof cover.

   (B) If within 2 feet of a sink, an outlet must not be GFCI protected.

   (C) If within 6 feet of a sink, an outlet must be GFCI protected.

   (D) If within 2 feet of a sink, an outlet must also be within reach of the bathtub.

8. The following symbol is a/an

© John Wiley & Sons, Inc.

   (A) lamp.

   (B) fuse.

   (C) inductor.

   (D) bell.

9. When a circuit breaker trips, in what position will you find the operating handle?

   (A) on position

   (B) off position

   (C) halfway between on and off

   (D) three-fourths of the way between the on position and the off position

10. Which wire is smallest?

   (A) 00 AWG

   (B) 4 AWG

   (C) 10 AWG

   (D) 12 AWG

11. Which of the following is the best conductor of electricity?

   (A) plastic

   (B) wood

   (C) aluminum

   (D) copper

12. How many paths of electrical flow can be found in a series circuit?

   (A) one

   (B) two

   (C) two or more

   (D) It can't be determined from the information given.

13. A microwave is rated at 1,200 watts. At 120 volts, how much current does it draw?

   (A) 1 amp

   (B) 10 amps

   (C) 100 amps

   (D) 1,440 amps

14. Electricians use the term *low potential* to refer to

   (A) electrical circuits with a low potential for overload.

   (B) building codes that reduce the risk of fire.

   (C) the likelihood of getting a raise this year.

   (D) 600 watts or less.

15. Which of the following isn't a conductor of electricity?

   (A) water

   (B) graphite

   (C) gold

   (D) glass

16. The ground wire is always

   (A) green.

   (B) black.

   (C) whitish.

   (D) blue.

17. What does AM mean?

   (A) amp metrics

   (B) alien mothers

   (C) amplitude modulation

   (D) anode matrix

18. Silver is a better conductor than copper. But copper is more often used because of

   (A) the cost of silver.

   (B) the brittleness of copper.

   (C) the low melting point of silver.

   (D) the tendency of silver to tarnish.

19. Electronic circuits that produce high frequencies are called

   (A) amplifiers.

   (B) regulators.

   (C) transformers.

   (D) oscillators.

20. If you plug an appliance designed for AC into a DC power source, the appliance

   (A) will operate normally.

   (B) will produce excessive heat.

   (C) won't operate.

   (D) will explode into tiny pieces.

Subtest 7: Auto & Shop Information

TIME: 11 minutes for 25 questions

DIRECTIONS: This test is about automobiles, shop practices, and the use of tools. Pick the best answer for each question and then mark the corresponding space on your answer sheet.

1. If a car uses too much oil, which of the following parts may be worn?

    (A) camshaft

    (B) connecting rods

    (C) fuel pump

    (D) piston rings

2. Clean air filters are important because

    (A) dirty filters can cause a decrease in fuel mileage.

    (B) they remove pollutants, which can decrease engine performance.

    (C) they keep the oil from becoming contaminated.

    (D) Both A and B.

3. The alternator

    (A) starts the engine.

    (B) supplies regulated power to the battery.

    (C) connects the ignition system to the engine.

    (D) can be used as an alternative to motor oil.

4. In which automotive system would you find a "wishbone"?

    (A) suspension

    (B) engine

    (C) exhaust

    (D) oil pan

5. If the electrolyte solution in a battery is too low, you should add

    (A) sulfuric acid.

    (B) antifreeze.

    (C) distilled water.

    (D) gasoline.

6. What area of your car should be flushed periodically to maintain optimum performance?

    (A) exhaust system

    (B) brake system

    (C) cooling system

    (D) ignition system

7. The primary purpose of a carburetor is to

    (A) maintain engine timing.

    (B) regulate oil pressure.

    (C) mix fuel and air.

    (D) monitor tire pressure.

8. Car restorers often seek NOS parts. What does NOS stand for?

    (A) Near Original Specifications

    (B) NASCAR Operating Standards

    (C) New Old Stock

    (D) none of the above

9. To make spark plugs work effectively, the coil and breaker

   (A) provide a gap between the electrodes.

   (B) ignite the spark.

   (C) transfer the electricity to the correct spark plug.

   (D) create a very high electrical voltage.

10. Schrader valves can be found in your car's

    (A) tires.

    (B) engine.

    (C) transmission.

    (D) electronic ignition.

11. A bent frame causes

    (A) improper tracking.

    (B) auto accidents.

    (C) poor visibility

    (D) excessive rust.

12. In the tire designation 205/55 R 15 92 H, what does the "H" signify?

    (A) tread type

    (B) tire height

    (C) maximum sustained speed

    (D) turning radius

13. When the tightness of screws and/or bolts is important, it's best to use

    (A) a screwdriver.

    (B) a torque wrench.

    (C) tin snips.

    (D) a coping saw.

14. Hammer faces are commonly made of each of the following materials EXCEPT

    (A) steel.

    (B) brass.

    (C) glass.

    (D) lead.

15. Hammers, mallets, and sledges are all striking tools, but mallets and sledges don't have

    (A) claws.

    (B) metal parts.

    (C) as much durability.

    (D) heads.

16. Round objects can be measured most exactly using a

    (A) rigid steel rule.

    (B) folding rule.

    (C) set of calipers.

    (D) depth gauge.

17. The best chisel to use when making a circular cut in metal is a

    (A) masonry chisel.

    (B) socket chisel.

    (C) butt chisel.

    (D) round chisel.

18. A Stillson wrench is a type of

    (A) strap wrench.

    (B) hammer.

    (C) plumb bob.

    (D) pipe wrench.

19. Painting on a surface with too much moisture

    (A) causes no problems.

    (B) causes bubbling.

    (C) requires an extra coat of paint.

    (D) takes longer.

20. A tool used to control the location and/or motion of another tool is called a

    (A) control tool.

    (B) jig.

    (C) nail.

    (D) static rectifier.

GO ON TO NEXT PAGE

21. An 8-point saw

(A) has 7 teeth per inch.

(B) weighs 8 ounces.

(C) can saw 8 kinds of material.

(D) is 8 inches long.

22. Concrete is made by mixing

(A) cement.

(B) cement and water.

(C) liquid cement and chemical additives.

(D) mineral aggregate, a binder, and water.

23. Which of the following tools isn't used to cut metal?

(A)

(C)

(B)

(D)

24. The following tool is used to

© John Wiley & Sons, Inc.

(A) cut tile.

(B) cut wire.

(C) turn screws.

(D) cut bolts.

25. The following tool is a(n)

© John Wiley & Sons, Inc.

(A) Phillips screwdriver.

(B) Allen wrench.

(C) socket wrench.

(D) offset screwdriver.

STOP

DO NOT TURN THE PAGE UNTIL TOLD TO DO SO   DO NOT RETURN TO A PREVIOUS TEST

Subtest 8: Mechanical Comprehension

TIME: 19 minutes for 25 questions

DIRECTIONS: This test is about mechanical principles. Many of the questions use drawings to illustrate specific principles. Choose the correct answer and mark the corresponding space on the answer sheet.

1. A simple fixed pulley gives a mechanical advantage of

   (A) 2

   (B) 3

   (C) 1

   (D) unknown

2. The baskets are balanced on the arm in the figure below. If cherries are removed from Basket B, then to rebalance the arm,

© John Wiley & Sons, Inc.

   (A) the fulcrum will have to be moved to the right.

   (B) Basket B will have to be moved to the right.

   (C) Basket A will have to be moved to the left.

   (D) Basket A will have to be moved to the right.

3. If both Wheel A and Wheel B revolve at the same rate in the figure below, Wheel A will cover a linear distance of 12 feet

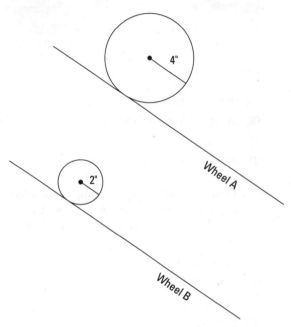

© John Wiley & Sons, Inc.

   (A) faster than Wheel B.

   (B) slower than Wheel B.

   (C) in about the same time as Wheel B.

   (D) half as quickly as Wheel B.

GO ON TO NEXT PAGE

4. If a force of 200 pounds is exerted over an area of 10 square inches, what's the psi?

 (A) 10

 (B) 15

 (C) 20

 (D) 200

5. In the following figure, if you move Anvil A toward the middle of the seesaw, Anvil B will

© John Wiley & Sons, Inc.

 (A) remain stationary.

 (B) move toward the ground.

 (C) rise in the air.

 (D) lose weight.

6. If a ramp measures 6 feet in length and 3 feet in height, an object weighing 200 pounds requires how much effort to move using the ramp?

 (A) 200 pounds

 (B) 100 pounds

 (C) 50 pounds

 (D) 300 pounds

7. A micrometer is used to measure

 (A) small changes in temperature.

 (B) changes in psi.

 (C) thicknesses to a few thousandths of an inch.

 (D) objects invisible to the unaided eye.

8. If the weight is removed from Side B of the seesaw, what happens to the weight on Side A?

© John Wiley & Sons, Inc.

 (A) The weight will never move from Side B.

 (B) The weight on Side A will move up in the air.

 (C) The weight on Side A will move toward the ground.

 (D) Nothing will happen.

9. The force produced when two objects rub against each other is called

 (A) gravity.

 (B) recoil.

 (C) magnetism.

 (D) friction.

10. Normally, atmospheric pressure is approximately

 (A) 14.7 psi

 (B) 23.2 psi

 (C) 7.0 psi

 (D) 10.1 psi

11. For Gear A and Gear B to mesh properly in the following figure,

© John Wiley & Sons, Inc.

(A) they must be the same size.

(B) they must turn at different rates.

(C) they must both turn in the same direction.

(D) their teeth must be of equal size.

12. Torsion springs

(A) produce a direct pull.

(B) exert no pull.

(C) produce a twisting action.

(D) coil but do not uncoil.

13. To move a 400-pound crate from the floor of a warehouse to the bed of a truck 4 feet off the ground, the most efficient device to use is a

(A) lever.

(B) inclined plane.

(C) fixed pulley.

(D) jackscrew.

14. Water in an engine can cause damage in winter weather because

(A) it can vaporize.

(B) water expands when it freezes.

(C) ice is heavier than water.

(D) cold water creates more steam than warm water.

15. The weight of the load is being carried on the backs of the two anvils shown in the figure. Which anvil is carrying the most weight?

Anvil A   Anvil B

© John Wiley & Sons, Inc.

(A) Anvil A

(B) Anvil B

(C) Both are carrying an equal amount of weight.

(D) It can't be determined without more information.

16. When the block-and-tackle arrangement shown in the figure is used to lift a load, all the following parts remain stationary except

Upper Block

Lower Block

LOAD

© John Wiley & Sons, Inc.

(A) the upper hook.

(B) the upper block.

(C) the lower block.

(D) All the parts move.

GO ON TO NEXT PAGE

17. In the following figure, what effort (E) must be applied to lift the anvil?

21–pound anvil

© John Wiley & Sons, Inc.

(A) 7.0 pounds

(B) 9.0 pounds

(C) 21.0 pounds

(D) 10.5 pounds

18. In the figure below, for each complete revolution the cam makes, how many times will the valve open?

cylinder

valve

cam

© John Wiley & Sons, Inc.

(A) 1

(B) 6

(C) 3

(D) 2

19. In the following figure, assume the valves are all open. Which valves need to be closed for the tank to fill up completely?

Water Supply

Valve 3

Valve 1

Valve 2

Valve 4   Valve 5

Drainage

© John Wiley & Sons, Inc.

(A) 3 and 4 only

(B) 3, 4, and 5

(C) 2, 3, and 4

(D) 4 only

20. If Gear A turns left in the figure below, Gear B

A

B

© John Wiley & Sons, Inc.

(A) won't turn.

(B) turns left.

(C) turns right.

(D) It can't be determined.

21. If Gear 1 makes 10 complete clockwise revolutions per minute in the figure below, then

© John Wiley & Sons, Inc.

(A) Gear 2 makes 10 complete clockwise revolutions per minute.

(B) Gear 2 makes 20 complete counterclockwise revolutions per minute.

(C) Gear 2 makes 5 complete counterclockwise revolutions per minute.

(D) Gear 3 keeps Gear 2 from making any revolutions.

22. For the fuel to travel from Reservoir A to Reservoir B, passing through Filters C and D on the way, which valves must be open?

© John Wiley & Sons, Inc.

(A) 1, 2, 4, and 8

(B) 1, 2, and 3

(C) 6, 7, and 8

(D) 4, 6, and 7

23. A yellow flame on a gas furnace indicates that

(A) everything is fine.

(B) the fuel-air mixture is too rich.

(C) the fuel-air mixture is too lean.

(D) the gas pressure is too low.

24. If a water tank on a toilet keeps overflowing, the problem is probably a

(A) defective float.

(B) clogged pipe.

(C) crimped chain.

(D) improper seal.

25. In the figure below, the board holds the anvil. The board is placed on two identical scales. Each scale reads

© John Wiley & Sons, Inc.

(A) 24

(B) 10

(C) 12

(D) 40

Subtest 9: Assembling Objects

TIME: 15 minutes for 25 questions

DIRECTIONS: The Assembling Objects subtest consists of questions that measure your ability to mentally picture items in two dimensions. Each question is comprised of five separate drawings. The problem is presented in the first drawing and the remaining four drawings are possible solutions. Determine which of the choices best solves the problem shown in the first picture; then mark the corresponding choice on your answer sheet.

13.

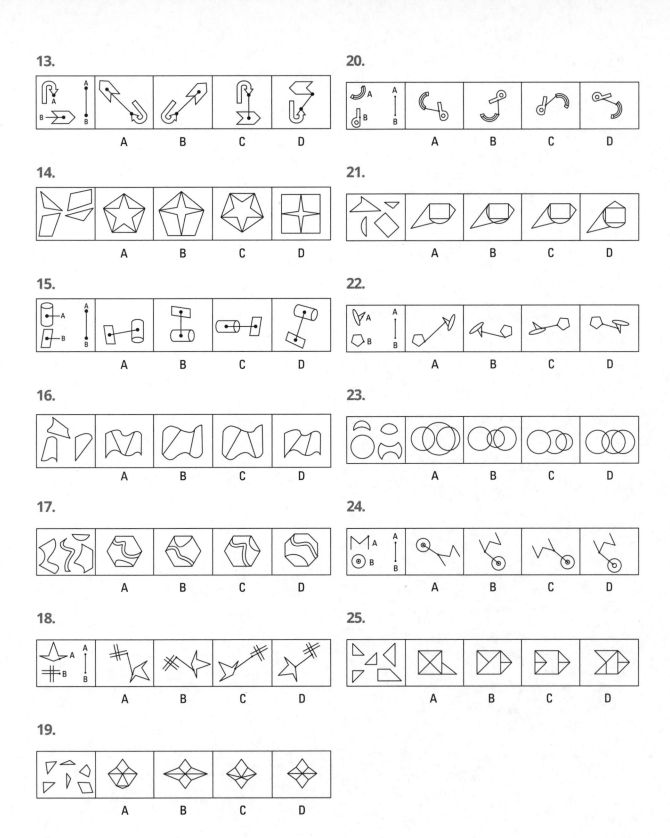

14.

15.

16.

17.

18.

19.

20.

21.

22.

23.

24.

25.

Chapter **21**

Practice Exam 2: Answers and Explanations

Here are the answers and explanations for the practice exam in Chapter 20. Read over each question from Chapter 20 as you check your answers. Doing so reminds you what the question is about and serves as a helpful review. If you look at each question and the possible answers, you can also identify some of the traps that you may run across on the ASVAB.

You don't have to be an algebra ace to determine whether you're making progress through your review efforts. Simply compare the number of wrong answers you got on Practice Exam 1 (Chapter 18) against the number of wrong answers you got on this test. If you put the work in, you'll probably find that you made fewer errors on Practice Exam 2.

By the time you've scored Practice Exam 2, you should have a good idea of your strengths and weaknesses. If some subjects or subtests still give you problems, keep studying — just follow the cross-references for some tips and additional practice questions. If you find you need in-depth study, check out the beginning of each subtest's chapter, where I name some books on various subjects covered in the subtests.

REMEMBER

The ASVAB is technically scored by comparing your raw score to the scores of other people, which produces a scaled score. Turn to Chapter 2 to find out how the ASVAB is scored.

Subtest 1: **General Science Answers**

The answers to the questions on the General Science subtest are fairly straightforward — you either know the answer or you don't. This can be a hard subject to study for because General Science includes the entire scope of scientific disciplines. The good news is you may not even have to score well on this subtest; it depends on the job you're interested in. See Appendix A for military jobs that require a good General Science score. You can find additional science practice questions in Chapters 10, 11, and 12.

1. **B.** *Metamorphosis* is the change an insect's body undergoes.

2. **D.** Each increase of 1 in magnitude means a quake is 10 times stronger. Therefore, an earthquake that registers as a 4 on the Richter scale is 100 times stronger than one that rates a 2.

3. **C.** Muscles connect to bone with connective tissue called *tendons.*

4. **A.** The *stamen* in a flower is the male part.

5. **D.** The lungs oxygenate the incoming blood.

6. **B.** At more than 4,100 miles, the Nile River is the longest of the rivers listed. Whether it's the longest in the world, as long thought, is now up for debate. In 2007, a group of scientists claimed to have found a new starting point for the Amazon River, which would give the Amazon about a 65-mile lead over the Nile.

7. **B.** Physics is the study of matter and its motion, energy, and force.

8. **A.** Any meteorologist will tell you that *nimbus* clouds mean rain.

9. **D.** Deoxyribonucleic acid — the stuff that genes are made of — is the full term for DNA.

10. **B.** *Anemos* is the Greek word for wind. An anemometer measures wind speed.

11. **A.** Electrical charges can be positive or negative, so Choice (A) is correct.

12. **C.** Jupiter is the planet with the most moons in the solar system, with a total of 63 (and possibly more to be categorized in the future).

13. **B.** Isaac Newton discovered the law of gravity.

14. **D.** The Apollo space program has put 12 men on the moon, with *Apollo* 11 being the first mission.

15. **C.** *Omni* is an English prefix for "all." Omnivores eat plants and animals.

16. **B.** Sharks have only cartilage (in place of bones).

17. **A.** The function of the liver is to remove toxins from the blood.

18. **C.** *Kinetic* comes from the Greek word *kinesis,* meaning to move.

19. **C.** Terrestrial planets are made up of materials other than just gases.

20. **A.** Calcium is a mineral found in dairy, green vegetables, and other foods.

21. **D.** The brain of a sperm whale is the largest and heaviest in the Animal kingdom.

22. **B.** Stars are classified by makeup, heat produced, and so on. Earth's sun is a G type star.

23. **C.** As an example, H_2O is two atoms of hydrogen combined with one oxygen atom.

24. **C.** A seed is a plant embryo enclosed in a casing.

25. **C.** *Vernal* means spring. *Equinox* means a point in time when day and night are of equal length. This equality occurs twice a year. The correct answer is the first day of spring.

Subtest 2: Arithmetic Reasoning Answers

This subtest is one of the most important because it makes up a portion of your AFQT score, the score that determines your overall mental qualifications to enlist in the military.

If you think you need more in-depth study, review Part 3 or see whether you can find some high school–level math textbooks at your local library.

1. **D.** For each die, the probability of rolling a 5 is 1 out of 6 $\left(\text{that is, } \frac{1}{6}\right)$, so the probability of not rolling a 5 is $1 - \frac{1}{6}$, or $\frac{5}{6}$. With two dice, the probability of not rolling a 5 is $\frac{5}{6} \times \frac{5}{6}$, or $\frac{25}{36}$.

2. **C.** Multiply $1,500 by 7%, or 0.07, and get $105. Then add $105 to $1,500 to find the answer, $1,605.

   Sometimes you can actually save time by not working the problem. In this problem, simply recognizing that the answer has to be more than $1,500 makes it obvious that Choices (A) and (B) are wrong. It also should be obvious that 7% of $1,500 has to be more than $7, so Choice (D) is also wrong. That only leaves the correct answer, Choice (C).

3. **A.** Two tons = 4,000 pounds; $4,000 \times \$0.12 = \$480$.

4. **C.** Expanding the equation $y = (a + b)^2$ results in $y = a^2 + b^2 + 2ab + b^2 = a^2 + b^2 + 2ab$. You are given that $a^2 + b^2 = 30$ and $ab = 10$. When you substitute these values into the equation, you get $y = 30 + 2(10)$. Simplifying, $y = 50$.

5. **C.** There are 2 pints in a quart, and 4 quarts make up a gallon; therefore, a gallon contains $2 \times 4 = 8$ pints, or 16 half-pints. One half-pint equals $\frac{1}{16}$ of a gallon.

6. **D.** First subtract the old cost from the new cost: $\$2.80 - \$2.50 = \$0.30$. Then divide the difference by the old cost to find the percent change: $\$0.30 \div \$2.50 = 0.12 = 12\%$.

7. **C.** The aircraft travels 120 miles in 12 minutes, which is $\frac{1}{5}$ of an hour. Therefore, in $\frac{5}{5}$ (or 1 hour), it would travel 5×120, or 600 miles. The aircraft is traveling 600 miles per hour.

8. **D.** Multiply 50 bushels by 8% to find the yield increase in bushels: $50 \times 0.08 = 4$. Add 4 bushels (the amount of the increase) to 50 bushels (the original yield) to determine that an 8% increase equals 54 bushels.

9. **B.** Convert the change to dollars and cents, then add:

$$
\begin{aligned}
14 \text{ dollars} &= \$14.00 \\
16 \text{ half dollars} &= \$8.00 \\
12 \text{ quarters} &= \$3.00 \\
8 \text{ dimes} &= \$0.80 \\
25 \text{ nickels} &= \$1.25 \\
\underline{10 \text{ pennies}} &= \underline{\$0.10} \\
&= \$27.15
\end{aligned}
$$

   Subtract the total from $30.00 to determine how much money Junior must borrow: $\$30.00 - \$27.15 = \$2.85$.

10. **B.** Her commission for the week was $40 (because $0.05 \times 800 = 40$). The ratio of her commission to her salary is 40:80, which can be reduced to 1:2.

11. **C.** A gallon consists of 4 quarts, and $4 \times 25 = 100$.

12. **D.** Four members is twice as many as two members. Multiply the number of days it would take four people to paint by 2 (that is, $3 \times 2 = 6$) to determine how long it would take two people to do the same task.

13. **A.** Brian's hourly wage is $24 \div 5 = \$4.80$. Christina's hourly wage is $10.95 \div 3 = \$3.65$. The difference is $\$4.80 - \$3.65 = \$1.15$.

14. **C.** The amount of time from 8:30 a.m. to 11:15 a.m. is 2 hours, 45 minutes. From 8:30 a.m. until 10:30 a.m. is 2 hours. From 10:30 until 11:15 is 45 minutes, or $\frac{3}{4}$ of an hour, for a total of $2\frac{3}{4}$ hours.

15. **C.** At a rate of 7 documents per minute, the employee can shred 630 documents in 90 minutes. How do you come up with that number? Multiply 7 by 90 (the number of minutes in 1½ hours). Subtract 630 from 900 total documents to determine that after $1\frac{1}{2}$ hours of shredding, 270 documents remain.

16. **A.** If the stereo depreciates 20%, the value of the stereo then becomes 80% of its original value. After depreciation, the value of the stereo the first year is $\$960\,(0.08 \times 1,200)$. The value of the stereo after the second year is $\$768\,(0.08 \times 960)$. $768 is Choice (A).

17. **A.** Divide the distance (135 miles) by the speed (45 miles per hour) to determine that Janet will take 3 hours to reach the city.

18. **D.** Multiply the price of the blouse by the amount of the discount: $\$18.50 \times 0.20 = \$3.70$.

19. **C.** Subtract the original salary from the new salary to get the difference in salary: $\$360 - \$320 = \$40$. Then divide the difference in salary ($\$40$) by the original salary ($\$320$) to determine the percent increase: $40 \div 320 = 0.125 = 12.5\%$.

20. **B.** A circle is 360 degrees, so 40 degrees is $\frac{1}{9}$ of a circle $\left(360° \div 40° = 9\right)$. To get the answer, multiply the circumference of the track by $\frac{1}{9}$: $\left(360 \text{ ft.} \times \frac{1}{9} = 40 \text{ ft.}\right)$.

21. **B.** Subtract $35.98 from $40.00 to get $4.02.

22. **B.** Subtract the time of the plane from the time of the balloon to determine how much longer it took the balloonist:

$$
\begin{array}{rllll}
& 13 \text{ days,} & 12 \text{ hours,} & 16 \text{ minutes,} & 13 \text{ minutes} \\
- & 4 \text{ days,} & 10 \text{ hours,} & 15 \text{ minutes,} & 7 \text{ minutes} \\
\hline
& 9 \text{ days,} & 2 \text{ hours,} & 1 \text{ minute,} & 6 \text{ minutes}
\end{array}
$$

23. **A.** Divide the total cost by the number of boxes purchased to determine the cost per box: $\$48 \div 12 = \$4$.

24. **D.** Multiply 20×0.05 to determine how many more miles per gallon the car will get. The answer is 1. Then add the number of additional miles per gallon the car will get to the original number of miles per gallon the car gets to reach the new average: $1 + 20 = 21$.

25. **A.** The minimum length of spike is equal to the diameter of the tree. To find the diameter of the tree, use the formula, $C = \pi d$, where $C = 43.96$ and $\pi \approx 3.14$: $43.96 \approx 3.14 \times d$; $d \approx 43.96 \div 3.14$; $d \approx 14$.

26. **D.** Divide 10½ by ¾. You can perform this operation by multiplying $10\frac{1}{2}$ by the reciprocal of $\frac{3}{4}$: $10\frac{1}{2}\times\frac{4}{3}=\frac{21}{2}\times\frac{4}{3}=\frac{84}{6}$. Divide 84 by 6, and the answer is 14.

27. **C.** First figure out how many stones will be needed along the 12-foot side of the patio and then how many stones will be needed along the 14-foot side of the patio. Then multiply those two numbers together to get the total number of stones required. Here's the math: Convert 12 feet to inches: 12 ft.×12 in./ft.=144 inches. The paving stones are 8 inches square, so divide 144 inches by 8 inches $(144\div8)$, which gives you 18 stones.

    Do the same math for the 14-foot length: 14 ft.×12 in./ft.=168 in., and 168÷8=21. Therefore, 21 stones are needed on the 14-foot side.

    Now multiply the stones: 18 stones×21 stones=378 stones, which is Choice (C).

28. **D.** Calculate the amount of the deduction by multiplying her salary by the percent deducted: $25,000×28%=$25,000×0.28=$7,000. Subtract that product from the salary to determine the net pay: $25,000−$7,000=$18,000.

29. **B.** When the sum of two angles is 180 degrees, the angles are said to be supplementary to each other. To find the supplement, subtract 55 from 180: 180−55=125.

30. **C.** Multiply the height of the stack in feet by 12 to determine the height of the stack in inches: 6×12=72 inches. Divide that number by 4 inches, the thickness of each board, to determine the number of pieces of lumber in the stack: 72÷4=18.

Subtest 3: Word Knowledge Answers

Keep in mind that your score on the Word Knowledge subtest counts toward your AFQT score (see Chapter 1), so make sure you're getting comfortable with this portion of the test.

If your score on the Word Knowledge subtest has improved since you took the first test, congratulations! If not, don't be too surprised. Improving your score on this subtest in a short period of time is difficult, but it can be done. Review the information from Chapter 4 and set aside time each day (maybe several times a day, depending on how soon you plan on taking the ASVAB) to memorize words, roots, prefixes, and suffixes. Make sure you sink your dictionary into the additional practice questions at the end of Chapter 4, too.

1. **C.** *Abeyance* is a noun that means a state of temporary disuse or suspension.

2. **A.** *Sturdy* is an adjective used to describe something that's strongly and solidly built.

3. **A.** *Bullock* is a noun that's used as a term for a young bull or steer.

4. **C.** *Brevity* is a noun that means the concise, exact use of words, whether in writing or speech. It can also mean shortness of time.

5. **B.** *Paradigm* is a noun that refers to a typical example or pattern of something; it can also mean a model.

6. **B.** *Facilitated* is the past tense of the verb *facilitate*, which means to make something easy or easier.

7. **D.** *Quiescence* is a noun that refers to a state of inactivity.

8. **B.** *Spectator* is a noun that refers to a person who watches something.

9. **B.** *Reclined* is the past tense of the verb *recline*, which means to lean or lie back in a relaxed position with the back supported.

10. **C.** *Cited* is the past tense of the verb *cite*, which means to quote something as evidence or to justify an argument or statement.

11. **C.** *Surround* is a verb that means to be all around something.

12. **B.** *Illustrious* is an adjective that means well-known, admired for past achievements, and respected.

13. **D.** *Inhabitant* is a noun that refers to a person or animal that lives in or occupies a place.

14. **B.** *Subterfuge* is a noun that means deceit used in order to achieve a goal.

15. **A.** *Ghastly* is an adjective that refers to something that causes great horror or fear.

16. **D.** *Rigid* is an adjective that means unable to bend or inflexible.

17. **A.** *Fraternal* is an adjective that means of or like a brother (or brothers).

18. **C.** *Deplore* is a verb that means to feel or express strong disapproval of something.

19. **B.** *Meager* is an adjective that means lacking in quantity or quality.

20. **A.** *Weal* is a noun that means well-being, happiness, or prosperity. Don't let Choice (B) throw you off; another definition of *weal* is a red, swollen mark left behind after a blow or pressure.

21. **C.** *Guileless* is an adjective that means innocent and without deception.

22. **C.** *Confiscate* is a verb that means to take or seize someone's property with authority.

23. **D.** *Dubious* is an adjective that means hesitating, doubting, or not to be relied upon.

24. **A.** *Illusion* is a noun that refers to something that is, or is likely to be, wrongly interpreted or perceived by the senses.

25. **D.** *Craving* is a noun that means a powerful desire for something.

26. **B.** *Enmity* is a noun that refers to feeling or being opposed or hostile to someone or something.

27. **B.** *Arbor* is a noun that means tree. It can also refer to the leafy, shady area that tree branches or shrubs create.

28. **D.** *Terminated* is the past tense of the verb *terminate*, which means to bring to an end.

29. **A.** *Buffoon* is a noun that means a ridiculous but amusing person.

30. **A.** *Null* is an adjective that means having or associated with the value zero; it also refers to something that has no legal or binding force or to something that is invalid.

31. **C.** *Indigent* is an adjective that means poor or needy. It's also a noun that refers to a needy person.

32. **C.** *Impertinent* is an adjective that means rude or not showing proper respect.

33. **D.** *Lustrous* is an adjective that means shining or glossy.

34. **B.** *Pardon* is a verb that means to forgive or excuse someone or something. It's also a noun that refers to the action of forgiving (or being forgiven) for something.

35. **D.** *Veracious* is an adjective that means speaking or representing the truth.

Subtest 4: Paragraph Comprehension Answers

Like Word Knowledge, the Paragraph Comprehension subtest also counts toward your AFQT score. If you're missing more answers than you should, review the info in Chapter 5 and concentrate on improving your analytical reading skills. For example, when you're reading a news story online, ask yourself what the main point of an article is. Or when you finish a news story, set the paper down and try to remember what the president said about the budget deficit. Think of this technique as a workout for your mind.

1. **B.** The author is describing a quaint country setting.

2. **B.** The passage states that the brooks in the village run south, so the answer is Choice (B). A few miles north, the brooks run in an opposite direction (north).

3. **B.** The passage states that Panama revolted against Colombia, not that they fought over the canal, so Choice (A) is incorrect. The passage states that the foreign companies were unsuccessful in building the canal, so Choice (C) is incorrect. The United States, not Panama, built the canal, so Choice (D) is wrong. In the next to last sentence, the passage states that the U.S. was given rights to the land the canal occupied, making Choice (B) the correct answer.

4. **D.** According to the passage, a torn U.S. flag can be professionally mended, but a severely torn flag should be destroyed. The preferred method of destruction is by burning.

5. **D.** The passage states that guilds had economic and social purposes, so Choice (A) is incorrect. The passage states that guilds were similar to labor unions, so Choice (B) is incorrect. The passage states that guilds protected merchants and craftspeople; it says nothing about exploiting workers, so Choice (C) is incorrect. The third sentence states that some guilds held considerable economic power, but even small guilds protected members, making Choice (D) the correct answer.

6. **D.** According to the passage, it took more than 4 years for the government to believe that anyone had flown a heavier-than-air craft. The historic flight was in December 1903, and the Wright brothers delivered the first aircraft to the government in August 1908, 4.5 years later. The passage supports all the other statements.

7. **C.** Freud comments on the characteristics of memory throughout the entire passage.

8. **A.** The passage describes how troy and common weights are different, so Choice (B) is incorrect. Common and avoirdupois are the same system, so Choice (C) is incorrect. A troy ounce is 480 grains, so Choice (D) is incorrect. Choice (A) is the correct answer because the second sentence states that a common ounce is 437.5 grains, which is just shy of 438 grains.

9. **B.** The passage doesn't address leading by example or use of technology by workers, so Choices (A) and (C) are incorrect. Maximizing worker performance is a result of leadership involvement, not a principle of leadership, making Choice (D) incorrect. The correct answer, showing interest in workers' problems, is in the third sentence of the passage.

10. **C.** The passage doesn't support Choices (A) or (B). The passage states that white blood cells are found in blood and bone marrow, so Choice (D) is wrong. The correct answer, Choice (C), can be found in the first sentence. The passage states that leukemia interferes with "the body's ability to produce red blood cells."

11. **C.** High intensity conflict is listed as a type of military operation (in the last sentence), not one of the four operational concepts.

12. **C.** The JV 2020 guides all the military services with its vision of future war fighting. Although Choice (D) is close, the passage doesn't specifically reference military training.

13. **B.** Cytogenetics is the study of the cellular basis of inheritance; the text doesn't support Choices (A), (C), or (D).

14. **A.** Nothing in the passage supports Choices (B) or (D). Although human genetics is an important subfield of genetics, nothing in the passage suggests that it's the only concern of geneticists. Microbial genetics, as the passage mentions, is a subfield in genetics that has nothing to do with humans, so Choice (C) is incorrect. Choice (A) is the correct answer — the second sentence mentions genes and their transmission to offspring.

15. **C.** Nothing in the passage supports Choices (A), (B), or (D). Choice (C) is the correct answer because the last sentence in the passage states, "[Genetic counselors] advise couples and families on the chances of their offspring having specific genetic defects." Note it does not state that genetic counselors use genetics to *prevent* offspring from inheriting defects, which is what Choice (D) states, making Choice (D) an incorrect answer.

Subtest 5: Mathematics Knowledge Answers

Although the military doesn't expect you to be the next Einstein, a solid grasp of mathematics is important because math skills make up half of your AFQT score. If you're still struggling on this subtest, it's time to hit the books. (Actually, as much as you may feel like it, I don't recommend that you literally hit the books — just study them.) See Chapters 6, 7, and 8 for some more fun practice questions.

1. **A.** If two exponents have the same base, you can multiply them by keeping the base and adding the exponents together: $x^2 \left(x^4 \right) = x^{2+4} = x^6$.

2. **A.** To find area, multiply length times width $\left(A = lw \right)$. You have the width, so you need to find the length. For a rectangle, $P = 2l + 2w$, so plug in the values you know and

solve for *l*. To determine the length, subtract two times the width from the perimeter: $36 - 2(4) = 36 - 8 = 28$. Divide the answer by 2 to determine the length of one side: $28 \div 2 = 14$. Then multiply length times width to determine the area: $A = 14 \times 4 = 56$.

3. **D.** The cube of 4 is $4 \times 4 \times 4 = 64$, so 4 is the cube root of 64.

4. **A.** To convert this number to scientific notation, move the decimal point to the left until it's to the immediate right of the first number, while counting the number of moves. In this case, you move it five places. The result is then multiplied by 10 raised to the power of the number of places the decimal point was moved. The exponent is positive here because the original number, 314,000, is larger than 3.14. Choice (B), 3.14×10^{-5}, is equal to 0.0000314, so it's incorrect.

5. **B.** A reciprocal is the number by which a number can be multiplied to produce 1. The reciprocal $\frac{1}{6}$ is 6, because $\frac{1}{6} \times 6 = 1$.

6. **A.** You start with $0.05 \div x = 1$. Multiply both sides of the equation by *x*: $0.05 = 1x$ or $x = 0.05$. Check by substituting 0.05 for *x* in the original equation.

7. **C.** $x^2 - 6x + 9 = (x-3)(x-3) = (x-3)^2$.

8. **C.** You start with $(3 \times 2)(7 - 2)(6 + 2) = (6 \times 4)x$. Solve the left side of the equation first. $(6)(5)(8) = (30)(8) = 240$. Therefore, $240 = (6 \times 4)x$, which equals $420 = 24x$. Now isolate *x* by dividing both sides of the equation by 24: $240 \div 24 = 24x \div 24$, or $10 = x$. Check your answer by substituting 10 for *x* in the original equation.

9. **B.** Isolate *x* on one side of the equation. Subtract *x* from both sides of the equation and then add 6 to both sides:

$$2x - 6 = x + 5$$
$$x - 6 = 5$$
$$x = 11$$

Check by substituting 11 for *x* in the original equation.

10. **D.** Solve for *I*. $I = (1,000)(7\%)(1)$, or $I = (1,000)(0.07)(1) = 70$.

11. **B.** Multiply out what's in parentheses. Then simplify and solve for *x*:

$$(x-7)^2 - 4 = (x+1)^2$$
$$(x-7)(x-7) - 4 = (x+1)(x+1)$$
$$x^2 - 14x + 49 - 4 = x^2 + 2x + 1$$
$$x^2 - 14x + 45 = x^2 + 2x + 1$$
$$-14x + 45 = 2x + 1$$
$$44 = 16x$$
$$2\frac{3}{4} = x$$

12. **A.** The area of a circle is $A = \pi r^2$, so $A = \pi 5^2$. The number π is approximately 3.14, so 3.14×25 means *A* is approximately 78.5 square inches.

13. D. Distribute the $\frac{2}{3}$, simplify, and solve for x. Note that when you divide by a negative number, you have to switch the direction of the inequality sign.

$$\frac{2}{3}(6x-9)+4>5x+1$$
$$4x-6+4>5x+1$$
$$4x-2>5x+1$$
$$-x>3$$
$$x<-3$$

14. B. For cylinders, Volume $= \pi r^2 h$. In this problem, $V = \pi(3)^2(5)$. Assume π is approximately 3.14. V is approximately equal to $(3.14)(9)(5)$, or 141 cubic inches.

15. A. A right triangle has one right angle (one 90-degree angle).

16. D. Parallelograms have opposite sides of equal length.

17. D. Angles measuring more than 90 degrees are obtuse angles.

18. B. This is a quadratic equation, which you solve by factoring. First factor out the -1; then factor the quadratic expression and solve for x:

$$-x^2 - x + 30 = 0$$
$$-(x^2 + x - 30) = 0$$
$$-(x+6)(x-5) = 0$$
$$x = -6, 5$$

19. B. Volume equals length times width times height ($V = lwh$). In this case, $V = 64$, so one edge of the box is 4 inches long (because 4 is the cube root of 64: $64 = 4 \times 4 \times 4$). Find the perimeter by adding the four sides together: $4 + 4 + 4 + 4 = 16$.

20. C. You calculate volume by multiplying length times width times height ($V = lwh$). Because the edges are equal on a cube, each edge is 3 inches (because $3 \times 3 \times 3 = 27$). The area of one face of the cube is $3 \times 3 = 9$ square inches, and because a cube has 6 sides, you multiply 9×6 to find the surface area of the cube, 54 square inches.

21. C. $(x^3)^3$ is the same as $(x^3)(x^3)(x^3)$. If two exponents have the same base, you multiply them by keeping the base and adding the exponents together: $(x^3)(x^3)(x^3) = x^{3+3+3} = x^9$.

22. D. $4!$ (4 factorial) $= 4 \times 3 \times 2 \times 1 = 24$.

23. B. You start with $a^3 + b^3 = a^3 + x^3$. To solve, subtract a^3 from both sides of the equation and then take the cube root:

$$a^3 + b^3 = a^3 + x^3$$
$$b^3 = x^3$$
$$\sqrt[3]{b^3} = \sqrt[3]{x^3}$$
$$b = x$$

24. B. The formula to find the sum of a finite arithmetic sequence is $S = \frac{n}{2}(a+b)$, where n is the number of terms, a is the first term in the sequence, and b is the last term in the sequence. In this case, there are 300 terms (n), and the first term is 1 and the final term is 300.

$$S = \frac{n}{2}(a+b)$$
$$= \frac{300}{2}(1+300)$$
$$= 150(301)$$
$$= 45{,}150$$

25. B. $\left(y^2\right)^3$ is the same as $\left(y^2\right)\left(y^2\right)\left(y^2\right)$. Multiply exponents with the same base by keeping the base and adding the exponents: $\left(y^2\right)\left(y^2\right)\left(y^2\right) = y^{2+2+2} = y^6$. The second $\left(y^2\right)$ in the equation cannot be added into the first term because now they are not like terms, so the answer is Choice (B), $y^6 + y^2$.

Subtest 6: Electronics Information Answers

If you're having difficulty defining the difference between AC and DC, you may want to spend some additional time studying basic electronic information. Reviewing Chapter 16 can help. You can also wrap your wires around the practice questions in that chapter as well.

On the other hand, you may not be interested in a military job that requires a decent score on this subtest (see Appendix A), in which case, try not to worry too much. Your main goal is to score well in all areas of the ASVAB. The better you do on each subtest, the more desirable you become as a candidate for all the available jobs.

1. **A.** A multimeter includes several pieces of test equipment, including an ammeter, which measures inline current.

2. **A.** Rotor bars are only on AC induction motors, not DC motors.

3. **A.** NTSC stands for National Television System Committee and, although it's gradually being replaced by ATSC (Advanced Television Systems Committee), NTSC is currently the broadcast standard in the U.S. Choice (B) is incorrect because RGB stands for red, green, and blue — the colors of light used to create an image. Although most televisions use this standard, it is not a broadcast standard. Choice (C) is incorrect because SECAM (*Séquentiel-couleur avec mémoire*, or sequential color with memory) is a standard used in other countries. Choice (D) is RTSC, which stands for Raytheon Technical Services Company and is therefore not the correct answer.

4. **A.** In a closed circuit, one terminal is always positive, and the other is always negative.

5. **C.** Amperes (or amps) are the unit of measure of electric current. Hertz is the unit of measurement of frequency, not current. Current equals voltage divided by resistance. Resistance is measured in ohms. Therefore, neither voltage nor ohms can be the unit of measure for current.

6. **B.** The symbol is a fuse. Fuses are designed to *blow* (melt) if the current flowing through them exceeds a specified value.

7. **C.** This is code prescribed by the NEC (National Electric Code). Outlets within 6 feet of a sink need to be GFCI protected for safety reasons.

8. **A.** The symbol is a lamp. A *lamp* is a transducer that converts electrical energy to light.

9. **C.** Conventional circuit breaker handles have three positions: on, off, and trip. When tripped, the handle moves between the on and off positions. To reset the breaker, move the handle to the off position and then to the on position.

10. **D.** The smaller the wire, the larger the number.

11. **D.** Plastic does not conduct, and wood is a poor conductor. Aluminum is a good conductor but not better than copper.

12. **A.** A series circuit has only one path, so if you break the circuit's path at any point, electricity stops flowing. An example of a series circuit is a string of Christmas lights that no longer works if a single bulb burns out.

13. **B.** I (current) = Power (watts) ÷ Effort (volts). In this case, $I = 1{,}200 \div 120 = 10$ amperes.

14. **D.** *Potential* equals voltage; *low potential* is anything less than 600 watts.

15. **D.** Glass is an insulator. Other insulators include plastics, paper, and rubber.

16. **A.** Ground wires are always green.

17. **C.** Amplitude modulation (AM) was the first type of audio modulation to be used in radio. It works well with high frequency (HF) and Morse code.

18. **A.** Silver is a better conductor, but it's more brittle than copper and more expensive.

19. **D.** Oscillators produce high frequencies. An *amplifier* changes the amplitude of a signal. A *regulator* is a circuit that maintains a constant voltage. A *transformer* is a device that changes (transforms) the voltage at its input side to a different voltage on its output side.

20. **B.** When DC is applied to an AC appliance, the amount of resistance is less, so more current flows through the wire and heat builds up.

Subtest 7: Auto & Shop Information Answers

You need to do well on this subtest to qualify for certain military jobs (see Appendix A). If you care about those jobs and you're missing more than a few questions on this subtest, it's time for more extreme measures — like taking your mother's car apart and putting it back together (or going back over Chapters 13 and 14).

1. **D.** Using too much oil is a symptom of piston ring wear.

2. **D.** Clean air filters allow your engine to breathe. Air filters remove airborne pollutants from the engine, such as microscopic dirt that can damage cylinder walls, pistons, and piston rings. They also filter out smoke, fumes, and odors. A dirty filter can decrease engine performance and cause a decrease in fuel mileage.

3. **B.** The alternator recharges (or supplies power to) the battery.

4. **A.** You can find a wishbone in a car's suspension.

5. **C.** For a non-sealed battery, if the electrolyte solution is too low, you need to add distilled water.

6. **C.** For optimum performance, you should flush an automobile's cooling system periodically.

7. **C.** In a combustion engine that has a carburetor, the purpose of the carburetor is to mix fuel and air.

8. **C.** In the world of automobile restorers, NOS stands for New Old Stock.

9. **D.** To fire, spark plugs need a very high electrical voltage, supplied by the coil and breaker.

10. **A.** The valve you use when filling your car's tires with air is a type of Schrader valve.

11. **A.** A bent frame causes improper tracking, which means that the right angle between the centerline and axles is not maintained.

12. **C.** The *H* signifies the maximum sustained speed at which the vehicle is stable.

13. **B.** When specific tightness of screws and/or bolts is required, use a torque wrench.

14. **C.** Hammer faces aren't made of glass.

15. **A.** Mallets and sledge hammers don't have claws.

16. **C.** A set of calipers is the most accurate widely used tool to measure round objects.

17. **D.** You use a round chisel to make circular cuts in metal.

18. **D.** A Stillson wrench is a type of a pipe wrench.

19. **B.** Paint will bubble if the surface you're painting has too much moisture in it.

20. **B.** A *jig* is a tool you use to control the location and/or motion of another tool.

21. **A.** Saws have one fewer tooth than they have points per inch.

22. **D.** A mineral aggregate (such as sand, gravel, or crushed stone), a binder-such as natural or synthetic cement, and water make concrete. The mix sometimes contains chemical additives as well.

23. **B.** Choice (B) is an image of a hand saw (carpentry saw), which you wouldn't use to cut metal.

24. **D.** The image is of a bolt cutter.

25. **B.** The image is of an Allen wrench.

Subtest 8: Mechanical Comprehension Answers

If you need to do well on the Mechanical Comprehension subtest (as in you're hoping for a military career that requires a score for this subtest) but you're still missing more answers than you should be, ask yourself whether your math skills need work. Go back to Chapters 6, 7, and 8 if they do. Many of the formulas you need to know for this subtest require an understanding of arithmetic and basic algebra. If the math isn't the problem, revisit Chapter 15 for more practice with Mechanical Comprehension principles.

TIP

Usually, improving your arithmetic and basic algebra skills will improve your score on the Mechanical Comprehension subtest. Improving your knowledge of physics is also beneficial. Take a look at Chapter 11.

1. **C.** A simple fixed pulley gives no mechanical advantage, although it does make work easier by directing the applied force. The mechanical advantage is 1.

2. **D.** Moving Basket A to the right counterbalances the loss of cherries from Basket B.

3. **A.** Wheel B has to make more revolutions to cover the same ground as Wheel A, so it covers the distance more slowly.

4. **C.** You can calculate psi as Pressure = Force ÷ Area. In this problem, $P = 200 \div 10 = 20$.

5. **B.** If you move Anvil A toward the center, Anvil B will move toward the ground.

6. **B.** The formula to determine mechanical advantage of an inclined plane is Length of Ramp ÷ Height of Ramp = Weight of Object ÷ Effort. Plugging in the numbers gives you

$$\frac{6}{3} = \frac{200}{E}$$
$$6E = 600$$
$$E = 100$$

7. **C.** Micrometers measure very small but not microscopic objects.

8. **C.** Reducing the weight on Side B will cause Side A to move toward the ground.

9. **D.** Objects rubbing together produce friction.

10. **A.** Normal atmospheric pressure (the average atmospheric pressure at sea level) is 14.7 psi.

11. **D.** Gears of unequal size can mesh properly as long as their teeth are of equal size.

12. **C.** Torsion springs coil or uncoil and produce a twisting action, not a direct pull; in other words, torsion springs apply torque.

13. **B.** To move a heavy object a few feet in height, the inclined plane is the most efficient device (of those listed) to use. *Note:* The mechanical advantage of an inclined plane is equal to the slope of the plane divided by the height. The longer the slope is (compared to the height), the greater the mechanical advantage will be.

14. **B.** Water expands when it freezes, possibly damaging engine components.

15. **A.** The load is closer to Anvil A, so it's carrying the greater portion of the weight.

16. **C.** All the listed parts remain stationary except the lower block.

17. **A.** Apply the leverage formula: Length of Effort Arm ÷ Length of Resistance Arm = Resistance Force ÷ Effort Force:

$$\frac{9}{3} = \frac{21}{E}$$
$$3 = \frac{21}{E}$$
$$3E = 21$$
$$E = 7$$

18. **C.** The valve will open each time a high point of the cam hits it. The cam has three high points, so the valve will open three times per revolution.

19. **A.** Closing only Valves 3 and 4 keeps the water from leaving the tank.

20. **C.** Gears in mesh always turn in opposite directions.

21. **B.** If Gear 1 turns at 10 rpm, then Gear 2, which is half the size, turns twice as fast, at a rate of 20 rpm.

22. **A.** Opening Valves 1, 2, 4, and 8 allows the fuel to travel through the filters. Opening Valves 1, 2, and 3 doesn't allow the fuel to travel through Filter D. Opening Valves 6, 7, and 8 doesn't allow the fuel to travel through the filters. Opening Valves 4, 6, and 7 doesn't allow fuel to travel to Reservoir B.

23. **B.** A yellow flame indicates too much fuel or not enough air. More air should be allowed to enter and mix with the gas. Thus, the fuel–air mixture is too rich.

24. **A.** The float measures the water level in the tank. If the tank overflows, the float is probably defective.

25. **C.** The 20-pound anvil and the 4-pound board weigh 24 pounds total or, divided by 2, 12 pounds per scale.

Subtest 9: Assembling Objects Answers

So far, only the Navy has elected to use scores from the Assembling Objects subtest and only for a few jobs. If you're planning to join the Navy and you're interested in a Navy career that requires a score on this subtest (see Appendix A), review Chapter 17 for help on improving your score.

TIP

Sometimes the fastest (and most accurate) way to choose the right answer on Assembling Objects questions is to eliminate choices that can't be right. You can always strategically determine the correct answer if it's not obvious right away.

1. **B.** Pay attention to where the points are in the original diagram. Point A is located on one of the three spikes in the uppermost figure, and Point B is located near the center of the triangle with a line extending at a 90-degree angle from its shortest side. You can rule out Choices (A), (C), and (D) because of the line coming from Point B.

2. **A.** Match each possible answer with the figures in the original diagram. Choices (B), (C), and (D) don't depict the original figures.

3. **C.** Point A is attached to a line that leaves the X-shaped figure on what's depicted as the right side. Rotate the X-shaped figure about 45 degrees and rotate the figure containing Point B 180 degrees, and you'll have Choice (C). Choices (A) and (D) can't be right; Point A's line comes out of the figure at the wrong angle. Choice (B) is incorrect because it shows Point A directly on the shape.

4. **D.** Each of the answer choices you're given in this problem is in the shape of a double-lined heart, so look at the shape inside the heart. The only one that matches that extra shape is Choice (D).

5. **C.** You can immediately rule out Choices (B) and (D) because the figure containing Point A is inverted in both of them. (Assembling Objects questions feature two-dimensional figures, not three-dimensional figures!) Choice (A) is wrong because the figure containing Point B has the point on the wrong side, which leaves you with Choice (C), a rotated and connected version of the original figures.

6. **A.** Choices (B), (C), and (D) are essentially the same, but the lines that enclose each figure are missing from the original image. That leaves you one choice: Choice (A).

7. **B.** Check out the locations of Point A and Point B. Point A comes out of the first amoeba (they look like amoebas, don't they?) through its rounded top. Point B is attached to the second one in a specific spot, too. The only choice that features accurate depictions of the points is Choice (B).

8. **C.** You need to make sure the pieces of this figure fit together properly, like the pieces of a puzzle. The easiest way may be to count the shapes (there are four) in the original diagram and compare them to each of the answer choices. Choices (A), (B), and (D) each only show three puzzle pieces. The only one that shows all four (and happens to be the correct answer) is Choice (C).

9. **D.** If you start by paying attention to the points and the lines that are attached to them, you'll see that Point A's line comes right out of the point of the triangle. You can fast-forward through all the other answers and skip to Choice (D), which is the only one that depicts the line coming from the triangle in the correct place.

10. **D.** Do some detective work and compare the shapes in the original diagram with those in the answer choices. Choice (A) shows six shapes, and only one of the shapes depicted matches with one in the original diagram. Choice (B) shows eight shapes, and none of them match the original shapes. Choice (C) doesn't match any of them, which leaves you with only one possible answer: Choice (D).

11. **C.** Look at where the points lie on each of the original figures, and pay attention to where the lines exit the figures, too. You can rule out Choices (A), (B), and (D) immediately because the points are in the wrong places on each figure.

12. **B.** Match up the shapes in the original figure and those in each answer choice. Choice (A) depicts a few shapes that don't appear in the original diagram, and so does Choice (C). Choice (D) doesn't add up to what you'd get by rearranging the original figures, but Choice (B) does.

13. **A.** Each figure in the answer choices depicts Point A in the correct place, but if you look closely, you'll see that the figure Point A is on is inverted in Choices (B) and (D). You can rule out the final incorrect choice by noting where the line from Point B extends from the shape — it's right through the middle of the angle, which means Choice (C) is wrong. The only possible answer is Choice (A).

14. **B.** Glance at the question, and then look at each answer choice. All the answer choices require the shapes to be identical in size and shape, but that's not the case with the original figures. For example, in Choice (A), you'd need to have five equally sized triangles to make the figure work, and Choice (C) is the same; it's simply rotated. Choice (D) also requires you to have four identical shapes, leaving Choice (B) as the correct answer.

15. **D.** Choices (A), (B), and (C) are wrong, although you'll have to look closely to determine why. Choice (A) is wrong because of the angle at which each line extends from each figure and because the figure that contains Point B is inverted. Choice (B) is incorrect because the figure with Point A in its center is inverted rather than simply rotated, and Choice (C) is wrong because the line coming from Point A comes from the top of the cylinder, not out of its side.

16. **D.** This question simply asks you to match the original shapes with those in the answer choices. Compare each and you'll see that the only figure that contains each of the shapes is Choice (D).

17. **C.** Put a big mental X over Choice (B), because it's obviously wrong (look at the thinnest wavy shape inside the figure, and you'll see that it doesn't match the one in the diagram). That means Choice (D) is wrong, too. Where did the largest shape in Choice (A) come from? It's not in the original diagram, which means you'd be wrong if you picked that one. But you'd be right if you picked Choice (C), because all the shapes in that figure match those in the original figure.

18. **B.** You'll have to wrap your brain around rotating versus inverting for this problem. Choice (D) is clearly wrong because Point A is in the wrong place, so just focus on Choices (A), (B), and (C). Point B is on the right side of the original figure, which looks like an intersection; it's on the southeast side, if that helps you visualize it. Tilt your head if you have to; you'll see that Choice (A) can't be correct because in that figure, Point B is on the northwest side of the intersection. Choice (C) shows the point in the northwest quadrant, too, which means only Choice (B) is correct.

19. **C.** This puzzle question is tough, so the best way to solve it is by matching the shapes in each answer choice with those in the original diagram. Start with the kite on the upper right of the original figure (sometimes it's easiest to start with shapes that are clearly out of place among the rest). The only figure it appears in is Choice (C). For the record, you could also base your decision on the two thin triangles in the original depiction; they also appear only in Choice (C).

20. **C.** Point A on the rainbow (you don't see a rainbow?) lies on the end of the center line in the figure, so forget about Choices (B) and (D). Now look at the lowercase *d.* In Choice (A), you're looking at a lowercase *b,* and you know that Assembling Objects questions want you to rotate, *not invert,* figures; that means the correct answer is Choice (C).

21. **A.** The crafty test-question writers who work on the ASVAB will throw plenty of these puzzle problems your way, so use the tried-and-true matching strategy. The only figure among the answer choices that depicts the four-sided, angular shape you see in the original diagram is Choice (A).

22. D. The pentagon in this figure isn't going to help you; whether you invert it, twist it, or turn it, Point B will always be in the right place. The other figure — the one containing Point A — is what will lead you to the right answer. Choice (C) is a no-go (that's military slang for "failure") because the point is in the wrong place. Choices (A) and (B) are also wrong, because the figure containing Point A is inverted, not rotated.

23. C. If you look at each of the answer choices, you'll see that there's an odd shape in each; it's one that resembles an apple core, and it occurs in the middle of each diagram, where the circles overlap. Compare the similar shape in the original diagram with each of the answer choices, and you'll see that it appears only in Choice (C).

24. B. Choices (A), (B), and (D) can't be right because of where Point A lies on the M-shaped figure, so eliminate those from the pool right away. The only one left is Choice (B), which shows Point A in the correct spot on the figure.

25. D. The odd figure out among the triangles is the trapezoid, so look through the answer choices to find it. The only one that contains it is Choice (D), which is the correct answer.

Chapter 22
Practice Exam 3

I suggest you take the third practice exam at least a week (or more, if you're following the study timeline outlined in Appendix B) before you're scheduled to take the real ASVAB. Use it to refresh your memory of the material or to increase your knowledge on any of the subtests that you have to do better on than you've been doing.

REMEMBER

Don't forget to use the test-taking strategies and the guessing tips in each of the subtest chapters earlier in this book. Chapter 3 provides additional information on how to improve your score just by using smart test-taking strategies.

This sample test features nine subtests and follows the same format as the actual paper–and–pencil ASVAB. To get the most out of this sample test, take it under the same conditions as the real ASVAB:

>> Allow yourself about 3 hours to take the entire exam, and take the whole thing at one time.

>> Find a quiet place where you won't be interrupted.

>> Bring a timer that you can set for various lengths of time, some scratch paper, and a pencil.

>> At the start of each subtest, set your timer for the specified period of time. Don't go on to the next section until the timer has gone off, and don't go back to a previous section. If you finish early, check your work for that section only.

>> Use the answer sheet that's provided.

>> Don't take a break during any subtest. You can take a short one- or two-minute break between subtests if you need it.

After you complete the entire test, check your answers against the answer keys and explanations in Chapter 23. Then compare the results to your results on Practice Exams 1 and 2. You should see some improvement.

Answer Sheet for Practice Exam 3

Subtest 1: General Science

1. Ⓐ Ⓑ Ⓒ Ⓓ   6. Ⓐ Ⓑ Ⓒ Ⓓ   11. Ⓐ Ⓑ Ⓒ Ⓓ   16. Ⓐ Ⓑ Ⓒ Ⓓ   21. Ⓐ Ⓑ Ⓒ Ⓓ
2. Ⓐ Ⓑ Ⓒ Ⓓ   7. Ⓐ Ⓑ Ⓒ Ⓓ   12. Ⓐ Ⓑ Ⓒ Ⓓ   17. Ⓐ Ⓑ Ⓒ Ⓓ   22. Ⓐ Ⓑ Ⓒ Ⓓ
3. Ⓐ Ⓑ Ⓒ Ⓓ   8. Ⓐ Ⓑ Ⓒ Ⓓ   13. Ⓐ Ⓑ Ⓒ Ⓓ   18. Ⓐ Ⓑ Ⓒ Ⓓ   23. Ⓐ Ⓑ Ⓒ Ⓓ
4. Ⓐ Ⓑ Ⓒ Ⓓ   9. Ⓐ Ⓑ Ⓒ Ⓓ   14. Ⓐ Ⓑ Ⓒ Ⓓ   19. Ⓐ Ⓑ Ⓒ Ⓓ   24. Ⓐ Ⓑ Ⓒ Ⓓ
5. Ⓐ Ⓑ Ⓒ Ⓓ   10. Ⓐ Ⓑ Ⓒ Ⓓ   15. Ⓐ Ⓑ Ⓒ Ⓓ   20. Ⓐ Ⓑ Ⓒ Ⓓ   25. Ⓐ Ⓑ Ⓒ Ⓓ

Subtest 2: Arithmetic Reasoning

1. Ⓐ Ⓑ Ⓒ Ⓓ   7. Ⓐ Ⓑ Ⓒ Ⓓ   13. Ⓐ Ⓑ Ⓒ Ⓓ   19. Ⓐ Ⓑ Ⓒ Ⓓ   25. Ⓐ Ⓑ Ⓒ Ⓓ
2. Ⓐ Ⓑ Ⓒ Ⓓ   8. Ⓐ Ⓑ Ⓒ Ⓓ   14. Ⓐ Ⓑ Ⓒ Ⓓ   20. Ⓐ Ⓑ Ⓒ Ⓓ   26. Ⓐ Ⓑ Ⓒ Ⓓ
3. Ⓐ Ⓑ Ⓒ Ⓓ   9. Ⓐ Ⓑ Ⓒ Ⓓ   15. Ⓐ Ⓑ Ⓒ Ⓓ   21. Ⓐ Ⓑ Ⓒ Ⓓ   27. Ⓐ Ⓑ Ⓒ Ⓓ
4. Ⓐ Ⓑ Ⓒ Ⓓ   10. Ⓐ Ⓑ Ⓒ Ⓓ   16. Ⓐ Ⓑ Ⓒ Ⓓ   22. Ⓐ Ⓑ Ⓒ Ⓓ   28. Ⓐ Ⓑ Ⓒ Ⓓ
5. Ⓐ Ⓑ Ⓒ Ⓓ   11. Ⓐ Ⓑ Ⓒ Ⓓ   17. Ⓐ Ⓑ Ⓒ Ⓓ   23. Ⓐ Ⓑ Ⓒ Ⓓ   29. Ⓐ Ⓑ Ⓒ Ⓓ
6. Ⓐ Ⓑ Ⓒ Ⓓ   12. Ⓐ Ⓑ Ⓒ Ⓓ   18. Ⓐ Ⓑ Ⓒ Ⓓ   24. Ⓐ Ⓑ Ⓒ Ⓓ   30. Ⓐ Ⓑ Ⓒ Ⓓ

Subtest 3: Word Knowledge

1. Ⓐ Ⓑ Ⓒ Ⓓ   8. Ⓐ Ⓑ Ⓒ Ⓓ   15. Ⓐ Ⓑ Ⓒ Ⓓ   22. Ⓐ Ⓑ Ⓒ Ⓓ   29. Ⓐ Ⓑ Ⓒ Ⓓ
2. Ⓐ Ⓑ Ⓒ Ⓓ   9. Ⓐ Ⓑ Ⓒ Ⓓ   16. Ⓐ Ⓑ Ⓒ Ⓓ   23. Ⓐ Ⓑ Ⓒ Ⓓ   30. Ⓐ Ⓑ Ⓒ Ⓓ
3. Ⓐ Ⓑ Ⓒ Ⓓ   10. Ⓐ Ⓑ Ⓒ Ⓓ   17. Ⓐ Ⓑ Ⓒ Ⓓ   24. Ⓐ Ⓑ Ⓒ Ⓓ   31. Ⓐ Ⓑ Ⓒ Ⓓ
4. Ⓐ Ⓑ Ⓒ Ⓓ   11. Ⓐ Ⓑ Ⓒ Ⓓ   18. Ⓐ Ⓑ Ⓒ Ⓓ   25. Ⓐ Ⓑ Ⓒ Ⓓ   32. Ⓐ Ⓑ Ⓒ Ⓓ
5. Ⓐ Ⓑ Ⓒ Ⓓ   12. Ⓐ Ⓑ Ⓒ Ⓓ   19. Ⓐ Ⓑ Ⓒ Ⓓ   26. Ⓐ Ⓑ Ⓒ Ⓓ   33. Ⓐ Ⓑ Ⓒ Ⓓ
6. Ⓐ Ⓑ Ⓒ Ⓓ   13. Ⓐ Ⓑ Ⓒ Ⓓ   20. Ⓐ Ⓑ Ⓒ Ⓓ   27. Ⓐ Ⓑ Ⓒ Ⓓ   34. Ⓐ Ⓑ Ⓒ Ⓓ
7. Ⓐ Ⓑ Ⓒ Ⓓ   14. Ⓐ Ⓑ Ⓒ Ⓓ   21. Ⓐ Ⓑ Ⓒ Ⓓ   28. Ⓐ Ⓑ Ⓒ Ⓓ   35. Ⓐ Ⓑ Ⓒ Ⓓ

Subtest 4: Paragraph Comprehension

1. Ⓐ Ⓑ Ⓒ Ⓓ   4. Ⓐ Ⓑ Ⓒ Ⓓ   7. Ⓐ Ⓑ Ⓒ Ⓓ   10. Ⓐ Ⓑ Ⓒ Ⓓ   13. Ⓐ Ⓑ Ⓒ Ⓓ
2. Ⓐ Ⓑ Ⓒ Ⓓ   5. Ⓐ Ⓑ Ⓒ Ⓓ   8. Ⓐ Ⓑ Ⓒ Ⓓ   11. Ⓐ Ⓑ Ⓒ Ⓓ   14. Ⓐ Ⓑ Ⓒ Ⓓ
3. Ⓐ Ⓑ Ⓒ Ⓓ   6. Ⓐ Ⓑ Ⓒ Ⓓ   9. Ⓐ Ⓑ Ⓒ Ⓓ   12. Ⓐ Ⓑ Ⓒ Ⓓ   15. Ⓐ Ⓑ Ⓒ Ⓓ

Subtest 5: Mathematics Knowledge

1. Ⓐ Ⓑ Ⓒ Ⓓ   6. Ⓐ Ⓑ Ⓒ Ⓓ   11. Ⓐ Ⓑ Ⓒ Ⓓ   16. Ⓐ Ⓑ Ⓒ Ⓓ   21. Ⓐ Ⓑ Ⓒ Ⓓ
2. Ⓐ Ⓑ Ⓒ Ⓓ   7. Ⓐ Ⓑ Ⓒ Ⓓ   12. Ⓐ Ⓑ Ⓒ Ⓓ   17. Ⓐ Ⓑ Ⓒ Ⓓ   22. Ⓐ Ⓑ Ⓒ Ⓓ
3. Ⓐ Ⓑ Ⓒ Ⓓ   8. Ⓐ Ⓑ Ⓒ Ⓓ   13. Ⓐ Ⓑ Ⓒ Ⓓ   18. Ⓐ Ⓑ Ⓒ Ⓓ   23. Ⓐ Ⓑ Ⓒ Ⓓ
4. Ⓐ Ⓑ Ⓒ Ⓓ   9. Ⓐ Ⓑ Ⓒ Ⓓ   14. Ⓐ Ⓑ Ⓒ Ⓓ   19. Ⓐ Ⓑ Ⓒ Ⓓ   24. Ⓐ Ⓑ Ⓒ Ⓓ
5. Ⓐ Ⓑ Ⓒ Ⓓ   10. Ⓐ Ⓑ Ⓒ Ⓓ   15. Ⓐ Ⓑ Ⓒ Ⓓ   20. Ⓐ Ⓑ Ⓒ Ⓓ   25. Ⓐ Ⓑ Ⓒ Ⓓ

Subtest 6: Electronics Information

1. Ⓐ Ⓑ Ⓒ Ⓓ   5. Ⓐ Ⓑ Ⓒ Ⓓ   9. Ⓐ Ⓑ Ⓒ Ⓓ   13. Ⓐ Ⓑ Ⓒ Ⓓ   17. Ⓐ Ⓑ Ⓒ Ⓓ
2. Ⓐ Ⓑ Ⓒ Ⓓ   6. Ⓐ Ⓑ Ⓒ Ⓓ   10. Ⓐ Ⓑ Ⓒ Ⓓ   14. Ⓐ Ⓑ Ⓒ Ⓓ   18. Ⓐ Ⓑ Ⓒ Ⓓ
3. Ⓐ Ⓑ Ⓒ Ⓓ   7. Ⓐ Ⓑ Ⓒ Ⓓ   11. Ⓐ Ⓑ Ⓒ Ⓓ   15. Ⓐ Ⓑ Ⓒ Ⓓ   19. Ⓐ Ⓑ Ⓒ Ⓓ
4. Ⓐ Ⓑ Ⓒ Ⓓ   8. Ⓐ Ⓑ Ⓒ Ⓓ   12. Ⓐ Ⓑ Ⓒ Ⓓ   16. Ⓐ Ⓑ Ⓒ Ⓓ   20. Ⓐ Ⓑ Ⓒ Ⓓ

Subtest 7: Auto & Shop Information

1. Ⓐ Ⓑ Ⓒ Ⓓ	6. Ⓐ Ⓑ Ⓒ Ⓓ	11. Ⓐ Ⓑ Ⓒ Ⓓ	16. Ⓐ Ⓑ Ⓒ Ⓓ	21. Ⓐ Ⓑ Ⓒ Ⓓ
2. Ⓐ Ⓑ Ⓒ Ⓓ	7. Ⓐ Ⓑ Ⓒ Ⓓ	12. Ⓐ Ⓑ Ⓒ Ⓓ	17. Ⓐ Ⓑ Ⓒ Ⓓ	22. Ⓐ Ⓑ Ⓒ Ⓓ
3. Ⓐ Ⓑ Ⓒ Ⓓ	8. Ⓐ Ⓑ Ⓒ Ⓓ	13. Ⓐ Ⓑ Ⓒ Ⓓ	18. Ⓐ Ⓑ Ⓒ Ⓓ	23. Ⓐ Ⓑ Ⓒ Ⓓ
4. Ⓐ Ⓑ Ⓒ Ⓓ	9. Ⓐ Ⓑ Ⓒ Ⓓ	14. Ⓐ Ⓑ Ⓒ Ⓓ	19. Ⓐ Ⓑ Ⓒ Ⓓ	24. Ⓐ Ⓑ Ⓒ Ⓓ
5. Ⓐ Ⓑ Ⓒ Ⓓ	10. Ⓐ Ⓑ Ⓒ Ⓓ	15. Ⓐ Ⓑ Ⓒ Ⓓ	20. Ⓐ Ⓑ Ⓒ Ⓓ	25. Ⓐ Ⓑ Ⓒ Ⓓ

Subtest 8: Mechanical Comprehension

1. Ⓐ Ⓑ Ⓒ Ⓓ	6. Ⓐ Ⓑ Ⓒ Ⓓ	11. Ⓐ Ⓑ Ⓒ Ⓓ	16. Ⓐ Ⓑ Ⓒ Ⓓ	21. Ⓐ Ⓑ Ⓒ Ⓓ
2. Ⓐ Ⓑ Ⓒ Ⓓ	7. Ⓐ Ⓑ Ⓒ Ⓓ	12. Ⓐ Ⓑ Ⓒ Ⓓ	17. Ⓐ Ⓑ Ⓒ Ⓓ	22. Ⓐ Ⓑ Ⓒ Ⓓ
3. Ⓐ Ⓑ Ⓒ Ⓓ	8. Ⓐ Ⓑ Ⓒ Ⓓ	13. Ⓐ Ⓑ Ⓒ Ⓓ	18. Ⓐ Ⓑ Ⓒ Ⓓ	23. Ⓐ Ⓑ Ⓒ Ⓓ
4. Ⓐ Ⓑ Ⓒ Ⓓ	9. Ⓐ Ⓑ Ⓒ Ⓓ	14. Ⓐ Ⓑ Ⓒ Ⓓ	19. Ⓐ Ⓑ Ⓒ Ⓓ	24. Ⓐ Ⓑ Ⓒ Ⓓ
5. Ⓐ Ⓑ Ⓒ Ⓓ	10. Ⓐ Ⓑ Ⓒ Ⓓ	15. Ⓐ Ⓑ Ⓒ Ⓓ	20. Ⓐ Ⓑ Ⓒ Ⓓ	25. Ⓐ Ⓑ Ⓒ Ⓓ

Subtest 9: Assembling Objects

1. Ⓐ Ⓑ Ⓒ Ⓓ	6. Ⓐ Ⓑ Ⓒ Ⓓ	11. Ⓐ Ⓑ Ⓒ Ⓓ	16. Ⓐ Ⓑ Ⓒ Ⓓ	21. Ⓐ Ⓑ Ⓒ Ⓓ
2. Ⓐ Ⓑ Ⓒ Ⓓ	7. Ⓐ Ⓑ Ⓒ Ⓓ	12. Ⓐ Ⓑ Ⓒ Ⓓ	17. Ⓐ Ⓑ Ⓒ Ⓓ	22. Ⓐ Ⓑ Ⓒ Ⓓ
3. Ⓐ Ⓑ Ⓒ Ⓓ	8. Ⓐ Ⓑ Ⓒ Ⓓ	13. Ⓐ Ⓑ Ⓒ Ⓓ	18. Ⓐ Ⓑ Ⓒ Ⓓ	23. Ⓐ Ⓑ Ⓒ Ⓓ
4. Ⓐ Ⓑ Ⓒ Ⓓ	9. Ⓐ Ⓑ Ⓒ Ⓓ	14. Ⓐ Ⓑ Ⓒ Ⓓ	19. Ⓐ Ⓑ Ⓒ Ⓓ	24. Ⓐ Ⓑ Ⓒ Ⓓ
5. Ⓐ Ⓑ Ⓒ Ⓓ	10. Ⓐ Ⓑ Ⓒ Ⓓ	15. Ⓐ Ⓑ Ⓒ Ⓓ	20. Ⓐ Ⓑ Ⓒ Ⓓ	25. Ⓐ Ⓑ Ⓒ Ⓓ

Subtest 1: General Science

TIME: 11 minutes for 25 questions

DIRECTIONS: This test challenges your knowledge of general science principles usually covered in high school classes. Pick the best answer for each question and then mark the space on your answer sheet that corresponds to the question number and the letter indicating your choice.

1. The moon completes a revolution around Earth approximately every

   (A) 28 days.

   (B) 365 days.

   (C) 24 hours.

   (D) 7 days.

2. Carcinogens are chemicals that cause

   (A) high blood pressure.

   (B) gene mutations.

   (C) blood clots.

   (D) diabetes.

3. A paramecium is

   (A) a one-celled organism.

   (B) algae.

   (C) bacteria.

   (D) a many-celled organism.

4. What substance is essential for the function of the thyroid gland?

   (A) potassium chloride

   (B) hemoglobin

   (C) calcium

   (D) iodine

5. The brainstem controls

   (A) vision.

   (B) voluntary muscle movements.

   (C) your sense of balance.

   (D) some involuntary activities.

6. Which element is the most abundant one in the atmosphere?

   (A) oxygen

   (B) nitrogen

   (C) helium

   (D) hydrogen

7. Minerals are necessary for

   (A) respiration.

   (B) eliminating waste.

   (C) preventing night blindness.

   (D) metabolic function.

8. What's the only metallic element found as a liquid at room temperature?

   (A) bromine

   (B) tellurium

   (C) mercury

   (D) silver

9. Which of the following isn't a type of telescope?

   (A) reflecting

   (B) convexing

   (C) refracting

   (D) catadioptric

10. A dekagram

    (A) is larger than a kilogram.

    (B) is smaller than a kilogram.

    (C) is the same as a kilogram.

    (D) doesn't exist.

GO ON TO NEXT PAGE

11. The aurora borealis can be seen only in the
    (A) winter.
    (B) summer.
    (C) Southern Hemisphere.
    (D) Northern Hemisphere.

12. The three important properties of sound waves are
    (A) wavelength, speed, and crest.
    (B) speed, frequency, and reflection.
    (C) wavelength, frequency, and vibration.
    (D) wavelength, frequency, and speed.

13. Between which two planets can most of the asteroids in the solar system be found?
    (A) Mars and Jupiter
    (B) Saturn and Jupiter
    (C) Earth and Mars
    (D) Mercury and Venus

14. At room temperature, an element can be a
    (A) gas.
    (B) liquid or gas.
    (C) gas or solid.
    (D) liquid, gas, or solid.

15. The elements hydrogen and helium comprise what percentage of almost all matter in the universe?
    (A) 75%
    (B) 82%
    (C) 90%
    (D) 98%

16. Compounds are created when
    (A) atoms of two or more like elements are combined.
    (B) atoms of two or more different elements are combined.
    (C) two or more molecules are combined.
    (D) a molecule decomposes.

17. What theory suggests the universe will come to an end when its ever-increasing rate of expansion causes all matter to fly apart?
    (A) The Big Rip
    (B) The Big Bang
    (C) The Big Crunch
    (D) The Big Easy

18. A watt-hour measures
    (A) the amount of work performed or generated.
    (B) the number of electrons moving past a specific point.
    (C) resistance.
    (D) voltage.

19. Which of the following planets, known as *gas giants*, has no rings?
    (A) Neptune
    (B) Jupiter
    (C) Uranus
    (D) They all have rings.

20. Gas particles move
    (A) more slowly than liquid particles.
    (B) more slowly than solid particles.
    (C) more quickly than liquid particles.
    (D) at the same rate as all other particles.

21. Absolute zero is
    (A) 0 degrees Fahrenheit.
    (B) 0 degrees Celsius.
    (C) −273 degrees Celsius.
    (D) −32 degrees Fahrenheit.

22. Radiology is employed when doing which of the following?
    (A) using a Magnetic Resonance Imaging machine
    (B) using a blood pressure cuff
    (C) blood typing
    (D) breathing

23. Which of the following statements is not true?

(A) The human female chin is usually more rounded or pointed than the human male chin.

(B) The human female pelvis is usually narrower than the human male pelvis.

(C) The human male skull is usually larger than the human female skull.

(D) The human male skull has a larger brow ridge than the human female skull.

24. A lunar eclipse occurs when

(A) Earth moves into the moon's shadow.

(B) the sun blocks the moon from view.

(C) Earth moves into the sun's shadow.

(D) the moon moves into Earth's shadow.

25. What chemical can be used to detect blood, even if it's been wiped from a surface?

(A) luminol

(B) cyanide

(C) ninhydrin

(D) alcohol

Subtest 2: Arithmetic Reasoning

TIME: 36 minutes for 30 questions

DIRECTIONS: This test is about arithmetic. Each question is followed by four possible answers. Decide which answer is correct and then mark the space on your answer sheet that has the same number and letter as your choice. Calculators are not permitted. Use scratch paper for any figuring you need to do.

1. A baker sells a dozen donuts for $3.99. The cost to make three donuts is $0.45. How much is the total profit on 5 dozen donuts?

(A) $17.70

(B) $13.20

(C) $2.19

(D) $10.95

2. Your piggy bank contains $19.75 in dimes and quarters. There are 100 coins in all. How many dimes are there?

(A) 25

(B) 30

(C) 35

(D) 40

3. A bricklayer charges $8 per square foot to lay a patio. How much would it cost for the bricklayer to lay a 12-foot-by-16-foot patio?

(A) $960

(B) $192

(C) $224

(D) $1,536

4. Terry earns three times more per hour than Tim. Tim earns $2 more per hour than Angie. As a group, they earn $43 per hour. What's Angie's hourly wage?

(A) $7.00

(B) $8.00

(C) $9.00

(D) $10.00

5. If four people can run eight machines, how many machines can two people run?

(A) 2

(B) 4

(C) 1

(D) 3

6. The price of daily admission at an amusement park is $36. The park sells an unlimited season pass for $240. How many trips would you need to make with the season pass in order for it to cost less than paying the daily admission rate?

(A) 6

(B) 7

(C) 8

(D) 9

7. A plumber needs four lengths of pipe, each 3 feet, 6 inches long. Pipes are sold by the foot. How many feet does he need to buy?

(A) 15

(B) 16

(C) 14

(D) 12

8. The product of two consecutive odd numbers is 399. What are the numbers?

(A) 17 and 19

(B) 19 and 21

(C) 21 and 23

(D) 25 and 27

9. A personal trainer earns a 65% commission on her training sales. If she sells $530 worth of training, how much commission does she make?

(A) $874.50

(B) $34.45

(C) $344.50

(D) $185.50

10. A rectangle is 1 inch longer than it is wide. Its diagonal is 5 inches. What's the width of the rectangle?

(A) 2 inches

(B) 3 inches

(C) 4 inches

(D) 5 inches

11. A treasure map is drawn to a scale of 2 inches equals 3 miles. On the map, the distance between Point A and X-marks-the-spot is $9\frac{1}{2}$ inches. How many actual miles does this represent?

   (A) $20\frac{1}{2}$ miles

   (B) $14\frac{1}{4}$ miles

   (C) $6\frac{1}{3}$ miles

   (D) 19 miles

12. A painter has painted a picture on a piece of canvas that measures 10 by 14 inches. To accommodate a frame, he has left an unpainted margin of 1 inch all the way around. What part of the canvas has been painted?

   (A) 96%

   (B) 91%

   (C) 65%

   (D) 69%

13. A dog trainer is building a rectangular dog run that measures 9 by 16 feet. If she wants to fence the perimeter of the run, how many feet of chain link fence will she need?

   (A) 144 feet

   (B) 25 feet

   (C) 32 feet

   (D) 50 feet

14. A rectangle is $1\frac{1}{2}$ times as long as it is wide. The perimeter of the rectangle is 100 inches. What's the length of the rectangle?

   (A) 20 inches

   (B) 30 inches

   (C) 40 inches

   (D) 45 inches

15. Miguel passed seven of his history quizzes and failed three. The fraction of quizzes he passed is correctly expressed as

   (A) $\frac{7}{3}$

   (B) $\frac{3}{7}$

   (C) $\frac{7}{10}$

   (D) $\frac{3}{5}$

16. A 3-yard-long ribbon was used to trim four dresses. Each dress used the same amount of ribbon. How much ribbon was used for each dress?

   (A) 1 yard

   (B) $\frac{2}{3}$ yard

   (C) $\frac{1}{2}$ yard

   (D) $\frac{3}{4}$ yard

17. Kelly bought a painting at an antiques sale for $500, and the following day she was able to sell it for an additional $30. What percentage of the sale price was her profit?

   (A) 5%

   (B) 6%

   (C) 7%

   (D) 4%

18. A bin of bolts at the hardware store contains 7 dozen bolts when full. The stock clerk is supposed to reorder bolts when the bin is $\frac{1}{6}$ full. How many bolts are in the bin when it's time to reorder?

   (A) 14 bolts

   (B) 1 bolt

   (C) 84 bolts

   (D) 12 bolts

19. Two bicyclists head toward each other from the opposite ends of Main Street, which is 6 miles long. The first biker started at 2:05 going 12 mph. The second biker began peddling 4 minutes later at a rate of 14 mph. What time will they meet?

   (A) 2:13

   (B) 2:24

   (C) 2:21

   (D) 2:34

20. A recipe calls for 8 ounces of black beans or red beans. The cheapest option to buy and use would be

   (A) two 4-ounce cans of black beans at $0.79 each.

   (B) one 8-ounce can of red beans at $1.49.

   (C) two 3-ounce cans of black beans at $0.59 each.

   (D) three 3-ounce cans of red beans at $0.65 each.

GO ON TO NEXT PAGE

21. A street vendor sells $25.70 worth of pretzels on Friday, $32.30 on Saturday, and $31.80 on Sunday. He spends a fourth of the money over the weekend. How much money does he have left?

(A) $89.80

(B) $22.45

(C) $44.90

(D) $67.35

22. A recruit has $30.00. He saw some camouflage socks for $3.95 a pair. How many pairs of socks can he buy?

(A) 9

(B) 7

(C) 6

(D) 4

23. A crate containing a puppy weighs 60 pounds, 5 ounces. The puppy weighs 43 pounds, 7 ounces. How much does the crate alone weigh?

(A) 16 pounds, 8 ounces

(B) 16 pounds, 2 ounces

(C) 17 pounds

(D) 16 pounds, 14 ounces

24. In a manufacturing plant that produces new computers, a 0.15 probability exists that a computer will be defective. If five computers are manufactured, what's the probability that all of them will be defective?

(A) 7.6

(B) 0.60

(C) 0.00042

(D) 0.000076

25. A house contains one 12-foot-x-14-foot bedroom, one 12-foot-x-10-foot bedroom, and one 8-foot-x-12-foot bedroom. What's the total amount of carpeting needed to carpet all three bedrooms?

(A) 383 square yards

(B) 128 square yards

(C) 88 square yards

(D) 43 square yards

26. Rafael can type 9 pages an hour. How long will it take him to type 126 pages?

(A) 14 hours

(B) 9 hours

(C) 7 hours

(D) 16 hours

27. In a 60-minute gym class, 48 girls want to play volleyball, but only 12 can play at a time. For each player to get the same amount of playing time, how many minutes should each person play?

(A) $1\frac{1}{2}$ minutes

(B) 6 minutes

(C) 30 minutes

(D) 15 minutes

28. The public library charges $2.00 for the first day a borrowed DVD is overdue and $1.25 for each day after that. If a person paid $8.25 in late fees, how many days was the DVD overdue?

(A) 7 days

(B) 6 days

(C) 4 days

(D) 5 days

29. A half-cup of pudding has 150 calories. The same amount of broccoli has 60 calories. How much broccoli can a person eat to equal the same number of calories in the $\frac{1}{2}$ cup of pudding?

(A) 2 cups

(B) $2\frac{1}{2}$ cups

(C) $1\frac{1}{2}$ cups

(D) $1\frac{1}{4}$ cups

30. The neighbor's dog barks at a raccoon every 15 minutes at night. If he first barks at 10 p.m., when you're trying to fall asleep, how many times will he have barked by 2 a.m., when you give up trying to sleep and decide to read a book instead?

(A) 16 times

(B) 132 times

(C) 17 times

(D) 15 times

DO NOT TURN THE PAGE UNTIL TOLD TO DO SO   STOP   DO NOT RETURN TO A PREVIOUS TEST

Subtest 3: Word Knowledge

TIME: 11 minutes for 35 questions

DIRECTIONS: This test is about the meanings of words. Each question has an underlined word. You may be asked to decide which one of the four words in the choices most nearly means the same thing as the underlined word or which one of the four words means the opposite. If the underlined word is used in a sentence, decide which of the four choices most nearly means the same thing as the underlined word as used in the context of the sentence. Mark the corresponding space on your answer sheet.

1. <u>Lackadaisical</u> most nearly means

   (A) flowerless.

   (B) listless.

   (C) promiscuous.

   (D) suitable.

2. The fruit was <u>edible</u>.

   (A) waxy

   (B) expensive

   (C) foreign

   (D) digestible

3. Universities and colleges should be designed to cater to the <u>philomaths</u>.

   (A) athletes

   (B) scholars

   (C) teachers

   (D) faculty

4. <u>Pretense</u> most nearly means

   (A) politeness.

   (B) dishonesty.

   (C) stress.

   (D) appearance.

5. At an early age Jane showed a <u>proclivity</u> for music and dancing.

   (A) predisposition

   (B) interest

   (C) dislike

   (D) fever

6. Her conversation was <u>incoherent</u>.

   (A) eloquent

   (B) succinct

   (C) unintelligible

   (D) amusing

7. The week following Joe DiMaggio's death was filled with often <u>mawkish</u> eulogies.

   (A) long

   (B) sentimental

   (C) boring

   (D) detailed

8. She <u>established</u> proof.

   (A) offered

   (B) invented

   (C) demanded

   (D) demonstrated

9. <u>Ephemeral</u> most nearly means

   (A) short-lived.

   (B) mythical.

   (C) dead.

   (D) exceptional.

10. <u>Avocation</u> most nearly means

    (A) hobby.

    (B) occupation.

    (C) vacation.

    (D) education.

11. <u>Kvetch</u> most nearly means

    (A) assert.

    (B) yell.

    (C) complain.

    (D) argue.

12. Her eyesight was <u>acute</u>.

    (A) sharp

    (B) poor

    (C) unusual

    (D) tested

GO ON TO NEXT PAGE

13. Inamorata most nearly means
    (A) boyfriend.
    (B) mistress.
    (C) best friend.
    (D) acquaintance.

14. Her thoughts on the matter were inconsequential.
    (A) profound
    (B) disturbing
    (C) irrelevant
    (D) confused

15. Debouch most nearly means
    (A) emerge.
    (B) fight.
    (C) relax.
    (D) capture.

16. He was an amateur astronomer.
    (A) veteran
    (B) novice
    (C) interested
    (D) pleased

17. She had no idea how to react to her ludic boyfriend.
    (A) playful
    (B) cheating
    (C) crazy
    (D) lazy

18. The rose was crimson.
    (A) blooming
    (B) colorful
    (C) fragrant
    (D) red

19. The word most opposite in meaning to benison is
    (A) theft.
    (B) replaceable.
    (C) curse.
    (D) heavy.

20. She was exempt from gym class.
    (A) banned
    (B) excused
    (C) tired
    (D) refreshed

21. The eldritch light of the desert can play tricks on your eyes.
    (A) bright
    (B) wavering
    (C) strange
    (D) yellow

22. Defective most nearly means
    (A) flawed.
    (B) noticeable.
    (C) rare.
    (D) durable.

23. Allot most nearly means
    (A) plow.
    (B) assign.
    (C) property.
    (D) test.

24. The doctor gave the patient a cursory examination.
    (A) in-depth
    (B) painful
    (C) unnecessary
    (D) superficial

25. Arcanum most nearly means
    (A) rare.
    (B) secret.
    (C) tangible.
    (D) false.

26. Her answer was terse.
    (A) defensive
    (B) angry
    (C) lengthy
    (D) brief

27. The <u>dulcet</u> songs of the band got the attention of the audience.

   (A) harmonious

   (B) love

   (C) jazzy

   (D) loud

28. He was arrested on a <u>misdemeanor</u> charge.

   (A) theft

   (B) serious

   (C) petty crime

   (D) bogus

29. <u>Embonpoint</u> most nearly means

   (A) plumpness.

   (B) height.

   (C) quickness.

   (D) cold.

30. He <u>concocted</u> a story about me.

   (A) told

   (B) rehearsed

   (C) invented

   (D) remembered

31. He spent his days searching fruitlessly for that <u>chimera</u>, his true self.

   (A) personality

   (B) enigma

   (C) talent

   (D) monster

32. Her <u>former</u> home was in Colorado.

   (A) previous

   (B) current

   (C) second

   (D) abandoned

33. <u>Mulct</u> most nearly means

   (A) complain.

   (B) play.

   (C) work.

   (D) fleece.

34. My voice is <u>strident</u>.

   (A) soft

   (B) melodious

   (C) harsh

   (D) baritone

35. <u>Raffish</u> most nearly means

   (A) clean.

   (B) serene.

   (C) tawdry.

   (D) expensive.

DO NOT TURN THE PAGE UNTIL TOLD TO DO SO STOP DO NOT RETURN TO A PREVIOUS TEST

Subtest 4: Paragraph Comprehension

TIME: 13 minutes for 15 questions

DIRECTIONS: This test measures your ability to understand what you read. This section includes paragraphs of reading material followed by incomplete statements or questions. Read each paragraph and select the choice that best completes the statement or answers the question. Mark your choice on your answer sheet by using the correct letter with each question number.

Because leadership is charged with bringing new ideas, methods, or solutions into use, innovation is inextricably connected with the process of being an effective leader. Innovation means change, and change requires leadership. Leaders must be the chief transformation officers in their organizations and learn everything there is to know about the change before it even takes place. Furthermore, they must learn how to deal with the emotions that result from the chaos and fear associated with change.

1. According to the passage,

   (A) leaders should resist making changes that subordinates are likely to resist.

   (B) innovation and change are distinctly different processes.

   (C) it's not necessary for the leader to know everything about a change before it's implemented.

   (D) change is often associated with panic and disorder.

Cougars are the most wide-ranging big cats in North America, inhabiting a wide variety of environments. A cougar, also called a puma or a mountain lion, lives about 18 years in the wild, can jump 20 feet (in distance) at a time, and can range 50 miles when on the prowl for food.

2. According to this passage,

   (A) a cougar isn't the same thing as a mountain lion.

   (B) cougars are an endangered species.

   (C) cougars live in many areas of North America.

   (D) cougars live only a few years in the wild.

A helping relationship refers to interactions in which the counselor makes a determined effort to contribute in a positive way to the counselee's improvement. In counseling, the counselor establishes a helping relationship by drawing on practices that help the counselee live more in harmony with himself or herself and others and with a greater self-understanding. The relationship develops because the counselee needs assistance, instruction, or understanding.

3. Which of the following statements is not supported by the passage?

   (A) Successful counseling requires developing a relationship.

   (B) Most counselees initially reject advice given by the counselor.

   (C) Counseling helps a counselee develop a greater understanding of him/herself.

   (D) Counseling relationships are developed by relying on helpful practices.

Many small cities and towns rely on volunteer fire departments to put out fires. A professional fire department, however, has more training, more expertise, and more experience in fighting fires and investigating their causes. In many cases, it's worthwhile for even very small towns to hire professional firefighters.

4. According to this passage, it's reasonable to assume that

   (A) volunteer firefighters have less training, expertise, and experience than professional firefighters.

   (B) volunteer firefighters have the skills and resources to investigate the causes of fires.

   (C) professional firefighters don't know what causes fires.

   (D) a professional fire department is cost-prohibitive for small towns.

The idea being an alarming one, he scrambled out of bed and groped his way to the window. He was obliged to rub the frost off with the sleeve of his dressing-gown before he could see anything and could see very little then. All he could make out was that it was still very foggy and extremely cold and that there was no noise of people running to and fro and making a great stir, as there unquestionably would've been if night had beaten off bright day, and taken possession of the world.

5. This story takes place

   (A) in Ireland.

   (B) on a calm summer evening.

   (C) on a winter night.

   (D) both A and C.

Epidemiology is the study of what causes diseases, injuries, and other physiological damage to humans and why such problems occur. Epidemiologists examine where and when disease outbreaks occur. By using statistics and other scientific methods, epidemiologists determine what factors affect the frequency and severity of disease patterns. The primary goal of epidemiology is to control or prevent outbreaks of disease — other goals are subordinate.

6. What would be the best title for this passage?

   (A) "Epidemiology: The Study of Disease Patterns"

   (B) "Goals for the Future of Epidemiology"

   (C) "Using Statistical Methods in Epidemiology"

   (D) "Employment Outlook for Epidemiologists"

Buddhism is a religion that must be viewed from many angles. Its original form, as preached by Gautama in India and developed in the early years succeeding and as embodied in the sacred literature of early Buddhism, isn't representative of the actual Buddhism of any land today.

7. According to this passage,

   (A) most Buddhists live in India.

   (B) Buddhist teachings have changed over the years.

   (C) Buddhism draws its teachings from early Christianity.

   (D) Buddhist temples can be found in any land of the world.

Questions 8 and 9 are based on the following passage.

Many criminal-law statutes permit more severe punishment of a person convicted of a crime if he or she intended to harm another person. For example, voluntary manslaughter carries a heavier penalty than involuntary manslaughter in most states. Planned crimes are also punished more severely than spur-of-the-moment crimes.

The problem is that juries find it difficult to know what the intent of a person was at the time he or she committed a crime. Many defendants will deny that they intended to harm the other person and claim that any harm that occurred was "accidental." The law asks too much of juries when it expects them to determine what a person was thinking. Juries should only be asked to weigh objective evidence.

8. The author of this passage would agree that

   (A) laws should not punish people based on intention.

   (B) juries aren't intelligent enough to weigh evidence.

   (C) more laws should distinguish between crimes committed with intent and crimes committed on the spur of the moment.

   (D) lawyers will lie about anything.

9. According to this passage,

   (A) most states don't distinguish between voluntary and involuntary manslaughter.

   (B) punishing people more severely for voluntary manslaughter is unconstitutional.

   (C) it's difficult for juries to determine a defendant's intentions at the time a crime was committed.

   (D) prosecutors can, through careful questioning, show a defendant's intention at the time a crime was committed.

Questions 10 through 12 are based on the following passage.

Ergonomics is the science of designing and arranging workspaces so that people and objects interact efficiently and safely. Lack of attention to ergonomics causes thousands of workers to suffer repetitive stress injury, eye fatigue, muscle soreness, and many other medical problems each year.

Adequate lighting, well-designed chairs, and clutter-free work areas contribute to effective ergonomic design. The opportunity to take short breaks every hour or two, especially for desk-bound workers, is also helpful. It's also important for workers to avoid performing the same movements over and over for hours at a time. Variety in the type of work being done can decrease the chance of injury.

10. According to this passage,

   (A) ergonomics can cause injuries.

   (B) ergonomics is about designing and arranging workspaces efficiently and safely.

   (C) ergonomics is expensive and time-consuming.

   (D) few people experience problems due to poor ergonomics.

11. According to this passage,

   (A) adequate lighting and well-designed chairs, although important, have nothing to do with ergonomics.

   (B) repetition in the type of work people do helps them accomplish their tasks safely and efficiently.

   (C) short breaks aren't important for desk-bound employees because they do little heavy labor.

   (D) ergonomic design also includes keeping work areas well-lit and clutter-free.

12. According to this passage, it's reasonable to assume that

   (A) employers should invest in ergonomic design to protect workers.

   (B) lack of ergonomic design isn't dangerous.

   (C) labor unions have opposed ergonomic design.

   (D) poor design is responsible for most employee accidents.

Questions 13 through 15 are based on the following passage.

Electricity is the most inefficient and costly way to heat a home. One kilowatt-hour of electricity creates about 3,400 British thermal units (BTUs). (BTUs are a standard heat measurement.) The price of electricity per kilowatt-hour is between $0.10 and $0.25 or between $29.35 and $73.13 per million BTUs.

In contrast, fuel oil, which produces 140,000 BTUs per gallon, costs about $8.33 to $13.89 per million BTUs. Natural gas, which produces 100,000 BTUs per therm, can be purchased for $5.00 to $22.50 per million BTUs. Oak firewood, which produces 26,000,000 BTUs per cord, costs $5.77 to $13.46 per million BTUs.

Choosing the right heating method for your home, based on the cost of fuel, may be more expensive at installation but will be cheaper in the long run.

13. According to the passage, a BTU

   (A) is an unusual method of measuring heat.

   (B) stands for "British thermal unit."

   (C) is the abbreviation for a "big thermal unit."

   (D) can heat a 9-x-12 room.

14. According to the passage,

   (A) heating with fuel oil is always cheaper than other methods.

   (B) oak firewood produces fewer BTUs per dollar than the other types of fuel.

   (C) natural gas costs more than all other fuels except oak firewood.

   (D) electricity is always the most expensive way to heat a house.

15. The title of this passage should be

   (A) "Choosing the Right Heating Method"

   (B) "Heating Methods for Houses"

   (C) "Know Your BTUs"

   (D) "Price List for Fuel"

STOP

DO NOT TURN THE PAGE UNTIL TOLD TO DO SO   DO NOT RETURN TO A PREVIOUS TEST

Subtest 5: Mathematics Knowledge

TIME: 24 minutes for 25 questions

DIRECTIONS: This section tests your ability to solve general mathematical problems. Select the correct answer from the choices given and then mark the corresponding space on your answer sheet. Use scratch paper to do any figuring.

1. If $y = 6$, then $2y \times y =$
   - (A) 12
   - (B) 72
   - (C) 18
   - (D) 242

2. If $0.05x = 1$, then x equals
   - (A) $\frac{1}{20}$
   - (B) 20
   - (C) 10
   - (D) 5

3. Simplify: $\sqrt{25x^2}$
   - (A) x
   - (B) x^2
   - (C) $5x$
   - (D) $-5x^2$

4. Factor: $9x^3 + 18x^2 - x - 2$
   - (A) $(9x^2 - 1)(x + 2)$
   - (B) $(9x^2 + 1)(x - 2)$
   - (C) $(9x^2 + 2)(x - 1)$
   - (D) $(9x^2 - 2)(x + 1)$

5. Solve for x: $5x + 7 = 6(x - 2) - 4(2x - 3)$
   - (A) 1
   - (B) -1
   - (C) 2
   - (D) -2

6. Simplify: $x(x^2) =$
   - (A) x^2
   - (B) $2x$
   - (C) $2x^2$
   - (D) x^3

7. Simplify: $\sqrt{(5 + x)^2} =$
   - (A) $5 - x$
   - (B) $5 + x$
   - (C) $\sqrt{5} - \sqrt{x}$
   - (D) $\sqrt{5} + \sqrt{x}$

8. $(3 \times 3)(5 - 3)(6 + 2) = x^2$. What's the value of x?
   - (A) 6
   - (B) 12
   - (C) 144
   - (D) 64

9. If $-5x = 25$, x equals
   - (A) -5
   - (B) 5
   - (C) 10
   - (D) 0

10. A circle measures 12 feet in diameter. What's its area to the nearest foot?
    - (A) 452
    - (B) 24
    - (C) 113
    - (D) 48

11. A square box has 6-inch sides. What's its volume?
    - (A) 18 cubic inches
    - (B) 216 cubic inches
    - (C) 12 cubic inches
    - (D) 36 cubic inches

GO ON TO NEXT PAGE

12. A circle has a diameter of 10 inches. What's its approximate area?

(A) $\pi(10)^2$

(B) $\pi(25)$

(C) $\pi(5)$

(D) $\pi(10)^2(10)$

13. A cylinder has a diameter of 12 inches and a height of 10 inches. What's its approximate volume?

(A) 4,521 cubic inches

(B) 120 cubic inches

(C) 1,130 cubic inches

(D) 1,440 cubic inches

14. Triangle *ABC* is a(n)

© John Wiley & Sons, Inc.

(A) equilateral triangle.

(B) right triangle.

(C) scalene triangle.

(D) isosceles triangle.

15. The interior angles of the following quadrilateral

© John Wiley & Sons, Inc.

(A) are all right angles.

(B) each equals 45 degrees.

(C) are all unequal.

(D) total 180 degrees.

16. In the following figure, the sum of Angles 1 and 2 equals

© John Wiley & Sons, Inc.

(A) 180 degrees.

(B) 90 degrees.

(C) 45 degrees.

(D) 360 degrees.

17. Solve for x: $3(2x-5)-2(4x+1)=-5(x+3)-2$.

(A) 0

(B) 1

(C) 2

(D) 3

18. A cube has a volume of 64 cubic inches. What's the length of one side of the cube?

(A) 4 inches

(B) 16 inches

(C) 8 inches

(D) 32 inches

19. Simplify: $\left(x^3\right)^2 =$

(A) x^5

(B) x^6

(C) x^9

(D) $2x^3$

20. If r inches of rain fall in one minute, how many inches fall in h hours?

(A) $rh \div 60$

(B) $60 - h$

(C) rh

(D) $60rh$

21. If $x = y$, then $6 + 4(x-y) =$

(A) $6xy + 4$

(B) $6 + 4xy$

(C) $10x - 10y$

(D) 6

22. $\sqrt{820}$ is a number between

(A) 20 and 30.

(B) 10 and 20.

(C) 80 and 90.

(D) 40 and 50.

23. Simplify: $(x+2)(x+2) =$

(A) $x^2 + 2x + 4$

(B) $x^2 + 4x + 4$

(C) $x^2 + 4x + 2$

(D) $x^2 + 2x + 0$

24. Evaluate the expression $6a - 3x - 2y$ if $a = -3$, $x = -7$, and $y = 4$.

(A) -5

(B) -40

(C) 31

(D) 40

25. Simplify: $(x+4)(3x+5) =$

(A) $3x^2 + 9x + 20$

(B) $3x^2 + 17x + 15$

(C) $3x^2 + 17x + 20$

(D) $3x^2 + 9x + 15$

Subtest 6: Electronics Information

TIME: 9 minutes for 20 questions

DIRECTIONS: This section tests your knowledge of electrical, radio, and electronics information. Select the correct response from the choices given and then mark the corresponding space on your answer sheet.

1. What effect does a speaker wire's gauge have on speaker sound quality?

   (A) Higher gauge wires are thicker with better sound quality.

   (B) Lower gauge wires are thicker with better sound quality.

   (C) Lower gauge wires are thicker with lesser sound quality.

   (D) Higher gauge wires are thicker with lesser sound quality.

2. What's the primary advantage of a quad-band cellphone over a dual-band cellphone?

   (A) transmission strength

   (B) coverage area

   (C) reception strength

   (D) smaller phone size

3. When working with electricity, you should assume that all electrical equipment is alive unless you know for certain otherwise. This prevents

   (A) damage to circuits.

   (B) personal injury.

   (C) unnecessary labor.

   (D) overheating the equipment.

4. The heat effect of current occurs

   (A) when the pressure of the current in the wire breaks up impurities in the wire, creating heat.

   (B) when the current in the wire decays electrons, causing them to move more quickly, creating heat.

   (C) when the current overcomes resistance in the wire, creating heat.

   (D) The heat effect of current is only theoretical; it has never been proven to exist.

5. What special type of diode is commonly used to regulate voltage?

   (A) capacitor

   (B) transistor

   (C) Zener

   (D) LED

6. This symbol means

   © John Wiley & Sons, Inc.

   (A) ohm.

   (B) ampere.

   (C) high voltage.

   (D) wattage.

7. Electromotive force is another way of saying

   (A) frequency.

   (B) watts.

   (C) cycles per second.

   (D) voltage.

8. A primary advantage of using a Li-Ion battery instead of a NiMH battery in your cellphone is

   (A) Li-Ion batteries are lighter.

   (B) Li-Ion batteries last longer.

   (C) Li-Ion batteries don't interfere with signal quality.

   (D) none of the above.

9. Transistors contain at least three terminals called the

   (A) base, emitter, and collector.

   (B) base, positive terminal, and negative terminal.

   (C) emitter, amplifier, and collector.

   (D) base and two gates.

10. To control a light fixture from two different wall switches, you should use

   (A) a single-pole switch and a four-way switch.

   (B) two three-way switches.

   (C) two four-way switches.

   (D) two single-pole switches.

11. A transistor is also called a(n)

   (A) rectifier.

   (B) cathode.

   (C) amplifier.

   (D) semiconductor.

12. This symbol means

   © John Wiley & Sons, Inc.

   (A) ground.

   (B) resistor.

   (C) diode.

   (D) battery.

13. To decrease capacitance, capacitors

   (A) should have less voltage applied to them.

   (B) should be connected in parallel.

   (C) should be connected in series.

   (D) should be eliminated.

14. A resistor marked 2.5K ohms has the value of

   (A) 2.5 ohms.

   (B) 250 watts.

   (C) 2,500 ohms.

   (D) 25,000 ohms.

15. A 9-volt battery contains

   (A) 1 cell.

   (B) 6 cells.

   (C) 9 cells.

   (D) 3 cells.

16. The hot wire is always

   (A) purple.

   (B) green.

   (C) whitish.

   (D) black.

17. How wide is the full AT motherboard?

   (A) 11 inches

   (B) 11.5 inches

   (C) 12 inches

   (D) 12.5 inches

18. The following symbol represents a(n)

   © John Wiley & Sons, Inc.

   (A) relay.

   (B) on-off switch.

   (C) push switch.

   (D) connected wire.

19. If a 120-volt current is protected by a 25-amp circuit breaker, what's the largest number of watts an appliance can safely use?

   (A) 1,200 watts

   (B) 1,800 watts

   (C) 3,000 watts

   (D) 3,600 watts

20. The following symbol represents a

   © John Wiley & Sons, Inc.

   (A) rheostat.

   (B) capacitor.

   (C) relay.

   (D) potentiometer.

Subtest 7: Auto & Shop Information

TIME: 11 minutes for 25 questions

DIRECTIONS: This test contains questions about automobiles, shop practices, and the use of tools. Pick the best answer for each question and then mark the corresponding space on your answer sheet.

1. A symptom of worn piston rings is
   - **(A)** a knocking and pinging sound when driving.
   - **(B)** soft and spongy acceleration.
   - **(C)** the smell of exhaust in the car.
   - **(D)** an engine using excessive amounts of oil.

2. What term refers to the rebuilding of an engine to precise factory specifications?
   - **(A)** blueprinting
   - **(B)** speccing
   - **(C)** gold rebuild
   - **(D)** silver rebuild

3. The number of cranks a crankshaft has on a V-8 engine is
   - **(A)** 6.
   - **(B)** 4.
   - **(C)** 3.
   - **(D)** 8.

4. When an engine runs on after the ignition key is turned off, it's called
   - **(A)** dieseling.
   - **(B)** sputtering.
   - **(C)** ignition recharge.
   - **(D)** ignition malfunction.

5. If a radiator fails, the engine
   - **(A)** will idle roughly.
   - **(B)** may burn fuel less efficiently.
   - **(C)** works hard to maintain speed.
   - **(D)** can quickly overheat.

6. On modern automobile engines, what's the purpose of the intake manifold?
   - **(A)** It regulates airflow to the cooling system.
   - **(B)** It provides airflow to the air-conditioner and heater.
   - **(C)** It distributes air evenly between each cylinder.
   - **(D)** It regulates fuel pump pressure.

7. Brake systems work by
   - **(A)** applying friction to the wheels to stop their rotation.
   - **(B)** reversing power to the wheels.
   - **(C)** applying pressure to the axle.
   - **(D)** interrupting power to the transmission.

8. Which of the following isn't a component of the cooling system?
   - **(A)** heater core
   - **(B)** radiator
   - **(C)** thermostat
   - **(D)** hydrator

9. A catalytic converter
   - **(A)** combines the fuel-air mixture.
   - **(B)** reduces dangerous exhaust emissions.
   - **(C)** converts the up-and-down motion of the pistons to rotary motion.
   - **(D)** charges the battery when the engine is in operation.

10. If the steering wheel vibrates at high speeds, the most likely problem is
    - **(A)** front end alignment.
    - **(B)** front tire balance.
    - **(C)** cracked steering column.
    - **(D)** overinflated tires.

11. During the compression stroke on a four-cycle engine,

   (A) the intake valve opens to fill the cylinder with fuel.

   (B) the burning fuel mixture forces the piston to the bottom of the cylinder.

   (C) the intake valve closes, and the piston moves to the top of the cylinder.

   (D) the exhaust valve releases the burned gas.

12. On older cars with carburetors, the air filter can be found

   (A) on top of the engine.

   (B) under the engine.

   (C) behind the engine.

   (D) on the left or right side of the engine.

13. Glazing is the process of

   (A) cutting glass to size.

   (B) using putty to hold glass to a window frame.

   (C) polishing glass before using.

   (D) removing glass from a window.

14. A wrench with fixed, open jaws is called a(n)

   (A) adjustable wrench.

   (B) Allen wrench.

   (C) socket wrench.

   (D) open-end wrench.

15. All hammers have a

   (A) head, face, and handle.

   (B) head, toe, and handle.

   (C) head and foot.

   (D) head and claw.

16. To determine the number of threads per inch on a fastener, use a

   (A) depth gauge.

   (B) thread gauge.

   (C) thickness gauge.

   (D) wire gauge.

17. To chip or cut wood in close, the best tool is a

   (A) screwdriver.

   (B) butt chisel.

   (C) framing chisel.

   (D) paring chisel.

18. Machine screws

   (A) are made by machines.

   (B) can be used interchangeably with wood screws.

   (C) have uniform threads from top to bottom.

   (D) are machined to fine tolerances.

19. Double-headed nails are used

   (A) to reinforce a joint.

   (B) on temporary construction.

   (C) to make frames for furniture.

   (D) when a larger striking surface is needed.

20. To thin oil-based paint, use

   (A) turpentine.

   (B) baby oil.

   (C) benzene.

   (D) varnish.

21. When finishing a piece of wood, it's best to sand

   (A) diagonal to the grain.

   (B) against the grain.

   (C) with the grain.

   (D) in small circles.

22. To transfer an angle, the best tool to use is a

   (A) square.

   (B) caliper.

   (C) level.

   (D) sliding T-bevel.

GO ON TO NEXT PAGE

23. The following tool is a(n)

(A) pipe wrench.

(B) socket wrench.

(C) adjustable crescent wrench.

(D) box-end wrench.

24. Which of the following screw heads requires a Phillips screwdriver?

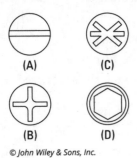

(A)　　　(C)

(B)　　　(D)

25. The following tool is used to

(A) punch holes.

(B) drive nails.

(C) measure thickness.

(D) set nails.

Subtest 8: Mechanical Comprehension

TIME: 19 minutes for 25 questions

DIRECTIONS: This test is about mechanical principles. Many of the questions use drawings to illustrate specific principles. Choose the correct answer and mark the corresponding space on the answer sheet.

1. Helical gears have

(A) straight teeth.

(B) slanted teeth.

(C) teeth of unequal size.

(D) no advantage over spur gears.

2. In the following figure, which pillar supports the greater load of the anvil?

© John Wiley & Sons, Inc.

(A) Pillar A

(B) Pillar B

(C) Both pillars support the anvil equally.

(D) It's impossible to determine from the information given.

3. Wheel A has a diameter of 10 feet. Wheel B has a diameter of 8 feet. If both wheels revolve at the same rate, Wheel B will cover a linear distance of 16 feet

(A) at the same time as Wheel A.

(B) more slowly than Wheel A.

(C) in twice the time as Wheel A.

(D) faster than Wheel A.

4. What effort must be used to lift a 30-pound anvil (see the following figure) using a first-class lever? (Don't include the weight of the lever in your calculations.)

© John Wiley & Sons, Inc.

(A) 10 pounds

(B) 15 pounds

(C) 50 pounds

(D) 5 pounds

5. What mechanical advantage does the block-and-tackle arrangement in the following figure give?

© John Wiley & Sons, Inc.

(A) 1

(B) 3

(C) 2

(D) 4

GO ON TO NEXT PAGE

6. If a ramp is 8 feet long and 4 feet high, how much effort is required to move a 400-pound object up the ramp?

(A) 35 pounds

(B) 150 pounds

(C) 800 pounds

(D) 200 pounds

7. 33,000 foot-pounds of work done in one minute is called

(A) a job for an enlisted soldier.

(B) 1 horsepower.

(C) 330 psi.

(D) meaningful force.

8. A 130-pound woman is wearing shoes with high heels that measure 1-inch square. If the woman is standing on one heel, what psi does the heel exert as it rests on the ground? (Disregard atmospheric pressure in your calculations.)

(A) 130

(B) 65

(C) 260

(D) 11

9. Clothes from the dryer stick together because of

(A) gravity.

(B) magnetism.

(C) friction.

(D) static electricity.

10. An aneroid barometer measures

(A) atmospheric pressure.

(B) water pressure.

(C) hydraulic-fluid pressure.

(D) the ambient temperature.

11. If Gear A is revolving in a clockwise manner, as in the following figure, Gear B

© John Wiley & Sons, Inc.

(A) remains stationary.

(B) revolves in a clockwise manner.

(C) revolves in a counterclockwise manner.

(D) turns more slowly than Gear A.

12. Springs are used for all of the following purposes EXCEPT

(A) to store energy for part of a mechanical cycle.

(B) to force a mechanical component to maintain contact with another component.

(C) to reduce shock or impact.

(D) to increase the weight of a mechanism.

13. The floats in Tubes A and B measure specific gravity. Which tube contains the liquid with the higher specific gravity?

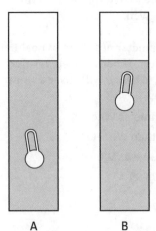

A   B

© John Wiley & Sons, Inc.

(A) Tube A

(B) Tube B

(C) It can't be determined.

(D) Both Tube A and Tube B have the same specific gravity.

14. Universal joints are used to

(A) connect ball bearings.

(B) fix two shafts so they don't pivot or rotate.

(C) connect shafts in a U–shape.

(D) couple two shafts set at different angles.

15. The try-cock in the following schematic measures

© John Wiley & Sons, Inc.

(A) temperature of water.

(B) pressure of water.

(C) pressure of steam buildup.

(D) level of water.

16. The steel plate below is held in place by different machine screws, each indicated by different symbols. How many different types of machine screws have been used?

© John Wiley & Sons, Inc.

(A) 6

(B) 15

(C) 5

(D) 9

17. The amount of force (*F*) needed to balance the lever in the following figure is most nearly

© John Wiley & Sons, Inc.

(A) 15 pounds.

(B) 13 pounds.

(C) 7.5 pounds.

(D) 20 pounds.

18. With one complete revolution of the cable winch shown below, the load will move

© John Wiley & Sons, Inc.

(A) 12 inches.

(B) 6 inches.

(C) 24 inches.

(D) 36 inches.

GO ON TO NEXT PAGE

19. In the following figure, assume the valves are all closed. Which valves need to be open to fill the tank entirely?

© John Wiley & Sons, Inc.

(A) 1 and 2 only

(B) 1 only

(C) 1, 2, and 3

(D) 2 only

20. If Gear 1 in the following figure makes 10 complete clockwise revolutions per minute, then

© John Wiley & Sons, Inc.

(A) Gear 2 makes 2 clockwise revolutions per minute.

(B) Gear 3 makes 8 clockwise revolutions per minute.

(C) Gear 3 makes 30 clockwise revolutions per minute.

(D) Gear 3 makes 9 counterclockwise revolutions per minute.

21. A gear and pinion have a ratio of 1 to 4. If the gear makes 200 revolutions per minute, the speed of the pinion is

(A) 50 rpm.

(B) 800 rpm.

(C) 400 rpm.

(D) 200 rpm.

22. The gas gauge in an automobile relies on what mechanical device to measure the amount of gas in the tank?

(A) ball and cock

(B) automatic valve

(C) float

(D) mechanical switch

23. Using a runner gives you a mechanical advantage of

(A) 4.

(B) 2.

(C) 3.

(D) 1.

24. For the valve shown in the figure below to open once each second, the cam must revolve at a rate of

© *John Wiley & Sons, Inc.*

(A) 6 rpm.

(B) 10 rpm.

(C) 15 rpm.

(D) 3 rpm.

25. The following figure represents a water tank. Which of the following statements is not true?

© *John Wiley & Sons, Inc.*

(A) If Valves 1 and 2 are open and Valves 3, 4, and 5 are closed, the tank will eventually overflow.

(B) If all valves are open, the water will remain at a constant level as long as the rate of intake is equal to the rate of discharge.

(C) Water in the tank will rise if Valves 1 and 2 are open and Valves 3 and 4 are closed.

(D) The tank will empty entirely if Valves 1 and 2 are closed and Valves 4 and 5 are open.

Subtest 9: Assembling Objects

TIME: 15 minutes for 25 questions

DIRECTIONS: The Assembling Objects subtest consists of questions that measure your ability to mentally picture items in two dimensions. Each question is comprised of five separate drawings. The problem is presented in the first drawing and the remaining four drawings are possible solutions. Determine which of the choices best solves the problem shown in the first picture, and then mark the corresponding choice on your answer sheet.

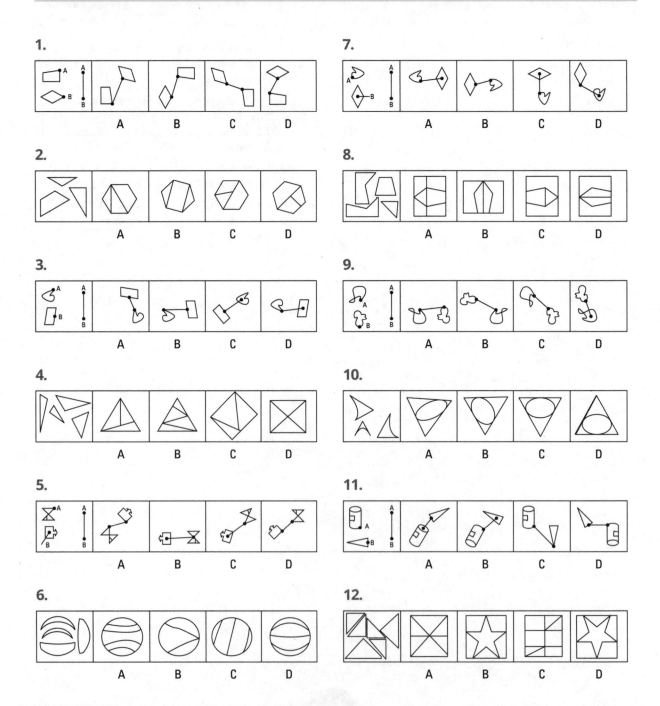

13.

14.

15.

16.

17.

18.

19.

20.

21.

22.

23.

24.

25.

Chapter 23

Practice Exam 3: Answers and Explanations

Read over each question from Chapter 22 as you check the answer key. I hope you did well on this practice exam. If you find you need to study more for any subtest, follow the cross-references. (And for in-depth study, check out some of the book recommendations in Chapter 19.)

Subtest 1: General Science Answers

If you're still having problems figuring out the difference between an isotope and an ion, remember you may not have to do well on this subtest. It depends on the military career you're interested in. (See Appendix A for a list of military jobs that require a good General Science score.) If this subtest is important to your military career aspirations, consider putting in some extra study. You can find additional information and practice questions in Chapters 10, 11, and 12.

1. **A.** The moon orbits the Earth approximately every 27.3 days. The closest answer is Choice (A).

2. **B.** *Carcinogens* cause gene mutations and can cause cancer.

3. **A.** A *paramecium* is a slipper-shaped one-celled organism.

4. **D.** Iodine is necessary for the thyroid gland to function.

5. **D.** The brainstem controls some involuntary muscle activities.

6. **B.** The element most abundant in the atmosphere is nitrogen (about 78%), followed by oxygen (about 21%).

7. **D.** Minerals are essential for various bodily functions, including the metabolic processes that turn food into energy.

8. **C.** Mercury, found in older-style thermometers, is the only metal that is in its liquid state at room temperature. Bromine is liquid at room temperature, but it's not a metallic element (be careful to read every word of the questions you see on the ASVAB).

9. **B.** Reflecting, refracting, and catadioptric are all types of telescopes, so Choice (B) is correct.

10. **B.** A dekagram is 10 grams, and a kilogram is 1,000 grams, so a dekagram is smaller than a kilogram.

11. **D.** The aurora borealis can be seen only in the Northern Hemisphere — hence the nickname Northern Lights.

12. **D.** Characteristics of sound waves include wavelength, frequency, velocity (speed), and amplitude. *Crests* are the high points of longitudinal waves, like the up-and-down waves in a string. Reflection (echoing) is a behavior of sound waves, but it isn't considered a wave property.

13. **A.** Most asteroids in our solar system are in a belt between Mars and Jupiter.

14. **D.** Substances can be liquid (for example, water), gas (for example, oxygen), or solid (for example, iron) at room temperature.

15. **D.** About 98% of all matter in the universe is composed of hydrogen and helium.

16. **B.** When unlike atoms combine, the result is a *compound* (for example, iron and oxygen become iron oxide). If atoms of the same element come together (such as if two hydrogen atoms combine), they form elemental molecules, which aren't considered compounds.

17. **A.** The Big Bang is the most widely accepted scientific theory on the origin of the universe. The Big Rip is a theory regarding the end.

18. **A.** A watt-hour measures the amount of work performed or generated, such as in household appliances.

19. **D.** All the gas giants (planets) listed have rings.

20. **C.** Gas particles move more quickly than liquid particles, which move more quickly than solid particles, which makes Choice (C) correct.

21. **C.** *Absolute zero* is 0 kelvin, which is the same measure as −273.15 degrees Celsius.

22. **A.** Magnetic Resonance Imaging (MRI) machines employ radiology (dealing with radiation) to produce images.

23. **B.** The human female pelvis is usually wider than the male pelvis. (The question asks which choice isn't true, and paying attention to detail can make the difference in getting a question right or wrong on the ASVAB.)

24. **D.** A *lunar eclipse* occurs when the moon passes behind the Earth, so the moon is in the shadow of the Earth.

25. **A.** Luminol is used to detect minute traces of blood. Cyanide, ninhydrin, and alcohol can't do that.

Subtest 2: Arithmetic Reasoning Answers

You have to do well on this subtest to qualify for military enlistment — your score from the Arithmetic Reasoning subtest counts toward your AFQT score. If you're still doing poorly on this test, you may want to postpone taking the ASVAB until you have more study time under your belt (and perhaps take a math class or two). You may also want to review Part 3 of this book.

1. **D.** Multiply $0.45 (the cost of making three donuts) by 4 to find the cost of making a dozen donuts: $0.45 \times 4 = $1.80. Then subtract the cost of making one dozen donuts from the selling price of one dozen donuts to get the profit on one dozen donuts: $3.99 - $1.80 = $2.19.

   Because the baker sold five dozen donuts, multiply the profit on one dozen donuts times 5 to determine the profit on five dozen donuts: $2.19 \times 5 = $10.95.

2. **C.** Let x equal the number of dimes. Then $100 - x$ represents the number of quarters. You have $0.10x in dimes and $0.25(100 - x)$ in quarters, so set up your equation and solve for x:

$$0.10x + 0.25(100 - x) = 19.75$$
$$0.10x + 25 - 0.25x = 19.75$$
$$-0.15x = -5.25$$
$$x = 35$$

3. **D.** First determine the square footage of the patio: $12 \text{ feet} \times 16 \text{ feet} = 192$ square feet. Then multiply this number by the cost per square foot to determine what the bricklayer charges: $192 \times $8 = $1,536.

4. **A.** Let x equal Angie's hourly wage; $x + 2$ would then represent Tim's hourly wage, and $3(x + 2)$ would represent Terry's hourly wage. Set up your equation and solve for x:

$$x + (x + 2) + 3(x + 2) = 43$$
$$x + x + 2 + 3x + 6 = 43$$
$$5x + 8 = 43$$
$$5x = 35$$
$$x = 7$$

5. **B.** Two people is half as many as four people. Multiply the number of machines four people can run by $\frac{1}{2}$ to determine how many machines two people can run: $8 \times \frac{1}{2} = 4$.

6. **B.** Let x equal the number of daily tickets you would purchase; $36x$ equals the daily ticket cost:

$$240 < 36x$$
$$\frac{240}{36} < x$$
$$6\frac{2}{3} < x$$

   You would need to use the ticket more than $6\frac{2}{3}$ times (or 7 times) for it to be cheaper to use the season ticket.

7. **C.** You can convert the lengths of the pipes from feet and inches to inches and then divide the total inches needed by 12 to get the total number of feet of pipe needed. However, the easiest and fastest way to do this problem is to realize that 3 feet, 6 inches is 3.5 feet. Multiply the number of pipes needed by 3.5 feet to get the number of feet of pipe needed.

$$4 \times 3.5 = 14$$

8. B. The fastest way to solve this is to simply multiply some possible pairs of consecutive odd numbers. Since $20 \times 20 = 400$, try the odd numbers closest to that: $19 \times 21 = 399$. However, you can also solve this with algebra. Let x equal the first number and $x + 2$ equal the second number:

$$x(x+2) = 399$$
$$x^2 + 2x = 399$$

This is a quadratic equation that you can solve by setting it equal to zero and factoring.

$$x^2 + 2x - 399 = 0$$
$$(x - 19) + (x + 21) = 0$$
$$x - 19 = 0 \quad \text{or} \quad x + 21 = 0$$
$$x = 19 \qquad\qquad x = -21$$
$$x + 2 = 21 \qquad\qquad x + 2 = -19$$

Two solutions are possible: 19 and 21, and −21 and −19. Because the latter pair isn't one of the answer choices, the first pair is the correct answer.

9. C. Multiply her total sales by her percent commission to find her commission: $\$530 \times 0.65 = \$344.50$. You could also start with an estimate: $500 \times 0.7 = 350$. Choice (C) is the only value that's close.

10. B. The formula for the length of the diagonal of a rectangle is $d^2 = l^2 + w^2$ (this is the Pythagorean theorem, where l and w are the sides of a right triangle and d is the hypotenuse). In this case, $d = 5$ and $l = w + 1$. Substituting the known values into the formula results in $5^2 = (w+1)^2 + w^2$.

$$5^2 = (w+1)(w+1) + w^2$$
$$25 = w^2 + 2w + 1 + w^2$$
$$25 = 2w^2 + 2w + 1$$

This equation is a quadratic equation, which you can solve by setting it equal to zero and factoring.

$$0 = 2w^2 + 2w - 24$$
$$\tfrac{1}{2}(0) = \tfrac{1}{2}(2w^2 + 2w - 24)$$
$$0 = w^2 + w - 12$$
$$0 = (w - 3)(w + 4)$$
$$w - 3 = 0 \quad \text{or} \quad w + 4 = 0$$
$$w = 3 \qquad\qquad w = -4 \text{ (not a possible solution)}$$

11. B. If 2 inches = 3 miles, then 1 inch equals 1.5 miles: $3 \div 2 = 1.5$. Multiply 1.5 miles $\times$ 9.5 inches to determine the actual distance: $1.5 \times 9.5 = 14.25$, or $14\frac{1}{4}$ miles.

12. D. The area of the entire piece of canvas = 10 inches $\times$ 14 inches = 140 square inches. The portion painted on equals 8 inches $\times$ 12 inches = 96 square inches. (This is determined by subtracting 2 inches — 1 inch on each side — from the length of each side to account for the margins.) Divide 96 by 140 to determine that about 68.5% of the canvas is covered with paint. You can round up to 69%.

13. D. Calculate perimeter by adding the lengths of all four sides of a quadrilateral: $9 + 9 + 16 + 16 = 50$ feet.

14. **B.** The formula for the perimeter of a rectangle is $P = 2l + 2w$. In this case, $P = 100$ and $l = 1.5w$. Set up your equation and solve for w:

$$100 = 2(1.5w) + 2w$$
$$100 = 3w + 2w$$
$$100 = 5w$$
$$w = 20$$

The width of the rectangle is 20 inches. Because the length is $1\frac{1}{2}$ times the width, $1.5 \times 20 = 30$.

15. **C.** The total number of quizzes is 10. If he passed seven of them, the fraction would be expressed as $\frac{7}{10}$.

16. **D.** Divide the amount of ribbon (in yards) used by the number of dresses to determine how much ribbon (in yards) was used in each dress: $3 \div 4 = \frac{3}{4}$. Three-quarters of a yard of ribbon was used to make each dress.

17. **B.** Divide \$30 by \$530 $(\$500 + \$30)$ to determine the percentage of the sale price that the profit comprised: $30 \div 530 = 0.056 = 6\%$.

18. **A.** First find how many bolts a full bin contains: $7 \times 12 = 84$ bolts. Then multiply the total number of bolts in a full bin by $\frac{1}{6}$ to find how many bolts are in the bin when it's $\frac{1}{6}$ full: $84 \times \frac{1}{6} = \frac{84}{6} = 14$ bolts.

Tip: A shortcut is to find $\frac{1}{6}$ of a dozen first and then multiply by 7, the number of dozens. That is, $12 \times \frac{1}{6} = 2$ bolts, and $2 \times 7 = 14$ bolts. You can do this because multiplication is commutative — you can multiply the numbers in any order.

19. **C.** The first bike got a $\frac{4}{5}$–mile head start $\left(12 \text{ mph} \times \frac{4}{60} \text{ hr.} = \frac{48}{60} = \frac{4}{5} \text{ mi.}\right)$. Therefore, by the time the second bike leaves, there are $5\frac{1}{5}$ miles between them $\left(6 - \frac{4}{5}\right)$. Their combined rate of travel is $12 + 14 = 26$ mph. Let t = the number of hours the second bike travels.

$$26t = 5\frac{1}{5}$$
$$26t = \frac{26}{5}$$
$$t = \frac{26}{5} \div \frac{26}{1}$$
$$t = \frac{26}{5} \times \frac{1}{26}$$
$$t = \frac{1}{5}$$

One-fifth of an hour equals $60 \div 5 = 12$ minutes. The second bike left at 2:09, so both bikes will meet at 2:21.

20. **B.** Choice (B) is the cheapest option that gives you enough beans. Calculate each answer option and compare:

- **Choice (A):** $2 \times \$0.79 = \$1.58$
- **Choice (B):** \$1.49
- **Choice (C):** Two 3-ounce cans give you less than 8 ounces, so this answer can't be correct.
- **Choice (D):** $3 \times \$0.65 = \$1.95$

21. **D.** Add the sales amounts together: $25.70 + $32.30 + $31.80 = 89.80. Then multiply the total sales by $\frac{3}{4}$ to determine how much money he has left: $89.80 \times 0.75 = 67.35.

22. **B.** Divide $30.00 by $3.95. The whole number is the number of pairs of socks the recruit could buy: $30.00 \div $3.95 = 7.59$, or 7 pairs of socks. In cases like this, you could also start with an estimate: $30 \div 4 \approx 7$, which is the only one that comes close to Choice (B).

23. **D.** Subtract 43 pounds, 7 ounces (the weight of the puppy) from 60 pounds, 5 ounces (the weight of the crate). Converting an additional pound of the crate to ounces makes the subtraction possible. Sixteen ounces make a pound, so 60 pounds, 5 ounces is the same as 59 pounds, 21 ounces. Do the subtraction:

$$\begin{array}{r} 59 \text{ pounds, } 21 \text{ ounces} \\ - 43 \text{ pounds, } 7 \text{ ounces} \\ \hline 16 \text{ pounds, } 14 \text{ ounces} \end{array}$$

24. **D.** The probability that all five computers will be defective is $0.15 \times 0.15 \times 0.15 \times 0.15 \times 0.15 = 0.0000759$ (round up to 0.000076). If you start with an estimate, like $(0.1)^5 = 0.00001$, you'll see that only Choice (D) is close to that value.

25. **D.** Find the area of each bedroom and add them together: $12 \times 14 = 168$; $12 \times 10 = 120$; $8 \times 12 = 96$; and $168 + 120 + 96 = 384$ square feet. Then, because 9 square feet make up a square yard, divide the total area in square feet by 9 to determine the number of square yards needed: $384 \div 9 = 42.6$ square yards. You can round up to 43 square yards.

26. **A.** Divide the total number of pages to be typed by the number of pages Rafael can type per hour to find the number of hours it will take him to type the pages: 126 pages $\div 9$ pages per hour $= 14$ hours.

27. **D.** Divide the group of 48 girls by the number of girls who can play at the same time: $48 \div 12 = 4$. This means four groups of girls have to share the 60 minutes: 60 minutes $\div 4 = 15$ minutes. Thus, each girl plays for 15 minutes.

28. **B.** Subtract the first day's late charge from the total: $8.25 - $2.00 = 6.25. Then divide that amount by $1.25 to determine the number of additional days the movie was overdue: $6.25 \div $1.25 = 5$. Add those 5 days to the first day the movie was late to find that the movie was 6 days overdue.

29. **D.** Divide the number of calories in the pudding by the number of calories in the broccoli: $150 \div 60 = 2.5$. The calorie-counter can eat 2.5 times the amount of broccoli as they can eat pudding for the same number of calories. Multiply 2.5 by 0.5 cup (the amount of pudding that contains 150 calories) to find how many cups of broccoli this person can eat for 150 calories:

$$2.5 \times 0.5 = 1.25 = 1\frac{1}{4} \text{ cups}$$

30. **C.** The dog is barking every 15 minutes, or 4 times per hour. The time between 10 p.m. and 2 a.m. is 4 hours. Multiply the total number of hours in the time period by 4 barks per hour. Then add 1 because the dog barked at the beginning of the period also: $(4 \times 4) + 1 = 16 + 1 = 17$.

Subtest 3: Word Knowledge Answers

The Word Knowledge subtest is another one of the "big four" that counts toward your AFQT score. If you're not seeing the improvement in your scores that you need to see, work with a partner who can quiz you on vocabulary. Review your vocabulary words intensely, even several times a day, to ensure your success on this subtest. See Chapter 4 for more help on improving your word knowledge. You also have a chance to practice this subtest topic in the practice AFQTs in Chapters 24 and 26.

1. **B.** *Lackadaisical* is an adjective that means carelessly lazy or lacking enthusiasm and determination.

2. **D.** *Edible* is an adjective that means fit to be eaten.

3. **B.** *Philomath* is a noun that refers to a person who enjoys learning new things.

4. **B.** *Pretense* is a noun that means an attempt to make something that isn't true appear to be true. (It's related to the word *pretend.*)

5. **A.** *Proclivity* is a noun that means a tendency to choose or do something regularly; it's an inclination or predisposition toward something.

6. **C.** *Incoherent* is an adjective that describes spoken or written language as being expressed in a confusing, unclear way.

7. **B.** *Mawkish* is an adjective that means sentimental in a feeble or sickly way.

8. **D.** *Established* is an adjective that means having been in existence for a long time, recognized, and accepted.

9. **A.** *Ephemeral* is an adjective that means lasting for a very short time.

10. **A.** *Avocation* is a noun that means a minor occupation or a hobby.

11. **C.** *Kvetch* is a verb that means to complain; it's also a noun used to refer to a person who complains a lot.

12. **A.** *Acute* is an adjective that means having or showing a perceptive understanding or insight; it also means shrewd.

13. **B.** *Inamorata* is a noun that means a person's female lover. (Not surprisingly, *inamorato* is a noun that means a person's male lover.)

14. **C.** *Inconsequential* is an adjective that means unimportant or not significant.

15. **A.** *Debouch* is a verb that means to emerge from a narrow or confined space into an open area. (Don't confuse *debouch* with *debauch,* which means to corrupt something.)

16. **B.** *Amateur* is a noun that refers to a person who engages in something on an unpaid basis. It's also an adjective that means engaging or engaged in something without payment or nonprofessionally.

17. **A.** *Ludic* is an adjective that means showing spontaneous playfulness.

18. **D.** *Crimson* is an adjective that means of a rich, deep red color that leans toward purple on the color spectrum.

19. **C.** *Benison* is a noun that means a blessing, so the opposite is a curse.

20. **B.** *Exempt* is an adjective that means free from an obligation imposed by others.

21. **C.** *Eldritch* is an adjective that means weird and sinister, or ghostly.

22. **A.** *Defective* is an adjective that means imperfect or faulty.

23. **B.** *Allot* is a verb that means to give something to someone as a share or task.

24. **D.** *Cursory* is an adjective that means hasty and therefore not detailed or thorough.

25. **B.** *Arcanum* is a noun that refers to a deep secret or mystery.

26. **D.** *Terse* is an adjective that means abrupt or sparing in the use of words.

27. **A.** *Dulcet* is an adjective that usually refers to sound and means sweet and soothing.

28. **C.** *Misdemeanor* is a noun that means a minor wrongdoing.

29. **A.** *Embonpoint* is a noun that refers to the plump, fleshy part of a person's body.

30. **C.** *Concocted* is the past tense of the verb *concoct*, which means to make something by putting together various ingredients. It also refers to creating or devising a story or plan.

31. **D.** *Chimera* is a noun that means a thing that is hoped or wished for but is illusory or impossible to achieve.

32. **A.** *Former* is an adjective that means having previously filled a role or been a particular thing.

33. **D.** *Mulct* is a verb that means to extract money from someone by fining or taxing.

34. **C.** *Strident* is an adjective that means harsh and loud. It also means presenting a certain point of view in an unpleasant and excessive way.

35. **C.** *Raffish* is an adjective that means unconventional and slightly disreputable, especially in an attractive way.

Subtest 4: Paragraph Comprehension Answers

Because the military uses the Paragraph Comprehension subtest to determine whether you even qualify for enlistment (it counts toward your AFQT score), you need to do well here. If you're still struggling, remember to take your time when you read the passages. And after you read each question, you can quickly reread the passage just to make sure you're on the money. The information is in the paragraph; you just have to concentrate to pull it out. Turn to Chapter 5 if you still need additional help to pull off a good score on this subtest. Additional opportunities to practice taking this subtest are in Chapters 24 and 26.

1. **D.** The last sentence in the passage states that chaos and fear are associated with change, making Choice (D) the correct choice. The passage states that leaders must learn to deal with negative emotions connected with change, making Choice (A) incorrect. The second sentence makes it clear that innovation means change, so Choice (B) is incorrect. The third sentence clearly states that leaders must learn everything there is to know about the change, making Choice (C) the wrong choice.

2. **C.** The first sentence says cougars are wide-ranging big cats in North America, making Choice (C) correct. The passage states that pumas, mountain lions, and cougars are the same thing, so Choice (A) is incorrect. Nothing in the passage supports Choice (B), which says cougars are endangered. The passage states that cougars live about 18 years in the wild, so Choice (D) is incorrect.

3. **B.** The counseling process works because the counselee feels the need for assistance, instruction, or understanding. Therefore, Choice (B) — counselees initially reject the advice of their counselors — isn't supported by the passage. The other three choices are all supported by the content of the paragraph.

4. **A.** The second sentence says that professional fire departments have more training, expertise, and experience. Therefore, the reader can infer that volunteer departments have less training, expertise, and experience than professionals. The passage says that professionals, not volunteers, have the skills needed to investigate fires, so Choice (B) is incorrect. The passage states that professional firefighters have more experience investigating the causes of fires, so Choice (C) is incorrect. The passage states that hiring professional firefighters is worthwhile, so Choice (D) is incorrect.

5. **C.** The passage doesn't state the locale of the story, so Choices (A) and (D) are incorrect. The references to extreme cold and lack of light make Choice (B) an incorrect answer. In sentence three, the author says it was still very foggy and extremely cold, so Choice (C) is the answer.

6. **A.** The main point of the passage is to define epidemiology, as evidenced by the opening sentence. Epidemiology is the study of what causes diseases. Choices (B), (C), and (D) aren't the main points of the passage.

7. **B.** The only statement that's supported by the passage is Choice (B), which says Buddhist teachings have changed. In fact, this sentence is the primary theme of the passage. The other choices aren't supported by information contained in the paragraph.

8. **A.** Choice (B), which questions jurors' intelligence, isn't supported by the passage. Choice (C), which asks for more laws that take intent into consideration, is the opposite of what the author argues. The text doesn't support Choice (D), which calls lawyers liars. The first line of the passage states that statutes permit more severe punishment of a person convicted of a crime if he or she intended to harm another person. The last sentence says juries should only be asked to weigh objective evidence, so the author would no doubt agree that laws should not punish people based on intention, Choice (A).

9. **C.** The passage says that most states punish voluntary manslaughter more severely than involuntary manslaughter, so Choice (A) is incorrect. The argument that punishing people more severely for voluntary manslaughter is unconstitutional isn't made in the passage, so Choice (B) is incorrect. The passage doesn't support Choice (D), which says prosecutors can establish intent. The first sentence of the second paragraph states that juries find it difficult to know what the intent of a person was at the time he or she committed a crime, so Choice (C) is correct.

10. **B.** Lack of attention to ergonomics, not ergonomics itself, can cause injury, so Choice (A) is incorrect. The passage doesn't support Choice (C), which discusses cost and time. The passage states that many people suffer injuries when sufficient attention isn't paid to ergonomics, so Choice (D) is incorrect. The first says, "Ergonomics is the science of designing and arranging workspaces so that people and objects interact efficiently and safely," so Choice (B) is correct.

11. **D.** The passage states that adequate lighting and well-designed chairs are part of ergonomic design, so Choice (A) is incorrect. The passage states that repetitious work can cause injury, so Choice (B) is incorrect. The passage states that desk-bound workers should take breaks, so Choice (C) is incorrect. The first sentence in the second paragraph states that adequate lighting, well-designed chairs, and clutter-free work areas contribute to effective ergonomic design, so Choice (D) is correct.

12. **A.** The passage makes it clear that lack of ergonomic design is dangerous, so Choice (B) is incorrect. Nothing in the passage supports Choice (C), which brings up labor unions. Although the passage claims that lack of ergonomic design causes injury, nothing in the passage supports Choice (D). The passage's second sentence says that lack of attention to ergonomics causes thousands of workers to suffer repetitive stress injury, eye fatigue, muscle soreness, and many other medical problems, so it's reasonable to assume that employers should invest in ergonomic design to protect workers, which makes Choice (A) correct.

13. **B.** The passage says that BTUs are the standard measure of heat, so Choice (A) is incorrect. BTU stands for British thermal unit, so Choice (C) is incorrect. Nothing in the passage supports Choice (D), which names room dimensions.

14. **D.** The passage shows that fuel oil can be more expensive than other heating methods, so Choice (A) is incorrect. Oak firewood is sometimes less expensive than other types of fuel, so Choice (B) is incorrect. Natural gas can sometimes cost less than firewood, so Choice (C) is incorrect. The first sentence states that electricity is always the most inefficient and costly way to heat a home, which makes Choice (D) correct.

15. **A.** The main point of this passage deals with choosing the right fuel based on price; only Choice (A) summarizes this point. Choices (B), (C), and (D) are less important points. The final sentence makes Choice (A) correct.

Subtest 5: Mathematics Knowledge Answers

The Mathematics Knowledge subtest is used to determine whether you qualify for enlistment, so you need to do well. If you're still missing too many questions, you may need to take more drastic measures, such as enrolling in a basic algebra class at a local community college. If your scores are improving, keep hitting the books and testing yourself up until the day of the ASVAB. Turn to Chapters 6, 7, and 8 for more information. The practice AFQTs in Chapters 24 and 26 also give you a chance to gauge your progress.

1. **B.** Substitute 6 for y in the equation: $2(6) \times 6 = 12 \times 6 = 72$.

2. **B.** Divide both sides of the equation by 0.05 to solve for x: $0.05x \div 0.05 = 1 \div 0.05$, or $x = 20$. To check your answer, substitute 20 for x in the original equation.

3. **C.** The radical symbol represents the nonnegative square root, so $\sqrt{25x^2} = \sqrt{(5x)^2} = 5x$.

4. **A.** $9x^3 + 18x^2 - x - 2 = 9x^2(x+2) - 1(x+2) = (9x^2 - 1)(x+2)$. The fully factored answer is $(3x+1)(3x-1)(x+2)$, but that's not what the question asks. Make sure you look for the answer to the question. Another method: Try multiplying the pieces. All the answer choices feature $9x^2 \times x = 9x^3$, and the constant is always -2. Only Choice (A) multiplies to have a positive $18x^2$.

5. **B.** Solve for x:

$$5x + 7 = 6(x-2) - 4(2x-3)$$
$$5x + 7 = 6x - 12 - 8x + 12$$
$$5x + 7 = -2x$$
$$7x + 7 = 0$$
$$7x = -7$$
$$x = -1$$

6. **D.** If two powers have the same base, they can be multiplied by keeping the base and adding the exponents together. In this case, x is the same as x^1: $x \cdot x^2 = x^{1+2} = x^3$.

7. **B.** This is so easy that it may tempt you to think that the correct answer is too obvious. The square root of $(5+x)^2$ is simply $5+x$.

8. **B.** You start with $(3 \times 3)(5-3)(6+2) = x^2$. First solve the left side of the equation: $(9)(2)(8) = 144$. So $x^2 = 144$. Find the square root of each side: $x = 12$.

9. **A.** You start with $-5x = 25$. Isolate x by dividing each side of the equation by -5: $x = -5$.

10. **C.** The area of a circle equals π times the radius squared. The radius is half the diameter, which is 12 in this problem. Plug in the known values: $A = \pi r^2$; $A = \pi 6^2 = 36\pi$. If π is approximately 3.14, the area of the circle is approximately 3.14×36, or 113 square feet.

11. **B.** Volume equals length $\times$ width $\times$ height $(V = lwh)$: $6 \times 6 \times 6 = 36 \times 6 = 216$ cubic inches.

12. **B.** The area of a circle is $A = \pi r^2$. Radius is half the diameter, so the radius is 5. In this problem, $A = \pi 5^2 = 25\pi$.

13. **C.** For cylinders, Volume $= \pi r^2(h)$. Because the radius is half the diameter, you can calculate the problem this way: $V = \pi(6^2)10 = \pi(36)10$. If π is approximately 3.14, then $3.14 \times 36 \times 10 = 1{,}130$ cubic inches.

14. **D.** In an isosceles triangle, sides a and c are equal, and angles 1 and 2 are equal.

15. **A.** Rectangles have four equal angles, and all angles are right angles.

16. **A.** The sum of the measures of supplementary angles always equal 180 degrees.

17. **A.** Solve for x:

$$3(2x-5) - 2(4x+1) = -5(x+3) - 2$$
$$6x - 15 - 8x - 2 = -5x - 15 - 2$$
$$-2x - 17 = -5x - 17$$
$$3x - 17 = -17$$
$$3x = 0$$
$$x = 0$$

18. **A.** Volume equals length × width × height $(V = lwh)$. Finding the cube root of 64 shows that each edge measures 4 inches $(4 \times 4 \times 4 = 64)$.

19. **B.** $(x^3)^2$ is the same as $(x^3)(x^3)$. To multiply exponents with the same base, keep the base and add the exponents: $(x^3)(x^3) = x^{3+3} = x^6$.

20. **D.** To find out how much rain falls in an hour, multiply the amount that falls in one minute by 60, because 60 minutes make up an hour. In h hours, the amount of rain is $60rh$.

21. **D.** Because $x = y$, you can plug in x for each y in the problem. Therefore, $6 + 4(x - x) = 6 + 4(0) = 6 + 0 = 6$.

22. **A.** The problem asks for the square root of 820. You know that $20^2 = 400$ and $30^2 = 900$, so the range of 20 to 30 is correct.

23. **B.** The problem asks you to find $(x + 2)(x + 2)$. Using the FOIL method (First, Outer, Inner, Last), systematically multiply each term in the first set of parentheses by each term in the second set of parentheses:

   - Multiply the First terms: $x(x) = x^2$.

   - Multiply the Outer terms: $x(2) = 2x$.

   - Multiply the Inner terms: $2(x) = 2x$.

   - Multiply the Last terms: $2 \times 2 = 4$.

   Now add all the products together, and you get $x^2 + 2x + 2x + 4$. Add like terms to get the final answer of $x^2 + 4x + 4$.

24. **A.** Replace the unknowns with the numbers given: $(6)(-3) - 3(-7) - 2(4) = -18 + 21 - 8 = -5$.

25. **C.** The problem asks you to find $(x + 4)(3x + 5)$. Use the FOIL method:

   - **Multiply the First terms:** $x(3x) = 3x^2$.

   - **Multiply the Outer terms:** $x(5) = 5x$.

   - **Multiply the Inner terms:** $4(3x) = 12x$.

   - **Multiply the Last terms:** $4(5) = 20$.

   Now add all the products together, and you get $3x^2 + 5x + 12x + 20$. Add like terms to get the final answer, $3x^2 + 17x + 20$.

Subtest 6: Electronics Information Answers

If you need to do well on the Electronics Information subtest to qualify for a certain military career (see Appendix A) and you're still missing questions, review Chapter 16 and spend some time memorizing key electronics concepts, including the mathematical formulas (like Power = Voltage × Current) that help you solve all kinds of electronics problems.

1. **B.** Unless a specific gauge is specified by the speaker manufacturer, you should always choose lower gauges for better sound quality.

2. **B.** There are four frequency bands used throughout the world. A quad-band cellphone would be able to access any of these frequency bands.

3. **B.** The greatest concern when dealing with electricity is personal injury.

4. **C.** *Heat effect* occurs when electrical current must overcome the resistance of the wire. Heat effect can be quite obvious or very subtle.

5. **C.** Like other diodes, Zener diodes allow current in only one direction, except if the voltage across it is greater than a threshold voltage (called *breakdown voltage*), at which point current also flows through the Zener diode in the opposite direction. This action allows the Zener diode to regulate voltage.

6. **A.** The symbol stands for *ohm*.

7. **D.** *Electromotive force* is the difference of potential, so the term is another way of saying *voltage*.

8. **A.** Lithium-ion (Li-Ion) batteries are much lighter than nickel metal hydride (NiMH) batteries.

9. **A.** The three terminals a transistor must have are the base, emitter, and collector.

10. **B.** To control a light fixture from two different positions, use two three-way switches.

11. **C.** *Amplifier* is another name for *transistor*.

12. **A.** The symbol means *ground*.

13. **C.** Capacitance is the ability to hold an electrical charge. Connecting capacitors in series reduces the capacitance.

14. **C.** 2.5K ohms is 2,500 ohms. K = 1 kilo, or 1,000.

15. **B.** A cell is equal to about 1.5 volts, so $9 \div 1.5 = 6$.

16. **D.** Primary live wires are black.

17. **C.** A motherboard is the physical arrangement in a computer that contains the computer's basic circuitry and components. Motherboards come in various sizes and component arrangements referred to as form factors to fit standard case sizes, components required, and so on. AT is a standard form factor that has a width of 12 inches and a length of 13.8 inches.

18. **B.** An on-off switch allows current to flow only when it's in the closed (on) position.

19. **C.** Determine the wattage that could cause the circuit breaker to trip with this formula: Watts = Volts × Amps, or $120 \times 25 = 3,000$ watts.

20. **D.** A *potentiometer* is a type of variable resister with three contacts that's used to control voltage.

Subtest 7: Auto & Shop Information Answers

If you have your heart set on fixing Jeeps and tanks or doing other related military jobs (see Appendix A) and you're still struggling on this test, review Chapters 13 and 14 and go through the practice questions at the end of those chapters.

1. **D.** The function of piston rings is to keep oil in the cylinders. When the rings are worn, more oil is used.

2. **A.** An engine is said to be *blueprinted* when the builder has double-checked all tolerances and used custom specifications for the vehicle to ensure manufacturer's rated power (or greater) is achieved.

3. **D.** A V-8 engine cranks (or rotates) 8 times.

4. **A.** Dieseling occurs when an engine continues to run due to fuel in the cylinders after the compression stroke.

5. **D.** A radiator is part of the cooling system, and if any part of that system fails, an engine can quickly overheat, Choice (D).

6. **C.** The intake manifold distributes air evenly between each of an engine's cylinders.

7. **A.** Calipers cause brake pads to press on the wheels, slowing the rotation and slowing or stopping the car.

8. **D.** The heater core, radiator, and thermostat are all part of the cooling system.

9. **B.** A *catalytic converter* is part of the emissions control system; it reduces dangerous exhaust emissions.

10. **B.** If the steering wheel vibrates, the front wheels may need balancing, or you may have a bent rim.

11. **C.** In a cylinder, the intake valve closes and the piston moves to the top during the compression stroke.

12. **A.** On older cars, you can find the air filter on top of the carburetor, on the top of the engine.

13. **B.** *Glazing* is a process used when replacing a pane of glass in a window frame.

14. **D.** A wrench with fixed open jaws, usually listed in a standard or metric size, is called an *open-end wrench.*

15. **A.** All hammers (such as ball peen, mallet, and so on) have a handle and a head with a face.

16. **B.** You use a thread gauge when determining the threads per inch on a threaded fastener.

17. **B.** You use a butt chisel (which has a short blade) to chip or cut wood in close quarters.

18. **C.** Machine screws have uniform threads that maintain the exact same diameter over the entire length of the fastener, unlike other screws with tapered threads.

19. **B.** Double-headed (or duplex-headed) nails are easier to remove and are used in temporary construction.

20. **A.** You can thin oil-based paint by using turpentine.

21. **C.** To make a smoother finish, sand wood with the grain.

22. **D.** To transfer an angle, you use a sliding T-bevel.

23. **C.** The tool shown is an adjustable crescent wrench.

24. **B.** Choice (B) shows a screw that requires a Phillips (also called Phillips-head) screwdriver.

25. **A.** The tool shown in the figure is used to punch holes.

Subtest 8: Mechanical Comprehension Answers

If you need to do well on the Mechanical Comprehension subtest, don't forget to apply your math skills to the concepts. (A little extra physics study wouldn't hurt, either.) But simply using your common sense can help you quite a bit, too. For example, you may not know exactly why a metal spoon feels colder than a wooden spoon when they're at the same temperature, but at least you know that it feels colder. And knowing that may help you answer a question correctly. Check out Chapter 15 for more information on the Mechanical Comprehension test and Chapter 11 for more in-depth discussion of physics.

1. **B.** The teeth of helical gears are slanted.

2. **B.** The anvil is closer to Pillar B, so Pillar B bears more weight.

3. **B.** Wheel B is smaller. It has to make more revolutions than Wheel A to cover the same amount of distance, so it will take longer.

4. **A.** E stands for *effort needed.* Here's how to set up the equation: 30 (weight of the anvil) $\times$ 2 (length of resistance arm) $= x(6)$ (length of effort arm). Do a little multiplication, and you get $60 = 6x$. To isolate x, divide each side by 6: $10 = x$.

5. **A.** A fixed, simple pulley gives no mechanical advantage, so its mechanical advantage number is 1.

6. **D.** The formula to determine the mechanical advantage of an inclined plane is Length of Ramp ÷ Height of Ramp = Weight of Object ÷ Effort:

$$\frac{8}{4} = \frac{400}{E}$$
$$8E = 400(4)$$
$$8E = 1{,}600$$
$$E = 200$$

7. B. One horsepower equals 33,000 foot-pounds per minute.

8. A. Pressure = Force ÷ Area. *Psi* stands for *pounds per square inch,* so you don't have to change the units of measurement. Just plug in your numbers: $P = 130$ lb. $\div 1$ in.$^2 = 130$ psi.

9. D. *Static electricity* is the buildup of electrical charge on surfaces, which causes materials to "stick" together this way.

10. A. An aneroid barometer measures atmospheric pressure.

11. C. Meshed gears always turn in opposite directions.

12. D. Springs are used for all the listed purposes except to add weight.

13. B. *Specific gravity* is a comparison between the density of a liquid and the density of water. The liquid with the higher specific gravity will have a float that rises higher.

14. D. Universal joints are used to connect shafts that aren't in the same plane.

15. D. Try-cocks are valves that measure water level. Water seeks a level throughout a system, so in the schematic, the try-cock correctly indicates the water level.

16. A. There are six different symbols, so six different types of machine screws were used.

17. B. To determine the amount of force the anvils exert, first multiply the length of the resistance arm (as it applies to the anvil) by the weight of each anvil and add the products together. The 10-pound anvil is supported by the entire weight of the resistance arm, so $5 \times 10 = 50$. The 5-pound anvil is being supported by 3 feet of the resistance arm, so $3 \times 5 = 15$. Add 'em up: $50 + 15 = 65$. This number is equal to the length of the resistance arm times effort (force), or $65 = 5F$. To isolate F, divide both sides by 5: $13 = F$.

18. C. One revolution of the winch will move the weight 24 inches, the circumference of the winch drum.

19. A. Valves 1 and 2 need to be open to fill the tank.

20. B. The number of revolutions a gear makes is inversely proportional to its difference in size from the gear that's turning it. Gear 1 makes 10 clockwise revolutions per minute. Gear 2 is half the size of Gear 1, so to determine the number of revolutions it makes, multiply the number of revolutions Gear 1 makes by the inverse (reciprocal) of $\frac{1}{2}$, which is $\frac{2}{1}$ (or just 2): $10 \times 2 = 20$. Therefore, Gear 2 makes 20 counterclockwise revolutions per minute. Gear 3 is 2.5 times (or $\frac{5}{2}$ times) the size of Gear 2. To determine the number of revolutions Gear 3 makes, multiply the inverse of $\frac{5}{2}$ the number of revolutions Gear 2 makes: $\frac{2}{5} \times 20 = \frac{40}{5} = 8$ revolutions per minute.

21. B. The pinion turns four times as often as the gear: $4 \times 200 = 800$ rpm.

22. C. A float indicates the level of liquid in a container.

23. B. Using a runner (a single, moveable pulley) gives a mechanical advantage of 2.

24. **A.** Because 60 seconds comprise a minute, the valve must open 60 times per minute. The cam will open the valve 10 times per revolution, and $60 \div 10 = 6$. The cam must make 6 revolutions per minute to raise the valve 60 times per minute.

25. **D.** Because Valve 4 is above the bottom of the tank, some water will remain in the tank below the level of the valve, so the tank will never be completely empty.

Subtest 9: Assembling Objects Answers

At present, only the Navy uses the scores from this subtest. If you plan to sail the Seven Seas and you want one of the few Navy jobs that requires you to put parts A and B together, you may want to go over the practice subtests again. For additional practice questions, see Chapter 17.

TIP

Try to rearrange the original figure in your head so it matches an answer choice. If the right answer isn't readily apparent, rule out incorrect choices before you decide on one.

1. **C.** As with many Assembling Objects questions, this one requires you to pay attention to where the points are located on each figure. You can immediately rule out Choices (A), (B), and (D) because Point B is in the wrong place on each of them.

2. **A.** You know Choice (B) is wrong because it depicts four shapes, and there are only three in the original diagram. Choice (C) is incorrect because it depicts two four-sided shapes, and there's only one four-sided shape in the question. Choice (D) is also wrong because it doesn't even contain the triangles the original diagram shows you, leaving only Choice (A) as the correct answer.

3. **A.** The first answer to rule out is Choice (C) because it depicts Point A in the center of the figure rather than on its point. Choice (D) can go, too, because Point B is in the wrong place. Finally, you can eliminate Choice (B) because it requires you to invert the figure that contains Point A. Choice (A) is the only figure that rotates the original figures and has the points in the right places.

4. **B.** Choices (A) and (C) aren't contenders in this question because they depict only three triangles, whereas the original figure shows four. Choice (D) is wrong because all the triangles are the same size with the same dimensions, so Choice (B) must be correct.

5. **C.** Make a mental note of where Point A lies on its figure in the original diagram; it's opposite the small triangle in the lower-left corner. That tells you Choices (B) and (D) are wrong. Now note where Point B lies and where its line leaves its figure. Choice (A) is incorrect because the Point B is outside the figure, not inside it (as it is in the original diagram).

6. **D.** Counting shapes tells you that Choice (A) is incorrect (it shows five shapes rather than four) and that Choice (B) is incorrect (it shows only three shapes, and one of them resembles a triangle). Choice (C) can't be right, either, because there are no figures in the original diagram that have parallel sides.

7. **C.** It's obvious that Choices (B) and (D) are incorrect because Point B lies on the outside of the diamond rather than inside it. Choice (A) is incorrect for two reasons: The angle of the line exiting the diamond is wrong, and it inverts the shape that Point A lies on instead of simply rotating it.

8. **C.** Pick a shape that stands out in the original diagram, such as the triangle. The triangle doesn't appear anywhere in Choice (B) or (D), so those are out. Choice (A) shows the two largest shapes as four shapes stuck together. The only answer choice that matches the exact shapes from the original diagram is Choice (C).

9. **B.** Start with the figure that includes Point A. Point A is in the wrong place in Choice (D), so even if you guess between the remaining answers, you have a better chance of getting this question right. Look at the original figure containing Point B next, which is depicted incorrectly in Choice (C). (Your chances have improved to 50-50!) Rotate the figure containing Point A; it's the opposite of what's depicted in Choice (A). You now have a 100 percent chance of answering this question correctly by choosing Choice (B).

10. **A.** The two larger figures in the problem appear to be the same size, so you can rule out Choices (B), (C), and (D), because each of those shows two smaller figures of the same size. The only answer choice that uses two large figures and one small one is Choice (A).

11. **D.** The points are dead giveaways on this question. Check out Point A, and you'll see that in Choice (A), it's in the wrong place. Point B is in the wrong place in Choices (B) and (C), which leaves you with the right answer: Choice (D).

12. **A.** Rule out Choices (B), (C), and (D) because they include shapes that aren't in the original diagram, which includes only triangles. Choice (A) is the only figure that uses two triangles that are larger than the remaining four.

13. **C.** Point A and its line leave the box at what appears to be a right angle, so you can rule out Choices (B) and (D) right off the bat. Without rotating the shape, you can see that the correct answer is Choice (C), but if you do rotate it, you'll see that Choice (A) is incorrect because it requires you to flip, not rotate, that figure.

14. **B.** Choices (A) and (D) are the same, so if one's right, the other is, too. That's not possible on the ASVAB, so eliminate those two from your choices. Besides, their shapes don't match those in the original diagram. Now compare the shapes in Choices (B) and (C), and you'll find out that those depicted in Choice (C) don't match those in the original diagram, either; that makes Choice (B) correct.

15. **D.** Ignore Choice (C) because it shows Point B in the center of the shape (the original diagram shows the point on a corner). In Choice (B), the figure containing Point B is inverted rather than rotated, so that can't be correct. Now look at the figure that contains Point A, which is inverted in Choice (A) but not in Choice (D). That means Choice (D) is the one you should choose.

16. **C.** Compare the shapes in this puzzle problem. The shapes in Choices (A), (B), and (D) don't match those in the original diagram, so Choice (C) is the clear winner.

17. **A.** Choice (C) depicts a triangle, and there's no triangle in the original diagram, so it's incorrect. Choice (D) depicts another shape that doesn't appear in the original image. Choices (A) and (B) are close, but if you look at the dimensions of the largest shape, you'll see that Choice (A) is the correct answer.

18. **B.** Forget Choices (A) and (D), because Point A's location doesn't match the original image in either. You can ignore Choice (C) because Point B is in the wrong place, too. Your last remaining choice, Choice (B), is the right answer.

19. **A.** By now, you probably know the best strategy for puzzle questions (find an odd shape and look for it in each answer choice). In this case, it's the pair of corner pieces that appear on the left side of the diagram. The only pieces that match those two show up in Choice (A), and you can be sure because each one features a pointed end and an end with a straight edge — it's almost as if the point were cut off.

20. **C.** Point A lies on the outer edge of the diamond-shaped figure where the shorter line meets the edge. The only answer choice that depicts that accurately is Choice (C). Don't let Choice (B) throw you off; it contains an inverted version of the shape containing Point A, and on the ASVAB, you'll rotate but never invert.

21. **B.** Choice (C) doesn't feature a triangle at all, but there's one in the original diagram, so scratch that one off your list of possibilities. Choice (D) shows four separate pieces making up the pentagon's perimeter, but the original figure gives you only three; that one's out, too. Choice (A)'s borders have the wrong dimensions (particularly the largest border piece), so the only possible answer is Choice (B).

22. **D.** Choice (C) is automatically wrong because Point A isn't in the same place as it is in the original diagram. Choices (A) and (B) show the figure containing Point B as a mirror image of the original (it's inverted), so neither of those can be correct. That leaves you with Choice (D), which depicts the original figures slightly rotated and connected.

23. **D.** Start comparing puzzle pieces to see what matches. Choice (A)'s largest triangle isn't a match for the original figure's largest triangle, so it's incorrect. Choice (B) features an odd shape (the third one in from the left) that doesn't appear in the original, so that's also incorrect. Choice (C) shows two thin triangles, and neither of them appears in the original diagram. However, Choice (D) has everything the original diagram has, so it's the right answer.

24. **A.** The pentagon isn't going to give you any help on this question (neither the one in the figure nor the official Pentagon in Arlington, Virginia), so you'll have to look at Point A and its figure to find the right answer here. Point A is on the lower corner of the straight edge, which doesn't match up with Choice (C) or (D). Look closely at Choice (B), and you'll see that the figure is inverted, which leaves you with Choice (A) as the correct answer.

25. **C.** The double-lined outer edge in Choice (B) is a continuous shape, which isn't possible given the original image, so rule that one out right away. Choice (A) depicts shapes inside the border with dimensions that don't match the original diagram, and if you look even more closely, you'll see that the interior shape on the bottom of the figure isn't a match at all. Choice (D) has two curved shapes on the upper part of the figure, but that's not possible with the original figures. Choice (C) has all the right ingredients, and in this case, it's the winning recipe.

Chapter 24

AFQT Practice Exam 1

I f you're wondering what in the world this exam is doing in a book on the ASVAB, don't be confused. The *Armed Forces Qualification Test*, or AFQT, is part of the ASVAB — in a way, it's a test within a test. Your scaled AFQT score is derived from four subtests of the ASVAB, and it determines your overall mental qualification to join the service branch of your choice. Each branch of military service has set its own minimum AFQT score in order to qualify for enlistment. The four subtests that can make or break your chances of joining the military are Arithmetic Reasoning (AR), Word Knowledge (WK), Paragraph Comprehension (PC), and Mathematics Knowledge (MK).

Because I like you (and because you were kind enough to buy this book), I've included a couple of extra chances for you to evaluate your communication and math skills before you head over to the MEPS (Military Entrance Processing Station), your school, or the local National Guard Armory for the real deal.

After you complete the entire practice test, check your answers in Chapter 25. If you decide you want even more practice on the AFQT, head to Chapter 26.

REMEMBER

Your goal here is to determine where you may still need to spend some more time studying. If you miss only one question on the Word Knowledge subtest but you miss 15 on Arithmetic Reasoning, you may want to dedicate some extra study time to further develop your math skills before you take the actual ASVAB.

Answer Sheet for AFQT Practice Exam 1

Subtest 1: Arithmetic Reasoning

1. Ⓐ Ⓑ Ⓒ Ⓓ   7. Ⓐ Ⓑ Ⓒ Ⓓ   13. Ⓐ Ⓑ Ⓒ Ⓓ   19. Ⓐ Ⓑ Ⓒ Ⓓ   25. Ⓐ Ⓑ Ⓒ Ⓓ
2. Ⓐ Ⓑ Ⓒ Ⓓ   8. Ⓐ Ⓑ Ⓒ Ⓓ   14. Ⓐ Ⓑ Ⓒ Ⓓ   20. Ⓐ Ⓑ Ⓒ Ⓓ   26. Ⓐ Ⓑ Ⓒ Ⓓ
3. Ⓐ Ⓑ Ⓒ Ⓓ   9. Ⓐ Ⓑ Ⓒ Ⓓ   15. Ⓐ Ⓑ Ⓒ Ⓓ   21. Ⓐ Ⓑ Ⓒ Ⓓ   27. Ⓐ Ⓑ Ⓒ Ⓓ
4. Ⓐ Ⓑ Ⓒ Ⓓ   10. Ⓐ Ⓑ Ⓒ Ⓓ   16. Ⓐ Ⓑ Ⓒ Ⓓ   22. Ⓐ Ⓑ Ⓒ Ⓓ   28. Ⓐ Ⓑ Ⓒ Ⓓ
5. Ⓐ Ⓑ Ⓒ Ⓓ   11. Ⓐ Ⓑ Ⓒ Ⓓ   17. Ⓐ Ⓑ Ⓒ Ⓓ   23. Ⓐ Ⓑ Ⓒ Ⓓ   29. Ⓐ Ⓑ Ⓒ Ⓓ
6. Ⓐ Ⓑ Ⓒ Ⓓ   12. Ⓐ Ⓑ Ⓒ Ⓓ   18. Ⓐ Ⓑ Ⓒ Ⓓ   24. Ⓐ Ⓑ Ⓒ Ⓓ   30. Ⓐ Ⓑ Ⓒ Ⓓ

Subtest 2: Word Knowledge

1. Ⓐ Ⓑ Ⓒ Ⓓ   8. Ⓐ Ⓑ Ⓒ Ⓓ   15. Ⓐ Ⓑ Ⓒ Ⓓ   22. Ⓐ Ⓑ Ⓒ Ⓓ   29. Ⓐ Ⓑ Ⓒ Ⓓ
2. Ⓐ Ⓑ Ⓒ Ⓓ   9. Ⓐ Ⓑ Ⓒ Ⓓ   16. Ⓐ Ⓑ Ⓒ Ⓓ   23. Ⓐ Ⓑ Ⓒ Ⓓ   30. Ⓐ Ⓑ Ⓒ Ⓓ
3. Ⓐ Ⓑ Ⓒ Ⓓ   10. Ⓐ Ⓑ Ⓒ Ⓓ   17. Ⓐ Ⓑ Ⓒ Ⓓ   24. Ⓐ Ⓑ Ⓒ Ⓓ   31. Ⓐ Ⓑ Ⓒ Ⓓ
4. Ⓐ Ⓑ Ⓒ Ⓓ   11. Ⓐ Ⓑ Ⓒ Ⓓ   18. Ⓐ Ⓑ Ⓒ Ⓓ   25. Ⓐ Ⓑ Ⓒ Ⓓ   32. Ⓐ Ⓑ Ⓒ Ⓓ
5. Ⓐ Ⓑ Ⓒ Ⓓ   12. Ⓐ Ⓑ Ⓒ Ⓓ   19. Ⓐ Ⓑ Ⓒ Ⓓ   26. Ⓐ Ⓑ Ⓒ Ⓓ   33. Ⓐ Ⓑ Ⓒ Ⓓ
6. Ⓐ Ⓑ Ⓒ Ⓓ   13. Ⓐ Ⓑ Ⓒ Ⓓ   20. Ⓐ Ⓑ Ⓒ Ⓓ   27. Ⓐ Ⓑ Ⓒ Ⓓ   34. Ⓐ Ⓑ Ⓒ Ⓓ
7. Ⓐ Ⓑ Ⓒ Ⓓ   14. Ⓐ Ⓑ Ⓒ Ⓓ   21. Ⓐ Ⓑ Ⓒ Ⓓ   28. Ⓐ Ⓑ Ⓒ Ⓓ   35. Ⓐ Ⓑ Ⓒ Ⓓ

Subtest 3: Paragraph Comprehension

1. Ⓐ Ⓑ Ⓒ Ⓓ   4. Ⓐ Ⓑ Ⓒ Ⓓ   7. Ⓐ Ⓑ Ⓒ Ⓓ   10. Ⓐ Ⓑ Ⓒ Ⓓ   13. Ⓐ Ⓑ Ⓒ Ⓓ
2. Ⓐ Ⓑ Ⓒ Ⓓ   5. Ⓐ Ⓑ Ⓒ Ⓓ   8. Ⓐ Ⓑ Ⓒ Ⓓ   11. Ⓐ Ⓑ Ⓒ Ⓓ   14. Ⓐ Ⓑ Ⓒ Ⓓ
3. Ⓐ Ⓑ Ⓒ Ⓓ   6. Ⓐ Ⓑ Ⓒ Ⓓ   9. Ⓐ Ⓑ Ⓒ Ⓓ   12. Ⓐ Ⓑ Ⓒ Ⓓ   15. Ⓐ Ⓑ Ⓒ Ⓓ

Subtest 4: Mathematics Knowledge

1. Ⓐ Ⓑ Ⓒ Ⓓ   6. Ⓐ Ⓑ Ⓒ Ⓓ   11. Ⓐ Ⓑ Ⓒ Ⓓ   16. Ⓐ Ⓑ Ⓒ Ⓓ   21. Ⓐ Ⓑ Ⓒ Ⓓ
2. Ⓐ Ⓑ Ⓒ Ⓓ   7. Ⓐ Ⓑ Ⓒ Ⓓ   12. Ⓐ Ⓑ Ⓒ Ⓓ   17. Ⓐ Ⓑ Ⓒ Ⓓ   22. Ⓐ Ⓑ Ⓒ Ⓓ
3. Ⓐ Ⓑ Ⓒ Ⓓ   8. Ⓐ Ⓑ Ⓒ Ⓓ   13. Ⓐ Ⓑ Ⓒ Ⓓ   18. Ⓐ Ⓑ Ⓒ Ⓓ   23. Ⓐ Ⓑ Ⓒ Ⓓ
4. Ⓐ Ⓑ Ⓒ Ⓓ   9. Ⓐ Ⓑ Ⓒ Ⓓ   14. Ⓐ Ⓑ Ⓒ Ⓓ   19. Ⓐ Ⓑ Ⓒ Ⓓ   24. Ⓐ Ⓑ Ⓒ Ⓓ
5. Ⓐ Ⓑ Ⓒ Ⓓ   10. Ⓐ Ⓑ Ⓒ Ⓓ   15. Ⓐ Ⓑ Ⓒ Ⓓ   20. Ⓐ Ⓑ Ⓒ Ⓓ   25. Ⓐ Ⓑ Ⓒ Ⓓ

Subtest 1: Arithmetic Reasoning

TIME: 36 minutes for 30 questions

DIRECTIONS: This test contains questions about arithmetic. Each question is followed by four possible answers. Decide which answer is correct and then mark the space on your answer sheet that has the same number and letter as your choice. Use scratch paper for any figuring you need to do. Calculators are not allowed.

1. If a barber is capable of cutting the hair of 35 people per day and he works 7 days per week, how many haircuts could he give during the months of April, May, and June?

   (A) 3,185

   (B) 3,150

   (C) 2,545

   (D) 2,555

2. If you type 45 words per minute, how many words can you type in 12 minutes?

   (A) 490

   (B) 540

   (C) 605

   (D) 615

3. Tom is flying a kite at the end of a 500-foot string. His friend Kathy is standing directly under the kite 300 feet away from Tom. How high is the kite flying?

   (A) 300 feet

   (B) 350 feet

   (C) 400 feet

   (D) 450 feet

4. Amy wants to fence in a yard using 400 feet of fencing. If she wants the yard to be 30 feet wide, what will its length be?

   (A) 170 feet

   (B) 175 feet

   (C) 180 feet

   (D) 185 feet

5. A three-digit code must be used to access a computer file. The first digit must be an A or a B. The second digit must be a number between 0 and 9. The final digit is a single letter from the alphabet from A to Z. How many possible access codes can there be?

   (A) 38

   (B) 468

   (C) 520

   (D) 640

6. The sun is 93 million miles from Earth, and light travels at a rate of 186,000 miles per second. How long does it take for light from the sun to reach Earth?

   (A) 5 minutes

   (B) $6\frac{1}{2}$ minutes

   (C) 7 minutes

   (D) $8\frac{1}{3}$ minutes

7. A tanning-bed pass for unlimited tanning costs $53 per month this year, but it was only $50 per month last year. What was the percentage of increase?

   (A) 5%

   (B) 5.5%

   (C) 6%

   (D) 6.5%

8. Eleven plus forty-one is divided by a number. If the result is thirteen, what's the number?

   (A) 2

   (B) 4

   (C) 6

   (D) 8

GO ON TO NEXT PAGE

9. Mark received an hourly wage of $9.25. His boss gave him a 4% raise. How much does Mark make per hour now?

    (A) $9.29

    (B) $9.62

    (C) $9.89

    (D) $9.99

10. How many pounds of nails costing $7 per pound must be mixed with 6 pounds of nails costing $3 per pound to yield a mixture costing $4 per pound?

    (A) 2 pounds

    (B) 2.5 pounds

    (C) 3 pounds

    (D) 3.5 pounds

11. Theodore has 24 baseball cards. He sells $\frac{1}{4}$ of his cards to Tom and $\frac{1}{3}$ of his cards to Larry, and his mom accidently throws away $\frac{1}{6}$ of his cards. How many baseball cards does Theodore have left?

    (A) 2

    (B) 18

    (C) 12

    (D) 6

12. Theresa bought five karaoke CDs on sale. A karaoke CD normally costs $24, but she was able to purchase the CDs for $22.50 each. How much money did Theresa save on her entire purchase?

    (A) $7.50

    (B) $1.50

    (C) $8.00

    (D) $22.50

13. On a trip to the beach, you travel 200 miles in 300 minutes. How fast did you travel?

    (A) 30 mph

    (B) 40 mph

    (C) 50 mph

    (D) 60 mph

14. Twenty-one students, or 60% of the class, passed the final exam. How many students are in the class?

    (A) 45

    (B) 40

    (C) 35

    (D) 30

15. Joan invests $4,000 in an account that earns 3% simple interest. How much will Joan have in the account in 10 years?

    (A) $4,500

    (B) $4,800

    (C) $5,200

    (D) $5,400

16. A rectangle has a perimeter of 36 inches. Its length is 3 inches greater than twice the width. What's the rectangle's length?

    (A) 5 inches

    (B) 13 inches

    (C) 18 inches

    (D) 20 inches

17. A backyard is 50 feet by 100 feet. What's its area?

    (A) 150 square feet

    (B) 300 square feet

    (C) 500 square feet

    (D) 5,000 square feet

18. Eric is driving a car in which the speedometer displays speed in kilometers per hour (kph). He notes that his car is traveling at a rate of 75 kph, when he passes a speed limit sign stating the limit is 40 miles per hour (mph). He knows that a kilometer is about $\frac{5}{8}$ of a mile. If a police officer stops him at this point, how many miles per hour over the limit will the ticket read?

    (A) 5

    (B) 7

    (C) 9

    (D) 11

19. Three apples and twice as many pears add up to one-half the number of grapes in a fruit basket. How many grapes are in the basket?

(A) 8

(B) 18

(C) 28

(D) 38

20. Apples are on sale for "Buy 2 pounds, get 1 pound free." How many pounds must Janet purchase to get 2 pounds free?

(A) 2 pounds

(B) 4 pounds

(C) 6 apples

(D) 3 pounds

21. If four pipes of equal length measure 44 feet when they're connected together, how long is each pipe?

(A) 11 feet

(B) 4 feet

(C) 22 feet

(D) 9 feet

22. A German shepherd and an Alaskan malamute are both headed toward the same fire hydrant. The German shepherd is 120 feet away from the hydrant, and the Alaskan malamute is 75 feet away from the hydrant. How much closer to the hydrant is the Alaskan malamute?

(A) 45 feet

(B) 25 feet

(C) 75 feet

(D) 195 feet

23. A recruit reporting to boot camp took a bus from her home to the military processing center in another city. The trip took 14 hours. If she left at 6 a.m., what time did she arrive at the processing center?

(A) 7 p.m.

(B) 12 a.m.

(C) 8 p.m.

(D) 9 p.m.

24. A farmer sold 3 pints of strawberries for $1.98 each, 5 pints of raspberries for $2.49 each, and a bushel of peaches for $5.50 at his roadside stand. How much money did the farmer make?

(A) $9.97

(B) $23.89

(C) $18.39

(D) $18.91

25. A librarian wants to shelve 532 books. If four books fit on a 1-foot length of shelving, how many feet of shelving does she need to shelve all the books?

(A) 13

(B) 45

(C) 33

(D) 133

26. A student buys a science textbook for $18.00, a math textbook for $14.50, and a dictionary for $9.95. What's the total cost of the books?

(A) $27.95

(B) $42.45

(C) $41.95

(D) $38.50

27. Debra works an 8-hour shift on Friday. How many minutes does she work on Friday?

(A) 480 minutes

(B) 800 minutes

(C) 240 minutes

(D) 400 minutes

28. Six people can run three machines in the factory. How many machines can 18 people run?

(A) 7

(B) 9

(C) 6

(D) 8

GO ON TO NEXT PAGE

29. On a map drawn to scale, $\frac{1}{2}$ inch equals 1 mile. What length on the map equals 5 miles?

    (A) 2.5 inches

    (B) 5.0 inches

    (C) 10.0 inches

    (D) 1.5 inches

30. A man bought a pair of jeans for $23.00, a shirt for $14.95, and two ties for $7.98 each. What was the total cost of his clothing?

    (A) $53.91

    (B) $45.93

    (C) $51.99

    (D) $54.50

Subtest 2: Word Knowledge

TIME: 11 minutes for 35 questions

DIRECTIONS: This test has questions about the meanings of words. Each question has an underlined word. You need to decide which one of the four words in the choices most nearly means the same thing as the underlined word and then mark the corresponding space on your answer sheet.

1. The <u>abhorrent</u> smell from the lake overpowered the picnickers gathered on the shore.

   (A) strong

   (B) pleasant

   (C) offensive

   (D) tantalizing

2. <u>Belie</u> most nearly means

   (A) pleasure.

   (B) rule.

   (C) pretend.

   (D) misrepresent.

3. The water was calm that day with <u>detritus</u> slowly moving in the small eddies.

   (A) fish

   (B) lily pads

   (C) plants

   (D) debris

4. The prime minister was always cautious about leaving his <u>redoubt</u> in Belgrade.

   (A) city

   (B) stronghold

   (C) house

   (D) country

5. Mike was afraid he might be <u>ostracized</u> for stepping out of line.

   (A) banished

   (B) scolded

   (C) assaulted

   (D) arrested

6. The hotel was specifically designed for the <u>wayworn</u> traveler.

   (A) lost

   (B) weary

   (C) demanding

   (D) happy

7. The park has no showers and no <u>potable</u> water.

   (A) usable

   (B) clear

   (C) drinkable

   (D) tasty

8. <u>Decamp</u> most nearly means

   (A) to backpack.

   (B) to leave.

   (C) to doubt.

   (D) to act with abandon.

9. <u>Glorious</u> most nearly means

   (A) splendid.

   (B) particular.

   (C) delayed.

   (D) contentious.

10. <u>Duplicity</u> most nearly means

    (A) hyperactivity.

    (B) godlike.

    (C) deception.

    (D) criticalness.

11. <u>Mallet</u> most nearly means

    (A) sermon.

    (B) participate.

    (C) hammer.

    (D) fish.

12. <u>Hosiery</u> most nearly means

    (A) dangerous.

    (B) illegal.

    (C) stocking.

    (D) automatic.

GO ON TO NEXT PAGE

13. Hale most nearly means

   (A) old.

   (B) healthy.

   (C) customary.

   (D) uninformed.

14. Magnitude most nearly means

   (A) importance.

   (B) peculiar.

   (C) alone.

   (D) tantamount.

15. His vapid presentation earned him a C in the class.

   (A) difficult

   (B) plagiarized

   (C) dull

   (D) polished

16. Percival was unpopular at the meeting because he imparted so much extraneous data.

   (A) extensive

   (B) unwelcome

   (C) superfluous

   (D) radical

17. She was often solicitous of her father's feelings.

   (A) careful

   (B) ignorant

   (C) forgetful

   (D) abusive

18. I could never get over her liquid blue, limpid eyes.

   (A) bright

   (B) clear

   (C) attentive

   (D) dull

19. The goal of the treaty is to develop international amity and reciprocal trade.

   (A) agreement

   (B) friendship

   (C) standards

   (D) understanding

20. He often bragged about the bravery of his favorite cohort.

   (A) person

   (B) teacher

   (C) companion

   (D) employee

21. Speechless most nearly means

   (A) well-spoken.

   (B) silent.

   (C) restless.

   (D) talkative.

22. Indigenous most nearly means

   (A) poor.

   (B) rich.

   (C) immigrant.

   (D) native.

23. Illusive most nearly means

   (A) insignificant.

   (B) deceptive.

   (C) useful.

   (D) hidden.

24. Hesitate most nearly means

   (A) slam.

   (B) slow to act.

   (C) foreclose.

   (D) end.

25. Gravity most nearly means

   (A) planet.

   (B) relationship.

   (C) earn.

   (D) seriousness.

26. Fondle most nearly means

   (A) stir.

   (B) handle.

   (C) ogle.

   (D) radiate.

27. <u>Fete</u> most nearly means

    (A) festival.

    (B) criticize.

    (C) approve.

    (D) eat.

28. <u>Encore</u> most nearly means

    (A) play.

    (B) applause.

    (C) repetition.

    (D) excite.

29. <u>Diverse</u> most nearly means

    (A) various.

    (B) hidden.

    (C) nestled.

    (D) pastime.

30. <u>Detest</u> most nearly means

    (A) anger.

    (B) hate.

    (C) surprise.

    (D) excite.

31. Mike was known as a smart aleck, able to deliver <u>acerbic</u> one-liners with no effort.

    (A) funny

    (B) cheap

    (C) sharp

    (D) poetic

32. It took a great degree of <u>inexorable</u> force to break into the cavern.

    (A) strong

    (B) unyielding

    (C) acute

    (D) powerful

33. Attendants were stationed at intervals, with the obvious intent to <u>hector</u> those who moved too slowly.

    (A) hurry

    (B) harass

    (C) encourage

    (D) note

34. Reggie was as <u>gauche</u> in this group of polite company as he always had been.

    (A) funny

    (B) entertaining

    (C) tactless

    (D) embarrassed

35. <u>Confident</u> most nearly means

    (A) assured.

    (B) positive.

    (C) intelligent.

    (D) educated.

Subtest 3: Paragraph Comprehension

TIME: 13 minutes for 15 questions

DIRECTIONS: This test contains items that measure your ability to understand what you read. This section includes one or more paragraphs of reading material followed by incomplete statements or questions. Read the paragraph and select the choice that best completes the statement or answers the question. Mark your choice on your answer sheet by using the correct letter with each question number.

On June 22, 1944, President Franklin Delano Roosevelt signed into law one of the most significant pieces of legislation ever produced by the United States government: The Servicemembers' Readjustment Act of 1944, commonly known as the GI Bill of Rights. By the time the original GI Bill ended in July 1956, 7.8 million World War II veterans had participated in an education or training program, and 2.4 million veterans had home loans backed by the Veterans Administration (VA).

1. The GI Bill provided

(A) free housing, training, and education.

(B) medical coverage, education, and assistance to veterans.

(C) home loan guarantees, training, and education for many former military members.

(D) a means to exempt veterans from Social Security taxes.

You can put up to $3,000 a year into an individual retirement account (IRA) on a tax-deductible basis if your spouse isn't covered by a retirement plan at work or as long as your combined income isn't too high. You also can put the same amount tax-deferred into an IRA for a nonworking spouse if you file your income tax return jointly.

2. The maximum amount that a married couple could possibly save in a tax-deferred IRA during a year is

(A) $3,000.

(B) $6,000.

(C) $9,000.

(D) The question can't be answered based on the information contained in the passage.

Presidential appointments are an ongoing effort. Some of a president's appointments require Senate confirmation. These appointments are for positions throughout the federal government, for the Cabinet and subcabinet, for members of regulatory commissions, for ambassadorships, for judgeships, and for members of numerous advisory boards.

3. Which of the following statements is not true?

(A) All presidential appointments require Senate confirmation.

(B) A position on a regulatory commission is an example of a presidential appointment.

(C) Presidential appointments happen throughout the president's term in office.

(D) All of the above statements are true.

A link between advertising and alcohol consumption is intuitively compelling but hasn't been consistently supported by research. Because alcohol advertising is pervasive, econometric studies may not be sensitive to change or assess in a range where change actually makes a difference. In dealing with advertising, partial bans aren't likely to be effective, and total bans aren't practical. Advertising bans in one medium also are weakened by substitution of increased advertising in alternative media and/or other promotions.

4. The author of this passage believes that

(A) advertisement of alcoholic beverages should be illegal.

(B) partial bans on alcohol advertising could be effective in some cases.

(C) bans on alcohol advertising aren't likely to work.

(D) clear links have been established between alcohol consumption and advertising.

The etymology of the word or name *Alabama* has evoked much discussion among philological researchers. It was the name of a noted southern Indian tribe whose habitat when first known to Europeans was in what is now central Alabama. One of the major waterways in the state was named for this group and from this river, in turn, the name of the state was derived. According to some investigations, the tribal name Alabama must be sought in the Choctaw tongue, because it isn't uncommon for tribes to accept a name given them by a neighboring tribe.

5. The state of Alabama was named after

(A) a Choctaw Indian tribe.

(B) European settlers.

(C) a river.

(D) an Indian chief.

Each of the 94 federal judicial districts handles bankruptcy matters, and in almost all districts, bankruptcy cases are filed in the bankruptcy court. Bankruptcy cases can't be filed in state court. Bankruptcy laws help people who can no longer pay their creditors get a fresh start by liquidating their assets to pay their debts or by creating a repayment plan. Bankruptcy laws also protect troubled businesses and provide for orderly distributions to business creditors through reorganization or liquidation.

6. Which of the following statements is not supported by the passage?

(A) Bankruptcy must be filed in a federal court.

(B) Bankruptcy is designed to help individuals and protect businesses.

(C) Businesses can be reorganized or liquidated through bankruptcy.

(D) Bankruptcy must be filed in the bankruptcy court.

Questions 7 and 8 are based on the following passage.

The U.S. Department of Justice has prepared a report about hate crimes in the United States between 1997 and 1999. In 60% of hate crime incidents, the most serious offense was a violent crime, most commonly intimidation or simple assault. The majority of incidents motivated by race, ethnicity, sexual orientation, or disability involved a violent offense, while two-thirds of incidents motivated by religion involved a property offense, most commonly vandalism. Younger offenders were responsible for most hate crimes. Thirty-one percent of violent offenders and 46% of property offenders were under age 18.

7. Most property offense hate crimes were motivated by

(A) religion.

(B) race.

(C) sexual orientation.

(D) abortion.

8. The majority of hate crimes during this period can be classified as

(A) property offenses.

(B) violent crimes.

(C) assault.

(D) intimidation.

Linewatch operations are conducted near international boundaries and coastlines in areas of Border Patrol jurisdiction to prevent the illegal entry and smuggling of aliens into the United States and to intercept those who do enter illegally before they can escape from border areas. Sign cutting is the detection and the interpretation of any disturbances in natural terrain conditions that indicate the presence or passage of people, animals, or vehicles.

9. The activity that's designed to detect changes in the natural environment, which may indicate passage of undocumented aliens, is called

(A) linewatching.

(B) sign cutting.

(C) Border Patrol Operations.

(D) Terrain Observation.

GO ON TO NEXT PAGE ▶

Wales was in ancient times divided into three parts nearly equal, consideration having been paid, in this division, more to the value than to the just quantity or proportion of territory. They were Venedotia, now called North Wales; Demetia, or South Wales, which in British is called Deheubarth, that is, the southern part; and Powys, the middle or eastern district. Roderic the Great, or Rhodri Mawr, who was king over all Wales, was the cause of this division. He had three sons, Mervin, Anarawt, and Cadell, amongst whom he partitioned the whole principality.

10. Wales was divided into divisions because

(A) natural boundaries such as rivers and mountains made the division necessary.

(B) Wales was too large for the king to over-see personally.

(C) the King of Wales wanted his sons to rule.

(D) all of the above.

Questions 11 and 12 are based on the following passage.

The fierce and warlike tribe, called the Huns, who'd driven the Goths to seek new homes, came from Asia into Southeastern Europe and took possession of a large territory lying north of the River Danube. During the first half of the fifth century, the Huns had a famous king named Attila. He was only 21 years old when he became their king. But although he was young, he was very brave and ambitious, and he wanted to be a great and powerful king. As soon as his army was ready, he marched with it into countries, which belonged to Rome. He defeated the Romans in several great battles and captured many of their cities. The Roman Emperor Theodosius had to ask for terms of peace. Attila agreed that there should be peace, but soon afterwards he found out that Theodosius had formed a plot to murder him. He was so enraged at this that he again began war. He plundered and burned cities wherever he went, and at last the emperor had to give him a large sum of money and a portion of the country south of the Danube.

11. A good title for the above paragraph would be

(A) "The Burning of Rome"

(B) "Emperor Theodosius"

(C) "Attila the Hun"

(D) "Rome for Dummies"

12. After terms of peace were offered, Attila resumed the war against Rome because

(A) he discovered the emperor wanted to assassinate him.

(B) he wanted to further expand his kingdom.

(C) the emperor of Rome offered too little money in the peace terms.

(D) Danube, his second-in-charge, advised him not to accept the peace terms.

Questions 13 through 15 are based on the following passage.

In the military, as in all professions, the issue of competence is directly relevant to professional integrity. Because human life, national security, and expenditures from the national treasury are so frequently at issue when the military acts, the obligation to be competent isn't merely prudential. That obligation is a moral one, and culpable incompetence here is clearly a violation of professional integrity. Part of the social aspect of professional integrity involves the joint responsibility for conduct and competence shared by all members of the profession. Only fellow professionals are capable of evaluating competence in some instances; hence, fellow professionals must accept the responsibility of upholding the standards of the profession. Fellow military members can spot derelictions of duty, failures of leadership, failures of competence, and the venalities of conduct that interfere with the goals of the military mission. Often, the obligations of professional integrity may be pitted against personal loyalties or friendships; and, where the stakes for society are so high, professional integrity should win out.

13. One word that best describes the primary theme of this passage would be

(A) proficiency.

(B) equality.

(C) evaluations.

(D) relationships.

14. Professional competence is

(A) a moral obligation.

(B) directly relevant to professional integrity.

(C) essential because military operations impact human life, national security, and use of taxpayer funds.

(D) all of the above.

15. The author of the passage would agree that

(A) friendship must often take a back seat to professional integrity.

(B) only fellow professionals should evaluate competence.

(C) professional competence is a direct result of effective training programs.

(D) all of the above.

Subtest 4: Mathematics Knowledge

TIME: 24 minutes for 25 questions

DIRECTIONS: This section is a test of your ability to solve general mathematical problems. Select the correct answer from the choices given and then mark the corresponding space on your answer sheet. Use scratch paper to do any figuring. Calculators are not allowed.

1. Solve for x: $5x - 2x = 7x + 2x - 24$

(A) 2

(B) −2

(C) 4

(D) −4

2. The cube of 6 is

(A) 125

(B) 225

(C) 216

(D) 238

3. In the graph $3x + 7y = 21$, at what point is the x-axis intersected?

(A) $(7, 0)$

(B) $(0, 7)$

(C) $(0, 4)$

(D) $(4, 0)$

4. $x + y = 6$ and $x - y = 4$. Find the value of x.

(A) 3

(B) 5

(C) 7

(D) 8

5. Solve for y: $4(y + 3) + 7 = 3$

(A) 2

(B) −2

(C) 4

(D) −4

6. $(12 \text{ yards} + 14 \text{ feet}) \div 2 =$

(A) 25 feet

(B) 12 feet

(C) 50 feet

(D) 8 feet

7. $x^3(x^3) =$

(A) x^9

(B) $2x^9$

(C) $2x^6$

(D) x^6

8. $4\frac{1}{5} + 1\frac{2}{5} + 3\frac{3}{10} =$

(A) $6\frac{1}{5}$

(B) $8\frac{9}{10}$

(C) $5\frac{1}{2}$

(D) $7\frac{1}{5}$

9. $1.5 \times 10^2 =$

(A) 45

(B) 150

(C) 1,500

(D) 15

10. The average of 54, 61, 70, and 75 is

(A) 50

(B) 52

(C) 55

(D) 65

11. 2 feet, 4 inches + 4 feet, 8 inches =

(A) 6 feet, 8 inches

(B) 7 feet

(C) 7 feet, 2 inches

(D) 8 feet

12. If $x = 4$, then $x^4 \div x =$

(A) 12

(B) 36

(C) 64

(D) 72

13. Solve for x: $5 - 3x \geq 14 + 6x$

(A) $x \geq -1$

(B) $x \leq -1$

(C) $x > -1$

(D) $x < -1$

14. $(900 \times 3) \div 6 =$

(A) 45

(B) 450

(C) 55

(D) 550

15. If $x = 2$, then $x^x(x^x) =$

(A) 16

(B) $2x^x$

(C) 8

(D) 24

16. Solve for x: $x^2 - 2x - 15 = 0$

(A) 4, −2

(B) 3, −3

(C) 5, −3

(D) −1, 1

17. $\sqrt{49} \div \sqrt{64} =$

(A) $\frac{1}{4}$

(B) $\frac{1}{2}$

(C) $\frac{1}{3}$

(D) $\frac{7}{8}$

18. If $5y^2 = 80$, then y is

(A) a positive number.

(B) a negative number.

(C) either a positive or negative number.

(D) an imaginary number.

19. If $2 + x \geq 15$, what's the value of x?

(A) $x < 13$

(B) $x > 13$

(C) $x \geq 13$

(D) $x \leq 13$

20. If a circle has a radius of 15 feet, which is the best estimate of its circumference?

(A) 24 feet

(B) 72 feet

(C) 94 feet

(D) 36 feet

21. What's the volume of a box measuring 12 inches long by 8 inches deep by 10 inches high?

(A) 960 cubic inches

(B) 128 cubic inches

(C) 42 cubic inches

(D) 288 cubic inches

22. The following figure is a(n)

© John Wiley & Sons, Inc.

(A) parallelogram.

(B) obtuse triangle.

(C) trapezoid.

(D) rectangle.

23. The sum of the measures of the interior angles of a parallelogram is

(A) 360 degrees.

(B) 540 degrees.

(C) 180 degrees.

(D) 720 degrees.

24. What is the prime factorization of 100?

(A) 2×50

(B) $2^2 \times 5^2$

(C) 4×25

(D) 25^2

25. $\sqrt{-9}$ is an example of a(n)

(A) real number.

(B) imaginary number.

(C) irrational number.

(D) rational number.

DO NOT TURN THE PAGE UNTIL TOLD TO DO SO **STOP** DO NOT RETURN TO A PREVIOUS TEST

Chapter 25

AFQT Practice Exam 1: Answers and Explanations

U se this answer key to score the Practice AFQT Exam in Chapter 24. Note that the actual AFQT is scored by comparing your raw score to other people's scores, which produces a scaled score. Turn to Chapter 1 to find out how the AFQT score is derived from the Arithmetic Reasoning, Word Knowledge, Paragraph Comprehension, and Mathematics Knowledge subtests. Keep in mind that these four subtests determine whether you can even get into the military. If you find you're still struggling in any of these subtest areas, you may want to concentrate some additional study effort before knocking on your recruiter's door to say, "I'm ready!"

Subtest 1: Arithmetic Reasoning Answers

Mathematical word problems can be tough for some people. You have to zero in on relevant facts, turn those facts into a mathematical formula, and reach the correct solution. Yikes! No wonder there are so many math books on the market. If you still need work on this subtest, I recommend reviewing the chapters in Part 3. Running through the additional practice questions at the ends of those chapters may also help.

1. **A.** There are 30 days in April, 31 days in May, and 30 days in June for a total of 91 days. Multiply the number of days by the number of haircuts per day: $91 \times 35 = 3,185$.

2. **B.** Multiply the number of words you can type per minute (45) by the number of minutes you'll be typing (12): $45 \times 12 = 540$.

3. C. Visualize a right triangle, where the kite string represents the hypotenuse and the line between Tom and Kathy represents one of the legs. The Pythagorean theorem states that if you know the length of two sides of a right triangle, you can determine the length of the third side using the formula $a^2 + b^2 = c^2$. In this case, $300^2 + b^2 = 500^2$. Solve for b:

$$90,000 + b^2 = 250,000$$
$$b^2 = 250,000 - 90,000$$
$$b^2 = 160,000$$
$$b = \sqrt{160,000}$$
$$b = 400$$

4. A. The formula used to determine the perimeter of a rectangle is $P = 2(l + w)$. The width is 30, and the perimeter is 400. Plug in the numbers and solve for l:

$$400 = 2(l + 30)$$
$$400 = 2l + 60$$
$$340 = 2l$$
$$l = 170$$

5. C. There are two possibilities for the first digit (A or B), 10 possibilities for the second digit (0 to 9), and 26 possibilities for the third digit. Using the multiplication principle, $2 \times 10 \times 26 = 520$ possible access codes.

6. D. The distance formula is distance equals rate times time, or $d = rt$. Substitute the known values: $93,000,000 = 186,000t$. Therefore, $t = 500$ seconds. Divide 500 by 60 to convert to minutes: 500 seconds ÷ 60 seconds/minute $= 8\frac{1}{3}$ minutes.

7. C. The difference in the price is $3, so divide the difference by the original price: $3 ÷ $50 = 0.06$, or 6%.

8. B. Let x = the unknown number. Set up the equation as $\frac{11 + 41}{x} = 13$. Then solve for x:

$$\frac{11 + 41}{x} = 13$$
$$\frac{52}{x} = 13$$
$$52 = 13x$$
$$x = 4$$

9. B. Mark received a 4% raise, so to calculate the new wage, start off by finding the raise: $9.25 \times 0.04 = 0.37. Then add that number (the amount of Mark's raise) to his original hourly wage. Mark's new hourly wage is $9.25 + $0.37 = 9.62.

10. A. Let x = the weight of nails costing $7 per pound. The total cost of the mixture *(M)* equals the sum of the cost for each type of nail, or $M = A + B$, where $A = 7x$, $B = 3(6)$, and $M = 4(6 + x)$. Substitute the known values into the equation and solve for x:

$$4(6 + x) = 7x + 18$$
$$24 + 4x = 7x + 18$$
$$24 - 18 = 7x - 4x$$
$$6 = 3x$$
$$x = 2$$

11. D. You need to add the fractions, so convert the different denominators to a common denominator — 4, 3, and 6 all divide evenly into 12, so use 12 as the common denominator.

$$\frac{1}{4} \times \frac{3}{3} = \frac{3}{12} \qquad \frac{1}{3} \times \frac{4}{4} = \frac{4}{12} \qquad \frac{1}{6} \times \frac{2}{2} = \frac{2}{12}$$

To add the fractions, first add the new numerators together: $3 + 4 + 2 = 9$. Place the added numerator over the new denominator, 12, and you can see that $\frac{9}{12}$ of the cards have been sold or lost. You can reduce $\frac{9}{12}$ to $\frac{3}{4}$, so $\frac{1}{4}$ of the cards remain. $\frac{1}{4}$ of 24 is $\frac{1}{4} \times 24 = 6$, so 6 cards remain.

12. A. Subtract the sale price from the regular price: $\$24.00 - \$22.50 = \$1.50$. Multiply the difference by the number of CDs to find out how much Theresa saved altogether: $\$1.50 \times 5 = \$7.50$.

13. B. First convert the 300 minutes to hours by dividing by 60 (300 minutes ÷ 60 minutes/ hour = 5 hours). Use the distance formula ($d = rt$) and substitute the known values: $200 = 5r$; $r = 40$ mph.

14. C. Let x = the number of people in the class; 60% of $x = 21$, so $0.60x = 21$, and $x = 35$.

15. C. Use the interest formula ($I = Prt$) to determine the amount of interest earned, where the principal (P) is 4,000, the rate (r) is 0.03 (3%), and the time (t) is 10. $I = 4,000(0.03)(10)$, or $I = \$1,200$. Add the interest earned to the original amount invested: $\$4,000 + \$1,200 = \$5,200$.

16. B. A rectangle's perimeter is determined by the formula $P = 2(l + w)$. The length of this rectangle is $3 + 2w$. Substituting the known values into the formula results in

$$36 = 2(w + 3 + 2w)$$
$$36 = 2(3w + 3)$$
$$18 = 3w + 3$$
$$15 = 3w$$
$$w = 5$$

The length is $3 + 2w$, so $l = 3 + 2(5) = 13$.

17. D. The area of a rectangle is the length times the width of the rectangle, or $A = lw$: $50 \times 100 = 5,000$ square feet.

18. B. A kilometer is $\frac{5}{8}$ of a mile, so multiply $75 \times \frac{5}{8} = \frac{375}{8}$. Divide 375 by 8 to determine that Eric was traveling at about 47 miles per hour, 7 mph over the 40 mph posted limit.

19. B. Let x = the number of grapes; 3 apples and 6 pears (twice the number of apples) equals $\frac{1}{2}$ of x, or

$$3 + 6 = \frac{1}{2}x$$
$$9 = \frac{1}{2}x$$
$$2(9) = x$$
$$x = 18$$

20. B. If Janet must purchase 2 pounds of apples to get 1 free pound, then to get 2 free pounds, she would need to purchase twice as many apples, or 4 pounds of apples.

21. **A.** All pipes are equal in length, so divide the total length, 44 feet, by the total number of pipes, 4. The answer, 11, is the length of each individual pipe. You can check this answer by multiplying: $4 \times 11 = 44$.

22. **A.** Subtract the Alaskan malamute's distance from the German shepherd's distance $(120 - 75 = 45)$ to determine how much closer the Alaskan malamute is to the hydrant.

23. **C.** Simply add 14 hours to 6 a.m. to reach 8 p.m. Twelve hours from 6 a.m. is 6 p.m., and two hours after that brings you to 8 p.m.

24. **B.** Multiply 3 pints of strawberries at \$1.98 ($3 \times \$1.98 = \$5.94$), 5 pints of raspberries at \$2.49 ($5 \times \$2.49 = \$12.45$), and 1 bushel of peaches at \$5.50 ($1 \times \$5.50 = \$5.50$). Add the products together to determine the amount of cash the farmer earned: $\$5.94 + \$12.45 + \$5.50 = \$23.89$. You can also start with an estimate by rounding the prices and multiplying, like this: $(3 \times 2) + (5 \times 2.5) + 5.5 = 6 + 12.5 + 5.5 = 24$. Choice (B) is the only value close to the estimate.

25. **D.** Divide 532 by 4 to determine how many feet of shelving will be needed: $532 \text{ books} \div 4 \text{ books/foot} = 133 \text{ feet}$.

26. **A.** Simply add the cost of all the books: $\$18.00 + \$14.50 + \$9.95 = \$42.45$.

27. **A.** $8 \text{ hours} \times 60 \text{ minutes/hour} = 480 \text{ minutes}$.

28. **B.** Eighteen people can run three times the number of machines 6 people can run, because $18 = 3 \times 6$ (divide 18 by 6). Six people can run 3 machines, so multiply $3 \times 3 \text{ machines} = 9 \text{ machines}$. Therefore, 18 people can run 9 machines.

29. **A.** Multiply the scale measurement for 1 mile $\left(\frac{1}{2} \text{ inch per mile} \right)$ by 5 miles: $\frac{1}{2} \times 5 = \frac{1}{2} \times \frac{5}{1} = \frac{5}{2}$. Divide 5 by 2, and you get 2.5 inches.

30. **A.** Simply add the cost of all the items: $\$23.00 + \$14.95 + \$7.98 + \$7.98 = \$53.91$. To save time, you can also round up the cost of each item to the next-highest dollar amount and add the rounded numbers. Your answer (\$54) is a little higher than Choice (A), which makes it the right answer.

Subtest 2: Word Knowledge Answers

I hope you did well on this subtest. (I was crossing my fingers the whole time!) If not, you may want to take another gander at Chapter 4.

1. **C.** *Abhorrent* is an adjective that means repugnant or inspiring disgust and loathing.

2. **D.** *Belie* is a verb that means to fail to give a true impression of something. It also means to disguise, contradict, or betray.

3. **D.** *Detritus* is a noun that refers to waste or debris.

4. **B.** *Redoubt* is a noun that refers to a temporary or supplementary fortification that usually doesn't have flanking defenses.

5. **A.** *Ostracized* is the past tense of the verb *ostracize*, which means to exclude someone from a group or society.

6. **B.** *Wayworn* is an adjective that means weary from traveling.

7. **C.** *Potable* is an adjective that means safe to drink. (In basic training, you'll see huge water tanks spray-painted with "Potable Water," so that's where you'll go to rehydrate.)

8. **B.** *Decamp* is a verb that means to depart secretly or suddenly, especially to relocate to another area.

9. **A.** *Glorious* is an adjective that means having exceptional beauty that evokes feelings of admiration. It also means having, bringing, or worthy of fame or admiration.

10. **C.** *Duplicity* is a noun that means deceitfulness.

11. **C.** *Mallet* is a noun that refers to a hammer with a large head.

12. **C.** *Hosiery* is a noun that refers to stockings, pantyhose, and socks collectively.

13. **B.** *Hale* is an adjective that means strong and healthy (when referring to a person).

14. **A.** *Magnitude* is a noun that refers to the great size or extent of something; it also means great importance or consequence.

15. **C.** *Vapid* is an adjective that means offering nothing stimulating or challenging.

16. **C.** *Extraneous* is an adjective that means unrelated or irrelevant to the current subject, and one of its synonyms is *superfluous* (which means unnecessary, especially when something is in abundance).

17. **A.** *Solicitous* is an adjective that means showing interest or concern.

18. **B.** *Limpid* is an adjective that means clear and unclouded.

19. **B.** *Amity* is a noun that refers to a friendly relationship.

20. **C.** *Cohort* is a noun that means a group of people banded together as a group or treated as a group.

21. **B.** *Speechless* is an adjective that means temporarily unable to speak, refraining from speech, or lacking the ability to speak.

22. **D.** *Indigenous* is an adjective that means native or originating or occurring naturally in a certain place.

23. **B.** *Illusive* is an adjective that means deceptive (like an illusion). Don't confuse *illusive* with *elusive*, which means difficult to find, catch, or achieve.

24. **B.** *Hesitate* is a verb that means to pause before doing or saying something or to be reluctant to do something.

25. **D.** *Gravity* is a noun that refers to extreme or alarming importance or seriousness. (It's also what keeps you from floating into space, which is pretty serious *and* important.)

26. **B.** *Fondle* is a verb that means to stroke or caress lovingly or erotically.

27. **A.** *Fete* is a noun that refers to a celebration or festival. It can also be a verb that means to honor or entertain someone lavishly.

28. C. *Encore* is a noun that means a repeated or additional performance of something.

29. A. *Diverse* is an adjective that means showing a substantial amount of variety. It also means very different.

30. B. *Detest* is a verb that means to dislike intensely.

31. C. *Acerbic* is an adjective that means sharp and forthright, especially when referring to a comment or a style of speaking.

32. B. *Inexorable* is an adjective that means impossible to prevent or stop. It also means unyielding or unalterable.

33. B. *Hector* is a verb that means to talk to someone in a bullying way.

34. C. *Gauche* is an adjective that means lacking grace, unsophisticated, and socially awkward.

35. A. *Confident* is an adjective that means feeling or showing confidence in oneself. It also means self-assured.

Subtest 3: Paragraph Comprehension Answers

If you still need to boost your score, engage in some more reading practice. Improving your vocabulary can also help improve your reading comprehension skills. See Chapter 5 for some tips.

1. C. According to the passage, millions of veterans received home loan guarantees, education, and training, making Choice (C) the correct answer. Be careful here, because Choice (A) is tempting, but nothing in the passage indicates that the housing, education, and training were totally free.

2. B. The paragraph states that the maximum amount one can place into a tax-deferred IRA is $3,000, plus an additional $3,000 if the spouse isn't employed. The question asks about a couple, so add $3,000 + $3,000 to get $6,000.

3. A. Although many presidential appointments require Senate confirmation, not all do. The passage mentions only some appointments, so Choice (A) is an incorrect statement.

4. C. The author specifically states that partial bans on alcohol advertising aren't likely to be effective and that total bans wouldn't be practical.

5. C. According to the passage, a river was named after the Alabama Indian tribe, and the state derived its name from this river.

6. D. The question here is looking for the incorrect (unsupported) statement. The first sentence states that bankruptcy is usually (not always) filed in bankruptcy court, making Choice (D) an incorrect statement.

7. A. The second sentence states that most violent crimes were motivated by such factors as race and sexual orientation, and most property crimes were motivated by religion. The question refers to property crimes, so Choice (A) is the right answer.

8. **B.** Sixty percent of all hate crimes during the period were violent crimes. Assault and intimidation are examples of violent crimes.

9. **B.** The last sentence in the passage describes the sign cutting operation.

10. **C.** The rationale for the division is explained in the final sentence, which mentions the king's sons. The passage makes no reference to the size of Wales or the natural boundaries.

11. **C.** The primary subject of this paragraph is Attila, who was king of the Huns.

12. **A.** Attila agreed to peace but soon after discovered that the Roman emperor had launched a plot to kill him.

13. **A.** The primary theme of the passage is stated in the first sentence. *Proficiency* is closest in meaning to the word *competence*, which is the primary theme of the passage.

14. **D.** The passage directly supports all the statements.

15. **A.** The author specifically states that when pitted against friendship, professional integrity should win out. The author explains that only fellow professionals can evaluate other professionals in some (not all) cases, making Choice (B) incorrect. Choice (C) isn't supported by information in the passage.

Subtest 4: Mathematics Knowledge Answers

If you didn't do as well as you'd hoped on the Mathematics Knowledge subtest, review Chapters 6, 7, and 8.

1. **C.**

$$5x - 2x = 7x + 2x - 24$$
$$3x = 9x - 24$$
$$-6x = -24$$
$$6x = 24$$
$$x = 4$$

2. **C.** The cube of 6 is $6^3 = 6 \times 6 \times 6 = 216$.

3. **A.** The equation $3x + 7y = 21$ is the equation for a line, and a line intersects the x-axis at the point where the y-coordinate is 0 ($y = 0$). Substitute 0 for y in the equation to find the value for x at the intersection point:

$$3x + 7y = 21$$
$$3x + 7(0) = 21$$
$$3x = 21$$
$$x = 7$$

The point's coordinates are (7, 0).

4. B. This problem gives you a system of equations — two equations with two variables. You can find x by solving one of the equations for y and plugging that value into the other equation. First, $x + y = 6$, so $y = 6 - x$. Substitute this known value for y in the second equation and solve for x:

$$x - y = 4$$
$$x - (6 - x) = 4$$
$$x - 6 + x = 4$$
$$2x - 6 = 4$$
$$2x = 10$$
$$x = 5$$

5. D.

$$4(y + 3) + 7 = 3$$
$$4y + 12 + 7 = 3$$
$$4y + 19 = 3$$
$$4y = -16$$
$$y = -4$$

6. A. Convert 12 yards, 14 feet to feet:

$$(12 \text{ yards} \times 3 \text{ feet/yard}) + 14 \text{ feet}$$
$$= 36 \text{ feet} + 14 \text{ feet}$$
$$= 50 \text{ feet}$$

Divide by 2 as instructed: 50 feet $\div 2 = 25$ feet.

7. D. If two powers have the same base, the numbers can be multiplied by keeping the base the same and adding the powers (exponents) together: $x^3 \left(x^3 \right) = x^{3+3} = x^6$.

8. B. Convert to the lowest common denominator (which is 10), and then add: $4\frac{1}{5} + 1\frac{2}{5} + 3\frac{3}{10} = 4\frac{2}{10} + 1\frac{4}{10} + 3\frac{3}{10} = 8\frac{9}{10}$.

9. B. Following the order of operations, you have to find the power (10^2) before multiplying: $1.5 \times 10^2 = 1.5 \times (10 \times 10) = 1.5 \times 100 = 150$.

10. D. Add the numbers and then divide by the number of terms to find the mean. The sum is $54 + 61 + 70 + 75 = 260$. You have four numbers, and $260 \div 4 = 65$.

11. B. 2 feet + 4 feet = 6 feet, and 4 inches + 8 inches = 12 inches (the equivalent to 1 foot). Therefore, you have a total of 7 feet.

12. C. Your first reaction may be to substitute 4 for each x and then do the math. But you can save yourself some work (and time) by first dividing x^4 by x, which is x^3. Then substitute 4 for each x, and you find that the equation is now $4 \times 4 \times 4$. Then multiply: 4×4 is 16, and 16×4 is 64, which is your final answer.

13. B. As you solve this inequality, remember that when you multiply or divide an inequality by a negative number, you need to reverse the direction of the inequality sign:

$$5 - 3x \geq 14 + 6x$$
$$5 - 3x - 6x \geq 14$$
$$-9x \geq 14 - 5$$
$$-9x \geq 9$$
$$x \leq -1$$

14. B. $(900 \times 3) \div 6 = 2,700 \div 6 = 450$.

15. A. Substitute 2 for all the x's: $x^x(x^x) = 2^2 \times 2^2 = 4 \times 4 = 16$.

16. C. This is a quadratic equation that you can solve by factoring and setting each factor equal to zero:

$$x^2 - 2x - 15 = 0$$
$$(x - 5)(x + 3) = 0$$
$$x - 5 = 0 \quad \text{or} \quad x + 3 = 0$$
$$x = 5 \qquad\qquad x = -3$$

17. D. Find the square roots before dividing. The square root of 49 is 7, and the square root of 64 is 8. Now divide: $7 \div 8 = \frac{7}{8}$.

18. C. The square root of a positive number can be either positive or negative. For instance, the square root of 16 is ± 4, because 4^2 and $(-4)^2$ both give you the positive number 16.

19. C. Solving this inequality doesn't require multiplying or dividing by a negative number, so the inequality sign remains the same: $2 + x \geq 15$; $x \geq 13$.

20. C. Circumference equals π times diameter, and diameter is equal to two times the radius. In other words, $C = \pi d$, and $d = 2r$. Thus, $C = \pi(2)(15) = \pi 30$. If you round π to 3.14, the answer is 94.2, or about 94 feet.

21. A. Volume equals length times width times height ($V = lwh$). Plug in the numbers and solve: $V = 12 \times 8 \times 10 = 960$ cubic inches.

22. C. In a trapezoid, two of four sides are parallel to each other.

23. A. All quadrilaterals have angles that total 360 degrees.

24. B. A *prime number* only has 1 and itself as factors. You can find the prime factors of 100 by factoring until you can't factor any value further:

$$100 = 4 \times 25 = 2 \times 2 \times 5 \times 5 = 2^2 \times 5^2$$

25. B. The square root of a negative number doesn't exist as far as real numbers are concerned. In mathematics, this is called an *imaginary number*, and it's represented by the letter i.

Chapter 26

AFQT Practice Exam 2

The Armed Forces Qualification Test (AFQT) consists of four of the subtests on the Armed Services Vocational Aptitude Battery (ASVAB). The four subtests used to determine your AFQT score are Arithmetic Reasoning, Word Knowledge, Paragraph Comprehension, and Mathematics Knowledge.

The AFQT score is very important. Although all the ASVAB subtests are used to determine which military jobs you qualify for, the AFQT score determines whether you're even eligible to join the military. All the military service branches have established minimum AFQT scores, according to their needs (see Chapter 2 for more information).

The AFQT is not a stand-alone test (it's part of the ASVAB), but in this chapter, I present the subtests applicable to the AFQT in the same order in which you'll encounter them when you take the actual ASVAB.

After you complete the entire practice test, check your answers against the answer key in Chapter 27.

REMEMBER

The test is scored by comparing your raw score to the scores of other people, which produces a scaled score. So just because you missed a total of 20 questions doesn't mean that your score is 80. (That would be too simple.) Turn to Chapter 1 to find out how the AFQT score is derived from these four subtests.

Your goal in taking this practice test is to determine which areas you may still need to study. If you miss only one question on the Word Knowledge subtest but 15 questions on Arithmetic Reasoning, you probably want to devote some extra study time to developing your math skills before you take the ASVAB.

Answer Sheet for AFQT Practice Exam 2

Subtest 1: Arithmetic Reasoning

1. Ⓐ Ⓑ Ⓒ Ⓓ
2. Ⓐ Ⓑ Ⓒ Ⓓ
3. Ⓐ Ⓑ Ⓒ Ⓓ
4. Ⓐ Ⓑ Ⓒ Ⓓ
5. Ⓐ Ⓑ Ⓒ Ⓓ
6. Ⓐ Ⓑ Ⓒ Ⓓ

7. Ⓐ Ⓑ Ⓒ Ⓓ
8. Ⓐ Ⓑ Ⓒ Ⓓ
9. Ⓐ Ⓑ Ⓒ Ⓓ
10. Ⓐ Ⓑ Ⓒ Ⓓ
11. Ⓐ Ⓑ Ⓒ Ⓓ
12. Ⓐ Ⓑ Ⓒ Ⓓ

13. Ⓐ Ⓑ Ⓒ Ⓓ
14. Ⓐ Ⓑ Ⓒ Ⓓ
15. Ⓐ Ⓑ Ⓒ Ⓓ
16. Ⓐ Ⓑ Ⓒ Ⓓ
17. Ⓐ Ⓑ Ⓒ Ⓓ
18. Ⓐ Ⓑ Ⓒ Ⓓ

19. Ⓐ Ⓑ Ⓒ Ⓓ
20. Ⓐ Ⓑ Ⓒ Ⓓ
21. Ⓐ Ⓑ Ⓒ Ⓓ
22. Ⓐ Ⓑ Ⓒ Ⓓ
23. Ⓐ Ⓑ Ⓒ Ⓓ
24. Ⓐ Ⓑ Ⓒ Ⓓ

25. Ⓐ Ⓑ Ⓒ Ⓓ
26. Ⓐ Ⓑ Ⓒ Ⓓ
27. Ⓐ Ⓑ Ⓒ Ⓓ
28. Ⓐ Ⓑ Ⓒ Ⓓ
29. Ⓐ Ⓑ Ⓒ Ⓓ
30. Ⓐ Ⓑ Ⓒ Ⓓ

Subtest 2: Word Knowledge

1. Ⓐ Ⓑ Ⓒ Ⓓ
2. Ⓐ Ⓑ Ⓒ Ⓓ
3. Ⓐ Ⓑ Ⓒ Ⓓ
4. Ⓐ Ⓑ Ⓒ Ⓓ
5. Ⓐ Ⓑ Ⓒ Ⓓ
6. Ⓐ Ⓑ Ⓒ Ⓓ
7. Ⓐ Ⓑ Ⓒ Ⓓ

8. Ⓐ Ⓑ Ⓒ Ⓓ
9. Ⓐ Ⓑ Ⓒ Ⓓ
10. Ⓐ Ⓑ Ⓒ Ⓓ
11. Ⓐ Ⓑ Ⓒ Ⓓ
12. Ⓐ Ⓑ Ⓒ Ⓓ
13. Ⓐ Ⓑ Ⓒ Ⓓ
14. Ⓐ Ⓑ Ⓒ Ⓓ

15. Ⓐ Ⓑ Ⓒ Ⓓ
16. Ⓐ Ⓑ Ⓒ Ⓓ
17. Ⓐ Ⓑ Ⓒ Ⓓ
18. Ⓐ Ⓑ Ⓒ Ⓓ
19. Ⓐ Ⓑ Ⓒ Ⓓ
20. Ⓐ Ⓑ Ⓒ Ⓓ
21. Ⓐ Ⓑ Ⓒ Ⓓ

22. Ⓐ Ⓑ Ⓒ Ⓓ
23. Ⓐ Ⓑ Ⓒ Ⓓ
24. Ⓐ Ⓑ Ⓒ Ⓓ
25. Ⓐ Ⓑ Ⓒ Ⓓ
26. Ⓐ Ⓑ Ⓒ Ⓓ
27. Ⓐ Ⓑ Ⓒ Ⓓ
28. Ⓐ Ⓑ Ⓒ Ⓓ

29. Ⓐ Ⓑ Ⓒ Ⓓ
30. Ⓐ Ⓑ Ⓒ Ⓓ
31. Ⓐ Ⓑ Ⓒ Ⓓ
32. Ⓐ Ⓑ Ⓒ Ⓓ
33. Ⓐ Ⓑ Ⓒ Ⓓ
34. Ⓐ Ⓑ Ⓒ Ⓓ
35. Ⓐ Ⓑ Ⓒ Ⓓ

Subtest 3: Paragraph Comprehension

1. Ⓐ Ⓑ Ⓒ Ⓓ
2. Ⓐ Ⓑ Ⓒ Ⓓ
3. Ⓐ Ⓑ Ⓒ Ⓓ

4. Ⓐ Ⓑ Ⓒ Ⓓ
5. Ⓐ Ⓑ Ⓒ Ⓓ
6. Ⓐ Ⓑ Ⓒ Ⓓ

7. Ⓐ Ⓑ Ⓒ Ⓓ
8. Ⓐ Ⓑ Ⓒ Ⓓ
9. Ⓐ Ⓑ Ⓒ Ⓓ

10. Ⓐ Ⓑ Ⓒ Ⓓ
11. Ⓐ Ⓑ Ⓒ Ⓓ
12. Ⓐ Ⓑ Ⓒ Ⓓ

13. Ⓐ Ⓑ Ⓒ Ⓓ
14. Ⓐ Ⓑ Ⓒ Ⓓ
15. Ⓐ Ⓑ Ⓒ Ⓓ

Subtest 4: Mathematics Knowledge

1. Ⓐ Ⓑ Ⓒ Ⓓ
2. Ⓐ Ⓑ Ⓒ Ⓓ
3. Ⓐ Ⓑ Ⓒ Ⓓ
4. Ⓐ Ⓑ Ⓒ Ⓓ
5. Ⓐ Ⓑ Ⓒ Ⓓ

6. Ⓐ Ⓑ Ⓒ Ⓓ
7. Ⓐ Ⓑ Ⓒ Ⓓ
8. Ⓐ Ⓑ Ⓒ Ⓓ
9. Ⓐ Ⓑ Ⓒ Ⓓ
10. Ⓐ Ⓑ Ⓒ Ⓓ

11. Ⓐ Ⓑ Ⓒ Ⓓ
12. Ⓐ Ⓑ Ⓒ Ⓓ
13. Ⓐ Ⓑ Ⓒ Ⓓ
14. Ⓐ Ⓑ Ⓒ Ⓓ
15. Ⓐ Ⓑ Ⓒ Ⓓ

16. Ⓐ Ⓑ Ⓒ Ⓓ
17. Ⓐ Ⓑ Ⓒ Ⓓ
18. Ⓐ Ⓑ Ⓒ Ⓓ
19. Ⓐ Ⓑ Ⓒ Ⓓ
20. Ⓐ Ⓑ Ⓒ Ⓓ

21. Ⓐ Ⓑ Ⓒ Ⓓ
22. Ⓐ Ⓑ Ⓒ Ⓓ
23. Ⓐ Ⓑ Ⓒ Ⓓ
24. Ⓐ Ⓑ Ⓒ Ⓓ
25. Ⓐ Ⓑ Ⓒ Ⓓ

Subtest 1: Arithmetic Reasoning

TIME: 36 minutes for 30 questions

DIRECTIONS: This test contains questions about arithmetic. Each question is followed by four possible answers. Decide which answer is correct and then mark the space on your answer sheet that has the same number and letter as your choice. Use scratch paper for any figuring you need to do. Calculators are not allowed.

1. Mike has $5.25 in quarters and dimes. He has exactly 15 dimes. How many quarters does he have?

   (A) 6
   (B) 12
   (C) 15
   (D) 21

2. Kelly used to pay $500 a month for rent. Now she pays $525 a month for rent. By what percent did her rent increase?

   (A) 0.5 percent
   (B) 5 percent
   (C) 10 percent
   (D) 12.5 percent

3. A bag has 8 pennies, 5 dimes, and 7 nickels. A coin is randomly chosen from the bag. What is the probability that the coin chosen is a dime?

   (A) $\frac{1}{20}$
   (B) $\frac{1}{4}$
   (C) $\frac{1}{3}$
   (D) $\frac{3}{10}$

4. There are 2 pints in 1 quart and 4 quarts in a gallon. How many pints are in 2 gallons?

   (A) 32 pints
   (B) 16 pints
   (C) 8 pints
   (D) 4 pints

5. Paul invests $2,000 in an account that pays 4 percent annual interest. How much will he earn in interest in one year?

   (A) $160
   (B) $80
   (C) $120
   (D) $800

6. One mile is equal to 5,280 feet. Sergeant Jeffries walked 1.2 miles. What distance (in feet) did he walk?

   (A) 7,392 ft.
   (B) 1,056 ft.
   (C) 5,780 ft.
   (D) 6,336 ft.

7. A total of 200 people attended a conference. Use the chart to determine how many attendees were women.

Conference Attendance

Men 47%

Women 53%

© John Wiley & Sons, Inc.

   (A) 94
   (B) 212
   (C) 53
   (D) 106

GO ON TO NEXT PAGE

8. Suppose you have $88 in your checking account. You use your debit card to pay $22 for a sweater and $8 for lunch, and then you deposit a $38 check. What is the balance in your account?

   (A) $58

   (B) $96

   (C) $20

   (D) $156

9. There are 24 right-handed students in a class of 30. A student is chosen from the class at random. What is the probability that the student is left-handed?

   (A) $\frac{1}{2}$

   (B) $\frac{1}{5}$

   (C) $\frac{4}{5}$

   (D) $\frac{1}{4}$

10. At a laundromat, it costs $1.75 to wash each load of laundry and $1.50 to dry each load of laundry. How much will you pay to wash and dry four loads of laundry?

    (A) $2.25

    (B) $20.00

    (C) $20.25

    (D) $13.00

11. Delia has been walking at a constant speed of 2.5 miles per hour for 12 minutes. How many miles has she walked?

    (A) 0.2 mile

    (B) 0.5 mile

    (C) 2 miles

    (D) 4.8 miles

12. A rectangular deck is 6 meters long and 8 meters wide. What is the distance from one corner of the deck to the opposite corner?

© John Wiley & Sons, Inc.

    (A) 10 m

    (B) 12 m

    (C) 14 m

    (D) 15 m

13. Tom is going to hang three framed pictures side by side on a wall. How many different ways can he arrange the pictures?

    (A) 9

    (B) 5

    (C) 6

    (D) 27

14. A cleaning company charges by the square foot. The company charged $600 to clean 4,800 square feet of space. How much would the company charge to clean 12,000 square feet of space?

    (A) $950

    (B) $1,200

    (C) $1,400

    (D) $1,500

15. Kendra earns $12 an hour. Her employer pays 1.5 times her normal pay rate for overtime. Last week, she worked 40 hours plus 4 hours overtime. How much did she earn last week?

    (A) $552

    (B) $528

    (C) $1,400

    (D) $480

16. A hot tub is 75 percent full with 600 gallons of water. How many gallons of water are in the hot tub when it's half full?

(A) 200 gallons

(B) 400 gallons

(C) 800 gallons

(D) 300 gallons

17. Angela has 15 coins (quarters and dimes) in the cash register. The total value of the quarters and dimes is $2.55. How many dimes are in the cash register?

(A) 8 dimes

(B) 7 dimes

(C) 3 dimes

(D) 10 dimes

18. A rectangular table top measures 48 inches long by 36 inches wide. A square game board that is 18 inches on each side is on the table top. Which amount of the table top's area is not covered by the game board?

(A) 1,710 in.²

(B) 1,404 in.²

(C) 1,656 in.²

(D) 96 in.²

19. A map of Texas has a scale of 1 cm = 11 km. The actual distance between Dallas and San Antonio is about 440 km. How far apart are the cities on the map?

(A) 11 cm

(B) 44 cm

(C) 40 cm

(D) 22 cm

20. Jake is four years older than Kenneth. Alicia is two years younger than Kenneth. The sum of Jake's, Kenneth's, and Alicia's ages is 38. What is Kenneth's age?

(A) 9

(B) 15

(C) 12

(D) 10

21. Mrs. Jacobs is making a large circular rug with a radius of 10 feet. Every square foot of material used to make the rug costs her $0.50. Approximately how much will the material for the entire rug cost?

(A) $157

(B) $167

(C) $628

(D) $314

22. John's quiz scores in science class are 8, 6, 10, 7, 9, and 5. What is John's average quiz score?

(A) 6

(B) 8

(C) 7.5

(D) 8.5

23. Robert charges a flat fee of $15 plus $20 per half-hour to repair computers. He started one job at 8:45 a.m. and worked until he finished. The total charge for that job was $75. What time did he finish the job?

(A) 12:15 p.m.

(B) 11:45 a.m.

(C) 10:15 a.m.

(D) 9:30 a.m.

24. The measure of angle P is 44°. Angle Q is 12° less than half the measure of the supplement of angle P. What is the measure of angle Q?

(A) 136°

(B) 80°

(C) 124°

(D) 56°

25. Rose and Carla play on the same basketball team. During the last game, Rose scored $\frac{3}{5}$ of the team's points. Carla scored 16 percent of the team's points. What percentage of the team's points were not scored by either Rose or Carla?

(A) 76 percent

(B) 66 percent

(C) 24 percent

(D) 34 percent

GO ON TO NEXT PAGE

26. John and Garret are running in a marathon. John runs at a steady rate of 3.5 miles per hour, and Garret runs at a steady rate of 4.25 miles per hour. How far apart will they be 2 hours after the race starts?

   (A) 0.75 mile

   (B) 2.5 miles

   (C) 1.5 miles

   (D) 2.25 miles

27. Jim can repair a heating unit in 2 hours. Kyle can repair the same unit in 3 hours. How long will they take to repair the unit if they work together?

   (A) 1 hour and 10 minutes

   (B) 1 hour and 12 minutes

   (C) 48 minutes

   (D) 50 minutes

28. A square has an area of 121 cm². What is the perimeter?

   (A) 121 cm

   (B) 22 cm

   (C) 33 cm

   (D) 44 cm

29. How many gallons of water should you add to 4 gallons of a juice that is 20 percent water so the final mixture is 50 percent water?

   (A) 2.2 gallons

   (B) 2 gallons

   (C) 2.4 gallons

   (D) 1.4 gallons

30. David is at a car dealership trying to decide between buying a truck or a sedan. The truck is available in three colors, and the sedan is available in four colors. Each vehicle also has both a 2-wheel-drive and a 4-wheel-drive option in all available colors. How many different choices does he have?

   (A) 48

   (B) 14

   (C) 12

   (D) 6

Subtest 2: Word Knowledge

TIME: 11 minutes for 35 questions

DIRECTIONS: This test has questions about the meanings of words. Each question has an underlined word. You need to decide which one of the four words in the choices most nearly means the same or opposite thing as the underlined word and then mark the corresponding space on your answer sheet.

1. Kindle most nearly means
   - (A) devise.
   - (B) ignite.
   - (C) boil.
   - (D) expire.

2. The word most opposite in meaning to burnout is
   - (A) successful.
   - (B) ruined.
   - (C) enthusiasm.
   - (D) fatigue.

3. Blatant most nearly means
   - (A) obvious.
   - (B) overdrawn.
   - (C) certain.
   - (D) hidden.

4. Hasten most nearly means
   - (A) delay.
   - (B) anxious.
   - (C) rush.
   - (D) stabilize.

5. Objective most nearly means
   - (A) massive.
   - (B) favored.
   - (C) neutral.
   - (D) dependent.

6. No one could convince the headstrong teen that he was wrong.
   - (A) cruel
   - (B) stubborn
   - (C) friendly
   - (D) unaffected

7. The thought of dissecting the frog made me cringe in disgust.
   - (A) recoil
   - (B) volunteer
   - (C) wail
   - (D) rally

8. Despite her wild past, Bobbi prefers to live a more domestic lifestyle these days.
   - (A) native
   - (B) homebound
   - (C) foreign
   - (D) elaborate

9. Grandma always taught us to be frugal and grateful for what we had.
   - (A) careless
   - (B) excessive
   - (C) cheap
   - (D) thrifty

10. I wanted to curtail the date because of Bob's cat obsession.
    - (A) develop
    - (B) shorten
    - (C) postpone
    - (D) continue

11. The captain received many accolades for her bravery during the battle.
    - (A) honors
    - (B) criticisms
    - (C) presents
    - (D) promotions

GO ON TO NEXT PAGE

12. Covert most nearly means

  (A) tiresome.

  (B) popular.

  (C) secret.

  (D) unruly.

13. Abhor most nearly means

  (A) commence.

  (B) embrace.

  (C) remove.

  (D) dislike.

14. The mandate to report at exactly 9 a.m. the next day was written on my boss's personal stationery.

  (A) invitation

  (B) greeting

  (C) command

  (D) permission

15. The word most opposite in meaning to assortment is

  (A) variety.

  (B) difference.

  (C) mixture.

  (D) consistency.

16. Credible most nearly means

  (A) cynical.

  (B) rehearsed.

  (C) genuine.

  (D) vague.

17. Reprieve most nearly means

  (A) on hold.

  (B) complete.

  (C) final.

  (D) justice.

18. Tedious most nearly means

  (A) fresh.

  (B) dreary.

  (C) difficult.

  (D) annoying.

19. Jackson's music was so loud he was oblivious to the honking car behind him.

  (A) cognizant

  (B) superfluous

  (C) ignorant

  (D) perceptive

20. The coach knew how to bolster the team's morale in the final moments.

  (A) recruit

  (B) demean

  (C) allude

  (D) encourage

21. The word most opposite in meaning to abstract is

  (A) exclusive.

  (B) realistic.

  (C) imaginative.

  (D) far-fetched.

22. The rain hampered the runner's ability to break the record.

  (A) facilitated

  (B) eased

  (C) forced

  (D) hindered

23. Cower most nearly means

  (A) attack.

  (B) celebrate.

  (C) cringe.

  (D) sublime.

24. Tangent most nearly means

  (A) detour.

  (B) wavering.

  (C) focus.

  (D) perfect.

25. Nullify most nearly means

  (A) suggest.

  (B) cancel.

  (C) perform.

  (D) promote.

26. Tangible most nearly means

(A) theoretical.

(B) fragile.

(C) possessive.

(D) physical.

27. Absolution most nearly means

(A) condemnation.

(B) owing a debt.

(C) assurance.

(D) forgiveness.

28. Abrogate most nearly means

(A) materialize.

(B) terminate.

(C) embark.

(D) constitute.

29. I wanted to temper the dinner conversation so Grandpa wouldn't walk out.

(A) ignore

(B) irritate

(C) soothe

(D) anger

30. Plethora most nearly means

(A) scarcity.

(B) infection.

(C) unique.

(D) abundance.

31. Mary was tentative about buying the more expensive car.

(A) unhappy

(B) optimistic

(C) hesitant

(D) certain

32. The word most opposite in meaning to retaliation is

(A) vengeance.

(B) forgiveness.

(C) recognition.

(D) payback.

33. Jennifer tried to admonish me about asking Mr. Michelson questions because of his long-winded nature.

(A) encourage

(B) punish

(C) spurn

(D) warn

34. The memo was more like a diatribe of all the things Kathy hated about work.

(A) novel

(B) tirade

(C) compliment

(D) dispute

35. The word most opposite in meaning to memento is

(A) rubbish.

(B) souvenir.

(C) jewel.

(D) prize.

DO NOT TURN THE PAGE UNTIL TOLD TO DO SO STOP **DO NOT RETURN TO A PREVIOUS TEST**

Subtest 3: Paragraph Comprehension

TIME: 13 minutes for 15 questions

DIRECTIONS: This test contains items that measure your ability to understand what you read. This section includes one or more paragraphs of reading material followed by incomplete statements or questions. Read the paragraph and select the choice that best completes the statement or answers the question. Mark your choice on your answer sheet by using the correct letter with each question number.

Terry always wanted to move back to Chicago, the city of her birth, because of fond childhood memories. After convincing her husband, Jim, to leave sunny California, her dream was coming true. They moved in the fall, just in time to catch the leaves changing. However, the worst winter in the city's history was too much for their beach bum mentality, and Terry soon regretted her decision. Her dream wasn't the same as reality, and she realized you can't always go back.

1. Why does Terry feel like "you can't always go back"?

   (A) Chicago is too far.

   (B) She is no longer a child.

   (C) California had changed her.

   (D) Winter was her favorite season.

Questions 2 and 3 refer to the following passage.

A new study shows that since the 1970s, the number of households with pets has almost tripled. Yet despite this increased pet ownership, the number of animals euthanized at shelters each year is still between 2.5 and 3 million. In fact, according to the Humane Society of the United States, in 2012, only 30 percent of the 62 percent of households with pets got the animals from shelters or rescue organizations. Furthermore, many of the euthanized animals are healthy, and 25 percent of the dogs euthanized are purebred. There is still a lot of work to do to spread the word about rescue pets to ensure healthy animals don't meet this fate.

2. What is the main point of the passage?

   (A) Americans have more pets than ever before.

   (B) More households should adopt rescue animals.

   (C) More cats are adopted than dogs.

   (D) Shelters house only sick or hurt dogs.

3. Of the households that had pets in 2012, how many of them got their pets from a shelter or rescue organization?

   (A) 62 percent

   (B) 25 percent

   (C) 3 percent

   (D) 30 percent

Christo and Jeanne-Claude were an artistic couple known for their elaborate and grandiose projects. Their projects involved giant sheets of nylon wrapped or hanging in an unlikely environment. They achieved notoriety for their artistic installations, such as Valley Curtain, which displayed a 200,200-square-foot curtain hanging between two Colorado mountains. Although their unconventional penchant for wrapping monuments and buildings wasn't understood by everyone, no one can dispute that their work was respected nonetheless.

4. In this passage, penchant means

   (A) inclination.

   (B) disinterest.

   (C) incompetence.

   (D) experience.

Despite having used her new shoes for only three months during her frequent marathon training, Tara was having pains in her feet while running. All the articles she read said that running shoes should last at least six months if used an average of two to three times a week. Tara decided she had bought the wrong shoes.

5. Based on the passage, what other reason could Tara's shoes be worn out sooner than six months?

(A) She runs with bad form.

(B) The shoes are cheap.

(C) She runs more than average.

(D) She damaged her shoes on rough terrain.

Robert De Niro may never have won his first Academy Award if he had gotten the role he wanted as Michael Corleone in *The Godfather*. In 1975, he received his first nomination and win for his role as young Vito Corleone in *The Godfather: Part II*. By 2013, he'd scored six more nominations (including another win in 1981).

6. According to the passage, how many Academy Awards has Robert De Niro been nominated for?

(A) 3

(B) 6

(C) 7

(D) 0

Questions 7 and 8 refer to the following passage.

Tiffany often wished her family lived closer to another airport. It seemed like her flights were always either canceled or delayed due to weather. In fact, she missed Christmas one year because of a blizzard, and her flight home from her grandma's birthday celebration was postponed for five hours because of a thunderstorm. But she couldn't do anything about it. The region just had terrible weather sometimes.

7. What is the main point of the passage?

(A) Tiffany doesn't like visiting her family.

(B) The region's weather is unpredictable.

(C) Tiffany's local airport is terrible.

(D) Tiffany has bad luck.

8. In this passage, <u>postponed</u> means

(A) ruined.

(B) over.

(C) expedited.

(D) delayed.

Historical battle reenactments date back to the Middle Ages, when actors would perform scenes from Ancient Rome to entertain a public audience. The most famous reenactments, of course, are those pertaining to the American Civil War, which became popular during the war's centennial celebration in 1961. Almost 50,000 people gathered to commemorate the beginning of the Civil War, which started on April 12, 1861. These days, anywhere from 500 to 20,000 people will congregate to reenact a famous battle from the war. Both the Confederate and Union armies are equally represented.

9. How many years does a centennial celebration recognize?

(A) 20,000

(B) 100

(C) 500

(D) 1,861

Questions 10 and 11 refer to the following passage.

When you're driving in snow, a few bits of knowledge can be the difference between a safe trip and an accident. Never slam on the brakes in the snow. Tapping the brakes helps you slow down without skidding. If you are skidding, turn into the direction of the skid, not away from it. This approach will help you gain control of the vehicle.

10. The author wrote this passage to

(A) convince the reader to drive in the snow.

(B) provide driving tips for snowy conditions.

(C) make sure your brakes are tuned.

(D) scare the reader about driving in the snow.

GO ON TO NEXT PAGE ▶

11. Driving safely in snowy conditions means

(A) understanding the results of your actions.

(B) avoiding braking.

(C) avoiding busy roads.

(D) relinquishing control.

The crowd at the store was growing quickly. Children reached for their favorite-colored backpack. Notebooks flew off the shelves, and pencils of different shapes and sizes were running low in stock. Back-to-school shopping had definitely begun.

12. What is the author telling the reader in the passage?

(A) that school supplies are scarce

(B) that the store isn't prepared

(C) that parents spend too much money on supplies

(D) that the beginning of school is approaching

Questions 13 and 14 refer to the following passage.

The 70-year career of Frank Lloyd Wright is one of the most remarkable and renowned in the architecture world. He designed 1,141 buildings, and 532 of those designs were actually developed. The 409 that remain are considered individual works of art. His name is as famous as Bruce Springsteen's in modern-day society.

13. How many buildings were constructed from Frank Lloyd Wright's designs?

(A) 532

(B) 1,141

(C) 70

(D) 409

14. In this passage, renowned means

(A) common.

(B) popular.

(C) misunderstood.

(D) famous.

Sailors don't like to share the water with motorboaters because of the massive wake left by the high-speed boats. The waves disrupt the easy flow of the sailboats, causing them to twist and turn in the wind. The sentiment between sailors and speedboaters is similar to that between skiers and snowboarders.

15. How do skiers feel about snowboarders?

(A) They think snowboarders are a great addition to the slopes.

(B) They hate snowboarders.

(C) They don't like to share the mountain with snowboarders.

(D) They think snowboarders lack a high level of skill.

Subtest 4: Mathematics Knowledge

TIME: 24 minutes for 25 questions

DIRECTIONS: This section is a test of your ability to solve general mathematical problems. Select the correct answer from the choices given and then mark the corresponding space on your answer sheet. Use scratch paper to do any figuring. Calculators are not allowed.

1. $(-5)^3 =$

(A) −125

(B) −15

(C) 15

(D) 125

2. If $42 < 2x$, which is true about the value of x?

(A) x is less than 21.

(B) x is greater than 21.

(C) x is less than or equal to 21.

(D) x is greater than or equal to 21.

3. $473 + 220 + 27 =$

(A) 710

(B) 620

(C) 720

(D) 711

4. In the decimal 45.21, which digit is in the tenths place?

(A) 4

(B) 5

(C) 2

(D) 1

5. What are the coordinates of point P?

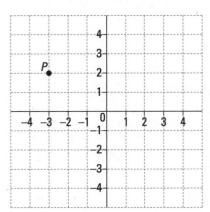

© John Wiley & Sons, Inc.

(A) $(-3, -2)$

(B) $(3, -2)$

(C) $(-3, 2)$

(D) $(2, -3)$

6. Express $\frac{11}{4}$ as a decimal.

(A) 2.25

(B) 2.5

(C) 2.75

(D) 3.25

7. If $-2 + y = 8$, then $y =$

(A) −10

(B) −6

(C) 6

(D) 10

GO ON TO NEXT PAGE

8. A circle has a circumference of 9.24 centimeters. What is the diameter of the circle?

(A) 1.5 cm

(B) 3 cm

(C) 3.14 cm

(D) 6 cm

9. What is 28 percent of 40?

(A) 9.4

(B) 10.2

(C) 11.2

(D) 12.5

10. Which is equal to $10^3 \times 10^{-6} \times 10^2$?

(A) 10

(B) 100

(C) 0.1

(D) 0.01

11. Simplify: $2 + 2y + 4 + y$

(A) $3y + 6$

(B) $3y + 8$

(C) $8y$

(D) $2y^2 + 6$

12. What is the value of x?

© John Wiley & Sons, Inc.

(A) 54°

(B) 34°

(C) 58°

(D) 38°

13. $(5 - 2)! =$

(A) 118

(B) 12

(C) 6

(D) 3

14. $\frac{1}{2} + \frac{1}{16} + \frac{1}{4} =$

(A) $\frac{3}{22}$

(B) $\frac{13}{22}$

(C) $\frac{13}{16}$

(D) $\frac{7}{16}$

15. How many factors does the number 51 have?

(A) Four

(B) Three

(C) Two

(D) One

16. The number 0.405 is what percent of 0.9?

(A) 4.5 percent

(B) 45 percent

(C) 25 percent

(D) 50 percent

17. The measure of angle P is $m°$. What is the measure of the complement of angle P?

(A) $(180 - m)°$

(B) $(90 - m)°$

(C) $(m - 90)°$

(D) $(m - 180)°$

18. What is the length b in the right triangle?

© John Wiley & Sons, Inc.

(A) 4 cm

(B) 5 cm

(C) 6 cm

(D) 7 cm

19. Translate the following sentence into an equation: "x decreased by 11 is twice x."

(A) $11 - x = 2x$

(B) $x - 11 = 2$

(C) $11 - x = 2$

(D) $x - 11 = 2x$

20. The mean of 5, 7, 8, 10, 4, and x is 7.5. What is the value of x?

(A) 7

(B) 8

(C) 10

(D) 11

21. $(9-3\cdot2)^2 - 0.5(-2) =$

(A) 10

(B) 145

(C) 8

(D) 143

22. Simplify: $9 - 4(5x - 2)$

(A) $17 - 20x$

(B) $25x - 2$

(C) $7 - 20x$

(D) $25x - 10$

23. The height, h, of a cylinder is twice the radius r. What is the volume of the cylinder?

(A) πr^3

(B) $4\pi r^3$

(C) $2\pi r^3$

(D) $8\pi r^2$

24. Find the area of the entire region shown.

7.5 cm

2 cm

10 cm

11 cm

© John Wiley & Sons, Inc.

(A) 85 cm²

(B) 89 cm²

(C) 125 cm²

(D) 719 cm²

25. Of 260 students at a local elementary school, 140 are boys. Express the ratio of girls to boys as a simplified fraction.

(A) $\frac{6}{7}$

(B) $\frac{7}{6}$

(C) $\frac{13}{7}$

(D) $\frac{7}{13}$

Chapter 27

AFQT Practice Exam 2: Answers and Explanations

Did you do well on this practice exam? I sure hope so! Use this answer key to score the practice exam in Chapter 26.

REMEMBER

The AFQT isn't scored based on number correct, number wrong, or even percent of questions correct. Instead, the score is derived by comparing your raw score with the raw score of others who have taken the test before you. In determining the raw score, harder questions are worth more points than easier questions. (For more on scoring, turn to Chapter 1.)

Don't waste time trying to equate your score on this practice test with your potential score on the actual AFQT. It can't be done. Instead, use the results of this practice test to determine which areas you should devote more study time to.

Subtest 1: Arithmetic Reasoning Answers

How'd you do on this subtest? If you don't feel so good about the results, you may want to put off taking the real ASVAB until you feel more confident about your math skills. In addition to reviewing Part 3, you may want to find a tutor or a class that can help you brush up on the basics. I can't stress enough how important it is to score well on this subtest.

1. **C.** If Mike has 15 dimes, he has $(15)($0.10) = 1.50 in dimes. Subtract that from the total to find out how much he has in quarters: $5.25 - $1.50 = 3.75. Then, divide that result by $0.25 to determine how many quarters he has: $3.75 \div $0.25 = 15$.

2. **B.** The percent increase is the amount of increase, $25, divided by the original amount, $500: $25 \div 500 = 0.05$. Convert 0.05 to a percent by multiplying 0.05 by 100 to get 5 percent.

3. **B.** The probability of randomly selecting a dime is equal to the number of dimes in the bag, 5, divided by the total number of coins in the bag, 20: $5 \div 20 = \frac{1}{4}$.

4. **B.** If 1 gallon contains 4 quarts, 2 gallons contain 8 quarts. Multiply that number by the number of pints per quart, 2, to get 16 pints in 8 quarts.

5. **B.** Use the interest formula $I = Prt$, where I is the interest, P is the principal, r is the interest rate (as a decimal), and t is the time in years.

$$I = \$2,000(0.04)(1) = \$80$$

6. **D.** Convert miles to feet by multiplying 1.2 miles by the conversion factor, 5,280 feet: $1.2(5,280) = 6,336$ ft.

7. **D.** According to the chart, 53 percent of the attendees were women. Multiply the percent of women (0.53) by the number of attendees (200): $0.53(200) = 106$.

8. **B.** Subtract the purchase amounts (\$22 and \$8) from the amount in your checking account: $\$88 - \$22 - \$8 = \$58$. Then add the amount of deposit: $\$58 + \$38 = \$96$.

9. **B.** The probability of choosing one of the six left-handed students in the class (remember, it's a class of 30, and 24 students are right-handed) is easy to find. Because $\frac{6}{30}$ students are left-handed, reduce the fraction to come up with the probability. $\frac{6}{30} = \frac{1}{5}$. You have a one-in-five chance of randomly choosing a leftie.

10. **D.** Each total load costs $\$3.25 \left(\$1.75 + \$1.50\right)$. Multiply that by 4 to get the total cost of all your laundry: $\$3.25 \times 4 = \$13$. You might be better off taking it to your parents' house, where it's free (and your mom feeds you)!

11. **B.** Convert the minutes to hours by dividing 12 by 60: $12 \div 60 = 0.2$ hours. Use the distance formula, $d = rt$, to find the distance in miles that she walked: $d = 2.5(0.2) = 0.5$ mile.

12. **A.** Use the Pythagorean theorem, $a^2 + b^2 = c^2$, to find the length of the diagonal, c:

$$6^2 + 8^2 = c^2$$
$$36 + 64 = c^2$$
$$100 = c^2$$
$$\pm\sqrt{100} = c^2$$
$$\pm 10 = c$$

Use the positive answer because length is always positive.

13. **C.** For the first picture to be hung on the wall, there are three choices. After he hangs the first picture, there are two choices left for the second picture, and then one choice left for the last picture. Multiply to find the number of different ways he can arrange the three pictures: $(3)(2)(1) = 6$ ways.

14. **D.** The easiest way to figure out how much the cleaning company would charge is to first determine how much it charges per square foot. Divide \$600 by 4,800 to find that out: $\$600 \div 4,800 = \$0.125$ per square foot. You want the company to clean 12,000 square feet, so multiply that number by the per-square-foot rate: $12,000 \times \$0.125 = \$1,500$.

15. **A.** Kendra earned $12(40) = \$480$ for the 40 hours she worked. Her overtime pay rate is $1.5(\$12) = \$18$ per hour. She earned an additional $\$18(4) = \$72$ in overtime pay. Her total pay last week was $\$480 + \$72 = \$552$.

16. **B.** Seventy-five percent of the total amount of water the tub will hold, x, is equal to 600 gallons. You can represent this fact with the equation $0.75x = 600$. Solve the equation to determine how many gallons the tub holds when full:

$$0.75x = 600$$
$$x = \frac{600}{0.75}$$
$$x = 800$$

The full hot tub holds 800 gallons of water. Half of 800 gallons is 400 gallons.

17. **A.** Let q equal the number of quarters and d equal the number of dimes. The value of the quarters is $25q$, and the value of the dimes is $10d$. So the value of dimes and quarters is $25q + 10d = 255$.

You also know that the total number of coins is 15, so $q + d = 15$. You can rearrange this equation to isolate q: $q = 15 - d$. Now you can substitute that for the q in the first equation and solve for d:

$$25(15 - d) + 10d = 255$$
$$375 - 25d + 10d = 255$$
$$375 - 15d = 255$$
$$15d = -120$$
$$d = 8$$

18. **B.** Use the formula for a rectangle, $A = lw$, to find the area of the table top: $A = (48)(36) = 1{,}728$ in.^{2} The formula for the area of a square is $A = s^2$, where s is the length of one side. Use it to find the area of the game board: $A = 18^2 = 324$ in.^{2} Then you can find the amount of area not covered by the game board by subtracting the area of the game board from the area of the table top: $1{,}728$ in.$^2 - 324$ in.$^2 = 1{,}404$ in.^{2}

19. **C.** Let x represent the distance between the cities on the map. Write and solve an equation to find x:

$$\frac{x}{440} = \frac{1}{11}$$
$$11x = 440$$
$$x = 440 \div 11$$
$$x = 40$$

20. **C.** Let x represent Kenneth's age. You can then write Jake's age as $x + 4$ and Alicia's age as $x - 2$. The sum of their ages is 38. Write and solve an equation to find x:

$$x + x + 4 + x - 2 = 38$$
$$3x + 2 = 38$$
$$3x = 36$$
$$x = 12$$

21. **A.** The area of a circle is $A = \pi r^2$. If the radius is 10 feet, then the area is $A = \pi r^2 \approx 3.14(10)^2 \approx 3.14(100) \approx 314$ ft.^{2} Multiply the area by the cost per square foot: $3.14(\$0.50) = \$157$.

22. C. John took six quizzes in science class. To find his average, first add all his scores together: $8 + 6 + 10 + 7 + 9 + 5 = 45$. Then, divide that number by 6 (the number of quizzes John took):

$$\frac{45}{6} = 7.5$$

His average score was 7.5.

23. C. Subtract the $15 base fee from $75 to find Robert's total hourly earnings: $75 − $15 = $60. Divide $60 by $20 to find the number of half-hours that he worked: $60 ÷ $20 = 3 half-hours. Three half-hours equal 1.5 hours, so add this amount of time to 8:45 a.m. to discover that he finished the job at 10:15 a.m.

24. D. If two angles are supplementary, the sum of their measures is equal to 180°. To find the supplement of angle P, subtract its measure from 180°: $180° − 44° = 136°$. Angle Q is 12° less than half the supplement of angle P, so divide 136° by 2 and then subtract 12°:
$\frac{136°}{2} − 12° = 68° − 12° = 56°$.

25. C. Write the fraction of points scored by Rose as a percent: $\frac{3}{5} = 0.6 = 60\%$.

Together, Rose and Carla scored 60 percent + 16 percent = 76 percent of the points scored by the team. So the percentage of points not scored by either player is 100 percent − 76 percent = 24 percent.

26. C. This problem uses the distance formula: $d = rt$. John's distance is the product of his rate (3.5 mph) and the time (2 hours): $d = 3.5(2) = 7$ miles. Garret's distance is the product of his rate (4.25 mph) and the time (2 hours): $d = 4.25(2) = 8.5$ miles. After 2 hours, they're 8.5 miles − 7 miles = 1.5 miles apart. You can solve this problem another way, too: Figure out John and Garret's speed difference, which is 0.75 mph. Multiply that by 2 hours of running and you can see that they're 1.5 miles apart.

27. B. Use the formula $\frac{a \times b}{a + b}$, where a is the amount of time Jim takes to repair the unit and b is the amount of time Kyle takes to repair the unit:

$$\frac{2 \times 3}{2 + 3} = \frac{6}{5} = 1\frac{1}{5}$$

To figure out how many minutes are in $\frac{1}{5}$ of an hour, multiply that fraction by 60 minutes:

$$\frac{1}{5}\left(\frac{60}{1}\right) = \frac{60}{5} = 12$$

An alternate way to solve this problem is by finding out how much Jim and Kyle can do in the same unit of time, such as 1 hour. Jim can do half of a heating unit in 1 hour, while Kyle can do one-third of a heating unit in 1 hour. Adding their times in a formula like this can be very useful:

$$\frac{\frac{1}{2}}{1} + \frac{\frac{1}{3}}{1} = \frac{\frac{5}{6}}{1}$$

Together, they can do $\frac{5}{6}$ of a unit in 1 hour, leaving $\frac{1}{6}$ of the unit to go. It takes 12 minutes longer for them to finish the unit (1 hour = 60 minutes; 60 ÷ 5 = 12), which tells you that they need 12 more minutes.

28. D. To find the length of one side of the square, find the square root of the area: $\sqrt{121} = 11$. Multiply the side length by 4 to find the perimeter: $4 \times 11 = 44$.

29. **C.** Let *x* represent the amount of water to be added to the 20 percent mixture, and then make a chart to help solve the problem.

	# gallons	% water	Amount water
Water	*x*	100	100*x*
Juice	4	20	4(20)
Mixture	*x* + 4	50	50(*x* + 4)

© John Wiley & Sons, Inc.

From the table, you know that the amount of added water is 100*x*, and the amount of juice is $4(20)$. The sum of these two amounts is equal to the amount of mixture, $50(x+4)$. Write and solve an equation to find *x*:

$$100 + 4(20) = 50(x+4)$$
$$100x + 80 = 50x + 200$$
$$50x = 120$$
$$x = 2.4$$

30. **B.** The number of different trucks David can choose from is the product of the number of colors (3) and the number of drive options (2). So he has $3(2) = 6$ choices of trucks.

Similarly, the number of sedans he can choose from is the product of the number of colors (4) and drive options (2). So he has $4(2) = 8$ choices of sedans.

The total number of options is the sum of the number of choices of trucks and sedans: $6 + 8 = 14$.

Subtest 2: Word Knowledge Answers

As with all AFQT subtests, the Word Knowledge subtest determines whether you qualify for enlistment. If you're not seeing improvement in your scores, work with a partner who can quiz you on vocabulary words. I also recommend reviewing the tables in Chapter 4 and Appendix C several times a week.

1. **B.** *Kindle* is a verb that means to light or set on fire. It also means to arouse or inspire an emotion or feeling.

2. **C.** *Burnout* is a noun that means physical or mental collapse due to overwork or stress.

3. **A.** *Blatant* is an adjective that refers to something that's very obvious or completely lacking in subtlety.

4. **C.** *Hasten* is a verb that means to be quick to do something, to move or travel in a hurry, or to make something happen sooner than it otherwise would.

5. **C.** *Objective* is an adjective that means not influenced by opinions or personal feelings when considering and representing facts. It's also a noun that refers to a goal.

6. **B.** *Headstrong* is an adjective that means self-willed and obstinate.

7. **A.** *Cringe* is a verb that means to bend the head or body in fear or in a servile manner.

8. **B.** *Domestic* is an adjective that means of or relating to the running of a home or family relations.

9. **D.** *Frugal* is an adjective that means sparing or economical when it comes to money or food.

10. **B.** *Curtail* is a verb that means to reduce in quantity or extent or to impose a restriction on something.

11. **A.** *Accolade* is a noun that means an award or privilege granted as a special honor or as an acknowledgment of merit.

12. **C.** *Covert* is an adjective that means not openly acknowledged.

13. **D.** *Abhor* is a verb that means to regard with disgust and hatred.

14. **C.** *Mandate* is a noun that means an official order to do something. It's also a verb that means to give someone authority to act in a certain way.

15. **D.** *Assortment* is a noun that means a miscellaneous collection of things or people, so the word most opposite in meaning is *consistency.*

16. **C.** *Credible* is an adjective that means able to be believed or convincing.

17. **A.** *Reprieve* is a verb that means to cancel or postpone someone's punishment. It's also used as a noun to refer to the cancellation or postponement of a punishment.

18. **B.** *Tedious* is an adjective that means too long, slow, or dull. It can also mean tiresome or monotonous.

19. **C.** *Oblivious* is an adjective that means not concerned about or not aware of what is happening.

20. **D.** *Bolster* is a verb that means to support, strengthen, or prop up.

21. **B.** *Abstract* is an adjective that means existing in thought or as an idea but without a physical or concrete existence.

22. **D.** *Hamper* is a verb that means to hinder or impede movement or progress of someone or something.

23. **C.** *Cower* is a verb that means to crouch down in fear.

24. **A.** *Tangent* is a noun that means a completely different line of thought or action. It also means a straight line or plane that touches a curve (or curved surface) at a point but, if extended, doesn't cross it at that point.

25. **B.** *Nullify* is a verb that means to invalidate or to make legally null and void. It also means to cancel out something or make something useless or valueless.

26. **D.** *Tangible* is an adjective that means perceptible by touch.

27. **D.** *Absolution* is a noun that means a formal release from guilt, punishment, or obligation.

28. **B.** *Abrogate* is a verb that means to do away with or repeal.

29. **C.** *Temper* is a verb that means to serve as a neutralizing or counterbalancing force to something. It's also a noun that refers to a person's state of mind as it relates to being angry or calm.

30. **D.** *Plethora* is a noun that means a large or excessive amount of something.

31. **C.** *Tentative* is an adjective that means done without confidence or hesitant. It also means not certain or fixed, or provisional.

32. **B.** *Retaliation* is a noun that refers to the action of harming someone in an act of revenge. It also refers to a counterattack. The word most opposite in meaning is *forgiveness*.

33. **D.** *Admonish* is a verb that means to warn or reprimand someone firmly or to advise or urge someone earnestly.

34. **B.** *Diatribe* is a noun that refers to a forceful and bitter verbal attack against someone or something.

35. **A.** *Memento* is a noun that means an object kept as a reminder or souvenir of a person or event, so the word most opposite in meaning is *rubbish*.

Subtest 3: Paragraph Comprehension Answers

If you're struggling with this subtest, remember to take your time when you read the passages. Then read the question and go back and skim the passage to confirm that you're choosing the correct answer. Check out Chapter 5 for more review on this subtest.

1. **C.** The author doesn't explicitly state that California changed Terry, but you can infer the correct answer from the phrase "too much for their beach bum mentality." Based on that phrase and the distinction between sunny California and the worst winter, you can determine that the weather in California had ruined her ability to handle cold weather. The other answer choices can't be inferred from the limited information given in the paragraph.

2. **B.** You may think that the paragraph is about the increased number of pets in American households, but that's only a small piece of information. The other information about pets in shelters and rescue facilities dominates the rest of the paragraph, with the main idea presented in the last sentence. All the information supports the idea that Americans need to adopt more rescue pets.

3. **D.** You'll notice that all the percentage numbers fall within the middle two sentences. You may be tempted by Choice (A), but read carefully and you'll see that it's the total number of households with pets, not the number with rescue pets.

4. **A.** The paragraph describes how the artists were known for their preference, or inclination, for undertaking these large and unconventional projects.

5. **C.** The passage states that shoes last six months for average use, so that's the only information that could lead to a logical assumption about Tara or her shoes. The other answers aren't related to the presented information.

6. **C.** The passage says that De Niro was nominated for six other awards in addition to the Oscar he won in 1975. That makes seven nominations in all.

7. **B.** Although Tiffany certainly seems to have bad luck with flights, the passage describes the different inclement weather conditions for her region. The use of "sometimes" at the end signifies its unpredictability.

8. **D.** The passage states that the thunderstorm caused her flight to be delayed for five hours, which is the meaning of *postponed.*

9. **B.** The term *centennial* means 100 years, but even if you didn't know this fact, you read that the people gathered in 1961 to celebrate a war that started a hundred years earlier, in 1861.

10. **B.** The passage provides safe driving tips for snowy conditions in order to prevent safety hazards. The first part of the first sentence states the focus.

11. **A.** The passage describes what to do and what not to do when driving in snow. The author explains the results of each action. Therefore, you can infer that knowing what actions are dangerous in the snow will help you drive more safely.

12. **D.** If back-to-school shopping has begun, the beginning of school must be around the corner. Nothing in the passage suggests any of the other answers is correct.

13. **A.** The passage states that 532 of his designs were developed.

14. **D.** The last sentence of the passage says that Frank Lloyd Wright is as famous as Bruce Springsteen. You can infer that his career is famous as well.

15. **C.** The passage states that sailors and skiers share similar feelings toward their respective fellow athletes. Sailors don't like to share the water with motorboaters, so the inference you can draw is that skiers don't like to share the mountain with snowboarders.

Subtest 4: Mathematics Knowledge Answers

If you're missing too many math questions, keep studying (see Chapters 6, 7, and 8 for more information on each subject), and consider asking someone who excels in math to help you grasp the basic concepts. If your scores are improving, keep doing what you're doing right up until test day.

1. **A.** The value of $(-5)^3$ is equal to -5 multiplied by itself three times:
$$(-5)^3 = (-5)(-5)(-5) = 25(-5) = -125$$

2. **B.** To get x alone on one side of the inequality, divide both sides of the inequality $42 < 2x$ by 2:
$$42 < 2x$$
$$\frac{42}{2} < x$$
$$21 < x$$
$$x > 21$$

3. **C.** This one is simple addition.

4. C. The digit 4 is in the tens place, the digit 5 is in the ones place, the digit 2 is in the tenths place, and the digit 1 is in the hundredths place.

5. C. Locate point *P* by starting at the origin and moving along the *x*-axis until you're even with point *P*. That's the −3 mark, so −3 is your *x* coordinate. Now move along the *y*-axis until you reach point *P*. It's at the 2 mark, so 2 is the *y* coordinate.

6. C. Divide 11 by 4 using long division.

$$
\begin{array}{r}
2.75 \\
4\overline{)11.00} \\
\underline{-8} \\
30 \\
\underline{-28} \\
20 \\
\underline{-20} \\
0
\end{array}
$$

7. D. To get *y* by itself on one side of the equal sign, add 2 to both sides of the equation: $-2 + y + 2 = 8 + 2$. The −2 and 2 on the left side cancel each other, so $y = 10$.

8. B. The formula for the circumference of a circle is $C = \pi d$. Substitute 9.24 for *C* and 3.14 for π and then solve for *d* by dividing both sides by 3.14.

$$9.42 = 3.14d$$
$$\frac{9.42}{3.14} = d$$
$$3 = d$$

9. C. Write 28 percent as a decimal: 28 percent $= 28 \div 100 = 0.28$. Multiply: $0.28(40) = 11.2$.

10. C. To multiply terms with the same base, add the exponents:

$$10^{3 + (-6) + 2} = 10^{-1}$$

Simplify:

$$10^{-1} = \frac{1}{10} = 0.1$$

11. A. This expression has two pairs of like terms. First, 2 and 4 are like terms and have a sum of 6. The terms 2*y* and *y* are also like terms and have a sum of 3*y* (remember that *y* is the same as 1*y*).

12. D. The sum of the angles of a triangle is always equal to 180°. To find the value of *x*, subtract 34° and 108° from 180°: $180° - 34° - 108° = 38°$.

13. C. Using the order of operations, simplify inside the parentheses first: $(5 - 2)! = 3!$. The expression 3! is the product of all whole numbers from 3 down to 1: $3! = (3)(2)(1) = 6$.

14. **C.** To add these fractions, you have to find their common denominator, which is the least common multiple (LCM) of all three denominators. In this case, the common denominator is 16. Multiply the numerator and denominator of each fraction by the number that makes each denominator 16. (You don't have to do anything to the middle fraction because it already has the common denominator.)

$$\frac{1 \times 8}{2 \times 8} + \frac{1}{16} + \frac{1 \times 4}{4 \times 4} = \frac{8}{16} + \frac{1}{16} + \frac{4}{16}$$
$$= \frac{8 + 1 + 4}{16}$$
$$= \frac{13}{16}$$

15. **A.** The factors of a number are all the numbers, including the number and 1, that divide into the number without a remainder. The number 51 has four factors: 1, 3, 17, and 51.

16. **B.** Write this sentence as an equation, using x to represent the percent you're trying to find: $0.405 = 0.9x$. Divide both sides by 0.9 to get x alone on one side of the equal sign.

$$0.405 = 0.9x$$
$$\frac{0.405}{0.9} = x$$
$$x = 0.45$$

You convert the decimal 0.45 to a percent by multiplying 0.45 by 100: $0.45(100) = 45$ percent.

17. **B.** If two angles are complementary, the sum of their measures is 90°. Because the measure of angle P is $m°$, you find the complement of angle P by subtracting its measure from 90°.

18. **D.** Because the triangle is a right triangle, you need the Pythagorean theorem: $a^2 + b^2 = c^2$. You know the lengths of side a and the hypotenuse (c), so plug those values into the theorem and solve for b:

$$24^2 + b^2 = 25^2$$
$$576 + b^2 = 625$$
$$b^2 = 49$$
$$b = \pm 7$$

Use the positive answer because a length is never negative.

19. **D.** When you decrease something, you're subtracting from it. In this instance, you're taking 11 away from x; that means you have $x - 11$. "Is" means "*equals*" in mathematical terms (and you know that every equation must have an equal sign). "Twice x" means $2x$. Your equation will look like this: $x - 11 = 2x$.

20. **D.** The mean is the sum of all values divided by the number of values, or the average. First, find the sum of the values: $5 + 7 + 8 + 10 + 4 + x = 34 + x$. Because there are six values, you'll set this side of the equation up as a fraction:

$$\frac{34 + x}{6}$$

You already know the answer to the equation is 7.5, so your equation will look like this:

$$\frac{34 + x}{6} = 7.5$$
$$34 + x = 45$$
$$x = 11$$

21. **A.** Use the order of operations: Simplify inside the parentheses first, compute all exponents next, multiply and divide from left to right after that, and then add and subtract from left to right:

$$(9-3\cdot2)^2-0.5(-2)=(9-6)^2-0.5(-2)$$
$$=(3)^2-0.5(-2)$$
$$=9-0.5(-2)$$
$$=9-(-1)$$
$$=9+1$$
$$=10$$

22. **A.** First, use the distributive property to remove the parentheses: $9-20x+8$. Then simplify by adding 9 and 8 to get $17-20x$.

23. **B.** The formula for the volume of a right cylinder is $V=\pi r^2h$. Substitute $h=2r$ into the formula:

$$V=\pi r^2h$$
$$=\pi r^22r$$

Reorder the terms:

$$V=2\pi\cdot r^2\cdot r$$
$$=2\pi r^3$$

24. **B.** You can break the figure down into a rectangle on the left with dimensions 7.5 cm by 10 cm and a right triangle on the right whose base is $11-7.5=3.5$ cm and whose height is $10-2=8$ cm.

© John Wiley & Sons, Inc.

The area of the rectangle is $A=lw=(10)(7.5)=75$ cm², and the area of the triangle is $A=\dfrac{bh}{2}=\dfrac{(3.5)(8)}{2}=14$ cm². Add the two areas to find the total area: $75+14=89$ cm².

25. **A.** The problem only gives you the number of boys, so first you must find the number of girls by subtracting 140 from 260: $260-140=120$. When you need to express the number of girls to boys as a fraction, there are 120 girls for every 140 boys; that means 120:140 or $\dfrac{120}{140}$, which simplifies to $\dfrac{6}{7}$.

On the ASVAB, you have to pay close attention to wording; if the question had asked for the ratio of boys to girls, Choice (B) would've been correct. If the question had asked for the ratio of boys to total students, Choice (D) would've been correct.

7

The Part of Tens

Find out what mistakes to avoid as you prepare to take the ASVAB on testing day.

Get hints for maximizing your score on the all-important AFQT.

Discover ways to improve your English and math skills.

Chapter **28**

Ten Surefire Ways to Fail the ASVAB

Technically, you can't fail the ASVAB — it's not a pass/fail test. It's a tool the military uses to measure your potential for learning military jobs and military duties. But realistically, each of the branches has established minimum Armed Forces Qualification Test (AFQT) scores applicants need to qualify for enlistment and minimum line scores to qualify for certain military jobs. If you don't qualify to join the service branch of your choice or don't qualify for the job you want, you haven't technically failed, but you have to take the test again (after a few study sessions) and pass to get into the branch of service you want to join.

If you avoid the mistakes outlined in this chapter, you can improve your chances of qualifying for enlistment and getting the military job of your dreams.

Choosing Not to Study at All

Many people think that they don't need to study for the ASVAB. They assume that because they studied many of the subjects in high school, they'll do fine if they just wing it.

This train of thought isn't correct (and it's kind of off the tracks). Why wouldn't you study? At the very least, brushing up on vocabulary and math concepts definitely helps you score higher on the ASVAB. Using a calculator is a no-no on the ASVAB, so you may want to revisit some math tricks for doing calculations by hand. Auto, Shop, and Mechanical Comprehension aren't required high school courses, so these subjects may be completely new to you and require additional attention.

Using study guides like this one gives you an idea of what to expect *and* allows you to sharpen some skills that may have gotten a little dull. Even better, you won't have to retake the ASVAB if you want to change jobs a few years down the road.

Failing to Realize How Scores Are Used

The military powers that be use the subtests on the ASVAB to determine which military jobs you qualify for. If you don't know how the scores are used, you can't decide which parts of the exam are most important for you to study.

Check out Chapters 1 and 2 for an explanation of how the military uses ASVAB subtest scores to determine your qualifications. Also head to Appendix A to see the scores you need to get into the military career you want.

Studying for Unnecessary Subtests

If you don't want to be a mechanic in the military, why would you study Auto & Shop Information? You should be spending your time on the subjects you need to score well on to land your dream job. Don't forget the math and vocabulary review, because the military uses those ASVAB subtests to compute the all-important AFQT score, which determines whether you can join the branch of your choice.

TIP

It's easier to study subject areas that you find easy or have an interest in, but if you're already an electronics whiz, don't waste your time studying for that subtest. Spend your time studying subject areas that you know you need to work on.

Losing Focus

I'm not going to sugarcoat this: The ASVAB is tiring. You have to take nine or ten subtests (depending on the version) that cover some really diverse subjects. You have about three hours to complete the actual test, which is plenty of time for most people. If you lose focus while you're taking the test, time can slip away, and you may not get to all the questions. It's hard, but stay focused on the task at hand throughout the whole test. It'll be over soon.

TIP

Here are some tips that can help you maintain focus:

>> **Arrive at the test location with time to spare.** This gives you a few minutes to sit and relax before you have to dive into the test questions. (Most recruiters bring their recruits directly to the testing location, so you'll arrive early enough.)

>> **Leave your baggage at the door.** Don't worry about whether you'll get the military job you want or whether you'll pass the physical when you see a military doctor. You'll have plenty of time to worry about that after you finish the test.

>> **Concentrate on one subtest at a time.** Don't waste time rehashing the questions on the previous subtest or trying to anticipate the questions on the next subtest. Focus on the subtest you're taking at the time.

>> **Take a few moments to relax and refocus between subtests.** If you finish a subtest with time to spare, close your eyes for a bit and take some deep breaths before you begin the next subtest.

When you answer the final question on one subtest on the CAT-ASVAB, you move immediately to the next subtest. If the timer on the computer screen says you have a few minutes of time left on the subtest, use that time to relax and refocus before submitting that final answer.

Panicking over Time

Yes, you have only a limited time to take the test, but don't worry about it. The more you panic, the more likely you are to make mistakes. Just work at a steady pace, and you'll do fine. Most people have plenty of time to answer all the questions in each subtest.

REMEMBER

Don't spend too much time on any single question. If you're drawing a blank, make a guess and move on. (See "Making Wild Guesses or Not Guessing at All" later in this chapter.)

The CAT-ASVAB shows both a timer on the computer screen, counting down the number of minutes you have to finish that subtest, and the number of questions you have remaining. If you're taking the pencil-and-paper version of the test, check the clock on the wall. The proctor will generally write the start and finish times for the current subtest on a whiteboard. Keep your eye on the time remaining, but don't panic over it.

Deciding Not to Check the Answers

You should always double-check your answers before you commit to them — you don't want silly mistakes to trip you up. Don't mark your answer and then check your work. Check your work first.

Do not second-guess yourself (see "Changing Answers" later in this chapter). Just check for accuracy (like in mathematical equations). Be sure to mark your answer sheet correctly, too, verifying that the number of the question matches the number on your answer sheet (you don't have to worry about this with the computerized version of the ASVAB). Getting just one question off can mess up the rest of your answer sheet.

TIP

If you're taking the paper and pencil version of the test, mentally say to yourself, "The answer to Question 22 is Choice (C)" as your pencil moves. That can help you avoid filling in the wrong circle.

Making Wild Guesses or Not Guessing at All

Take the time to eliminate answers you know are incorrect before choosing among the remaining answer options. And here's the number one rule: Don't leave any blank spaces. In most cases, guessing if you have to is the way to go — at least you have a higher chance at getting the right answer, as opposed to a 0 percent chance if you leave the answer blank. If you can eliminate answers you know are wrong before guessing, you increase your chances of answering correctly even more. For tips on smart guessing, see Chapter 3.

WARNING

Even though you've likely read this before, I'm still going to say it one last time: If you're running out of time at the end of a subtest while taking the CAT-ASVAB, be careful about guessing your way through the last questions. If you don't finish a subtest, you'll be scored as if you'd guessed randomly on the remaining questions. It's in your best interest to guess smart if you're running out of time.

Changing Answers

After you double-check your math, decide that Choice (C) is correct, and mark it on the answer sheet, don't change your answer on the paper version of the ASVAB! You're almost certain to change a right answer to a wrong one when you play that game. Plus, you can drive yourself crazy by second-guessing (and third- and fourth-guessing) your decision. Mark the answer and move on.

WARNING

You can't change an answer on the CAT-ASVAB. After you submit an answer, that's it; the computer moves you on to the next question, and you can't go back.

Memorizing the Practice Test Questions

Don't waste your time trying to memorize the practice questions in this book. I can almost guarantee you won't see any of the practice questions in this book (or any other study guide) on the actual ASVAB. Military test materials are highly controlled items, and no author of an ASVAB preparation book has access to them. In fact, military members and military civilian employees who disclose actual ASVAB test questions or answers can go to jail — and I'm not planning on doing time!

Just use the practice questions in this book as a measurement tool of which subject areas you should spend your time concentrating on.

Misunderstanding the Problem

Make sure that you know what the question wants from you and then give the question what it wants. Pay close attention to detail, because you can easily confuse a division sign for an addition sign or miss a key element that can lead you to the wrong answer. By familiarizing yourself with the types of questions on the ASVAB, you'll be able to zero in on what you're supposed to do a lot more quickly than those poor folks who didn't have the brilliant idea to buy this book.

Chapter 29

Ten Tips for Doing Well on the AFQT

Commonly referred to as the ASVAB score, the Armed Forces Qualification Test (AFQT) score is actually computed only from the reading and math skills subtests of the ASVAB. The AFQT score determines whether you're even qualified to enlist in the service of your choice. (For the full scoop, see Chapter 1.) The ten concepts presented in this chapter help you score better on the four subtests of the ASVAB that are used to calculate your AFQT score.

As Soon as the Test Starts, Write Down What You're Likely to Forget

TIP

You can't bring your own scratch paper to the test, but the test proctors will give you as many sheets of scratch paper as you want. Not only is your scratch paper useful to take the place of the calculator you're not allowed to use, but you can also use it to write notes at the very beginning of the test — things that you're worried you may forget. For example, if you're worried that you'll forget the math order of operations, write it down first thing.

Read All the Answer Choices before Deciding

I think the people who write ASVAB test questions must go through a special course that tells them they have to keep you on your toes. Many of the answer choices given on the ASVAB are "close, but no cigar." In other words, question-writers try to sneak in incorrect answers that are *almost* correct . . . but not quite. You may even notice that the practice exam questions in Chapters 18, 20, 22, 24, and 26 have those types of answers. The military has found that realistic training is the most effective.

The best defense against this type of trickery is to read each answer choice completely, even if you think the first or second choice looks plausible. You're looking for the answer that's *most correct.*

Don't Expect Perfect Word Matches

REMEMBER

The Word Knowledge subtest of the ASVAB contains questions that ask you to find the word that is *closest in meaning* to a given word. Don't get confused and think that you have to find the word that means *exactly* the same thing as the given word. Just follow the directions. Because some of the answer options may have similar meanings, you need to choose the answer that's closest in meaning to the given word — the answer that's *most* right.

Read the Passages before the Questions

Some of the Paragraph Comprehension questions can be tricky. Often, a question asks you to come to a conclusion based on the information presented in a paragraph. The only way to do this effectively is to understand the entire paragraph and what the author wants to convey. If you instead read the question first, you may find yourself wasting time by looking for information that isn't directly stated.

Reread to Find Specific Information

The Paragraph Comprehension subtest often asks you to find specific information in a passage. Go back and reread the paragraph. You shouldn't have to guess what this information is — it's in the passage, or you can easily deduce it from the passage. For instance, if a paragraph includes the sentence, "Six out of ten smokers will contract some form of cancer," and a question asks, "How many smokers *won't* contract some form of cancer?" you can easily deduce that four is the correct number.

Base Conclusions Only on What You Read

You may have to draw inferences or conclusions from what you've read. You must use only the information presented in the paragraph to reach this conclusion instead of relying on your own ideas and opinions. In other words, ask yourself, "Would the author agree with this statement, based on what he or she has written in this paragraph?" Apply this test to each answer option to choose the best answer.

Change Percents to Decimals

To perform math operations, you often have to change a percent to a fraction or a decimal.

To change a percent to a fraction, multiply the percent by $\frac{1}{100}$ and drop the percent sign:

$$5\% = 5 \times \frac{1}{100} = \frac{5}{100}$$

To change a percent to a decimal, move the decimal point two places to the left and drop the percent sign:

$$5\% = 0.05$$

Understand Inverses

Inverse operations are opposite operations. The opposite of addition is subtraction, and vice versa. And the opposite of multiplication is division, and vice versa.

But when it comes to numbers, the term *inverse* is not the same as *opposite*. The *opposite* of 5 is -5, but the *inverse* of 5 is $\frac{1}{5}$. When you deal with numbers, think of writing the inverse of a number as standing the number on its head: The inverse (reciprocal) of 5, or $\frac{5}{1}$, is $\frac{1}{5}$.

Remember How Ratios, Rates, and Scales Compare

You need to understand the differences among ratios, rates, and scales:

>> **Ratio:** A ratio represents any relationship between two objects. If Luis invests \$10 in Lotto tickets and Joe invests \$20 in Lotto tickets, then for every dollar Luis invests, Joe invests two. That's a ratio of 1:2.

>> **Rate:** Rate is an expression of the relationship between two unlike elements. For example, if Anna's car can travel a distance of 450 miles per tank of gas and her gas tank holds 15 gallons, then her car consumes gas at a rate of 30 miles per gallon, or 30 mpg (miles and gallons being unlike elements). Mathematically, 450 (miles) ÷ 15 (gallons in the tank) = 30 miles to the gallon.

>> **Scale:** A scale expresses a relationship between two like elements, although the units of measure may differ. A map drawn to scale may use 1 inch to represent 1 mile. Although an inch and a mile aren't the same unit of measure, they measure the same thing (distance).

Make Sure Your Answers Are Reasonable

On the Mathematics Knowledge and Arithmetic Reasoning subtests, you have very limited time to answer each question (flip to Chapters 6 and 9, respectively, for more on the exact timings). If you use your time wisely, you should have plenty of time to double-check and make sure you've chosen the correct answer.

REMEMBER

Your answers should make sense, or they're probably wrong. For example, if you're required to compute the average speed that a car maintains during a 2,000-mile trip and your answer is 2,000 mph, your answer is probably not correct. If a question includes a formula (such as $2 + x = 10$), plug in your answer for the variable and see whether both sides are equal. If you answered 8, plug in 8 for x and find that $10 = 10$. That means your answer checks out.

The people who design ASVAB test questions often include wrong answers that you may choose if you make a common mistake when solving the problem, such as using a formula incorrectly. Double-checking your answers allows you to catch your errors.

» Knowing key rules and formulas

» Expanding your vocabulary

» Becoming a better reader

Chapter **30**

Ten Ways to Boost Your Math and English Skills

The ASVAB includes two math and two English subtests: Mathematics Knowledge, Arithmetic Reasoning, Word Knowledge, and Paragraph Comprehension. These four subtests are probably the most important subtests of the ASVAB, because they make up your AFQT score, which is the score that determines whether you qualify to join the branch of your choice. (Check out Chapter 1 for more info on the AFQT and Chapters 24 and 26 for sample AFQTs. You can also peruse the latest editions of *ASVAB AFQT For Dummies* and *1,001 ASVAB AFQT Practice Questions For Dummies* by yours truly, both published by Wiley.)

Because these four subtests are so important, this chapter includes ten surefire ways to build your skills in these critical areas before you take the test.

Practice Doing Math Problems

The best way to get a firm grasp of certain types of math is by doing math problems and not simply reading them. Take advantage of the practice math questions in this book, and visit the public library to see what kind of high school math textbooks it has to lend. The more you do math, the better you'll get at it.

Put Away Your Calculator

You're not allowed to use a calculator when you take the ASVAB, so now is the time to get used to solving basic math problems without one. Practice working out problems by hand, and make sure you know your multiplication tables and other basic calculations. The ASVAB math questions are written by people who know how to compute 2 + 2 in their heads.

TIP

As you solve math problems by hand, you can get a feel for what works and what doesn't. For instance, some questions ask you to find the square root of a number, which you may find hard without a calculator. But a little logic can help. If you know the square root of 9 is 3 ($3 \times 3 = 9$) and you know the square root of 16 is 4, then you can conclude that the square root of 12 falls between 3 and 4.

Memorize the Order of Operations

Mathematical equations with multiple steps must be solved in a specific order. Otherwise, you won't get the correct answer. Memorize the order in which you do certain calculations when you're solving equations, and practice applying these rules well before test day.

REMEMBER

When solving an equation involves multiple steps, the correct order of operations is

1. **Whatever's within parentheses (and other grouping symbols)**

If you have multiple parentheses nested inside each other, do the innermost set first. On the ASVAB, the other grouping symbols you run across are the fraction bar and the square root sign. Do what's beneath the square root bar before taking the root. Do any operation above the fraction bar and any operation below the fraction bar before dividing.

2. **Exponents**

3. **Multiplication and division**

Operate from left to right.

4. **Addition and subtraction**

Again, work from left to right.

For example, $3 + 2 \times 3$ isn't equal to 5×3, or 15. The correct answer is 9. You first do the multiplication and then the addition. You can remember the order of operations as "Please Excuse My Dear Aunt Sally," or PEMDAS. Check out Chapter 6 for more explanation.

Know Your Geometry Formulas

You encounter some math questions that require you to calculate area, perimeter, and volume on the ASVAB. Memorize the following area formulas:

>> **Area of a rectangle:** For any rectangle, Area = Length × Width: $A = lw$.

>> **Area of a triangle:** For triangles, Area = Base × Height (or altitude) divided by 2: $A = \frac{1}{2}bh$.

>> **Area of a circle:** For circles, area is π (approximately 3.14) times the radius squared: $A = \pi r^2$.

Know these perimeter and circumference formulas:

>> **Perimeter of polygon (a shape with straight sides):** Calculate the perimeter of any quadrilateral (four-sided figure) or triangle by adding the lengths of all the sides together.

>> **Circumference of a circle:** Find the circumference of a circle by multiplying π times the diameter: $C = \pi d$. **Note:** Diameter equals 2 times the radius.

And know these formulas for the volume of 3-D solids:

» **Volume of a box:** Find the volume of a rectangular solid by multiplying Length × Width × Height: $V = lwh$.

» **Volume of a cylinder:** Find the volume of a cylinder by multiplying the area of the circular base (π times the base's radius squared) by the cylinder's height: $V = \pi r^2 h$.

Keep a Word List

The English language is packed with words, and nobody expects you to know them all. However, the ASVAB writers do expect you to have a good grasp of many vocabulary words. One way to improve your vocabulary is to keep a word list.

TIP

How does a word list work? As you read, write down the words that you don't know. Quickly look them up in the dictionary (you can even look them up from your smartphone). You can then apply your word list in your day-to-day life. Of course, you can't remember every single word, but you can focus on mastering one new word every day and using it in conversation. Check out Chapter 4 for more tips on building your vocabulary.

REMEMBER

Don't waste your time by choosing little-known words, such as *absquatulate* (which means to leave hurriedly or secretly). You're unlikely to see obscure words on the ASVAB, but you should make a practice of learning the meaning of as many common English words as possible.

Study Latin and Greek

You can skip the grammar and pronunciation, but you should get to know some of the roots, prefixes, and suffixes that English has borrowed from Latin and Greek. These word parts are the building blocks of much of the English language, and they can give you clues about what words mean.

If you see an unfamiliar word on the Word Knowledge section, try to figure out its root. For example, if you know the meaning of *mercy*, you can figure out the meaning of *merciful*. Remember that prefixes and suffixes can be added onto a root to change the word's meaning or function. Here are some examples:

» **Changing meaning:** The prefix *a-* usually means *opposite,* so the word *atypical* means the opposite of *typical,* not a typical thing.

» **Changing parts of speech:** *Establish* is a verb meaning *to make stable* or *to prove,* whereas *establishment* (with a suffix) is a noun meaning *a thing that has been established.*

For a list of common word parts you should know, check out Chapter 4 and Appendix C.

Use Flashcards

Flashcards help you remember important facts through the process of spaced repetition. Learning psychologists agree that this is one of the most effective methods of memorizing new information. Plus, it's cheap — all you need is a set of blank index cards and a pen to create your very own studying machine.

You can use flashcards to improve both your mental math and vocabulary — write down vocab words, roots, prefixes, and suffixes; practice matching square roots and square numbers; or just make sure you know your math formulas.

Read More, Watch TV Less

The best way to improve your reading comprehension is simple: Read more. If you spend two hours a day watching TV and posting pictures on social media, you can instead use those two hours to read a novel or the newspaper or a book about car repair — whatever interests you the most. You'll be surprised at how fast your reading speed and comprehension improve with just a little daily practice.

Practice Finding Main and Supporting Points

All writing should have a point. The main point is the thing that the writer wants you to take away from his or her words. Some passages include more than one point. Usually, such passages have one main point and one or more subpoints that support the main idea. As you're reading passages on the ASVAB (and in real life), you want to be able to easily identify the main point. You should practice identifying the points during your own reading sessions. Read each paragraph and then ask yourself what information the author is trying to convey to you.

Use a Study Guide

In my humble opinion, there is no better commercial ASVAB study guide available than this one. Read the chapters carefully and then use the practice tests to determine where you need more study.

WARNING

Use the practice questions only to test your own knowledge of the subject. Don't expect to see the same questions on the actual ASVAB. The people who write the actual ASVAB tests keep a close eye on commercial study guides, like this one, and try to avoid having the same questions. What they can't do is defeat a well-prepared applicant like you, so commit yourself and knock it out of the park!

Appendixes

Appendix A

Matching ASVAB Scores to Military Jobs

The military has hundreds of enlisted job opportunities, ranging from decontaminating chemical detection equipment to interpreting foreign languages. Each of the military services has established its own individual *line score* requirements (a combination of various ASVAB subtest scores) for specific enlisted jobs. The tables in this appendix show the minimum line scores that the services have established for entry-level enlisted jobs.

REMEMBER

Just because you achieve the minimum ASVAB line score for the job of your choice doesn't mean you'll absolutely get that job. The military considers other factors, including the current needs of the service (vacant positions), whether you're eligible for a security clearance, and your medical exam results.

The charts in this appendix are as accurate as they can be at press time. However, military jobs and qualification standards are subject to change with little or no notice. For the most up-to-date information and for complete job descriptions and qualification factors, see your local military recruiter or visit your desired branch's official website:

>> **Army:** www.GoArmy.com

>> **Air Force and Space Force:** www.AirForce.com

>> **Navy:** www.Navy.com

>> **Marines:** www.Marines.com

>> **Coast Guard:** www.GoCoastGuard.com

Army Enlisted Jobs

The Army calls its enlisted jobs *Military Occupational Specialties* (MOSs), and more than 150 such specialties exist for entry-level recruits. Table A-1 shows entry-level Army MOSs and the ASVAB line scores required to qualify for the jobs. Scan the table and see if you find a job that interests you.

Line scores are abbreviated as follows: Clerical (CL), Combat (CO), Electronics (EL), Field Artillery (FA), General Maintenance (GM), General Technical (GT), Mechanical Maintenance (MM), Operators and Food (OF), Surveillance and Communications (SC), and Skilled Technical (ST). See Chapter 2 for an explanation of which ASVAB subtest scores are used to calculate each of the line scores.

TABLE A-1 Army Enlisted Jobs and Required ASVAB Scores

MOS	Title	Score	MOS	Title	Score	MOS	Title	Score
09L	Interpreter/ Translator	N/A**	**11B**	Infantry	CO-87	**11C**	Indirect Fire Infantryman	CO-87
12B	Combat Engineer	CO-87	**12C**	Bridge Crewmember	CO-87	**12D**	Diver	ST-106 or GM-98 and GT-107
12G	Quarrying Specialist (Reserves only)	GM-93	**12K**	Plumber	GM-88	**12M**	Firefighter	GM-88
12N	Horizontal Construction Engineer	GM-90	**12P**	Prime Power Production Specialist	ST-107, EL-107, and GT-110	**12Q**	Power Distribution Specialist	EL-93
12R	Interior Electrician	EL-93	**12T**	Technical Engineer	ST-101	**12V**	Concrete and Asphalt Equipment Operator	GM-88
12W	Carpentry and Masonry Specialist	GM-88	**12Y**	Geospatial Engineer	ST-100 or GT-100	**13B**	Cannon Crewmember	FA-93
13F	Joint Fire Support Specialist	FA-96	**13J**	Fire Control Specialist	FA-93	**13M**	Multiple Launch Rocket System Crewmember	OF-95
13R	Field Artillery Firefinder Radar Operator	SC-98	**13T**	Field Artillery Surveyor/ Meteorological Crewmember	EL-93	**14E**	Patriot Fire Control Enhanced Operator/ Maintainer	MM-100
14G	Air Defense Battle Management System Operator	GT-98 and MM-96	**14H**	Air Defense Early Warning System Operator	GT-98 and MM-99	**14P**	Air and Missile Defense (AMD) Crewmember	OF-95
14S	Avenger Crewmember (Reserves only)	OF-85	**14T**	Patriot Launching Station Enhanced Operator/ Maintainer	OF-95	**15B**	Aircraft Powerplant Repairer	MM-104

MOS	Title	Score	MOS	Title	Score	MOS	Title	Score
15D	Aircraft Powertrain Repairer	MM-104	15E	Unmanned Aircraft Systems Repairer	EL-93 and MM-104	15F	Aircraft Electrician	MM-104
15G	Aircraft Structural Repairer	MM-104	15H	Aircraft Pneudraulics Repairer	MM-104	15J	OH-58D/ARH Armament/ Electrical/ Avionics Systems Repairer	EL-93 and MM-104
15N	Avionic Mechanic	EL-93	15P	Aviation Operations Specialist	ST-91	15Q	Air Traffic Control Operator	ST-101
15R	AH-64 Attack Helicopter Repairer	MM-99	15S	OH-58D Helicopter Repairer	MM-99	15T	UH-60 Helicopter Repairer	MM-104
15U	CH-47 Helicopter Repairer	MM-104	15W	Unmanned Aircraft Systems Operator	SC-102	15Y	AH-64D Armament/ Electrical/ Avionics Systems Repairer	EL-98 and MM-104
17C	Cyber Operations Specialist	GT-110 and ST-112	17E	Electronic Warfare Specialist	SC-105, EL-105, and ST-105	18X	Special Forces Candidate**	CO-100 and GT-110
19D	Cavalry Scout	CO-87	19K	M1 Armor Crewman	CO-87	25B	Information Technology Specialist	ST-95
25C	Radio Operator/ Maintainer	SC-98 and EL-98	25D	Cyber Network Defender	GT-105 and ST-105	25L	Cable Systems Installer/ Maintainer	SC-89 and EL-89
25M	Multimedia Illustrator	EL-93 and ST-91	25N	Nodal Network Systems Operator/ Maintainer	EL-102 and SC-105	25P	Microwave Systems Operator/ Maintainer	EL-107
25Q	Multichannel Transmission Systems Operator/ Maintainer	EL-98 and SC-98	25R	Visual Information Equipment Operator/ Maintainer	EL-107	25S	Satellite Communication Systems Operator/ Maintainer	EL-117
25U	Signal Support Systems Specialist	SC-92 and EL-93	25V	Combat Documentation/ Production Specialist	EL-93 and ST-91	27D	Paralegal Specialist	CL-105
31B	Military Police	ST-91	31D	Criminal Investigations Special Agent	ST-107 and GT-110	31E	Internment/ Resettlement Specialist	ST-95

(continued)

MOS	Title	Score	MOS	Title	Score	MOS	Title	Score
31K	Military Working Dog Handler	ST-91	**35F**	Intelligence Analyst	ST-101	**35G**	Geospatial Intelligence Imagery Analyst	ST-101
35L	Counterintelligence Agent*	ST-101	**35M**	Human Intelligence Collector	ST-101	**35N**	Signals Intelligence Analyst	ST-101
35P	Cryptologic Linguist	ST-91	**35Q**	Cryptologic Cyberspace Intelligence Collector/ Analyst	ST-112	**35S**	Signals Collection Analyst	ST-101
35T	Military Intelligence Systems Maintainer/ Integrator	ST-112	**36B**	Financial Management Technician	CL-101	**37F**	Psychological Operations Specialist**	GT-107
38B	Civil Affairs Specialist	GT-107	**42A**	Human Resources Specialist	GT-100 and CL-90	**42R**	Musician	N/A**
42S	Special Band Musician	N/A**	**46S**	Public Affairs Mass Communication Specialist	GT-107	**56M**	Religious Affairs Specialist	CL-90
68A	Biomedical Equipment Specialist	EL-107	**68B**	Orthopedic Specialist	ST-101 and GT-107	**68C**	Practical Nursing Specialist	ST-101 and GT-107
68D	Operating Room Specialist	ST-91	**68E**	Dental Specialist	ST-91	**68F**	Physical Therapy Specialist	ST-101 and GT-107
68G	Patient Administration Specialist	CL-90	**68H**	Optical Laboratory Specialist	GM-98	**68J**	Medical Logistics Specialist	CL-90
68K	Medical Laboratory Specialist	ST-106	**68L**	Occupational Therapy Specialist	ST-101 and GT-107	**68M**	Nutrition Care Specialist	OF-95
68N	Cardiovascular Specialist	ST-101 and GT-107	**68P**	Radiology Specialist	ST-106	**68Q**	Pharmacy Specialist	ST-95
68R	Veterinary Food Inspection Specialist	ST-95	**68S**	Preventive Medicine Specialist	ST-101	**68T**	Animal Care Specialist	ST-91
68U	Ear, Nose, and Throat (ENT) Specialist	ST-101 and GT-107	**68V**	Respiratory Specialist	ST-102	**68W**	Combat Medic Specialist	ST-101 and GT-107
68X	Behavioral Health Specialist	ST-101	**68Y**	Eye Specialist	ST-101 and GT-107	**74D**	Chemical, Biological, Radiological, and Nuclear Operations Specialist	ST-100

MOS	Title	Score	MOS	Title	Score	MOS	Title	Score
88H	Cargo Specialist	GM-88	88K	Watercraft Operator	MM-99	88L	Watercraft Engineer	MM-99
88M	Motor Transport Operator	OF-85	88N	Transportation Management Coordinator	CL-95	88P	Railway Equipment Repairer (Reserves only)	MM-97
88T	Railway Section Repairer (Reserves only)	MM-87	88U	Railway Operations Crewmember (Reserves only)	MM-92	89A	Ammunition Stock Control and Accounting Specialist	ST-91
89B	Ammunition Specialist	ST-91	89D	Explosive Ordnance Disposal (EOD) Specialist	GM-105	91A	M1 Abrams Tank System Maintainer	MM-99 or MM-88 and GT-92
91B	Wheeled Vehicle Mechanic	MM-92 or MM-87 and GT-85	91C	Utilities Equipment Repairer	GM-98 or GM-88 and GT-83	91D	Power Generation Equipment Repairer	GM-98 or GM-88 and GT-88
91E	Allied Trade Specialist	GM-98 or GM-88 and GT-95	91F	Small Arms/ Artillery Repairer	GM-93 or GM-88 and GT-85	91G	Fire Control Repairer	EL-98 or EL-93 and GT-88
91H	Track Vehicle Repairer	MM-92 or MM-87 and GT-85	91J	Quartermaster and Chemical Equipment Repairer	MM-92 or MM-87 and GT-85	91L	Construction Equipment Repairer	MM-92 or MM-87 and GT-85
91M	Bradley Fighting Vehicle System Maintainer	MM-99 or MM-88 and GT-92	91P	Artillery Mechanic	MM-99 or MM-88 and GT-88	91S	Stryker Systems Maintainer	MM-92 or MM-87 and GT-85
92A	Automated Logistical Specialist	CL-90	92F	Petroleum Supply Specialist	CL-86 and OF-85	92G	Culinary Specialist	OF-85
92L	Petroleum Laboratory Specialist	ST-91	92M	Mortuary Affairs Specialist	GM-88	92R	Parachute Rigger	GM-88 and CO-87
92S	Shower/ Laundry and Clothing Repair Specialist	GM-84	92W	Water Treatment Specialist	GM-88	92Y	Unit Supply Specialist	CL-90
94A	Land Combat Electronic Missile System Repairer	EL-102	94D	Air Traffic Control Equipment Repairer	EL-102	94E	Radio and Communications Security Repairer	EL-102

(continued)

MOS	Title	Score	MOS	Title	Score	MOS	Title	Score
94F	Computer/ Detection Systems Repairer	EL-102	**94H**	Test Measurement and Diagnostic Equipment Maintenance Support Specialist	EL-107	**94M**	Radar Repairer	EL-107
94P	Multiple Launch Rocket System Repairer	EL-93	**94R**	Avionic and Survivability Equipment Repairer	EL-98	**94S**	Patriot System Repairer	EL-107
94T	Short Range Air Defense System Repairer	EL-98	**94Y**	Integrated Family of Test Equipment Operator and Maintainer	EL-107			

* Soldiers must be at least 21 years old at time of graduation.

** Soldiers must pass one or more assessment and selection programs.

Air Force Enlisted Jobs

The United States Air Force has about 120 entry-level enlisted jobs for new recruits. The Air Force refers to enlisted jobs as *Air Force Specialty Codes* (AFSCs). Table A-2 shows the Air Force entry-level AFSCs and the line scores required to qualify for each job. The table is organized by AFSC number, so browse the table and see which AFSCs pique your interest.

Line scores are abbreviated as follows: General (G), Electronic (E), Mechanical (M), and Administrative (A). See Chapter 2 for information on which ASVAB subtest scores are used by the Air Force to calculate the various line scores.

TABLE A-2 **Air Force Enlisted Jobs and Required ASVAB Scores**

AFSC	Title	Score	AFSC	Title	Score	AFSC	Title	Score
1A0X1	In-Flight Refueling Specialist	G-55	**1A1X1**	Flight Engineer	G-55	**1A2X1**	Aircraft Loadmaster	G-57
1A3X1	Airborne Mission Systems Specialist	G-55	**1A6X1**	Flight Attendant**	G-55	**1A8X1**	Airborne Cryptologic Language Analyst	G-72
1A8X2	Airborne Intelligence, Surveillance, and Reconnaissance	G-55	**1A9X1**	Special Missions Aviator	G-60 and M-60	**1B4X1**	Cyber Warfare Operations*	G-64
1C0X2	Aviation Resource Management	G-55	**1C1X1**	Air Traffic Control	G-55 and M-55	**1C2X1**	Combat Controller	G-44

AFSC	Title	Score	AFSC	Title	Score	AFSC	Title	Score
1C3X1	Command and Control Operations	G-49	1C4X1	Tactical Air Control Party Specialist	G-49	1C5X1	Command and Control Battle Management Operations	G-49
1C6X1	Space System Operations	E-60	1C7X1	Airfield Management	G-50 and M-40	1C8X1	Radar, Airfield and Weather Systems	E-70
1C8X2	Airfield Systems	E-70	1N0X1	All Source Intelligence Analyst	G-57	1N1X1	Geospatial Intelligence	G-57
1N2X1	Signals Intelligence Analyst	G-62	1N3XX	Cryptologic Language Analyst	G-72	1N4X1	Fusion Analyst	G-49
1N7X1	Human Intelligence Specialist	G-49	1N8X1	Targeting Analyst	G-50 and E-50	1P0X1	Aircrew Flight Equipment	M-40
1S0X1	Safety	G-55	1T0X1	Survival, Evasion, Resistance, and Escape*	G-55	1T2X1	Pararescue	G-44
1U0X1	Remotely Piloted Aircraft Sensor Operator	G-64 and E-54	1U1X1	Remotely Piloted Aircraft Pilot	G-64 and E-54	1W0X1	Weather	G-66 and E-50
2A0X1	Avionics Test Stations and Components	E-70	2A2X1	SWF/PR Integrated Communication/ Navigation/ Mission Systems	E-70	2A2X2	SOF/PR Integrated Instruments and Flight Control Systems	E-70
2A2X3	SOF/PR Integrated Electronic Warfare Systems	E-70	2A3X3	Tactical Aircraft Maintenance	M-47	2A3X4	Fighter Aircraft Integrated Avionics	E-70
2A5X1	Airlift/Special Mission Aircraft Maintenance	M-47	2A5X2	Helicopter/ Tiltrotor Aircraft Maintenance	M-56	2A5X3	Mobility Air Forces Electronic Warfare Systems	E-70
2A6X1	Aerospace Propulsion	M-60	2A6X2	Aerospace Ground Equipment	M-47 and E-28	2A6X3	Aircrew Egress Systems	E-70
2A6X4	Aircraft Fuel Systems	M-47	2A6X5	Aircraft Hydraulic Systems	M-56	2A6X6	Aircraft Electrical and Environmental Systems	E-61 and M-41
2A7X1	Aircraft Metals Technology	M-47	2A7X2	Nondestructive Inspection	M-42	2A7X3	Aircraft Structural Maintenance	M-47

(continued)

TABLE A-2 *(continued)*

AFSC	Title	Score	AFSC	Title	Score	AFSC	Title	Score
2A7X5	Low Observable Aircraft Structural Maintenance	M-47	2A8X1	Mobility Air Forces Integrated Communication/ Navigation/ Mission Systems	E-61	2A8X2	Mobility Air Forces Integrated Instrument and Flight Control Systems	E-61
2A9X1	Bomber/Special Integrated Communication/ Navigation/ Mission Systems	E-61	2A9X2	Bomber/Special Integrated Instrument and Flight Control Systems	E-61	2A9X3	Bomber/Special Electronic Warfare and Radar Surveillance Integrated Avionics	E-61
2F0X1	Fuels	M-47 and G-38	2G0X1	Logistics Plans	A-56	2M0X1	Missile Maintenance	E-70
2M0X2	Missile and Space Systems Maintenance	M-47	2M0X3	Missile and Space Facilities	E-70	2P0X1	Precision Measurement Equipment Laboratory	E-70
2R0X1	Maintenance Management Analysis	G-70	2R1X1	Maintenance Management Production	G-44	2S0X1	Materiel Management	A-41 or G-44
2T0X1	Traffic Management	A-35	2T1X1	Ground Transportation	A-28 and M-47	2T2X1	Air Transportation	M-47 and A-28
2T3X1	Mission Generation Vehicular Maintenance	M-47	2T3X2	Vehicle Management	M-56	2T3X7	Fleet Management and Analysis	A-41
2W0X1	Munitions Systems	G-57 or M-60	2W1X1	Aircraft Armament Systems	M-60 or E-45	2W2X1	Nuclear Weapons	M-60
3D0X1	Knowledge Operations Management	A-47	3D0X2	Cyber Systems Operations	G-64	3D0X3	Cyber Surety	G-64
3D0X4	Computer Systems Programming	G-64	3D1X1	Client Systems	E-60	3D1X2	Cyber Transport Systems	E-70
3D1X3	Radio Frequency Transmission Systems	E-70	3E0X1	Electrical Systems	E-35 and M-35	3E0X2	Electrical Power Production	E-40 and M-56
3E1X1	Heating, Ventilation, Air Conditioning, and Refrigeration	M-47 or E-28	3E2X1	Pavement and Construction Equipment	M-40	3E3X1	Structural	M-47
3E4X1	Water and Fuel Systems Maintenance	M-47 and E-28	3E4X2	Liquid Fuel Systems Maintenance	M-47	3E4X3	Pest Management	G-38
3E5X1	Engineering	G-49	3E6X1	Operations Management	G-44	3E7X1	Fire Protection	G-38

AFSC	Title	Score	AFSC	Title	Score	AFSC	Title	Score
3E8X1	Explosive Ordnance Disposal*	G-64 and M-60	**3E9X1**	Emergency Management	G-62	**3M0X1**	Services	G-24
3N0X2	Broadcast Journalist	G-72	**3N0X5**	Photojournalist	G-72	**3N1X1**	Regional Band*	G-24 or A-21
3P0X1	Security Forces	G-33	**3S0X1**	Personnel	A-41	**4A0X1**	Health Services Management	G-44
4A1X1	Medical Materiel	G-44	**4A2X1**	Biomedical Equipment	E-70 and M-60	**4B0X1**	Bioenvironmental Engineering	G-49
4C0X1	Mental Health Services	G-55	**4D0X1**	Diet Therapy	G-44	**4E0X1**	Public Health	G-44
4H0X1	Cardiopulmonary Laboratory	G-44	**4J0X2**	Physical Medicine	G-49	**4M0X1**	Aerospace and Operational Physiology	G-44
4N0X1	Aerospace Medical Services	G-44	**4N1X1**	Surgical Service	G-44	**4P0X1**	Pharmacy Technician	G-44
4R0X1	Diagnostic Imaging	G-44	**4T0X1**	Medical Laboratory	G-62	**4T0X2**	Histopathology	G-44
4V0X1	Optometry	G-55	**4Y0X1**	Dental Assistant	G-44	**4Y0X2**	Dental Laboratory	G-66
5J0X1	Paralegal	G-51	**5R0X1**	Religious Affairs	G-51 or A-35	**6C0X1**	Contracting	G-72
6F0X1	Financial Management and Comptroller	G-57	**9S100**	Scientific Applications Specialist	M-88 and E-85			

* Candidates must pass additional tests to qualify for this job.

** Candidates must be over the age of 21.

Navy Enlisted Jobs

The Navy calls its enlisted jobs *ratings* and uses an alphanumeric system to categorize each Navy Occupational Specialty, or NOS. The Navy offers about 80 types of jobs to entry-level recruits. This branch doesn't use line scores for job-qualification purposes. Instead, the Navy combines scores from the various ASVAB subtests for each of its enlisted ratings. Many enlisted sailors don't have their jobs guaranteed; instead, they join an enlisted program and are later assigned a job within that program.

Table A-3 (in ratings order) shows combinations of ASVAB subtest scores that are required to qualify for Navy enlisted jobs. Peruse the list and see which jobs may best suit you. The ASVAB subtests are abbreviated as follows: General Science (GS), Arithmetic Reasoning (AR), Word Knowledge (WK), Paragraph Comprehension (PC), Auto & Shop Information (AS), Mathematics Knowledge (MK), Mechanical Comprehension (MC), Electronics Information (EI), and Assembling Objects (AO). Verbal Expression (VE) is the sum of your Word Knowledge and Paragraph Comprehension scores.

TABLE A-3 Navy Enlisted Jobs and Required ASVAB Scores

Rating	Title	Score	Rating	Title	Score	Rating	Title	Score
AIRR	Navy Aviation Rescue Swimmer	VE + AR + MK + MC = 210 or VE + AR + MK + AS = 210	**AB**	Aviation Boatswain's Mate, Handling	VE + AR + MK + AS = 184	**ABE**	Aviation Boatswain's Mate, Equipment	VE + AR + MK + AS = 184
ABF	Aviation Boatswain's Mate, Fuels	VE + AR + MK + AS = 184	**AC**	Air Traffic Controller	VE + AR + MK + MC = 220 or VE + MK + MC + CS = 220	**AD**	Aviation Machinist's Mate	VE + AR + MK + AS = 210 or VE + AR + MK + MC = 210
AE	Aviation Electrician's Mate	AR + EI + GS + MK = 222 or AR + MK + MC + VE = 222	**AG**	Aerographer's Mate	VE + MK + GS = 162	**AM**	Aviation Structural Mechanic	VE + AR + MK + AS = 210 or VE + AR + MK + MC = 210
AME	Aviation Structural Mechanic, Equipment	VE + AR + MK + AS = 210 or VE + AR + MK + MC = 210	**AO**	Aviation Ordnance	VE + AR + MK + AS = 185 or MK + AS + AO = 140	**AS**	Aviation Support Equipment Technician	VE + MC + AR + MK = 210
AT	Avionics Electronics Technician	AR + MK + EI + GS = 222 or VE + AR + MK + MC = 222	**AW**	Naval Aircrew	VE + AR + MK + MC = 210 or VE + AR + MK + AS = 210	**AZ**	Aviation Maintenance Administration	VE + AR = 103
BM	Boatswain's Mate	VE + AR + MK + AS = 163 or MK + AS + AO = 126	**BU**	Builder	AR + MC + AS = 145	**CE**	Construction Electrician	AR + MK + EI + GS = 201
CM	Construction Mechanic	AR + MC + AS = 162	**CS**	Culinary Specialist (Surface)	VE + AR = 88	**CSS**	Culinary Specialist (Submarine)	AR + MK + EI + GS = 200 or VE + AR + MK + MC = 200
CTI	Cryptologic Technician – Interpretive	VE + MK + GS = 162	**CTT**	Cryptologic Technician – Technical	VE + MK + GS = 162	**CTM**	Cryptologic Technician – Maintenance	VE + MK + EI + GS = 223
CTN	Cryptologic Technician – Networks	AR + 2MK + GS = 255 or VE + AR + MK + MC = 235 or AR + 2MK + GS = 235 and CT = 65*	**CTR**	Cryptologic Technician – Collection	VE + AR =109	**DC**	Damage Control	VE + AR + MK + AS = 205 or VE + AR + MK + MC = 205
EA	Engineering Aide	AR + 2MK + GS = 207	**EM**	Electrician's Mate	VE + AR + MK + MC = 210 or AR + MK + EI + GS = 210	**EN**	Engineman	VE + AR + MK + AS = 200 or VE + AR + MK + AO = 205

Rating	Title	Score	Rating	Title	Score	Rating	Title	Score
EO	Equipment Operator	AR + MC + AS = 145	EOD	Explosive Ordnance Disposal	AR + VE = 109 and MC = 51 or GS + MC + EI = 169	ET	Electronics Technician	Varies based on specialty
FC	Fire Control	AR + MK + EI + GS = 222	FT	Fire Control Technician	AR + EI + GS + MK = 223	GM	Gunner's Mate	AR + MK + EI + GS = 205
GSE	Gas Turbine System Technician – Electrical	VE + AR + MK + MC = 210 or AR + MK + EI + GS = 210	GSM	Gas Turbine System Technician – Mechanical	VE + AR + MK + AS = 200 or VE + AR + MK + AO = 205	HM	Hospital Corpsman	VE + MK + GS = 156
HT	Hull Maintenance Technician	VE + AR + MK + AS = 205 or VE + AR + MK + MC = 205	IC	Interior Communications Electrician	AR + MK + EI + GS = 213	IS	Intelligence Specialist	VE + AR = 107
IT	Information Systems Technician (Surface)	AR + 2MK + GS = 222 or AR + MK + EI + GS = 222	ITS	Information Systems Technician (Submarine)	AR + 2MK + GS = 222 or AR + MK + EI + GS = 222	LN	Legalman	VE + MK = 105 or VE + MK + CS = 157 (minimum VE = 52)
LS	Logistics Specialist (Surface)	VE + AR = 102	LSS	Logistics Specialist (Submarine)	AR + MK + EI + GS = 200 or VE + AR + MK + MC = 200	MA	Master-at-Arms	AR + WK = 98 (minimum WK = 43)
MC	Mass Communications Specialist	VE + AR = 115 (minimum VE = 55)	MN	Mineman	VE + AR + MK + MC = 210 or VE + AR + MK + AS = 210	MM	Machinist's Mate (Surface)	VE + AR + MK + AS = 200 or VE + AR + MK + AO= 205
MMA	Machinist's Mate (Submarine)	VE + AR + MK + MC = 210	MR	Machinery Repair	VE + AR + MK + AS = 205 or VE + AR + MK + MC = 205	MT	Missile Technician	AR + MK + EI + GS = 222 or VE + AR + MK + MC = 222
MU	Musician	No line score criteria, but must score 35 on AFQT	ND	Navy Diver	AR + VE = 103 and MC = 51	OS	Operations Specialist	VE + MK + CS = 157 or AR + 2MK + GS = 210
PS	Personnel Specialist	VE + MK = 105 or VE + MK + CS = 157	PR	Aircrew Survival Equipmentman	VE + AR + MK + AS = 185 or MK + AS + AO = 140	QM	Quartermaster	VE + AR = 96
RP	Religious Program Specialist	VE + MK = 105 or VE + MK + CS = 157	SECF	Submarine Electronics/ Computer Field	AR + MK + EI + GS = 222 or VE + AR + MK + MC = 222	SH	Ship's Serviceman	VE + AR = 95

(continued)

Rating	Title	Score	Rating	Title	Score	Rating	Title	Score
SO	Special Warfare Operator (SEAL)	GS + MC + EI = 170 or VE + MK + MC + CS = 220 or VE + AR = 110 and MC = 50***	**ST**	Sonar Technician (Surface)	AR + MK + EI + GS = 223	**STS**	Sonar Technician (Submarine)	AR + MK + EI + GS = 222 or VE + AR + MK + MC = 222
SW	Steelworker	AR + MC + AS = 145	**UCT**	Underwater Construction Team	VE + AR = 103 and MC = 51	**UT**	Utilitiesman	AR + MK + EI + GS = 201
YN	Yeoman	VE + MK = 105 or VE + MK + CS = 157						

* Applicants must also pass the Navy's Cyber Test.

** Applicants must also take the Navy Advanced Programs Test unless they achieve VE + AR + MK + MC = 252 or AR + MK + EI + GS = 252.

*** Applicants must pass additional screening.

Marine Corps Enlisted Jobs

The United States Marine Corps needs a few good men (and women) to fill about 140 enlisted entry-level job specialties. Like the Army, the Marine Corps calls its enlisted jobs *Military Occupational Specialties* (MOSs). The Marine Corps uses the following line scores, and they're abbreviated in Table A-4 as follows: Mechanical Maintenance (MM), Electronics (EL), General Technical (GT), Verbal Expression (VE), and Clerical (CL).

TABLE A-4   **Marine Corps Enlisted Jobs and Required ASVAB Scores**

MOS	Title	Score	MOS	Title	Score	MOS	Title	Score
0111	Administrative Specialist	CL-100	**0161**	Postal Clerk	CL-100	**0211**	Counterintelligence/ Human Intelligence Specialist	GT-110
0231	Intelligence Specialist	GT-100	**0241**	Imagery Analysis Specialist	GT-100	**0261**	Geographic Intelligence Specialist	GT-100
0300	Basic Infantry Marine	GT-80	**0311**	Rifleman	GT-80	**0313**	Light Armored Reconnaissance Marine	GT-90
0321	Reconnaissance Marine	GT-105	**0331**	Machine Gunner	GT-80	**0341**	Mortarman	GT-90
0351	Infantry Assault Marine	GT-100	**0352**	Antitank Missile Gunner	GT-100	**0411**	Maintenance Management Specialist	GT-100

MOS	Title	Score	MOS	Title	Score	MOS	Title	Score
0431	Logistics/ Embarkation Specialist	GT-100	0451	Airborne and Air Delivery Specialist	GT-100	0471	Personnel Retrieval and Processing Specialist	N/A
0472	Personnel Retrieval and Processing Technician	N/A	0481	Landing Support Specialist	GT-95 and MM-100	0511	MAGTF Planning Specialist	GT-110
0612	Tactical Switching Operator	EL-105	0621	Transmissions System Operator	EL-105	0627	Satellite Communications Operator	EL-105
0631	Network Administrator	EL-105	0651	Cyber Network Operator	GT-110	0671	Data Systems Administrator	EL-105
0800	Basic Field Artillery Marine	GT-90	0811	Field Artillery Cannoneer	GT-90	0842	Field Artillery Radar Operator	GT-105
0844	Field Artillery Fire Control Marine	GT-105	0847	Field Artillery Sensor Support Marine	GT-105	0861	Fire Support Marine	GT-100
1141	Electrician	EL-90	1142	Engineer Equipment Electrical Systems Technician	MM-105 and EL-100	1161	Refrigeration and Air Conditioning Technician	MM-105
1171	Water Support Technician	MM-95	1721	Cyberspace Defensive Operator	GT-110	1316	Metal Worker	MM-95
1341	Engineer Equipment Mechanic	MM-95	1345	Engineer Equipment Operator	MM-95	1361	Engineer Assistant	GT-100
1371	Combat Engineer	MM-95	1391	Bulk Fuel Specialist	MM-95	1812	Armor Marine	GT-90
1833	Assault Amphibious Vehicle Crewmember	GT-90	1834	Amphibious Combat Vehicle Crewmember	GT-90	2111	Small Arms Repairer/ Technician	MM-95
2131	Towed Artillery Systems Technician	MM-95	2141	Assault Amphibious Vehicle Repairer/ Technician	MM-105	2146	Main Battle Tank Repairer/Technician	MM-105
2147	Light Armored Vehicle Repairer/ Technician	MM-105	2161	Machinist	MM-105	2171	Electro-Optical Ordnance Repairer	EL-115 and MM-105
2311	Ammunition Technician	GT-100	2621	Special Communications Signals Collection Operator/ Analyst	GT-110	2631	Electronic Intelligence Analyst	GT-110

(continued)

TABLE A-4 *(continued)*

MOS	Title	Score	MOS	Title	Score	MOS	Title	Score
2641	Cryptologic Linguist Operator/Analyst	GT-105	2651	Intelligence Surveillance Reconnaissance Systems Engineer	GT-110 and EL-110	2831	Digital Wideband Systems Maintainer	EL-115
2841	Ground Electronics Transmission Systems Maintainer	EL-115	2847	Ground Electronics Telecommunications and Information Technology Systems Maintainer	EL-115	2871	Calibration Technician	EL-115
2887	Artillery Electronics Technician	EL-115	3043	Supply Chain and Materiel Management Specialist	CL-105	3051	Inventory Management Specialist	CL-95
3052	Packaging Specialist	CL-90	3112	Distribution Management Specialist	GT-90	3381	Food Service Specialist	GT-90
3432	Finance Technician	CL-105	3451	Financial Management Resource Analyst	GT-110	3521	Automotive Maintenance Technician	MM-95
3531	Motor Vehicle Operator	MM-85	4421	Legal Services Specialist	CL-110 and GT-105	4512	Combat Graphics Specialist	GT-110 and VE-45
4531	Combat Mass Communicator	GT-110 and VE-45	4541	Combat Photographer	GT-110 and VE-45	4571	Combat Videographer	GT-110 and VE-45
55XX	Band	N/A	5711	Chemical, Biological, Radiological and Nuclear Defense Specialist	GT-110	5811	Military Police	GT-100
5831	Correctional Specialist	GT-100	5939	Aviation Communication Systems Technician	EL-115	5948	Aviation Radar Technician	EL-115
5951	Aviation Meteorological Equipment Technician	EL-110	5952	Air Traffic Control Navigational Aids Technician	EL-110	5953	Air Traffic Control Radar Technician	EL-110
5954	Air Traffic Control Communications Technician	EL-110	5974	Tactical Data Systems Technician	EL-115	5979	Tactical Air Operations/Air Defense Systems Technician	EL-115

MOS	Title	Score	MOS	Title	Score	MOS	Title	Score
6042	Individual Material Readiness List Asset Manager	CL-105	6046	Aircraft Maintenance Data Specialist	EL-100	6048	Flight Equipment Technician	MM-105
6062	Aircraft Intermediate Level Hydraulic/ Pneumatic Mechanic	MM-105	6073	Support Equipment Electrician/ Refrigeration and Engine/ Gas Turbine Technician	MM-105	6074	Cryogenics Equipment Operator	MM-105
6092	Aircraft Intermediate Level Structures Mechanic	MM-105	6111	Helicopter/ Tiltrotor Mechanic-Trainee	MM-105	6112	Helicopter Mechanic, CH-46	MM-105
6113	Helicopter Mechanic, CH-53	MM-105	6114	Helicopter Mechanic, UH/AH-1	MM-105	6116	Tiltrotor Mechanic, MV-22	MM-105
6122	Helicopter Power Plants Mechanic, T-58	MM-105	6123	Helicopter Power Plants Mechanic, T-64	MM-105	6124	Helicopter Power Plants Mechanic, T-400/T-700	MM-105
6132	Helicopter/ Tiltrotor Dynamic Components Mechanic	MM-105	6152	Helicopter Airframe Mechanic, CH-46	MM-105	6153	Helicopter Airframe Mechanic, CH-53	MM-105
6154	Helicopter Airframe Mechanic, UH/AH-1	MM-105	6156	Tiltrotor Airframe Mechanic, MV-22	MM-105	6172	Helicopter Crew Chief, CH-46	MM-105
6173	Helicopter Crew Chief, CH-53	MM-105	6174	Helicopter Crew Chief, UH-1	MM-105	6176	Tiltrotor Crew Chief, MV-22	MM-105
621X	Fixed-Wing Aircraft Mechanic	MM-105	622X	Fixed-Wing Aircraft Power Plants Mechanic	MM-105	6242	Fixed-Wing Aircraft Flight Engineer, KC-130	MM-105
624X	Fixed-Wing Transport Aircraft Specialist	MM-105	625X	Fixed-Wing Aircraft Airframe Mechanic	MM-105	6276	Fixed-Wing Aircraft Crew Chief, KC-130	MM-105 and GT-110
628X	Fixed-Wing Aircraft Safety Equipment Mechanic	MM-105	631X	Aircraft Communications/ Navigation/ Radar Systems Technician, EA-6	EL-105	6314	Avionics/ Maintenance Technician, Unmanned Aircraft System	EL-105
631X	Aircraft Communications/ Navigation/ Radar Systems Technician	EL-105	632X	Aircraft Communications/ Navigation/ Electrical Systems Technician	EL-105	6332	Aircraft Avionics Technician, AV-8B	EL-105

(continued)

MOS	Title	Score	MOS	Title	Score	MOS	Title	Score
633X	Aircraft Electrical Systems Technician	EL-105	**6386**	Aircraft Electronic Counter measures Systems Technician, EA-6B	EL-105	**6423**	Aviation Electronic Micro/Miniature Component and Cable Repair Technician	EL-105
6432	Aircraft Electrical/Instrument/Flight Control Systems Technician	EL-105	**6469**	Reconfigurable Transportable Consolidated Automated Support System Technician	EL-105	**6483**	Communication/Navigation/Cryptographic/Countermeasures Systems Technician	EL-105
6492	Aviation Precision Measurement Equipment Calibration/Repair Technician	EL-110	**6499**	Mobile Facility Technician	EL-105	**6531**	Aircraft Ordnance Technician	GT-105
6541	Aviation Ordnance Systems Technician	GT-105	**6672**	Aviation Supply Specialist	CL-100	**6694**	Aviation Logistics Information Management System Specialist	GT-110 and EL-115
6842	METOC Analyst Forecaster	GT-105	**7011**	Expeditionary Airfield Systems Technician	MM-95	**7041**	Aviation Operations Specialist	CL-100
7051	Expeditionary Firefighting and Rescue Specialist	MM-95	**7212**	Low Altitude Air Defense (LAAD) Gunner	GT-90	**7236**	Tactical Air Defense Controller	GT-105
7242	Air Support Operations Operator	GT-100	**7257**	Air Traffic Controller	GT-110	**7314**	Unmanned Aircraft System Operator	GT-110
7372	Tactical Systems Operator/Mission Specialist*	GT-110						

Applicants must also complete SERE School.

Coast Guard Enlisted Jobs

Although it's part of the Department of Homeland Security, the Coast Guard operates similarly to the military branches that fall under the Department of Defense. Like the Navy, the Coast Guard calls its enlisted jobs *ratings*. Also like the Navy, the Coast Guard doesn't use line scores for job qualification purposes. Instead, it uses the sums of various ASVAB subtest scores.

Table A-5 shows combinations of ASVAB subtest scores that are required to qualify for Coast Guard enlisted jobs. The ASVAB subtests are abbreviated as follows: General Science (GS), Arithmetic Reasoning (AR), Word Knowledge (WK), Paragraph Comprehension (PC), Auto & Shop Information (AS), Mathematics Knowledge (MK), Mechanical Comprehension (MC), Electronics Information (EI), and Assembling Objects (AO); Verbal Expression (VE) is your combined Paragraph Comprehension and Word Knowledge score.

TABLE A-5 Coast Guard Enlisted Jobs and Required ASVAB Scores

Rating	Title	Score	Rating	Title	Score	Rating	Title	Score
AET	Avionics Electrical Technician	MK + EI + GS = 171	**AMT**	Aviation Maintenance Technician	AFQT = 65 or AR + MC + AS + EI = 220 and minimum AR = 52	**AST**	Aviation Survival Technician	AFQT = 65 or VE + MC + AS = 162 and minimum AR = 52
BM	Boatswain's Mate	AR + VE = 100	**CS**	Culinary Specialist	VE + AR = 106	**DC**	Damage Controlman	VE + MC + AS = 155
EM	Electrician's Mate	MK + EI + GS = 153 and minimum AR = 52	**ET**	Electronics Technician	AFQT = 65 or MK + EI + GS = 172 and minimum AR = 52	**GM**	Gunner's Mate	AR + MK + EI + GS = 209
HS	Health Services Technician	VE + MK + GS + AR = 207 and minimum AR = 50	**IT**	Information Systems Technician	AFQT = 65 or MK + EI + GS = 172 and minimum AR = 52	**IS**	Intelligence Specialist	AR + VE = 109
ME	Maritime Enforcement Specialist	VE + AR = 100	**MK**	Machinery Technician	AR + MC + AS = 154 or VE + AR = 105	**MST**	Marine Science Technician	VE + AR = 114 and minimum MK = 56
MUS	Musician	N/A*	**OS**	Operations Specialist	VE + AR = 105	**PA**	Public Affairs Specialist	VE + AR = 109 and minimum VE = 54
SK	Storekeeper	VE + AR = 105 and minimum VE = 51	**YN**	Yeoman	VE + AR = 105			

* Interested applicants must audition for the position.

Appendix B

Countdown to Taking the ASVAB

The ASVAB isn't an intelligence test, although you'll need to tap into your knowledge reserves when you take it. It's actually designed to tell the military where you'll shine as a service member based on your current knowledge and your aptitude for learning more. The military uses carefully calculated line scores to determine which jobs will be a good fit for you within the branch you choose.

This appendix gives you a study plan to prepare for the ASVAB based on how many weeks you have until you take the test.

How Much Time Do You Have to Prepare?

Your recruiter will call MEPS to find out when you can take the ASVAB, but ultimately, you control when you take the test. Let your recruiter know if you feel rushed. Landing the military job you want depends on your scores, so if you need more time to prepare, ask for it. It's important that you study at your own pace so you can absorb all the information you need.

REMEMBER

Knowing math and English concepts is an important prerequisite to taking the ASVAB — but it's also important that you learn and review these topics over time. You can't put off studying until the night before you take the test; you'll end up being frazzled on test day, and it'll show in your scores.

Outline Your ASVAB Study Strategy

Use the tables in Appendix A to determine what scores you need to get the job you want. If your dream job involves working on helicopter engines, you'll need to devote extra time to brushing up on your Auto & Shop Information (AS), Mechanical Comprehension (MC), and Electronics Information (EI) knowledge.

Each branch has a baseline AFQT score (see Chapter 1 for each branch's current minimum AFQT score) that you must meet or exceed to enlist.

TIP

It's a good idea to have a backup job in mind, just in case your first choice isn't available. The military's needs change on an almost daily basis, so even if your recruiter is fairly certain your dream job will be available when you sign on the dotted line, it's best to get used to adapting to the unexpected; you'll face it often during the course of your military career.

Every section of the ASVAB is important because each branch gauges your overall ability based on various combinations of your scores (and if you want to switch jobs after you get some rank on your chest, you won't have to retake the ASVAB to improve your scores).

If you don't have three months to prepare, which the following schedule outlines, you can accelerate your pace so it corresponds to how much time you *do* have. Simply count how many weeks (or days) you have between today and test day, and then try to schedule the plan at even intervals.

12 weeks out: Identify your weak spots

Take Practice Exam 1 in Chapter 18 so you get a good idea of which areas need a little spit-and-polish (that's an old military term that refers to shining boots). Make sure you're in a quiet place where others are unlikely to disturb you, and keep a stack of scratch paper handy.

Score each subtest according to the answers in Chapter 19. Take an objective look at your scores and determine which subtests you performed well on. If they correspond with the job you want in the military, that's great — but as the military always says, don't become complacent. You still need to study, right up to the day before the test, to make sure you're on the right track to ace the ASVAB.

If you didn't perform very well on some of the subtests, you'll know exactly where to focus. However, at this point, it's most important to determine how you stack up against military standards on the AFQT portion of the test. The scores that matter most include

>> Word Knowledge

>> Paragraph Comprehension

>> Arithmetic Reasoning

>> Mathematics Knowledge

It's usually helpful to create your own flashcards using blank index cards. Studies have shown that flashcards help people memorize new information, and even the act of writing down information can go a long way toward helping you remember.

10 weeks out: Dust off your strengths

When you took the first practice test, you were able to see where you need improvement and where you're already strong. The good news is that you don't have to learn anything new at this point. Instead, keep strengthening your grasp on your weak spots and revisit your strongest areas.

TIP

You can use this opportunity to take the practice exam in Chapter 20 to find out how much all your hard work has paid off in those not-so-spectacular areas. Before you take it, review Chapter 29 and apply the strategies outlined there — you may be surprised at the progress you've made.

8 weeks out: Studying with your recruiter

Find out which subjects you need to devote your attention to and, if possible, rule out everything that counts toward your AFQT score. You can see how far you've come by taking the AFQT Practice Exam 1 in Chapter 24.

Determine which subjects you need to improve based on your results this time around.

Talk to your recruiter about scheduling time to study together. Many recruiting stations will set up study sessions for groups of enlistees if enough people are interested in participating. (Here's a little secret: The better you do on the test, the better you make your recruiter look to his or her superiors.)

TIP

Most recruiters have the ability to give you practice tests that reflect a potential AFQT score.

Continue working on the weaknesses you identified when you took the first two practice tests.

6 weeks out: Retest yourself

Take the third practice exam in Chapter 22. It's time to reevaluate where you are, so after you grade the exam, rank the subtests based on your performance. Pay special attention to your scores on the AFQT subtests (Word Knowledge, Paragraph Comprehension, Mathematics Knowledge, and Arithmetic Reasoning).

Spend most of your time over the next two weeks studying for the two subtests you need to improve most.

TIP

Alternate studying your two subjects so you don't become overwhelmed. If you get tired of studying one, switch to the other — and make sure you let your recruiter know where you need the most help.

4 weeks out: Zeroing in on your targets

Retake the first practice exam from Chapter 18. At this point, you should be able to see major progress in your weakest areas (and if you've been staying on top of studying, you'll see improvement on the AFQT subtests, too).

Rank your scores again, just like you did two weeks ago. Test day is just a month away, so focus on

>> Strengthening your abilities in Word Knowledge and Paragraph Comprehension

>> Pushing yourself in Mathematics Knowledge and Arithmetic Reasoning

>> Studying the subtest area that will help you get the job you want, even if you're already confident in your ability

2 weeks out: Flashcards, practice tests, and more flashcards

Ask a friend to quiz you with your flashcards, and determine what's most important for you to study. It's crunch time, so you don't want to spend too much time learning new material; focus on a well-rounded study plan that reinforces everything you've already learned.

TIP

Review the online cheat sheet (go to www.dummies.com and search for "ASVAB cheat sheet") to make sure you understand the strategies it outlines, including its tips on what to do when you're unsure about an answer.

The day before the test

Tomorrow's the big day, and you're as prepared as you'll ever be. Before you settle in for one last study session, pack up everything you need to bring to MEPS: your ID card, your glasses, and anything else your recruiter has told you to bring.

TIP

Most MEPS locations adhere to a specific dress code, even for those taking the ASVAB. Ask your recruiter beforehand what the facility allows.

Don't be too hard on yourself during your last study session. Break up your time into two 1-hour blocks, and during the first hour, focus on the subjects you need to ace to get your dream job.

During the second hour, review all the notes you've taken, flip through this book to look for highlights, and make sure you're familiar with the time constraints you'll face when you're sitting in front of the computer at MEPS (see Chapter 1).

REMEMBER

It's going to be tough to relax the day before you take the test, but give it your best shot. You'll perform best if you

» **Hydrate.** Shoot for eight glasses of water, and steer clear of energy drinks, coffee, and soda.

» **Relax.** You don't need built-up stress interfering with your test-taking abilities, so do what you need to do to relax. Curl up with *Relaxation For Dummies* by Shamash Alidina (Wiley), watch a funny movie, or spend time with family and friends — whatever works for you.

» **Sleep.** Get at least 8 hours of sleep the night before the test so you're on your toes when you arrive at MEPS. That means going to bed early because the military starts operating at zero-dark-thirty (*zero-dark-thirty* translates to "all the civilians are still snug and warm in their beds . . . and will be for 2 more hours").

Appendix C

Word Knowledge Resources

Word Knowledge makes up a big chunk of your overall ASVAB score — and it's part of the AFQT, or Armed Forces Qualification Test, so it determines whether you're even eligible to enlist in any branch of the U.S. Armed Forces. Your Word Knowledge score also factors into many military jobs (see Appendix A to match up job codes with the ASVAB line scores you need to land your dream job).

This appendix gives you exhaustive lists of word roots, prefixes, and suffixes that you can study to ace the Word Knowledge subtest on the ASVAB. Use the far-right column to jot down your own words, which may help you remember specific word parts on test day.

Digging Down to Word Roots

Not all the words you'll see on the ASVAB have their roots in Greek or Latin, but because so many do, you're likely to see at least a handful of them on the test. Knowing the word roots in Table C-1 can help you figure out what words mean, helping boost your Word Knowledge score.

TABLE C-1 **Word Roots**

Word Root	Meaning	Examples	Your Words
ac or acr	sharp, bitter, or sour	acid	
		acute	
		exacerbate	
act or ag	to do, to force, or to lead	activate	
		agitate	
		enact	

(continued)

TABLE C-1 *(continued)*

Word Root	Meaning	Examples	Your Words
al, ali, or alter	other or another	alias alien alternative	
am	love	amiable amorous enamored	
ambi or amphi	both, on both sides, or around	ambidextrous ambiguous amphibian	
ana	up, back, against, again, or throughout	analysis analytic anatomy	
anim	of the life, mind, soul, or breath	animal animosity unanimous	
anthro or andr	man or human	android anthropologist philanthropy	
aqua or aque	water	aquarium aquatic aqueduct	
arch, archi, or archy	chief, ruler, or principal	anarchy architect monarch	
astro or aster	stars	astronaut astronomer asterisk	
auto	self, same, or one	autocrat autograph automatic	
bell or belli	war	bellicose belligerent rebel	
ben or bene	good or well	benefactor beneficial benevolent	

Word Root	Meaning	Examples	Your Words
bio	life or living matter	biography	
		biohazard	
		biology	
cant or chant	to sing	cant	
		enchant	
		recant	
capt, cept, or ceive	take or hold	captor	
		intercept	
		perceive	
carn	flesh	carnage	
		carnivore	
		reincarnation	
caust or caut	to burn	cauterize	
		caustic	
		holocaust	
cede, ceed, or cess	go or yield	access	
		exceed	
		recede	
centr	center	central	
		concentrate	
		eccentric	
cern, cert, cret, crim, or crit	to separate, to distinguish, to judge, or to decide	ascertain	
		certainty	
		hypocrite	
chron	time	chronic	
		chronology	
		synchronize	
cis	to cut	incision	
		precise	
		scissors	
claim or clam	shout or speak out	clamor	
		exclaim	
		proclaim	
corp	body	corporation	
		corps	
		corpse	

(continued)

TABLE C-1 *(continued)*

Word Root	Meaning	Examples	Your Words
cred	to believe or trust	credit credo incredibly	
crypt or crypto	hidden or secret	crypt cryptic encrypt	
dem	people	academy democracy epidemic	
di	day	dial diary dismal	
dole	to suffer or grieve	condolences doleful indolence	
don, dot, or dow	to give	antidote donate pardon	
dur	to harden, to last, or lasting	durable duration endure	
equ	equal or even	adequate equation equivalent	
esce	becoming	adolescent coalesce incandescent	
fab or fam	to speak	defame fable famous	
fac, fic, fig, fait, feit, or fy	to do or make	configure deficient factory	
fer	to bear, bring, or carry	confer ferry transfer	

Word Root	Meaning	Examples	Your Words
fi or fid	faith or trust	confide	
		fidelity	
		infidel	
fin	end	confine	
		final	
		infinity	
fus	to pour	diffuse	
		infuse	
		profuse	
gen	birth, production, or formation	genealogy	
		generation	
		genes	
geo	earth or soil	dungeon	
		geography	
		geology	
gn or gno	to know	agnostic	
		ignorant	
		ignore	
grad or gress	to step	aggressive	
		digress	
		progress	
gram or graph	to write or draw	diagram	
		grammar	
		graph	
hap	by chance	happen	
		happy	
		mishap	
her or hes	to stick	adhere	
		coherent	
		inherent	
herb or herbi	grass or plant	herbicide	
		herbivorous	
		herbal	
idio	peculiar, personal, or distinct	idiosyncrasy	
		idiot	
		idiotic	

(continued)

TABLE C-1 *(continued)*

Word Root	Meaning	Examples	Your Words
it or iter	way or journey	ambition itinerary reiterate	
ject	to throw or throw down	eject inject project	
jud	to judge	judgment judicial prejudice	
jur	law or to swear	jurisdiction jury perjury	
lab	work	collaborate elaborate labor	
lang or ling	tongue	bilingual language linguistics	
lav, lau, or lu	to wash	dilute laundry lavatory	
lec, leg, or lex	to read or speak	lecture legend legible	
lect or leg	to choose or select	collect elect select	
lev	to lift, rise, or lighten	alleviate elevate relevant	
liber	free	deliver liberal liberty	
loc, log, or locu	word, speech, or thought	colloquialism dialogue prologue	

Word Root	Meaning	Examples	Your Words
luc, lum, or lus	light	lucid illuminate translucent	
mag or max	big or great	magnify magnitude maximum	
mand or mend	to command, order, or entrust	commend demand mandatory	
mob, mot, or mov	to move	automobile demote movable	
mut	to change	commute mutation transmute	
nau or nav	ship or sailor	astronaut nautical navy	
noc or nox	harm	innocent noxious obnoxious	
pac or peac	peace	appease pacify pact	
pas, pat, or path	feeling, suffering, or disease	compassion empathy sympathetic	
ped	child or education	encyclopedia pediatric pedagogy	
ped or pod	foot	pedal pedestrian podium	
pel	to push or drive	compel expel propel	

(continued)

TABLE C-1 *(continued)*

Word Root	Meaning	Examples	Your Words
pet	to seek or strive	appetite	
		compete	
		petition	
phob	fear	claustrophobic	
		phobia	
		xenophobia	
phys	nature, medicine, or the body	physical	
		physician	
		physique	
ple or plen	to fill or be full	complete	
		implement	
		supplement	
port	to carry	export	
		import	
		portable	
pri or prim	first	primary	
		primal	
		pristine	
put	think	computer	
		dispute	
		input	
que or quis	to seek	acquire	
		inquisition	
		query	
rect	straight or right	correct	
		erect	
		rectangle	
salv	to save	salvage	
		salvation	
		salve	
sci	to know	consciousness	
		omniscient	
		science	
sed, sess, or sid	to sit or settle	dissident	
		preside	
		residue	

Word Root	Meaning	Examples	Your Words
sens or sent	to feel or be aware	resent	
		sensory	
		sentinel	
sol	alone	desolate	
		isolated	
		solitary	
sourc, surg, or surrect	to rise	insurgents	
		resurrect	
		source	
spec or spic	to look or see	inconspicuous	
		retrospect	
		spectrum	
sum	total	sum	
		summary	
		summit	
tact, tag, tam, or tang	to touch	contact	
		contaminate	
		intact	
tain, ten, tent, or tin	to hold	abstain	
		detain	
		tenacious	
test	to bear witness	attest	
		contest	
		testament	
tor, torq, or tort	to twist	contort	
		distort	
		torque	
ult	last or beyond	ultimate	
		ultimatum	
		ultraviolet	
vail or val	strength, worth, or use	avail	
		equivalent	
		invalid	
ver	truth	veracious	
		verdict	
		verify	

(continued)

TABLE C-1 *(continued)*

Word Root	Meaning	Examples	Your Words
vid or vis	to see	adviser video visual	
voc or vok	word or calling	advocate evoke vocation	
volu or volv	to roll or turn	evolve revolution volume	
vor	to eat	carnivore omnivore voracious	

Pointing Out Prefixes

Not all words have prefixes, but those that do put them right in the front of the word (and suffixes go at the end). A prefix can change the entire meaning of a word, as Chapter 4 demonstrates. Understanding the relationships between the prefixes in Table C-2 and the root words listed in Table C-1 can help you settle on the correct answers when you're taking the Word Knowledge subtest.

TABLE C-2   **Prefixes**

Prefix	Meaning	Examples	Your Words
a- or an-	not or without	agnostic anomaly atypical	
ab-	away from, apart from, or down	abnormal abolish abstract	
ad-	toward or near	address adjacent advocate	
ambi- or amphi-	both, or on both sides	ambidextrous ambiguous amphibian	
ant- or ante-	before	antecedent antenatal anteroom	

Prefix	Meaning	Examples	Your Words
anti-	against	antibiotic antidepressant antifreeze	
bi-	two	bilingual binoculars bipartisan	
cent- or centi-	hundred or hundredth	centiliter centimeter centipede	
circu- or circum-	around	circuit circumference circumstance	
co-, col-, com-, or con-	together or with	collaborate cooperate compatible	
contra-, contro-, or counter-	against	contradict controversial counterculture	
de-	away from, off, down, or reversal	defrost derailed devalue	
deca-	ten	decade decahedron decathlon	
dis-	opposite of	disagree disappear disintegrate	
dys-	faulty or abnormal	dysfunction dyslexic dystrophy	
e- or ex-	out of or from	evade exclude expire	
em- or en-	cause to or put into	embed encode engulf	

(continued)

TABLE C-2 *(continued)*

Prefix	Meaning	Examples	Your Words
extra-	outside or beyond	extract extracurricular extraordinary	
fore-	before	forecast foremost foresight	
hex- or sex-	six	hexagon hexadecimal sextet	
hyper-	over or above	hyperactive hyperbole hyperventilate	
hypo-	beneath, less than, or under	hypochondriac hypocrite hypothesis	
in- or im-	not or without	immoral inactive innocuous	
in- or im-	inside or into	implicit indigenous intrinsic	
inter-	among or between	interim intermittent interstate	
mal- or male-	bad or wrong	malady malfunction malicious	
med- or medi-	middle	medieval mediocre medium	
mega-	very large	megabyte megalomania megaphone	
mis-	wrongly	misinterpret mistake misunderstand	

Prefix	Meaning	Examples	Your Words
mono-	one	monologue monopoly monotone	
multi-	many	multiple multiply multitude	
non-	not or without	nonabrasive noncarcinogenic nonsense	
nov-, neo-, or nou-	new	neoclassical neonatal neophyte	
oct-	eight	octagon octane octopus	
omni-	all	omnipotent omnipresent omnivore	
para-	beside	paradox parallel paranoid	
pan- or pant-	all or everyone	pandemic panorama pantheon	
pent-	five	pentagon pentagram pentathlon	
poly-	many	polygamy polygon polytheist	
post-	after	posterior post-mortem postpone	
pre-	before or in front	predetermined prefix premonition	

(continued)

TABLE C-2 *(continued)*

Prefix	Meaning	Examples	Your Words
pro-	to go forth or put forth	proceed proclaim proponent	
quad-, quar-, or quat-	four	quadrant quart quartet	
quin- or quint-	five	quintet quintile quintuplet	
re-	back or again	recline rediscover reunite	
se-	apart or away	seduce segregate separate	
semi-	half	semicircle semiconscious semifluid	
sept-	seven	septennial septet septuplet	
sub- or sup-	under	submarine subterfuge subtitle	
super- or sur-	above or over	supersede surpass surveillance	
sym- or syn-	together or the same	symmetry synonym synthetic	
trans-	across or beyond	transaction transcontinental transit	
un-	not	undone unknown unseen	

Spotting Hard-Working Suffixes

Thousands of words have suffixes that change their meaning. Suffixes always come at the end of a word, as I explain in Chapter 4. Suffixes can also help you identify what type of word (a noun, a verb, or something else) you're working with. When you understand how suffixes hitch themselves to root words, you'll have an easier time answering tough questions on the ASVAB. Table C-3 shows you some of the most common suffixes in the English language.

TABLE C-3 **Suffixes**

Suffix	Part of Speech It Indicates	Meaning	Examples	Your Words
-able	adjective	able to be	agreeable available portable	
-ac	adjective	pertaining to	cardiac insomniac maniac	
-acity or -ocity	noun	quality of	audacity incapacity ferocity	
-age	noun	action or process	advantage blockage pilgrimage	
-al	adjective	relating to	bacterial frugal natural	
-an or -ian	adjective or noun	relating to or one who is skilled at	comedian theologian urban	
-arian	noun	a person who	Aquarian librarian vegetarian	
-ate	adjective or verb	state or quality of; can make a word a verb	affectionate fixate medicate	
-ative	adjective	tending to	creative fixative talkative	

(continued)

TABLE C-3 *(continued)*

Suffix	Part of Speech It Indicates	Meaning	Examples	Your Words
-cide	noun	killing	homicide insecticide suicide	
-cy	noun	condition or state	efficiency lunacy privacy	
-dom	noun	condition of or state of	boredom freedom kingdom	
-ed	verb	past tense	chased laughed zipped	
-en	verb	makes a word a verb	frighten sweeten thicken	
-ence	noun	state or condition	absence negligence sequence	
-ent	adjective or noun	causing or one who performs or causes	competent correspondent incident	
-escence	noun	process or state	adolescence evanescence florescence	
-est	adjective	most	craziest healthiest stillest	
-ful	adjective	having the quality of	disrespectful hopeful thoughtful	
-ible	adjective	able to be	convertible flexible legible	
-ic	adjective	relating to or having the quality of	apologetic genetic magnetic	

Suffix	Part of Speech It Indicates	Meaning	Examples	Your Words
-ify	verb	to transform something into something else	magnify objectify simplify	
-ing	noun or verb	materials or an action or process	bedding dancing writing	
-ity	noun	state of or quality of	density fertility plausibility	
-ive	adjective or noun	having a quality, or a person or thing with the quality of	competitive explosive negative	
-ize	verb	cause or become	characterize hospitalize personalize	
-less	adjective	without	directionless heartless senseless	
-ly	adverb	makes a word into an adverb	bravely motherly quickly	
-ment	noun	action or result	establishment movement shipment	
-ness	noun	state or quality	fullness kindness thinness	
-or	noun	a person who	advisor inventor translator	
-ous	adjective	full of	dangerous hazardous porous	
-tion or -sion	noun	act or process, result of a process, state, or condition	motion navigation tension	

(continued)

TABLE C-3 *(continued)*

Suffix	Part of Speech It Indicates	Meaning	Examples	Your Words
-tude	noun	state, condition, or quality	fortitude gratitude solitude	
-ty	adjective or noun	state, condition, or quality	ability meaty scanty	
-uous	adjective	state or quality of	arduous strenuous voluptuous	
-y	adjective	having or resembling	dirty guilty sporty	

Index

mirroring, 301

misunderstandings, 528

mitosis, 170

mixed numbers, 83–84

mixture, 181

MK subtest. *See* Mathematics Knowledge (MK) subtest

mode, 80

molecules, 177

moons, 208–209

Moore, John T. (author), 175

mortising chisel, 238, 239

motor, 289, 290

muffler, 224

multimeter, 279

multiple-choice questions, 28–29

multiplying/multiplication, 79, 82–83, 85, 100

multistep equations, solving, 100–101

muscular system, 160, 162–163

N

nails, 240–241

naming angles, 117

National Oceanic Atmospheric Administration (NOAA), 201

Navy. *See* U.S. Navy

needle-nosed pliers, 237

negative numbers, 106

nervous system, 160, 161

neutrons, 177

Newton, Isaac (scientist), 251

newtons, 177

Newton's laws of motion, 183–185

nitrogen, 199

notes, making, 529

noun, 46

Nuclear Field (NUC) line score, Navy/Coast Guard and, 23

nucleus, 168, 277

number sequences, 79–80

numerator, 81

nuts, 241–242

O

observations, using as a test-taking technique, 265–266

obtuse angle, 116

obtuse triangle, 118

oceans, 197–198

octane ratings, 221

offset screwdriver, 236

ohms, 276, 279, 293

Ohm's law, 279, 293

oil filter, 223

oil galleries, 223

oil pan, 223

oil pump, 223

omnivores, 157

1,001 ASVAB AFQT Practice Questions For Dummies (Johnston), 76

one-step equations, solving, 99–100

on/off switch, 289, 290

open-end wrench, 235–236

operations, 77, 78–79, 534

Operations (OPS) line score, Navy/Coast Guard and, 23

Operators and Food (OF) line score, Army and, 22

orbit, 207

order, 158, 159

order of operations, 78–79, 534

osmosis, 169

ossification, 163

outside calipers, 234

oxyacetylene welding, 237

oxygen, 199

P

paleobotany, 203

paleoclimate, 201

paleoecology, 203

paleomagnetism, 205

paleontology, 203–205

palynology, 203

paper test, 25–28

Paragraph Comprehension (PC) subtest

about, 9, 55

in AFQT, 12

analyzing paragraphs, 62

answers and explanations, 70–71

breaking down paragraphs, 60–61

components of, 56

example questions, 57–59, 62

importance of, 55–56

practice questions, 66–69

Q&A for Practice Exam 1 (AFQT), 476–479, 488–489

Q&A for Practice Exam 1 (ASVAB), 324–326, 350–351

Q&A for Practice Exam 2 (AFQT), 504–506, 517–518

Q&A for Practice Exam 2 (ASVAB), 376–378, 401–402

Q&A for Practice Exam 3 (ASVAB), 426–428, 452–454

question types, 56–59

slow readers, 63–64

test-taking tips for, 64–65

parallel circuit, 282

parallel lines, 117

parallelograms, 119–120

parentheses, in order of operations, 78

parts of speech, 46–47

pascals, 177

passages, 60–61, 530

patterns, finding, 79–80

PC subtest. *See* Paragraph Comprehension (PC) subtest

penny system, 240

pepsin, 162

percentile score, 11

percents, 84, 86–87, 530

perfect squares, 89

perimeter, 118, 534

periodic table, 177–178

permutations, 77

pH, 181–182

phagocytosis, 170

phanerozoic, 04

pharynx, 162

Phillips screwdriver, 236

photosynthesis, 167, 170

phylum, 158, 159

physics, 182–190

Physics I For Dummies (Holzner), 175, 247

Physics II For Dummies (Holzner), 175

physiological effect, 286

pi, 121

pickup tube/screen, 223

pipe cutters, 238

pipe vise, 240

pipe wrench, 236

piston rings, 220

pistons, 220

pivot joints, 163

About the Author

Angie Papple Johnston joined the U.S. Army in 2006 as a Chemical, Biological, Radiological, and Nuclear (CBRN) Specialist, ready to tackle chemical weapons in a Level-A HAZMAT suit. During her second deployment as part of Operation Iraqi Freedom, Angie became her battalion's public affairs representative, covering breaking news from Tikrit to Kirkuk. She has earned a Combat Action Badge, several Army Commendation medals and Army Achievement medals, and numerous accolades for her work in Iraq.

Angie also served as the Lead Cadre for the Texas Army National Guard's Recruit Sustainment Program (RSP), teaching brand-new privates how to survive Basic Combat Training, Advanced Individual Training, and the Army before becoming the CBRN noncommissioned officer-in-charge in an aviation battalion in Washington, D.C. She currently resides in South Korea with her husband (another noncommissioned officer in the U.S. Army), their son, and two dogs.

Dedication

This book is for everyone brave enough to stand up, raise your right hand, and put on a uniform. It's also for Davy Johnston, who means everything to me, and CBRN pro David Robert Johnston, Jr., who keeps a stack of *For Dummies* books on his desk and takes pictures of the best shelf in the bookstore for me, even when I'm not there.

Author's Acknowledgments

Thank you, Lindsay Lefevere, for making this possible. You inspire me!

Chrissy Guthrie, as always, you are so much fun to work with . . . and you make everything look so easy. Thank you so much for everything you do.

MAJ Jonathan Kralick, I can't thank you enough for your help on this book and for the things you do every day to ensure our military moves forward in the right direction. Alison Kralick, thank you for coming to the rescue and making this connection — and I, like the rest of your friends, can't wait to see next year's costumes.

Thank you, Megan Knoll, for the wonderful contributions you made to ensure this book is a great resource for our future military leaders.

Kathleen Bienenstein and Bonnie Swadling, thank you for supporting me in everything I do. You're always there for me and I love you.

Mom, Dad, Darl, Tina, and Jesse: I love you guys. Jesse, I'm not even going to say it this year. You already know.

Publisher's Acknowledgments

Executive Editor: Lindsay Sandman Lefevere

Editorial Project Manager and Development Editor:
  Christina N. Guthrie

Copy Editor: Megan Knoll

Technical Editor: MAJ Jonathan Kralick, P.E.

Proofreader: Debbye Butler

Production Editor: Mohammed Zafar Ali

Cover Image: © scyther5/Getty Images